The United States Congress in Comparative Perspective

The United States Congress in Comparative Perspective

John E. Schwarz
University of Arizona

L. Earl Shaw
University of Minnesota

The Dryden Press
Hinsdale, Illinois

Copyright © 1976 by The Dryden Press
A Division of Holt, Rinehart and Winston
All rights reserved
Library of Congress Catalog Card Number: 73-19245
ISBN: 0-03-079430-7
Printed in the United States of America
6789 038 987654321

For Judi and Betty —
   two exemplary human beings
   and loving companions.

To the memory of Louise Lasker Schwarz,
   whose influence on the writing
   of this book was profound.

Acknowledgements

Our thanks and appreciation go to many who helped us at various stages in the research and writing of this book. Among these include Richard Blue, John Crow, Lawrence Dodd, Helen Ingram, Henry Kenski, Geoffrey Lambert, Gerhard Loewenberg, Lowell Noonan, Daniel O'Neil, Steven Seitz, Thomas Volgy, and Oliver Woshinsky. We also enjoyed the assistance of William Muggli, Lee Ridgeway, Betsy Rieke, Bonnie Stewart, Manfred Stinnes, and Bruce Wright. The support and counsel of two special friends, David and Sara Lasker, were of continuing benefit to us as well. Helpful, too, were research funds made available by both The University of Arizona and the Institute of Government Research at The University of Arizona. To all these persons and organizations, and to many others, we are greatly indebted. For the weaknesses and errors that remain, we take full responsibility.

Contents

	Introduction	1
Chapter 1	A Theoretical Overview	11
Chapter 2	The Institutional Setting	21
Chapter 3	The Policy Process in Action: Four Case Studies	96
Chapter 4	Legislators and Their Political Parties	118
Chapter 5	Legislators and Their Political Parties: Another Perspective	159
Chapter 6	Legislative-Executive Relations in the Making of Legislation	192
Chapter 7	The Legislative and Supervision of Executive Action	257
Chapter 8	Executive-Legislative Relations: Some Explanations	292
Chapter 9	Interest Groups and the Legislature	325
Chapter 10	Representing Citizen Opinion in the Legislative	366
Chapter 11	Conclusion	394
	Bibliographical Notes	400
	Credits	407
	Index	409

Introduction

Every modern society faces issues that affect the interests of large numbers of people. Many of the issues are quite divisive and bring various groups in the society into direct conflict. How much should society spend on its defenses relative to its expenditures for education and housing? What is to be done to clean up the environment, and who is to pay? How far should the political system go in attempting to provide equal rights and opportunities for each of its citizens? How should the system of health care be organized: should it be run under public or private enterprise or a combination of the two? Should further nationalization of industry take place? Have trade unions become too powerful—should their organization and powers be altered? These are just a sampling of the issues that many modern societies face today. The resolution of each of these issues—what is decided and how it is decided—will affect, sometimes very deeply, often in quite different ways, the lives of almost all individuals within these societies.

The methods used to resolve issues such as these vary from society to society. The history of politics could be written as an examination of the various methods of decision-making developed to reach binding decisions for the whole society. One method for reaching such decisions is a democracy, which theoretically maximizes the participation of all the citizens of society in the decision-making process. However, practical considerations prevent the continuous participation in every decision of all citizens in a large population or a large geographical locale; thus, as developed in many Western societies, the idea of representative democracy has been offered as the nearest approximation possible under contemporary circumstances.

Central to the idea of representative democracy as a method of decision-making has been the representative legislature. Examples of representative legislative bodies are the United States Congress, the British House of Commons, the French National Assembly, and the West German Bundestag.

This study examines the operation of one of these legislatures, the United States Congress, from a perspective that draws upon experiences of the European legislative bodies (reasons for selecting the three European legislatures will be outlined later in this chapter). The study describes how members of these legislative bodies, in making decisions, have acted toward other major forces in the political system. The study also attempts to develop understanding of why members behave as they do. In this regard, we discuss a variety of goals legislators pursue along with certain elements of the political setting as these in combination help us understand behavior in Congress as compared to the European legislatures. Finally, we come to some evaluative judgments. Here our analysis suggests that the Congress has compiled a record of representing national public opinion that equals and perhaps surpasses what can ordinarily be accomplished by the major structural alternatives, often drawn from European experience, that critics of the Congress have proposed. And, despite claims of legislative decline, the Congress has also retained substantial influence in the making of public policy, including a record of policy initiative that critics of Congress have frequently failed to recognize. It is important to add that the Congress has accomplished these ends despite, indeed partly because of, two characteristics often thought to be major defects. These are the comparatively undisciplined nature of Congressional parties and the fragmented character of the Congressional power structure.

In this introductory chapter, we commence with a definition of the representative legislature and make some brief remarks about the decision-making authority of the legislature. We then outline the major questions addressed in the study and describe, in general terms, the various theoretical approaches upon which the study will build.

In its modern form, the representative legislature can be defined as combining the following characteristics: first, its members are chosen by the enfranchised citizenry of the society in open, contested, and periodic elections; second, it has a plural membership, with members formally equal to one another; and third, it is an institution that by itself, or in conjunction with other governmental institutions, is able to make authoritative decisions for the territorial society it collectively represents.

Several aspects of this definition should be kept in mind. As the definition implies, the authority of the representative legislature rests on its claim that it represents collectively the larger political community of which it is a part.[1] The usual institutional procedure by which modern democratic societies believe representation is assured is the procedure of election.[2] When we speak of a representative legislature, we mean by the word "representative" a legislature which, at minimum, has been elected.

The election process, as the term is used here, needs to meet several requirements. Each of the legislative bodies we treat meets these requirements (see Chapter 2). First, elections signify that legislators are not appointed by another official or set of officials. Nor are members of a representative legislature self-selected. Rather, they must place themselves *directly* before the general public. Therefore, we would not consider the United States Senate a representative legislature prior to 1913. For the same reason, we would not consider the British House of Lords, French Senate or West German Bundesrat to be representative legislatures. Implicit here, too, is the idea that legislators are not chosen for life but are accountable to the public again in periodic elections. Elections must not only permit opposition and free debate, but in at least the majority of instances alternative candidates do run.[3] Furthermore, the concept of having received a "larger share of the popular vote" must be integral to the determination of who wins the election. And, in an effort to provide a minimally agreeable definition as opposed to one we would regard as perfect, we have referred to members of the legislature as having been elected by the enfranchised citizenry. While the enfranchised citizenry now includes almost the entire legally defined adult population for each of the assemblies we consider, some writers have stipulated that if as little as 25 percent of the citizenry were enfranchised, the system might still be designated as electoral.[4]

The representative legislature is also a collegial body. It not only has a plural membership, but when the legislature comes together to make a collective decision, it votes on the basis of formal equality of members, thereby distinguishing the representative legislature from formal, hierarchically ordered organizations.

Finally, we have suggested that a governmental institution that possesses the previous characteristics must by itself, or in conjunction with other governmental institutions, be able to make authoritative decisions for the territorial society it collectively represents. Thus we have included not only structural characteristics but also a functional characteristic in our definition. That is, we have defined a representative legislature not only in terms of what it looks like but also in terms of what it can and does do.

Certainly there are instances in which executives or courts can act or have acted without legislative approval or authority in each of the systems we consider. Nevertheless, it remains the case that each of the legislatures has been integral, at minimum as an arena of authorization and legitimization or, at maximum, as the central arena of policy development, to the making of public decisions in many areas of policy (see Chapter 6). Perhaps the best illustration is the French National Assembly. Though we will find its formal decision-making powers to be the most circumscribed of the four legislatures, still the Assembly's approval lay behind the authorization of over thirteen hundred statutes from 1959 through 1973. Nor have these statutes dealt simply with insignificant matters or narrow concerns. As a noted commentator has observed, "if one weighs their content, the parliaments of the Fifth Republic have enacted statutes of great importance for all aspects of national life."[5] This statement would apply equally to the other three legislatures.

Because the popularly elected legislature has been an institution central to the development of democratic systems, the constitutional or formal authority of the legislature to make decisions in these systems is ordinarily very great indeed. Let us take the American Congress to illustrate just a few dimensions of the authority and power that it and legislatures in most Western societies are capable of exercising. In the United States, the taxes that are required to finance the national budget account for a substantial portion of the gross national product (about 20 percent, provided for mainly out of citizens' pockets). For the most part, it has been the Congress which has had the final formal authority to accept, reject, or alter federal budgets and to determine how much each citizen will pay in taxes. The courts consistently have sustained Congressional authority in these areas. Congress' decisions on budgetary and tax matters alone help shape the whole range of our material lives; for example, our incomes, our housing, the quality of education, the availability of jobs and the types of jobs available, and the quality of our health care.

In addition, the legislature has authority to determine societal decisions in numerous areas outside those bearing mainly on the raising and using of taxes. The employment of these powers can also have serious implications, as legislation during the past decade on civil rights, crime control, and environmental pollution in the United States readily suggests. Also what could have a more immediate effect on a person's private life than the power to authorize military conscription whereby an individual may be sent away from his family and friends into a way of life totally foreign to his previous experience.

Because of the impact that decisions of the legislature can have on individual lives and on the life and spirit of the wider society in which individuals live, it is proper that we should want to know *how* this institution operates and, especially, the forces and pressures to which members in it respond. Such an examination is one of the purposes of this book. We will look at the behavior of legislators as they make decisions that affect how the legislature responds to the issues before society, and we will investigate some of the reasons that prompt legislators to behave the way they do.[6]

We will also use our study of the way legislators behave to help us achieve another objective. This is the provision of a base of knowledge that can aid us in evaluating and making some critical judgments about legislators and the way they act, especially members of the United States Congress.

This latter objective is of special relevance in the context of contemporary times. As we pointed out previously, the popularly elected legislature has been an integral part of the historical development of democratic systems in the Western world and is intended to be a key instrument in giving citizens a voice in the decision-making process. Yet increasingly the legislature has come under attack from a variety of sources as having perhaps lost the potential to act as an effective vehicle of democratic government. This view has often been expressed about Congress.[7]

One fundamental kind of criticism is that, despite being popularly elected, the Congress has not been sufficiently reflective of the general public, that many of its members have come mainly to be dominated by special interests, and that the decision-making structure within Congress has, itself, been undemocratic. Another element of the indictment is that the Congress has lost the ability to undertake positive action to solve the problems of contemporary society. As a consequence, it has either become subservient to Presidential leadership or has been capable of exerting power almost exclusively in the sense of frustrating and blocking proposals for positive action.

These criticisms, if valid, are substantial. They have led many people to ask, in the words of one author, "Can representative government do the job?"[8] Not only have many scholars and journalists been highly critical of Congress, but the general public also seems to share this view. During recent years, for example, national opinion polls have ordinarily recorded less than a majority of the American public as having confidence in the Congress. This figure dropped to below 30 percent in the wake of events surrounding Watergate.

It is in the context of such skepticism that it is essential to examine the criticisms that have been raised and to attempt to judge how valid these criticisms are. The descriptions and explanations of legislative behavior that we develop as the study proceeds should help us in this endeavor.

Although the primary object of our attention in this study is the United States Congress, our interest in the Congress as a representative legislature also leads us to want to know how it compares with other legislatures,[9] some of which are used as models for Congressional reform. As a consequence, we will bring into our analysis of the Congress the experience of three European legislatures. Which of these three legislatures we compare to the Congress will depend on the particular topic of inquiry and the availability of sufficient evidence to undertake reasonably sound comparisons.

One of the legislatures used for comparison is the British House of Commons. We selected this legislature because its practice, and particularly the practice of party responsibility, has frequently been cited as a model for Congressional reform. Inspection of the House of Commons can give us added perspective on the Congress and help us avoid parochial description, explanation, and evaluation of the Congress. The other two legislatures are the National Assembly of the French Fifth Republic and the West German Bundestag. Each of these legislatures is of interest not only in its own right, but also because in a number of respects each is a variant of both American practice and British practice (see Chapter 2). The experiences of these legislatures should thus help us gain further perspective on the operation of both the American Congress and the British House of Commons.

Some readers of this book will perhaps have little acquaintance with one or more of the four legislatures or the political systems of which they are a part. After outlining a framework in Chapter 1 to guide our analysis of legislators' behavior, we introduce the basic structure of the four legislatures and political systems in Chapters 2 and 3. The purpose of these chapters is to offer readers an overview of the formal workings of the legislatures and to provide background material for more focused description and analysis of legislators' behavior, which commences in Chapter 4. In Chapter 2, we sketch the constitutional powers of the legislatures, modes of election to the legislature, and the organization of the four legislatures. In Chapter 3, we examine a case study in policy-making for each of the political systems with special reference to the part played by the respective legislatures.

We then turn our attention to the major analytical subjects of the study. The first of these subjects concerns the influence political parties have on the decisions members of the Congress and the European legislatures make. How significant is one's party to the way members of Congress behave and what differences are there in this regard between members of Congress and members of major parties in the European legislatures? What factors help to explain differences in party behavior revealed by the American and European legislative experiences? Are the particular factors that shape party behavior unique to each legislature or are there significant commonalities across the four legislatures? We take up these questions in Chapters 4 and 5.

A second area of study concerns relations between the legislature and the executive in the policy-making process. What is the place of the four legislatures in the policy formulation, deliberation, and implementation stages of policy-making? Have legislatures become weak and subservient before the power of the executive, as some critics assert? Has legislative power, when utilized, been almost entirely "negative" in character (that is, blocking action) as others contend to be the case? Are some of the legislatures considerably more influential in the policy-making process and, if so, in what ways and why? How important are legislative committees as a source of legislative influence? Are they able, as is frequently argued in the context of Congressional politics, to frustrate executive leadership despite potential support for executive proposals on the floor? On the whole, what factors seem to determine how much influence the legislature and the executive exert and do these determinants bperate across the four systems, or are they different in each system? We take up such questions in Chapters 6, 7, and 8.

A third set of questions we address deals with how members of the Congress and of other legislatures compare insofar as their behavior toward interest groups is concerned. What strategies do interest groups use in attempting to influence the behavior of legislators? How successful are these strategies? Is the influence of interest groups on legislators practically unlimited, or are there limits to the extent to which legislators are likely to respond to pressure applied by interest groups? Are some legislatures more resistant to interest group pressures than others? What factors appear to determine the extent and limits of interest group influence and how does this relate to the representation of public opinion? We will investigate these questions in Chapter 9.

Building on the questions just outlined, the discussions of Chapters 4 through 9 have two overall objectives that complement one another. One objective is to describe in broad terms the place of the legislature in the decision-making process and how legislators behave toward major political forces such as their own party, the executive, and interest groups. The other objective of these chapters is to explain why legislators behave as they do.

In the process of addressing this second objective, we will draw upon four different approaches to analyze legislative behavior. These approaches are known as role theory, incentive theory, power theory, and systems analysis. Some introductory comments here about the four approaches will provide background material helpful to understanding both our general framework, which we present in the following chapter, and the discussions using the framework in Chapters 4 through 9.

In attempting to explain why legislators behave as they do, the four approaches center on different variables. Some of the approaches concentrate on the dispositions and orientations of the legislators themselves as the central variables that explain legislative behavior. Other approaches emphasize the kinds of resources that politically relevant actors use and the influence particular resources have on how legislators behave. Still other approaches focus on how the structures within which legislators operate are organized and the effect of that organization on how legislators behave. An analysis of legislative behavior needs to build on and encompass each of these approaches.

Role theory and incentive theory are two approaches that attempt to explain legislative behavior by reference to the dispositions and orientations of the legislators themselves. One of the central concerns of researchers using role theory has been to examine legislative behavior as a product of what legislators' roles are. The theory formally postulates that legislators' roles derive both from the expectations of others who are relevant to the legislator and from the legislators' own beliefs. As applied empirically by students of legislative politics, however, roles have usually been defined and described primarily in terms of legislators' own beliefs about what their roles are, that is, what they consider their job to be.[10]

There are many kinds of roles legislators may attempt to act out. For instance, of the variety of roles legislators can play, one kind of role is that of being a representative. But how ought a representative act? The answer to this question is not immediately obvious because there is no single feeling or belief as to how a representative should act. Rather, there is a number of different ideas about what a representative should do. For example, should a representative act mainly on his own judgment as a trustee, or should he act mainly on citizen opinion? If he acts on citizen opinion, should he use national opinion, the opinion of his constituency, or a combination of the two as a guide for his actions? Studies have shown that legislators from different legislatures, and even within the same legislature, do not answer questions such as these in a uniform way. That is, there are various ways legislators think they should play the role of representative. This is true regarding other roles, too. It is by reference to the legislator's own conception of the various roles he plays in being a legislator, what he believes his job to be, and how he feels a legislator ought to act that researchers applying role theory have attempted to understand how legislators behave and how the legislature works.

An assumption behind role theory, stated concisely by the authors of the *Legislative System*, is that

[A] significant proportion of legislators' behavior is role behavior, that this behavior is substantially congruent with their role concepts, and that insight into the workings of legislative bodies can therefore be gained by ascertaining their role concepts.[11]

By looking at legislators' own role concepts as these regard action toward others, such as constituents, interest groups, party, other legislators, or the executive, a great deal of insight into the workings of legislatures can be gained. Even so, there are other factors to be considered. Legislators' feelings about their roles must be looked at in relation to other variables, including other dispositions they may have as well as the characteristics of the particular situation in which they must act.

This point can be illustrated by reference to incentive theory. It is fairly easy to move from the idea behind role theory to incentive theory, which also emphasizes the motivations and orientations of legislators. Indeed, at many points the two approaches overlap. Incentive theory focuses on the needs or drives that lead men into politics and on the way these needs shape their behavior within a particular political institution, say, the legislature. Do legislators seek status or fame? Do they have strong desires to further particular policy programs? Do they become legislators solely to satisfy feelings of obligation to their party or community when no one else was available or acceptable? Or do they wish, as legislators, to further some great cause or ideology to which they have devoted much of their lives? These are just some of the needs (or incentives) that lead people to run for the legislature. The purpose of incentive theory is to uncover the relationship between the behavior of legislators and the motives that have led them into politics.[12] Like role theory, incentive theory emphasizes the motivations and perspectives of the legislators themselves in trying to explain legislative behavior, although it departs from role theory by delineating and focusing on a wide variety of different motives some of which are treated only implicitly in role theory. Still, both theories concentrate on forces inside the legislator himself—goals and attitudes—as opposed to theories which stress outside forces, such as interest group pressures.

Theories of power, on the other hand, stress the outside forces that press upon legislators and induce them to follow a certain path of action rather than other available alternatives. The outside forces acting upon a legislator may be another legislator or some group or person outside the legislature.

A critical question raised by power theorists is, "who gets what they want and why" (and how do they do it?).[13] Dahl expressed his own idea of power as follows: "A has power over B to the extent that he can get B to do something that B would not otherwise do."[14]

The focus of research on the part of those using the power framework is often on the resources (or power base) people have and the use of their resources to influence the behavior of an actor, for instance, a legislator. Generally the activation of these resources is what results in "exercising" power (as opposed to "having" power). A resource might be money to help run a campaign, votes to help win elections, or the ability to affect the fate of either a legislator's career advancement or his policy proposals in the legislature. Even one's reputation for power or expertise may be a power resource.

For a resource to be useful, it must be meaningful to the legislator. At minimum, the legislator himself must think that the resource is available and has some *relevance* for the achievement of his own goals and purposes. Despite this, studies of power generally have not focused on the goals and purposes or perceptions of legislators as explicitly as they have attempted to describe who was influential and the resource bases of the influential.[15]

A fourth approach by which legislative behavior can be examined is systems analysis. The aspect of systems analysis most relevant to our purpose is its focus on the transformation of demands made by individuals and groups (called inputs) into concrete kinds of activities by the political system (called outputs). Some types of outputs from legislatures are the activities of legislators as representatives, the substance of the policies or laws they agree upon, and the actions they undertake to oversee the executive and bureaucracy.[16]

In between the demands directed to the legislature and the outputs that the legislature produces is the legislature itself. One object of systems analysis is to discover what it is about the legislature that transforms demands into particular kinds of legislative decisions and activities. This question is somewhat similar to the one raised by power theorists, but while power theory looks to the resources or power of the various pertinent actors, systems analysis stresses more how the system is organized to meet demands placed on it. That is, how legislators act is seen to be a function partly of particular features of the organizational setting within which legislators operate. Examples of organizational factors that might affect legislative behavior are whether the political system is essentially a parliamentary or separation-of-powers system, the size of the legislature, the type of committee system the legislature uses, how parties are organized in the legislature, and the level of staffing available to legislators.[17]

As the above remarks suggest, the four approaches offer a number of variables to explain legislative behavior. However, broadly speaking, the variables can be categorized in terms of three kinds of factors lying behind how legislators behave. These are: the dispositions and orientations of the legislators themselves; the resources (power) of those making demands and their relationship to legislators' dispositions; and the particular organizational setting (the organization of both the broader political system and of the legislature itself) within which this relationship takes place and political responses occur.

The framework we present in the following chapter to help us understand why legislators behave toward others as they do builds upon these three factors. In turn, we will then use this framework in the analytical sections of Chapters 4 through 9 to help us account for legislators' behavior toward their party, the executive, and interest groups.

Our investigation of how legislators behave culminates in Chapter 10, which concentrates on one of the primary functions the legislature is supposed to serve. This is the function of representing citizen opinion in the decision-making process. Our attention focuses on the United States Congress and on comparing the Congress to an alternative representational system often advocated by critics of Congress. This is the party-responsibility system, especially as it has operated in Great Britain and the House of Commons. How has representation of the national citizenry in Congress compared to the level of opinion representation a party-responsibility system, like that of Great Britain, is capable of achieving? Has the Congress accomplished this end well or has it been deficient when placed alongside the party-responsibility alternative? This topic will lie at the heart of our discussion in Chapter 10.

Chapter 11 closes the analysis by providing a general summary. The summary serves to review the study in two ways. First, it recapitulates the major variables treated in the study. It brings together the variety of goals legislators pursue in combination with particular components of the political setting as these were found pertinent to understanding behavior in Congress and the European parliamentary bodies.

The summary also brings together the results of the analysis as they apply to certain key criticisms of the Congress. Here we find that the criticisms do not accurately portray either the contemporary record of Congress or how the Congress functions as compared to the major alternatives the critics have proposed. This is not to suggest that the critics are wholly wrong (they are not in some areas and in some cases) or that the Congress is completely free of faults and needs no change. It is to suggest that the critics of Congress have tended to exaggerate, sometimes greatly, the problems they have cited and have simultaneously depreciated a number of the contributions the Congress has made. We will see, too, that the critics have not recognized the extent to which some of the problems they wish to avoid are possibly more inherent in the institutional and organizational alternatives they have proposed.

Notes

[1] See the discussions in James Clarke Adams, *The Quest for Democratic Law* (New York: Thomas Y. Crowell, 1970); Gerhard Loewenberg, ed., *Modern Parliaments: Change or Decline* (Chicago: Aldine-Atherton, 1971), pp. 3-4; idem, "Comparative Legislative Research," in *Comparative Legislative Behavior: Frontiers of Research*, ed. Samuel Patterson and John Wahlke (New York: John Wiley and Sons, 1972).
[2] See Hanna Pitkin, *The Concept of Representation* (Berkeley: University of California Press, 1967), and A. H. Birch, *Representation* (New York: Praeger, 1971).
[3] If they are open and competitive, we would regard primaries within a party as a substitute for competition between parties.
[4] Fred W. Riggs, "Legislative Structures: Some Thoughts on Elected National Assemblies," in *Legislatures in Comparative Perspective,* ed. Allan Kornberg (New York: David McKay, 1973), p. 42.
[5] Henry W. Ehrmann, *Politics in France* (Boston: Little, Brown, 1971), p. 284.
[6] Our interest thus centers principally on the individual legislator or inferences we can make about individual legislators from larger sets or subsets of legislators. Understanding adequately the decisions of the legislature as an institution requires that we focus first on individual units of the legislature—what the individual legislators do, how they do it, and why they individually behave as they do. For a similar view see: John Wahlke and Heinz Eulau, eds., *Legislative Behavior: A Reader in Theory and Research* (Glencoe, Ill.: The Free Press, 1959), especially pp. 3-8 and p. 242; Roderick Bell, "Notes for a Theory of Legislative Behavior," in *Comparative Legislative Systems*, ed. Herbert Hirsch and M. Donald Hancock (New York: The Free Press, 1971), especially

p. 22; J. W. Thibaut and H. H. Kelley, *The Social Psychology of Groups* (New York: John Wiley and Sons, 1959), p. 5; James Buchanan, "An Individualistic Theory of Political Process," in *Varieties of Political Theory*, ed. David Easton (Englewood Cliffs, N. J.: Prentice-Hall, 1966). For a different position on the central problems and priorities in the study of legislatures, see Robert A. Packenham, "Legislatures and Political Development," in *Legislatures in Developmental Perspective*, ed. Allan Kornberg and Lloyd Muslof (Durham, N. C.: Duke University Press, 1970), pp. 521-82.

[7]A listing of major literature making these criticisms is presented in the bibliographic note at the end of this book.

[8]Thomas K. Finletter, *Can Representative Government Do the Job?* (New York: Reynal and Hitchcock, 1945).

[9]An excellent review and bibliography on the meaning and advantages of the comparative approach are found in the discussion and citations of Arend Lijphart, "Comparative Politics and the Comparative Method," *American Political Science Review* 65 (September 1971): 682–93.

[10]See Roger Davidson, *Role of the Congressman* (New York: Pegasus, 1969); John Wahlke, et al., *The Legislative System: Explorations in Legislative Behavior* (New York: John Wiley and Sons, 1962); and Allan Kornberg, *Canadian Legislative Behavior: A Study of the 25th Parliament* (New York: Holt, Rinehart and Winston, 1967), especially pp. 105-13. See also Edwin Thomas and Bruce Biddle, "The Nature and History of Role Theory," in *Role Theory: Concepts and Research*, ed. Bruce Biddle and Edwin Thomas (New York: John Wiley and Sons, 1966), pp. 3-19.

[11]Wahlke et al., *The Legislative System*, p. 29. See also Davidson, *Role of the Congressman*.

[12]The first full-fledged presentation of incentive theory can be found in James L. Payne, *Patterns of Conflict in Colombia* (New Haven, Conn.: Yale University Press, 1968). See, also, Payne, *Incentive Theory and Political Process: Motivation and Leadership in the Dominican Republic* (Lexington, Mass.: D.C. Heath and Company, 1972); Oliver H. Woshinsky, *The French Deputy: Incentives and Behavior in the National Assembly* (Lexington, Mass.: D. C. Heath and Company, 1973); and James Payne and Oliver Woshinsky, "Incentives for Political Participation," *World Politics* 24 (July 1972): 518-46. For another work which takes a very similar approach, see James Barber, *The Lawmakers* (New Haven, Conn.: Yale University Press, 1965).

[13]This is similar to the title of Harold Lasswell's classic *Politics: Who Gets What, When, How?* (New York: McGraw-Hill, 1936). Lasswell and Abraham Kaplan in *Power and Society* (New Haven, Conn.: Yale University Press, 1950) define the role of political science as an empirical discipline as the "study of the shaping and sharing of power" (p. XIV). See also Max Weber, *The Theory of Social and Economic Organization*, ed. Talcott Parsons (Glencoe, Ill.: The Free Press, 1968).

[14]Robert A. Dahl, "The Concept of Power," *Behavioral Science* 2 (July 1957): 202-3; see, also, his article on "Power" in the *International Encyclopedia of the Social Sciences*, vol. 12, where he states, "At the most general level, power terms in modern social science refer to subsets of relations among social units such that the behaviors of one or more units (the responsive units—R) depend in some circumstances on the behavior of other units (the controlling units—C)" (p. 407). Note especially the bibliography in the *IESS* article.

[15]An overview of some of the key literature utilizing the power approach and an assessment of the utility of power in empirical analysis is found in James March, "The Power of Power," in ed. Easton *Varieties of Political Theory*, pp. 39-70.

[16]A general presentation of systems theory, as it applies to the inputs and outputs of political structures, is found in David Easton, *A Systems Analysis of Political Life* (New York: John Wiley and Sons, 1965). For use of systems analysis in organizing knowledge about the Congress, see Leroy N. Rieselbach, *Congressional Politics* (New York: McGraw-Hill, 1973).

[17]Leroy N. Rieselbach, ed., *The Congressional System: Notes and Readings* (Belmont, Calif.: Wadsworth, 1970), pp. 12–14.

Chapter 1
A Theoretical Overview

In the last two decades, political scientists have sought to create a more conceptually systematic, dynamic, and empirically based comparative method of analysis. Some have focused on whole political systems; others have sought to compare political sub-units (for example, parties, interest groups, bureaucracy, and so on) or processes (for example, political socialization, political development, and the like). Noticeably few have been cross-national studies of legislatures, and as Gerhard Loewenberg commented in a review of the literature on non-American legislatures, "No common theory or set of concepts is accepted in legislative research and despite repeated appeals for 'accelerated theoretical advance,' little effort has been devoted to that end."[1]

Wahlke and Eulau's observation is still pertinent:

Research on legislative behavior has been disproportionately sensitive to problems of technique. . . . Yet, the most sophisticated technical developments . . . are meaningless unless research findings are presented in a theoretically, or at least conceptually, viable framework which will give more than *ad hoc* significance to the great variety of factors that constitute the legislative process.[2]

The purpose of this chapter is to outline a framework that can help to organize knowledge about legislative behavior in the four systems we will consider. In developing this framework, our desire is to provide a mechanism that will integrate a set of pertinent variables and will also allow us, during the course of the study, to tie an extensive body of findings and differing approaches on legislative politics together from the research of others along with our own.

How a legislator behaves toward the actors and groups surrounding him is obviously a complex phenomenon. However, at least in part, a legislator's behavior toward other actors can be viewed as a product of his own goals and attitudes and the way these goals and attitudes orient him to other actors within a given political setting.

As this statement implies, an analysis of legislative behavior must consider a number of factors. First, it must consider factors having to do with the legislator personally. In our study these factors center on the legislator's own goals and attitudes, or dispositions. A second factor that analysis must consider is how the legislator's dispositions orient him to other actors desiring a favorable legislative response. This, in turn, can be influenced by a third consideration: the organization of the surrounding political setting within which legislative responses occur. How the surrounding setting is organized can not only affect a legislator's orientation toward other actors but also his capacity to act on the goals and attitudes that motivate him.

One factor that is central to an understanding of how a legislator acts toward others is his own dispositions. Dispositions are the motivations that underlie human behavior, the basic goals, purposes, attitudes, and feelings that point and move people in various directions. In a sense, they are the foci around which each legislator organizes his political life and his responses to other individuals and groups.[3]

A variety of different dispositions can move and shape how a legislator acts. We distinguish three general types of dispositions: ambition, or status, dispositions; affective, or identicative, dispositions; and normative dispositions. Each of these is pertinent to our analysis.

Ambition, the first of the dispositions, can take an economic (private gain), social, or political status form. Political ambition, in particular, has been thought by some to be the principal motive lying behind how a legislator acts.[4] In its political form, which we will focus upon, a legislator's actions can be seen as arising out of a concern for his or her political career and a desire to further that career. A popular illustration familiar to most readers is the argument that members of Congress often key how they act to the needs of their major campaign contributors because of their own need for such contributions to win elections and remain in office. Another illustration is the notion that members of the House of Commons usually vote loyally behind their parliamentary party because such behavior is necessary to attain important political office.

We will investigate some of the ways political ambition might help us understand the way a legislator behaves toward other actors, including his party, the executive, and interest groups. Our examination will take into account two aspects of political ambition. These are career survival and career advancement. By career survival (for a legislator) we mean the desire to hold or maintain a place (seat) in the legislature. Successful selection to membership is, of course, also a precondition for the pursuit of goals originating in the other various dispositions within the legislator's framework. By career advancement, we mean the legislator's desire to raise his political status —that is, to secure a "higher" (more preferred or powerful) political office within the legislature or the executive.[5]

Legislators are probably not driven solely by calculations and goals relating to their own career ambitions. A second kind of disposition that might move a legislator is *affective* or *identicative* in nature. This disposition is based on feelings of friendship (or dislike) for another individual, or it can be based on a sense of identification with and of belonging to particular groups of persons or organizations. Such feeling for others may well influence a legislator's behavior, career motives aside. And, while affective feelings may enter explicitly into the legislator's calculations as to how he should behave, they may also prompt an almost instinctive or reflexive kind of a response. One legislator's comments about relations among his fellow colleagues illustrates the relevance the affective disposition, even if only one facet of it, can have: "Those who don't drink and don't socialize with the others are respected, but there is no camaraderie. They are not as effective."[6]

Study of a legislator's affective attachments to others can encompass a number of areas. Legislators not only have friendships both inside and outside the legislature, but a legislator's background and socialization experiences with various groups (such as party, race, religious, or regional groupings) may produce feelings of strong identification that can influence how he behaves. Of the various friendships and identifications legislators have, attention has been focused on their sense of identification with their party and party colleagues and the bearing such feelings may have on their behavior. Party identification will also be a principal object of our attention.

As suggested above, affective attachments to a group of people, such as party identification, imply that the legislator sees the group as more than a vehicle for achieving career goals. These attachments also carry a meaning for the legislator beyond the policy principles for which the group or organization stands. Although career and policy motives may also be reasons for which the legislator supports the group, and may even help to produce identification, they differ from a sense of identification with or of belonging to the group. That is, the legislator's feelings of belonging and of being a part of the group may itself shape his response toward that group.

Although we contend that a legislator's affective attachments are analytically distinct from his political career calculations or policy commitments, they can be quite difficult to isolate for investigation of their impact on political behavior.[7] When we come to analyze them, we will utilize both direct and indirect measures in an effort to show that affective attachments to a particular organization or group of people lead a legislator to move in a particular direction more so than political career calculations or policy goals would dictate.

A third type of disposition is *normative* or *ideological* in nature. This set deals with the legislator's views about how he should act—his commitments to or beliefs in certain principles or ideas as well as the criteria for justifying the action he takes. Among other considerations, this disposition has to do with the desire to make good public policy.

Included here are the legislator's own attitudes regarding what the goals of public policy ought to be.[8] For example, the legislator may hold the attitude that government should generally give priority to redistributing wealth or, more specifically, that government ought to see to it that no person goes hungry or that rates of taxation be made more progressive. Whether general or specific, the point is that the legislator's attitudes about the goals of these as well as other policies may help direct his behavior on the various issues and demands coming before him.[9]

Interacting with such attitudes is the concern, more or less important depending on the legislator, that the policies he backs be supportable by information and expertise. In modern, developed societies, reference to information and expertise is often central to justifying policy stances, both to oneself and to others. Information (and the organization and presentation of that information) is usually critical to support or deny the claim that there is a problem to be solved. Information is also critical to discovering various alternatives and defending a particular alternative as the best solution to a problem. Our contention is that in attempting to justify policy positions, many legislators, if not all, are moved to seek information (and to require information from other legislators or groups outside the legislature) either to develop a rationality for or to confirm the rationality of the positions they take. As a consequence of this disposition, factors such as who controls information and expertise or whom the legislator perceives to be expert, can become quite important to the way the legislator behaves towards others.[10]

Also part of the normative disposition is the legislator's beliefs about how government *ought* to operate. That is, aside from a particular policy a legislator wants to see adopted, he may have a commitment as to how (that is, the proper procedures through which) that policy is to be adopted and the proper "role" for him to play.[11] For example, he may believe that the legislature ought to play a dominant role in the lawmaking process, or he may feel that the executive should dominate. He may think that a legislator should support his party; on the other hand, he may feel that a legislator should act as a delegate from his district. Such normative commitments a legislator has to the "roles" of various positions and institutions can shape how he views his relationship to others and how he ought to behave toward others.

Of course, the role expectations of others may influence the legislator's own conceptions and how he behaves. By way of socialization, for example, the legislator himself may have come to believe in certain roles that fit the expectations others have. In such cases it would make little difference whether one investigated the legislator's own role concepts or, instead, the role expectations of others.

However, a legislator may adopt others' role expectations not because he has been socialized into them but because meeting others' expectations might be relevant to achieving goals that stem from his career ambitions, affective attachments, or policy attitudes. For example, if behaving loyally to his legislative party is expected in order to attain career survival and advancement, the legislator may adopt and behave according to a party-oriented role in order to further these other goals. In such a case, however, we need to examine these other goals rather than focus solely on the legislator's role conceptions if we are adequately to uncover why the legislator behaves as he does.

As is true with each of the goals then, a legislator's role conceptions are distinguishable from the other goals he pursues, and it is quite possible for conflict to occur among them. For instance, a legislator may believe his role should be to act as delegate from his district but may simultaneously identify with a particular group, such as his legislative party, whose interests conflict with those of his district on a particular set of issues. In such an instance of conflict, one can expect a legislator to follow a different, less uniform pattern of behavior than he would if his dispositions reinforced or complemented one another.

Thus, our analysis of behavior will not focus on one disposition but on a variety of different dispositions. Our reference will be to three kinds of dispositions based on political ambition, affective orientation, and normative outlook. Within these general types, our analysis will concentrate more specifically on the relevance of legislators' desires for career survival and advancement (ambition dispositions), their feelings of party identification (an affective disposition), and their policy attitudes, desires to make informed decisions, and role conceptions (normative dispositions).

In examining the three dispositions during the course of the study, we will bring together a combination of different types of data and evidence. Where possible, we will use systematic interview or questionnaire surveys of legislators. However, evidence of this kind, while available, is not plentiful. As a consequence, our investigation will also rely on other kinds of evidence. For example, we will utilize published statements of individual legislators or groups of legislators as well as judgments of respected analysts. Sometimes we will also need to discern the effects of particular variables by indirect means. For instance, in the absence of direct knowledge about a disposition from surveys, it might be possible to indicate the disposition indirectly by certain kinds of experiences legislators have had in the past about which knowledge is available. It is important to note that the use of such indicators will require us to infer a link between the indicator and the disposition. As we do this, we will provide support for the inferences we make in the base of the study.

If the three dispositions shape a legislator's behavior, his behavior toward other actors and groups in the political system (party colleagues, public opinion, interest groups, and the executive) should result from the relationship or connection these actors and groups have to his dispositions. As Lowi has put it, "The types of relationships to be found among people are determined by their expectations—by what they hope to achieve or get from relating to others."[12]

The relationship another actor has to the legislator's dispositions, and the legislator's resultant behavior, may or may not involve outside inducements. If induced, the legislator's behavior can be seen as an outgrowth of rewards or sanctions that attach to or are controlled by the other actor. In turn, the rewards or sanctions gain meaning from the legislator's affective, career, or normative dispositions. For example, a legislator may decide to support the policies of another actor in order to avoid social pressures from colleagues in groups with which he identifies or in order not to create strains in his friendships. As another illustration, the legislator may act supportively because he thinks such support might have implications for certain career goals that he wants to achieve.

But how a legislator behaves toward others need not be predicated on outside inducement. For example, a legislator may decide to support another actor not because he anticipates rewards or fears sanctions but because there is a broad commonality between his own policy views and the policy objectives of the other actor. Or, the legislator may support a certain actor simply because he believes it is a proper part of his role to do so.

Whether action is induced by particular rewards and sanctions or is essentially volunteered, the question remains: do the legislator's dispositions orient him to the actor so as to raise the probability of supportive behavior? If they do, then by definition the bases for the legislator's support (either the particular rewards and sanctions or the reasons for voluntary support) can be viewed as resources of that actor. They are resources because they help the actor gain a favorable response from the legislator. However, it is important to note that in either case these resources gain meaning from the legislator's own dispositions and the goals and attitudes flowing from these dispositions. Indeed, it is not only the legislator's own goals that are relevant but also his perception of how the other actors relate to the achievement of these goals.[13]

As the legislator deals with the various pressures and objectives of the actors and groups surrounding him, the decision-making process can become quite complex. Partly through conscious thought and partly without reflection, he will need to weigh priorities and evaluate alternatives. His own purposes, which stem from his dispositions, may reinforce each other, or they may contradict one another (and the legislator may not give equal weight to each of the dispositions). Added to this, he will often have to react to many different issues almost simultaneously.

Because of these complexities, the legislator may seek shorthand methods to make decisions. One of a number of methods helpful to accomplishing this end is known as cueing. Cueing is when a legislator looks to (or "cues" upon) another, frequently other legislators, to decide how to act on a particular issue or set of issues.

Consistent with the idea of a legislator's dispositions mentioned above, whom the legislator decides to cue upon can be seen as a consequence of how his dispositions orient him to other legislators. As an example, let us take a member of the House of Representatives and assume that he is motivated in part by a desire to survive elections back home, a sense of identification with his party, a certain attitude about policy, and a desire to make informed decisions. If these motives are relevant to his behavior, we would expect them to play an important part in defining his pattern of cueing. Hence, if he uses cueing in a particular policy area, we ought to find him turning mainly to other legislators of his party whom he perceives face rather similar election problems to his back home, have a broadly similar policy attitude, and have greater expertise than he has in the policy area. Since characteristics such as these are relevant to the legislator's own goals, cueing on other legislators who combine these characteristics enables him to act consistently on his goals without having to become highly involved in the particular policy area.

This illustration returns us to the overall point that understanding a legislator's behavior toward other actors requires specification and knowledge both of the legislator's own dispositions and of the other actor's particular relevancy to the goals and attitudes that stem from these dispositions. This is true whether a legislator is cueing, otherwise reacting to other legislators, or responding to actors outside the legislature.

At the same time, relations between a legislator and other actors do not exist in a vacuum. They exist in the context of a political setting that itself can affect how the legislator behaves.[14]

A central element of the political setting is the kind of political structure within which the legislator operates and his response occurs. The structure can shape a legislator's behavior in two principal ways. First, how the structure is organized can affect his capacity to act effectively on the goals he wants to achieve. Second, again in light of the legislator's goals, the way the structure is organized can affect the costs and benefits to the legislator of making certain decisions as opposed to others.

There are various ways political structures differ that can be relevant to the legislator's *capacity* to act effectively on his goals. How much authority the legislature has to make decisions differs across both legislatures and different policy areas. Also, power to make certain kinds of decisions within the legislature (over agenda, the gathering of information, the introduction and amending of proposed legislation, and so on) is distributed in different ways across different legislatures and different policy areas. The mode of legislative party and committee organization also differs across legislatures; so do resources given to legislators, such as staffing.

The level and distribution of formal powers, the particular modes of legislative organization that prevail, and the resources given individual legislators can have an impact on whether the legislature enables them to pursue certain goals effectively or not. To illustrate, the extent to which a legislature provides its members with the capacity to gather and coordinate information independently of executive or interest group input can affect how dependent a legislator becomes on these other actors and, therefore, how he will relate to these actors. In this as well as other respects detailed in the study, by virtue of the presence of particular powers, modes of organization, and other resources, a legislator may be able to act toward others in ways that would not be possible, despite his goals, if the powers, modes of organization, or resources were not available to him.

A second way the political structure can be relevant in light of the legislator's goals is through its influence on the *costs and benefits* of the decisions he must make. For example, suppose a legislator of the majority party knows that by voting against his party's position on an important policy issue, the party may be forced to leave government office (as is possible in some parliamentary systems). In such a case, the costs to the legislator of a decision to vote against his party would be rather different than if his vote meant only that the particular piece of legislation he disliked would be defeated. For this reason, as we will detail more fully in Chapter 4 and subsequent chapters, whether the legislator operates in the context of a parliamentary system or instead operates in a separation-of-powers system can be quite pertinent to how he behaves.

The structure of the system can affect the costs and benefits of a legislator's decisions in other ways as well. It can do so particularly by how it allots control over certain rewards, such as career rewards, pertinent to the legislator. Control over the achievement of important career objectives varies from structure to structure. To illustrate, the seniority system in Congress has divorced advancement to committee chairmanships from the control of party leaders in Congress and from the President, while advancement to preferred political offices has not been divorced from the control of equivalent actors in Great Britain. Quite obviously, the extent to which the structure gives or denies others control over the achievement of important career goals, and to whom it gives control, can have ramifications for a legislator's relationships with other actors by virtue of its influence on the costs and benefits that may result from how he behaves toward these actors.

At this juncture, it would be useful to bring together the points outlined above. The approach we use assumes, as is implicit in most approaches, that behavior is a joint result of characteristics of the person and of his situation or environment. The contribution of both the person and his situation must be considered if analysis is to be adequate.

As Figure 1.1 suggests, knowledge of what a legislator wishes to achieve is basic to understanding his behavior. It is not ordinarily the case that a single disposition, such as political ambition, underlies legislative behavior. Some legislators may individually be motivated by one particular disposition, but in the aggregate, a variety of different dispositions moves legislators to act as they do. Along with political ambition, we will also look to dispositions having an affective and normative character.

According to Figure 1.1, a legislator's behavior toward other actors can be viewed as an outgrowth of his own dispositions and how these dispositions orient him toward other actors within the context of a given political setting. The impact of the setting can be examined in terms of the capacity it affords the legislator to act effectively on his goals and the way it influences the costs and benefits that accrue from alternative

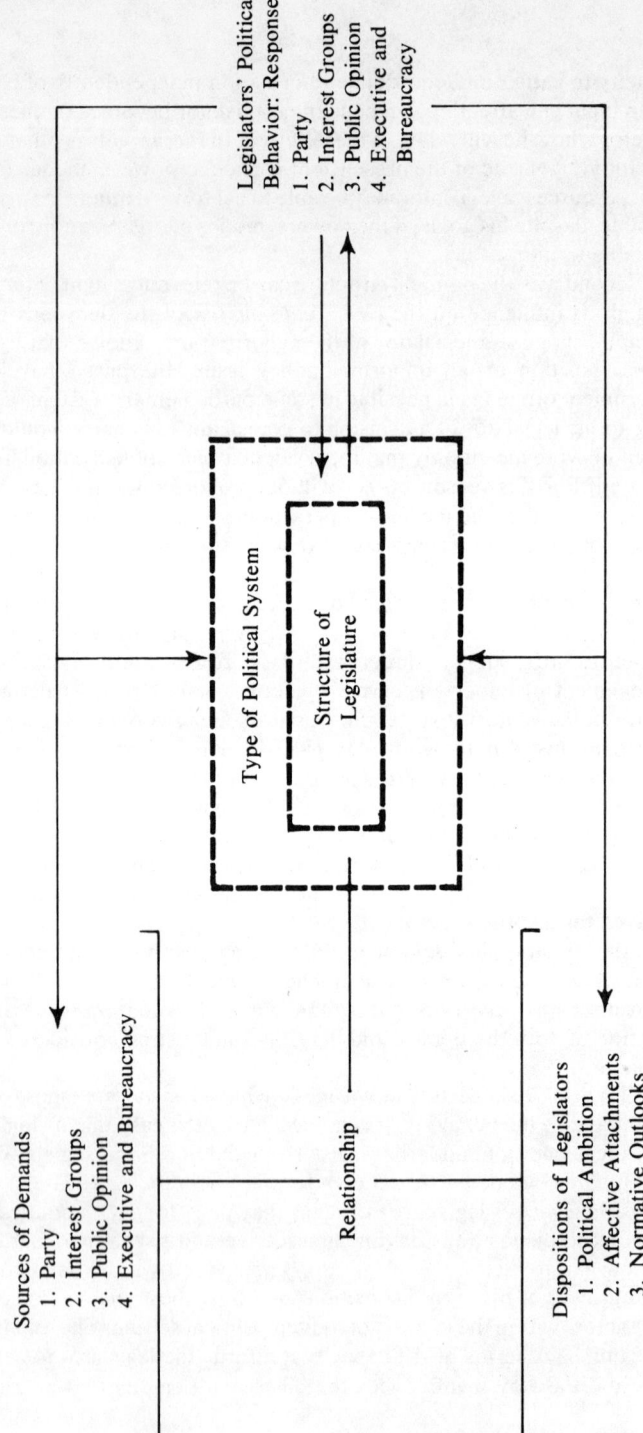

Figure 1.1
A Framework for the Study of Legislative Behavior

courses of action he may take. Drawing upon these ideas, the study will investigate legislators' behavior toward their party, the executive and bureaucracy, and external opinion.

There are also various feedback paths in Figure 1.1. We do not treat feedback in detail in this study, but we wish to underline the point that relationships among the main factors are dynamic and ongoing. A legislator's behavior can influence which political actors will make demands on him and can even affect his own dispositions.[15] It can also affect the nature of the political system and/or the legislature itself. Illustrations may be cited to clarify each of the feedback paths. The legislator may vote consistently probusiness, thus leading some actors in the surrounding setting, such as labor pressure groups, to minimize direct lobbying efforts at him to avoid wasting time. To illustrate the second path, a legislator who initially votes with his party for career reasons ultimately may come to develop a feeling of affective attachment to his fellow party members as a result of his actions. In turn, this may work further to intensify behavior supportive of his party. Finally, in some instances, the results of a legislator's behavior may affect the relatively stable dimensions of the political and legislative structure such as the resources that will be made available to legislators. The Legislative Reorganization Act of 1946 along with the Budget Reorganization Act of 1974 in the United States and the changing committee structure in the House of Commons in Britain in the latter 1960s are examples of legislative actions that, in varying degrees, altered the resources legislators would have available to engage in behavior appropriate to the realization of their individual goals.

Notes

[1] Gerhard Loewenberg, "Comparative Legislative Research" in *Comparative Legislative Behavior: Frontiers of Research,* ed. Samuel Patterson and John Wahlke (New York: John Wiley, 1972), p.5. Several years earlier, Robert Peabody similarly noted of legislative research that "Despite...significant advances, political scientists have not yet produced a conceptually clear and comprehensive theory of Congressional behavior," in Ralph K. Huitt and Robert L. Peabody, *Congress: Two Decades of Analysis* (New York: Harper & Row, 1969) p.3.

[2] John Wahlke and Heinz Eulau, eds., *Legislative Behavior: A Reader in Theory and Research* (Glencoe, Ill.: The Free Press, 1959), p.355.

[3] For citation and a general discussion of some of the relevant literature, see articles on "Attitude," "Personality," and "Self" in the *International Encyclopedia of the Social Sciences (IESS),* ed. David L. Sills (New York: Macmillan and The Free Press, 1968). See also M. Brewster Smith, "Personality in Politics," *Political Research and Political Theory,* ed. Oliver Garceau (Cambridge, Mass.: Harvard University Press, 1968). For a summary of neobehavioral literature dealing with variables intervening between the stimulus and the response, see Albert Bandura and Richard H. Walters, *Social Learning and Personality Development* (New York: Holt, Rinehart and Winston, 1963). See also Arthur Kalleberg, "Concept Formation in Normative and Empirical Studies," *American Political Science Review* 63 (March 1969): 26-39.

[4] See Joseph A. Schlesinger, *Ambition and Politics: Political Careers in the United States* (Chicago: Rand McNally, 1960); David Mayhew, *Congress: The Electoral Connection* (New Haven, Conn.: Yale University Press, 1974); and Morris Fiorina, *Representatives, Roll Calls, and Constituencies* (Lexington, Mass.: D. C. Heath, 1974).

[5] The career advancement motive parallels the goals Fenno refers to as attempting to gain and maintain political "influence," "power," or "prestige" within or beyond the legislature. See Richard F. Fenno, Jr., *Congressmen in Committees* (Boston: Little, Brown, 1973), pp. 1-5, 139.

[6] John Wahlke et al., *The Legislative System: Explorations in Legislative Behavior* (New York: John Wiley and Sons, 1962), p. 216.

[7] It may be that the principal significance of affective attachments is their reinforcement of other dispositions.

[8] For a view of this in terms of a general value scheme or outlook on life which guides response, see Milton Rokeach, "Attitudes: Nature," *IESS,* vol. 1, p. 454-55; idem, *The Nature of Human Values* (New York: The

Free Press, 1973); for an interpretation of ideology as a style of approach rather than a specified set of central values, see Robert D. Putnam, "Studying Elite Political Culture: The Case of 'Ideology'," *American Political Science Review* 65 (September 1971): 651-81.

[9]See Oliver Woshinsky, *The French Deputy: Incentives and Behavior in the National Assembly* (Lexington, Mass.: D.C. Heath, 1973), especially pp. 61-67; John W. Kingdon, *Congressmen's Voting Decisions* (New York: Harper & Row, 1973), especially 72-79, 245-54; and Robert A. Bernstein and William W. Anthony, "The ABM Issue in the Senate, 1968-1970: The Importance of Ideology," *American Political Science Review* 68 (September 1974): 1198-1206.

[10]See, for example, Donald Matthews and James Stimson, "Decisionmaking by U.S. Representatives: A Preliminary Model," in *Political Decision-Making*, ed. S. Sydney Ulmer (New York: Van Nostrand Reinhold, 1970), pp. 14-43.

[11]Definitions and methods of measuring legislators' role conceptions can be found in Wahlke et al., *The Legislative System*, and Roger Davidson, *The Role of the Congressman* (New York: Pegasus, 1969).

[12]Theodore Lowi, "American Business, Public Policy, Case Studies, and Political Theory," *World Politics* 16 (July 1964): 688.

[13]For a general discussion of the importance of perceptions, see Bernard Berelson and Gary Steiner, *Human Behavior: An Inventory of Scientific Findings* (New York: Harcourt, Brace and World, 1964), Chapter 4 and pp. 130-31 (which cites additional sources), and Floyd H. Allport, *Theories of Perception and the Concept of Structure* (New York: John Wiley and Sons, 1955).

[14]Richard F. Fenno, "The Internal Distribution of Influence: The House," in *The Congress and America's Future*, ed. David B. Truman (Englewood Cliffs, N.J.: Prentice-Hall, 1973), pp. 63-68, and Philip M. Williams, *The French Parliament: Politics in the Fifth Republic* (New York: Praeger, 1968).

[15]Leon Festinger, *A Theory of Cognitive Dissonance* (Stanford, Calif.: Stanford University Press, 1957); M. Brewster Smith, Jerome S. Bruner, and Robert White, *Opinions and Personality* (New York: John Wiley and Sons, 1956).

Chapter 2
The Institutional Setting

Before we can discuss and understand the legislative behavior of members of the Congress and of the European parliaments, it is important to describe the basic structures and processes within which that behavior takes place. As we shall show in the study, the structure, organization, and formal legislative powers characteristic of a particular legislature have an effect on how legislators act, particularly how they respond to pressures and appeals from the executive, bureaucracy, interest groups, public opinion, and their own parties.

This chapter will provide an overview of the structural and procedural aspects of the four legislatures. The main categories of discussion will be: the constitutional powers and limitations of the legislatures, the election process, and the organization of the legislature, including a description of the basic features of the parties and committees. We will discuss the United States Congress first and then turn to the Western European legislatures, drawing comparisons with the Congress and with each other. The discussion in this chapter combined with a description of the dynamics of the policy processes seen in the case studies of the next chapter should help to give the reader a "feel" for the four legislatures. In so doing, the two chapters also provide basic material helpful to a more focused analysis of legislative behavior, which commences in Chapter 4.

The United States Congress

Congress and the Constitution: Introduction and Overview of Formal Powers

The allocation of formal powers in the written Constitution of the United States placed the bicameral legislature at the center of the government. It is not without significance that the *first* article of the Constitution states: "all legislative powers. . .shall be vested in a Congress." The Senate and House of Representatives, are relatively equal in authority[1]. Both must concur, along with Presidential approval (except in instances where two-thirds of each house, voting separately, override a Presidential veto), before proposed legislation is enacted. The Constitution specifically *delegated* numerous significant powers to the Congress, particularly in the area of domestic policy, including: the right to lay and collect taxes; to borrow on the credit of the United States; to coin money and regulate standards of weights and measures; to establish post offices and post roads; to create and support an army and navy; to regulate commerce with foreign nations and among the states; to create federal courts; to declare war, ratify treaties, and establish a government for the capital district. In addition Congress was given *implied powers* to make any laws "necessary and proper" for the execution of those delegated powers.[2] Laws enacted by Congress are supreme over the laws of state governments, and both state and federal judges are obligated to strike down state policies that conflict with federal laws.

Although the powers of Congress are extensive, they are not unlimited. Specific prohibitions on Congressional action are made in the Constitution and in the Bill of Rights to safeguard individual rights. Not only was this kind of formal limitation placed upon Congress by the Founding Fathers in the hope of preventing tyranny, but also a government of separation of powers with checks and balances was created. This dispersal of power, checking power with power, ambition with ambition, was regarded as the means to bring about genuinely free and responsible government. The separation-of-powers system emphasizes both separation of personnel and overlapping powers.

The separation of personnel can be seen clearly in the differing tenure and constituencies to which members of government are responsible. The President is elected nationally by popular vote (formally through an electoral college) to a four-year term; Senators are elected to six-year terms in statewide popular elections; and House members are elected to two-year terms from districts whose sizes are based on population distribution within the states. The election for the Presidency is always held on the same day and year as elections for Congress. Every two years, there is an "off-year" election for the House of Representatives and approximately one-third of the Senate when the Presidency is not at stake. Federal judges are appointed for life by the President and confirmed by the Senate.

The overlapping of powers also operates as a check and balance within the system. Although *"all* legislative powers" were vested in the legislature by the Constitution, that same Constitution provided resources for the President in the policy-making process. The President is required to give Congress information on the state of the Union and recommend measures he considers necessary and expedient. He may veto bills enacted by Congress. In the area of foreign policy, the Constitution gives both the President and Congress potentially expansive powers, depending on how they are interpreted. The President makes treaties, receives ambassadors, and is "commander in chief " of the armed forces. Congress was given the power to declare war and organize and regulate military personnel, and the Senate must ratify treaties. Since all appropriations must go through Congress, considerable influence can be exerted on foreign policy via the power of the purse.

The President is both chief of state and chief of government. He is not, however, politically responsible to the legislature. That is, he is not elected by either or both houses of the legislature, and he is not dependent upon the legislature for continuance in office; however, the President can "be removed from office on impeachment for and conviction of treason, bribery, or other high crimes and misdemeanors." Constitutionally the House brings the impeachment charges to the Senate, which has sole power to try impeachments. The concurrence of two-thirds of the Senators present is necessary for conviction. The placement of the impeachment process in Congress instead of in the Supreme Court indicates the political rather than simply juridical nature of impeachment. The recent impeachment inquiry of President Nixon brought this seldom-used but awesome Congressional power to public attention and raised numerous questions regarding its proper interpretation and use.[3] For example, the term "high misdemeanors" is interpreted by some to include misconduct in office, gross impropriety, and the like, while others insist that it is limited to strictly criminal offenses. The proper use of impeachment is also questioned because some fear that the abuse of that power by Congress would undermine the separation-of-powers system by placing the Presidency in a position of complete subservience to the Congress.

The federal judiciary also participates in the policy-making process by overseeing Congressional and state laws and executive actions to determine their constitutionality. In some cases, judicial interpretations, for example in the desegregation decisions, have had the effect of establishing national policy. Congress, on the other hand, has the power to create as well as to regulate the size, composition, and jurisdiction of the lower courts. In addition, it can regulate the size, composition, and appellate jurisdiction of the Supreme Court. Federal judges are also subject to the impeachment process.

Thus, though the Constitution placed the Congress in a central position to deal with matters involving domestic policy and gave it important powers in foreign policy, in neither area can it act alone. Effective government demands coordination of both houses of the legislature and all branches of government. While there is legal separation of powers, there is at the same time clear interdependence of the three branches in establishing effective public policy. The Constitution of 1787 did not create a system of separate powers; rather, it attempted to create "a government of separated institutions *sharing* powers."[4]

The Election Process

Formal and Informal Qualifications for Membership Formal constitutional qualifications for membership in each house of Congress deal with age, citizenship, and residence. A Senator must be at least thirty years of age, have been a citizen at least nine years, and be an inhabitant of the state in which he is elected. The Representative's qualifications are slightly less restrictive: he must be at least twenty-five years old, a citizen for at least seven years, and an inhabitant of the state from which he is chosen. Although the residence rule for the Senate was circumvented somewhat with the appointment of Democrat Pierre Salinger, a former aide to John F. Kennedy, to be Senator from California (due to a loose interpretation of what constitutes an "inhabitant") and the election of Senator Robert F. Kennedy from New York in 1966, it is still almost impossible to get elected from a state unless you are a "local man." While the Constitution does not require it, almost all Representatives since 1842 have come from the single-member Congressional districts within each state and have been elected by gaining a plurality in the general election. Political prudence and expediency dictate nomination and election of a "local" man from each district. All 435 members of the House of Representatives are legal residents or inhabitants of the district within the state they represent.

It is not the Constitutional rules, but other informal requirements (for example, class, race, education, sex,, and so on) which provide the major restrictions on the chances to serve in Congress. Donald Matthews, in a study of the Senate, observed that the "informal requirements" operate to include only about 5 percent of the American people.[5] The informal requirements are not invariable criteria, and there is always the possibility that a woman, a member of a minority group, or a person with little education or low socioeconomic background will be elected. In fact, in a few districts, minority group membership may be necessary for election, because the national minority may be a "majority" in a given district. But, generally speaking, these informal requirements exist, as evidenced by the fact that only nineteen women and seventeen blacks are in the Ninety-fourth Congress. Congress is clearly not a demographic microcosm of the American people. The "typical" member of Congress—if we could construct such a creature—would be a well-educated, white, Protestant male, a veteran in his early fifties, with a background in law, business or banking.[6] Informal requirements are significant in that they, among other factors, structure political opportunities and thus guard the gateway to Congress.[7]

Apportionment As we noted above, legislators in both the Senate and the House are today popularly elected within the fifty states. The Senate is composed of two Senators from each state, a provision of the Constitution which is "theoretically" unamendable despite its "undemocratic" effects and overtones. Equality in the Senate was part of the price of union, a condition for membership required by the smaller states of the country to balance the House. The lower house—the House of Representatives—is based on population, the number originally not to exceed one Representative for every thirty thousand persons but with each state to have at least one. For a while the House took the easy way out and continued simply to expand itself with the growth of population. In 1911, size clearly had become a hindrance to coordination and decision-making, and a ceiling on membership was set at 435. The number was allowed to increase temporarily to 437 in 1959 when Hawaii and Alaska were admitted to the Union. It was agreed that the number would revert to 435 after the 1960 census. As the popular base for each house is different, so is the term of election. A Senator is elected for a six-year term. Approximately one-third stand for reelection every two years so that never is the entire Senate up for election. On the other hand, the entire House membership stands for reelection every two years. There are no limits on the number of times Senators or Representatives can be reelected. It has been suggested by some that the two-year terms and the electoral base of the House have made it more responsive to rural and conservative interests than the Senate, which has a longer tenure and a statewide constituency that allows for maximum impact of urban and liberal interests.[8]

A special word needs to be said about reapportionment of the House of Representatives.[9] The Constitution specifically requires the "enumeration" of Representatives from the states within every ten-year period, but the decision on districting within states was left to individual state legislatures. During the early years, members were elected at-large in the states. Not until 1842 did Congress begin to provide guidelines, and it was not until 1872 that Congress set forth the following criteria: single-member districts, compact and contiguous districts, and, as nearly as possible, uniformity in the population of districts. However, the last apportionment act to have such criteria was in 1911, so that state legislatures later became free to draw lines as they pleased. The 1929 Apportionment Act provided for "automatic" reapportionment after each subsequent decennial census, that is, a redistribution of each state's fair share of the total 435 seats based on its share of the total U. S. population, each state having at least one Representative. However, within each state the popular size of districts varied widely. After nearly half a century of "unequal" districts, the Supreme Court entered the "political thicket" of apportionment. This culminated in the 1964 decision (*Wesberry* v. *Sanders*), which declared that each Congressional district should contain approximately the same number of people. This was seen as necessary to bring about equality in the weight of a citizen's vote—"the one man, one vote" principle. (As late as 1950, three-fifths of the total representatives in the House were from rural districts.) Most state legislatures responded promptly to the new criteria. Others were ordered by federal courts to comply. Obviously, the legislatures still have great latitude in how they draw or gerrymander these equal districts; many districts are unusually shaped and artificial for political purposes, but they are approximately equal in population.[10]

The "one man, one vote" decision did not provide the anticipated increase in urban and Democratic seats, for by the 1960s the population movement, relatively speaking, was away from the cities to the suburbs. According to the 1970 census figures, urban centers have not only lost population to the suburbs in a relative sense (meaning a smaller "share" of the 435 Congressmen), but at least half of the twenty-five largest cities have suffered a net population loss. Most of the changes due to reapportionment in districts tended to favor the Republicans because, according to *Congressional Quarterly,* many of the new districts "were placed in fast-growing Republican suburbs and because legislatures in several key states drew the lines to partisan Republican advantage."[11] Seventeen of the twenty-four seats that switched in party control in 1972 to the Republicans did so largely because of redistricting or reapportionment, whereas Democrats won only eight of their new seats for that reason. However, in general, it can be said that the reapportionment brought about by the one man, one vote decision has not had a dramatic impact upon party fortunes.[12]

The Election Process and Election Results Even if relatively equal-sized districts for the House of Representatives prevail, there likely will be some difference between votes received by a party and its number of seats in Congress. Thus, even if constituents were highly aware and issue-oriented and the parties were fully programatic in style, the composition of the legislature might not exactly reflect opinion in the entire country. This is due in part to the nature of the election process; that is, the single-member-district (SMD) system used to elect members of the House and the fact that each state has two Senators regardless of population. Table 2.1 shows the relationship between total votes for the various parties in the House districts in which Democrats opposed Republicans and the number of seats won by each party. Obviously, the votes were not translated into seats with complete precision by the SMD system.[13] In each instance where seats were contested, the Democratic party received somewhat more seats than was its "share" according to the overall vote it received nationwide for those seats. Democrats gained from 2 percent (1972) to 8 percent (1964) more of the contested seats than they deserved.

Since each state, regardless of population size, has two Senators, the *potential* for misrepresentation of total voter preferences in party choice for Senators is obvious. New York, with sixty times the population of Alaska, has the same number of Senators. Milton Cummings has observed that, according to the 1970 census figures, the twenty-six states (with fifty-two Senators) having the smallest populations comprise only one-sixth of the total U. S. population.[14] Theoretically, then, about one-twelfth of the American people (in other words, razor-thin majorities of slightly over 50 percent in each election in each of those twenty-six states) could elect a majority of the Senate. Such an occurrence is, of course, unlikely. Although not exactly comparable to the House data, Table 2.2 gives us a rough picture of how popular votes for the parties' Senatorial candidates within the states have been translated into Senate seats. The closest correspondence is for 1972, when the popular votes divided almost evenly. The seats were also as even as they could be, given an uneven number up for election. The 1970 election shows the greatest distortion. The Republicans garnered 44.5 percent of the popular vote but only received 33 percent of the contested seats. If we combine all three years selected, thus including every Senate seat (two are included twice due to special elections for vacancies), we will get some idea of how well the Senate composition as a whole reflects party popular vote. Again, as in the House, there appears to be a slight Democratic bias. As we cautioned earlier, we must be careful not to equate the Senate data and the House data, for we are including three different elections taking place under widely varying circumstances, with approximately one-third of the seats up each election. Nevertheless, rough overall tendencies can be observed that allow some degree of comparability to the findings on the House.

Table 2.1
Party Popular Vote and Seats in
House of Representatives (in percent)

Year	Percent Popular Votes of Two-Party Vote for Congress in Contested Districts[a]	Percent of Contested Seats Won	Percent of Total Vote[b]	Percent of Total Seats Won
1964 Democrats	56.7	64.7	62.3	67
Republicans	43.3	35.3	38.7	33
1968 Democrats	49.7	52.7	53.4	56
Republicans	50.3	47.3	46.6	44
1972 Democrats	49.9	51.8	52.3	56[c]
Republicans	50.1	49.2	47.7	44

a Some seats were not contested by both major parties. In 1964 the Democrats won all thirty-eight noncontested seats. In 1968 the Democrats won thirty-nine noncontested seats. In 1972 the Democrats won forty-three; the Republicans eight.

b Includes averaging-out of expected votes where no actual votes were reported by the state due to lack of opposition.

c Includes one seat won by an Independent and three seats in which the candidate was endorsed by both the Republicans and Democrats. All four caucus with the House Democrats.

Table 2.2
Party Popular Vote and Seats in Senate (in percent)

Year		Percent Popular Vote of Two-Party Vote for Senate in Contested States[a]	Percent of Contested Seats Won	Percent of Total Seats Up For Election Won
1968	Democrats	50.1	53.1	52.9
	Republicans	49.9	46.9	47.1
1970	Democrats	55.5	66	62.9[b]
	Republicans	44.5	33	31.4
1972	Democrats	49.6	48.5	48.5
	Republicans	50.4	51.5	51.5
All Three Elections Combined[c]	Democrats	52.6	56.1	54.9
	Republicans	47.8	43.9	43.2

[a] Two seats in 1968 were not contested by both parties. These figures also exclude votes cast in states in which both a Democrat and a Republican ran and lost.
[b] Two states won by other than a Democrat or Republican.
[c] There were more than 100 seats total since there had been vacancies filled by election.

Nomination Nomination, usually by a popular party primary, is the initial step in getting or remaining elected. Most primaries allow only members of the party to cast votes.[15] However, in most states a mere declaration of party membership at voting time permits a voter to participate. In general, the popular primary, a relatively recent phenomenon in American politics, inhibits a prominent role for the party organization, though in numerous instances the primary is circumvented by preprimary endorsement of a consensus choice by party leaders.[16] Rarely is there intervention by the national party organization. As Price capsulizes the situation, "In American parties the local primary is generally an open contest, to be won by a local candidate campaigning on issues of local concern."[17]

Unfortunately, the hoped-for increase in democracy only partially occurred with the triumph of the direct primary. Citizen participation in the primary election (except in some one-party states, such as those in the South, where often the primary *is* the election for all practical purposes) is quite a bit smaller than the turnout for the general election, generally only 20 to 25 percent of the potential adult voting-age population.[18] Also, the rate of competition has not been high in primaries, especially outside the South, and rarely are incumbents beaten. One study of the 1968 primaries found that, of the 302 House seats outside the South, incumbents were running for reelection in 274 instances. Only 87 (39.2 percent of the 302 incumbents) faced *any* primary opposition; in only 23 of the 302 contests was the winner's margin less than two to one. Even in the instances where there was no incumbent, in less than half was there opposition.[19]

Jewell and Patterson point out that from 1952 to 1970, only 5 percent of the incumbent Senators were defeated in primaries,[20] whereas Jones's study shows that, from 1956 to 1966, less than 2 percent of incumbent Representatives seeking renomination were denied it.[21] Primary competition is greatly dependent on the party's prospects for success in the general election.[22] "Safe party seats encourage competition in the primary of the major party and discourage competition in the minority party. However, if an incumbent is running—particularly one with a few years seniority—it also tends to deter primary competition in his party. Still, Keefe and Ogul observe: "Contests for nominations to Congress, even when incumbents are involved, occur in virtually all southern Democratic primaries."[23] Not only are southerners more likely to face opposition, but they also are more likely to lose than their counterparts in the North. A study of Senate nominations from 1920 to 1954 found a one-third loss rate for southern Senators, whereas nonsouthern Senators lost less than 2 percent of the time.[24] Finally, the high cost of campaigning for a nomination may also limit the democratic consequences of primaries by significantly limiting the gateway to Congress to a very few.

Individual Margins of Victory and Turnover in General Elections An examination of general election results reveals (as with primaries) that individual House races are usually characterized by large margins of victory, low turnover, and high survival rates for incumbents seeking reelection. What appears as a competitive two-party system nationally, when we look at Presidential votes or the makeup of the Congress, actually occurs alongside rather lopsided victories within the House districts. Although the large majority of seats are contested by at least two candidates, the number of House "marginal" districts, in which one party's candidate narrowly wins over the other party's candidate (that is, by less than a 10 percent margin) is small. Whereas about 60 percent of Senate elections are won with 55 percent or less of the two-party vote, only about 20 percent of the House contests are this close.[25] In 1970 and 1972, over 70 percent of House winners received at least 60 percent of the two-party vote. In the Senate elections of 1968, 1970 and 1972, the winner received 60 percent or more of the vote only about a third of the time. Nearly all of the Senate seats are now contested, whereas the number of House seats not contested, though having declined since World War II, is still about 10 percent of the total. Not surprisingly, the major portion of these are in the South, though the rise of the Republican party there promises to decrease further the number of uncontested seats.

Contrary to popular belief, safe seats (not equivalent to uncontested seats) are found in all sections of the country, including the big urbanized industrialized states which may in fact be closely contested in statewide elections. H. Douglas Price points out that there are roughly as many safe districts in the eight most populous and competitive states as in the eleven states of the South.[26] Raymond Wolfinger and Joan Hollinger have traced the number of noncompetitive Democratic districts in each Congressional election from 1946 through 1968.[27] They define a "noncompetitive" election as one in which the Democratic candidates receive 65 percent or more of the major party vote. There was a steady increase in the number and share of noncompetitive districts in the North, which peaked at about 64 percent in 1964. Thus only about a third of the

Democratic safe seats came from the South in 1964. This was no doubt in part due to the Goldwater debacle. A look at the 1966 and 1968 elections reveals that 1964 was an "abnormal" year, yet for these two elections there was still a majority of Democratic safe seats outside the South. The figures for the northern Democrats are 53 percent and 52 percent in 1966 and 1968 respectively, with the corresponding southern Democratic share at 47 percent and 48 percent. Furthermore, in 1970 and 1972 the northern Democrats' share was over 55 percent in each instance. Wolfinger and Hollinger's research also reveals that no longer do safe districts have a heavily rural bias.

Besides closeness of vote, party turnover (that is, the change in control of a seat from one party to another) is another way of looking at competition. In a study of interparty competition for Congressional seats from 1914 to 1960, Jones points out that not only has competition for Congressional seats never been very high but also that it is decreasing.[28] Table 2.3 summarizes his findings. The percentage of "fluidity" is the percent of change in party control in each district as compared to the total possible number of changes (in other words, 1740 in the four elections between 1952 and 60, or 4 x 435). The other measure of party competition simply records the percentage of elections in which there was no change in party control of a district in the time period studied. (For example, from 1942 to 1950, 74 percent of all Congressional districts were won by the same party.)

Table 2.3
Interparty Competition for Congressional Seats

Time Period	Percent Fluidity	Percent of No. Change Dist.	Actual No. of Changes
1914-1926	11.8	62.1	308
1932-1940	10.6	69.9	184
1942-1950	11.9	74.0	199
1952-1960	7.8	78.2	135

Source: Charles O. Jones, "Inter-Party Competition for Congressional Seats," *Western Political Quarterly* 17 (September 1964): p. 465.

Keefe and Ogul, interpreting Jones's study, sum it up this way: "Viewed broadly, the chances are that the same party will win five consecutive elections in about three-fourths of all congressional districts."[29] In the 1952 through 1960 Congressional elections, only 1 of the 435 House districts changed party control in each election. Over 200 stayed Democratic throughout, while 135 remained Republican.

In recent years, in both chambers (but especially in the House) a significantly large share of races has involved incumbents who have had a high rate of survival. Thus, personnel turnover as well as party turnover is low. Table 2.4 indicates the average turnover (that is, new persons elected) for the House membership in various time periods since 1940.

Table 2.4
Average Turnover in the House of Representatives

Date	Average Turnover (Number)	Percent of House Membership
1940-48	96	22
1950-58	68	16
1960-68	66	15
1970-74	73	17

Included in the table are *all* new members regardless of whether an incumbent was beaten or not. In most instances, the incumbent retired. But even including those seats vacated voluntarily by incumbents, we see that the average Congress since 1950 included about 85 percent incumbents. Due to the staggered terms of Senators, it is difficult to compare turnover since only one-third of the Senate is up for reelection each two years. In the three elections from 1968 to 1972, more than one-third of the Senators elected were not incumbents.

But how many incumbents actually run, and what is their rate of success in the general elections? Normally, 85 to 95 percent of the House incumbents seek reelection. For example in 1974, 391 initially sought reelection (8 lost in primaries). Similarly, from 1964 to 1972 (in five regular elections), nearly 90 percent of the Senators occupying seats up for reelection ran again (about 6 percent of those lost in primaries). In 1974, 27 of the 34 incumbents initially sought reelection (2 lost in primaries). In the ten election years from 1952 to 1970, only 16 percent of incumbent Senators who actually sought reelection were defeated in the general election. As we noted earlier, an additional 5 percent had been defeated in the primaries; so that, in all, 21 percent failed in their reelection effort. Or to put it another way, four out of five incumbent Senators running were successfully reelected. For the eight election years from 1956 to 1970, only 6 percent of the incumbent Representatives who actually sought reelection were defeated in the general election. A disproportionate number were freshman incumbents.[30] Combined with the less than 2 percent who lost in the primaries, that means a survival rate of over 92 percent. The average member of the House in the Ninety-fourth Congress (1975-76) had served 5.2 terms.[31] Slightly more than 40 percent of the members elected had served at least four previous terms; about 14 percent of those elected would serve at least their tenth term. However, with the addition of 92 new faces in the House for the Ninety-fourth Congress, the largest number since the Eighty-first, the average member's seniority dropped to 8.5 years at the beginning of the session as compared to 9.0 for the previous Congress.

Election Costs and Campaign Finance The double election, consisting of the direct primary and the general election, usually makes running for Congress quite expensive.[32] Costs have ballooned since 1950, partly as a result of greater utilization of the mass media, especially television. Total *cash* costs for a Senate race by all candidates in states with moderate size population (for example, Oregon, North Carolina, Minnesota, Massachusetts, and Indiana) can easily run from $500,000 to over $1 million. For example, in 1972 in Minnesota, each of the two major party candidates (Mondale and Hansen) spent about $500,000. One example of election costs in the more populous states is the general election for the 1970 New York Senate contest. Republican Goodell spent $1.3 million (more than half on television); Democrat Ottinger spent $4 million (including primary expenses); and both of them lost. Conservative James Buckley, the winner, spent at least $2 million. Interestingly, as the Nader project reports, of the total of fifteen major candidates for the Senate seats of the seven most populous states in the 1970 general elections, eleven were millionaires. The four who were not lost.[33]

Costs are smaller for candidates who run for the House, but even here the final bill for a campaign in a competitive urban seat can run from $50,000 to $100,000. Costs normally drop somewhat for a rural or suburban seat or for a noncompetitive seat, but an election bill of $250,000 for a particular candidate is not unheard of. The average investment required of a serious candidate is probably somewhere between $30,000 and $60,000. However, it should not be forgotten that Representatives must run three times as often as Senators.

Based on the figures of the highly responsible Citizen's Research Foundation Reports for the 1970 elections for the House (435) and Senate (35), we calculate that the *average* cost per House seat was *a minimum* of $60,000, whereas the average cost per Senate seat was $1.9 million.[34] Despite our earlier observation on the 1970 Senate election in the seven most populous states, it should not be assumed that personal wealth guaranteed victory. But it was surely an advantage, especially in providing the "opportunity" to run. New spending limits and limits on the contributions by the candidate and his family to his own campaign may lessen somewhat the advantage of wealth.

Most of the fund-raising, significantly, is local, and most of that is "individual candidate" oriented. National party support, relatively speaking, is usually meager (except in a few key races) when compared to the magnitude of the total cost of the campaign.[35] In general the Republican candidates, due to the success of the Republican Booster's Club, have received more assistance from the national party instruments than Democrats have. Herbert Alexander, perhaps the foremost authority on campaign financing, reports that in 1970 Democratic House candidates taken as a whole received $344,000 from all party committees compared with $1.7 million for Republican House candidates. Democratic party committees gave their Senatorial candidates $428,000 compared with $956,000 for Republicans.[36] The money is not spent randomly or equally but rather where it will "do the most good." Incumbents in marginal districts and freshmen are likely to receive larger shares. Incumbents in general receive more than nonincumbents; often nonincumbents receive no support.[37]

The high cost of campaigning in order to build a successful electoral coalition,[38] coupled with the low dollar input of the national party organizations, necessitates local and individual fund-raising. These costs contribute to decentralization in the electoral process and can militate against national party unity and the "discipline" of Congressional parties. Further, this lack of national party assistance usually works to the advantage of the incumbent, who has the "visibility," "contacts" with key interests on both the local and national level, his own personal Congressional staff and the right to make free mailings, and is continually building up goodwill in his "errand boy" role for constituents who have special needs or gripes against the government, especially the bureaucracy. Fishel notes with respect to House races that

Since there is normally an *inverse* relationship between time spent in office and out of pocket campaign costs, combined with the increasing ease most incumbents have in raising money, the impact of this inequality falls heavily on potential challengers.[39]

Congressmen fully recognize the advantages of incumbency in both the primary and the general election. One study which is based largely on roundtable discussions of members of the House concluded that

Although members of Congress are inclined to talk about reelection campaigns in terms of the problems involved, they argue that as incumbents they possess extraordinary advantages over their opponents. There is a tendency to believe that, aside from isolated instances, where an overriding issue is present, there is little excuse for defeat.[40]

In 1971 and 1974 the first substantial campaign reforms since 1925 were adopted. Previous legislation had been totally ineffective in regulating campaigns. The provisions in the 1971 act for reporting contributions and expenditures have led to a number of disclosures upon which prosecutions have been based. Some of the principal provisions of the act broadened the definition of election to include primaries, tightened the requirements for reporting both contributions and expenses, and defined more strictly the roles unions and corporations can play in political campaigns. The 1974 Campaign Reform Act radically overhauled the system of campaign financing by limiting contributions and, for the first time ever, established expenditure ceilings for Congressional and Presidential primaries and general elections. Effective January 1, 1975,* Senatorial candidates are limited to $100,000 or 8 cents per voter, whichever is greater, in primaries and $150,000 or 12 cents per eligible voter, whichever is greater, in general elections. House candidates are limited to $70,000 in primaries and $70,000 in the general election. Fund-raising costs of up to 20 percent of the candidate's spending limit are exempted from the general spending limits. The 1974 act also provided for the first use of public funds to cover Presidential campaign costs. It also created a full-time eight-member bipartisan Federal Elections Commission to be responsible for administering the election laws and the public financing of Presidential elections.[41]

Party Composition of Congress Table 2.5 reveals the party composition of the Congress and the Presidents since World War II. Through the Ninety-fourth Congress, the Republicans controlled the Presidency sixteen of those years (eight Congresses), yet they controlled the Congress only twice (a total of four years), in 1946, the first election after the war, and in the Eisenhower landslide of 1952. The Democrats have controlled both houses of Congress since 1954. Eight times the Congress and the Presidency have been in opposite party hands. The party winning the Presidency normally picks up House seats (note the exceptions of 1956 and 1960).[42] Almost invariably, that same party loses House seats in the off-year elections as voter participation drops. In fact, only once in this century (1934) has the President's party picked up House seats in an off-year election. The average loss in an off-year election in the last two decades has been about 30 seats. Party gains and losses in both the Senate and the House in either Presidential or off-year elections are likely to occur in "marginal" states or districts (about 100), most often when freshmen incumbents are running or when there is no incumbent in the race.

*In 1976 the Supreme Court declared the Congressional spending limits unconstitutional.

Table 2.5
Election Results for Congress and Presidency, 1946-1974

Election Year	Congress Elected	Dem.	House Rep.	Other	Dem	Senate Rep.	Other	President
1946	80th[b]	188	246	1	45	51	0	Truman (D)[d]
1948[a]	81st	263	171	1	54	42	0	Truman (D)
1950	82nd	234	199	2	48	47	1	Truman (D)
1952[a]	83rd	213	221	1	47	48	1	Eisenhower (R)
1954	84th[b]	232	203	0	48	47	1	Eisenhower (R)
1956[a]	85th[b]	234	201	0	49	47	0	Eisenhower (R)
1958	86th[b]	283	154	0	66	34	0	Eisenhower (R)
1960[a]	87th	263	174	0	64	36	0	Kennedy (D)
1962	88th	258	176	1[c]	68	32	0	Kennedy (D)
1964[a]	89th	295	140	0	67	33	0	Johnson (D)
1966	90th	248	187	0	64	36	0	Johnson (D)
1968[a]	91st[b]	243	192	0	58	42	0	Nixon
1970	92nd[b]	255	180	0	55[e]	45[f]	0	Nixon (R)
1972[a]	93rd[b]	244	191	0	57	43	0	Nixon (R)
1974	94th[b]	291	144	0	61	38	1[g]	Ford (R)[h]

[a] Also a Presidential election year.
[b] Congress and Presidency in control of opposing parties.
[c] Vacancy—Clem Miller (D., Calif.) died on October 6, 1962, but his name remained on the ballot and he received a plurality.
[d] Replaced Roosevelt (D) who was elected to fourth Presidential term in 1944.
[e] Includes Harry Byrd (Va.) elected as an Independent but caucuses with Democrats.
[f] Includes Buckley (N.Y.) elected as a Conservative but caucuses with Republicans.
[g] Vacancy—The New Hampshire election results were so close that no one was seated at the beginning of the Congress. Democrat John Durkin defeated Republican Louis Wyman in a special election, Sept. 16, 1975.
[h] Succeeded to Presidency Aug. 9, 1974 with Nixon's resignation.

Vacancies The importance of incumbency gives added significance to the method used to fill vacancies that may occur in Congress. House vacancies are usually filled by the Governor of the state in which the vacancy occurs by calling for a special election. Sometimes, particularly if a regular election is near, the decision will be put off until then. As for the Senate, the Governor, on the authority of the Seventeenth Amendment to the Constitution, ordinarily appoints a temporary replacement until the next election. When the vacancy is filled in an election, the new Senator completes the rest of the former Senator's term. A study of Senate vacancies from 1919 to 1965 reveals that a surprising 18 per cent of *all* Senate terms during that period were not completed by the person originally elected to the office.[43]

The Organization of Congress

We turn now to discuss the organization of Congress. Special attention will be given to the structure of parties and the committee system in Congress. Of course, each of these elements of Congressional organization will enter our analysis again in later chapters. Our purpose here is to provide general description and background discussion of the organization members find once they reach Congress.

Congressional Parties For purposes of discussing the Congressional parties, it is useful to remember that, besides the "party in government" or in Congress, parties also have an organizational apparatus outside the Congress and have an electoral following that one might call the "party in the electorate."[44] Within the party in government there are numerous subsectors, as well, since the President, Senate, and House all have different electoral bases and all play a significant role in policy-making. There is no coordinating or hierarchical party organization even for those in public office. Each sector and subsector has a different clientele or constituency, resources, incentives and goals, some of which may and do conflict.

Party Conferences, Caucuses, and Major Party Committees Members elected to the House or Senate who bear the party label, Democrat or Republican (as practically all do), automatically become members of their respective legislative parties if they wish to attend the party conference or caucus. However, neither of the parties in Congress enjoys a concentration of power sufficient in either the House or the Senate that will allow a party majority automatically to translate a program into legislation. The power of the majority as well as the minority party in each house is highly dispersed, which has been a target of persistent criticism of the Congress and of American parties.

In both parties in each chamber the basic unit of legislative party organization is the conference or caucus, which comprises all members of the party. A principal function of the party conference or caucus is to select the party leaders and, in the case of the majority party in the House, to select the Speaker of the House (who, unlike his counterpart in Great Britain, is also a partisan leader). But, in many of these instances, the selections are almost "automatic" as occurs in most cases of "reelection" or "promotion" (for example when Thomas O'Neill simply moved from majority whip up to Democratic majority leader in the House after the death of Hale Boggs).

The conference or caucus is theoretically also supposed to develop and promote a "party policy" binding on all members to support it. There have been periods in American history (for example, the Democratic House Caucus from the fall of Speaker Joe Cannon in 1911 until 1918) in which the caucus has played such a role, that is, "binding" members and thereby delivering a high proportion of the vote. This is not the present situation. Once the chambers and parties are organized, the influence of the party caucus usually fades into the background.

Starting in 1969, the House Democrats voted to have regular monthly caucuses, but the vast majority of the caucuses called under the new rule failed to produce the necessary 50 percent attendance and so were not held. Eight were held during the first two and a half years of operation under the new rule. In a recent instance, in May 1973, the House Democratic Caucus, despite some conservative opposition, met to endorse an antiwar position formulated by party leaders through the Steering and Policy Committee (examined below). The caucus voted 144 to 22 to reject Nixon's request for funds to assure enough money to continue bombing in Cambodia. This was a rare instance in which the Caucus made a position the policy of the entire House majority. Recent votes by the House and Senate Democratic caucuses against additional military aid to Cambodia and South Vietnam are other atypical examples. In the last few years, the caucus or conference has also been a principal focus of reform efforts, particularly by liberal House Democrats, to modernize and democratize Congress.

The Legislative Reorganization Act of 1946 (LRA) originally included a provision to set up policy committees in each House for each party "to formulate overall legislative policy for the two parties." Though it was approved by the Senate, it was omitted by the House. A year later, in an independent action, the Senate acted to establish and fund policy committees for the Senate parties. House Republicans in 1949 decided to make their Steering Committee a Policy Committee. The House Democrats, though they had a Steering Committee which played a largely inactive role in policy formulation, did not follow suit, partly because of the intense opposition of Speaker Sam Rayburn. However, in early 1973, with the blessings of Speaker Carl Albert (D., Okla.), the Democratic Caucus voted to establish a new Democratic Steering and Policy Committee to give greater coherence and direction to the party's legislative strategy. Thus, each party in each house now has a policy committee.

The Senate Republican Policy Committee, chaired by John Tower (Tex.), has ranged from nine to twenty-three members. Today there are fifteen members who serve a two-year term and are elected at the party Conference. Of these, party leaders are ex officio members. The smaller Senate Democratic Policy Committee (and a small Legislative Review Committee) is appointed for an indefinite period by the floor leader but subject to caucus confirmation. The floor leader, Mike Mansfield (Mont.), is chairman, and the party whip and Conference secretary are ex officio members. The Democrats in the past had a disproportionate share of Senators from the southern and western states, but successful attempts have been made to have the committee better reflect the ideological and regional diversity of the party. The Senate Republicans have made continuing attempts to be representative (as is also true for the House Republicans). Both have institutionalized their policy committees more than the Democrats, whose committees until recently were instruments of personal leadership for the party leaders. Unlike both Democratic policy committees, neither Republican policy committee is chaired by the floor leaders of the respective houses. The House Republican Policy Committee, headed by Barber Conable (N.Y.), usually includes members selected biennially from geographical zones and from recent "classes" of Republicans. It also includes party leaders and ranking Republican members of several key committees such as the House Rules Committee. The new Democratic Steering and Policy Committee is comprised of the party leaders, including deputy whips, twelve other members elected by the Caucus membership on a regional basis, and a few others to be appointed at-large by the top party leader (now the Speaker), presumably to go to members of groups that may be left out by the other elections.

But policy committees have not lived up to their proposed role, for they cannot overcome the root problem—party disunity. Hugh Bone, a leading scholar of the Senate Policy Committees, has concluded:

> They have never been "policy" bodies, in the sense of considering and investigating alternatives of public policy, and they have never put forth an over-all congressional party program. The committees do not assume leadership in drawing up a general legislative program . . . and only rarely have the committees labelled their decisions as "party policies."[45]

The simple creation of a policy committee did not upset the old patterns of power and authority within the legislature, nor could it change some of the other characteristics of American politics that militate against the formulation and implementation of an overall party position. Though they have failed to formulate and enforce party positions, the party committees have "served as a focus for discussion, compromise, and communication," and to some extent coordination.[46]

Each party in each house has a campaign committee ostensibly concerning itself with assisting and possibly enlarging its party's membership in Congress. It provides technical services, public relations material, research assistance, and money. Money is always scarce and, thus, must be rationed. This provides a potential political resource for the party leadership (and contributors). Yet only a few hard-pressed Senators get much significant help, though Republicans get more than Democrats. A House Democrat may get only $1,000 or $2,000 and Republican $2,000 or $3,000, with $5,000 being the maximum. As we have seen, this is only a fraction of the amount needed to wage a successful campaign. Both House campaign committees consist of one representative designated by each state's delegation, with the Democrats including several party leaders such as the Speaker, chief and deputy whips, and chairman of the caucus. The Democratic Senate leader appoints about fifteen members of the Democratic Senate Campaign Committee for two-year terms. The chairman of the Republican Campaign Committee in the Senate is appointed by the Republican Conference. He, in turn, appoints the relatively large committee. Responsibility for raising funds for the Republicans' campaign committees is left in the hands of the Republican National Committee, but once funds are granted, the campaign committees have absolute authority. The Democrats are more erratic and less consistent about fundraising, demonstrating far less cooperation with the national party than the Republicans.

The other major type of party committee, the Committee on Committees, selects which party members will sit on which Congressional committee. We discuss the Committee on Committees of the parties at greater length later in this chapter.

It is also important to note that there is a series of informal groups and subgroups in each party, especially within parties in the House. Depending upon the particular state, party members from the state delegation may meet regularly to discuss common problems and strategies. There also are groups within parties organized along lines of ideology. The largest of these, known as the Democratic Study Group, includes most members of the liberal wing of the Democratic party in the House and numbered over 200 in the Ninety-fourth Congress. One of its central purposes is to facilitate communication among its members and especially to maximize voting on the floor. In reaction southern Democratic conservatives formed the Democratic Research Group, and in 1973 a centrist group of about 50 moderates formed the very loose United Democrats. There is a small group of approximately 30 liberals organized in the House Republican party. It is known as the Wednesday Group. There is an even smaller Republican Wednesday Club in the Senate.

Elective Leaders Of course, each of the parties also has a leadership (referred to also as "elective leaders"), whose election we mentioned earlier is the principal task of the party caucus or conference. Unified leadership for the total legislative party is virtually impossible because of the bicameral system with its different electoral bases and lack of party cohesion. Each party in each house selects its own leaders and determines their powers. Crucial in the selection of a leader is his influence and friends within that particular chamber in which he serves, not his prestige "outside."[47] Recruitment patterns of party leaders tend to favor moderates over those at the extremes. A party leader "leads from the center." However, "formal powers" are few, and much depends upon the individual's own personality and political skills.

Once one has made it into the elective leadership "in group," one quite often moves up as those above retire.[48] For example, John McCormack, formerly floor leader, moved up to Speaker of the House with the death of Speaker Sam Rayburn. Carl Albert, who moved up to floor leader when McCormack became Speaker, later moved to Speaker when McCormack retired. Mike Mansfield moved up when Lyndon Johnson left the Senate. This does not mean there are not challenges to the existing elective leaders. Most attempts simply are not successful. However, following election fiascos, one may find a real challenge to party leaders in the caucuses. For example, it was at such times that Republican Charles Halleck unseated Joseph Martin as minority floor leader in the House, and later Gerald Ford unseated Halleck. Great concern over the future and image of the Democratic party (as well as dissatisfaction with the incumbent leadership) prompted Senate Democrats to drop Russell Long as majority whip in the Senate for the younger and more liberal northeasterner—Teddy Kennedy. Robert Byrd (W. Va.), then secretary to the caucus, later successfully challenged Kennedy after the Chappaquiddick incident. Democrats in the House seem much more likely than Republicans to resolve questions of leadership change through noncontested election or appointment. Furthermore, they are more likely to develop clearer patterns of succession. The distinctions and patterns in the Senate seem less clear.

The leader of the majority party in the House is the Speaker of the House—the legislator with the greatest potential for influence in the chamber. Often he is referred to as the "second most powerful man in Washington," but that depends on who holds the position. Though formally chosen by the whole House, the Speaker, who is presiding officer of the House, is in effect decided on beforehand in the majority party caucus. Party members, though they may have disagreed with his selection in caucus, vote with the party with almost complete unity on the floor in selection of the Speaker. It is one of the few such demonstrations of party unity.

The Speaker's influence lies in his position as both presiding officer and leader of the majority party. He assigns bills to committees, announces the order of business and schedules the votes, interprets the rules, can set significant precedents, puts questions to a vote and repeats the vote, has the power of recognition of members from the floor, appoints members of conferences and special committees, can speak and debate on the floor (which he does sparingly on crucial bills), serves as a bridge to the President and the Senate, and helps members with their special projects. One of his potential sources of power is his impact on the committee assignments of his party. Of particular significance is the recent decision by House Democrats to allow its top party leader (now the Speaker) to nominate (in effect to select) all Democratic members of the House Rules Committee.

But none of these potentials for power taken separately accounts for the great influence of the Speaker. It is rather the "scope" of his powers and the particular personality and knowledge of the individual holding the position. Skill is also an important factor, including the feel the Speaker has for whom to approach for added support and when he can effectively use both the Whip system and the information he holds by virtue of his position at the center of the communication network of the majority party in the House.[49]

The current Speaker, Carl Albert, is assisted by the majority leader or floor leader (now Thomas O'Neill, D., Mass.) and the majority whip. The opposition party selects a minority leader (now John Rhodes, R., Ariz.) and a minority whip. The majority leader, who works closely with and "under" the Speaker, leads his party's efforts on the floor and works to arrange the daily schedule of the House. The minority party leader is usually considered his party's chief spokesman and key strategist in the House. He combines many of the political roles of the Speaker and floor leader of the majority party. He strives to develop, to the degree possible, a coherent and responsible opposition position. He is the chief link or liaison to the majority party and negotiates such matters as scheduling, support, numbers and party shares of committee membership, and so on. Often because of the lack of united parties in the House, he can attack, criticize, and delay the majority party and thus assure that the minority position is not only heard but possibly accommodated. He can even lead in the development of coalitions with some dissident members of the majority party that may result in significant amendment, delay, or even defeat of majority party legislation. The minority leader's role of course takes on a more positive stance if his party occupies the White House.[50]

The majority whip (as well as the minority whip) has the assistance of a deputy whip and assistant whips, each covering party members from an area or region. The Democratic floor leader chooses his own whip who in turn selects his deputy whip. However, the eighteen assistant whips for the Democrats are chosen in a rather decentralized way, primarily by the deans of the state delegations for which an assistant whip would be responsible. The Republican whip is chosen by the Republican Committee on Committees; he, in turn, picks his deputy and assistants—three of whom are "regional whips."

Randall Ripley's excellent study of the whip organization in the House concludes that the House Whips are (1) responsible for the presence on the floor of their fellow party members, but they must also (2) transmit certain information to them, (3) ascertain how they will vote on selected important pieces of legislation, and (4) gently apply pressure to change the minds of the recalcitrant and stiffen the wills of the wavering.[51] The whip organization lies at the core of party influence and party solidarity in the House. Ripley also points out that the importance and role of the whip organization varies with the style or mode of leadership of the Speaker or minority leader and even with the role of the chairman of the House Rules Committee.

In the Senate the key men are the floor leaders, who are the chief spokesmen and strategists for their party. The President of the Senate, the constitutionally provided presiding officer, is the Vice-President of the United States. But he is perceived as a member of the executive branch, both by the legislative parties and by himself, and thus his influence with the legislature is practically nonexistent. He usually presides only for the opening of the session and on various ceremonial occasions. The President pro tem of the Senate is also primarily honorary and goes to the most senior member of the majority party. He is thus usually one of the elder statesman in the Senate whose power or influence will rest upon his seniority, committee assignments, and chairmanship, certainly not in his role as President pro tem. The Majority Leader in the Senate (now Mike Mansfield, D., Mont.) combines the partisan political roles of the Speaker and majority leader in the House, but he lacks some of the formal powers of the Speaker. The role of the minority leader in the Senate, Hugh Scott (R., Pa.), is quite comparable to his counterpart in the House. The smaller size of the Senate makes the elaborate type of whip organization one finds in the House unnecessary. However, both party leaders do have a whip organization to aid in gathering intelligence and to assist in managing a bill on the floor and marshalling votes in support.

Donald Matthews found that whereas the Senate Democratic leadership is "highly personalized, informal and centralized in the hands of the floor leader," the Republicans are more "formalized, institutionalized and decentralized."[52] Such centralization means that, compared to Senate Republicans, the Democratic leader is in a more advantageous position to exercise leadership. In addition to being floor leader, he is chairman of the Policy Committee, which schedules legislation in the Senate, chairman of the Steering Committee, which serves as the Democratic Committee on Committees to make committee assignments (those prized plums from which legislative power later derives), and the chairman of the Conference. Since the Conference meets irregularly, he thus provides whatever general and central leadership there is for the Democratic party. In the Senate Republican party, the jobs of floor leader, chairman of the Conference, chairman of the Policy Committee, and chairman of the Committee on Committees will go to different men. Republican leadership is therefore less individualized and more "corporate," with even the Conference being more active among Republicans.

Effective party leadership is made more difficult in the Senate than in the House partly because each member of the 100-man Senate is relatively more powerful than each member of the 435-man House. Nor is the presiding officer of the Senate a leader. Thus, for both the Democratic and Republican party leaders in the Senate, leadership is often dependent on personal kinds of factors. Much is dependent upon the particular skills, personality, and influence of the men who occupy these positions. The majority leader's sum total of influence depends upon the skill with which he combines and emphasizes the "fragments of power" that are available to him.[53] Some of the "fragments of power" he can use in attempting to forge a source of leverage are: his impact upon committee assignments, his ability to help a Senator with special projects or pet legislation; his ability to provide little favors such as office space and location; his role in scheduling (which he shares with the Policy Committee); his ability to debate and his individual skill as parliamentarian; his potential for skillfully manipulating the mass media; his links to the President and to the leadership of the House; and his position in his party's communication network. He must try to gather all these fragments of power and forge them into an instrument of power. But as Lyndon Johnson, generally regarded as the most effective party leader of recent years in the Senate, was fond of pointing out, the only real power available is the "power of persuasion." Ralph Huitt, a leading scholar on Congress, suggests "that the successful senatorial leader is one who (1) can and does help individual Senators to maximize their effectiveness in playing their personal roles in the Senate, and (2) structures roles and alternatives so that a maximum of senators can join in support of the preferred solution of an issue."[54]

In the selection and performance of a party leader, a premium is thus put upon location within the party, for he must be able to work with all factions of the party; a pragmatist who has the ability to play the negotiator or broker rather than an ideologue or commander normally is selected. What Fenno observes in speaking of the requirements of leadership in the House is a relevant comment on all the party leaders in the legislature, whether of the majority or minority party. The requirements he notes have been those of the negotiator. Principal among them has been the recognized ability to command the trust, confidence and respect of various party factions to the end that the tasks of informal negotiation among them will be facilitated.[55] Thus, rather than being creators or enforcers of predetermined policy, party leaders are brokers of majorities and agents of compromise. Being a good leader is, in part, being a good follower.

The party leaders will be in a stronger position if their party occupies the White House. Even though the party may be the majority party in a house, without the Presidency much more time must be spent on attack, delay, criticism, and so on, for the Presidency is an important focus of policy initiation in the American political system. But party leaders in both houses, regardless of which party holds the Presidency, have difficult times forging binding party positions partly because of the paucity of rewards and deprivations available to them and the competitive power base given to Congressional committees. Further discussion and analysis of party in the Congress, as it compares to the European legislatures, will be taken up in Chapters 4 and 5.

Committees Writing in 1885, Woodrow Wilson described the role of Congressional committees (to be distinguished from party committees) in making policy:

The House sits, not for serious discussion, but to sanction the conclusions of its Committees as rapidly as possible. It legislates in its committee-rooms; not by the determinations of majorities, but by the resolutions of specially-commissioned minorities; so that it is not far from the truth to say that Congress in session is Congress on public exhibition, whilst Congress in its committee-rooms is Congress at work.[56]

In many respects Congress's committees are, indeed, "little legislatures." Though having no constitutional basis, the committee system in Congress has continued to play a crucial role in the development of public policy. The growing volume, range, and complexity of legislation necessitate some sort of division of labor and specialization in order to give careful, competent attention to each major piece of legislation. By so doing, the committee system enhances the position of the legislature vis-á-vis the President and the bureaucracy. It allows not only for close inspection and review of legislative proposals in pursuit of its legislative tasks but also serves to enable "oversight" of executive actions by legislators who have considerable experience and expertise in a given area. Although there has been a trend toward open committee and subcommittee meetings (now over 90 percent), the committee system and mode of operation continue to facilitate political compromise, accommodation, and negotiation. The committee room and committee atmosphere are conducive to a "meeting of the minds"—building some sort of consensus acceptable to the major interests affected.

The committees perform the same tasks as the legislature itself: sorting and analysis, evaluation, deliberation, reporting, deciding priorities, and oversight. The most important committees are the standing or permanent committees (and their fractional subdivisions, subcommittees), to which nearly all legislation initially goes for study and recommendation. At many points in Congressional history these committees have grown to unreasonable numbers (for example, 73 in the Senate in 1913) with overlapping and conflicting jurisdictions. The Legislative Reorganization Act of 1946 attempted to rationalize and streamline the committee system by reducing the number of committees (the House was cut from 48 to 19 and the Senate from 33 to 15) and dividing their jurisdiction along policy/subject lines to minimize overlap. Since then, each chamber has added a Budget Committee and a committee to deal with science, space, and aeronautics matters. In addition the Senate has created a Veteran's Affairs Committee; the House has added an ethics committee and Small Business Committ- while dropping the controversial Internal Security Committee.

Occasionally, there are overlaps in jurisdiction. In such cases it may be crucial to a bill's success as to which standing committee it is assigned. Another possible point of conflict over a bill is due to the "double consideration" a bill gets because of the distinction between "authorization" and "appropriation." A subject area standing committee, such as Senate Labor and Public Welfare, or House Education and Labor, may report out favorably a bill for a given program, and the Senate or House may approve or "authorize" it. But it still needs "funding." At this point the Appropriations Committee enters the picture. The Committee holds the purse strings and has considerable impact upon the substantive content of legislatio. Besides the authorization and appropriations process, the Rules Committee in the House, originally intended to be a sort of "traffic cop," has often turned out to be a third round of committee consideration. This committee decides which nonrevenue bills will get to the floor and what kind of rules will apply to the amending of a bill on the floor.

Since 1910-11, the period of the rebellion against the dictatorial Speaker, Joe Cannon, the committees "have won solid institutionalized independence from party leaders both inside and outside Congress."[57] In both the House and the Senate, standing committees are integral to the decision-making process, leading to considerable dispersal or fragmentation of power in Congress. Each committee has wide latitude to set its own rules and organize itself internally. Moreover, committees are given substantial powers regarding which bills to report and in what form to report them. Of course, there are ways to get around committees and to relieve a committee of a bill. The discharge motion in the Senate (requiring only a majority vote on the floor, although this can be subject to a filibuster which requires three-fifths of the total Senate membership to terminate) and the discharge petition in the House (requiring a majority of House members to sign the petition) are examples. Yet these and other available procedures have seldom been used successfully. This is partly because the procedures can be cumbersome to employ. Since the spirit of reciprocity is strong, they may also be politically inadvisable to use. Another possibility is that committees have been broadly sensitive to the views and needs of the wider body, thereby reducing the possibility that majorities strongly opposed to a committee can be generated. These possibilities are examined in greater detail in Chapter 8.

By dispersing powers among the standing committees, problems of policy coordination across committees can arise. Congress addressed this problem in 1974 by establishing Budget Committees for each house. These committees are charged with recommending overall budgetary targets and priorities. They are also charged with making ensuing recommendations on spending and revenue over the year to assure that the Congress either adheres to the targets or changes them only with knowledge of the relationship between the totality of spending programs and revenues. To carry out these tasks, the Budget Committees have been given a sizable staff through the newly created Congressional Budget Office.

We must be careful not to oversimplify or overgeneralize our comments on committees. Committees are markedly different from one another both within the same chamber and across the two chambers. They differ in a number of respects, such as degree of autonomy, the kinds of members on the committee, degree of integration with party leadership, influence on Congressional decision-making and success on the floor, the role of the chairman, and so on. Furthermore, perhaps primarily because of the larger size of the House, committees are more important to the internal procedures of the House than of the Senate. Thus in comparing the two houses, Fenno notes:

Senate committees are less important as a source of chamber influence, less preoccupied with success on the chamber floor, less autonomous within the chamber, less personally expert, less strongly led, and more individualistic in decision-making then are House committees.[58]

Committee Membership and Assignments The party ratio in each standing committee is roughly comparable to the ratio in the whole chamber; that is, if the Republicans have about 40 percent of the House seats, then on a committee of ten they would have about four members. The exact numbers are worked out between party leaders. Although efforts are made by the majority leaders to be reasonable and fair, the majority party, whether Republican or Democrat, has in the past taken a disproportionate share on such key committees as Ways and Means, House Rules, and Appropriations. These are the most important committees, and thus attempts are made to head off potential trouble in which a coalition of minority party members and renegades or mavericks of the majority party might be able to forge a dominating coalition.

It is important to take a look at the Committee on Committees, which has the discretion to make judgments about the relative weight of various factors (including seniority) in determining who shall be nominated to particular committees from their respective parties. Until the Ninety-fourth Congress, the House Democratic Committee on Committees was made up of the Democratic members of Ways and Means and the top party leaders. The reform-minded Caucus of the Ninety-fourth Congress, with seventy-five new faces, transferred most of the powers of nomination from Ways and Means to the Steering and Policy Committee chaired by Carl Albert. (Albert himself nominates to the Caucus the party's members for the Rules Committee.) Each Democratic Steering and Policy Committee member is responsible for screening committee assignment applications from Representatives in a designated number of states or zones. Since 1971, the Democratic Caucus has also permitted nominations by home state delegations so as not to be limited to Steering Committee input. Competition is enhanced, of course, if there are numerous applications for the same committee from the same zone. The Caucus has the final right of formal approval of the nominees or challengers.

The House Republican Committee on Committees, unlike the Democratic side, has no other function than making committee assignments. Appointed and chaired by the floor leader, it consists of one member for each state (unlike the Democrats) with at least one Republican representative in Congress. Because such a large group is unwieldy, an Executive Committee is designated. Each state with at least seven Republicans in its House delegation is entitled to elect one member to the Executive Committee. The floor leader then selects one member to represent those states with six Republicans, one to represent those with five, and so on down to one. Two other members are elected by the two most recent "classes" of freshmen Republicans to represent them. Whereas in the Democratic Committee on Committees, every member casts one vote, the Republicans on the Executive Committee vote in proportion to their state or states' Republican strength. The full Committee and Conference must formally approve assignments.

Both House Democrats and Republicans rank the twenty-two House standing committees in categories of importance. Congressmen who serve on one of the most important committees (for example, Ways and Means) rarely serve on any other standing committee. Congressmen who serve on committees of lesser importance may serve on more than one committee.

In the Senate, the procedures are less formal because the smaller size of the Senate makes the assignment process a less difficult task, since there are fewer requests and all Senators are usually on two or three committees. In the Senate, the Democratic Committee on Committees consists of the Democratic Steering Committee, which is appointed and chaired by the floor leader. Before Mansfield, members were selected from the established Democratic members of the Senate. The Senate Republican Committee on Committees consists of six to nine Senators appointed by the chairman of the Republican Conference. Both the Democratic and Republican Committee on Committees are subject to approval by the conference.

Since 1953, the Democratic Steering Committee has followed the policy instituted by Lyndon Johnson of giving each freshman Democrat an assignment on one major committee before granting senior Senators a second or third assignment. The Republicans later instituted a similar procedure. Existing procedure allows a Senator membership on not more than two major committees of a list of the fourteen more important committees (except for senior members who in 1970 were already serving on three committees on the list) and one of the less desirable committees. Of the most important committees, the top ones (for example, Appropriations) are designated exclusive, meaning a Senator may serve on only one of them.

Committees vary in importance, and most Representatives and Senators desire to be placed in what they presume to be the most important committees. By observing the committee transfer patterns, one could develop a ranked list of prestigious committees.[59] In the House, Ways and Means, Appropriations, and Rules are clearly the top committees, whereas few House members seek the Post Office and Civil Service or District of Columbia committees. In the Senate the most prestigious committees are Foreign Relations, Finance, and Appropriations, with the least interest expressed by Senators in Post Office and Civil Service, Rules and Administration, Government Operations, and District of Columbia committees. The new budget committees will likely become highly desirable in both houses.

Whereas committee seniority normally determines a committee's chairmanship, appointment to a committee is influenced by several factors. Masters' study of committee assignments in the House from 1947 to 1959 indicates the tendency to appoint experienced (two or more terms) Congressmen who are responsible legislators to the most prestigious and powerful committees. (This is true also in the Senate, where seniority seems to play a larger role in committee transfers, especially for the Republicans.) They represent districts which are not only relatively safe but will not require them to take inflexible or uncompromising positions on controversial issues. "The Committee on Committees wants to feel that the district will not only re-elect him but also allow him to operate as a free agent, enabling him to make controversial decisions on major policy questions without constant fear of reprisals at the polls."[60] In addition to experience, "legislative responsibility," and the right type of district, geographical area or balance is a factor in major committee assignments in the House. For example, each party's Committee on Committees tends to follow the "state seat" philosophy of selecting a member from the same state party delegation as the vacating member in order to preserve the existing geographical balance. Each party regards it as especially important to maintain geographical balance, that every section of the nation be represented, on the Ways and Means and Appropriations committees. Attempts are also made to limit each state's membership on the committee to one, except in the case of very large state delegations such as California, New York, and Illinois. Perhaps the most important single factor in assignments below the major committee category is whether a particular post will help insure reelection of the member assigned or not. Most members of a party are concerned about the reelection of other party members because a large party contingent maximizes their own influence.

Of crucial importance in both the House and the Senate are the personal desires, backgrounds, and political situations of the individual Congressman. Clearance with the chairman of the committee to which the candidate aspires is usually followed. Approval of the party leader normally is needed on key appointments. Often major interest groups' views may be taken into consideration, for example, what the Farm Bureau feels is important for agricultural assignments. Seniority is another of the factors in committee assignment, especially when there is competition between two men with comparable credentials except seniority. Although high seniority is not the only criterion for key committee assignments, it is crucial for continuation on such a committee if the Congressman's party loses seats in the election following his assignment. Committee members with the least seniority lose their assignments first.

The committee assignment process is one of the few points of intralegislative power for the astute legislative party leader; it can be the chief party weapon. It is difficult to make generalizations about or to define precisely the actual role played by party leaders, but the leaders certainly exert great influence on the selection of the members of of their respective Committee on Committees. In practice, the leadership in both parties focuses on assignments to the major committees and pays less attention to the minor committees. The leaders have virtual veto over important committees (see Chapter 5). The party leaders in both parties and both houses have influence, but they use it with a light, not a heavy, hand. Party leaders try to get members on committees who will agree with their concepts of "responsible legislators" and party responsibility, and by being instrumental in initial assignments they have a potential point of future leverage in appealing to that legislator on particular bills.

Committee Chairmen By Congressional custom the selection of the standing committee chairman is determined by seniority.[61] The majority party member with the longest consecutive period of membership on the committee normally becomes committee chairman if he so wishes. A similar condition prevails for selection of the ranking member from the minority party on each committee. As a consequence, if a member can stay alive and continue to get reelected, he can move up to the powerful position of chairman or ranking minority member. We should note that it is committee seniority, not seniority in the Congress, that determines the top positions. Thus, early assignment to a good committee is important if one does not wish to "waste" seniority by switching.

The Ninety-fourth Congress provides dramatic exceptions to the seniority rule, which from 1925 to 1974 had been violated only once. With the transfer of the committee assignment powers to the Democratic Steering and Policy Committee also came its power to place nominations of committee chairmen (and the subcommittee chairmen of the Appropriations Committee) before the whole House Democratic party Caucus, which had been increased by large numbers of newly elected liberals. In secret, recorded, separate Caucus ballots, three chairmen (all long time Southern chairmen) lost their chairmanships by narrow margins. Henry Reuss (Wis.), the third-ranking committee member in terms of seniority, replaced Wright Patman (Tex.) as Chairman of Banking, Currency and Housing; second-ranking Thomas Foley (Wash.) replaced W. R. Poage (Tex.) as top man on Agriculture; and second-ranking Melvin Pierce (Ill.), a "northerner," but of similar defense philosophy, replaced Edward Hebert (La.) as head of Armed Services. In addition, Wayne Hays (Ohio) of the House Administration Committee escaped removal after a bitter contest with Frank Thompson (N.J.), who actually had been nominated by the Democratic Steering and Policy Committee. We should also note that Wilbur Mills, who appeared on stage in Boston with stripper Fanne Foxe and later entered the hospital for exhaustion and alcoholism, resigned his chairmanship of the Ways and Means Committee when it became apparent to him, at the urging of close friends, party leaders, and fellow committee members, that he would be deposed.

The principle has been established that a chairmanship is not "automatic," that the chairman and ranking minority member owe their expected or continued service in their respective roles to their party caucus. Voicing a feeling shared by many of the reformers, one Democratic House member interviewed by the authors noted that, though the same Congressmen normally may be elected to be committee chairmen that would have succeeded to them by seniority, the new procedures and recent removals will make those chairmen more "responsive" to the committee membership and the wider Democratic party membership.

Turning now to the House Republicans, their top-ranking member on each committee is elected individually by the full party Conference. The Republican Committee on Committees nominates a member for the top spot on each committee (not necessarily on the basis of seniority). In 1973, there were two challenges in the party Conference in which alternative candidates to the most senior committee members of the respective committees received about a third as many votes as the senior winner.

In 1973, the Senate Republicans also made an important change in their procedure for election of ranking minority members (or chairmen if they are ever in the majority).

It gives an important role to committee members in that the ranking minority member is nominated by a vote of the Republicans on the individual committees. The full party Conference must then confirm the nominee. Senate Democratic candidates for the top spot are nominated by their Steering Committee and voted on individually by the party Conference. Significantly, the Senate Democrats in January, 1975, voted to select committee chairmen by *secret* ballot in the future if one-fifth of the Conference requests it. However, for each committee for both parties in the Senate of the Ninety-fourth Congress, the top positions are held by committee members with the greatest committee seniority.

This seniority norm would not be very controversial if a chairman was simply a neutral presiding officer over committee meetings. This is not the case; there is concentration of power in committee chairmen, which, of course, is magnified by the central role played by standing committees in the legislative process. There is no standardization of operations of committees and committee chairmen; this varies from committee to committee and chairman to chairman. The power of the committee chairman has not always been as great as it is today. With the demise of Speaker Joe Cannon in 1911 and the subsequent curtailment of the Speaker's power to appoint committee chairmen and committees, the power of the committee chairmen in the House increased significantly over the next fifty years.

The chairman has a broad range of formal and informal powers. He has considerable power over subcommittee membership and the committee's utilization of subcommittees. He can decide whether to refer a bill to subcommittee or not or to give a bill to a particular subcommittee, perhaps one which he may chair himself, and in this way influence the fate of the bill.[62] He has control of the agenda and thus can determine priorities of bill consideration. His influence can affect not only substantive bills desired by a member but also the power relationships among committee members and their power in Congress as a whole. In many instances, he can prevent full committee meetings if he wishes, or he can decide when to have them. However, in both houses a majority of the committee can call a meeting and act if the chairman refuses to do so. This is highly unusual, for the legislators fear the ire and power of the chairman, respect the general mode of operation, or think in terms of their future chairmanships. Once a meeting is held, the chairman's own views, personal influence, potential for rewards and punishment in the future, and the way in which he presides can alter the outcome.

In the House, the committee chairman is the one who appears before the Rules Committee to defend the committee action and request a "rule" to clear the bill's way to the floor. Also, in both houses, the committee chairman is usually the leader (or appoints someone) in floor debate on legislation reported from his committee. Again in the House, where debate is limited, the chairman can allot debating time to whomever he pleases, can open or close debate on bills reported from his committee, and can move the "previous question" when he thinks appropriate. He usually also serves on the Conference committee (discussed below) on bills originating in his committee and typically decides who the other representatives of his chamber will be. Finally, he appoints and assigns much of his party's committee staff, which can be a valuable resource, given the limited time and voluminous work load of Congressmen. Thus, a Congressional committee chairman, despite recent curtailments, still has numerous weapons in his arsenal to reward and punish other Congressmen who support or obstruct the working of his will. The power, of course, varies with the abilities, skills, and desires of the particular man who occupies the position, and varying styles, prestige, knowlege, and so on can affect the chairman's influence.

However, we must be careful not to exaggerate the powers of the chairman, for his influence is very much dependent upon the total context and specifically the nature of his relationships with his colleagues on his committee. John Manley's study of former chairman Wilbur Mills and the Ways and Means Committee views influence as very much a reciprocal phenomenon. The support of his fellow committee members was a necessary condition of Mill's "power": He was as "responsive" to the committee as the committee was to him.[63] Mills' influence was partly a function of sharing views of the Committee members (and to some degree the wider House membership) and giving the members what they wanted.

Similarly, in his comparative study of six House committees, Fenno concluded that the most critical fact about any chairman was his relationship to the "strategic premises" espoused by a substantial majority of his committee's members. He found that only one of the six chairmen he examined operated in a manner contrary to the strategy and goals of a sizable majority of the committee. This was Tom Murray of the Post Office Committee, and eventually he lost control of his committee. That is, due to formal rule changes and informal negotiations, the committee members were able to effectively circumvent him.

These findings suggest that a chairman must retain the support of the bulk of the committee members if he is to be successful; he must be sensitive to the pressures, demands, and needs that arise inside the committee in order to avoid circumvention or revolt. A cohesive and determined majority on the committee may over time successfully restrict a chairman who flagrantly rejects its views.[64] To this now is added the possibility of defeat in the caucus or conference.

The way in which committee chairmen are chosen, especially the importance of seniority, has some rather obvious consequences for the characteristics of those who hold power. It has the tendency to place in chairmanships men familiar with the committee's work, but who are older than the average Representative or Senator. At the beginning of the Ninety-fourth Congress the average chairman's age in both houses was 63 whereas the overall average age was 50 in the House and 55.5 in the Senate. This is especially true for the major committee chairmanships. Younger and more recent additions to the legislature must "wait their turn" before assuming key committee leadership roles. Not only is older age reflected in the legislative power structure, but also there develops a bias against those from competitive districts or states. "Safe" seats gain the chairmanships.

Many critics have charged that a sectional bias thus results. They point out that Democratic chairmen, especially among the top committees, have been concentrated in the South and that the Republican pattern favors the Midwest and, to a lesser extent, the East. George Goodwin, in a study of the distribution of committee chairmanships by geographical regions from the 1947 through 1968 Congresses, showed that southerners had 60 percent of the Senate chairmanships and 62 percent of the House chairmanships during that time (while having only about a quarter of the population). When the Republicans were in power, Midwesterners had 58 percent of the Senate chairmanships and 66 percent of the House chairmanships.[65] In the Ninety-fourth Congress the southern Democratic share of chairmanships in the Senate was 33 percent (a 17 percent drop from the Ninety-third Congress) and in the House, 41 percent (a 2 percent drop from the previous Congress). Overall there seems to be some dropping off in comparison to Goodwin's figures cited above. Southerners until recently had continued to chair nearly 70 percent of the most prestigious committees in both Houses, but they lost control of the powerful House Rules Committee for the Ninety-third Congress when William Colmer (D. Miss.) retired. With Mills' resignation in the Ninety-fourth Congress and three southern chairmen deposed, only one powerful committee (Appropriations) is chaired by a southerner. There are several studies that have argued quite persuasively that the southern Democrats' institutional base of power has reached its peak and is now declining.

Barbara Hinckley's recent study of the seniority system challenges many myths that have been propagated by scholars, journalists, critics, and even practitioners of Congressional politics. She concludes that one cannot trace southern dominance in the Democratic party simply to the seniority system. She contends that there is no evidence that application of the seniority rule automatically results in regional bias. The effect of the seniority system is at most "limited" or "marginal." She notes:

> Democratic committee chairmen or ranking minority members, taken as a group, reflect with fair accuracy the composition of the Democratic members in Congress, and the Republican leaders even more accurately reflect their party's membership. Thus Southerners have filled more than 50 percent of the Democratic committee chairs in the past two decades, and Southerners have usually comprised more than 50 percent of the Democratic membership of the House and Senate.[66]

She indicates that the seniority requirement of continuous service can be met by a majority of the Congressmen and Senators; that is, most are from "safe seats" and have "average" tenure. Seen in this way, the seniority rule requires long service from a membership where long service is the rule not the exception. Our earlier figures on turnover and the advantages of incumbency support Hinckley's findings. Thus other factors such as distribution of members in the party, "luck of the seniority draw," initial committee assignments and subsequent reassignments, and so on influence the distribution of committee chairmanships. However, Hinckley notes that the seniority system may distort somewhat, as, for example, the bias against the small number of competitive states and districts alluded to above. There is also a "time lag" in the distribution of chairmanships and ranking members. For example, only recently has the Midwest strength in the Democratic party that began in the late 1950s started to show up in the redistribution of chairmanships. The seniority system also has a "magnifying effect; it gives a 'bonus' to the plurality or majority faction in the party, whether majorities are reckoned on the basis of North versus South, rural versus urban, or liberal versus conservative.... But in practice the group with the longest tenure has tended also to be the largest and strongest group."[67]

The trends cited above and increasing seniority of northern Democrats suggests an important shift in the direction of power in the Democratic party in the near future. Wolfinger and Hollinger indicate:

> The northern wing of the congressional party is just now recovering the ground lost in the

Republican sweep of 1946. The enormous losses in that election were confined almost entirely to the North. One of the long term consequences of the Republican landslide then was the beginning of a "seniority generation" dominated by Southerners.[68]

With the increasing number of noncompetitive and safe seats in the North and the increasing thrust of the Republican party in the South, northern Democrats' "useful seniority" will soon surpass southerners'. Thus, within a few years, as southerners retire or die off, northerners will begin to realize in turn the fruits of the seniority system. There will be a resulting decline in the power of the most deviant wing of the Democratic party and therefore a possible increase in party cohesion. A greater party "responsibility" will likely result, and the tension between Congressional seniority leaders and Democratic Presidents and party leaders will likely decrease.

Subcommittees The last two decades have seen a remarkable growth in the number and rise of subcommittees.[69] By 1970 over 250 subcommittees were operating, nearly 200 of which were "standing" subcommittees carrying over from session to session with fairly stable membership. Many Senators serve on upwards from five subcommittees and the average Representative on three or four. The principal advantage and/or need of subcommittees is the greater specialization they allow in handling the complex and various aspects of legislation assigned to the full committee. Legislative effectiveness is also increased in its encounter with and oversight of executive agencies. In the Senate, the subcommittee system has given younger members the chance to exercise their talents and possibly earn recognition well before their chance would come as a senior member of a committee. Men with two to four years of service can become chairmen of important subcommittees and, if so inclined and endowed, make an invaluable contribution to the performance of the committee's tasks.

Recent rule changes have already resulted in a greater distribution of the subcommittee chairmanships. The main beneficiaries appear to have been the liberals. The principal danger or disadvantage in the proliferation of subcommittees is the further fragmentation of power that may develop, thus making a coherent and efficient legislative program more difficult. Most House subcommittee chairmen are senior members of the related committee. In about two-thirds of the committees, this norm has operated almost without exception; in the other third, the same norm was used more often than not. Ironically, the fact that seniority was not always followed in subcommittee assignments in the past often worked to the advantage of southerners, for they could then serve over more senior northerners. Where the committee chairman makes assignments, he may be somewhat limited by previous subcommittee assignments and chamber rules. Once an individual gains a subcommittee chairmanship, he holds on to it with almost the same tenacity one holds on to a full committee chairmanship. However, in the past, a skillful chairman could make the subcommittee a tool for an integrated power structure. The new Subcommittee Bill of Rights adopted recently by the House Democrats, with its emphasis on fixed subcommittee jurisdictions, elected subcommittee chairmen, more subcommittee autonomy and adequate staffing, and greater protection given its subcommittee members regarding retention of their assignments, could severely erode House chairmen's power.

The degree of choice a Congressman has in subcommittee placement varies. At the extreme, the Agriculture Committee often accords a member his choice; he thus serves on the subcommittee handling his district's commodity, thereby "representing" his constituency and enhancing his reelection chances. The chairmen of most full committees normally consult with the ranking minority members before deciding on the subcommittee ratio and the actual assignments of the opposing parties.

The relationship of subcommittees to parent committees and to chairmen of parent committees varies a great deal. It may range from the thirteen highly independent and important subcommittees of the House Appropriations Committee to the rather insignificant Subcommittee on Restaurants of the Senate Rules and Administration Committee. Some committees, such as the Senate Budget and House Rules, do not use subcommittees at all. Others, such as the prestigious Senate Foreign Relations Committee, give them minor tasks. Subcommittees may be standing or special (the latter appointed from bill to bill or session to session); they may have clearly defined jurisdiction or vague jurisdiction.

Subcommittee autonomy and power is shaped considerably by the full committee chairman's personality, his view of his role, and the nature or thrust of his policy objectives. The full committee task (including the degree of consensus on that task) and the nature of the legislation are also important variables. The full committee chairman willing, a subcommittee with a strong chairman and dealing with a complex, specialized piece of legislation virtually makes the full committee decision. In the Appropriations Committee and the Senate Judiciary Committee, subcommittees have been granted clearly defined jurisdictions and, within these, a rather free hand. The full committee usually defers to the subcommittee's decision.

Select Committees   Another type of committee found in Congress is the select or special committee, which is theoretically a temporary committee created by resolution to undertake a particular legislative task.[70] They usually are disbanded after they report. They are formally appointed by the presiding officer, though they are, in effect, appointed by party leaders, with the majority party having the majority share of members. Their general function is one of investigation and study of specific problems. Undoubtedly the most famous recent select committee was the Senate Select Committee on Presidential Campaign Activities (chaired by Senator Sam Ervin) created to investigate the Watergate affair as well as the broader question of Presidential campaigns. They report directly to the full House or Senate, but they are not authorized to report on legislation for consideration on the floor. While select committees have had only slight impact on public policy, they often are the forerunners of standing committees as in the case of the new House Small Business Committee and the space committees in each house. The combined total of select committees in both houses is usually no more than ten.

Select committees serve a multiplicity of purposes. They may serve certain interest groups (as the Select Committees on Small Business have) who lack, or think they lack, access to standing committees. They are thereby assured of some input, however ineffective, into the legislative process. Select committees also serve as an additional instrument of legislative oversight of the executive. In some instances, select committees, as with subcommittees, serve individual Congressmen, making use of their talents and giving them a forum. This circumvents the seniority system and thrusts young men into leadership roles, as in the cases of Estes Kefauver and Harry Truman.

Membership, and especially chairmanship, may be a vehicle for an individual legislator to solidify support in his home constituency. Select committees may also be a way of evading "undersirable" standing committees or avoiding jurisdictional fights in areas of overlapping standing committee jurisdictions. Select committees have served as institutions for "self-education" of the respective houses or for the education of the citizenry. The impact on public policy of select committees depends primarily on the prestige and influence of members appointed to the committee and the gravity of the issue considered, but important issues are normally referred to regular standing committees. The 1947 Herter committee is an example of a select committee with influential personnel considering a crucial problem, the Marshall Plan.

Joint Committees Joint Committees, which are formed through concurrent resolutions or legislative acts, consist of members from both legislative chambers. Joint committees may be: *select* (usually given some minor administrative task); *conference* (which we shall discuss later); and *standing* (which are more or less permanent). Their principal duty is to achieve coordination between the two houses and avoid duplication of effort or overspecialization. Examples of standing joint committees are the Joint Economic Committee, Joint Committee on Internal Revenue, and the numerous joint housekeeping committees (operations, library, and others). The best known and most powerful of the few existing joint committees is probably the Joint Committee on Atomic Energy, the chairmanship of which rotates between chambers every two years. It is the only joint committee to which legislation is referred and is thus the only one that can report bills. However, this is not the major source of its power. Its close surveillance of and interaction with the executive branch often enable it to get the AEC to adopt committee recommendations. Even so, the impact of the Joint Committee on Atomic Energy is partly traceable to the early postwar period in which it developed and the nature of the subject matter considered.[71]

On the whole, while some degree of coordination has taken place in the past three decades (since 1946), the spirit of bicameralism and house pride fosters jealousy and difficulties, especially for House members, that make effective coordination next to impossible.

Conference Committees Conference committees are ad hoc joint committees appointed for the clearly defined purpose of working out differences in House and Senate versions of bills approved by the two chambers. It is not unusual for 40 to 45 percent of the total number of public laws passed to have gone through conference; most of these laws are major rather than minor pieces of legislation. Members are appointed by the presiding officers of each house, but it is customary to appoint members recommended by the committee chairmen and ranking minority members involved. This usually means that the committee chairmen and senior committee members of both parties are appointed. If a subcommittee played a key role, its senior members are normally recommended. The Senate usually includes all members of the interested subcommittee. Such a pattern of selection gives the conference committees the political cast of the committee system in the Congress, resulting in opponents to a bill or provision of a bill being included on the conference committee. However in 1974, the House approved a requirement that the Speaker appoint a majority of members who "genuinely support" the House's position. Normally three to nine members in each house from both parties are appointed. Each house need not appoint the same number. However, a majority of *each* house's contingent must agree to the conference report before it is returned to the two houses, where its reports are *not* subject to amendment and are usually adopted. Significantly since 1975 at the urging of the House, conferences are opened unless a majority of either chamber's conferees vote in public to close a session.

Conference committee representatives theoretically seek a "middle ground" or compromise bill between differing versions. Sometimes (though still in a minority of instances) new material is introduced that may substantially change the bills, and they are often adopted in the revised form by both houses during the rush for adjournment. However, careful research does not support a charge of irresponsibility on the part of conference committees. Rarely do completely new bills emerge from the conference. Each contingent is expected to represent the position of its respective house (sometimes it has specific instructions) but not to be so rigid as to make some compromise impossible.

Who "wins" in the conference committees—the House or the Senate? Fenno's monumental study of the appropriations committees (covering 1947-62) indicates that Senate conferees have tended to dominate. In terms of "dollar outcomes" in the final version of the bills in the 331 appropriations conferences, the Senate "won" 187 times, the House 101 times; there were 43 "draws" or fairly equal compromises. Fenno surmises that this is at least partly traceable to "more direct" and "more complete" support of the Senate for its conferees. Fenno writes: "When Senate conferees go to the conference room, they not only represent the Senate—they are the Senate. The position they defend will have been worked out with a maximum of participation by Senate members and will enjoy a maximum of support in that body."[72] Support for the House Appropriations Committee is more tenuous partly because its members are more economy-oriented than the rest of the House members. Also a smaller proportion of the House members than the much smaller Senate have been involved in their respective versions. The reader should be reminded that here we are only talking about Senate dominance in appropriations conference committees, for Fenno and others suggest that the House in general has more influence on the total appropriations process. David Vogler's study of the relative chamber influence in 596 conference committees in five Congresses found that the Senate "won" 65 percent of the time to the House's 35 percent. He suggests: "Senate predominance similar to that found by Fenno in appropriations is discovered in almost all policy areas and in most intercommittee subsystems. This pattern of greater Senate influence is found to obtain in both Democratic and Republican Congresses."[73] However, since we do not have a zero-sum situation and judgments of winners, especially on substantive policy, have an element of arbitrariness, we must be cautious in accepting exact conclusions. Nevertheless, a pattern does seem to be present.

Committee Staffs In addition to the individual staffs of Congressmen (which are greatly concerned with housekeeping, communications, and political tasks), Congress also has committee staffs available and, often separate subcommittee staffs. The Legislative Reorganization Act (LRA) of 1946 initially provided for the employment of professional staff members and clerks. The LRA of 1970 and actions since then have expanded the professional staff and encouraged the use of temporary consultants. Some committees, most notably the Appropriations Committee, have been given disproportionate assistance. Today a 30 member staff is not unusual for most committees; a few have 50 or more persons. Each house has over 300 professional staff people.

The increasing volume and complexity of legislation, coupled with the pressures of time and fear of executive domination of the information-gathering process, prompted the decision to improve committee staffing. Some independent countervailing expertise was deemed necessary if the legislative branch was to maintain even a semblance of its constitutional prerogatives. Though still understaffed, these stopgap attempts have produced a fairly high-quality staff that has aided in the maintenance of a dynamic role for the legislative branch in public policy-making, primarily by strengthening the committee system. The staff helps to collect, analyze, and evaluate data; suggest problems to be considered or implications of existing proposals; possibly suggest a solution or a variety of alternative solutions to problems; draft bills and suggest "legislative strategy"; and aid in investigations, especially in putting on public hearings.[74]

According to the Legislative Reorganization Act of 1846, staffs were to be hired by a majority vote of the committee on the basis of merit or "fitness" and not by political affiliation. They then were to be assigned to the chairman and ranking minority member but to carry out the directives of the committee. This desire to create a "nonpartisan" staff has *not* developed in most committees. However, the House Foreign Affairs (renamed in 1975 the International Relations Committee) and Senate Foreign Relations Committees have been fairly successful in fulfilling the mandate. Most partisan are probably those committees with major ideological and interest conflicts such as Agriculture, Education and Welfare, and Labor and Public Welfare. In practice, for most committees, the committee chairman controls the staff. Even in "nonpartisan" staffs, the chairman makes the decision about whom to hire, though he consults with the ranking minority member. Until recently, examinations of the staffing patterns of most committees, including select committees, indicated not only a partisan bias for the majority party, but an overwhelming basis.[75] However, in 1975 the House acted to guarantee the minority party a share of the statutory staff for committees.

Congress also has at its disposal the General Accounting Office (GAO) and the Congressional Research Service (CRS). The GAO furnishes staff aides to committees on request and conducts special audits, investigations, and management studies requested by Congress and its committees. It periodically is called to give reports on proposed bills or even to testify before committees. The primary function of the CRS as indicated in the Legislative Reorganization Act of 1970 is to serve as a research arm of Congress instead of being a reference service (as its forerunner, the Legislative Reference Service). Sufficient time has not elapsed to ascertain whether the CRS will be as isolated from Congressmen or their staff or if it will be as ineffectively utilized as was the Legislative Reference Service.

The Western European Parliaments

Having outlined some of the major features of the Congress, we are in a position to take up the three European systems—Great Britain, France, and West Germany. The structures of these sustems are different from the American political system in a number of respects. One of the most important differences is that each European system is either fully or partially a parliamentary system, whereas the American system is not. Another important difference is that the upper legislative house in each system is not elected directly by the public and some are also clearly less potent than the lower house, whereas both the House and the Senate in the United States are elected directly by the public and, with few exceptions (particularly regarding nominations and treaties), are equal in their authority.

The European systems, especially those of France and West Germany, also share a number of characteristics with the American system. For instance, France is, in part, a Presidential system in which the President and legislature are entirely separate institutions with separate powers. Each is also elected separately, even in different years. West Germany, too, has a tradition of the executive and the legislature being independent (if not electorally separate) institutions. Moreover, like the United States, West Germany is a federal system and is characterized in some respects by decentralizing political forces similar to those in the United States.

Our discussion of the three European legislative systems will follow the general outline we used for the United States. After briefly introducing the major political institutions in each system (the executive, the lower house, and the upper house) and the formal relations of these institutions to each other, we will look at the authority the legislatures have to make decisions in each of the three systems and at the kinds of limits placed on this authority. We will then turn to a discussion of the process by which members are nominated and elected to the three legislatures. Finally, we will describe the internal organization of the three legislatures.

An Overview of the Political Institutions

We commence with an introductory sketch of some basic features of the three European systems, starting with Great Britain.[76] Great Britain is a parliamentary system, with the British House of Commons serving as the parliamentary body. Because it is a parliamentary system, the equivalent of the chief executive in Great Britain (the Prime Minister, who heads the cabinet and government) is not elected in popular elections separately from the House of Commons. Instead, the electorate votes for the House of Commons, which, in turn, selects the Prime Minister.

In practice, however, the system has worked in such a way that the electorate in effect votes for the House of Commons and the Prime Minister simultaneously. In the past thirty years, except for 1974, the leader of the political party that won an absolute majority of seats in elections to the House of Commons became the Prime Minister and formed the cabinet and government.

Formally, the Prime Minister and the other government ministers are appointed to their offices by the monarch. In appointing a Prime Minister, the monarch will select the candidate who led the victorious party in the parliamentary elections (or, if no victorious party emerges, the monarch selects whom the House will support). The monarch then accepts the Prime Minister's appointments of the other government ministers. In a case where a Prime Minister has resigned and where the parliamentary party in power cannot agree on a successor (and this would be an unlikely possibility) the monarch might play a part in selecting a new Prime Minister.

Unless extended by Parliament, elections to the House of Commons occur periodically during intervals of no more than five years.[77] In contesting parliamentary elections, the two British political parties with the greatest strength are the Conservative and Labour parties. The Liberal party is a smaller third party which, since 1945, has received from 6 to about 20 percent of the popular vote and from 1 to 4 percent of the seats in the House of Commons. There are also other, even smaller, parties.

As pointed out previously, each election from 1945 to 1974 produced an absolute majority in the House of Commons for one of the major parties, enabling that party simultaneously to control both the executive (government) and the legislature. The Conservatives won in 1951 under Winston Churchill, in 1955 under Anthony Eden, in 1959 under Harold Macmillan, and in 1970 under Edward Heath. Labour victories were in 1945 and 1950 under Clement Atlee and in 1964 and 1966 under Harold Wilson. In 1974, a general election held early in the year did not produce an absolute majority for any party in the House. After several weeks of negotiations among the parties, no coalition emerged, and Harold Wilson became the Prime Minister of a minority government. Under Wilson, Labour later went on to win an absolute majority of the Commons in a second election during 1974.

Political parties are crucial in linking the Prime Minister and government to the majority in the House of Commons. Within the House of Commons, these parties are called parliamentary parties (the parties outside Parliament are called extraparliamentary parties).[78] Each parliamentary party selects its own leader who, in turn, becomes the leader of the party before the nation and the electorate. In this way, the parliamentary party plays a critical part in determining its nominee for the premiership. How the parliamentary parties are organized and how they go about selecting their leaders will be described in greater detail later in this chapter and in Chapter 6.

In a parliamentary system the executive is politically responsible before the legislature. In the British system this means that the government is politically responsible before the House of Commons. Unlike the separation-of-powers system in the United States, the British government can be voted out of power by a majority of the House of Commons at any time and for almost any reason, thereby leading to new elections. Under the principle of collective responsibility, however, the House may not vote any single minister out of power; it must vote the government out collectively.

The House of Commons has not used this power for some time because of the workings of party support for the government. More informally, however, members belonging to the majority parliamentary party can put pressure on the Prime Minister to resign. If the Prime Minister does resign without a formal censure from the Commons, the party may then replace him with another Prime Minister. We will discuss the politics of resignation and replacement of Prime Ministers more fully when we examine leadership selection in Chapter 6.

The Prime Minister also has the right to dissolve Parliament at any time and call for another mandate through new elections. Prime Ministers have used this power in order to have elections at the most advantageous time possible. The Prime Minister may also try to use the power to dissolve Parliament and call new elections for purposes of keeping members of his parliamentary party in line. However, if the Prime Minister's electoral position is not secure, to follow through with this threat may cost him greatly.

The Prime Minister and his cabinet ministers[79] (together with junior ministers, etc.) constitute the government. Individual ministers remain in office as long as they retain the Prime Minister's support, and the Prime Minister (as well as the government) remains in office in between elections as long as he retains the support of his parliamentary party (since ordinarily his party has a majority in the House of Commons).

The government, in turn, is responsible for coordinating and effectuating the administration of legislation passed by the House of Commons as well as making decisions under powers the House of Commons delegates to it. Furthermore, and also very important, is that the government plays a leading part in the initiation of legislation into the House of Commons, including all financial bills.

Besides the institutions mentioned thus far, there is also the upper house of Parliament, the House of Lords. Unlike the American system, the upper house in the British system is not the equal of the lower house. This is especially the case regarding the power to reject legislation. The House of Lords can only reject legislation *provisionally*, for the House of Commons can overrule the Lords after one year has passed (or, after thirty days on money bills). In fact, insofar as concerns government bills, the Lords has not used its delaying power since this power was limited to one year in 1949. Nor has it often used its right of amendment to obstruct legislation desired by the government and the House of Commons.

Moreover, the Lords is not representative in the minimal sense we used the term in our introductory chapter. Unlike the House of Commons (or the United States House and Senate), the members of the House of Lords are not subject to periodic popular elections. Rather, the members serve as a consequence of hereditary title or as a consequence of being given a title by the monarch.

One value attributed to the House of Lords is that it can force reconsideration of a bill. The House of Lords frequently uncovers weaknesses in aspects of a bill and pressures the government and the House of Commons to adopt its amendments. Furthermore, some government ministers are drawn from the Lords. Finally, the House of Lords provides a platform from which the views of its members can gain public attention.[80]

With these preliminary remarks about the British system in mind, we can turn for a moment to West Germany which, like Britain, has a parliamentary system.[81] The Bundestag serves as the parliamentary body and, acting as a parliamentary body, selects the political leader of the executive, the Chancellor. It does so, formally, upon recommendation of the President.[82] Somewhat akin to the monarch's role in Britain, the recommendation of the President in selecting the Chancellor has reflected the outcome of popular elections and the leadership choice made by the parliamentary parties in the Bundestag.

Once chosen, the Chancellor selects his ministers, who are appointed by the President to form the government (see Chapter 6). They remain in office as long as they continue to retain the support of the Chancellor.

As in Britain, the German government plays a leading part in initiating legislation into the Bundestag. It makes decisions under powers delegated to it by Parliament, as well, and along with the states of the West German federal system, plays a part in the administration of federal legislation.

The German Chancellor is politically responsible before the Bundestag, although in a somewhat circumscribed sense compared to Great Britain. The Bundestag, on its own initiative, can defeat the Chancellor and force him from office. But, it can do so only if there is a successor whom a majority of members in the Bundestag is prepared to support (the House of Commons does not have to meet this condition in order to defeat a government). The Chancellor must also resign if he is defeated after having asked for the confidence of the Bundestag. If defeated in this situation, the Chancellor is empowered to dissolve the Bundestag and call for new elections.[83]

Elections to the Bundestag, which occur periodically within at least a four-year period, have been an important determinant of who forms the government and who becomes Chancellor. The major parties competing to win elections to the Bundestag, and thereby also to gain control of the executive, are the Christian Democratic Union/Christian Social Union (CDU/CSU) and the Social Democratic Party of Germany (SPD). The Free Democratic party (FDP, a liberal party) is a third party whose success in winning seats, unlike that of the British Liberal party, has been sufficient usually to prevent either of the two major parties from winning an absolute majority of the seats in the Bundestag. Because of this, the formation of coalition governments has been necessary. It has been normal for the party winning a plurality of the seats in the Bundestag to provide the Chancellor[84] and for this party and another to form a coalition government. This has usually been done by the CDU/CSU or the SPD (whichever is larger) forming a coalition government with the FDP.[85]

As in the case of the British system, political parties in West Germany are a crucial factor serving to link the government to the majority in the Bundestag. Although the party's Chancellor-designate to lead the national party in elections to the Bundestag is chosen by the extraparliamentary party, the parliamentary party and its leaders have in practice generally been integral in this choice.[86] Moreover, the Chancellor continues in office until the next election only as long as his parliamentary party, its leaders (including cabinet members), and the other parliamentary party in the coalition continue to support him. Since 1960, two CDU/CSU Chancellors have resigned because support for them from these quarters had withered. Ludwig Erhard replaced Konrad Adenauer, who stepped down in 1963 (Adenauer had been Chancellor since 1949), and then, in late 1966, Erhard was forced to resign and was replaced by Kurt-Georg Kiesinger. In both cases, the CDU/CSU parliamentary party, after negotiations with the other party with which it would form a majority coalition, selected a new leader who then became Chancellor. This enabled the CDU/CSU to retain power and to change Chancellors without needing to go to the electorate.[87]

A somewhat different situation arose in 1972 under the Chancellorship of Willy Brandt of the SPD (who became Chancellor after the elections of 1969). Although Brandt retained the support of most of his parliamentary party, the combination of a narrow Bundestag majority and of some dissidents within the SPD and its coalition partner, the FDP, made it difficult for Brandt to lead. He chose the strategy of going to the electorate by losing a vote of confidence and dissolving the Bundestag. This tactic proved to be successful, for the 1972 elections produced an increased Bundestag majority behind Brandt and the coalition parties. With his increased majority, Brandt continued as Chancellor. However, amid embarrassing disclosures about an aide, Brandt resigned office in 1974 and Helmut Schmidt of the SPD became the Federal Republic's fifth Chancellor.

Alongside the government and the Bundestag, a third major national political institution in West Germany is the Bundesrat. The Bundesrat is the upper legislative house which represents the states of the federal system. The purpose of the Bundesrat is to feed into the legislative process the interests of the states.[88] It reviews government legislative proposals both before and after they are introduced into the Bundestag. If the proposals pass the Bundestag, they may be rejected by the Bundesrat. The Bundesrat's rejection is final if the legislative proposal involves certain matters (relating especially to the powers of the state governments). In this way, about 50 percent of the legislation passed by the Bundestag is subject to veto by the Bundesrat.[89] For legislation in these areas to be adopted, then, it must pass both the Bundestag and the Bundesrat. Other legislation does not require the consent of the Bundesrat, and on this legislation the Bundestag can override the Bundesrat.

When there are differences between the Bundestag and Bundesrat, a meeting of the Joint Mediation Committee can be convened. This committee, like the conference committees of the United States Congress, consists of an equal number of members of the two houses and has the purpose of settling policy differences between the houses (unlike the American conference committee, however, the members of the Joint Mediation Committee are permanent members and do not change according to the bill under consideration). Meetings of the committee are usually requested by the Bundesrat; on legislation over which it has a final veto, the Bundesrat generally requests the committee meet when it has reason to feel that its position on the piece of legislation will prove acceptable to the Bundestag.[90] From 1949 to 1973, the Joint Mediation Committee met on 311 bills and was able to mediate successfully in 271 of the cases.

The committee report on a bill is not final and must be submitted to each house. If the bill is one over which the Bundesrat has a final veto, both the Bundesrat and the Bundestag must adopt the bill in the same form before it can become law. If the Bundesrat does not have a final veto, then the text as adopted by the Bundestag becomes law. However, within a week after the Joint Mediation Committee has completed its work, whether it has been able to reach agreement or not, the Bundesrat can enter a protest, or a suspensive veto. If it has done so by two-thirds vote, the Bundestag needs a two-thirds vote to override the suspensive veto.

Due to its absolute and suspensive veto, the Bundesrat is a powerful institution, certainly more so than the British House of Lords, and nearly equal to the Bundestag in terms of legislative authority. However, unlike the members of the Bundestag, who are elected directly by the public, the members of the Bundesrat are selected by and politically responsible to the *land* (state) governments. The public plays an indirect rather than direct part in this through elections to the state parliaments, which in turn provide the basis for the formation of the state governments.

These brief remarks about the German system are sufficient to suggest that it is a complex system, even in its very basic aspects. So, too, is the French system. Indeed, the basic political structures of the French political system are perhaps somewhat more complex than the others being discussed.[91] Part of the reason for this lies in the history of the French Fourth Republic (1946-58). There was a great deal of cabinet instability under the parliamentary system of the Fourth Republic because Premiers and their governments were not able to maintain the support of the Assembly. As a consequence, from 1946 to 1958 there was a total of twenty-seven Premiers, each lasting an average of less than six months.[92]

In an effort to build a stronger executive while simultaneously maintaining a parliamentary system, the framers of the Constitution of the Fifth Republic called for *two* executives, both of whom would be capable of playing a major part in the policy process, and serve as political leaders. One is the President of the Republic. The President is elected by popular vote in periodic elections that take place separately (even in different years) from elections to the legislature.[93] Moreover, the President is not politically responsible to the legislature. In these ways, the French President is somewhat similar to the American President. The major powers of the President (as well as those of the Premier and government) in relation to the French Parliament will be described in the following section.[94]

The second executive, the Premier, is selected by the President and is, along with his government, politically responsible to the lower house of the French legislature, the National Assembly. In this latter sense, the Premier and government are somewhat similar to the parliamentary executive such as in Great Britain or West Germany.

The National Assembly can force the Premier and government from office in one of two ways. One of these is for an Assembly member, supported by a petition signed by 10 percent of the Assembly, to call for a motion of censure and to gain the support of an absolute majority of the Assembly when the motion is put to a vote.[95] The second way is for the Premier and government to be defeated by an absolute majority after asking for the confidence of the Assembly. If the government asks for a vote of confidence on a bill, the bill is considered adopted unless Assembly members petition for a motion of censure and file their petition within twenty-four hours. If the motion of censure is adopted, both the bill and the government are defeated.

The fact that there are two politically significant executives and that one executive (the President) is not politically responsible before the legislature while the other (the Premier) is can create certain problems. For example, if the President wishes to exercise leadership by selecting a Premier of his own choice, but an absolute majority of the National Assembly opposes the Premier, a stalemate can occur. In an attempt to resolve the stalemate, the President can opt to dissolve the National Assembly and call for new elections (with the hope that the voters will send back an Assembly majority which agrees with him).[96] If the stalemate persists after the election, the Constitution of the Fifth Republic contains no provisions for resolving the stalemate, for the President cannot dissolve the Assembly again for at least one year.

The potential problem we cite has not yet been realized in the Fifth Republic because the Assembly has thus far been willing to support the premiers the Presidents have selected. Until 1974, Presidents were Gaullist (Charles de Gaulle, 1959-69 and George Pompidou, 1969-74) and the current President, Valéry Giscard d'Estaing, is the leader of the Republican Independents, who have frequently been allied with the Gaullists both in elections and in governments. During these years, there were only six Premiers, all Gaullist, and only one motion of censure was successful in the Assembly during the entire period.

An important reason why the Assembly has supported the President is that the

Gaullists have won the largest percentage of seats in the National Assembly in each election since 1958, regularly winning over 40 percent of the seats. The large majority of Gaullists have been from the Union of Democrats for the Fifth Republic (UDR) or, before 1968, the Union for the New Republic (UNR).[97] Other political parties of consequence have been the Independent Republicans (which has provided a generally supportive coalition partner for the Gaullist party), the Catholics (the Centre Démocrate, the Mouvement Républicain Populaire), the Radicals, the Socialists, and the Communists. In an effort to defeat the Gaullists in the 1960s, segments of the Radical and Socialist parties formed electoral coalitions during the Presidential and Assembly elections. The purpose of this strategy was to run one coalition candidate, the strongest candidate, rather than to have the parties fighting each other in individual races against the Gaullists or Gaullist supporters (for example, Independent Republicans). In the Assembly elections of 1973, the Socialists and the Communists combined to form an electoral coalition led by François Mitterand. By so doing, they managed to win a plurality of the popular vote.[98] Even so, the Gaullist party and its allies again managed to gain a majority (although a much reduced majority) of the seats in the Assembly.

A secondary reason sometimes given as to why the Assembly has supported the President and the governments is the constitutional provision that members of the legislature cannot simultaneously be in the government (called the incompatability rule). This rule does not apply either in Great Britain or West Germany. Most members of the government (always including the Prime Minister in Great Britain) in these two systems are also members of the House of Commons or the Bundestag. The framers of the French Fifth Republic felt that if members of the Assembly could not also be in the government, and the Assembly became a less important route to achieving government office, it would reduce the incentive to defeat the government. In fact, however, French Premiers have looked to Assembly members when forming their governments. An Assembly member simply resigned his seat upon appointment to the government. Since 1962, over half of the members of the government in major posts have served in the Assembly prior to their appointment.[99]

In addition to the two executives and the National Assembly, there is the Senate, the upper house of the French legislature. The government is not politically responsible before the Senate as it is before the Assembly. However, all legislation which the Assembly adopts must go to the Senate and must be adopted by the Senate before it becomes law unless the government intervenes. When a disagreement occurs between the two houses, a joint committee may be called by the government to iron out the differences. If the differences are not settled, the Assembly is empowered, if requested by the government, to make the definitive ruling. Otherwise, the two houses are equal in legislative authority and the Assembly cannot override the Senate. However, like the upper house in West Germany, the members of the French Senate are not elected directly by the public, but are elected indirectly. The electoral college which votes for the Senate is based on the grographical *departements* of France and consists mainly of delegates elected by the town and municipal councils.

Constitutional Powers of the Legislature

Having sketched the three European systems in outline fashion, we turn to the powers of the legislatures. We focus our attention particularly on the houses that are elected directly by the public (that is, the British House of Commons, the West German Bundestag, and the French National Assembly), the houses central to our study.

Alongside their parliamentary functions of determining the executive,[100] the House of Commons, the National Assembly, and the Bundestag are also primary legislative decision-making bodies. Because of the idea of "the supremacy of Parliament," it may be that there are no limits to the Parliament's legislative authority in the British system. The essence of the idea of parliamentary supremacy is that Parliament has the authority to make any decision about any matter falling within the jurisdiction of the political system. In theory, at least, this could be interpreted to mean everything and that there is no matter that falls outside the competence of Parliament.

On the other hand, as in the United States, there are formal constitutional constraints imposed on legislative authority in West Germany and France. First, the constitutions specify that certain kinds of decisions are entirely outside the scope of the political system. For example, Article 2 of the French Fifth Republic Constitution states that laws cannot differentiate between citizens on the basis of origin, race, or religion, and Article 4 specifies that laws may not abridge the right of political parties and groups to form or to carry on their activities freely (a limit is placed on these freedoms in that parties and groups must respect the principles of national sovereignty and democracy). Furthermore, no law can deprive suffrage to persons who are otherwise qualified under the Constitution. Decisions as to whether laws are valid according to the provisions of the Constitution on these or other matters are made by the Constitutional Council, a body chosen equally by the President, the President of the Assembly, and the President of the Senate.[101]

The German Constitution (Basic Law) also contains a series of provisions limiting the powers of the political system. Articles 1 through 19 of the Basic Law deny authority to the political system to abridge freedom of the press, religion, expression, organization, and movement.[102] They also restrict the authority of the political system to search private homes or to separate families. Furthermore, no law can limit the right of persons to own property, except for purposes of eminent domain (requiring like compensation), or freely to choose their occupation.

A second constitutional limit is placed on the Bundestag because, as in the case of the American Congress, it is part of a federal system. In West Germany, the federal system cannot lay sole or determining claim on revenues from personal or corporate taxes, since this is by right also a claim of the states (*länder*). Furthermore, on educational and cultural matters, primary powers are given to the state governments. For other policy areas where there are concurrent federal and state powers, however, the states may legislate only in the absence of federal legislation. And, there is a number of powers which the federal system exercises exclusively.[103] Exclusive and concurrent powers taken together give the federal system, and the Bundestag, broad authority to legislate, for example, in the areas of economic and social policy, criminal law, agricultural policy, transportation policy, competition policy, tariffs, foreign policy and defense, and federal financial and appropriations policies.[104]

Third, both the German and the French constitutions delineate certain decisions which the central system can make but which may be made without the approval of the legislature. For example, the French Constitution enumerates certain powers that are "legislative powers." While the enumeration is quite broad, those powers not enumerated are outside the scope of the Assembly; they are subject to the rule-making power of the executive. The enumeration of legislative powers under Article 34 and Article 35 of the Fifth Republic Constitution includes the general organization of the national defense; property rights; legislation pertaining to employment, unions, and social security; education; civil rights; criminal law; national planning to determine economic and social action; taxation; and declaring war. In the first four areas cited, legislation determines fundamental principles rather than implementation of the principles. Moreover, under conditions of emergencies (determined by the French President after consultation),[105] the French President may make decisions during the emergency by decree. Finally, legislation in France can bypass the legislature if enacted by public referendum called for by the President on proposal of the government.[106]

The Basic Law of West Germany also gives some decision-making powers to the executive without requiring the immediate approval of the Parliament. For example, with the consent of the Finance Minister, the German cabinet can undertake expenditures exceeding those the Parliament previously authorized (Article 112). Further, under Article 81, the West German President may, by declaring an emergency in regard to a particular bill, secure the adoption of the bill by approval of the Bundesrat, without consent of the Bundestag. However, this may be done only in a limited set of circumstances.[107]

Fourth, constitutions may set limits to the powers of the legislature even in regard to some matters over which the legislature does have the right to make authoritative decisions. This type of limit applies particularly to legislative authority over the budget, both in France and Germany. The French Constitution places the right of decision on the budget in the hands of the legislature. Nevertheless, it goes on to limit this right. If the Assembly has not passed the budget within seventy days, the budget as proposed by the executive automatically becomes law. Also, Assembly amendments cannot have the consequence of either raising the total amount of expenditures or reducing the total amount of revenue proposed by the government. A similar practice applies in West Germany (the West German Basic Law enables the German government to veto such decisions of Parliament) and in Great Britain.[108]

Fifth, constitutions frequently make some specifications as to the organization of the legislature. While these specifications ordinarily do not limit the legislature in its ability to act in the making of legislation, an exception is found in the Constitution of the French Fifth Republic. In another effort to develop a strong executive, the French Constitution gives the Premier and cabinet considerable legal authority over matters such as the agenda of the legislature, and it also seeks to limit the ability of committees in the legislature to control legislation. (We will review these particular provisions of the French Constitution on pages 83-84.)

Finally, as we saw earlier, each of the constitutions (and constitutional practice as well in Great Britain) limits the lower house in the sense that the executive can dissolve it and call for new elections. In Great Britain, this power belongs to the Prime Minister, while, in France, it is available to the President after consultation with the Premier and the Presidents of the Assembly and the Senate. In West Germany, the power of dissolution is held by the Federal President upon the proposal of the Chancellor. However, the Chancellor is empowered to make such a proposal only if he has been defeated by the Bundestag in a vote of confidence.

While the National Assembly and the Bundestag are subject to a number of constitutional restraints, they still have far reaching authority to make legislation and are potentially very powerful institutions. This is also the case for the House of Commons, for which there are even fewer formal restraints. The core of the powers of these three legislatures over the budget and over a wide range of substantive policy areas gives each of them the potential to play a determining part in the making of a great many public decisions.

Beyond the variety of formal constraints we have discussed, there may also be informal limits. Practice has served to limit the use the popularly elected legislative bodies make of certain of their powers. For example, the primary initiator of successful legislation has not been the legislature. Rather it has been the executive in each of the systems we are examining. Thus, in Great Britain, the government initiated 77 percent of the legislation adopted by the Commons from 1957 to 1969.[109] Governments of the French Fifth Republic initiated about 90 percent of the legislation passed by the Assembly from 1959 to 1968.[110] And about 75 percent of the legislation passed by the Bundestag from 1949 to 1969 was initiated by the government.[111]

The legislature has also limited itself through the practice of delegating legislation. The notion of delegated legislation involves a decision of the legislature to allow the executive to make decisions on specified policy matters; that is, the legislature delegates legislative authority to the executive. In general, these cover comparatively narrow policy matters, and the legislature places some restraints on its delegations of power. Not only will the legislature carefully denote the policy area, but it often will prescribe a time limit (this is required by the Fifth Republic Constitution, for example) or will reserve the right of review and veto.[112] Nevertheless, the amount of delegated legislation is considerable. The number of executive orders issued on the basis of delegated legislation in West Germany accounted for about 67 percent of the total legislation (laws plus executive orders) during the period 1949-61.[113] For Britain, both the amount of delegated legislation and the extent to which it is brought before the House of Commons for debate is detailed in Table 2.6. Although many executive decisions based on delegated legislation were reviewed by a committee of the House (the Committee on Statutory Instruments), few received attention before the entire House.

Table 2.6
Statutory Instruments in Great Britain Examined by the Committee on Statutory Instruments of the House of Commons and by the House of Commons, 1959-65

Session	Total of Instruments Examined by the Committee	Number Brought to Special Attention of the House
1959-60	495	9
1960-61	617	4
1961-62	594	2
1962-63	713	5
1963-64	760	7
1964-65	1088	4

Source: Frank Stacey, *The Modern Government of Britain* (Oxford: The Clarendon Press, 1968), p. 208.

The Election Process

Despite the rise in delegated legislation over the years, the legislation and budgets upon which the three legislatures vote and make a determination remain broad in the range of substantive areas they cover and significant in policy content.[114] Moreover, except where specified by the constitution, delegated powers must themselves be explicitly approved by the legislatures before decisions made under such powers can be authoritative. Finally, to the extent that the executive retains these powers, this too is within the authority of the legislature to decide.

The power to make authoritative decisions constitutes one component of our definition of a representative legislature. Another component is that the members of the legislature be selected directly by the enfranchised citizens in open and periodic elections. In this section, we examine the election process for the House of Commons, the National Assembly, and the Bundestag—the three houses which meet this condition.

In each system, elections to these houses are periodic in the sense that they must occur within a certain number of years (Britain, five years; West Germany, four years; France, five years). When elections occur, almost all seats are contested by at least two and often three or more different candidates. Nominations for by far the great majority of candidates standing for election take place through political parties (we have referred above to the nomenclature of the major parties in the three systems). The importance of the party structure for nomination in the three systems is such that the rules for getting on the ballot sometimes slightly favor nominees from those parties that have previously exhibited some electoral strength. The law in West Germany requires that independent candidates and candidates of parties not holding seats in the Parliament each must submit a petition with 200 names; however, the parties with representation in Parliament can nominate candidates without submitting a petition. The law in Great Britain requires each candidate to deposit the equivalent of $360, which will be forfeited if the candidate fails to win one-eight of the vote in his constituency. This is not a small amount of money for most individuals and might be a determining consideration in whether an independent would forward himself or not. It is less likely to be a determining factor for an organized political party.

The nomination process for individual candidates in most European parties differs in two important ways from the nomination process in American parties. First, nominations are not decided through primaries. Second, the central party apparatus usually has greater formal power to intervene.

Rather than primaries, in most of the parties nominations to run for election to the legislature are officially made by the party organization in each constituency or district or federation, usually by elected or appointed delegates.* Nominations might be made by the executive committee of the local party or a separate selection committee. If a selection committee makes the nominations, its members may be chosen either by the executive committee of the local party organization or by the constituency party members.[115]

The exact mechanism for selecting nominees differs both across parties and even within parties. For example, some Conservative constituency associations use a

---

*State list nomination practices in West Germany are excluded from treatment here.

selection committee that reports to the executive committee while others use only the executive committee.

In *most* parties the local level is an important component of the nomination process. The local party committee may review numerous potential nominees submitted to it by its own members, by prospective candidates, or by other persons.[116] Generally, after discussion, the committee will choose to consider seriously only a few of the candidates. The selection committee, or the executive committee, will then interview the candidates, or gain personal contact with them in other ways, as a basis upon which to select the nominee. Depending upon the party and the circumstances, the nominees of the committee may need to gain approval in general meeting of the constituency party members.

When the local party associations are important determinants of nominees to run under the party label, this does not mean that local political considerations will be a critical factor in the nomination process. As we will see in Chapter 4, when we examine this at greater length, local considerations can be of importance in the nomination process in some parties, such as the West German CDU/CSU.[117] But, in other parties, such as the British Conservative and Labour parties, local political considerations usually are less significant.[118] Indeed, the local associations in these parties have sometimes gone in the other direction by denying renomination to a parliamentarian who has rebelled against or otherwise been disloyal to the leadership of the national party in the House of Commons.

A second characteristic that distinguishes the nomination process in a number of Western European parties from the process in American parties is that there may be some degree of formal control over nominations given to the central-level party organization. For example, in the French Communist party the powers accorded to the central level are considerable and not infrequently employed. Direct intervention by the central organization may prevent a local party from nominating a particular candidate or may even impose a particular candidate upon a local party. In other cases, such as the Gaullist party, the central party has great power and employs it, although less frequently than does the Communist party and, even then, usually in conjunction with the local party. In still other cases, such as the British Conservative and Labour parties, the powers at the central level are potentially wide-reaching but are only rarely employed.

Because nomination of party candidates is by the party organization, whether local or national, there is no need for expensive primary campaigns. Unlike the situation in the United States, the possibility that a candidate might need to spend enormous sums of money to gain nomination (almost $2 million in the case of the United States Senatorial primary campaign of Richard Ottinger of New York) is not present in any of the European legislative systems. On the other hand, primaries have the advantage of opening the nomination process to the wider public (hundreds of thousands of voters for certain primaries). A much smaller group of people participates in the selection of nominees in the three European legislative systems.

Moreover, despite the absence of primaries, the costs of running a party organization and of competing in general elections remain considerable. Since 1960, the lowest cost for a major party during an election year in West Germany was in 1961 when the national SPD organization spent over $3 million. With the addition of local expenditures and services, the SPD figure rose to approximately $7 million.[119] The CDU/CSU is reported to have expended approximately $8 million during the same year.[120] According to reported expenditures, the British parties spend approximately $3 to 4 million fighting a general election (this is outside most local expenditures and the free time they receive over the communications media).

These sums place most European parties in a position of requiring financial support outside that provided by the normal party dues. Despite the presence of some public subsidies in West Germany, about half of the $8 million the CDU/CSU expended in 1961 came from contributions from the business community.[121] In 1969, despite larger public subsidies, the CDU/CSU received $6 million in private contributions. Running its own campaign, British industry spent almost $4 million before the 1959 election; the iron and steel industry alone spent over $600,000 before the 1959 election opposing nationalization and another $1.5 million during the twelve months preceding the 1964 election.[122] The financial support available directly to the Conservative party is suggested by its ability, when in opposition in 1947, to raise over $3 million in five months. Included in these contributions were single gifts of over $30,000.[123]

Thus, a main disadvantage of primaries—that they require an inordinate amount of financing—is reduced in the Western European systems by not having primaries. But the problems of financing are by no means eliminated in the European systems. It is still expensive to run a party and to fight general elections. Private individuals and organizations in these systems, as in the United States, make sizable contributions to political parties to finance these costs. Moreover, we have observed organizations undertaking expensive campaigns of their own preceding elections. We will examine in some detail the impact of money as a resource to influence election outcomes and to influence legislators in Chapter 9.

Another important element of the election process is the system used to determine who wins election to the legislature. As applied to our legislatures, we can speak broadly of three kinds of electoral systems. A single-member-district system (SMD) divides the country into a certain number of districts or constituencies, each of which elects one member to the legislature. The principle is simple: the candidate in the district who wins a plurality (in some cases an absolute majority) of the popular vote wins the election. The single-member-district system, or a variation of it, is used in Great Britain and the French Fifth Republic (as observed earlier, it is also used in the United States). A proportional representation system (PR) also divides the country into a certain number of districts, but each of the districts elects more than one member. Each party puts forth a list of candidates in the district, with the number of candidates elected from each party list being determined on the basis of the relative numerical size of the vote each party won in the election. This system was used in France under the Fourth Republic. Finally, the SMD and PR systems may be combined, as in West Germany. In this system, half of the members to the Bundestag are elected from single-member districts. The other half are elected by proportional representation on the basis of lists of candidates submitted at the state level by each state party.

When elections are determined according to the single-member-district system, there usually is not a stiff battle between parties in most of the districts. Although candidates from different parties compete, most districts are relatively safe for one party or another. We have already seen this to be the case in Congressional elections, in which about 75 percent of Congressional districts do not change party hands even over five consecutive elections. One finds this also to be true in Great Britain. From 1950 to 1964, for example, 87 percent of the constituencies did not change party hands over the four elections during that period. In the 1959 elections, over 70 percent of the constituencies were won by more than 10 percent of the vote.[124] A similar pattern is present in West Germany, although there is somewhat greater turnover. For example, 76 percent of the Bundestag members elected from constituencies in 1953 were reelected in 1957, and 77 percent elected in 1957 were reelected in 1961.[125]

Among the Western European legislative systems, an SMD system is used as the sole method of election in both Great Britain and the French Fifth Republic. It has had some significant political effects worthy of note in each of these systems.

Except for the first 1974 elections in Britain (see Table 2.7), British parliamentary elections since 1945 have produced absolute majorities for one of the parties in the Commons, even though that party did *not* win an absolute majority of the popular vote. Thus, the electoral system usually worked to overrepresent the largest party (the party having a plurality of the popular votes) and to give that party an absolute majority of seats in the Commons (see Tables 2.7 and 2.8). However, only in 1951 did the system enable a party not winning a *plurality* of the popular vote (the Conservatives) to gain an absolute majority in the Commons.

Table 2.7
Election Outcomes in Great Britain, 1945-74

Year	Government Party	Percent of Total Popular Vote	Percent of Seats in the House of Commons
1945	Labour	48.3	61.2
1950	Labour	46.1	50.6
1951	Conservative	48.0[a]	51.3
1955	Conservative	49.7	54.8
1959	Conservative	49.4	57.9
1964	Labour	44.1	50.3
1966	Labour	47.9	57.7
1970	Conservative	46.4	52.4
1974 (I)	Labour	37.2	47.4
1974 (II)	Labour	39.4	50.1

[a]This percentage did not amount to a plurality of the popular vote.

Table 2.8
The Second British General Election of 1974

Party	Percent of Popular Vote	Percent of Seats in the Commons
Labour	39.4	50.1
Conservative	35.8	43.4
Liberal	18.4	2.1
Other	6.4	4.4

In addition to the usual effect of producing absolute majorities from popular pluralities, the SMD system has worked in Great Britain to underrepresent the third party (the Liberals) and the other even smaller parties. For example, in 1974 these parties won 24.8 percent of the vote but only 6.5 percent of the seats in the House (see Table 2.8). That is, they were underrepresented by 18.3 percent. In 1970, these parties won 10.7 percent of the vote and 2.1 percent of the seats in the House, an underrepresentation of 8.6 percent.

The French Fifth Republic also uses an SMD system, although it is slightly different from that used in Great Britain. Elections to the National Assembly involve two runoffs in most districts. After the first election, a second election is held one week later in each district in which no candidate won an absolute majority of the vote during the first runoff. If no candidate won an absolute majority, each candidate who received more than 10 percent of the registered vote can stand in the second runoff, and the candidate winning a plurality of the vote in the second runoff wins the Assembly seat.

In France the SMD system has distorted the relationship between popular vote and Assembly seats to a greater extent than it has in Great Britain. The discrepancy between the popular vote for a single party and the percentage of seats it received in the House of Commons has not usually been greater than 10 percent in Britain. This is not the case in France. This can be seen in Table 2.9, which compares second election vote percentages to percentages of seats won by each party in the Assembly from 1958 to 1973. A discrepancy of more than 10 percent occurred in each election except for 1967.

As Table 2.9 illustrates, however, the SMD system as practiced in the French Fifth Republic has not damaged the smaller parties as it has in Great Britain. Rather, it hurt one of the largest parties, the Communist party. The discrepancy in the percentage

Table 2.9
The Results of Elections to the French
National Assembly, 1958-73 (in percent)

	1958 Votes	1958 Seats	1962 Votes	1962 Seats	1967 Votes	1967 Seats	1968 Votes	1968 Seats	1973 Votes	1973 Seats
Gaullists[a]	29	42[c]	43	57[c]	44	51	49	73[c]	38	53[c]
Conservative	21	26								
MRP	08	11								
Con-MRP[b]			13	12	08	09	08	07		
Centrists-Reform										
Radical	06	08	08	09						
Socialists	14	10	15	14						
Fédératés					26	25	22	12[c]	45	35[c]
Comm-Soc										
Communists	21	02[c]	21	08[c]	22	15	20	07[c]		

[a] After 1958, Gaullists include Independent Republicans along with the UNR (or UDR).
[b] Mouvement Républicain Populaire or Centre Démocrate.
[c] Discrepancies of 10 percent or greater between popular votes and Assembly seats.

Communist vote and the seats it won was -19 percent in 1958, -13 percent in 1962, -7 percent in 1967 and -13 percent in 1968.

One can also see from the table that in the elections of 1962, 1967, 1968, and 1973 the Gaullists and their allies won an absolute majority of the seats in the Assembly without having an absolute majority of the popular vote. While gaining only 43 percent of the popular vote in 1962 and 44 percent in 1967, the Gaullists and their allies managed to win 57 percent of the Assembly seats in 1962 and 51 percent in 1967. In 1968, with 49 percent of the popular vote, the Gaullists and their allies won 73 percent of the seats in the Assembly. Finally, in 1973, the Gaullists won about 53 percent of the Assembly with about 38 percent of the popular vote (this was the only occasion the Gaullists did not win a plurality of the popular vote). Thus, as in Great Britain, the electoral system in the French Fifth Republic has had the important political effect of producing an absolute majority governing coalition in the Assembly where no absolute majority existed in the electorate.

On the other hand, this type of effect has not been present in West Germany. The method of determining election victors in West Germany combines the SMD and the PR systems. Half of the 520 Bundestag members are elected from single-member constituencies, and half are elected by proportional representation. The geographical basis for the PR system are the *länder*, or states. The system works in such a way that a party's candidate can run in a constituency while simultaneously holding a place on the party's state list (the names on the party list and the order of names is determined by the state party). Thus, if the candidate is not elected in his constituency, he may be elected by virtue of holding a high position on the *land* PR list. On the other hand, if the candidate is elected by his constituency, his name is in effect withdrawn from the *land* PR list, and the candidate immediately below him on the list takes his place.

The technical method used to calculate the total number of seats each party wins is complicated, but its consequence is simple: the total number of seats a party wins is essentially proportional to its percentage of vote in each of the *länder*, regardless of how many constituencies the party won. That is, the effect of the German electoral system on the relationship between popular votes and seats in the Bundestag is essentially that of a PR system.

The result is that the percentage of party vote to percent of party seats in the Bundestag corresponds to a greater degree than in either Great Britain or the French Fifth Republic. The correspondence would be even closer except for the rule (to discourage very small parties) that those parties which do not gain at least 5 percent of the vote or three constituency seats have no right to any representation in the Bundestag. The correspondence between percentages of party vote and percentages of party seats from 1949 to 1972 is indicated for the three largest parties on Table 2.10.

The greatest distortion in distribution of party seats in seven elections was about 6 percent (SPD, 1949). After 1953, the greatest distortion was about 3 percent. This can be compared to the second 1974 British election, in which the Labour party was overrepresented in the House of Commons by almost 11 percent, or the 1959 election, which overrepresented the Conservatives in the House by almost 9 percent. Similarly, the outcome of the French elections found the Gaullists overrepresented in the Assembly by 13 percent in 1958, by 14 percent in 1962, by 24 percent in 1968, and by about 15 percent in 1973.

Table 2.10
West German Bundestag Election Returns for the Three Largest Parties, 1949-72 (in percent)

Party	1949	1953	1957	1961	1965	1969	1972[a]
CDU/CSU							
Vote	31.0	45.2	50.2	45.3	47.6	46.1	44.8
Seats	36.0	49.1	53.0	48.1	48.4	48.8	45.2
SPD							
Vote	29.2	28.8	31.8	36.2	39.3	42.7	45.9
Seats	35.0	31.8	34.9	38.9	41.9	45.2	46.4
FDP							
Vote	11.9	9.5	7.7	12.8	9.5	5.8	8.4
Seats	13.0	10.4	8.3	12.9	9.6	6.0	8.5

[a]not including Berlin

Because it tended to distort the electoral outcome less than would an SMD system, the West German electoral system has not produced a party majority in the Bundestag where no majority existed in the electorate. The only occasion upon which one party won an absolute majority of the seats in the Bundestag was the CDU/CSU victory of 1957, when the CDU/CSU also won an absolute majority of the popular vote.

Our discussion of the electoral systems of Great Britain, West Germany, and France suggests that there has been some distortion between percentage of party vote in the country and the representation of parties in the legislature, regardless of the type of electoral system chosen. The degree of distortion, however, has depended upon the type of system: a PR system has been more reflective of the vote than an SMD system. Another chief difference between the effects of legislative electoral systems has been whether or not the electoral system produced party majorities (for a single party or allied parties) in the legislature where no such majority existed in the electorate. Because of its greater distortion, the SMD system in Britain and France tended to produce artificial party majorities in the legislature more than did the PR system in West Germany.[126]

Still, it is important to note that with only two exceptions the government party or coalition in both Britain and the French Fifth Republic has always won a plurality of the popular vote. Furthermore, with only a single exception in Germany, the Chancellor has been chosen from the party that won a plurality of the popular vote and of the Bundestag seats (the only exception here was when the SPD, under Brandt, formed the government in 1969).

Because the SMD system in Britain and France has tended artificially to produce an absolute legislative majority from a popular plurality and because the PR system in West Germany (as well as in the French Fourth Republic) tended not to produce an absolute legislative majority of one party at all, there has been in effect no certain electoral linkage between the preferences of an absolute majority of the voters and the formation of a majority government under either system. This has been the case because of the presence in each country of third party and/or fourth parties that have won a fairly sizable percentage of the popular vote. The consequences of this situation for the representation of the public, and for theories of representation as applied to different legislative institutions, need to be explored. We will do so at some length in Chapter 10.

One final point about the electoral systems of the three nation's deals with how each replaces legislators who die or resign while in office. At present, Great Britain handles this problem by having an election in the constituency to replace the former MP (Member of Parliament). These are called by-elections. A number of these by-elections occur between general elections and become weathervanes of popular support for the government and the governing party. Moreover, if the government's majority in the House of Commons is small, by-elections can be of critical political portent, for every seat in the Commons is of great importance in this situation.

The French and the Germans use different and simpler methods. In the case of France, each deputy is elected with an alternate who replaces him if he leaves office. In West Germany, a member of the Bundestag who leaves office is replaced by the candidate of his party highest on the *land* list who did not win election to the Bundestag.

Legislative Organization

As we observed previously, each of the legislatures has rather broad authority in the field of legislation. In the end, many public policy decisions must receive the approval of the legislature before they become law. Even in the case of delegated legislation, the legislature must approve the delegation of power before the executive is authorized to make decisions which have the effect of law.

How do the legislatures organize themselves to carry out their legislative responsibilities? We will again focus our attention on the three popularly elected houses. Although these houses are parliamentary institutions, they each organize themselves somewhat differently from the others. In describing the main features of the three houses, we will turn first to the House of Commons, then to the Bundestag, and finally to the National Assembly.

The British House of Commons The legislative process in the House of Commons normally includes a number of different stages. Usually, the executive formulates and initiates legislation. There are several arenas in the House of Commons in which initiated legislation is then discussed and debated. Among these are the parliamentary parties, the standing committees of the House, and debate on the floor of the House. Initiated legislation typically receives a formal first reading on the floor (generally there is no debate at this stage) and is then discussed within each of the parliamentary parties.[127] Following this, the bill comes up for a second reading on the floor in which the principles of the bill are debated and a vote (division) takes place on whether the bill is, in principle, acceptable to the House. Once accepted, the bill then goes to a standing committee where amendments to the bill can be made, although the principle behind the bill cannot be altered. After the standing committee reports to the House, the House as a whole debates and votes on amendments. This is called the report stage. Finally, the bill receives a third reading on the floor of the Commons. Final House approval of the bill, as amended, takes place at the third reading.

A principal actor in this process is the government and administration. The legislative management functions carried out by the government, through its parliamentary party majority in the House, are many and varied. British parliamentarians expect the government to formulate and initiate most pieces of major legislation in the House. To do this, the government is given considerable control over the House of Commons agenda. There are approximately 160 sitting days in the average session. The main legislative time the government does not control includes the approximately 20 days for private member considerations, about 28 days on the proposed budget controlled by the opposition, and the question hour and adjournment debate which begin and end each sitting.[128]

Not only does the government exercise considerable control over the agenda, thus giving it a leading position in determining which bills the House will debate, but its parliamentary majority generally also enables it to exercise some control over the length of debates and the length of time a bill can be considered by the standing committees. A simple majority vote is required to close debate and, if necessary, a bill can be called up from committee by adoption of a guillotine motion, which also requires a majority of the House. Through the guillotine, the House instructs the committee to end its deliberations at a specific time and to report the bill back to the House. Indeed, the guillotine may be used to establish time limits for each stage of the process in the House.

The scheduling of the debate, itself, is accomplished by the government[129] in consultation with the opposition through regular meetings of the whips. The actual debate is chaired by the Speaker of the House.[130]

Beyond this, most parliamentary offices of substance to members of the majority party are dispensed by the Prime Minister or the government. These include ministerial, junior ministerial, secretarial, and whip posts, which have proliferated considerably during the twentieth century.[131] The Prime Minister also controls the honors list.[132] Finally, the government controls the administration of legislation. It can be helpful or fail to be helpful to particular parliamentary members by how it administers policies and the decisions it makes under delegated legislation.

The Prime Minister and the government constitute the main core of the leadership of the majority parliamentary party in the House (a discussion of leadership selection within the parliamentary parties is found in Chapter 6). The other major parliamentary party forms the opposition. Its leader, who is elected by the parliamentary party, is known as the shadow Prime Minister. He and the opposition or shadow ministers form what is known as the "shadow cabinet." When in opposition, the Conservative leader selects the other shadow ministers, while the Labour leader does so in the context of parliamentary party elections to the Parliamentary Committee of the Labour party. The purposes of the shadow cabinet are both to present the public with a potential alternative government and to provide the opposition with principal spokesmen responsible for critiquing the government, on and off the floor, in each ministerial sector of policy (such as foreign policy, defense policy, transportation, and so forth).[133] The shadow Prime Minister, if Conservative, also appoints his parliamentary party's chief whip and junior whips. Thus, even the opposition leader, especially if Conservative, but not excluding the Labour leader, has a number of parliamentary awards at his disposal.[134]

There are several institutional ways by which the leadership of the parliamentary party (whether the cabinet or shadow cabinet) can become acquainted with the views of other members of the parliamentary party (known as backbenchers).[135] Each of the major parliamentary parties contains a set of "backbench" committees. One type of committee is general; another type is specialized. These committees tend to be a focal point for the discussion of legislation within the parliamentary parties.

The general committee within the Conservative parliamentary party is called the "1922 Committee." It is composed of all Conservative backbenchers and meets once weekly principally to discuss important pieces of legislation and major issues that are either pending before the House or are being considered by the leadership. When in opposition, the leadership regularly participates in the committee. When in power, leaders (ministers) attend upon the request of the committee.

General meetings of the Parliamentary Labour Party (PLP) include the leaders as well as the backbenchers. There is also a Parliamentary Committee of the Labour party when in opposition which is chaired by the leader and consists of members elected by the parliamentary party. When in power, a Liaison Committee, chaired by a backbencher, is intended to serve as a communication link between the government and the backbenchers.

In addition, there is a set of specialized committees in each parliamentary party, generally numbering from fifteen to twenty committees for each party. They bring together backbench parliamentarians interested in particular sectors of policy, enabling them to specialize in a way not afforded by the standing committees of the House of Commons. They constitute another forum in which backbenchers can discuss policy with their leaders. The committees receive legislative initiatives before the second reading and sometimes even before the first reading. This allows backbench parliamentarians an opportunity to voice collective opinions on controversial policies at a much earlier stage than do the standing committees of the House.

These general and specialized parliamentary party committees provide mechanisms both for backbench members to influence one another and for the leaders to become acquainted with the views of the backbenchers in their party. Michael Foot, Labour MP,[136] has written:

The Labour MP who seeks to change or affect great decisions must persuade his colleagues in the secret conclave of the party meeting. True, he will have had the chance of pressing his view at an earlier meeting of a specialized official group. But if his powers of advocacy fail there. . . it is the party meeting, not on the floor of the House of Commons. . . that he will have the only opportunity to determine action.[137]

Another method by which backbench opinion is communicated to the leadership is through the whips' office. The chief whip and his assistants attempt to keep in close personal touch with each backbencher in the parliamentary party and attempt to get dissident backbenchers direct contact with the appropriate party leaders. According to Martin Redmayne, former chief whip of the Conservative party:

I have thirteen Whips plus my deputy, and each of those has, first of all, what we call an area—a geographical area of the country in which there are thirty or forty Conservative members. His business is to keep in contact with them, and not merely to keep in contact with them but to know them so well that he may in an emergency be able to give a judgment as to what their opinion will be without even asking them.

The explanation of policy is properly done by Ministers. It has always been my habit as Chief Whip to get the Minister concerned to talk to the backbenchers who have a complaint or criticism, because after all he is the man responsible for policy. My job is to see that the two sides are brought together.[138]

One usually thinks of the whip as acting to communicate the policies of the party leaders to the backbenchers and, in particular, to persuade backbenchers by various arguments and means to support their leaders' position. Since the whips' office is responsible to the leader of the parliamentary party, this is one of its major functions. It is even recognized in phraseology. Thus, when the leadership regards a vote (division) on a bill to be significant, it applies what is known as a "two-line whip" in communicating its position to backbenchers. On matters of greatest significance, the leadership applies what is called a "three-line whip."

Nevertheless, as Redmayne's comments suggest, the whips' office is also expected to know what backbenchers are thinking and to bring their views before the leadership. This, too, is a purpose that a well-functioning whips' office will serve. Intraparliamentary party communication is important and can sometimes be vital, because neither of the parliamentary parties is free of internal conflict. Indeed, there is considerable variation of opinion within each parliamentary party, and especially in the PLP (this will be explored further in Chapters 4 and 5).

Debate within the parliamentary parties and their committees begins before, sometimes well before, the second reading of a bill on the floor of the Commons. However, after passing the second reading, there is another forum in which the bill is discussed. This is the House committee stage, in which amendments to the bill are formally proposed. Of course, many of these amendments may have already been discussed and some agreed to by the government as a consequence, for instance, of the earlier deliberations of its parliamentary party.

During the committee stage, the bill can go to the committee of the whole by vote of the House. In this case, the House as a whole would be the committee, but this can be cumbersome since there is much legislation and only one committee of the whole. While the committee of the whole is still used, since 1945 the Commons has increasingly employed standing general committees on legislation to consider amendments. The standing committee then reports to the House (called the report stage), which discusses and votes upon the committee amendments and other amendments that were not considered in the standing committee.

There are usually six or seven standing general committees on legislation in the House, in addition to a standing committee on private members' bills and another on Scottish affairs. The membership on each committee varies, ranging from twenty to fifty members. The party membership on the committees is roughly proportional to the size of each of the parliamentary parties in the House.

The House of Commons' standing committees on legislation are similar to the legislation committees of the United States Congress in that both can amend bills. However, the committees of the House of Commons are not as potentially influential in the legislative process. Their ability to affect legislation is truncated in a number of ways. The justification for this limitation has been based partly on the theory that the government (and its policy) is responsible to the House as a whole rather than to a part of the House, which a standing committee would necessarily constitute.

One of the curbs on the power of the Commons' committees is that they normally get a bill after it has passed its first and second readings. Since debate and a vote of the House on the principles of a bill takes place on the second reading (the first reading involves mainly a statement of the bill's content), the House will have already adopted the principles of a bill before it reaches a standing committee. The result is that the committee has *no* jurisdiction over the major principles involved. It is limited to discussing matters such as exemptions, implementation, adjustment, and wording.

Another limitation is that the Commons' committees have no executive powers. Not only may they not treat the principles of the legislation before it, but they also may not inquire into matters which go beyond the *specific* legislative text. They do not carry out investigations and have no power to summon witnesses or papers.

Nor do the committees or their members have much in the way of staffing. Ordinarily, each committee will have only one clerk of the House available to it. Further, individual members have no research staffs of their own. Several together have an office room and may employ a secretary (each member is given a very limited amount of funds to do this). Members are also entitled to use the research staff of the House of Commons Library, but the staff at the library comprises so few professional persons that there is a ratio of MPs (excluding ministers) to staff of over forty to one.[140]

If these limitations were not enough, there are still others. The committees are not specialized. The assignment of bills works by rotation. A committee may receive a bill on transportation one week and on social policy the following week. However, in order to use the expertise of individual parliamentarians, often parliamentarians who are specialists on the piece of legislation are appointed to the committee. This insures somewhat greater expertise, but probably not to the degree found if the committees were actually specialized. Moreover, this procedure has the disadvantage of making each committee an essentially new one for each piece of legislation it discusses. In this sense they are no longer standing committees. They have become quasi-ad hoc committees.

As a result of these various considerations, the value of chairmanship posts and membership on the House standing general committees on legislation is very much reduced. It would be a mistake, however, to imply that the standing committees play no role. At times, the committee stage is intense and filled with political surprises. Party cohesion remains high in the committees, but amendments can still be pressed upon a government. This may result from the government acquiescing or from the absence of some members of the majority party, which can give a majority to the opposition. Amendments which are not acceptable to the government can, of course, be defeated by the House during the report stage.

Alongside the standing general committees in the Commons, there are also some specialist committees. The oldest, and most effective, is the Public Accounts Committee (first established in 1861). It reviews expenditures to assure that money has been spent as the Commons intended it to be spent. Its function is thus formally supervisory or administrative rather than legislative. An Estimates Committee (now called the Expenditures Committee) was created in 1912 with the purpose of examining economies in the use of intended expenditures. The two committees have undertaken a number of investigations. They have, for example, uncovered gross underestimations of projected costs for military and health programs and have discovered waste in the expenditure of funds.

Another committee was established in 1944 to review government decisions based on powers the House had delegated to it. The committee was established following the increase in delegated legislation at the beginning of World War II. It is known as the Committee of Statutory Instruments (see also page 63). Further, a Committee on Nationalized Industries was established in 1955. It, too, was intended essentially as a supervisory committee. Within its mandate, the committee has consistently influenced the managing boards of the nationalized industries in Great Britain. The success of the committee is in part indicated by the fact that the House created several other subject-matter type of committees in 1967, for example, the Committee on Science and Technology and one on agriculture. Also, the Committee on the Parliamentary Commissioner for Administration was formed in 1967 after passage of the Act setting up a British ombudsman. We shall have more to say about these committees in later chapters (see especially Chapter 7) when we examine the supervisory activities of the House of Commons.[141]

The reward value of the chairmanship of most of these specialized committees is greater than the chairmanships of the Commons' standing general committees. This has been especially the case for the two most effective specialist committees, Public Accounts (chaired traditionally by a member of the opposition party) and Nationalized Industries (chaired by a member of the government party). The influence these two committees have had and the information open to them have made their chairmanships attractive posts. In addition, the chairmen to these committees are often elevated to more prestigious positions. Harold Wilson, who became Prime Minister, was chairman of Public Accounts from 1959 to 1962, and his successor, Douglas Houghton, became a member of one of his cabinets. Most of the chairmen of the Committee on Nationalized Industries have been awarded peerages.

As the chairmanships of these two committees are valued awards, it is of some importance to note that each of the committees elects its own chairman, thus giving backbenchers the opportunity to fill significant positions. But, even here, parliamentary party leaders, acting through the whips, have a considerable voice in the assignment of the two posts.[142]

As our earlier remarks indicated, both the leaders of the majority parliamentary party (the Prime Minister and the cabinet) and the leaders of the opposition parliamentary party (the shadow Prime Minister and the shadow cabinet) have numerous avenues available to them in the House to express their policy positions and to take a leading part in debate. But there are also avenues open to backbenchers in the parliamentary parties. We have already discussed some of these avenues. They include participation by individual members in the general and specialized committees of their parliamentary party, in the standing and specialist committees of the House, and in debates on the floor.

Another kind of avenue is the oral and written question addressed to the government and to which the responsible minister must answer. The opposition and backbenchers from the governing party make great use of this means of expressing views, asking thousands of questions each year. An hour is given near the beginning of each day's sitting for members' oral questions (which are communicated to the government in advance), for the replies of the appropriate minister, and for rebuttal questions and answers on each side (see Chapter 7).[143]

In addition, individual members can publicize their views by raising motions under the ten-minute rule, which gives a member ten minutes of time on the floor of the Commons to speak in behalf of his motion. Members can also propose motions, which will be followed by debate, during times regularly scheduled for private member motions. Or, the individual member can voice a position through the early day motion. These motions are to be debated on the earliest available day, but, in fact, are rarely taken up in a formal debate. Instead, the motion is printed and individual members signify their support for the motion by signing it. The adjournment debate, which ends a day's sitting, is another way for the individual members to present their views on a particular topic (especially matters dealing with local concerns).

Finally, individual members can propose legislation, called private members' bills. Since 1957, about 25 percent of the public legislation which the House of Commons adopted has been in the form of private members' bills. Some of these have been of considerable importance, as in the case of the abolition of capital punishment, which was adopted on the basis of a private member bill. Some that did not pass have instead helped to press the government to propose its own legislation.[144]

In the British system, almost all public policy decisions require either the authorization or the explicit approval of the House of Commons. The government also needs the continued consent of the House, and particularly of its parliamentary party in the House, to remain in office. In this section we have reviewed some of the basic mechanisms of the legislative process in the House, including a number of ways both leaders and backbenchers have of expressing their positions and of attempting both to influence decisions on legislation and to scrutinize government actions. The House of Commons also provides the opposition party with a continuing forum for expressing its position to the public. Indeed, by offering such a forum, the House of Commons has become a principal battleground which the opposition uses to present the public with alternative or competing policies in its attempt to build a popular majority preparatory to the next election.

The West German Bundestag As the House of Commons in Britain provides a forum for the expression of views and the consideration of legislation, many of the same purposes are served by the West German Bundstag. Even so, it works quite differently from the House of Commons.[145] One of the most notable differences is that the Bundestag is organizationally separate from the government. This is the case both for the Bundestag as a body and for the governing parliamentary parties. Each has a leadership of its own that is separate from the government and from the party leaders in the government.

The Bundestag still depends on the government for the initiation of most legislation, and the Chancellor plays a leading part in distributing ministerial offices, which are coveted by more than a few parliamentarians. Hence, the Chancellor and the cabinet still have a formidable position in the Bundestag.[146] Nevertheless, the government does not serve as a management committee for the Bundestag to the degree that it does for the House of Commons.

Whereas the government in Great Britain constitutes the chief "committee" in organizing the work of the House of Commons, this function in the Bundestag is given to the Bundestag's Council of Elders rather than to the government. The purpose of the Council of Elders is, through interparty bargaining, to establish the agenda, determine the length of debate and the number of speakers, decide to which specialized legislation committees bills will be referred (both the primary committee to which a bill will be sent and the secondary committees), and determine the distribution of committee chairmanships among the parties. Although the Council of Elders has no final decision-making authority, as a forum for interparty bargaining it is an exceedingly important organ in the Bundestag.

The Council of Elders is chaired by the Bundestag President, who also functions (along with the Vice-Presidents) as Speaker of the House. The total membership of the Council is divided proportionally according to the strength of each of the parliamentary parties in the Bundestag. In the past the President, who also chairs the debates, has been chosen by the largest parliamentary party.[147] The number of Vice-Presidencies has been subject to considerable interparty dispute. Generally four have been selected and have been divided proportionally among the parties, beginning with the second largest party (since the largest party controlled the Presidency). The remaining positions on the Council of Elders have also been based on proportional party representation. As in the case of the Presidency and the Vice-Presidencies, each of the allotted party positions on the Council of Elders is chosen by the party itself. Those members selected by each party are then automatically elected by the Bundestag as a whole. The composition of the Council of Elders is thus dependent on the parliamentary strength of each of the Bundestag parties, and the decision of each party is paramount to selection to the Council.

We have already suggested that the parliamentary parties which form the government see themselves as being separate from the government[148] and, indeed, are separate in organizational terms. The implcation is that the management of the Bundestag in the end is in the hands of the parliamentary parties (working through the Council of Elders) and not the government, since the parliamentary parties control the Council of Elders. As a result, it has happened at times that government legislation has been left off the agenda and government desires in regard to committee chairmanship appointments and committee referral of bills have been ignored.

A second kind of management committee in the Bundestag is the specialized, standing committee on legislation.[149] The number of these committees has varied considerably since 1949 with a high of thirty-nine and a low of seventeen (as of 1973). Each covers a particular policy sector, such as agriculture or foreign policy or defense or social policy. Unlike the Congress, the chairmen of these committees are selected roughly proportionally in regard to the parliamentary membership of each of the Bundestag parties. Thus, the opposition parties will have a share of the committee chairmanships. In 1973, for example, the SPD (one of the governing parties) and the CDU/CSU (opposition party) each had eight committee chairmen, and the FDP (the other governing party) had one chairmanship. There was a similar distribution of deputy chairmen.

The chairmen and the particular party members chosen by the party to fill its allotted posts on the legislation committees are generally adopted automatically by the respective committees. Thus, as in the selection of the Council of Elders, parliamentary parties are also decisive to the selection of the chairmen and members of the Bundestag's standing committees.

The Bundestag's standing committees on legislation perform an internal policy management function which is considerably greater than that of the House of Commons' standing general committees on legislation and is closer to that of the standing committees of the United States Congress. The House of Commons' standing committees consider a bill only after the second reading vote in the Commons, which means the committees have no jurisdiction over the principles of the legislation since the principles have been adopted at the second reading vote. The Bundestag's committees, on the other hand, usually receive legislation after the first reading. The committees can therefore alter a bill completely or, in effect, substitute a bill of their own. It is the committee's bill which then comes before the Bundestag for the second reading. Thus, the prerogatives that are given to the Bundestag's standing committees to deal with legislation are greater than those of the standing committees in the House of Commons. And, they can initiate bills, which Commons' committees cannot.

After the committee reports the bill, it receives a second and a third reading in the Bundestag. Either reading may become the subject of a general debate on the principles of the bill or of amendments to the bill. The committee *rapporteur*, who has been responsible for formulating the committee text in conjunction with the committee deliberations, acts as the committee spokesman in the debates. The final vote on the bill, as amended, takes place at the third reading. The bill then goes to the Bundesrat (if the government introduced the bill, the Bundesrat will also have reviewed it prior to its introduction into the Bundestag).

Returning to the committee stage, the process of committee deliberation ordinarily begins by gathering information on the piece of legislation. The committee chairman selects from the committee membership a *rapporteur* who develops a working paper for the committee and outlines changes that ought to be made to the bill. Also, hearings may be held in which the views of interest groups, experts in the area, and representatives of the government are heard and considered. Then the committee debates the bill clause by clause, voting on the individual clauses and on amendments to them.

In dealing with legislation, each of the committees is specialized by subject matter, enabling each committee and its members to develop some competence in particular areas of legislation for which it is responsible. As a consequence, the German government may have to contend with a group of parliamentarians who have significant powers in the legislative process and who can also claim to have some expertise behind the competing policy recommendations they may present to the Bundestag.

However, until the reforms of 1969 doubled the staff, there was only minimal staffing for the committees or their members. Prior to 1969, the committee could draw upon a Bundestag research staff, enabling the committee to use one or two, and sometimes more, research specialists. It also had secretarial assistance. The committee chairman and the committee *rapporteur* were able to make use of this staff and receive additional help from research specialists available through their parliamentary party. Especially if compared to the United States Congress, however, staffing was modest. Even after the 1969 reforms, the staff available to the Bundestag's committees does not come close to matching the committees of the U.S. Congress. Moreover, individual Bundestag members have public funding sufficient only to secure the services of one assistant.

The chairmen of the Bundestag committees do not have quite the prerogatives in dealing with the committees that committee chairmen in the House of Representatives or the Senate have had. Even so, the position of the chairman gives him the initiative on such matters as the committee agenda, the appointment of *rapporteurs*, direction of the research staff, and leadership in the debate during committee meetings. The deputy chairman, who is always from another party, also can influence decisions in regard to these matters. As a result, according to Loewenberg, "in comparison to the ordinary committee member, the chairman and the deputy chairman are in a dominating position."[150]

Because of the significance of the Bundestag's committees, the chairmanships and deputy chairmanships of these committees are coveted awards. They are also positions from which a member might be appointed to the cabinet. From fifteen to twenty of these awards are usually open to the CDU/CSU and SPD parliamentary parties at the beginning of each Bundestag. Since seniority is not nearly as important a determining factor in allocating chairmanship or deputy chairmanship posts as it has been in the Congress, parliamentary parties can take into greater account factors such as loyalty and factional representation in making their committee chairmanship and deputy chairmanship assignments (see Chapter 4 for further discussion).

Another important element of the Bundestag organization is the parliamentary party (*fraktion*). The three parliamentary parties are the Christian Democratic Union-/Christian Social Union (CDU/CSU), the Social Democrats (SPD), and the Free Democrats (FDP). Activity on legislation within the parliamentary parties begins well before the first reading and continues throughout the legislative process. Discussions that take place in the various arenas of debate in the parliamentary parties, and particularly the governing parties, may have decided consequences for the final decisions of the Bundestag legislation committees and of the Bundestag itself. Further, we have already alluded to the prominent part of the parties play in such important functions as establishing the Bundestag's agenda or distributing chairmanship assignments.

The formal structure of each of the parliamentary parties is roughly similar. Let us look at the CDU/CSU and the SPD. Each of these parliamentary parties has an executive committee, a chairman, a deputy chairman or chairmen, whips, a set of specialized party committees, and a caucus. If the party is included in the government, it is important to note that the leadership of the parliamentary party, including the executive committee, is not the same as the party leadership in the government.

The executive committee of each parliamentary party plays a prominent part in the resolution of policy conflicts internal to the party and in formulating the positions the party will take in the Council of Elders, the Bundestag committees, and in debate. Its recommendations go before the parliamentary party caucus, which includes all members of the parliamentary party and is the ultimate authority within the party. Before making recommendations, the executive committee will generally take into account the policy positions of a wide variety of persons. These include the relevant party ministers, the members of the party's own specialized committees, and, especially in the CDU/CSU, the leaders of interested factions in the parliamentary party.

Because of the importance of the executive committee, election to it is viewed as a significant parliamentary award. The election of members to the executive committee of the parliamentary party in the CDU/CSU and the SPD is in many respects similar. In each case the outgoing executive committee presents the caucus with a list of nominees, which often is supplemented by nominations from members of the caucus. From one-half to two-thirds of the committee members are elected in this way. Although the nominees offered by the executive committee are in a distinctly favorable position, enough have been defeated so as not to make executive committee nominees certain winners. (The newly chosen CDU/CSU executive committee also has the right to select a specified number of additional members, subject to caucus approval.)

In addition, in both parties the executive committee includes the parliamentary party chairman, deputy chairmen, and whips. With few exceptions, each of these officers is also elected by the caucus.

As a consequence of these procedures, membership on the executive committee results from an interplay between the executive committee members and the caucus. This can be most clearly seen in the CDU/CSU. This parliamentary party has a number of organized factions within it. The parliamentary party is essentially a coalition of geographically, economically, and religiously based groups. The CSU is a Bavarian based organization which coalesced with the CDU. The parliamentary party also has within it organized groups of agricultural, small business, large business, and labor parliamentarians. Finally, there is the Catholic-Protestant dichotomy. The choice of executive committee members, as we have seen, is structured considerably by both the outgoing and the incoming executive committees, but their choice of nominees is shaped by the coalitional structure of the parliamentary party. Thus, usually the membership on the CDU/CSU executive committee is roughly proportional to the strength of each of the factions. The particular parliamentarians chosen for the executive committee is partly a result of bargaining between the executive committee and the factions.

The importance of factions within the CDU/CSU is also reflected in the persons elected by the caucus to the office of parliamentary party chairman and the office of chief whip. The party tends to shy away from placing these posts in the hands of members who are closely tied to particular factions within the party. It has instead generally chosen as leaders men who, by virtue of their independence, would not persistently give preference to any one faction at the expense of another. Since the SPD has not been composed of formally organized factions internal to the parliamentary party (until the left wing, desiring greater government involvement in the economy, formally organized in late 1972), the ability of the executive committee to control parliamentary awards of all types has been somewhat greater. This includes Bundestag committee chairmanships and deputy chairmanships, committee assignments internal to the party, as well as executive committee posts. Nevertheless, even before the left wing formally organized, the SPD caucus sometimes rejected the nominations forwarded by the executive committee. In 1957, for example, four of its nominees for the sixteen executive committee posts were rejected.[151]

Besides the apparatus we have discussed thus far, each of the parliamentary parties also has a set of specialized subject-matter committees, called working groups. There are six working groups in the CDU/CSU and eight in the SPD.[152] The policy position taken by these working groups on legislative matters is an integral element of each party's decision-making process on proposed legislation and feeds into the deliberations of the executive committee. The chairmen of the CDU/CSU's working committees are automatically members of the executive committee; the chairmen of the SPD's working groups are usually elected members to the SPD executive committee (for example, in 1972 six of the eight working group chairmen in the SPD were elected to the executive committee).

The membership of the specialized committees of both parliamentary parties parallels somewhat the membership on the specialized legislation committees in the Bundestag. For example, CDU/CSU members of the finance committee tend to be members of the CDU/CSU finance working group. This affords members a further opportunity to specialize and to gain expertise.

The specialized parliamentary party committees, the parliamentary caucus meetings, and the specialized Bundestag committees on legislation afford the individual members in the Bundestag a number of avenues of participation. Besides this, an individual member may address up to two verbal questions to the government each week. These questions must be answered during the daily question hour which begins each sitting, and the member can follow each question up with two supplementary questions. Members may also address questions to be answered in writing by the government. Members can participate in debate, as well, and 5 percent or more members can initiate a debate through an interpellation.[153] Finally, Bundestag members can initiate legislation. About 25 percent of the legislation adopted by the Bundestag has been initiated by "private" members (again, 5 percent or more Bundestag members are required to introduce nongovernmental legislation). Both the opposition party and backbenchers in the governing party have successfully gained passage of bills they initiated. They have also initiated legislation in an effort to press the government to make legislative proposals. Upon occasion, such tactics have been successful.[154]

It is important to note, too, the many avenues open to the opposition party in the Bundestag. The opposition party has direct access to all major points of the Bundestag's decision-making process. Negotiations in the Council of Elders have given the opposition a formal opportunity to influence the creation of the agenda. By tradition each major party is given rather equal time in debate. Also, the opposition can ask written questions and use the oral question hours. Moreover, the procedure in the Bundestag's specialized legislation committees gives a considerable weight to the committee chairman and deputy chairman, one of whom is likely to be from the opposition party. The *rapporteurs*, chosen by the committee chairman to develop the initial draft of committee reports on particular pieces of proposed legislation, are generally selected on the basis of neutrality toward that legislation. The norm, as well, is that the total *rapporteurs* for all committees are chosen in approximate proportion to party strength in the Bundestag. Thus, opposition parliamentarians receive a roughly proportional share of these assignments. Finally, the most important committee (Appropriations) has been chaired since 1949 by a member of the opposition.

Despite these possibilities, however, it was clear that SPD members felt the role of permanent opposition (until 1966) was insufficient. The result was that "many promising talents in the SPD . . . wandered off after years in the Bundestag . . ."[155] Only when the SPD entered the government did this process reverse itself.

The French Fifth Republic Assembly Let us turn now to the French Assembly. Like the West German system, the executive and the Parliament are not organizationally merged in the French Fifth Republic. Both the Assembly structure and the structure of the parliamentary parties within the Assembly are separate from the executive.

But the separation in the French case must be viewed in the context of the explicit attempt of the Fifth Republic Constitution to limit the power of the Assembly. Reacting to the influence and perhaps dominating position which the Fourth Republic Assembly held, the framers of the Fifth Republic Constitution attempted to assure that the executive could play a major role in managing the Assembly. Legislative management is vested in three sources: the executive, the Bureau and Presidents' Conference of the Assembly, and the Assembly's standing committees.

The purposes of the Bureau and the Presidents' Conference of the Assembly are quite similar to the purposes of the Council of Elders in the Bundestag. The Bureau is composed of Assembly members drawn proportionally from and selected by the Assembly parties (the Communists have been excepted from this). It is led by the President of the Assembly. Among its main functions are the direction of the Assembly's debates and the referral of bills to committee.[156] The Presidents' Conference, also chaired by the President of the Assembly, is composed of most of the Bureau members as well as additional representation from the party and committee leaders and a representative of the government. Its functions include organizing the agenda (which bills will be debated) subject to Assembly approval and organizing both the Assembly debates (who shall speak, the order of speakers, length of time, and so on), and the weekly question periods.[157]

The Constitution of the Fifth Republic, however, places many limits on the control of the Assembly over its own agenda and passes this control into the hands of the government. Although the Presidents' Conference organizes the agenda, priority on the agenda must be given to government bills and to private member bills accepted by the government, thereby making it difficult for a private member bill not accepted by the government even to receive a debate. Furthermore, the Assembly must follow an order of priority for bills initiated or accepted by the government. Thus, the government does not have to attempt to influence the Assembly as did governments of the Fourth Republic or as the German government has to attempt to influence the Bundestag and the Council of Elders. It can decide, and the government has used its powers to the fullest.[158] As Noonan has observed, "With respect to timetables, priorities and area of performance, the Parliament [has been] boxed in by the government."[159] The main activities escaping these governmental powers are motions of censure and the weekly question period, both of which receive priority over government business.

The Assembly's standing committees on legislation serve as another type of management committee. Unless a special committee is established, proposals for legislation must be sent to one of the six standing committees. Only after the committee reports does a debate in the Assembly take place.

These committees, like their counterparts in the United States Congress or West German Bundestag, played a most influential role in the management of legislation during the Fourth Republic, and their deliberations on legislation can still be intense and grueling. Once again, however, the framers of the Fifth Republic sought to limit what they felt were the excesses of Assembly influence in the Fourth Republic. A major restriction put on these committees in the Fifth Republic is that floor debate in the Assembly takes place not on the committee text but on the basis of the initial government proposal changed only by those amendments the government has accepted.

The committee or its members may and often do propose additional amendments, but, once again, the Constitution places some restrictions on the effect of amendments by giving the government the power to call for what is known as a package vote. According to Article 44, "If the Government so requests, the House shall decide by a single ballot on all or part of the bill under discussion *including only the amendments proposed or accepted by the Government.*"[160]

The standing committees on legislation have been altered in other ways as well. Instead of the nineteen committees of the Fourth Republic Assembly, the Constitution limits the number of committees in the Fifth Republic Assembly to six. As a consequence, each committee is large, ranging from 60 to about 120 members and averaging over 75 members. The subject matter covered by each committee is also far broader than was the case for the Fourth Republic committees. These limits were in part compensated for by the evolution of informal subcommittees having a smaller membership and covering a more specialized area of policy, although subcommittees fell into disuse in the latter 1960s.

The government's powers over the agenda and over the content of legislation to be voted upon, however, are not the totality of the situation. The government still must work through the Assembly. Despite its powers, it must retain the confidence of the Assembly, and it must be certain that the majority does not oppose its proposals. Thus, it must remain in contact and continue to communicate with the Assembly.

The main contact between the executive and the Assembly is through the parliamentary parties. Under a Gaullist President and government, the Gaullist parliamentary party has served as the major mechanism by which the executive and the Assembly are brought together. There is also a Liaison Committee that meets regularly linking the Premier to representatives of the coalition parties.

The highest authoritative body in the Gaullist parliamentary party is the caucus, composed of all members of the parliamentary party. It determines the political positions the party will follow in the Assembly debates and on the Assembly committees. It decides who will speak for the party and chooses the legislation the party will initiate. In effect, however, the decisions of the caucus may be highly structured through the intervention of the bureau of the Gaullist parliamentary party. Most members on the bureau, including the President of the parliamentary party, are elected each year by the parliamentary party according to a formula that assures representation to the various regions within France.

One of the main powers of the bureau is that the caucus' decisions can be based only on its proposals. Thus, "policy initiative and the power of decision belong to the bureau and not to the caucus,"[161] although the caucus may exert influence on these decisions. Moreover, no individual Gaullist member can submit a proposal for legislation or can pose oral questions having a policy content without the agreement of the parliamentary party bureau. Upon nomination by the President of the parliamentary party, the bureau also places a member on each of the six Assembly committees to convey its decisions to the other Gaullist members on the committee. These members are similar to whips. Finally, the bureau selects the leaders of each of the Gaullist parliamentary party specialized committees (known as "study groups"). Because of these powers, and due to the standing of the members making up the bureau, the major point of contact between the executive and the Gaullist parliamentary party has been the bureau of the parliamentary party.

Below the bureau are the study groups. Like the British and German parliamentary parties, the Gaullist parliamentary party contains a set of specialized committees. A decision of the bureau in 1968 reduced the number of parliamentary party specialized committees to six. In addition, there is a number of ad hoc policy committees. The specialized and ad hoc study groups can discuss legislation and forward recommendations to the bureau. Gaullist ministers may appear before the committees and have, upon occasion, presented to the committee the outlines of governmental proposals in advance of both their final draft and formal presentation to the Assembly. The extent to which this occurs appears to be a function of the willingness of the particular minister, the nature of the particular proposal, and the dynamism of the leaders of the parliamentary party committee. A study in 1965 found that of the fifteen study committees then operating, six were highly active, two were somewhat active, and seven were inactive.[162] Most of the active committees have had frequent contact with the appropriate government ministers, engaged in lengthy discussions, and successfully influenced more than a few policy proposals prior to debates in the Assembly.

The Gaullist parliamentary group is organizationally independent of the Gaullist President and government. Most of the leadership, such as the members of the bureau, is elected in elections by the parliamentary party rather than appointed by the executive. Many of these elections have been hotly contested. However, at least until 1969, both the person who became President of the parliamentary party and the Gaullist leaders in the Assembly's standing committees were chosen "in compliance with the wishes of the Prime Minister and the President of the Republic."[163]

The presence of a rather independently organized parliamentary party upon which the government depends does enable opposing viewpoints within that party to gain some hearing within governmental circles and some influence. On the other hand, the role of the opposition parties is more circumscribed, especially as compared to their role in the House of Commons or the Bundestag.

The main avenues typically available to opposition parties for expressing their views are their influence on the subjects to be debated (that is, influence over agenda), their role in debates, presentation of motions and proposals for legislation, amendments to legislation, participation on committees that discuss legislation, and the ability to ask written and oral questions. All of these avenues have been truncated in the Assembly of the Fifth Republic. The government has used its powers to control the topics on the Assembly agenda, often without serious regard for the interests and views of opposition parties. Moreover, through its control, only about one-quarter of the time given to debate has been put in the hands of the opposition parties. This control has also made it more difficult for opposition and private member proposals to gain a hearing in the Assembly. Amendments proposed by critics of the government, furthermore, may never come to a vote if the government insists on a package vote (the government did so on 118 occasions from 1962 to 1967). The participation of the opposition on Assembly committees has been reduced by the fact that, unlike the practice in the

Bundestag (or the Fourth Republic Assembly), the Assembly committee chairmen and the committee *rapporteurs* in the Fifth Republic have come from the majority. The Assembly committees have, in any case, lost some of their prerogatives since Assembly debate is based on the text of the government bill and not on the text proposed by the committee. Finally, the government, through the control of the majority on the Presidents' Conference, has been able to deter debate on oral questions that might embarrass the government. Thus, the government "has taken full advantage of both its political and procedural powers so as to ensure that all-out opposition has few opportunities to appeal to the country."[164] and so that it, rather than the opposition, can determine the timing of otherwise potentially effective opposition criticism.

Finally, we should say a word about the circumscribed role of the private member in the introduction of legislation. Significant procedural limits can be placed on a member who wishes to propose a bill. For example, in most of the parliamentary parties, such bills may need to be approved by the executive committee of the parliamentary party before they can be submitted to the Assembly's Bureau. Further, to gain a place on the Assembly's agenda, the government must be willing to accept the bill and to give it some priority. Finally, unless the government intervenes to call a conference committee, the Senate can block passage of the bill. Because of limits such as these, only about 10 percent of adopted legislation was a result of bills introduced by Assembly members from 1959 to 1968. In Great Britain and West Germany, on the other hand, about 25 percent of the legislation adopted over a similar period stemmed from bills introduced by nongovernmental members of the House of Commons and the Bundestag.

Summary

Our outline and overview of the four systems suggests both similarities and differences among the various legislatures. Each of the four legislatures is elected directly by the public in periodic elections. The elections are open to competition, and, with few exceptions, electors are presented with choices among alternative candidates or sets of candidates. Furthermore, pluralities of the popular vote are ordinarily related to the election of party or coalitional majorities in the legislature. Formally, each legislator is equal in the sense that each legislator has one vote. Also, each of the legislatures has authority to make decisions across a wide range of policy areas. In these respects, all related to the definition of a representative legislature (see Introduction), the four legislatures are broadly similar.

There are also important differences among the four legislatures. The greatest differences are between the American and British legislatures, while the French and German legislatures on some points are similar to the American legislature and other times more similar to the British legislature. A few examples will suffice to make this point.

One of the most important contrasts deals with the type of political system. The American Congress is part of a separation-of-powers system, while the British House of Commons functions in a parliamentary system. Here, the French and German legislatures are like the British in that they exist in a parliamentary system. On the other hand, as we have seen, the presence of an influential Presidency elected separately from the Assembly also gives the Fifth Republic some basic characteristics of a separation-of-powers system. The German Constitution, too, diverges to a degree from the British model by attempting more greatly to narrow the situations under which the legislature can censure the government. Nevertheless, even in the West German system, a major defeat of government policy on the floor of the Bundestag or several defeats on lesser issues, indicating that the government had lost its majority and would face further reversals, would likely lead the government to resign or to arrange for dissolution of the Bundestag. Only a party capable of maintaining sufficient cohesion on the floor can elect and make effective a Chancellor, the single greatest political prize in the federal system.

Another area of contrast is in the way legislative parties are organized in the Congress and the House of Commons. For example, the organization of parties in the Congress is rather simple in comparison to the British Labour and Conservative parties, with their intricate leadership structures, elaborate whip systems, and committees at various levels. On the other hand, in spite of its relative simplicity, party organization in the Congress has its own leadership independent of the President and his cabinet, while the Prime Minister and cabinet form the leadership of the governing party in the House of Commons. In these respects, we have pointed out that most German and French legislative parties are like those in Britain insofar as concerns organizational complexity, but share characteristics of Congressional parties in that they have leadership structures that are organizationally separate from the executive.

A third contrast deals with characteristics of the committee structure in the legislature. For example, most of the committees on legislation in the Congress are specialized by subject matter and have the ability either to change radically or to block proposed legislation. In contrast, committees on legislation in the House of Commons are more generalist in nature and, because they receive most legislation only after the second reading, cannot easily change in a fundamental manner the proposals they consider. In these respects, the committee system in the Bundestag is rather similar to that of the Congress. On the other hand, because of both the small number of committees and the powers the government has in the legislative process, the committee system in the Assembly has characteristics tending more in the direction of the British model.

Differences such as these across the four legislatures constitute important elements of the political setting within which the legislator operates and must relate to other political actors. As a consequence, they help to shape the legislator's behavior. Some of the ways in which these and other structural characteristics shape legislative behavior will be one object of our attention in Chapters 4 through 9 as we discuss how legislators act toward their party, the executive, and interest groups.

Notes

[1] Differences between the constitutional roles of the Senate and the House include: the election of the President (by the House) from the top three candidates and the Vice-President (by the Senate) from the top two candidates when there is no electoral college majority; their role in the impeachment process discussed below; the requirement that revenue bills originate in the House (subject to Senate amendments and House concurrence); and the power of the Senate to approve treaties and various Presidential appointments.

[2] William Keefe and Morris Ogul in their *The American Legislative Process* 3d. ed. (Englewood Cliffs, N.J.: Prentice-Hall, 1973), also call attention to related "but more obtuse or inferential, band of powers" referred to as *resulting* powers. "A resulting power cannot be traced directly to a specific authorization in the Constitution but results, or is fairly deduced, from a circumstance in which delegated powers are associated" (p. 34-35).

[3]See Raoul Berger, *Impeachment: The Constitutional Problems* (Cambridge, Mass.: Harvard University Press, 1973).
[4]Richard Neustadt, *Presidential Power* (New York: John Wiley and Sons, 1960), p. 33.
[5]Donald Matthews, *U.S. Senators and Their World* (New York: Random House, 1960), p. 44.
[6]See C. Q. *Guide to Current Amerian Government* (Washington, D. C.: Congressional Quarterly, Inc., Spring, 1973), pp. 25-26. For information on election opponents of Congressmen see: Jeff Fishel, *Party and Opposition: Congressional Challengers in American Politics* (New York: David McKay, 1973), especially Chapter 2; Robert Huckshorn and Robert Spencer, *The Politics of Defeat* (Amherst: University of Massachusetts Press, 1971).
[7]Literature relevant to motivation, opportunity, and legislative recruitment includes: Donald Matthews, *The Social Background of Decision-Makers* (Garden City, N. Y.: Doubleday, 1954); Herbert Jacob, "Initial Recruitment of Elected Officials in the U.S.—A Model," *Journal of Politics* 24 (November 1962): 703-16; Leo M. Snowiss, "Congressional Recruitment and Representation," *American Political Science Review* 60 (September 1966): 627-39; and Michael Mezey, "Ambition Theory and the Office of Congressmen," *Journal of Politics* 32 (August 1970); 563-79. For citations of other relevant literature, see Fishel, *Party and Opposition*.
[8]For example, Lewis Froman, *Congressmen and Their Constituencies* (Chicago: Rand McNally, 1963).
[9]Nelson Polsby, ed., *Reapportionment in the 1970's* (Berkeley: University of California Press, 1971), pp. 291-292 contains a brief but excellent bibliography on congressional reapportionment.
[10]For the Ninety-third Congress, the first under the 1970 census, the populations in 385 of the 435 House districts varied less than 1 percent from those of the average Congressional district. Contrast these figures to the Eighty-eighth Congress before *Wesberry v. Sanders* when only 9 of the 435 districts were within 1 percent of the average and in 236 districts the deviation was 10 percent or higher.
[11]*C.Q. Guide to Current American Government*, p. 10.
[12]This is not to say it has not had other impacts. Different kinds of Republicans may be elected. For example, whereas rural Republicans tend to be conservative, suburban Republican legislators cannot be classified as a group as either conservatives or liberals. David Mayhew has argued that reapportionment's effects have tended to favor incumbents (see David Mayhew "Congressional Representation: Theory and Practice in Drawing Districts," in *Reapportionment in the 1970's,* ed. Polsby, pp. 249-84).
[13]On the general topic of the relationship between the electoral system and legislative seats, see: Douglas Rae, *The Political Consequences of Electoral Laws,* 2d ed. (New Haven, Conn.: Yale University Press, 1973); Edward Tufte, "The Relationship Between Seats and Votes in Two-Party Systems," *American Political Science Review* 67 (June 1973): 540-54; Enid Lakeman, *How Democracies Vote* (London: Faber and Faber, 1970); and Maurice Duverger, *Political Parties: Their Organization and Activity in the Modern State* (New York: John Wiley and Sons, 1954).
[14]Milton Cummings, "Reapportionment in the 1970's: Its Effect on Congress," in *Reapportionment in the 1970's,* ed. Polsby, pp. 209-41.
[15]On reasons for the rise of the direct primary see Keefe and Ogul, *The American Legislative Process,* p. 93, and H. Douglas Price, "The Electoral Arena," in *"Congress and America's Future,* ed. David Truman (Englewood Cliffs, N. J.: Prentice-Hall, 1973), pp. 50-51. In a few states one or both parties still nominate by convention. See Leroy Rieselbach, *Congressional Politics* (New York: McGraw-Hill, 1973), p. 44. For a good brief discussion of primaries and their impact in the United States, see Frank J. Sorauf, *Party Politics in America* (Boston: Little, Brown and Co., 1972), Chapter 9.
[16]Sorauf, *Party Politics in America*, pp. 217-23.
[17]H. Douglas Price, "The Electoral Arena," p. 39.
[18]A related issue is the question of the "representativeness" of the primary. V. O. Key's earlier contention, in *American State Politics* (New York: Knopf, 1956), p. 153, that voters in primaries are "often" not representative of the party has been questioned and subjected to additional research by contemporary scholars. See for examples: Andrew J. DiNitto and William Smithers, "The Representativeness of the Direct Primary," *Polity* 5 (Winter 1972): 209-24; Austin Ranney, "The Representativeness of Primary Elections," *Midwest Journal of Political Science* 12 (May 1968): 224-38; Austin Ranney, "Turnout and Representation in Presidential Primary Elections," *American Political Science Review* 66 (March 1972): 21-37.
[19]Sorauf, *Party Politics in America*, pp. 226-27.
[20]Malcolm Jewell and Samuel Patterson, *The Legislative Process in the United States* (New York: Random House, 1973), p. 119.
[21]Charles O. Jones, *Every Second Year: Congressional Behavior and the Two Year Term* (Washington, D.C.: The Brookings Institution, 1967), p. 68.
[22]V. O. Key, *Politics, Parties, and Pressure Groups* (New York: Thomas Y. Crowell, 1964), pp. 451-52.
[23]Keefe and Ogul, *The American Legislative Process,* p. 95. See also p. 98.
[24]Key, *Politics, Parties and Pressure Groups*, pp. 451-52.
[25]See also Jewell and Patterson, *The Legislative Process in the United States,* Table 5.1, p. 122, which compares levels of two-party competition in the Senate (1952-70) and the House (1954, 1962, 1970); Keefe and Ogul, *The American Legislative Process,* Table 4.1, p. 98, which compares marginal, safer, and uncontested seats in the Senate and House from 1962 to 1970. However, Mayhew indicates that, viewed from the standpoint

of a career, the seats are not quite as safe as they first appear. In the Ninety-third Congress 58 percent of the House members and 70 percent of the Senators had at least one election in their career which they won with less than 55 percent of the total vote. See David Mayhew, *Congress: The Electoral Connection* (New Haven, Conn.: Yale University Press, 1974), p. 33.

[26]H. Douglas Price, "The Electoral Arena," p. 50. See also his Figure 2, which compares the margin of Democratic House and Senate (statewide) popular votes in 1962.

[27]Raymond E. Wolfinger and Joan Heifetz Hollinger, "Safe Seats, Seniority, and Power in Congress," in *Readings on Congress*, Raymond Wolfinger, ed. (Englewood Cliffs, N. J.: Prentice-Hall, 1971), pp. 36-57, especially Table 10, p. 53.

[28]Charles O. Jones, "Interparty Competition for Congressional Seats," *Western Political Quarterly* 17 (September 1964): 461-76. However, Leroy Rieselbach, *Congressional Politics*, p. 49 finds the percentage of fluidity for 1968-70 to be 4.7 percent. Frequent redistricting during the 1960s made it difficult to gain data comparable to Jones' for 1962-70.

[29]Keefe and Ogul, *The American Legislative Process*, p. 101. See also Joseph Schlesinger, "The Structure of Competition for the American States," *Behavioral Science* 5 (July 1960): 197-210.

[30]The figures on the Senate and House come from Jewell and Patterson, *The Legislative Process in the United States*, p. 122. See also Twentieth Century Fund, *Electing Congress* (New York, 1970), Charts 3 and 4.

[31]For relevant figures for the Ninety-second Congress see Keefe and Ogul, *The American Legislative Process*, pp. 125-26. See also Nelson Polsby, "The Institutionalization of the House of Representatives," *American Political Science Review* 62 (March 1968): 144-68. For an interesting study that examines changes in the character of the House from the end of the nineteenth century to the present and how these have changed the careers of members, see H. Douglas Price, "The Congressional Career: Then and Now," in *Congressional Behavior*, ed. Nelson Polsby (New York: Random House, 1971), pp. 14-27.

[32]Representative literature on the costs of campaigning includes: Herbert Alexander, *Money in Politics* (Washington, D.C.: Public Affairs Press, 1972); idem, "Links and Contrasts Among American Parties and Party Subsystems," in *Comparative Political Finance*, ed. A. J. Heidenheimer (Lexington, Mass.: D. C. Heath, 1970), pp. 73-106; *Congressional Quarterly, Dollar Politics* (Washington, D. C., 1971); Alexander Heard, *The Costs of Democracy* (Chapel Hill: University of North Carolina Press, 1960); Huckshorn and Spencer, *The Politics of Defeat*, Chapter 4; Fishel, *Party and Opposition*, Chapter 5; David Leuthold, *Electioneering in a Democracy* (New York: John Wiley and Sons, 1968); David Adamany, *Financing Politics* (Madison: University of Wisconsin Press, 1969); idem, *Campaign Finance in America*, (North Scituate, Mass.: Duxbury Press, 1972).

[33]Mark Green et al., *Who Runs Congress* (New York: Grossman Publishers, 1972), p. 10.

[34]Note that this is the average per seat, not the average per candidate. Alexander reports the figures in *Money in Politics*, pp. 24-26. Total known expenses of Senate candidates were $51.8 million; for the House they were $19.8 million. He further estimates that, due to underreporting and gaps in available information, "The survey must have missed at least 25 percent of the total outlay" (p. 26). Thus the final figure is closer to a total of $90 million. *Electing Congress* has a lower estimate of the costs for races for Congress in 1968—"probably more than $50 million" (p. 16).

[35]There has not been national government subsidization of Congressional campaigns in the United States. However, recent legislation provides tax credits, or tax deductions, for political contributions at all levels. Also now each taxpayer can earmark a one-dollar tax deduction to be channeled to the party of his choice to be used in *Presidential* elections. Nixon and the Republican members of Congress were able to postpone the effective implementation date until January 1973. However, this establishes the principle of government subsidization.

[36]Alexander, *Money in Politics*, p. 127. Note that this includes contributions to both incumbents and nonincumbents who are challenging. According to Fishel, *Party and Opposition*, pp. 103-4, it is the "luckiest" House candidates who receive one-sixth to one-tenth of their expenses from national party organizations or national interest groups associated with those parties. On aid from the Capitol Hill committees (The Senatorial and House Campaign Committees of each party), see Alexander, *Money in Politics*, pp. 120-28. See also Huckshorn and Spencer, *The Politics of Defeat*, pp. 120-32, and Fishel, *Party and Opposition*, pp. 100-110.

[37]Huckshorn and Spencer, *The Politics of Defeat*, p. 125; Fishel, *Party and Opposition*, pp. 101-3.

[38]On Congressional campaigns, including strategy and tactics in general, see: Fishel, *Party and Opposition*, Chapter 5; David Paletz, "The Neglected Context of Congressional Campaigns," *Polity* 3(Winter 1971): 195-217; John W. Kingdon, *Candidates for Office: Beliefs and Strategies* (New York: Random House, 1968); William J. Gore and Robert Peabody, "The Functions of the Political Campaign: A Case Study," *Western Political Quarterly* 11 (March 1958): 55-70; John C. Donovan, *Congressional Campaign: Maine Elects a Democrat* (New York: McGraw-Hill, 1960); and Charles O. Jones, "The Role of the Campaign in Congressional Politics" in *The Electoral Process*, ed. M. Kent Jennings and L. Harmon Zeigler (Englewood Cliffs, N.J.: Prentice-Hall, 1966), pp. 21-41.

[39]Fishel, *Party and Opposition*, p. 103. As we have noted above, what funds there are are biased in favor of incumbents' use. See also: H. Douglas Price, "The Electoral Arena," pp. 56-60.

[40]Charles Clapp, *The Congressman: His Work as He Sees It* (New York: Doubleday, Anchor, 1964), p. 374. However, see Robert Erikson, "The Advantage of Incumbency in Congressional Elections," *Polity* 3 (Spring

1971): 395-405. He suggests that the added increment for an incumbent as such may be only 2 percent of the vote, while the major explanation for incumbent House members almost always winning may be the safeness of the districts for one or the other party (pp. 404-5).

[41] For a fuller account of the two acts, see *Congressional Quarterly Almanac* (Washington, D. C., 1972), pp. 723-24, and *Congressional Quarterly Weekly Reports,* October 12, 1974, pp. 2865-70 and December 28, 1974, pp. 3442-43. An interesting case study on campaign financing legislation is Robert Peabody et. al. *To Enact a Law* (New York: Praeger, 1972).

[42] On the question of the impact of "Presidential coattails" (that is, Presidential impact on Congressional races), see Malcolm Moos, *Politics, Presidents and Coattails* (Baltimore, Md.: John Hopkins Press, 1951); Milton Cummings, *Congressmen and the Electorate* (New York: The Free Press, 1966); Warren Miller, "Presidential Coattails: A Study of Political Myth and Methodology," *Public Opinion Quarterly* 19 (Winter 1955-56): 353-68; Charles Press, "Voting Statistics and Presidential Coattails," *American Political Science Review* 52 (December 1958): 1041-40; John W. Meyer, "A Reformulation of the 'Coattails' Problem," in *Public Opinion and Congressional Elections,* ed. William McPhee and William Glaser (New York: The Free Press of Glencoe, 1962), pp. 52-64; Jewell and Patterson, *The Legislative Process in the United States,* pp. 124-31; Barbara Hinckley, "Incumbency and the Presidential Vote in Senate Elections," *American Political Science Review* 64 (September 1970): 836-42; and J. Vincent Buck, "Presidential Coattails and Congressional Loyalty," *Midwest Journal of Political Science* 16 (August 1972): 460-72.

[43] Alan L. Clem, "Popular Representation and Senate Vacancies," *Midwest Journal of Political Science* 10 (February 1966): 52-77.

[44] Sorauf, *Party Politics in America,* Chapter 1.

[45] Hugh A. Bone, "An Introduction to the Senate Policy Committees," *American Political Science Review* 50 (June 1956): 352. See also Hugh A. Bone, *Party Committees and National Politics* (Seattle: University of Washington Press, 1958); Charles O. Jones, *Party and Policy Making: The House Republican Policy Committee* (New Brunswick, N. J.: Rutgers University Press, 1964); Ralph K. Huitt, "Democratic Party Leadership in the Senate," *American Political Science Review* 55 (June 1961): 333-44; and, Malcolm Jewell, "The Senate Republican Policy Committee and Foreign Policy," *Western Political Quarterly* 12 (December 1959): 966-80.

[46] Keefe and Ogul, *The American Legislative Process,* p. 285. Until now, the House Republican Committee may have been used most profitably. Charles O. Jones points out that in 1959 it began to be useful as an instrument "to discover a basis (both substantive and procedural) for consensus or to discover that there is no such basis" (*Party and Policy Making,* p. 139). The new House Democratic Committee has some promise under Albert and O'Neill's leadership.

[47] See Nelson Polsby, "Two Strategies of Influence: Choosing a Majority Leader, 1962," in *New Perspectives on the House of Representatives,* ed. Robert Peabody and Nelson Polsby (Chicago: Rand McNally, 1969), pp. 325-58.

[48] On leadership change and succession, see: Robert Peabody, "Party Leadership Change in the House of Representatives," *American Political Science Review* 61 (September 1967): 675-93, and his "Senate Leadership Change, 1953-1970," Paper Presented at the 1970 American Political Science Association, especially p. 25. Much of the material in this paragraph is based on Peabody's work.

[49] Richard Fenno, "Internal Distribution of Influence: The House," in *Congress and America's Future,* 2nd ed. David B. Truman (Englewood Cliffs, N.J.: Prentice-Hall, 1973), p. 72. See, also, Randall Ripley, *Majority Party Leadership in Congress* (Boston: Little, Brown and Co., 1969), and his *Party Leaders in the House of Representatives* (Washington, D.C.: The Brookings Institution, 1967).

[50] See Charles O. Jones, *The Minority Party in Congress* (Boston: Little, Brown and Co., 1970).

[51] Randall Ripley, "The Party Whip Organizations in the House of Representatives," *American Political Science Review* 58 (September 1964): 561-76. For a comparison to the Senate see Walter J. Oleszek, "Party Whips in the United States Senate," *Journal of Politics* 33 (November 1971): 955-79.

[52] Matthews, *U. S. Senators,* pp. 123-24.

[53] David Truman, *The Congressional Party* (New York: John Wiley and Sons, 1959), Chapter 4.

[54] Ralph K. Huitt, "The Democratic Leadership in the Senate," p. 344. For a comparison of the differences in leadership styles between Mansfield and Johnson, see: John Stewart, "Two Strategies of Leadership: Johnson and Mansfield," in *Congressional Behavior,* ed. Polsby, pp. 61-92. On Everett Dirksen, the Republican party leader before Hugh Scott, see Jean Torcom, "Leadership: The Role and Style of Senator Everett Dirksen," in *To Be a Congressman: the Promise and the Power,* ed. Sven Groennings and Jonathon P. Hawley (Washington, D. C.: Acropolis Books Ltd., 1973), pp. 185-224.

[55] Fenno, "Internal Distribution," pp. 86-89. See also Ripley, *Party Leaders in the House of Representatives,* Chapters 3 and 5; idem, *Power in the Senate* (New York: St. Martin's Press, 1969), Chapter 4; idem, *Majority Party Leadership.*

[56] Woodrow Wilson, *Congressional Government* (New York: Meridian Books, 1956), p. 69. The committee system of Congress has received a great deal of attention by scholars in recent years. Some of the major books are: John Manley, *The Politics of Finance: The House Committee on Ways and Means* (Boston: Little, Brown and Co., 1970); Richard Fenno, *The Power of the Purse: Appropriations Politics in Congress* (Boston: Little, Brown and Co., 1966); Richard Fenno, *Congressmen in Committees* (Boston: Little, Brown and Co., 1973); Stephen Horn, *Unused Power: The Work of the Senate Committee on Appropriations* (Washington, D.C.: The

Brookings Institution, 1970); William Morrow, *Congressional Committees* (New York: Charles Scribner's Sons, 1969); David Price, *Who Makes the Laws: Creativity and Power in Senate Committees* (Cambridge, Mass.: Schenkman, 1972); John A. Ferejohn,*Pork Barrel Politics: Rivers and Harbors Legislation, 1947-1968* (Stanford, Calif.: Stanford University Press, 1974). Some of the key articles are: Ralph K. Huitt, "The Congressional Committee: A Case Study," *American Political Science Review* 48 (June 1954): 340-65; Charles O. Jones, "Representation in Congress: The Case of the House Agriculture Committee," *American Political Science Review* 55 (June 1961): 358-67; Richard Fenno, "The House Appropriations Committee as a Political System: The Problem of Integration," *American Political Science Review* 56 (June 1962): 310-24; and the special volume, "Changing Congress: The Committee System," *The Annals of the American Academy of Political and Social Science* 411 (January 1974). More specialized aspects of the literature on committees, such as committee assignments or supervisory activity, will be cited throughout the study as it becomes appropriate to do so.

[57] Polsby, "The Institutionalization of the House of Representatives," p 156.

[58] Fenno, *Congressmen in Committees*, p. 190; see also xiii. On other House-Senate differences, see Lewis Froman, *Congressional Process* (Boston: Little, Brown and Co., 1967).

[59] See Matthews, *U. S. Senators*, Chapter 7, and George Goodwin, *The Little Legislatures: Committees of Congress* (Amherst: University of Massachusetts Press, 1970), Chapters 3 and 4.

[60] Nicholas Masters, "Committee Assignments in the House of Representatives," *American Political Science Review* 55 (June 1961): 345-47. (This quotation appears on p. 353.) Much of the material in this paragraph is indebted to Masters and also to Goodwin, *The Little Legislatures*. We also draw upon the increasingly vast literature on committee assignment cited in Chapter 5.

[61] For material on the seniority system, see: Nelson Polsby, Miriam Gallaher, and Barry Runquist, "The Growth of the Seniority System in the U. S. House of Representatives," *American Political Science Review* 63 (September 1969): 787-807; George Goodwin, "The Seniority System in Congress," *American Political Science Review* 53 (June 1959): 412-36; Barbara Hinckley, *The Seniority System in Congress* (Bloomington: University of Indiana Press, 1971); Michael Abram and Joseph Cooper, "The Rise of Seniority in the House of Representatives,"*Polity* (Fall 1968) 52-85; Randall Ripley,*Power in the Senate* and, David Vogler, "Flexibility in the Congressional Seniority System: Conference Representation," *Polity* 1 (Summer 1970): 494-507.

[62] On January 23, 1973, the Democratic Caucus in the House approved a Subcommittee Bill of Rights that aims at fixed jurisdictions, more staff and autonomy, more favorable Democratic ratios, a greater role for seniority in determination of membership and chairmanships. There has been significant but not full compliance by the individual standing committees. See D.W. Rhode, "Committee Reform in the House of Representatives and the Subcommittee Bill of Rights," *The Annals of the American Academy of Political and Social Science* 411 (January 1974): 39-47. In the Ninety-fourth Congress, several House subcommittee chairmen were removed by internal subcommittee votes.

[63] Manley, *The Politics of Finance*, p. 150. Note also Chapter 4, especially pp. 100-101; 246; 380-84. For a similar position, see Hinckley, *The Seniority System*, pp. 92-93, 110-11.

[64] Fenno, *Congressmen in Committees*, especially Chapter III. See also his "Internal Distribution of Influence: The House," in Truman ed. *Congress and America's Future*, pp. 63-90. On the Senate, see Ripley,*Power in the Senate* and Ralph K. Huitt, "The Internal Distribution of Influence: the Senate," in Truman ed. *Congress and America's Future*, pp. 91-117.

[65] Goodwin, *The Little Legislatures*, p. 127; idem, "The Seniority System in Congress," p. 421. See also Hinckley,*The Seniority System*, especially, p. 37; Ripley,*Power in the Senate*, Chapter 3; and Keefe and Ogul, *The American Legislative Process*, p. 187-88.

[66] Hinckley, *The Seniority System*, p. 108.

[67] Hinckley, *The Seniority System*, p. 109. See also p. 108.

[68] Raymond Wolfinger and Joan Hollinger, "Safe Seats, Seniority and Power in Congress," p. 54. See also R. Ripley, "Power in the Post World War II Senate," *Journal of Politics* 31 (May 1969): 465-92.

[69] This section is especially indebted to George Goodwin, "Subcommittees: The Miniature Legislatures of Congress," *American Political Science Review* 56 (September 1962): 596-604; *The Little Legislatures*, and Charles O. Jones, "The Role of the Congressional Subcommittee," *Midwest Journal of Political Science* 6 (November 1962): 327-45.

[70] On select committees, see: V. Stanley Vardys, "Select Committees of the House of Representatives," *Midwest Journal of Political Science* 6 (August 1962): 247-65; Roy Hamilton, "The Senate Select Committee on National Water Resources: An Ethical and Rational Criticism," *Natural Resources Journal* 2 (April 1962): 45-54; and Dale Vinyard, "Congressional Committee on Small Business," *Midwest Journal of Political Science* 10 (August 1966): 364-77.

[71] See the study of this joint committee by Harold Green and Allan Rosenthal entitled *Government of the Atom* (New York: Atherton, 1963).

[72] Fenno,*Power of the Purse*, p. 669. The figures appear in Chapter 12. See also Jeffrey L. Pressman,*House vs. Senate* (New Haven, Conn.: Yale University Press, 1966).

[73] David Vogler, "Patterns of One House Dominance in Congressional Conference Committees," *Midwest Journal of Political Science* 14 (May 1970); 303-20; quotation on page 303. See also his *The Third House: Conference Committees in the United States Congress* (Evanston, Ill.: Northwestern University Press, 1971).

For a somewhat different conclusion on public works, see Ferejohn, *Pork Barrel Politics*, pp. 120-26. Gilbert Steiner, *The Congressional Conference Committees, Seventieth to Eightieth Congress* (Urbana: University of Illinois Press, 1951), found for an earlier period that the House dominated; of the 56 proposals analyzed the Senate "won" 15; the House 32; 9 were even.

[74] On the nature, purpose, and uses of professional staffs, see: Samuel Patterson, "Congressional Committee Professional Staffing: Capabilities and Constraints," in *Legislatures in Developmental Perspective*, ed. by Allan Kornberg and Lloyd Musolf (Durham, N. C., Duke University Press, 1970), pp. 391-428; James Robinson, "Staffing the Legislature," in *Legislatures in Developmental Perspective*, ed. Kornberg and Musolf, pp. 366-90; Kenneth Kofmehl, *Professional Staffs of Congress* (West Lafayette, Ind.: Purdue University Press, 1962); Gladys M. Kammerer, *Congressional Committee Staffing Since 1946* (Lexington, Ky.: Bureau of Government Research, 1951); David Price, "Professionals and 'Entrepreneurs': Staff Orientations and Policy Making on Three Senate Committees," *Journal of Politics* 33 (May 1971): 316-36; Norman Meller, "Legislative Staff Services: Toxin, Specific, or Placebo for Legislature's Ills," *Western Political Quarterly* 20 (June 1967): 381-89; John Manley, "Congressional Staff and Public Policymaking," *Journal of Politics* 30 (November 1968): 1046-67; Harrison W. Fox, Jr., and Susan Webb Hammond, "Congressional Staffs and Congressional Change," (Paper Presented to the 1973 Annual Meeting of the American Political Science Association).

[75] See James D. Cochrane, "Partisan Aspects of Congressional Committee Staffing," *Western Political Quarterly* 17 (June 1964): 338-48.

[76] A general description of the institutions of the contemporary British system may be found in John P. Mackintosh, *The Government and Politics of Britain* (London: Hutchinson and Co., 1970); R.M. Punnett, *British Government and Politics* (New York: W. W. Norton, 1968); and Frank Stacey, *The Government of Modern Britain* (Oxford: The Clarendon Press, 1968). The legislative process, both outside and within Parliament, is described in S. A. Wakland, *The Legislative Process in Great Britain* (New York: Praeger, 1968). See also Kenneth Bradshaw and David Pring, *Parliament and Congress* (London: Constable and Co., 1972) and Bernard Crick, *The Reform of Parliament* (London: Weidenfeld and Nicolson, 1970).

[77] The Parliament last extended its life beyond five years during World War II.

[78] The role of the extraparliamentary party in nominations and elections is discussed briefly on pp. 65-66 and in greater detail in Chapter 4 and Chapter 9. Insofar as policy-making is concerned, the parliamentary party has not been bound by the extraparliamentary party, although this has been the subject of greater question in the case of the Labour party's minority government than in the case of the Conservative party. Worthwhile studies on the subject are: Leon Epstein, "Who Makes Party Policy: British Labour, 1960-1961," *Midwest Journal of Political Science* 6 (1962): 165-82; Robert T. McKenzie, *British Political Parties* (New York: St. Martin's Press, 1963); and, S. Rose, "Policy Decision in Opposition," *Political Studies* 4 (June 1956): 128-38.

[79] The procedures of and politics behind the selection of the leader and the leader's selection of his ministers is described at length in Chapter 6. See also both McKenzie, *British Political Parties*, and G.W. Jones, "The Prime Minister's Power," in *European Political Processes: Essays and Readings*, ed. Henry Albinski and Lawrence Pettit (Boston: Allyn and Bacon, 1968), pp. 281-97.

[80] See Peter A. Bromhead, *The House of Lords and Contemporary Politics, 1911-1957* (London: Routledge, 1958).

[81] Review of the institutions of the West German political system may be found in Kurt Sontheimer, *The Government and Politics of West Germany* (New York: Praeger, 1972). An excellent study of the legislative process is Gerhard Loewenberg, *Parliament in the German Political System* (Ithaca, N.Y.: Cornell University Press. 1967). For detailed analysis of the political parties, including their parliamentary organization, see Heino Kaack, *Geschichte und Structur des deutschen Parteisystems* (Opladen: Westdeutscher Verlag, 1969).

[82] The President of West Germany is elected by a convention consisting of the members of the Bundestag and an equal number of members elected by the legislatures of the states of the West German federal system.

[83] This occurred in 1972 and produced an election victory for the Chancellor (Willy Brandt of the SPD). For dissolution to occur, the Chancellor must lose a vote of confidence at the same time that the Bundestag cannot agree on a successor. Further, both the Chancellor and the President must agree to the dissolution. On this, see George K. Romoser, "Change in West German Politics After Erhard's Fall," in *European Politics II: The Dynamics of Change*, ed. William G. Andrews (New York: Van Nostrand Reinhold, 1969), pp. 175-240, especially p. 205.

[84] Since 1949, the only exception to this rule was from 1969-72 when the SPD and the FDP formed a majority governing coalition even though the CDU/CSU was the largest individual party in the Bundestag.

[85] The one exception since 1949 was when the CDU/CSU formed a governing coalition, called the grand coalition, with the SPD from 1966 to 1969.

[86] For the relations between the parliamentary party and extraparliamentary party in the SPD and the CDU/CSU, see Douglas A. Chalmers, *The Social Democratic Party of Germany: From Working Class Movement to Modern Political Party* (New Haven, Conn.: Yale University Press, 1964), especially pp. 115-20; and Loewenberg, *Parliament in the German Political System*, pp. 175-76 and pp. 183-85.

[87] The CDU/CSU parliamentary party had approved Erhard to replace Adenauer some months before Adenauer resigned in 1963.

[88] On the Bundesrat, see Karlheinz Neunreither, *Der Bundesrat Zwischen Politik und Verwaltung* (Heidel-

berg: Quelle and Meyer, 1959), and Edward L. Pinney, *Federalism, Bureaucracy, and Party Politics in Western Germany* (Chapel Hill: University of North Carolina Press, 1963).

[89] The powers of the Bundesrat in this area are based on Article 84, paragraph 1 of the West German Basic Law.

[90] For a description of the operation of the Joint Mediation Committee, see Pinney, *Federalism, Bureaucracy, and Party Poltitics in Western Germany*, pp. 77-85.

[91] General descriptions of the institutions of the French Fifth Republic may be found in Roy Pierce, *French Politics and Political Institutions* (New York: Harper & Row, 1973); Henry W. Ehrman, *Politics in France* (Boston: Little, Brown and Co., 1971); and Maurice Duverger, *La Ve République* (Paris: Presses Universitaires de France, 1968). For a description of the legislature in the Fifth Republic, see Philip M. Williams, *The French Parliament: Politics in the Fifth Republic* (New York: Praeger, 1968).

[92] On the French Fourth Republic, see Philip M. Williams, *Crisis and Compromise: Politics in the Fourth Republic* (Garden City, New York: Doubleday, 1966)—the premiers are listed on pp. 526-27.

[93] The French President has been elected in national elections since a change in the Constitution in 1962. Elections occur every seven years, whereas the length of the Assembly can be no more than five years.

[94] Also see Duverger, *La Ve République*, pp. 41-167, and Malcolm Anderson, *Government in France: An Introduction to the Executive Power* (London: Pergamon Press, 1970).

[95] No member of the Assembly can sign more than one petition for a motion of censure during a session *unless* the motion of censure is in response to the govenment's initiation of a vote of confidence on a bill.

[96] According to Article 12 of the Fifth Republic Constitution, the President need only consult with the Premier and the Presidents of the two houses in making a decision on dissolving the Assembly.

[97] The development of this party from its foundations in the late 1950s (although it had been preceded by earlier Gaullist parties) is ably described in Jean Charlot, *L'U.N.R.: Étude du pouvoir au sein d'un parti politique* (Paris: Armand Colin, 1967).

[98] The Communists and the Socialists have had uneasy relations since the 1930s owing in part to fears on the part of many Socialists that the Communists would dismantle democratic institutions if they gained power. For relations between the Communists and the Socialists in France, see Charles A. Micaud, *Communism and the French Left* (New York: Praeger, 1963). For more recent commentary on the development of the democratic Left, see Harvey G. Simmons, *French Socialists in Search of a Role, 1956-1967* (Ithaca, N. Y.: Cornell University Press, 1970), and Frank L. Wilson, *The French Democratic Left: Toward a Modern Party System* (Stanford, Calif.: Stanford University Press, 1971). See, also, Georges Suffert, *De Defferre á Mitterrand: La campagne présidentielle* (Paris: Seuil, 1966).

[99] When a member resigns his Assembly seat, his seat is then taken by a member, called an alternate, who ran with him during the previous Assembly election.

[100] This applies to the head of the government or the cabinet in each of these systems and not to the head of state or the monarch. This is a particularly important distinction in France because the head of state, the President, has been a significant political actor.

[101] The creation of the Constitutional Council in the Fifth Republic had the effect of establishing a form of judicial review, which had not traditionally been a part of French political practice. One of the major functions of the Constitutional Council has been to rule on parliamentary actions especially in so far as they may affect the powers the Fifth Republic Constitution reserved to the President and government.

[102] As in France, these freedoms are limited insofar as they cannot be used to attack the basic democratic order. Furthermore, associations and groups are illegal if their object or their activities conflict with the criminal laws or with the concept of international understanding. The constitutionality of legislation in these and other matters is determined by the Federal Constitutional Court, half of which is elected by the Bundestag and half by the Bundesrat.

[103] These areas are cited in Article 73 of the German Basic Law, as amended. The powers include foreign policy, legislation on federal railroads and air traffic, industrial property rights, immigration, and defense policy.

[104] Recall that when legislation affects the powers of *land* administrations, they need to gain the approval of the Bundesrat as well as the Bundestag.

[105] The President must consult the Premier, the Presidents of the two houses, and the Constitutional Council (see p. 61). During the period of emergency, Parliament may meet by right and cannot be dissolved by the President. As it was applied in 1961, however, the Parliament was not allowed to discuss matters outside the cause or substance of the emergency.

[106] The Assembly and the Senate, by joint resolution, can also propose that the President initiate a public referendum on a bill. According to Article 11, a public referendum can be initiated on any bill dealing with the organization of the governmental authorities, entailing approval of agreements by the member states of the French community of nations, or providing for authorization to ratify a treaty that, without being contrary to the Constitution, might affect the functioning of the existing institutions. This has been interpreted in its widest sense to include bills having a constitutional or institutional portent and not solely bills of an ordinary kind.

[107] In particular, the Bundestag must have defeated the Chancellor in a vote of confidence without being dissolved, and the government must declare the bill to be urgent. See Article 81 of the Basic Law.

[108] This applies by a standing rule of the Commons in Great Britain. Furthermore, the standing rules of the

House of Commons require that all financial proposals be initiated by the executive.

[109]Punnett, *British Government and Politics*, p. 231; Peter G. Richards, *Honourable Members: A Study of the British Backbencher* (London: Faber and Faber, 1959), p. 112; and Bradshaw and Pring, *Parliament and Congress*, p. 295.

[110]André Chandernagor, *Un Parlement, pour quoi faire?* (Paris: Gallimard, 1967), p. 58; J. Grangé, "La Fixation de l'ordre du jour des Assemblées parlementaires," in *Études sur le Parlement de la Ve République*, ed. Eliane Guichard-Ayoub, Charles Roig, and Jean Grangé (Paris: Presses Universitaires de France, 1965), pp. 244-45; *Le Monde*, February 15, 1967; and Philip Williams and Martin Harrison, *Politics and Society in De Gaulle's Republic* (Garden City, N.Y.: Anchor, 1973), p. 267.

[111]German Bundestag, *Zeitschrift für Parlamentsfragen*, Jahrgang 4, Heft 1 (Bonn, 1973), p. 5.

[112]See, for example, the discussion in Hans Trossman, *The German Bundestag: Organization and Operation* (Darmstadt: Neue Darmstadter Verlagsanstalt, 1965), pp. 59-64.

[113]Loewenberg, *Parliament in the German Political System*, p. 278.

[114]A detailed discussion of relations between the executive and the legislature in the making of legislation and oversight will be found in Chapters 6 and 7.

[115]The West German Basic Law requires that party nominations at the constituency level be made either by secret vote in a general meeting of the constituency party members or by delegates they elect. Party nominations at the state level must be made by a party convention elected either directly or indirectly by party members in the state.

[116]In some parties, such as the Labour party, a candidate cannot propose his own name; his name must be formally submitted by an organization affiliated with or part of the constituency Labour association (party) or by the national party organization.

[117]See Karlheinz Kaufmann, et al. *Kandidaturen zum Bundestag* (Cologne: Kiepenheuer and Witsch, 1961), see also Bodo Zeuner, *Kandidatenaufstellung zur Bundestagswahl 1965* (The Hagne: Nijhoff, 1970).

[118]The political views of a candidate are likely to have more significance for his nomination in the Labour party than in the Conservative party. See Michael Rush, *The Selection of Parliamentary Candidates* (London: Nelson, 1969). Yet, Richard Rose found that on the question of British unilateral nuclear disarmament, a very heated issue in the Labour ranks in the arly and middle 1960s, there was only a slight relationship between the views of the constituency association and its candidate. See Richard Rose, "The Political Ideas of English Party Activists," in *Studies in British Politics: A Reader in Political Sociology*, ed. Richard Rose (New York: St. Martin's Press, 1966), pp. 285-307, especially pp. 302-3.

[119]Ulrich Duebber and Gerhard Braunthal, "West Germany," *The Journal of Politics* 25 (November 1963): 783.

[120]Duebber and Braunthal, "West Germany," p. 783. See also Uwe Schleth, "Germany," in *Comparative Political Finance*, ed. Arnold J. Heidenheimer (Lexington, Mass: D. C. Heath, 1970); and Arnold J. Heidenheimer and Frank C. Langdon, *Business Associations and the Financing of Political Parties* (The Hague: Martinus Nijhoff, 1968), pp. 14-88. For the SPD, see Chalmers, *The Social Democratic Party of Germany*.

[121]Duebber and Braunthal, "West Germany," p. 783.

[122]Richard Rose, *Influencing Voters: A Study of Campaign Rationality* (New York: St. Martin's Press, 1967), pp. 114-31. Altogether, the iron and steel industry spent about $3 million on electoral propaganda before the 1964 election (p. 130).

[123]Martin Harrison, "Britain," *The Journal of Politics* 25 (November 1963): 666.

[124]Charles O. Jones, "Inter-Party Competition in Britain—1950-1959," *Parliamentary Affairs* 17. (Winter 1963-64): 50-56.

[125]Loewenberg, *Parliament in the German Political System*, pp. 73-74.

[126]A more general investigation of the political effects of electoral systems covering eighteen countries is found in Rae, *The Political Consequences of Electoral Laws*.

[127]Discussion within the parliamentary parties may also precede the initiation of legislation.

[128]Each year begins with the Queen's speech, outlining the intentions of the government, and is followed by about a week of debate on the Queen's speech. Thus, this time is not used for actual government legislation. It is also not unusual for the government, in consultation with the opposition party, to allot days for debating currrent issues.

[129]The government acts through the Leader of the House, who is appointed by the Prime Minister.

[130]However, the Speaker does not also have the partisan political function of being leader of the majority party as does the Speaker of the House of Representatives.

[131]See Richard Rose, "The Making of Cabinet Ministers," *British Journal of Political Science* 1 (October 1971): 399. Ministerial and other governmental appointments have increased from 42 in 1900 to 122 in 1967 and 98 in 1970.

[132]Honors have been of somewhat greater significance to Conservative members than to Labour members.

[133]To aid it, the shadow cabinets has access to a rather substantial professional staff through the staff of the central extraparliamentary party organization.

[134]Although a Labour shadow Prime Minister must choose his shadow cabinet in the context of parliamentary party elections to the Parliamentary Committee of the Labour party, even he has considerable leeway in selecting his shadow cabinet both by naming additional shadow ministers and deciding who will serve in the chief frontbench positions. See R. M. Punnett, "The Labour Shadow Cabinet, 1955-1964," *Parliamentary*

Affairs 18, (Winter 1964-65): 61-70, and Punnett, *British Government and Politics*, pp. 116-17.

The procedures and politics behind selecting the shadow Prime Minister and behind his selection of the shadow cabinet are discussed in Chapter 6.

[135]The House of Commons is set up with rows of seats (benches) facing each other. Those in the government and shadow cabinet sit facing each other on the benches at the front. Those not in the government (government in the widest sense, including, for example, junior ministers and whips), or the shadow cabinet, sit on the benches behind their respective leaders (the backbenches) and are frequently referred to as backbenchers.

[136]Member of Parliament (MP).

[137]Quoted in S. E. Finer, H. B. Berrington, and D. J. Bartholomew, *Backbench Opinion in the House of Commons, 1955-1959* (Oxford: Pergamon Press, 1961), p. 3.

[138]Martin Redmayne and Norman Hunt, "The Power of the Whips," in *British Politics: People, Parties and Parliament*, ed. Anthony King (Boston: D. C. Heath and Company, 1966), p. 142.

[139]This is done on a written notice of Commons business sent weekly by the leadership to all members of the parliamentary party.

[140]Backbenchers also have some access to their party's professional staff at the extraparliamentary party central office, although less so if the party is in opposition (and its leaders therefore do not have the administration as an informational source at their disposal).

[141]For some excellent studies of these committees, see: Gordon Reid, *The Politics of Financial Control: The Role of the House of Commons* (London: Hutchinson, 1966); Nevil Johnson, *Parliament and Administration: The Estimates Committee, 1945-1965* (London: George Allen and Unwin, 1966); David Coombes, *The Member of Parliament and the Administration: The Case of the Select Committee on Nationalized Industries* (London: George Allen and Unwin, 1966); and Frank Stacey, *The British Ombudsman* (Oxford: The Clarendon Press, 1971), especially pp. 259-306.

[142]Reid, *The Politics of Financial Control*, pp. 102-3.

[143]Besides oral questions, the MP may also ask other questions for the government to answer in writing. The answers are then published in Hansard (the British equivalent of the *Congressional Record*).

[144]A study of the extent to which backbenchers make use of the various avenues available in the House is found in Malcolm J. Barnett, "Backbench Behavior in the House of Commons," *Parliamentary Affairs* 22 (Winter 1968-69): 38-61.

[145]Two excellent sources on the Bundestag are Loewenberg, *Parliament in the German Political System* and Trossmann, *The German Bundestag*. See also Friedrich Schäfer, *Der Bundestag* (Cologne and Opladen: Westdeutscher Verlag, 1967), and Kaack, *Geschichte und Structur des deutschen Parteisystems*.

[146]However, unlike the British Prime Minister, the Chancellor is not necessarily a member of the Bundestag.

[147]If the largest parliamentary party is not in the government, then the President of the Bundestag will be of a nongoverning party, as was the case from 1969 to 1972.

[148]See also Gerhard Lembruch, "The Ambiguous Coalition in West Germany," in *European Politics: A Reader*, ed. Mattei Dogan and Richard Rose (Boston: Little, Brown and Company, 1971), p. 558; and Loewenberg, *Parliament in the German Political System*, pp. 307-9.

[149]See Bruno Deschamps, *Macht und Arbeit der Ausschüsse* (Meisenheim am Glan: Westkulturverlag Anton Hain, 1954) and Trossman *The German Bundestag*, pp. 18-36.

[150]Loewenberg, *Parliament in the German Political System*, p. 148.

[151]Loewenberg, *Parliament in the German Political System*, p. 181.

[152]The FPD has generally had four working groups.

[153]German Bundestag, *Amtliches Handbuch des Deutschen Bundestages* (Darmstadt: Neue Darmstadter Verlagsanstalt, 1970), p. 166 and, on oral questions, p. 176. Chapter 7 will provide a more complete description of both oral questions and interpellations. For the rules applicable to the interpellation, see also Trossmann, *The German Bundestag*, pp. 70-71. For the uses and limits (especially the lengthy time intervening between the interpellation request and the debate), see Loewenberg, *Parliament in the German Political System*, pp. 408-9.

[154]Loewenberg, *Parliament in the German Political System*, pp. 267-68, and Jürgen Domes, *Mehrheitsfraktion und Bundesregierung* (Cologne-Opladen: Westdeutscher Verlag, 1964), pp. 136-51.

[155]Peter H. Merkl, "Party Government in the Bonn Republic," in *Lawmakers in a Changing World*, ed. Elke Frank (Englewood Cliffs, N. J.: Prentice-Hall, 1966), p. 81.

[156]See Duverger, *La Ve République*, pp. 123-24.

[157]Albert Mavrinac, *Organization and Procedure of the National Assembly of the Fifth Republic* (London: The Hansard Society for Parliamentary Government), pp. 8-18.

[158]See Grangé, "Fixation de l'ordre du jour des Assemblées parlementaires."

[159]Lowell G. Noonan, *France: The Politics of Continuity and Change* (New York: Holt, Rinehart and Winston, 1970), p. 324.

[160]Emphasis ours.

[161]Charlot, *L' U.N.R.*, p. 151.

[162]Charlot, *L' U.N.R.*, pp. 153-66 for an analysis of the study groups.

[163]Jean Charlot, *The Gaullist Phenomenon: The Gaullist Movement in the Fifth Republic* (London: George Allen and Unwin, 1971), p. 124.

[164]Philip Williams, "Parliament Under the French Fifth Republic: Patterns of Executive Dominance," in *Modern Parliaments: Change or Decline*, ed. Gerhard Loewenberg (Chicago: Aldine-Atherton, 1971), p. 101.

*Chapter 3*
The Policy Process In Action: Four Case Studies

In an effort to provide the reader with a more concrete grasp both of how proposed legislation becomes public law and of the use of strategies to promote or oppose legislation, it will be instructive to examine one specific case study of policy-making for each of the countries in our study. In this chapter, we will describe the legislative process as it has applied to a major piece of legislation from each country—cases which show each political system coping with a major substantive issue.

Of course, no single case study of a system can be typical because there is variation across issues in both the procedure legislation follows and the level of legislative involvement or legislative influence. But, for each of the legislatures, the case study does describe the various stages that are usually included in the process of policy-making and the use of strategies to promote or oppose legislation. The cases are fairly typical in these senses. Moreover, taken together, the cases also suggest the variety and range of issues that legislatures consider.

We should point out, as well, that the purpose of the case studies is to describe with substantive examples the stages of the legislative process rather than to explain why legislators behaved as they did. An analysis of why legislators behave the way they do toward such factors as political party, public opinion, interest groups, and the executive and bureaucracy in the making of legislation constitutes the major part of Chapters 4 through 10.

The United States: Civil Rights

In 1964, nearly a full century after the end of the American Civil War and a full decade after the Supreme Court declared segregated public school facilities unconstitutional, the United States Congress passed what Daniel Berman refers to as the "strongest civil rights bill since the Reconstruction."[1] Robert Dahl comments that this Civil Rights Act of 1964 "marks a milestone of profound significance for it meant nothing less than the closing of an era of Congressional impotence on civil rights legislation and the start of a new era of greater firmness."[2] The case study chronicled below tells us how this significant piece of legislation came to be.[3]

Though the Democratic party platform of 1960 made a firm commitment to the civil rights of black Americans, by 1963, the one-hundredth anniversary of the Emancipation Proclamation, it was clear that in fact civil rights was a low priority. The Kennedy administration felt there were other things that demanded more immediate attention and that to press on civil rights might scuttle or jeopardize other important pieces of legislation. It should be noted that President Kennedy's own convictions were probably in favor of an economic solution to the civil rights problems through tax and welfare legislation.

Raising the point of priorities suggests an important characteristic of the legislative process in the United States as well as in other countries. Despite a clear Democratic majority in both houses, President Kennedy felt that significant civil rights legislation could not be passed. He thus focused his push for civil rights on an increased use of executive powers and held to this policy in 1961 and 1962. In his January, 1963, State of the Union address, he touched on several aspects of civil rights, including extension of the life of the Civil Rights Commission, "technical and financial assistance to aid school districts in the process of desegregation," and amendments to voting provisions of the rather weak Civil Rights Acts of 1957 and 1960, but again these were not high-priority items for the administration. Berman notes that "administration spokesmen, in fact, let it be known in Congress that Mr. Kennedy wanted to avoid a fight over civil rights, for that might very well complicate the campaign for 'more pressing' legislation, such as the tax reduction bill which the President was promoting."[4]

However, events occurring outside Washington were to cause the administration to reassess its priorities. While a House Judiciary subcommittee was holding hearings on the Kennedy proposals, several dramatic racial incidents were occurring in the South. These, particularly the brutal occurrences in April, 1963, in Birmingham, Alabama (where Martin Luther King and Fred Shuttlesworth were leading a drive for equal rights), and the murder of Mississippi civil rights leader Medgar Evers in June, pushed the issue of civil rights to center stage. The reports of the incidents and the white reaction in the South, particularly as seen on television, helped develop greater northern support for and understanding of the difficulties of the southern black. The Kennedy administration reassessed its position and concluded that significant action by the national government (as opposed to the state or municipal governments) was needed to alleviate racial injustice and to thwart massive violence in the South.

In the aftermath of Birmingham, the Justice Department drew up a new and stronger bill to submit to Congress. The most controversial provision—no doubt a direct outgrowth of the sit-in movement and the Birmingham demonstrations—dealt with denial of "privately" owned or "commercial" public facilities to blacks. This "public accommodations" section was based on the constitutional power of the Congress "to regulate commerce . . . among the several states. . . ." The decision to base this section on the power to regulate commerce had a double purpose in the minds of the strategists. First, they wanted this section assigned to a Senate committee (the Commerce Committee) that was more likely to act favorably than the Judiciary Committee, chaired by a Mississippi Senator, thus assuring that a civil rights bill would come to the Senate floor. Second, this approach would avoid dependence upon the Supreme Court overturning an 1883 decision that the Fourteenth Amendment did not authorize Congress to make laws prohibiting racial discrimination carried on by private citizens. The proponents of the bill further realized that in the last quarter century the Court had not declared a single law unconstitutional that was based on the commerce power. Other provisions of Kennedy's new legislative package incorporated and/or expanded upon his previous proposals. Included was a provision empowering the Attorney General under certain circumstances to file suits for desegregation of public schools *before* private parties instituted a suit. Also, the general content of what had been known as the "Powell Amendment" (after Adam Clayton Powell, the black Congressman from New York) was included. Financial assistance could be withheld from any state by the administrator of a federal program if racial discrimination was being practiced.

Noteworthy also is what was left out of the Kennedy package. Kennedy and his strategists tried to anticipate what had a genuine chance of passage in Congress, choosing to focus their activity and power resources on items with probable payoff. Thus despite the 1960 Democratic plank and heavy lobbying on the part of civil rights and labor groups, a provision for a Fair Employment Practices Commission, though it received a favorable reference in the President's message accompanying the new bill, was not actually included as a part of the bill. Omitted also was another Democratic party plank to empower the Attorney General to institute suits to enjoin denials of constitutional rights. The new civil rights package was submitted to Congress on June 18, 1963.

In the meantime, the increased concern over civil rights precipitated an increase in the number and intensity of lobbying efforts. In addition to the activities of the usual civil rights organizations, the labor movement intensified its involvement, and principal churches entered in full force into the public arena not only to condemn racial discrimination but also to work for passage of laws to alleviate racial injustice. In July, representatives of all the major interest groups favoring strong civil rights legislation met and decided to coordinate their efforts and pool their resources. The Leadership Conference on Civil Rights, originally formed in 1949 and now consisting of seventy-nine groups, was the vehicle to do this.[5] Most of the lobbying of Congressmen was to be in favor of the civil rights bill.

The only organized lobby opposition to the bill (which was formed specifically for this purpose) was the Coordinating Committee for Fundamental American Freedom. A major portion of its funds came from the Mississippi Sovereignty Commission, a state agency that, however, accepted contributions from out of state. Of significance is the relative public indifference on the part of major business groups. They focused on other legislation, such as the tax bill. *If* the national business groups such as the National Association of Manufacturers and the Chamber of Commerce had decided to oppose sections of the bill, certain probusiness Congressmen, especially the conservative Republican House leadership, may have been deterred from favoring the civil rights bill and even activated to fight certain titles.[6] However, due to the lobbying lineup, most Congressmen were not to feel significant cross-pressures produced by lobbying activities.

From the standpoint of the administration's strategy, several things were now clear. First, the civil rights bill was of highest priority. Second, a bipartisan effort would be needed to assure passage. Though the Democrats had a clear majority in each house, party discipline was not strong, particularly on civil rights issues where constituency awareness was high.[7] Southern Democratic Senators and Representatives, many of whom were chairmen or key members on committees, would probably oppose the bill. Furthermore, two-thirds of the 100 Senators, assuming all would vote, would be needed to close off Senate debate. The need for Republican support caused the administration not to push for a stronger bill than was offered. Third, the likelihood of the southern filibuster and the fact that the Judiciary chairman in the Senate (James Eastland of Mississippi) and the three ranking Democrats were southerners seemed to favor a House-first strategy. Dahl explains:

Because the vote to close off debate would be so important, and because it would be much more difficult to get a cloture vote if Senators were not confident of the ultimate nature of the bill, it was advisable to obtain passage of the bill in the House first. Moreover, the difference in the relevant committees of the two houses also promised speedier action in the House.[8]

Emmanuel Celler of New York, long-time civil rights advocate, chaired the House Judiciary Committee and Subcommittee that would consider the bill. Of course, the Senate was simultaneously considering the bill, but administration efforts and party leadership pressure was on the House consideration.

House Judiciary Committee Consideration

In the House, the bill thus went to the Judiciary Committee chaired by Celler. Subcommittee Number 5, also chaired by Celler, held hearings on the bill. Although there were actually 158 bills relating to civil rights, the focus was on the administration package. Cabinet members Robert Kennedy (Attorney General), Willard Wirtz (Secretary of Labor) and Anthony Celebrezze (Secretary of Health, Education and Welfare) were among the impressive list of individuals offering testimony. Besides Celler, William McCulloch of Ohio (the ranking Republican) was a key figure in the subcommittee stage. The administration viewed McCulloch as the key to gaining the necessary bipartisan support in the Judiciary Committee and in the House. Assistant Attorney General Burke Marshall, head of the Justice Department's Civil Rights Division, and Nicholas Katzenbach, the Deputy Attorney General, began to work closely with and negotiate with him. McCulloch remained in close contact with his personal friend, House minority leader Charles Halleck, throughout negotiations. McCulloch demanded and received a firm commitment from the administration in exchange for his support that the administration would not weaken the bill passed by the House when faced with the southern power bloc in the Senate.[9] He did not want to get Republicans out on a limb unnecessarily. McCulloch wanted a bill that had a chance of surviving consideration intact.

Throughout the summer, while the administration was negotiating with the Republicans and sympathetic subcommittee hearings were taking place, racial incidents were continuing in the South, and there was an unprecedented march on Washington (August 28) by 200,000 persons to push for (among other things) the President's civil rights package. Meanwhile, the civil rights lobbyists were insisting on a stronger bill, and many liberal Congressmen were opposing Kennedy and his strategists' commitment (that is, to push only for provisions with a realistic chance of Senate passage) on both substantive and tactical grounds. The result was a countermove on the part of the subcommittee Democrats that actually resulted in strengthening the bill. It should be noted, however, that approval depended on northern Republicans (who felt that, if they did not go along, Democrats would get the credit for civil rights) and on some southern Democrats who felt the best way to assure final rejection of the bill on the floor was to strengthen it. Thus, the parent Judiciary Committee was sent a bill that included, in addition to JFK's requests: a strong Fair Employment Practices Commission (FEPC) provision in direct contradiction to the Kennedy strategy;[10] revival of the provision allowing the U.S. Attorney General to seek an injunction in federal court against violation of individuals' constitutional rights; recommendations that voting be protected in state as well as federal elections; and a provision to make the Civil Rights Commission a permanent agency.

The administration leaders were unhappy with this turn of events, for they felt the bill as reported could not pass. It clearly endangered the bipartisan coalition envisioned as a necessary requisite for passage. Republicans, especially McCulloch, felt betrayed. They felt they were being embarrassed publicly as the "conservatives" on civil rights. Southern Democrats were sure acceptance of the subcommittee bill was tantamount to southern victory. Only some liberal Democrats seemed to be happy with the bill. The Kennedy administration moved to restore close working relations with the Republicans through Halleck and McCulloch, who made it clear that "they would not continue to appear to be less favorable to civil rights than the Democrats."[11] Attorney General Robert Kennedy, a Democrat and the President's brother, testified against the new provisions of the bill reported by the subcommittee. Thus, intensive bipartisan negotiations were begun. Participating in the talks were top Democrats in the House, Speaker McCormack and majority leader Albert, Congressman Celler and McCulloch, and the principal Republican leaders. The President, in a rather unusual act, summoned the leaders, the rank-and-file committee members, and Vice-President Johnson to the White House, but the proponents of the strong bill could not be dissuaded.

The President was ready to compromise and, indeed, had to compromise. Deputy Attorney General Katzenbach, a key administration negotiator, told Halleck and McCulloch that the bill would have to be strengthened to include FEPC. Otherwise, the support of northern Democrats would be endangered.

Thus, some concession was the price of support. The negotiations resulted in a version that was milder than the House subcommittee report but stronger than the legislation originally proposed by the President. In October, the parent Judiciary Committee, with bipartisan support, reported out a civil rights bill that included FEPC, a mandatory (Kennedy had asked for discretionary authority) obligation on executive agencies to cut off federally funded programs in states and localities where there was racial discrimination, and a measure making the Civil Rights Commission a permanent agency (Kennedy had asked for a four-year extension). However, not everything the President proposed was strengthened. For example, the Attorney General, while empowered to initiate suits to protect some constitutional rights, did not have the broader provision of the earlier bill authorizing him to sue in order to prevent denial of *any* federal right. Also, though the public accommodations provision remained and prohibited discrimination in most facilities that had been at real issue it did not apply to *all* retail facilities, as the administration had proposed. The bill provided that the Attorney General could bring suits on his own to desegregate public facilities including public schools or he could intervene in suits brought by others alleging that they had been deprived of equal protection of the laws. Strategists felt that Title 6 (cutting off federal funds from state and local programs practicing racial discrimination) and Title 7 (which established an FEPC with certain enforcement powers) might have to be deleted or compromised to secure Senate passage. However, it was generally felt that the compromise bill which had firm and united bipartisan support would not be weakened by the whole House, if it made it to the floor.

In early November, the bill was sent to the historic graveyard of civil rights bills—the House Rules Committee (HRC), chaired by Howard Smith of Virginia, a staunch foe of civil rights. Two years earlier the President and Speaker Sam Rayburn had won a narrow victory to expand the size of the HRC in order to maximize chances of gaining favorable "rules" (which are necessary for all nonmoneyed bills to gain floor consideration). Carl Elliott of Alabama was one of the two Democrats (plus one Republican) added to the Committee. His economic liberalism was a key consideration, but economic liberalism did not necessarily make him liberal on civil rights. Chairman Smith stalled.

Senate Committee Consideration

Meanwhile, the original bill had been simultaneously introduced in the Senate by administration-chosen spokesmen[12] (only legislative members can formally introduce legislation, not the executive). In the Senate, the bill was referred to two separate standing committees. The public accommodations section (which we pointed out above was based on the constitutional power of Congress to regulate commerce) was referred to the Commerce Committee, chaired by Warren Magnuson (D., Wash.), who would be expected to be more friendly to civil rights legislation than James Eastland (D., Miss.), chairman of the Judiciary Committee, which had never voluntarily released a civil rights bill. Nevertheless, the Senate Judiciary Committee also got the bill.[13]

Magnuson, as expected, made it clear from the beginning that he intended to allow no obstruction and unnecessary delay. By early October, the Commerce Committee had concluded its hearings and was ready to report. Though their report dealt with only one section of the House Judiciary Committee's reported bill, it did provide the leadership a vehicle it needed to assure that the civil rights debate would get to the floor of the Senate, where amendments could be offered.

The Senate Judiciary Committee was a different matter. In eleven days of hearings, North Carolina's Senator Sam Ervin questioned Robert Kennedy. Efforts to speed up the proceedings were scuttled by Eastland. Though it was unlikely that the full bill would get to the floor in 1963, some action had to be taken on the Civil Rights Commission. A twelve-month extension was added to a private relief bill in the Senate, and then a parliamentary maneuver avoided the House Rules Committee when the bill was sent to the House. The Civil Rights Commission thus stayed alive.

LBJ Becomes President

The tragic assassination of President Kennedy occurred in November, 1963, thus placing a southerner and former majority leader of the Senate, Lyndon Johnson, in the

White House. Johnson lost no time in making it clear that he did not share the usual southern inclinations on civil rights and that civil rights was a priority on his agenda. In an address to the joint session five days after the assassination, Johnson said:

> We have talked long enough in this country about equal rights. We have talked one hundred years or more. It is time to write the next chapter and write it in the book of law. I urge you . . . to enact a civil rights law so that we can move forward to eliminate from this nation every trace of discrimination and oppression that is based upon race or color.

And he added:

> No memorial oration or eulogy could more eloquently honor President Kennedy's memory than the earliest possible passage of the civil rights bill for which he fought so long.

The agonizing national reappraisal and guilt resulting from the assassination served to push partisanship more and more into the background. New sympathy for the Kennedy legislative program helped LBJ muster bipartisan strength in his efforts to secure approval of many of those measures, especially civil rights. In his first State of the Union address, LBJ again gave civil rights top priority.

Discharge and House Floor Consideration

The strategy of making the Senate wait for the House action was continued. At the time of Kennedy's death, the bill was bottled up in the House Rules Committee (HRC), chaired by Smith, and efforts after the assassination to persuade him to release the bill failed. Therefore, in December Emmanuel Celler filed a discharge petition (which would require 218 signatures to release the bill from the Rules Committtee). It was clear that Johnson was sympathetic to efforts to discharge the bill. He even communicated directly, including personal phone calls, with certain "holdouts." The pro-civil rights lobbyists precipitated a bombardment of letters and other contacts with reluctant signers of the discharge petition. As the pressure mounted and more signed, Smith's close friend on the committee, Clarence Brown (R., Ohio), urged Smith to stop his delaying tactics. Finally, Smith announced he would hold scheduled hearings which, it turned out, produced additional delay, for the hearings and questioning seemed to drag on endlessly. Finally, proponents of the bill had to resort to a threat to use a procedure whereby three members of the HRC could formally request a committee meeting to decide whether to release the bill or not. If the chairman did not act within three days to call a meeting, within seven days a majority of the HRC could call the meeting and act. Seeing the handwriting on the wall, Smith capitulated and in an 11 to 4 vote (bipartisan) the committee in executive session on January 30, 1964, agreed to send the bill to the floor in early February.

The civil rights forces realized that to be successful they needed bipartisan support on the floor and an adequate number of favorable Congressmen when the House resolved itself into the Committee of the Whole (in which the House can conduct business with only 100 members present). Teller votes could be held at any point in a space of time too short for absent members to make it to the chamber to vote. Of particular significance was the role played by the Democratic Study Group (DSG), then made up of 125 liberal Democratic representatives, and the friendly lobbying organizations. The DSG in effect took over the role of the regular party whip organization (with the blessings of the leadership). In early summer of 1964, the DSG had set up a special twenty-two-man civil rights steering committee headed by Representative Richard Bolling (D., Mo.) which maintained liaison with the Justice Department and was instrumental in the successful effort to force the bill out of the HRC. When the bill reached the floor, Bolling and the DSG whip, Frank Thompson (D., N.J.), were present at all times. The elaborate DSG whip organization kept an eye on the floor and on sympathetic Congressmen, making sure they were there for critical quorum calls *and* voted the right way.

The intensive pressure tactics of the civil rights groups were coordinated by the Leadership Conference on Civil Rights.[14] They provided people to serve as "spotters" to keep tabs on a selected list of representatives. Though efforts were made to pair each spotter with Congressmen he knew personally so he could also call them off the House floor to solicit support and votes, this was not always the case. If a spotter saw one on his list was missing for an impending critical vote, he left the visitor's gallery and relayed the information to central headquarters which, in turn, relayed the information to aides who were strategically located in the offices of friendly Congressmen on each floor of the two House office buildings. In a matter of minutes from the initial spotting, an agent would be on the way to the office of the absent representative to request his presence on the floor. The pro-civil rights organizations also provided direct but gentle lobbying pressure on Congressmen. When union agents contacted representatives, representatives no doubt kept in mind the record of past or promise of future union help in their reelection bids. Significantly union representatives did not lobby Republicans or Democrats their unions had opposed in past elections. The task of calling on Republicans was carried out largely by representatives of religious groups.[15]

Legislative strategy was established by the floor manager of the bill (Celler) and Bolling's DSG civil rights steering committee. A strategy and planning meeting was held in Thompson's office each morning. Usually present were three or four key leaders of the Leadership Conference, Thompson, Bolling, and a key White House representative such as Lawrence O'Brien, the President's special assistant on Congressional relations. During debate on the House floor, Katzenbach, Marshall, and several other Justice Department attorneys, as well as Leadership Conference leaders, were in the gallery ready to be called down by Bolling or Thompson for a strategy session off the floor, sometimes in the Speaker's office. The favorable Republicans were led by McCulloch and other Republican members of the Judiciary Committee. Though various members of the Republican group were in periodic contact with the administration, Democrats, and Leadership Conference, they were not in the core strategy-mapping group.

The opposition in the House was quite meager compared to the past. The southern bloc in the House, led by Edwin Willis (D., La.), the ranking southerner on the Judiciary Committee and Smith (HRC Chairman), mounted a rather dispirited attack. The only organized lobby opposition, the Coordinating Committee for Fundamental American Freedoms, emphasized a public relations program and newspaper advertisements against the bill rather than direct lobbying and rounding up of votes.

On February 10, 1964, the bill was approved with a few amendments, mostly technical and none opposed by the bill's sponsors, in a bipartisan vote of the House, 290 to 130 (northern Democrats, 141 to 4; Republicans 138 to 34; and southern Democrats 11 to 92).

Senate Consideration

As the initial strategy had been designed, the bill was first approved by the House and sent to the Senate, where a parliamentary maneuver was used by the leadership to avoid sending the bill to the Judiciary Committee. The Senate has a seldom-used rule (16), which allows a House-passed bill to be "intercepted at the door" of the Senate and then be placed directly on the calendar without having to go to a standing committee. On February 26, Mansfield invoked the rule and was sustained by the Chair. Challenged by the chief southern strategist, Richard Russell (D., Ga.), the Senate upheld the Chair's ruling, 54 to 37.

After this encounter, there were actually two additional stages to the Senate consideration of the bill and thus two more opportunities for delaying or filibustering tactics on the part of southerners. First, there was the debate and vote on the motion by Mansfield to make the House-passed bill the pending business of the Senate by taking the bill from the calendar. In other words, there was a debate to see whether the bill should be debated or not. Second, if this first battle was won, there could be the consideration of the bill itself.

Both the proponents and the opponents of the bill were well organized. Majority whip Hubert Humphrey, long-time friend of civil rights, was supported by Johnson for the floor manager of the bill. The role of floor manager of a bill usually falls to the standing committee chairman reporting out the bill, but as indicated above, this bill did not go to a committee since the appropriate Democratic chairman, Eastland, was a key opponent. Several aspects of the proponents' strategy are clear. Most important was the effort to build bipartisan support in the Senate. The number of Senators needed for cloture was 67—thus necessitating such a strategy. Hubert Humphrey invited Thomas Kuchel of California, the Republican whip, to work with him. The two in turn assigned a pair of senators (one Democrat and one Republican) primary responsibility for defending and discussing each title of the bill and managing the amendment stage. These Senators, their staffs, and representatives of the Justice Department met daily to coordinate and plot strategy. Twice a week representatives of outside civil rights groups were allowed to attend the meetings. Never had the liberals of both parties been so well organized. However, lines of communication had to be kept open to minority leader Everett Dirksen. He was the key to cloture and, thus, to passage. Efforts were made by the Democrats to avoid stigmatizing him as an opponent of civil rights. The leadership hoped also to maintain a calm atmosphere, avoiding dramatic occurrences such as all-night sessions. It was also hoped (though not under the leadership's control, of course) that civil rights demonstrators would stay out of Washington during the Senate consideration.[16] Humphrey felt his tactics would minimize alienation of Senators.

The filibusterers were also well coordinated and organized. They divided themselves into three platoons, one scheduled to hold the floor while the others were off the floor, thus putting a heavier burden on the leadership for the bill in securing a quorum of 51 members which the southerners would call periodically. It should be noted that assurance of a quorum at all times was crucial for the liberals. In the first stage of the bill's consideration—that is, the motion to consider—each Senator could make no more than two speeches each legislative day. Unlike a calendar day, a legislative day lasts until formal adjournment of the Senate. To adjourn would mean each southerner would have two more chances on the floor. Adjournment is automatic if there is no quorum. Thus, if the liberals could avoid adjournment (as they did), the southerners would eventually run out of speakers. On March 26, nearly three weeks after the original Mansfield motion to make the House-passed bill the pending business, the Senate approved it, 67 to 17, with all opponents being from the South.

Now the second stage—consideration of the bill itself—began. Here again Humphrey and the proponents seized the initiative. Unlike in the past, when southern Senators talked on and on almost uninterrupted, the liberals took the lead in order to guide debate and drain off the media's attention from a narrower focus on the southerners. For example, southern speakers were frequently asked questions. Unlike the usual case when a bill reaches the floor, many Senators were not yet decided, and the debate could have an impact.

Throughout the floor debate, Humphrey and Kuchel led the bipartisan effort. Even a new bipartisan newsletter was circulated. A bipartisan alerting system for quorum calls was established (for the debate dragged on for weeks as southerners used their filibuster to prevent voting). Throughout this time, fence-sitting Senators, especially many Republicans from the Midwest and Rocky Mountain states, were visited by pro-civil rights lobbyists and inundated with pro-civil rights mail. Southerners who sought total victory hoped to delay voting as long as possible in hope that there would be internal dissension among the civil rights advocates and that public opinion might change. Governor Wallace of Alabama made strong showings in several Democratic primaries, and his success encouraged a stiffening of the "no compromise" southern position. They also held hopes that Dirksen would not negotiate with the administration and its legislative leaders. Their hope was not without some foundation in fact, for Dirksen was quite inconsistent. At one point he had objected to FEPC, noting correctly that JFK had promised a bill without an FEPC. They at least felt that Dirksen would seriously cripple the bill. The southerners, as well as the bill's sponsors, knew Dirksen was the key.

Every effort was made by the liberals to let Dirksen be the hero. Elizabeth Brenner Drew reports one leadership aide as saying, "We are carving out that statesman's niche and bathing it with blue lights and hoping that Dirksen will find it irresistible to step into it."[17] He did find it irresistible, but he took his own good time and numerous detours in getting there. Dirksen began to prepare amendments to the bill and discuss many of them within the Republican ranks. Humphrey repeatedly invited Dirksen to discuss his amendments with the bill's proponents, including the administration. Dirksen stalled—which, of course, dramatized *his* importance to the liberals in stopping a filibuster as well as enabling him to consolidate his position with Republicans as a critic and a man who could and likely would change the bill to make it more acceptable to them.

Finally on May 5 (the second filibuster had begun on March 30) Dirksen met with

Humphrey, Robert Kennedy (who remained as Attorney General for a while under Johnson), other Justice Department officials, and several other Senators and their aides. Dirksen offered over seventy amendments backed by considerable staff research and preparation. It later became clear that this was his "asking price" and that he would settle for much less. Dirksen was particularly concerned about the FEPC aspects of the bill and the amount of power given to the Attorney General to initiate suits and jump into local problems all over the country. Dirksen and the bill's proponents finally agreed on a position that allowed the Attorney General to sue where there was a "pattern or practice" of discrimination. Also, it was agreed that individuals with grievances would first work through local channels. If that failed and an individual filed suit, the Justice Department—the court permitting—could enter on the side of the individual. A few other minor changes were made, as well. Thus, a bipartisan package was drawn up that only slightly altered the House bill.

Some conservative Republicans and southerners were astonished at Dirksen's minimal concessions. Even many liberals and civil rights leaders who had actually feared Humphrey would concede too much were surprised. The compromise bill was presented at the party caucuses. Then, on May 26, Dirksen introduced the substitute bill to the Senate giving it his support. Though there was an initial retreat by a few conservative Midwest Republican Senators led by the chairman of the Republican Policy Committee, Burt Hickenlooper (R., Iowa), most—with minimal consideration on the handling of certain amendments—eventually agreed to support cloture. Even President Johnson, who played a rather muted though continuous and intensely interested role during Congress's deliberation on the fate of the civil rights bill, contacted a few reluctant Democrats in the final days to urge support of cloture.[18] Lobbyists, including representatives of steelworkers and other unions located in the West, the National Farmers' Union, church groups, and American Indians, made last minute appeals to key Senators.[19]

The petition for cloture was filed by Mansfield and Dirksen on June 8. On June 10, 1964, for the first time in history, a civil rights filibuster was ended. The vote was 71 (44 Democrats and 27 Republicans) to 29 (23 Democrats, of which 20 were southerners, and 6 Republicans, including Presidential candidate Barry Goldwater). The Senate went on to approve substantially the substituted bill hammered out by Dirksen and the Humphrey/Administration forces. Only a few minor amendments (of the 107 which had been offered before cloture) were accepted. The final vote of approval was 73 to 27 and occurred one year to the day after President Kennedy had submitted his civil rights bill to Congress.

The House and the President Go Along

But there was one last crucial step. In a parliamentary sense, the Senate had accepted a substitute for the House bill. Thus the bill had to go back to the House for approval and thus to Smith's committee, the House Rules Committee. Again Smith balked. Again to prod Smith to act, three committee members threatened to use the same device to schedule a committee meeting that they had used at an earlier stage. As was the case before, Smith relented and called the meeting for June 30. At the committee meeting, the members, rebelling against Smith, acted to expedite the House consideration and avoid last-minute voting just before the Republican National Convention. The Committee further voted 8 to 5 to take the presentation of the HRC's resolution out of Smith's hands and authorize Ray Madden (D., Ind.) to make it. Two days later, on July 2, the Senate version came to the floor of the House and was approved 289 to 126 without a single change (thus avoiding the conference committee obstacle). In a matter of hours, with a nationwide television audience looking on, President Johnson signed the bill and a new era in civil rights had its beginning.

The Western European Systems

As was our purpose with civil rights legislation, the three European cases to which we now turn provide us with illustrations of the stages and politics of the legislative process, this time of the three European systems. Since we are interested in representative legislatures in this study, we will focus our attention on the popularly elected house in each system, the House of Commons in Great Britain, the Bundestag in West Germany, and the National Assembly in France. When we speak of legislators (or parliamentarians) as opposed to the executive in the European context, it is important to recall that we are referring to members of the legislature who are not simultaneously members of the cabinet or executive.

The stages of the policy process in making legislation are rather similar for each of the houses we are examining. The focal point for the initiation of legislation is usually the executive, although we will cover one situation in which this was not the case. Once initiated, the proposed legislation goes through three stages of debate. These involve intraparty debate, debate in the legislative standing committees, and finally debate on the floor of the legislature. The stages do not necessarily follow in this order, but in each house each of the stages is a component of the policy process and this will be reflected in the case studies.

The case studies also provide examples of the politics that can surround each of the various stages. Politics varies according to the specific piece of legislation, so that no case is fully typical in this regard. Nevertheless, the case studies will enable us to get a taste of the activities and strategies of party, interest groups, and the executive surrounding the consideration of legislation and also enable us to observe the varying levels of involvement legislators can have in the making of legislation.

Great Britain: Resale Price Maintenance

In the latter 1950s, the British economy began to experience an inflationary push which, as it turned out, led in the 1960s to the highest rate of inflation among the Western, industrialized nations. A number of different policies were considered in an effort to avoid or depress this inflation. One of these proposals was to abolish resale price maintenance (RPM). However, the question of whether or not resale price maintenance ought to be abolished was one which seriously divided Conservative backbenchers. Through RPM, companies were able to control the prices at which their goods were sold, thus reducing the ability of larger retail outlets to lower their prices and thereby to undersell smaller shopkeepers. The Parliament banned collective RPM agreements between companies in 1956, but it was still legal for an individual company to enforce RPM for its own products. Although the effect of this practice was to put pressure on prices, a number of Conservative backbenchers in the Commons as well as in groups outside the Commons felt that to eliminate the practice might bring ruin to many small shopkeepers. Some of the Conservative backbenchers were also concerned about the electoral consequences for their party were it to abolish RPM.

By 1959, Sir David Eccles, who was then President of the Board of Trade, "began considering the possibility of abolishing RPM altogether, as the one concrete step which would encourage the lower prices which Ministers increasingly regarded as the prerequisite for the achievement of economic stability in 1960."[20] This prompted both supporters and opponents of RPM to raise questions in the House and led to the creation in 1960 of the Resale Price Maintenance Coordinating Committee, which brought together forty trade associations supporting RPM and which worked closely with Conservative backbenchers who also supported RPM. Aware of the opposition within the Conservative ranks to abolition of RPM, the Conservative government decided to buy time by calling for an inquiry to be conducted by the Board of Trade. The Board's report, which was confidential, maintained that there was an "overwhelming economic case for ending the practice."[21]

By now (1961), however, Eccles had been replaced at the Board of Trade, by Mr. Frederick Erroll, who had earlier opposed the abolition of RPM. Although he now supported abolition of RPM, it is uncertain how strongly he was committed to pressing the issue. Moreover, the division in the Conservative parliamentary ranks was apparent through debates taking place in the Conservative backbencher's Trade and Industry Committee. Appearing before this committee, Erroll was noncommittal. As a junior minister who had himself earlier supported RPM, confronted by opposition among many of his own backbenchers and by several senior ministers, including Prime Minister Macmillan,[22] it is not surprising that Erroll was unable in 1961 to summon sufficient pressure to obtain cabinet support for a scheme to abolish RPM. The cabinet again rejected the abolition of RPM as part of a consumer protection program in 1962.

A year later Sir Alec Douglas-Home became Prime Minister, and he chose as President of the Board of Trade a highly respected Conservative, Edward Heath.[23] Heath opposed RPM strongly, "totally convinced, intellectually, of the case for abolishing RPM as a result of his study of the information put before him by his department."[24] The government was also being pressed, due to the introduction of a private member bill to end RPM, to formulate a policy on the issue. The bill had been proposed in part because trading stamps given out by larger stores were making a mockery of RPM. Another private member bill was introduced by John Osborne, a Conservative, which proposed to regulate trading stamps.

As a result of these various considerations, Heath decided to act. His position in the cabinet was a strong one. This was in part due to the high regard in which he was held and in part due to the weakened position of Prime Minister Douglas-Home, whom many regarded as a caretaker leader. Heath brought his proposals to abolish RPM before the cabinet in January, 1964. Several lengthy cabinet discussions ended in compromise: RPM was to be prohibited, but manufacturers retained the right to apply for exemption before a judicial court. Applicants could maintain their RPM agreements until the case was decided.

Heath's announcement in the House of the government's pending proposals led to an outburst of opposition, indicating that the compromise was not acceptable to a number of Conservative backbenchers or to the trade associations. The Resale Price Maintenance Coordinating Committee appointed a public relations officer and a parliamentary agent for the purposes of examining the forthcoming proposed legislation and drafting amendments to it. Mass rallies were called for in several cities and members of trade associations were urged to see or correspond with their MPs. Within the Conservative parliamentary party, over 100 members attended discussions of the party's Trade and Industry Committee (which had not been consulted during the formulation of the bill[25]). Heath appeared before the committee on at least three occasions in order to defend his bill against mounting opposition from the backbenches. Leading members of the committee urged that no measure reach the statute book before the next election and that the measure should include exemptions of certain categories of industry. Heath also appeared before all Conservative backbenchers in the 1922 Committee, answering their questions for over two hours.

The proposed bill was published and had its first reading in the House on February 27. There were no concessions. Heath immediately met with the backbench Trade and Industry Committee in a gathering which over 200 Conservative backbenchers attended. Heath again conceded little, leading 17 of the strongest Conservative opponents of the bill to sign an early day motion to kill the bill on its second reading.

Before the main (second) reading of the bill on the floor of the House, the Conservative leadership made a concerted effort to persuade the Conservative backbenchers who opposed the bill to acquiesce. The Conservative chief whip, Martin Redmayne, met with the opponents but failed to convince them. Heath then made another attempt to persuade the opponents, again without success.

The second reading, upon which the principles of the bill are debated, ended with division (vote) supporting the government and the bill. But the division found 21 Conservatives voting against the bill and another 17 joining Labour by abstaining.

Heath's work was still far from over, for now the bill went to committee for amendment. To gain greater control over the situation, the bill was sent to the committee of the whole House rather than to a standing committee. In effect, this served to give the government a larger majority with which to work. Still, the committee stage promised to be grueling. Not only were some Conservatives prepared to advance crippling amendments, but Labour leaders indicated that the opposition would join the Conservative rebels on selected amendments. Exactly which amendments, of course, they did not announce in advance. As a result, the Conservative parliamentary party formed a working group in an attempt to achieve a united position. The group comprised members of the government, including Heath's representatives (Heath had approved the group's formation) and backbenchers who supported and opposed the bill. The group was chaired by the chairman of the backbench Trade and Industry Committee.

The working-group discussions led to some compromise but one in which the principles of the bill were left untouched. As one commentator put it, "Heath gave away form and retained substance."[26] With the government's approval, the compromise amendments were presented in the committee stage and adopted. Although the compromises satisfied some of the critics, other Conservative backbenchers remained opposed and continued to use the committee stage to press for significant amendment. On one of these amendments, to exempt the pharmaceutical industry, the government's majority fell to only one vote.

In effect, this was the final stage of the effort in the House of Commons to undermine the government bill. After the bill passed the committee stage, it went quickly through the third reading debate and was adopted by the House.

The RPM case provides an illustration of the legislative process in Great Britain with a rather high level of involvement by backbench parliamentarians. The activity of the Conservative backbenchers helped to stall legislation on abolishing RPM for several years and was of significance to the development of the compromise proposals that were contained in the bill the government originally initiated. Nevertheless, it is important to note that, despite some compromises, abolition of RPM remained the central feature of the government's proposals. Furthermore, once the government decided to act, it was able to secure the adoption of its bill including only minor further amendments. It did so within a period of but two months, notwithstanding the opposition to the bill.[27]

Of course, the selection of any single case catches certain elements of the political process and misses others. In particular, because Labour had decided to abstain on the second reading, the government did not face the problem that it might lose the second reading vote, which might have raised the question of the House's confidence in the government. However, this element and how it relates to parliamentary behavior will not be neglected as our analysis proceeds. It is covered in detail both in Chapter 4, where we treat the behavior of legislators toward party, and in Chapters 6 and 8, where we undertake a more extensive analysis of the relative influence of the executive and the legislature.

West Germany: The Reform of Public Health Insurance

At this point, let us turn to a case study that illustrates the legislative process in West Germany. The case deals with the politics of reforming the public health insurance system, especially as it relates to its financing.

Speaking before the Bundestag shortly after the 1953 elections, the Chancellor of West Germany, Konrad Adenauer of the Christian Democrats (CDU/CSU), called for a comprehensive reform of the public health insurance programs. At that time, the many programs operated by public authorities in West Germany cost about $2 billion. The need for reform was clear, and we mention here only one of the major problems. This problem was financial. The expenditures of the various programs were fast outstripping the programs' incomes, and both the trade unions and the SPD were demanding even added benefits from the programs. For example, they felt that a worker should receive 100 percent of his wages if he was sick, instead of the 65 percent then operative for nonsalaried workers. They also felt that a worker should not have to be sick for at least three days to receive benefits, as was the case under the existing legislation. Moreover, the SPD and the unions argued that the employers should assume greater responsibility for the financing of sickness insurance. Under the law operating in 1953, sickness funds, to which the workers and employers contributed equally, were responsible for financing 60 percent of the worker's wage, with the remaining 5 percent contributed by employer funds.[29]

After consulting a number of experts and interest groups through his advisory council, the Minister of Labor along with other government officials came to the conclusion that one necessary method for alleviating the financial problems the insurance programs faced was "cost-sharing." This solution would enable workers to receive more benefits. But, in return, workers would pay the first three to four dollars for their pharmaceuticals to the extent that they could afford it. Under the law operating in 1953, the entire cost of drugs was borne by the insurance programs. Academic advisors to the Chancellor reported in 1955:

A future health-insurance system can and must be freed from trivial cases. The overwhelming majority of the insured are in a position today to bear the costs of drugs up to the amount of 10 to 15 DM per month. . . . The present operation of the sickness funds is based on the fiction of the insolvency of all the insured.[30]

After further consultation with experts and interest groups, a government bill was finally presented to the Bundestag in late 1959. Cost-sharing for medical care and pharmaceuticals, based on income, was an essential feature of the bill, but along with this workers were promised both larger cash payments from the sickness funds (again we note that workers were equal contributors to these funds) and a reduction of the waiting period. The Minister of Labor, in presenting the proposals, was singularly optimistic. "A politician seldom has occasion for joy," he said. "But this is really a joyful day for me."[31]

The thrust of the policy, however, was unacceptable to both the SPD and the trade unions, as well as to medical groups. As important was the fact that the bill was unacceptable to many members in the labor wing of the CDU/CSU. This was partly a result of the efforts of German trade union leaders, who carried out an intensive public campaign and sent letters and telegrams to all Bundestag deputies in which it was indicated that deputies' positions would be followed closely.[32] As a consequence of this appeal

. . . a number of CDU deputies were quick to appear at Workers' rallies and to identify themselves with the demands of the trade unions. For example, at a delegates' assembly of Metal Workers in Hanover, Rudolph Werner, a CDU deputy, declared that the members of his party were not "insane" enough, especially in view of the general elections of the coming year, to assent to a bill so unequivocally rejected by a large part of the population.[33]

The cabinet, however, continued to defend its bill and showed itself willing only to make minor changes in its proposals even as late as February 9, 1960 (just as the CDU/CSU caucus in the Bundestag prepared to consider the bill).

The government's position was strengthened by the action of the Bundesrat in its preliminary consideration of the bill before the bill went to the Bundestag. Although the Bundesrat adopted numerous amendments to the bill, the principle of cost-sharing gained the consent of the Bundesrat toward the end of 1959.

The bill then went to the Bundestag. Committees within the CDU/CSU had been considering the question of reform for some time and had been unable to reach a unified stand. This was also the case for the CDU/CSU caucus, which met shortly prior to the first reading in the Bundestag on February 17. A lengthy debate occurred in the caucus with CDU labor deputies, among others, voicing opposition to the bill. In the end the CDU/CSU members were still divided and their main spokesmen in the first reading debate, although supporting the bill, did not do so enthusiastically. The CDU labor wing continued to be critical, and its two speakers joined the SPD speakers in opposition to the bill.

Following the first reading debate, the government bill went to the Bundestag Committee on Social Policy. This committee was comprised of twenty-nine members, of whom eleven were from the SPD and six were from the CDU labor wing (the CDU/CSU had a total of fifteen members). As a consequence, the SPD and the CDU labor-wing members together constituted a majority on the committee. They were opposed to the bill, although the CDU labor-wing members were willing to consider a less stringent cost-sharing system for the sake of party unity, whereas the SPD members were opposed to cost-sharing as a matter of principle. The opposition of these members to the bill as it stood found support in both the SPD Social Policy Committee and the CDU/CSU Social Policy Committee (also composed disproportionately of labor-wing members), which were considering the bill simultaneously with the Bundestag Committee on Social Policy.

The Bundestag Committee on Social Policy heard the testimony of a number of groups and engaged in a prolonged debate on the bill. But, because the contingent of fifteen CDU/CSU members never became unified, a majority on the committee favoring the bill could not be found. Even though the Minister of Labor in the end proposed a series of compromises to which Heinrich Krone (the Bundestag leader of the Christian Democratic parliamentary party) agreed, he was not able to save the bill. The bill never emerged from the committee. After deleting all cost-sharing provisions, the committee eventually dropped the bill from its agenda, thereby defeating the entire bill.

This defeat did not mean that the Bundestag adopted no reforms regarding health insurance. Two pieces of legislation were adopted, one in 1957 and the other in 1961. The Bundestag Social Policy Committee introduced a bill of its own in 1957 concerning cash benefits for workers even before the government bill had been introduced. The bill reflected a compromise between business and labor that was formulated within both the Bundestag Committee on Labor and the Bundestag Social Policy Committee. After a week of heated debate on the floor, the bill passed its second and third readings, substantially intact, and was approved in May, 1957. The bill increased the cash benefits to workers who were sick from 65 percent to 90 percent of the worker's wage. The contribution from the employer funds was raised from 5 percent to about 20 percent and the waiting period for eligibility was reduced from three days to two.

A second piece of legislation was also passed. After the major government initiative was killed in February, 1961, the CDU/CSU parliamentary party introduced its own compromise proposals. Its bill provided that workers would receive 100 percent of their wages for the first six weeks of illness and that the waiting period be reduced from two days to one. In addition, preventative care was to become an essential element of the services provided by the sickness funds. The first reading of the bill took place on February 21, 1961, and the SPD-CDU labor coalition assured the bill a smooth passage through the Committee on Social Policy. In May, 1961, the bill went through both the second reading debate and the third reading. It was passed by a show of hands and went into effect six weeks before the September, 1961, elections.

The case study on health insurance reform in West Germany is an example of the defeat of a government proposal even though the government continued to press for its own policy. In addition, the case provides an example of the control of compromise shifting from the hands of the executive into the hands of members of the Bundestag. In 1957, two Bundestag committees were primarily responsible for formulating the compromise between business and labor that allowed legislation to pass during that session. In 1961, it was the CDU parliamentary party that took the initiative in formulating proposals that successfully won the support of its labor wing, thereby enabling legislation to pass during that year.

We can briefly compare the British case study on RPM legislation to this case study on health insurance reform. In the British case, once the government decided to press for action against RPM, it was able to obtain the passage of legislation within a brief period of time. Such was not the fate of the German cabinet's proposals for health insurance reform in the Bundestag. Moreover, although the British cabinet made a number of important compromises in the process of obtaining its legislation, the control of compromise remained essentially in the hands of the cabinet. It was the cabinet that determined the shape of the compromise, except in the final stages when its representatives met in a special committee with representatives from the Conservative backbenches. Even this committee, however, did not attempt to impose on Mr. Heath any substantially different policy from the one he and the cabinet had originally proposed. In the health insurance legislation, on the other hand, the control of compromise twice fell primarily into the hands of Bundestag members, once in 1957 when two Bundestag committees acting together formulated the legislation that went on to be adopted and again in 1961 when the CDU parliamentary party drafted the legislation that prevailed.

France: Agricultural Policy[34]

French agriculture has been beset by many problems as France has become a more industrialized nation. The farmers of France, some employing techniques from the distant past, increasingly required artificially high prices and subsidies in order to live in a style commensurate with that of the industrialized sector of France and in order to compete on the world agricultural market. (One of the major reasons for French entry into the Common Market was that agricultural integration in the Common Market would open to French farmers the German market, since German farmers were on the whole even less efficient and competitive than French farmers.) Yet, although the agricultural problem in France was growing in proportion, as was indicated by rural protests and demonstrations in the early 1960s, there was little agreement even among farmers as to what form governmental action should take. Many members of the agricultural Fédération nationale des syndicats d'exploitants agricoles (ENSEA) took the view that the usual subsidies to farmers should continue to be the focal point of policy. The Centre national des jeunes agriculteurs (CNJA), on the other hand, argued that the most appropriate solution was structural reform—to enlarge farms and to mechanize the production and distribution processes considerably more than had been done in the past. Persons who supported continued subsidies contended, with justification, that structural reforms would force a sizable number of farmers off their land. Those who supported the reforms recognized this but felt that because subsidies would soon prove too costly there was no other alternative.

As it had usually done in the past, the FNSEA, which traditionally had been very influential in French legislative circles, pressed the Assembly in an attempt to limit the degree of acceptable structural reform. Given the receptive inclinations of many of the Assembly members from farm areas, the FNSEA was successful in arousing considerable Assembly support for its view. Its success, in effect, prompted Edgar Pisani, the Minister of Agriculture, to withdraw proposals stressing the structural reforms he had presented to the Assembly. He recognized that it was by no means certain that the Assembly would act favorably on the proposals.[35] Indeed, somewhat the same policy position Pisani was proposing had been, in the form of an amendment to another bill, defeated by the Assembly in 1960.

However, Pisani had become persuaded that structural reforms were necessary to alleviate French agricultural problems. He thus began the process of developing another set of proposals in which, though there would be compromises, structural reform would remain the guiding principle.

Pisani and his staff began by engaging in repeated informal discussions with the leaders of each agricultural association and followed up these discussions by formal negotiations with the leaders. He also met with many agricultural experts both within and outside his own ministry. The process of drafting the legislation, which had begun in 1961, ended in mid-1962. Hardly any contact was made at this stage with members of the National Assembly or other members of the cabinet.

The way for Pisani's proposals, however, was still by no means without possible obstruction either in the cabinet or in the Assembly. Several cabinet ministers, supported by some members of the Gaullist parliamentary party, continued to object to the structural reform principles of the proposals and forwarded amendments to reinstate subsidies to the position they had formerly held in French agricultural policies. The potential opposition of Gaullist farm deputies in the Assembly became particularly clear in several general debates the Agricultural Committee (working group) that the Gaullist parliamentary party had had on the matter.

As Pisani had sought to avoid parliamentary and cabinet critics in the drafting of his proposals—for he had not consulted with Assembly members or cabinet members—so he attempted now to maneuver around them by first seeking the support of de Gaulle. De Gaulle was attracted to the proposals because of the reasoning and technical advice behind them and because the proposals had been accepted enthusiastically by the CNJA, several other farmers' organizations, and organizations outside farming. Even the FNSEA had become partially persuaded. Still, de Gaulle took the precaution of having his own staff consult with the farm organizations as well as with a number of technical experts.

On the basis of these consultations, de Gaulle decided to support Pisani's proposals in the cabinet and to intervene in order to prevent it from adopting amendments that might undermine the proposals. The proposals were accepted by the cabinet almost intact during one meeting and sent to the Assembly.

In the Assembly, the proposals were considered by the specialized agricultural committees of the various parties, then by a special Assembly committee requested by the government, and finally on the floor.* Participating in the Gaullist meetings, the

---

*The government requested that a special Assembly committee consider the proposals so as to avoid the Assembly's Agricultural Committee, which had previously been resistant to reform efforts.

meetings of the Assembly committee, and the floor debate, Pisani agreed to a number of important substantive amendments to the original proposals dealing especially with the legal procedures for enlarging farms. But, given the support Pisani had enlisted from a variety of interest groups, from de Gaulle, and from the cabinet, the opposition in the Assembly was no longer capable of reversing the structural principles lying behind the proposals as it had done in 1960. Debate centered as much on the method Pisani had used to draft his proposals, and especially his persistent avoidance of the Assembly, as it did on the proposals themselves. Having aired these complaints in committee and then on the floor, the Gaullist deputies voted loyally behind their leaders and, combined with support of Gaullist allies, adopted the proposals. Formal consideration in the Assembly, from party and Assembly committee deliberations through debate on the floor, took only three weeks. The final vote on the bill found 316 deputies in favor and 91 opposed, with 35 deputies abstaining. In the end, only one Gaullist deputy voted against the bill.[36]

Conclusion

Taken together, the cases we have reviewed in this chapter are indicative of the variety and range of issues that legislatures consider and illustrate both the stages of the legislative process and the strategies used in the attempt to influence legislative outcomes. The four cases also present a variety of contrasts. For example, outcomes were determined by members of the majority party or majority coalition in two of the four cases (RPM and agricultural reform) but not in the other two cases (civil rights and health insurance). In the latter instances, coalitions between majority and opposition party legislators were crucial to the outcomes. Also, legislative outcomes essentially followed the executive's initial proposal with some modification in three of the cases (RPM, agricultural reform, and civil rights), whereas in the fourth case (health insurance) the final legislative outcome differed rather substantially from the executive's initiative. In each of the cases, however, the executive's initiative was itself partly shaped by political realities that executive officials anticipated they would face in the legislature.

Of course, the cases we have presented are a very small sample—only one from each country. No single case study can be said to be fully typical. If we wish to gain an idea of similarities and differences in how legislators behave or respond during the policy process and why legislators behave or respond the way they do, we need to examine a much greater body of evidence. This will be our objective in the following chapters.

Notes

[1] Daniel M. Berman, *A Bill Becomes a Law*, 2d ed. (New York: Macmillan, 1966), p. 134. Our case study of the Civil Rights Act of 1964 is especially indebted to this excellent book-length study of Congress's enactment of the 1960 and 1964 Civil Rights Acts.

[2] Robert A. Dahl, *Pluralist Democracy in the United States: Conflict and Consent* (Chicago: Rand McNally, 1967), p. 416.

[3] It is not within the scope of this work to analyze the judicial involvement in the civil rights revolution. Had it not been for the judicial activism of the Supreme Court in the civil rights field, particularly as typified by the 1954 *Brown* v. *Board of Education* decision which declared school segregation unconstitutional, the Congress and President might not have been considering this progressive piece of civil rights legislation in 1964. For a useful reference on the background and general discussion of civil rights policy in the United States, see Congressional Quarterly Service, *Revolution in Civil Rights* (Washington, D. C., 1968).

[4] Berman, *A Bill Becomes a Law*, p. 10. Also see Dahl, *Pluralist Democracy in the United States*, p. 419.

[5] Congressional Quarterly Service, *Revolution in Civil Rights*, p. 54-55.

[6] Congressional Quarterly Service, *Revolution in Civil Rights*, p. 56.

[7] See Warren Miller and Donald E. Stokes, "Constituency Influence in Congress," *American Political Science Review* 57 (March 1963): 45-56; and Charles F. Cnudde and Donald J. McCrone, "The Linkage Between Constituency Attitudes and Congressional Voting Behavior: A Causal Model," *American Political Science Review* 60 (March 1966): 66-72.

[8] Dahl, *Pluralist Democracy in the United States*, p. 421. Getting a bill from the House would enable the Senate leadership to circumvent its Judiciary Committee and make the House bill the pending business of the Senate. See the discussion below on Senate consideration.

[9] Dahl, *Pluralist Democracy in the United States*, p. 421-22.

[10] Actually the House Education and Labor Committee had held hearings and reported early in the summer on H.R. 405 which was an FEPC bill. However, that committee was dissuaded from pushing the Rules Committee to report that legislation by an agreement with the Judiciary Committee to consider the inclusion of their bill in the larger and more comprehensive legislation before Subcommittee Number 5 of that committee.

[11] Dahl, *Pluralist Democracy in the United States*, p. 423.

[12] This is the June administration bill, not the House Judiciary bill sent to the HRC. Democratic majority leader Mansfield introduced a measure including the whole administration package. He and Republican minority leader Everett Dirksen cosponsored another bill including everything but the public accommodations section. Warren Magnuson (D. Wash.) introduced a separate public accommodations bill which was actually the measure referred to the Interstate and Foreign Commerce Committee, which he chaired. See Stephen K. Bailey, *Congress in the Seventies* (New York: St. Martin's Press, 1970), p. 73.

[13] Berman, *A Bill Becomes Law*, p. 39; Bailey, *Congress in the Seventies*, p. 73. See also footnote 12.

[14] According to the Congressional Quarterly Service, "literally thousands" of persons associated with the groups in the Leadership Conference poured into Washington for the House debate. The key "leadership group" was: Clarence Mitchell (NAACP), Andrew Biemiller and Jack Conway (AFL-CIO), Joseph Rauh (ADA), and James Hamilton (National Council of Churches). *Revolution in Civil Rights*, p. 54.

[15] Congressional Quarterly Service, *Revolution in Civil Rights*, p. 55. We should also note that about halfway through the House debate, due to the rather good attendance and the expressed resentment of some members, this spot-and-call system was dropped. The DSG whip organization, which at first supplemented the system, replaced it.

[16] Elizabeth Brenner Drew, "The Politics of Cloture," *The Reporter* (July 16, 1964): 20.

[17] Drew, "The Politics of Cloture," p. 20.

[18] Congressional Quarterly Service, *Revolution in Civil Rights*, pp. 56-59; Drew, "The Politics of Cloture," p. 22.

[19] *Revolution in Civil Rights*, p. 59; Drew, "The Politics of Cloture," p. 22.

[20] Ronald Butt, *The Power of Parliament* (New York: Walker and Co., 1968), pp. 254-55.

[21] Butt, *The Power of Parliament*, p. 256.

[22] S. A. Wakland, *The Legislative Process in Great Britain* (New York: Praeger, 1968), p. 30.

[23] Edward Heath became leader of the Conservatives in 1965 and was elected Prime Minister in 1970.

[24] Butt, *The Power of Parliament*, p. 261.

[25] Wakland, *The Legislative Process in Great Britain*, p. 32.

[26] Samuel Finer, *Anonymous Empire: A Study of the Lobby in Great Britain* (London: Pall Mall, 1966), p. 71.

[27] For an assessment of the influence of the government in this case, see John P. Mackintosh, *The Government and Politics of Britain* (London: Hutchinson, 1970), pp. 54-55.

[28] This case is summarized from William Safran, *Veto-Group Politics: The Case of Health Insurance Reform in West Germany* (San Francisco: Chandler Publishing Company, 1967).

[29] Safran, *Veto-Group Politics*, p. 47.

[30] Safran, *Veto-Group Politics*, p. 32.

[31] Safran, *Veto-Group Politics*, p. 149.

[32] Deputies also may send letters of their own to other deputies. For example, deputy Ruf of the CDU/CSU sent a letter to each member of the CDU/CSU in which he enclosed a circular drafted by the Confederation of German Employers' Association and an article on health insurance reforms reprinted from a periodical. In retaliation, August Weimar distributed to all CDU/CSU members a working paper which he drafted himself and which attempted to refute the arguments which Ruf had made. See Jürgen Domes, *Mehrheitsfraktion und Bundesregierung* (Cologne and Opladen: Westdeutscher Verlag, 1964), p. 155.

[33]Safran, *Veto-Group Politics,* pp. 156-57.
[34]A longer and more complete description of this case may be found in Gaston Rimareix and Yves Tavernier, "L'Élaboration et le vote de la loi complémentaire à la loi d'orientation agricole," *Revue Française de Science Politique* 13 (June 1963): 389-425. We have relied heavily on this account.
[35]Rimareix and Tavernier, "L'élaboration et le vote," p. 393.
[36]Rimareix and Tavernier, "L'élaboration et le vote," p. 408.

Chapter 4
Legislators and Their Political Parties

Political parties are major links between the "people" and the decision-making processes in the modern, large-scale, democratic political system. Historically, there has been an intimate connection between the development of political parties and the extension and consolidation of representative democracy. Today parties of some kind (which offer candidates for election under their party label) compete for office not only in the four political systems under consideration but in every democratic nation. Parties help mobilize the electorate; they help structure and channel the political demands and resources of the public. As a consequence, parties continue to be important (some scholars even assert indispensable) instruments and "unofficial" institutions of contemporary democratic societies.[1]

Our analysis of legislative behavior begins with an examination of how legislators behave toward their party and particularly their legislative party. There are two reasons for beginning with an analysis of legislators' behavior toward their party. First, one's party serves as a major frame of reference for the voting responses of legislators to public issues in each of the four legislatures we are examining. To account for what leads to or detracts from party voting is thus central to any explanation of why legislators vote the way they do. Second, several of the variables by which party voting cohesion and dissidence can be explained are also useful in explaining other areas of legislative politics. These areas include the relative influence of the legislature and the executive in the making of policy, the activity of the legislature in its role of supervising the executive, and the relations between legislators and interest groups.

In this chapter we examine and try to explain the levels of voting cohesion that legislative parties maintain. After measuring levels of party voting cohesion in the first section of this chapter, we will attempt to account for the different levels of party voting we find. We will do so by making use of the framework presented and developed in Chapter 1—that is, by reference to the dispositions of the legislators and the political setting in which they operate. The dispositions with which we will deal (in the order we will discuss them) are the legislators' normative policy orientations, their feelings of identification with their party, their career ambitions, and their role orientations. Aspects of the political setting we bring into our account will be the way career rewards are distributed, the type of political system (parliamentary or separation of powers), and the level of intraparty organization of the legislative party.

Levels of Party Voting Cohesion

Party voting cohesion can be defined as the extent to which all members of a legislative party vote with that party. The most cohesive legislative party would be one in which all members of the party voted with their party all of the time. Obviously, most legislative parties are unable to maintain this level of cohesion, but the levels of cohesion do vary considerably from one party to another. This variation in levels of voting cohesion and the reasons for it are subjects we will examine in depth.

The test of voting cohesion we will use measures the percentage of divisions or roll call votes upon which 90 percent or more of the legislative party members voted with their party. That is, when 90 percent of the party members vote with their party, we define this as a *cohesive party vote*.

Table 4.1 shows, for twelve parliamentary and legislative parties, that three levels of party voting cohesion can be distinguished.[2] The most cohesive parties were consistently able to maintain cohesion on 95 percent or more of the roll call votes. Members of the British Conservative and Labour parties, the French Communist and Socialist parties, the French Gaullist party, and the German SPD consistently maintained this level of voting cohesion. During many years, members of these parties maintained cohesion on more than 99 percent of the roll call votes. The least cohesive parties generally were unable to achieve party voting cohesion on as much as 70 percent of the divisions. Examples include the Democratic and Republican parties of the United States and the French Radical party. In between these two groups are parties with a

Table 4.1
Levels of Voting Cohesion of Legislative Parties According to the Percentage of Votes Upon Which Ninety Percent of More of the Legislative Party Members Vote Together*

Party	Political System	Level of Cohesion
Communist	France	High[a]
Gaullist	France	High
Socialist (SFIO)	France	High
Social Democrats	West Germany	High
Conservative	Great Britain	High
Labour	Great Britain	High
Catholics (MRP)	France	Moderate[b]
CDU/CSU	West Germany	Moderate
FDP	West Germany	Moderate
Democrats (Senate, House)	United States	Low[c]
Republican (Senate, House)	United States	Low
Radical	France	Low

* The cohesion scores upon which this Table is based are presented in Table 4.10
[a] High cohesion equals cohesion on consistently more than 95 percent of the roll call votes.
[b] Moderate cohesion indicates cohesion generally on less than 95 percent and more than 80 percent of the roll call votes.
[c] Low cohesion equals cohesion generally on less than 70 percent of the roll call votes.

moderate level of voting cohesion. The members of these parties acted cohesively on about 85 percent of the divisions, although the percentage for any particular time period was sometimes higher than 90 percent and other times lower than 80 percent. Three parties that fall into this category ar the German CDU/CSU, the German FDP, and the French MRP (the French Catholic party).*

The results found in Table 4.1 should not lead us to conclude that voting cohesion has been entirely absent among members of parties at the lower end of the scale. Let us take as examples the Democratic and Republican Congressional parties in the United States. Compared to other parties, the members of the Democratic and the Republican parties have not voted cohesively if by cohesion we mean 90 percent unity. For instance, on the twenty *closest* votes during seven individual sessions of Congress over the 1947-70 period, the Congressional parties were able to muster 90 percent voting cohesion on less than 30 percent of these roll calls,[3] with the Republicans acting somewhat more cohesively than the Democrats. Or, looking at *key* roll call votes selected by *Congressional Quarterly*,[4] 90 percent or more of the Democrats voted together only 13 percent of the time over the twenty-year period 1949-69. Once again, the Republicans voted more cohesively but still were able to reach the 90 percent level on only 31 percent of the roll call votes.

Yet, if we reduce from 90 to 70 percent the measure of party members voting together and examine the twenty *closest* roll call votes for the years we covered, we find that Congressional party members voted together at that level on approximately 70 percent of these roll call votes. When votes were close, the American parties were obviously more than simply agglomerations of individuals in a free-floating political atmosphere.

Other measures suggest this as well. For example, analysis shows that, on *key* roll call votes, a majority of the Democrats voted against a majority of the Republicans nearly 70 percent of the time from 1949 to 1969. An apogee of 100 percent was reached in the 1962 House and in the Senate in 1950 and 1966.[5] Indeed, taking all roll call votes, members of Congress have supported their party's positions on the average approximately two-thirds of the time. Members opposed their party on the average less than 15 percent of the time.[6]

Moreover, there are between the Democratic and Republican Congressional parties a number of differences over issues, many of which have persisted over long time periods. Democrats more than Republicans have supported a larger economic role for the federal government, lower tariffs, legislation in favor of labor, farmers, blacks, and low-income groups, expanded health and welfare programs, and government regulation of business.[7] Each of these issues has separated the parties for a generation or more. As we would expect from differences such as these, each year the "average" Democrat in Congress has ranked markedly higher than has the "average" Republican on measures of liberalism, and the reverse has been true each year on measures of conservatism.[8] Thus, the absence of 90 percent party cohesion on roll call votes in Congress, which regularly occurs in both American parties, should not be interpreted to mean that parties in Congress are unimportant. While the American Congressional parties do not vote nearly as cohesively as do many other legislative parties, our discussion has suggested, and numerous other studies have concluded, that party

---

*The voting cohesion scores for each of the parties and for each of the years examined can be found on Table 4.10 at the end of this chapter.

affiliation is an important factor affecting the behavior of the members of Congress. Turner goes so far as to conclude in his *Party and Constituency* that

> Party pressure seems to be more effective than any other pressure in congressional voting, and is discernible in nearly nine-tenths of the roll calls examined. . . .Contrary to popular impression, the parties usually maintain their ranks on congressional votes, including those of headline significance, with sufficient solidarity so that voters may distinguish between the two points of view.[9]

Despite this cohesiveness, we have also seen that other legislative parties were able to maintain an even higher level—some a considerably higher level—of voting cohesion than did the American parties. To what can we attribute such differences? In attempting to answer this question, our analysis will focus on the American Congressional parties and on four legislative parties taken from the British, French, and West German experiences. These parties are the British Conservative and Labour parties, the French Gaullist party, and the West German CDU/CSU. Each was dominant in its legislature five years or more over the period 1946-74.[10]

The American and European legislative parties we will examine provide at least one case from each political system and at least one case from each of the three levels of party voting cohesion. This is shown in the following Table 4.2.

Table 4.2
Legislative Parties, Political Systems, and Party Voting Cohesion

Party	Political System	Level of Cohesion
Conservative	Great Britain	High
Labour	Great Britain	High
Gaullist	France	High
CDU/CSU	West Germany	Moderate
Democrat	United States	Low
Republican	United States	Low

Intraparty Cleavages and Legislators' Policy Orientations

Let us begin by looking at party voting cohesion as it is related to intraparty cleavages and legislators' own policy orientations. In general, a legislative party consists of members, most of whom have convictions about policy approaches that are closer to one another than they are to the convictions held by members of other parties. Our brief discussion above of the differences over policy that separate the voting records of most Congressional Democrats from most Congressional Republicans indicates that this conclusion is applicable to the members of Congress. Not only do voting records suggest such a conclusion, but research carried out by interview or questionnaire on the policy views of legislators in Congress also supports this conclusion as it generally does for the major opposing parties in the three European legislatures as well.[11] The relative commonality in the policy views of most members of a legislative party which research has revealed would surely seem to be an element helping to produce internal voting cohesion.

However, we are interested here primarily in the different levels of voting unity maintained by legislative parties, and this draws our attention to the other side of the coin. This is that the struggle to achieve voting unity in most legislative parties also takes place within the context of conflicts over policy direction among the legislative party members, conflicts resulting partly from the members' own differing views about the problems facing society. Legislators, even within the same party, may have different ideas regarding what the problems facing society are and how best to solve these problems. As a consequence, they may have different views about the required policy responses. These contrasting views about policy may be sufficiently consistent over a number of issues to create identifiable blocs or wings within the legislative party. When conflict occurs within the party, often the same members (policy subgroups) oppose each other, and the conflict between the subgroups can be defined in terms of differences over the policy direction the legislative party should take in a particular policy sector or a series of such sectors. In this section, we will examine the relationship between the presence of such cleavages, or policy subgroups, and the ability of legislative parties to maintain voting cohesion.

Policy Cleavages within Legislative Parties

Best known to Americans, of course, is the division in the Democratic party that separates most northern from southern members of Congress. It is not rare on Senate or House roll calls that a majority of northern Democrats opposes a majority of southern Democrats. From 1957 to 1974 this occurred yearly on a minimum of 21 percent of all roll call votes (1962) and on a maximum of 40 percent of the roll calls (1960). The conflict between northern and southern Democratic Congressmen on *key* roll calls was even more substantial, taking place on 64 percent of the key roll calls in the House from 1964 to 1969 and on 53 percent of the key roll calls in the Senate during the same period. Especially since the 1950s, the party loyalty scores of southern Democrats in the House have been markedly lower than those of northern or western Democrats.[12]

The persistent conflict between these two sizable groups within the Democratic Congressional parties reflects rather consistent differences in policy orientations along a liberal-conservative continuum, even when one considers constituency variables. Jewell and Patterson note: "There is no doubt . . . that Northern urban Democrats have a more liberal voting record than Southern urban Democrats, and the same distinction applies to Northern and Southern rural Democrats."[13] Each has had its own internal divisions, particularly the southerners, which enabled some members of one wing to support the other with varying degrees of frequency.[14] Nevertheless, as Price has shown, while "both Southern and non-Southern Democrats are split within their own ranks, . . . two out of three Southerners support the 'conservative-isolationist' view on labor-management policies, displaced persons, taxation and revenue policies, use of the treaty power, public housing, rent control, and some other economic issues, while two out of three non-Southern Democrats will support the 'liberal-internationalist' viewpoint."[15]

The liberal-conservative division between the North and the South in the Democratic party can be put in capsule form by referring to the liberal ADA Congressional voting scores. The 1971 ADA scores for members of the House serve as a representative example. During that year, almost 75 percent of the southern Democrats scored below

25 percent (out of a possible one hundred) on the ADA index of liberalism. Less than 5 percent of the northern Democrats scored that low. Indeed, a solid majority of northern Democrats scored above 50 percent on the index.[16]

Although less well known, the Republican party has also faced rather persistent regional divisions within its ranks.[17] For example, Ripley found that the party loyalty scores of Republican Congressmen from the Northeast were considerably lower than those of Republican Congressmen from the West, Midwest or South and border states.[18] This is reported for the Eighty-eighth Congress on Table 4.3, which also contains the party loyalty scores of Democratic Congressmen.

The division within the Republican party, as within the Democratic party, can be defined at least partly in terms of differences over the policy direction the party should take. For example, eastern Republicans as a group have taken a rather consistently more liberal stand on policies relating to labor than the remainder of their colleagues. Rieselbach uncovered differences between eastern and midwestern Republicans over foreign policy as well. Since 1945, eastern Republicans as a group were consistently less "isolationist" than midwestern Republicans in each of the three Congresses he examined.[19]

Cleavages over policy direction are also noticeable within parties that have maintained higher levels of party voting cohesion than the American parties. For example, divisions over policy direction have characterized the Parliamentary Labour Party (PLP) for a long time. In the 1950s, using motions signed by Labour parliamentarians, Finer was able to identify both a left and a right wing within the PLP. The members of these wings differed in their policy positions on a wide range of issues, including civil liberties, colonialism, pacifism, welfare benefits, and health and education.[20] Each of these wings contained a core of members who rather consistently supported motions identified with the policy stances of their respective wings. Finer reports fifty members who were furthest to the left in the Parliamentary Labour Party, although the hard core of the left wing has not been quite that large. Finer also identified fifty-five members

Table 4.3
Party Loyalty of Representatives by Region and Party for the Eighty-eighth Congress

	Democrats		*Republicans*
Region	*Party Loyalty Score**	*Region*	*Party Loyalty Score*
North (N 103)	77	Northeast (N 54)	34
West (N 58)	71	West (N 29)	60
South (N 95)	27	South & border (N 19)	68
		Midwest (N 76)	69
Average	57	Average	57

* Party Loyalty scores combine *Congressional Quarterly* support and opposition scores, the latter subtracted from the former.
Source: Randall Ripley, *Party Leaders in the House of Representatives* (Washington, D.C.: The Brookings Institution, 1967), p. 155.

who were furthest to the right. The exact size of either wing, beyond its core membership, tended, of course, to fluctuate with the issue.

Finer's results applied to the Labour party when it was in opposition. More recently, in the latter 1960s, Kornberg and Frasure undertook a questionnaire analysis of the policy attitudes of Labour MPs while Labour formed the government. The authors again uncovered conflicts in policy attitudes among the Labour parliamentarians. They concluded, "In the case of Labour, the differences [over policy] are significant between the leaders and the backbench as a whole, and also between the leaders and a left-wing group in the backbench."[21] Statistically significant differences were detected between the attitudes of leaders as compared to the attitudes of the backbenchers as a whole or the left-wing group on the backbench on six of the ten issues Kornberg and Frasure examined. Although Kornberg and Frasure did not find the left wing itself to be in conflict with the remainder of the party quite as sharply as did Finer, such conflicts were still apparent. Significant conflicts with the left wing centered principally on two of the domestic policy issues, trade union reform and prices and incomes policy, and on the foreign policy issue of entry into the Common Market.

Another party in which cleavage is to be found is the German CDU/CSU. As we observed in Chapter 2, the CDU/CSU is a coalition of rather distinct economic, religious, and regional groupings. These groupings are well represented in the CDU/CSU parliamentary party. The groups are often highly organized and, indeed, are given recognition in the form of office space and budgetary funds paid for by the parliamentary party.

For a party whose major opposition has been the Social Democrats, it is not surprising that a potentially highly dissident group in the CDU/CSU parliamentary party would be the labor group. This group has now been in existence over twenty years. The group, with a core of about thirty members and fringe of about an additional thirty members, has been active principally in regard to economic and social policies. It has had its own executive, office, staff, and regularized meetings and has not usually been open to all members of the parliamentary party but has determined for itself the parliamentarians who could become members of the group. Working-class background and union affiliation have been used as criteria for membership.

The potential difference in voting patterns between members of the labor group and the remainder of the CDU/CSU parliamentary party is indicated best by roll call votes during the 1953-57 Bundestag. Sixty-five percent of the members having a labor background (compared to 20 percent of all CDU/CSU members) were among the most dissident in the parliamentary party during that Bundestag. This is shown in Table 4.4.

Table 4.4
Party Voting in the Second Bundestag:
All CDU/CSU Members and the CDU/CSU
Labor Group (in percent)

	Number of Dissenting Votes			
	0-3	4-7	8+	Total
All CDU/CSU Members (N = 230)	54	26	20	100
Labor (N = 34)	22	13	65	100

An excellent example of the CDU/CSU labor group in action is the case study on the reform of health insurance in West Germany from 1953 to 1961, in which the CDU labor group frequently sided with the Social Democrats and against its own party leadership. A description of this case is found in Chapter 3.

Although the most highly organized, labor has not constituted the only organized economic grouping of CDU/CSU parliamentarians. Also of importance have been the farmers, who have formed their own group of about fifty members, and small business, with about thirty members. Like the labor group, these groups have had their own offices and staffs and have met quite regularly, generally once a week during sessions.

The Gaullists, too, have been faced with cleavages over policy within their ranks. From 1958 to 1962, a major source of division that consistently brought the same members into opposition with the party as a whole, as well as with the parliamentary party, was the Algerian question. Because of their policy views, at least thirteen parliamentarians who wished to retain a French Algeria were expelled from the party, forced to resign on this account, or were demoted. Among these parliamentarians were two founders of the UNR, Jacques Soustelle and Léon Delbeque.[22]

A more continuing source of conflict over policy direction, however, has centered principally in the areas of domestic economic and social policy. Although the Gaullist party has been generally moderate to conservative in its economic and social posture, the party has included a group of about thirty parliamentary members whose purpose has been to incorporate a more leftist orientation into the party's economic and social policies.[23] These parliamentarians have been highly organized, and, indeed, many were formally under a different nomenclature in the first Assembly. They were known as L'Union démocratique du travail (UDT), having their own executive, office, staff, and regular publications. Although they joined the Gaullist UNR in 1962, these parliamentarians continued to look upon themselves as a distinct group. This was recognized by the name the Gaullist party adopted, the UNR-UDT. It continues to be felt in the politics of the Gaullist parliamentary party, which still finds many of the left-wing members coming together and acting in concert in the parliamentary party committees specializing in social and industrial policy.

As is suggested by this description of the legislative parties, divisiveness has by no means been confined to the two American parties. Persisting cleavages, continually involving the same subgroupings of members, have been present within three of the four European parties as well. The conflicting subgroups of members within the parties have often been highly organized and have contained sizable numbers of party members. The smallest subgroup we have discussed consisted of about thirty core members.

Alone among the parliamentary parties, the British Conservative party appears not to have contained a consistency of internal division based upon persisting policy subgroups. To be sure, internal conflicts have existed within the Conservative parliamentary party, and we will cover several of these in the next chapter. But, Finer et al. found in their study of motions signed by Conservative members that policy divisions in the party tended to be shifting and dissipating ones rather than the persisting ones, frequently involving the same members, that have existed in the other parties. The authors remarked:

The Conservative party is not divided into wings, with each wing espousing a line or tendency of policy affecting all departments of national life. This alone goes far to explain the resilience and unity of the Conservative party. By their very nature, the internal quarrels of the party are temporary. They subside as the issues which gave them birth are resolved.[24]

Finer's research applied to the latter 1950s when the Conservatives were in power, but his conclusions have been corroborated by the research Kornberg and Frasure carried out on the policy attitudes of Conservative MPs in the latter 1960s, when the Conservatives were in opposition. Although Kornberg and Frasure detected a right-wing subgroup present, the core and fringes of this subgroup were not sufficient to produce significant cleavage within the parliamentary party as a whole. They concluded: "In the Conservative party, there are some differences . . . but these differences did not come close to attaining statistical significance."[25] Such homogeneity in the policy attitudes of Conservative MPs, as these studies point out, is one factor helping to account for the high voting cohesion the parliamentary party has been able to maintain.

Findings on the Relationship between Policy Cleavages and Legislators' Policy Views

However, we have seen that lines of cleavages over policy direction have been present in each of the other legislative parties. Persistent cleavages among legislators, whether between different parties or within the same party, have their roots in a number of factors. It is appropriate here to mention one of these factors. At the beginning of our discussion in this section, we pointed out that lines of policy cleavage among legislators are not likely to be entirely divorced from the policy views to which the legislators themselves adhere. Rather, it is likely that the cleavages will be reinforced by, if not sometimes principally due to, the legislators' own attitudes about policy. In making this point, we referred to research results based on legislators' responses to interviews and questionnaires. These findings uncovered a correspondence between many lines of policy cleavage dividing different parties and the legislators' own policy attitudes (see footnote 11). Kornberg and Frasure's questionnaire research, which allows us to look within an individual party (the PLP), found that some cleavages in this party could also be defined by the members' policy attitudes. Roll call voting research on the PLP lends further support to the conclusion that the lines of cleavage over policy direction among the PLP members have arisen partly from and have also been reinforced by the differing policy attitudes of the members themselves.[26]

Labour parliamentarians have not been unique in this regard. For example, let us look at the Democratic and Republican parties, two parties with significant internal cleavage over party direction. One of the consequences of the cleavages within the ranks of these parties has been the formation of the Conservative Coalition. The Conservative Coalition has brought together some Democrats and most Republicans in opposition to other Democrats and generally some Republicans. Definitionally, most of the Democrats in the Conservative Coalition have been from the South.[27] The conservatism of these members may have reflected the electoral constraints these members faced (the problems of career survival) and it is possible that similar considerations lay behind the actions of liberal Republicans who "defected" from their party and who voted against the Conservative Coalition.

Yet, it is also possible that one of the factors affecting levels of support for the Conservative Coalition has been the legislators' own policy views. We can attempt to determine this possibility by finding an indicator that might reflect the policy dispositions of legislators. For example, we can examine a particular background or socializing experience that research suggests should shape one's "ideological" orientation to questions of policy.

One socializing factor that may help shape this orientation is the size of one's home town or community. Previous research has shown that persons reared in small towns have tended to have outlooks relatively more conservative in direction than persons from large towns.[28] This conclusion has held not only for the population as a whole but also when region was held constant. A socializing factor that might have some bearing on a Congressman's policy orientations, then, is the size of the town in which he was reared. Based on the previous research findings, we would anticipate that Congressmen with a small town or rural background might be more likely to carry a conservative outlook into Congress, and would therefore be more likely to support the Conservative Coalition, than would Congressmen reared in larger towns or cities.

An analysis of this kind on members of the House was undertaken by Rieselbach, whose findings are reported on Table 4.5.[29] His analysis took into account not only the birthplace of a Congressman but also the region from which he came, the type of district (urban-rural) he represented, and his party affiliation.

Rieselbach found that the support of Congressmen for the Conservative Coalition was based mainly on region and party, but that the rural or urban character of the Congressman's birthplace also had a noticeable effect. Examining Table 4.5, we see

Table 4.5
Size of Birthplace, Constituency Type, and Support for the Conservative Coalition by Members of the House of Representatives (Ninetieth Congress*

Size of Birthplace	Northern Democrats Metropolitan	Northern Democrats Non-metropolitan	Southern Democrats Metropolitan	Southern Democrats Non-metropolitan	Republicans Metropolitan	Republicans Non-metropolitan
Rural, small town (under 10,000)	14.7	24.4	60.0	67.3	69.8	73.4
Urban (10,000 and over)	7.6	9.8	47.9	53.1	56.6	68.7

Source: Leroy N. Rieselbach, "Congressmen as 'Small Town Boys': A Research Note," *Midwest Journal of Political Science* Volume 14 Number 2 (May 1970), p. 328.

*The call entry is the mean percentage of support for the Conservative Coalition for each category of Congressmen.

that Congressmen reared in a small town or rural environment consistently gave greater support to the Conservative Coalition regardless of the region, party, or type of district represented. Moreover, Table 4.5 shows that the response of Congressmen to the Conservative Coalition was related to size of birthplace as *much* as it was to the type of district the Congressmen represented.

It is true that the significance of this indicator of the legislator's own policy orientation seems dwarfed by the impact of such considerations as region. Yet, it is possible that "region" itself is as much an indicator of the policy dispositions of American legislators as of the electoral constraints the members face. For instance, Hinckley points out:

The most dramatic example in the past two decades of defection from party is provided by southern Democrats, many of whom had never experienced a contested general election. Even southerners with little to fear from primary contests deserted the national party to represent their states' views on civil rights. While the threat of reprisal on election day cannot be discounted, . . . it seems likely that deep-rooted beliefs—the product of the socialization they and their constituents had experienced—[also] dictated southern Senators' filibuster against civil rights legislation and vote against the national government's assault on "states" rights.[30]

If members' own attitudes about policy are of significance to behavior in the Congress, we would anticipate that when an individual member consults or cues upon other members on issues about which he is insufficiently informed, the member's own policy attitudes would usually be basic to the choices he makes. Research indicates that this is true. The strong tendency is to look to someone whose policy orientation is similar to one's own. As Kingdon concluded from his detailed interviews with Representatives, the member "selects those he will follow according to his policy attitudes. . . . The quantitative evidence for this agreement being a fundamental decision rule is very strong."[31] Kingdon also found that the tendency for members sharing similar policy attitudes to cue upon one another worked to reinforce cleavages not only between members of different parties in the House, but also between subgroupings within parties, such as between northerners and southerners in the Democratic party.[32]

The findings to which we have referred suggest that some of the major lines of cleavage among party members in Congress have been partially rooted in the members' own policy attitudes. They do not appear to have been generated simply by the motive of survival. This conclusion complements the one reached with regard to the Parliamentary Labour Party which found that some of its internal divisions have been grounded in and encouraged by the members' own ideological predispositions. It is also consistent with the results of other research indicating a series of lines of policy cleavage among members of different parties that have been definable in terms of the members' own policy attitudes.

Another point that earlier discussion in this section suggests is that cleavages over policy direction have been more pervasive within some legislative parties than within others. The relative presence of cleavage might be broadly defined by addressing the following questions: first, were large policy subgroups present in a party and did they persist over time? Second, did these policy subgroups come into conflict over certain kinds of policy sectors or the entire spectrum of policy concerns? Employing these questions as guidelines, our earlier discussion indicates the Conservative parliamentary party to have been least divided by cleavages over policy direction. Research did not find this party to have experienced division among large policy subgroups that persisted over long periods of time. Following the Conservatives would be the Gaullists and the CDU/CSU. Each of these parties has been divided by sizable policy subgroups that persisted over time, but each of the subgroups appears to have focused more on certain sets of policy sectors than the entire spectrum of policy concerns. The parties that have been potentially the most divisive, according to these criteria, have been the American legislative parties and the British Labour party. Each of these legislative parties has not only been divided by sizable policy subgroups that persisted over time, but these subgroups did not confine themselves principally to particular kinds of policy sectors. Rather, they have been relevant, in the words of Finer et al., to "policy affecting all departments of national life."[33]

In the case of the Labour party, however, there is some question as to exactly how broad-ranged the cleavages involving the same policy subgroups have been. As we have observed, Kornberg and Frasure's research revealed somewhat less divisiveness between the left wing and the remainder of the parliamentary party than Finer's research found.

With these points in mind, we can discuss the relationship between the comparative level of cleavage over policy directions within each of the six legislative parties and the level of voting cohesion or dissensus these parties actually maintained. Table 4.6 looks at this relationship.

Table 4.6 suggests that the comparative level of cleavage over policy in four of the six legislative parties ran roughly parallel to the comparative level of voting dissensus the four parties were to experience. The four cases are the American Democratic and Republican parties, the West German CDU/CSU, and the British Conservative party. Moreover, in only one case, that of Labour, was there a marked divergence between the level of cleavage over policy direction and voting cohesion.

Nevertheless, Table 4.6 also suggests that there is more to party voting cohesion than the level of cleavage over policy direction that is present within a party. While

Table 4.6
Comparative Levels of Internal Cleavage and Voting Dissensus within Six Legislative Parties

Legislative Party	Internal Cleavage	Voting Dissensus*
Conservative	Low	Low
UDR (Gaullists)	Moderate	Low
Labour	Moderate to High	Low
CDU/CSU	Moderate	Moderate
Democrat	High	High
Republican	High	High

*.Voting dissensus is simply the reverse of voting cohesion. The ranking of the six parties regarding voting cohesion is found on Table 4.2

there seems to be a relationship between the two, there is not a complete correspondence, as the Labour and UDR examples indicate. The example of the Parliamentary Labour Party, in particular, points to the possibility that party voting cohesion in a comparative sense can be rather considerably higher than an examination of cleavages within the party would lead us to expect. Indeed, the absolute level of voting cohesion each of the six parties has maintained is probably higher than we would anticipate on the basis of the conflicts over policy within the parties. Even for the Conservative party, in which internal cleavages over policy direction are comparatively slight, still there is sufficient division among members on both domestic and foreign issues to create more voting deviation than has been the case, were these divisions allowed free reign.

Party Identification

If there is more to legislative party voting unity than the level of cleavage over policy among the party members, then an explanation of legislators' responses to party must reach beyond this factor alone. Another factor to which we might look is the extent to which the members of legislative parties feel a sense of identity with their party. Simply as a consequence of identifying with one's party, the legislator may find the act of going against his party distasteful. By virtue of his affective attachment to his party, the legislator may want to support his party despite disagreement he may have with particular policy stances taken by the party.

We observed in the first section of this chapter that party is a major frame of reference for the voting responses of legislators in each of the four legislatures we are examining, including that of the United States. As a consequence, we might expect that many legislators, even members of the Congress, would feel a sense of party identification. While we will treat this matter in greater detail in the following chapter, we ought also to spend a moment at this point in order to illustrate the presence of such feelings in parties of relatively low voting cohesion, such as the legislative parties in the American Congress.

The extent and importance of legislators' identification with their party, even in parties which do not maintain comparatively high levels of voting cohesion, should not be underestimated. Writing about the United States Senate, Matthews concluded that "most Senators do identify strongly with their party. They want to be 'good' Democrats or Republicans. . . . 'None of us,' one Senator remarked, 'likes to see the party split openly and repeatedly'."[34] Ripley attempted to uncover the extent of party feeling in the House by asking members, "Do you want to act in accord with party position?" Seventy-four percent of the Democratic respondents and seventy-two of the Republican respondents answered strongly in the affirmative.[35] Ripley also found that it was these members who in fact had the highest party voting scores.

This evidence suggests that many Representatives and Senators do identify with their parties. The presence of such feelings may help to explain why one's party has been an important focus for the voting behavior of legislators in the United States Congress, and we will go to some length to illustrate this in Chapter 5.

Nevertheless, it may still be the case that legislative parties differ in the degree to which the party leaders can draw upon especially strong feelings of attachment to party. Unfortunately, one of the problems we face in examining this possibility is that identification with the party as an organization and a group of people is not easily separable from support given the general policy principles or positions for which the party stands. Although the two are analytically distinguishable, they are in practice frequently interconnected. For example, the importance a legislator attaches to the general policy stances taken by his party may result partly from his longstanding identification with the group of people who make up the party; conversely, the legislator's attachment to the group of people making up the party may result partly from the feeling that these people (more than the people from other parties) share the basic ideas about policy that he has.

While we often cannot disentangle these two dispositions completely, we can examine a factor that might indicate feelings of party identification above and beyond support for the general policy principles for which the party stands. Locating such an indicator is necessary if only because there exists no comparative systematic interview or voting research to help us get at feelings of identification more directly.

Previous research findings in psychology and sociology have revealed that a person's affective identification with other individuals and groups, his feeling of belonging, is based partly on whether the person shares important attributes or characteristics of those other individuals and groups.[36] The approach we follow is based on this idea. First, we ask whether a legislator's party has the attribute we call a focused societal rooting (as indicated by the social or economic characteristics of its voting public); second, whether the legislators of that party share background characteristics common to or congruent with the societal rooting of their party; and, third, whether the legislators' background characteristics simultaneously contrast with the backgrounds of members of the major opposing party or parties. We suggest that legislators in this situation are likely to feel a strengthened sense of identity with one another and with their party. This idea, in turn, leads to the proposition that parties that contain high percentages of such legislative members also ought to find it easier to generate loyalty and support for the party than would parties that contain low percentages of such members.

How does this apply in practice? The British Labour, Conservative, and French Gaullist parties, the parties with the highest level of voting cohesion, have all had a large core of members whose own backgrounds reflected, or were congruent with,* the societal rootings of their party and whose backgrounds simultaneously contrasted with those of the members of the major opposing party or parties. Let us take up the British parties first. At least as indicated by voters' characteristics, British Conservatives have based their party on sectors of the population rooted strongly in the middle and upper classes.[37] These societal roots have also been reflected in the backgrounds of Conservative parliamentarians, almost all of whom were raised in middle- or upper-class families and have had business or professional occupations. The societal roots of the Labour party, on the other hand, have been in the working class and the trade unions.[38] Unlike the Conservative MPs, whose origins have been almost entirely from the middle and upper classes, a majority of Labour MPs, whether before or after 1945, have been raised in working-class families. Further, since 1945, more than one-third of the Labour backbenchers have themselves been nonsalaried manual

---

*What can be called "party-congruent" backgrounds.

workers or employees of trade unions. This is in contrast to less than 3 percent of the Conservative backbenchers over these years.

As in the case of the Conservative and Labour parties, the Gaullist party has also contained a large core of parliamentary members whose backgrounds have reflected the societal roots of the party. While including a working class element, the Gaullist party, like the Conservative party, has had societal roots among voters based mainly in the middle and upper classes that have distinguished the party sharply from its major opponents, the French Communist and Socialist parties.[39] These societal roots have also characterized the Gaullist parliamentary members, about 50 percent of whom have come from business, banking, military, and high civil servant backgrounds. Most of the remaining Gaullist parliamentarians have been doctors, lawyers, or other professionals. Approximately 70 percent of the Gaullist deputies were raised in upper- and middle-upper-class families. The deputies of the major opposing parties (Socialists and Communists), on the other hand, have come from quite different family backgrounds. Over 90 percent of these deputies were raised in lower-middle-class or lower-class families (see footnote 39).

Thus, for each of the three highly cohesive parties, there has existed a congruence between the party's societal roots and the backgrounds of a large core of the party's parliamentary members. Moreover, the backgrounds of the legislators in these parties have also contrasted with the backgrounds of the members of the major opposing party or parties.

Looking at evidence on the differing background characteristics of legislators *within* parties should also have some bearing on the points we are making. The evidence available on intraparty differences in members' backgrounds as these relate to their voting behavior pertains to the British Conservative and Labour parliamentary parties. The party-congruent backgrounds of most Conservative and Labour members combined with the simultaneous contrast in the backgrounds of the members of the two parliamentary parties have led us to expect, given our assumptions, that most members would feel a heightened sense of party identification, thereby helping to create a high level of voting cohesion. What we wish to suggest is that even the degree of party voting loyalty by MPs within these parties may be partly a function of particular party-congruent backgrounds and the group-orienting experiences normally associated with those backgrounds. For instance, middle- and upper-class conservatism has historically emphasized the right of the Conservative party to rule because its leaders are trained to rule. This image the party has of itself has been reflected in the high percentage of its parliamentary members who have attended the most prestigious public schools and universities.[40] Thus, it has been typical for over half of the Conservative backbenchers to have attended at least one of the following four highly esteemed British educational institutions: Eton, Harrow, Oxford, and Cambridge. Not only has this background been highly congruent with the image the party has had of itself, as we suggested above, but evidence indicates that the friendship networks established among the Conservative MPs who attended these educational institutions have acted further to reinforce a feeling of group identity among these MPs.[41] The importance of these Conservative members to maintaining the voting cohesion of the Conservative parliamentary party is illustrated by the fact that within the party, and even holding career factors constant, the voting records of these particular members have been consistently more loyal to the party than have those of other Conservative members who did not have such backgrounds. We will examine findings relating to this point in detail in Chapter 5.

In the case of the Parliamentary Labour Party, we can refer to members whose backgrounds were party-congruent as indicated by having risen into the parliamentary party by way of trade union occupations. While most Labour MPs have exhibited a high level of party voting support, those MPs who themselves rose through the trade union movement have been especially unswerving in their support of the party. Referring to the trade union MPs, Carter points out that voting loyalty has been "*the* central principle of their political lives [partly because] they grew up in the tradition of industrial unity and discipline, of solidarity as the essential price of survival."[42] These are group experiences we would expect to reinforce feelings of identification with one another and with the Labour party. The relevance of this type of background can be seen even in the declining relationship that has occurred recently between relative levels of voting loyalty within the Labour party and whether or not MPs were from working-class occupations. Older working-class Labour MPs have continued to be disproportionately loyal to the party, whereas this has been less the case for the newer and younger working-class MPs. One of the reasons that may help to account for the diminished relationship, according to an analysis undertaken by Holt and Turner, is that the newer and younger Labour MPs with working-class occupations have had "less trade union experience in rigorous industrial combat" than that which characterized their older working-class colleagues.[43]

Briefly recapitulating, each of the most cohesive parties in our study shared two characteristics relevant to the points we are making here. First, they each contained a large core of members whose own backgrounds were congruent with the societal rooting of the party. Second, these members' backgrounds contrasted quite sharply with the backgrounds of members of the major opposing party or parties. Given our assumptions, we would argue that these characteristics in combination were important to reinforcing members' feelings of identity with the party and with their colleagues, thus working to facilitate the high level of intraparty voting cohesion that each of these parties has maintained. We have also alluded to evidence on the voting behavior of parliamentarians *within* two of the parties which suggests that particular party-congruent backgrounds (i.e., educational background of Conservatives and trade union backgrounds of Labourites) have had a bearing on differential rates of voting loyalty within these parliamentary parties, as well.

We can now turn to the three legislative parties that have been less cohesive in their behavior. The three parties appear to have been in a different situation and one that, according to our assumptions, has not provided as firm a basis for developing especially strong feelings of identification among the members of the party. For example, let us look at the CDU/CSU. The backgrounds of CDU/CSU parliamentarians have contrasted with those of the members of the SPD. From 1953 to 1965, while normally over 70 percent of the SPD parliamentarians were members of trade unions, an average of only about 20 percent of the CDU/CSU parliamentarians were members of trade unions. Nevertheless, ever since its beginnings, the CDU/CSU has attempted to establish the image of a party based principally on heterogeneity and coalition across all classes and sectors in the society rather than a party located heavily in one class or sector. In this, the party has been rather successful. Indeed, although it has received disproportionate support from the middle and upper classes, it was able in only the second national election after its formation (1953) to win as large a percentage of the working-class vote as did the SPD. However, one consequence of this strategy may well have been that a focused societal rooting upon which to heighten members' feelings of party identification, based on congruency of background, could not be established in the case of the CDU/CSU to as great an extent as in the other parliamentary parties we considered.[44] In a similar vein, the two American parties have traditionally had a diverse rather than a crystalized societal rooting (see footnote 44). Furthermore, most members of both Congressional parties have shared broadly similar instead of contrasting socioeconomic occupations and backgrounds. Almost all members of both parties in the Senate have come from middle- or upper-class families and are businessmen, lawyers, or other professionals. The occupational backgrounds of the members of both parties in the House have also been broadly similar.[45] Compared with the more cohesive parties, then, there has been a less well-crystallized societal rooting upon which to heighten members' feelings of party identification in the CDU/CSU and the American legislative parties (see footnote 44); and, especially in the case of the American Congressional parties, feelings of identification have not been reinforced by sharp contrasts between the backgrounds of the members of the two parties.

We are not suggesting that there has been an absence of feeling of party identification among legislative members in the parties of lesser unity. To the contrary, we have argued otherwise in the beginning of this section and will do so again in the following chapter as we point to the relevance that feelings of party identification have had as a factor promoting voting cohesion in the American Congressional parties.

Nor do we wish to argue that high levels of voting cohesion cannot occur outside the presence of the conditions we have cited as helping to heighten feelings of party identification, if only because such feelings are not the only pertinent factors. Also of importance are factors such as members' policy and role outlooks, their career ambitions, and how these, in the context of the political setting, relate members to their party. Because other factors are relevant, they can in combination work to create high levels of party-orientated behavior even where party-congruency of members' backgrounds is not present.

However, feelings of identification with one's party may be of sufficient significance for the behavior of legislators that the stronger and more reinforced these feelings are, the more likely it is that legislators will respond to public issues along party lines. Our discussion has been based partly on this assumption. It has also been based on the assumption that members' feelings of identification would be increased if their party had a focused societal rooting and if the backgrounds of a sizable percentage of party members reflected this rooting, while simultaneously contrasting with the backgrounds of the members of the major opposing party or parties. Consistent with these assumptions, we have seen that the conditions outlined above held for each of the parties whose members maintained the highest levels of voting cohesion, whereas at least one of these conditions was absent for each of the parties which maintained lesser levels of voting cohesion.[46] Also consistent with our assumptions is evidence drawn from the two highly cohesive parties for which analysis was available suggesting that particular kinds of party-congruent backgrounds have had some bearing on differential rates of voting loyalty within these parties, as well.

Career Ambitions

Apart from the considerations offered thus far, there is another, political ambition, which more than a few observers feel is the principal motive lying behind how legislators behave. Schlesinger described this idea in the following terms: "The central assumption . . . is that a politician's behavior is a response to his office goals. Or to put it another way, the politician as office-seeker engages in political acts and makes decisions appropriate to gaining office."[47]

If this is true, the extent to which individual legislators must act loyally to their national party to achieve their office or career goals is a factor that one presumes would affect the voting loyalty of the individual legislators and therefore the voting cohesion of the legislative party. As Martin Redmayne, chief Conservative whip in the early 1960s put it, when reward of office is based on party loyalty, "the hope of office is an incentive to give support to the [party leadership]."[48]

In this section our analysis will focus on the relationship between evidences of loyalty to the national party and legislators' achievement of career ambitions. We will treat each of the six legislative parties in the order of their voting cohesiveness, taking up the British Conservative and Labour parties and the French Gaullists first, then the West German CDU/CSU, and finally the two American parties.

Two aspects of career ambition will be considered. One component deals with the maintenance of one's career, or career survival. The maintenance of a career in the legislature requires that the member be renominated and reelected. A second component is the enhancement of a legislator's career. Career enhancement concerns advancing to more influential political offices or posts either in the legislature or the executive.

Parties of High Voting Unity

Recall that the highest levels of voting cohesion were found in the British Conservative and Labour parties and the French Gaullist party. Data on these parties indicate that advancement of individual legislators to higher offices has been based to a significant extent on evidence of loyalty to the national party.

The Conservative leadership, when it forms the executive, has many rewards at its disposal. There are upwards of seventy-five governmental rewards composed of ministerial, junior ministerial, and whip offices. Loyalty to the Parliamentary party leadership is certainly not the sole criterion Conservative leaders have used to distribute these rewards, but it has been a significant one. Examining promotions during a twenty year period after World War II, Jackson concludes that "there is little doubt that a Member's former loyalty to his party and especially to the person who is Prime Minister are important factors. . . . Several Chief Whips have reported in interviews that they were consulted about all appointments of junior ministers and that the main question they were asked was whether or not the MPs had been loyal party supporters."[49] Martin Redmayne, as chief Conservative whip, once observed that "a regular rebel . . . is by definition not suitable for office. He can't be. It isn't a sensible attitude."[50]

The behavior of the Conservative leadership supports these statements. The period from 1959 to 1964, which we will discuss further in Chapter 5, is an example. Fifty-nine members of the Conservative backbench rebelled against the leadership twice or more on the seven major rebellions that took place during the 1959-64 Parliament. When it came time to appoint backbenchers to government office, the Conservative Prime Ministers practically ignored these rebels. Although the rebels comprised about 20 percent of all Conservative backbenchers, they comprised only 6 percent of the backbenchers who were appointed to higher office.[51]

The Parliamentary Labour Party leadership during its terms in governmental office also rewarded loyalists. The period from 1945 to mid-1947 provides an example. During this period, ministerial and junior ministerial replacements led to the appointment of twenty-eight backbenchers to governmental office. During the same period, over 30 percent of the Labour backbenchers had rebelled at least once.[52] In making its replacements, the Labour leadership saw fit to distribute only two of the twenty-eight appointments, or 7 percent, to those who had previously rebelled. The backbenchers who were consistently loyal comprised less than 70 percent of the backbenchers, but they received 93 percent of the promotions. While the relationship between promotions and voting loyalty in the Parliamentary Labour Party diminished during its second period in office (especially after 1966), a relationship was still present. Thus, although about 24 percent of the Labour backbenchers rebelled twice or more from 1966 through mid-1967, this group constituted only 12.5 percent of the governmental appointees from mid-1967 to the end of the Labour government in 1970.

The Gaullists, too, appear to have distributed ministerial and parliamentary party leadership posts on the basis of previous evidence of Gaullist loyalty. The most significant formative event of the Gaullist party was the resistance against German occupation during World War II. It was during this period of underground, clandestine activity that the bonds of loyalty were forged and the tests of loyalty most severe. Thus, participation in the Gaullist resistance was one indication of loyalty to Gaullism.

Table 4.7
Participation in the Resistance, the RPF, and the Social Republicans and the Distribution of Leadership Posts in the Gaullist Parliamentary Party, 1958-65 (in Percent)

Gaullist Background	*Percent of Party (1958-1962)*	*Percent of Group Becoming Leaders (1958-1962)*	*Percent of Group Becoming Leaders (1962-1965)*
3 background	13.5	55	70
2 background	25.5	47	54
1 background	32.5	37	38
no background	28.5	26	34

Source: Figures are based on Jean Charlot, *L'U.N.R.*, p. 215.

Beyond this evidence, a Gaullist could also indicate his loyalty by whether he was a member of the Gaullist RPF and whether he remained a member of the rather small band of Gaullist Social Republicans after the RPF split up in 1952 or not. From the onset in 1958 the Gaullist UNR party recognized such evidences of loyalty in distributing its rewards. Table 4.7 shows that the most highly rewarded group of UNR legislative members were those who had participated in the resistance and were members of both the RPF and the Social Republicans. The group rewarded least were legislators who had none of these evidences of loyalty. This pattern of rewards was followed during the entire 1958-65 period for which we have data.

Let us now turn to the renomination of Conservative, Labour, and Gaullist parliamentarians. Renomination in the Conservative Party is almost entirely in the hands of the local constituency associations. There are more than six hundred of these local associations, each having the primary responsibility for nominating or renominating Conservative parliamentary candidates for its own constituency. There has been some coordination from London in the form, for example, of suggesting candidates to local parties that desired such suggestions, but the national party has not exercised great control. Thus, Conservative MPs have needed to look primarily to their local constituency associations to gain renomination.

The renominations of some Conservative MPs have been contested by the constituency associations for failure to fulfill certain social obligations at the local level or to carry out administrative intervention and case work functions for the constituency. In fact, the major causes of failure to be renominated, besides voluntary retirement due to health or age, have dealt with factors such as obnoxious personal habits (drinking to excess, for example) or inadequate attention given to handling constituents' problems.

Another factor leading to denial of renomination by local associations has been the failure of an MP to remain loyal to the national parliamentary leadership. Even in a period that most often witnessed this factor at work (from 1956 to 1964), it is true that the candidacies of only about a dozen Conservative MPs were seriously challenged as a result of their disloyalty to the parliamentary party leadership. But seven of these challenges were successful. There were also some scattered challenges against the renomination of Conservative MPs on grounds that they supported particular policies of the parliamentary party leadership, yet in *no* case was such a challenge successful. For Conservative MPs, considerations of case work and personal habits aside, voting loyally behind the party leadership provided a strong presumption in favor of renomination.

Much the same can be said for the Labour party. The Labour national executive has usually deferred to constituency party decisions against incumbent Labour MPs when the constituency party wanted to drop MPs for disloyalty to the policies of the national leadership or for personal failings. Also, the national executive has occasionally intervened to prevent a constituency party from readopting an MP who was disloyal. So, some disloyal MPs were scuttled either by the local or by the national party. However, Labour MPs who have been loyal have been virtually assured of renomination. The occasions in which a constituency party seriously challenged its MP for remaining loyal have been few, and the central party successfully intervened in almost every case to secure readoption for the loyal MP.[53]

Nevertheless, even in the Labour party there has been a strong degree of local control over the selection of candidates running for the House of Commons. While the Labour national executive has intervened at times, it has not done so frequently. This is partly a result of the way local associations have used their control over candidate selection. As Ranney observes of both the Conservative and Labour local parties, while the local associations have rarely denied renomination to members who have opposed the national leaders by taking more extreme versions of the party's traditional ideology, such cannot be said about the renomination of rebels who supported the position of the opposition party in the lobbies. He goes on to say:

the local parties voluntarily continue to adopt candidates who, when elected, dutifully vote as the whips direct. Hence although the *de facto* local control of candidate selection resembles the *de jure* local control in the United States much more closely than is commonly supposed, it does not produce parliamentary parties of nearly so low cohesion as those in the United States.

Why? The fundamental answer lies in the fact that British constituency parties are not local in the same sense as American state and local parties. They are manned by activists primarily loyal to the national parties' leaders and causes. . . . Most local activists feel that giving aid and comfort to the opposition is the most grievous of political sins. Hence, they are far more prone than the national leaders to deny readoption to an MP who, by defying the whip, supports the other party's position.

In short, the national leaders do not need to control local candidate selection in order to maintain party cohesion in Parliament; the local activists do the job for them. . . .[54]

Thus, despite the presence of a high degree of local control over candidate selection in Great Britain, loyalty to the national parliamentary parties and leaders has been a meaningful criterion in the nomination and renomination of candidates by the local associations. This has been the case especially in the sense that the MP not support the position of the opposition in the lobbies. The result is that those candidates strongly predisposed not to support the opposition in the lobbies were apt to be nominated by the local associations and those MPs who did support the opposition were more likely to find their renomination the subject of successful challenge.

Let us now look at the Gaullists. While some challenges have occurred, deputies in the Gaullist party have not been denied renomination on grounds that they were loyal to the national party and its leadership.[55] Moreover, partly through central party initiative combined with the cooperation of local federations, and partly on the initiative of local federations, there have been cases in which members who opposed the national party were denied renomination. These cases have even included important political figures within the party such as Edgar Pisani. Furthermore, as we observed earlier, the central party has acted to expel some deputies who challenged the national party on vital issues and has forced some others to resign. The most celebrated cases, of course, were those dealing with the Algerian issue, but expulsion of several critics of the party's economic and social policy has also occurred. As for the effect of expulsion on the political careers of the Algerian dissidents, Ehrmann observes: "Anathema from the U.D.R. [Gaullist party] leadership ended the careers of the dissidents. Whenever they sought elective office, they were always soundly defeated. This was enough to discourage any further thought of defection among Gaullist deputies. . . ."[56]

Reviewing what we have said, the three legislative parties with the highest levels of voting cohesion appear to have dealt in a rather similar way with career goals. Our evidence suggests that the most loyal legislators have had a considerably greater chance of attaining positions of leadership. With few exceptions, they have also been assured that renomination to the legislature would not be denied them on grounds of their support for the policies of the national party and national party leadership.

Parties of Moderate and Low Voting Cohesion

Compared to the parliamentary parties, we have just reviewed, the voting cohesion of the CDU/CSU legislative party has been more moderate. If our hypothesis is correct, we should expect the achievement of career ambitions in the CDU/CSU to have been tied less to members' loyalty than we have seen to be the case for the Conservative, Labour, and Gaullist parliamentary parties.

The data indicate that party loyalty has been less significant as a condition for office-holding and for survival in the CDU/CSU. Table 4.8, for example, examines the 1953-57 period and the voting behavior of CDU/CSU members who were already holding office. The table covers the CDU/CSU appointees to ministerial and parliamentary offices (parliamentary party leaders, Bundestag officers, and Bundestag committee chairmen or vice-chairmen) in 1953 and the voting records of the appointees as compared to the remainder of the CDU/CSU members during the 1953-57 period. Governmental, or ministerial, appointees were very loyal, and this is significant. Yet, most of the officeholders were in parliamentary positions (forty-nine of sixty-one posts). The table shows that holding important parliamentary posts and voting loyalty were only moderately related. Again it is significant that the most loyal group of members (zero or one deviation) held parliamentary offices in disproportionate numbers. But, it is also important that the percentage of the most highly deviant group of CDU/CSU members (eight or more deviations) who held parliamentary offices was the same as the percentage of highly deviant members in the party. The group comprised 20 percent of all CDU/CSU Bundestag members and 20 percent of the members holding Bundestag or CDU/CSU parliamentary party offices.

Table 4.8
CDU/CSU Rewards* and Voting Loyalty
of CDU/CSU Bundestag Members,
1953-57 (in Percent)

Dissenting Votes	Total Membership** (N = 230)	Government Appointees (N = 12)	Parliamentary or Party Leaders (N = 49)
0-1	21	58	33
2-3	33	17	31
4-7	26	17	16
8+	20	8	20

*rewards distributed in 1953
**members serving entire four years

A somewhat similar pattern emerges if one looks at who was given office at the beginning of the third Bundestag (1957-61) and compares this to voting deviation in the previous Bundestag (1953-57). Although loyalty was emphasized to a somewhat greater degree, still the most rebellious parliamentarians from 1953 to 1957 were by no means excluded from rewards in 1957. A total of sixty-five CDU/CSU members were rewarded with government, Bundestag, and parliamentary party offices in 1957. Of the less rebellious of CDU/CSU members from 1953 to 1957 (seven or less deviations) who were reelected in 1957, 36 percent received offices in 1957. But 27 percent of the most rebellious group (eight or more deviations) also received office.

This type of pattern persisted into later years as well. For example, a total of approximately 10 percent of the CDU/CSU members deviated five or more times on the thirty-seven roll call votes during the Fourth Bundestag (1961-65). Of the CDU/CSU appointments to governmental, Bundestag, and CDU/CSU parliamentary posts at the beginning of the Fifth Bundestag (1965-69), about 9 percent were awarded to this group of parliamentarians, or almost exactly the percentage this group constituted of the parliamentary party as a whole.

Party voting loyalty also appears to have provided legislators less assurance of renomination in the CDU/CSU than in either British party or in the French Gaullist party. Local control over nomination and renomination of parliamentary candidates has been very strong in the CDU/CSU, as it has in most respects in the British parties and even the Gaullist party. However, favorable responses to local interests and pressures appear to have been a more important criterion to the deliberations and decisions of the CDU/CSU constituency parties than has been typical in the other parties. Some estimates suggest that about 20 percent of the incumbent CDU/CSU constituency members have not been renominated, including 10 percent of those incumbents who sought renomination.[57] What is significant to the discussion here is that it has not been unusual for nomination or renomination in the CDU/CSU to have been granted or denied on the basis of whether coalitions of economic interests in the constituency party supported or opposed the policies of the legislator, without great attention having been paid to the legislator's loyalty to the national parliamentary party. In an analysis of nominations, Kaufmann and his coauthors found a series of examples of constituency parties having nominated or renominated candidates principally because they had a record of support for policies particularly attractive to local economic interests.[58] They also cite other examples of constituency parties having denied nomination or renomination to CDU/CSU members because the members were insufficiently attentive to policies pertinent to local economic interests. Often important to the politics of nomination were conflicts between farming and labor interests in the local parties. The authors concluded:

When the [CDU/CSU] MP does not get on with his local constituency organization, he has to fight the struggle alone. It is important to his position that the local party members have the feeling that the deputy represents correctly their concerns and interests in the Bundestag.[59]

Those CDU/CSU members elected on the *land* or state lists, as a group, have been subject to even greater local pressures to secure renomination than have the constituency members. The *land* lists have reflected, in part, bargaining among contending groups within the CDU/CSU at the *land* level. Through this bargaining process, incumbents on the *land* lists have more frequently failed to gain renomination than have incumbents from constituencies. They also faced the problem, even if they gained renomination, of receiving a lower (and thereby more vulnerable) place on the list.

Given these local factors, it is not surprising that the CDU/CSU members elected from the *land* lists have been particularly prone toward disproportionate party voting deviation in the Bundestag, as Rueckert and Crane showed for the period they examined (1953-57).[60] Indeed, examining the same years they did, we found that the list members who voted most frequently against the parliamentary party were those constituting the bottom third of the elected list and who were therefore potentially in the most vulnerable position at the *land* level. Although the relationship between list membership and extent of deviation disappeared in the 1957-61 period, it reemerged with some force again in the 1961-65 period.[61]

Let us now turn to the American Congressional parties. In these parties, voting loyalty has not been terribly salient to the advancement of individual Congressmen to significant legislative offices. This is especially the case for holding committee and subcommittee chairmanships. There has been no relationship between advancing to or holding these offices and party voting loyalty. Until recently, the assumption of subcommittee chairmanships was under the control of individual committee chairmen, and the allocation of committee chairmanship offices was a function of seniority on the committee. The seniority system, which since 1921 has rarely been violated until the House Democrats unseated three incumbents in 1975, had the effect of moving most of the prestigious and powerful legislative posts outside the control of the party organization.

While we have seen that in West Germany party control of offices ensured their manipulation at least in part on the basis of party loyalty, the seniority system circumvented this possibility for the American Congressional parties. Indeed, as previously suggested, those Representatives and Senators who have occupied committee chairmanship offices have had voting records no different from the remainder of their colleagues. As one illustration, Table 4.9 shows for the Ninetieth Congress that the voting records of committee chairmen in support of their party leader, the President, were virtually the same as the voting records of Congressmen who had not received such posts. A similar conclusion would be reached by examining party voting loyalty scores over the years.[62]

Table 4.9
Average Presidential Support Scores for Democratic Committee Charimen and for All Democrats in the Ninetieth Congress (in percent)

	House		Senate	
	Support	Opposition	Support	Opposition
All Democrats	67	18	55	24
Chairmen	67	18	54	27

Source: *Congressional Quarterly Weekly Report,* February 7, 1969, pp. 226-27.

The main exceptions have been the two or three party posts that the legislative party as a whole or its leaders have dispensed. But, even these few posts have not usually been distributed to members with exceptionally high party voting records. Rather, they have been distributed to members whose party voting records have been moderately better than average.[63]

The absence of much positive relationship between advancement to significant legislative offices and party voting loyalty in the American parties coincides with a similar relationship between career survival and party voting loyalty. In the American parties, seldom has a legislator's party voting record been especially important to his renomination by his district party. In fact, the charge may be made, for example against a Democrat in the South, that a legislator has been *too* loyal to the national party position. Thus, in some instances party loyalty has become an issue *against* the incumbent. It has taken an unusual degree of deviation by a legislator from a typical or near typical Democratic constituency for party disloyalty to become an issue.[64]

Quite often, as a matter of fact, nomination or renomination of Congressional candidates has not even been entirely in the hands of the local party organization. It has been controlled through direct primaries in many of the American states. The significance of this method of renomination is that it has enabled incumbents to defy the organization's wrath; it has freed them from the party's discipline.[65]

This is not to say that loyalty to the legislative party has played no role in securing renomination or in gaining reelection. For example, Congressional party leaders have been able to help their party's members through committee assignments (see Chapter 5) and the passage of particular pieces of legislation of importance to the member's district. If the President was of the member's party, he could also be helpful in placing contracts and subsidies or patronage in the member's district. Such favors have been dispensed *partly* on the criterion of voting loyalty and may also have helped to heighten loyalty after a member received such favors.[66] For these reasons and others, such as party identification, party members have not voted against the party without serious consideration. As one southern Democrat said, "I try to find some way to be with the party. You like to be approved by the head of the family. You like to be remembered in the last will and testament."[67]

Nevertheless, party leaders recognize that the help they can give is often indirect and that members may well find it politically advisable to vote against the party. It has rarely been thought to be wrong for a member to act according to his perception of his constituency's welfare even if doing so led him to vote against his party in Congress. Thus, Joe Martin, when he was floor leader of the Republican party in the House, said: "Unless it was absolutely necessary, I never asked a man to side with me if his vote would hurt him in his district."[68]

The relevance of local political considerations to the career survival of American Congressmen applies not only to the problem of renomination but also to the problem of reelection. Congressmen and Senators, even of the President's party, have generally been quite free from him in regard to reelection. The coattails of the President may have had some bearing on members from marginal districts, but they have been less relevant to the reelection of most other Congressmen.[69]

Moreover, the effect of the President's coattails has varied rather greatly from election to election.[70] For example, consider the extent to which Congressional candidates of the winning Presidential party fared better, facing the same opposing candidate, during the Presidential election as compared to the preceding off-year election. We examined all House races from 1946 to 1968, covering a total of six Presidential elections. In only two of these six elections (1948 and 1968) did the incumbents of the *winning* Presidential party, facing the same candidate they had two years before, fare appreciably better, in a statistical sense, during the Presidential election than they had in the off-year election. In only three of the six elections (1948, 1956, and 1964) did nonincumbents of the winning Presidential party fare better than they had two years previously.

All in all, this suggests that the President may have coattails, but if he does, his coattails are very uneven from election to election. This is illustrated perhaps most strikingly by the results of the 1972 elections in which, despite President Nixon's landslide victory, the Republican party actually lost two seats in the Senate. Consistent with this fact of American political life, interviews with Congressmen show that most Congressmen themselves believe that their reelection back home is strongly a function of their own individual standing and record.[71]

The dependence of legislators on their own records to secure reelection back home has been greater for American Congressmen and Senators than for any of the other legislators we have examined, including the CDU/CSU members. Electoral patterns indicate that the individual CDU/CSU candidate has had little effect on the popular vote he obtained in his bid for election or reelection. Voters have not typically voted for the individual candidate outside the context of the national party and the national party leadership. While renomination of a CDU/CSU member may be affected by local considerations, his reelection has been almost entirely a function of the national appeal of the party and its leadership.[72]

This has also been the case for legislative members in the three other parliamentary parties. In Great Britain, for example, the level of national popular support for the parties has dominated constituency races to such an extent that it is a rule of thumb that the individual MP can personally influence the outcome in his constituency by only about five hundred votes (about 1 percent).[73] Similarly, Philip Williams has observed about the loyalty of the Gaullists to their national leadership: "The UNR deputies, like British MPs, usually voted with the government because they believed in its policies or because their constituents *sent* them to Parliament to support it . . . ."[74] Summed up by a Gaullist in perhaps too extreme but still essentially correct fashion, Michel Habib-Deloncle commented in the early 1960s, "Our deputies have been elected on one equation: UNR = de Gaulle."[75]

Let us briefly recapitulate. In examining the relationship between support for party and the achievement of career aspirations, we have taken the legislator's renomination, reelection, and advancement to higher office into account. The findings reported for the six legislative parties indicate a pattern which is consistent with our proposition that the more support for a party and its leadership helps legislators maximize the achievement of their career ambitions, the more they vote with their party. The three parties in which legislators have voted most cohesively are the Conservative, Labour, and Gaullist parties. These are the parties in which the achievement of career ambitions has been tied most closely both to the fortunes of the national party and to evidences of party loyalty. The members of the CDU/CSU have voted at a more moderate level of cohesion, and the achievement of career ambitions has been tied less to party support in the CDU/CSU than in the Conservative, Labour, and Gaullist parties. Finally, the achievement of career ambitions has been least dependent upon party support in the Democratic and Republican parties, and we observed voting cohesion to be at its lowest level in these two parties.

Earlier we alluded to Martin Redmayne's point about the significance of this variable for party voting. When he was chief whip for the Conservative-controlled government, he said of his party's backbenchers, "the hope of office is an incentive to give support to the government."[76] Although the leaders may understand and forgive a backbencher who opposes for good reason, the definition of "good reason" still remains in the hands of the leaders. It is they who control offices, and loyalty is an important consideration in their distribution of offices. As we have seen, a backbencher who rebels more than once may find himself in trouble, and the chief or junior whip can quietly remind him of this, if the need is there, before the division takes place. The difficulty a leader faces in maintaining party voting unity in an American Congressional party, on the other hand, was admirably indicated by a former leader when he said, "I didn't have anything to threaten them with."[77] While this perhaps understates the power available to Congressional party leaders, it is a rather accurate description of the position of American legislative party leaders in contrast especially to the position leaders have had in both British parties and the French Gaullist party.

However, even a leader of the Conservative, Labour, or Gaullist parties may have more difficulty with some of his followers than with others. For instance, a leader cannot make promotion seem terribly plausible if a member has repeatedly been passed by on previous occasions or if, for other reasons, the member feels his chances for promotion are slight. Were career aspirations important, we would expect that the members who feel their chances for promotion are slight would be less amenable to following the party leadership into the lobbies than would the remainder of the party members whose chances for promotion appear to be greater. This hypothesis is of sufficient interest that we wish to discuss it and the evidence relating to it in detail. We will do so in the following chapter in an examination of the Conservative backbenchers. Evidence presented there is quite consistent with the hypothesis. Thus, the rebels in the Conservative parliamentary party appear to have come disproportionately from the ranks of its members who either had previously been passed by or who had other reasons for feeling that they had little chance of gaining promotion.

Political Structure and Role Orientation

Our discussion thus far has considered party voting unity in the context of policy cleavages within the parties and legislators' policy attitudes, party identification, and achievement of career goals. These factors will be followed up in combination in the summary. At this juncture, we need to examine the possible effects of the type of political system in which legislators operate (the parliamentary as contrasted to the separation of powers system) and, alongside this consideration, take up evidence dealing with legislators' role orientations.

Party voting can be shaped by the kind of political structures that surround the legislators and within which legislators must operate. One feature of the political structure that may be quite significant for party voting is the type of political system. The significance of the type of political system for party voting has been summarized by Leon Epstein, who differentiated the effects of parliamentary and separation-of-powers systems:

The individual legislators of a governing (or potentially governing) party have an entirely rational motivation for cohesion in a parliamentary system that they do not have under the separation of powers. Each parliamentary vote on an important policy involves the question of whether the MP wants a cabinet of his party or of the opposition. Thus each vote becomes a party vote in a sense politically meaningful to the individual MP. . . .

No such incentive operates with sufficient force to impel American Congressmen, under the separation of powers, to be so cohesive (although Congressional party voting is by no means entirely uncohesive in degree or frequency.)[78]

The experience of the CDU/CSU suggests the effect a parliamentary system can have on the voting cohesion a legislative party achieves. On the basis of the way in which career rewards have been distributed by the party, the extent to which especially strong feelings of identity with the party have been present, and the cleavages over policy direction that have existed within the party, one would expect members of the CDU/CSU to have had a rather difficult time maintaining voting unity. And, indeed, its party voting record *has* been lower than that of the members of both British parties and the French Gaullists. At the same time, members of the CDU/CSU have maintained a markedly higher level of voting cohesion than have members of the American Congressional parties. One of the chief differences between the CDU/CSU and the American legislative parties is that CDU/CSU members have operated under a parliamentary system, whereas members of Congress have not. CDU/CSU members constantly had to achieve some semblance of party voting unity if they were to maintain a government of their party (or if they were to undermine an SPD controlled government). A major defeat of governmental policy on the floor of the Bundestag or several lesser defeats indicating that the government had lost its majority and would face further reversals would likely have led the government either to resign or to arrange for dissolution of the Bundestag. Indeed, each of the legislative parties we examined whose members maintained comparatively high or moderate levels of voting cohesion operated within a parliamentary context.

If a parliamentary system is to encourage party voting unity, however, it can do so only by building on the legislators' own goals and attitudes. Whether the legislator wants a cabinet of his party or of the opposition is a question that frequently arises in a parliamentary system but does not arise in a separation-of-powers system. The legislator is put in the position of weighing the salience a particular issue has for him against the importance for him of his party maintaining or gaining power. Therefore, the effectiveness of a parliamentary system in producing party voting cohesion depends upon the strength of the ties members have to their party.

These ties may be seen partly as a function of the various dispositions we discussed above. One obvious tie is that a legislator can enhance his career more easily if his party is in power than if it is not, but this is not necessarily the only politically meaningful disposition. Party identification can also be of importance. Then, too, there are the policy commitments of the members and the overall preference we have seen most members have for the policy direction of their party in comparison to the policy direction of the alternative party. In this regard, a parliamentary system can provide an increased incentive for party voting on an issue among potentially dissident members if the members feel that their differences with the particular policies of their party are less significant than the differences that separate their party from the opposition party on other issues.

One example of the effect the dispositions we examined can have on party voting cohesion in a parliamentary context is the Parliamentary Labour Party. We have seen that the Parliamentary Labour Party is divided into wings whose members espouse different policy views. The left-wing group has been particularly dissident. Nevertheless, because legislative voting in a parliamentary system can determine which party controls the government, party members may have to decide whether their attachment to the general policy objectives of their party (as compared to those of the alternative party) and their identification with their party are more critical to them than the differences they may have with their party or party leaders on any single issue or even set of issues. Despite their disenchantment with some of the policies of the PLP and the lower probability they have had of achieving governmental rewards, it is likely that even most left-wing members have stood to gain more in light of their overall policy objectives[79] and feelings of party identification by working to maintain or achieve a Labour government in preference to the Conservative alternative. To do this required that members of the left wing limit the extent and perhaps also the number of their rebellions, for the price of defeating their party might have been to enable the Conservatives either to gain or to sustain power.

All of this appears to be well recognized by the left wing itself. When Labour was in power, Michael Foot, one of the leaders of the left wing, said that none of the left-wing rebellions "has threatened to destroy the Government. [The left wing] knows how damaging that could be to the whole future of the Labour Party and the broader Labour movement."[80]

Considerations such as these would appear also to apply to the CDU/CSU. It is true that there are many subgroups of members in the CDU/CSU parliamentary party which have repeatedly come into conflict regarding particular policy sectors. Nevertheless, Barnes and Farah found through questioning Bundestag members that, in general, policy differences among CDU/CSU deputies have been less marked than those that divided CDU/CSU deputies from the SPD. They concluded: "It is clear that in general there is substantial agreement within the parties and substantial disagreement between them. Some of these differences lead to such unanimity on the part of the deputies that there is little or no variance to be explained."[81] Thus, except in the area of foreign policy, where members from both parties held rather similar attitudes, most CDU/CSU members agreed with the policy positions of their colleagues more so than they agreed with the policy positions and direction taken by the SPD. Given these policy ties (as well as other dispositions, such as career ambition), it is likely that the parliamentary context has served as an added incentive for members to support their party despite their disenchantment with party policy on a particular issue or a particular set of issues, for by voting to defeat their party might well have either brought in or helped maintain the SPD.[82]

Apart from the various dispositions already considered, there is another that may also be relevant in this context. This has to do with the role concepts of the legislators. To what extent do members feel it is their proper role to support their party and its leadership? Unfortunately, there is not as yet a great deal of evidence on legislators' role attitudes. What evidence is available on the parliamentary European parties we have considered deals primarily with the British parties and the French Gaullists. The evidence suggests that in the case of these parties many legislators have viewed support for their party in legislative battles to be both a proper and significant component of their parliamentary role.

Let us first take up the Gaullists by citing some of their major ideas and then reviewing supporting survey evidence. Urging a return to the administrative state, a number of Gaullists have accented the idea of strong government through which, and only through which, France could attain her greatness and her destiny. As a consequence, these Gaullists have emphasized the importance of maintaining unity within the parliamentary party. They saw a major consequence of disunity to be the return of the Fourth Republic's divisive legislative system and the "parties of yesterday," which they abhorred.[83] They also viewed the desire to "return to the pattern of the Fourth Republic" as the major factor that linked the anti-Gaullist parties.[84]

A return to the system and parties of yesterday, however, could be prevented only by the establishment of a stable government. For these Gaullists, then, the role of the parliamentary members became one primarily of supporting a stable government controlled by the Gaullist party. Toward this end, they urged the view that discipline should be "the primary quality required of the Gaullist deputy, cohesion the first objective assigned to the parliamentary party."[85]

This conception of the parliamentarian's role coincided with a theory of elections and of the electoral mandate. According to this theory, it was the Gaullist President and his policies that produced election victories and gained the popular mandate. If Gaullist parliamentarians were to be true to this mandate, the role of the parliamentarian needed to be one of supporting the President and the government that the President helped to select. As Habib-Deloncle put it, parliamentarians in Great Britain "do not seek to follow a doctrine of their own; their doctrine is the policy of the Government."[86] Under the Fifth Republic, members of the government party in the legislature ought to play a similar role. As this remark suggests, in developing their philosophy of the proper role of the legislator, a number of Gaullists have been influenced by their perceptions of the way the British system operates. To them, including many left-wing Gaullists, this meant that the Assembly should not only be supportive of Gaullist executive leadership; it also meant that "the legislature could no longer remain primarily a market-place where [interest] groups bargained and negotiated."[87]

It is little surprise, then, that surveys of Assembly members from different parties have found that Gaullist parliamentarians, more than most, look upon supporting party leaders and the executive as integral to the role of a parliamentarian. Such views have been found dominant in the Gaullist ranks.[88] Suggestive also is a comparison of Gaullist deputies to members of Congress. When asked whether they should support an important party bill even at the cost of some support in their constituencies, almost 80 percent of the Gaullist deputies interviewed thought they should support the party.[89] When American Congressmen were asked a similar question (with similar alternatives), only 35 percent of the Congressmen thought they should support the party.[90] The contrast in the responses of the Gaullist and American legislators speaks for itself.

The role conceptions to which we have referred appear to have lasted beyond the period of de Gaulle's own Presidency. Thus, Charlot commented in 1971: "The men have changed, de Gaulle himself has departed, but the philosophy concerning the power of the state, of parliament, and of the majority party remains the same as it was in 1962 and earlier in the new institutional context of the Fifth Republic."[91] Even the staunchest supporters of de Gaulle, men like Michel Debré, argued after de Gaulle's departure that the parliamentary party should be united behind its new President, Georges Pompidou, and his premier.[92]

Conceptions of the legislator's role in Conservative and Labour (particularly Socialist) theories of politics, although not documented by surveys, have been the subject of other scholarly analysis. Certain conceptions that are quite relevant to the point at hand have been nicely summarized by Samuel Beer and we will begin by briefly reviewing his presentation. In his discussion of the Conservative approach, Beer observes that the British system has not ordinarily been viewed as one "in which the active and originating element has been the voter, selecting a delegate to express his views in Parliament."[93] Rather, the voter chooses a government by electing a team of leaders heading a political party. The electoral or popular mandate is given to this team of party leaders and not to the individual parliamentarian. As a consequence, it is thought that the role of the parliamentarian of the governing party is to support the team of leaders the voters selected. Thus, Beer argues that by focusing the electoral mandate on the party leadership, the Conservative conception emphasizes party cohesion ordinarily based on the policies of the leadership.

The Socialist theory of elections attaches somewhat greater importance to the party as an electoral unit and to the parliamentarian as an agent of the party. In the Socialist view, Beer observes, the basic interests that compete for representation are social groups and "primarily the two major classes of industrial society."[94] It is the clash of differing class interests that defines the electoral battle. As in Conservative thought, an election does not result in individual parliamentarians being given a mandate. Rather, it results in a party representing a social class being given a mandate. Thus, the parliamentarians' electoral mandate is not thought to be a local mandate or one given to him individually, but rather a party mandate.[95] The role of the parliamentarian becomes, in essence, that of a party delegate.[96] Moreover, insofar as concerns the leaders within the parliamentary party, their role is to assure that the coherence of programs and policies gains acceptance in Parliament. To make certain this governing function is met, there needs to be unity of action among Labour parliamentarians. Beer alludes to this leadership role in Socialist and Labour thought more widely by pointing out that "a Socialist Government will need such control over its majority as will enable it to prevent amendments that muddle the purpose of a bill."[97]

The emphasis that not only the Labour view, but also the Conservative view, places on the governing function has implications for the role of parliamentarians in each of the parties and works to reinforce the conception that a basic component of the role of the party's parliamentarians is, at least in the end, one of acting cohesively as a unit. For, to govern effectively requires that members of the governing party maintain "effective unity." This is not only a role others expect of the parliamentarian but likely a role to which most parliamentarians ascribe themselve. To quote Epstein:

Each major British party, Conservative and Labour, maintains effective unity in its parliamentary ranks so that it is able,when a majority, to maintain a government in office, and able, when in opposition, to demonstrate its capacity to maintain a govenment if it became a majority. . . . [This] is a norm that is not seriously questioned even by the M.P.s who deviate from it. They and their leaders view parliamentary party cohesion as the essence of the contemporary British system.[98]

This does not mean that parliamentarians in no way attempt to influence the making of policy, but in the end the role of the parliamentarian is to support the parliamentary party. As Epstein noted, most parliamentarians accept this role. Extrapolating from his findings on the Canadian system, Kornberg similarly concluded: "In a parliamentary system of the British model concerted party action is part of the behavior ascribed to the legislative position. Thus, the individual legislator in such a system takes office expecting, and knowing significant others expect, that he will maintain party unity."[99]

To recapitulate, we have argued that the presence of a parliamentary setting can work to increase the incentives for the members of a parliamentary party to support their party. In so doing, a parliamentary system can place additional pressures on party members to close ranks and vote together. As observed earlier, each of the legislative parties we considered with comparatively high or moderate levels of voting cohesion operated within a parliamentary context. At the same time, to understand the party-unifying effect a parliamentary system can have, it is necessary to take into consideration the goals and attitudes, or dispositions, of the legislators and how these orient members toward their legislative party. Various dispositions are relevant. Pertinent here alongside career ambitions are members' role concepts and policy views (normative concerns) as well as their affective attachments. Indeed, there is growing evidence to suggest that affective and normative dispositions are for the usual member at least as determinative a source of voting loyalty as is career ambition.[100]

Because the members' own dispositions are critical, it may well be that the party-unifying effect of a parliamentary system works principally in regard to members of major legislative parties rather than to small or third parties. This is an important distinction. If a party's short-term potential to control the government alone or to dominate a coalition government is rather slim, this may alter the calculations parliamentarians make and diminish the effect a parliamentary setting can have on party voting cohesion. In this vein, Woshinsky has argued that were the size of the Gaullist party to decline appreciably in the Assembly, "especially to the point where they could no longer form the Government," fractionalization of the party could occur. One reason is that those members motivated primarily by career ambitions might desert the party and move to more successful parties. Also, doctrinal disputes within a Gaullist party unable to form a government could well prompt members motivated primarily by ideological considerations to defect and to form a new party.[101]

Party Organization

When the political context (such as the parliamentary system) places pressure on members of a party to act together despite the policy cleavages that divide them internally, we might expect the party to develop a more elaborate organization than would be the case when such pressures are less apparent, for the party will need instruments, which organization can provide, to facilitate the maximization of internal unity. As a consequence, we might expect that the parliamentary parties we have examined would be more highly organized internally than would legislative parties operating under a separation-of-powers system.

In looking to see whether our parliamentary parties have organized themselves to a higher degree than have the Congressional parties, we can refer back to our summary of party organization found in Chapter 2. As we observed in that chapter, each of the four European parties has been organized to a rather high degree. Two particular similarities emerged among the parliamentary parties. First, the equivalent of the caucus of each parliamentary party met quite frequently, at least once every other week and often once weekly. Second, there were numerous mechanisms besides the caucus to facilitate intraparty communication and interaction. For example, each of the parliamentary parties contained a series of specialized policy committees. In addition, each either had a large, representative, and well-organized legislative leadership structure separate from the cabinet leadership of the party or had a highly developed whip system that provided means for backbench views to flow to the leadership.

The relevance of such party organization to developing party voting unity is perhaps best revealed by the experience of the CDU/CSU. As our previous analysis has suggested, the various forces promoting party supportive behavior by CDU/CSU members, while not insubstantial, have not been as strong as in the cases of the three other European parties. On the other hand, partly because of those forces which did promote party-oriented behavior (and probably especially the parliamentary system), the CDU/CSU parliamentary party organized itself to a very high degree and its members made extensive use of this organization.[102] Constant interchange prevailed between the parliamentary party's executive committee, selected deliberately to represent the different groupings within the parliamentary party, and the specialized policy committees (work groups) of the caucus, which were themselves highly active. Loewenberg concludes that, partly as a consequence both of this collaboration and of the representativeness of the executive committee, the caucus adopted approximately 85 to 90 percent of the policy recommendations made to it by the executive committee.[103] His analysis also indicates that, without extensive use of its elaborate internal organization to work out consensus among the members, it is unlikely that the CDU/CSU parliamentary party would have been able to maintain the cohesion it did.[104]

The relevant point here is not only how highly a party is organized, but also how much its members can or are willing to use the internal mechanisms to communicate their views and settle their differences. In this regard, it is of interest to note differences that appear to have existed among the three parties of highest voting cohesion. Evidence on these parties indicates that members of the Conservative parliamentary party, the most consistently cohesive of the three parties (see Table 4.10 at the end of this chapter), tended to use intraparty mechanisms with somewhat greater regularity than did members of the Labour and Gaullist parties. Thus, Lynskey found that Conservative backbenchers went outside the parliamentary party organization to make their case public before the leadership (government) published its proposals on only two of the fourteen cases (14 percent) of dissidence he examined.[105] On the other hand, he found that Labour backbenchers went outside the parliamentary party organization somewhat more quickly. They did so on seven of eighteen cases (39 percent) he examined. [106] Insofar as concerns the Gaullist party, Charlot found in the mid-1960s that around half of the fifteen specialized committees then operative within the parliamentary party were not especially active.[107]

However, despite such differences among these three European parties, and the meaning they possibly have for cohesion in these parties, both the level of organization and the degree of organizational activity within each of the parties, as well as within the CDU/CSU, have been substantially greater than that found in the parties in either house of Congress. While rudiments of internal organization have been present in each of the Congressional parties, and undoubtedly have contributed to voting cohesion, organization has neither been as elaborate nor utilized as much as in the other parties under examination. The legislative parties of the United States have their own caucuses, for example, but until recently these caucuses met infrequently and irregularly, rarely more than three or four times a session. Even the general policy committees of the parties have met irregularly. It has not been unusual for this committee to meet at intervals of two months or more. Moreover, neither party has established a set of specialized policy committees, which all of the other parties have. Unlike the European parties, then, the organization that has functioned in a regularized manner in the American parties has generally been limited mainly to a handful of leaders and the whip system.

It is true that the rather low level of organization that has characterized parties in the Congress may have been due to the comparative absence of other forces motivating party-supportive behavior. On the other hand, where these other forces have been stronger, it is likely that the availability and use of an elaborate party organization has itself been a factor that contributed to party cohesion. Not only could such an organization serve members to help bring about agreement among conflicting viewpoints, which was in some cases its basic function, but it could also help to draw greater support from the remaining dissidents through the perception that they were given reasonable opportunity to express and to make their views felt on their party colleagues.[108]

Summary

A few conclusions are now in order. In broad outline, our examination of the behavior of legislators towards party has viewed behavior as resultant from certain goals and purposes of the legislators in combination with the political setting in which they operate. The types of goals and purposes brought into the analysis have included career ambitions, affective feelings of identification, and normative policy and role outlooks. As elements of the political setting, we examined especially the criteria employed in the system for distributing career rewards to members, the type of political system (parliamentary versus separation of powers), and the level and use of organization within the legislative party.

The sources of voting unity in the six legislaiave parties covered in our analysis appear to be many and diverse. We have seen that the struggle to achieve unity in most of the parties has taken place in the context of persistent cleavages among the members over policies the party should follow and that the success parties achieved in maintaining unity was associated to some extent with the level of cleavage within the party. Our analysis also presented evidence on several of the cleavages indicating they were generated partly by conflicts in the members' own policy predispositions.

At the same time, it is likely that the fractionalizing effect of persistent policy cleavages among members within a major party can be offset or muted by a combination of other factors. Thus, we found that parties tended to respond cohesively when they contained a sizable core of legislative members with backgrounds encouraging heightened feelings of identification with the party; when and to the extent members' achievement of their career ambitions would be served by remaining loyal to the national party leadership; when the political structure in which the members operated was a parliamentary system (thereby raising the costs of defeating the party to the extent that members' career ambitions, feelings of identification, or normative policy and role outlooks oriented and tied them to their own party); and when organizational channels of communication within the legislative party were both elaborate and utilized with some frequency.

The evidence presented in the analysis suggests that each of these conditions was, in essence, present in the three parliamentary parties that maintained the highest level of voting cohesion, regardless of the differing levels of persistent policy cleavage that were observed within these parties. These parties are the Conservative, Labour, and Gaullist parties. Furthermore, within contexts of persistent cleavages among the legislative party members, as the four conditions were relaxed, legislators' voting deviated more from party and party unity declined. The case of the CDU/CSU parliamentary party (a party of moderate voting cohesion) and of the American Congressional parties (parties of low voting cohesion) serve as examples.

Although lower than for the other parties, we emphasize the fact that voting unity among members of the American Congressional parties was by no means absent. As we observed at the outset of this chapter, party has been a rather significant correlate of voting behavior even in the Congress. Also, while members of other parties maintained higher levels of voting cohesion, even the most cohesive of these parties experienced some significant voting rebellions. An understanding of how and why legislators behave the way they do toward their party must consider voting loyalty from these perspectives as well. It is with this purpose in mind that our analysis of party voting continues in the next chapter.

Table 4.10
The Voting Cohesion of Twelve Legislative and Parliamentary Parties From the United States, Great Britain, France, and West Germany

Party	Level of Voting Cohesion	Percentage Voting Cohesion[a]	Periods[b]
Communist (Fr)	I	99, 99, 99, 99, 99	46-51, 51-55, 55-58, 63, 66-68
Conservative (Br)	I	99, 99, 99, 99, 99	51-55, 55-59, 59-64, 64-66, 66-68
Gaullists (Fr)	I	86[c], 99, 97	51-53, 63, 66-68
Labour (Br)	I	98, 99, 99, 95	46-50, 59-64, 64-66, 66-68
Socialists (Fr)	I	97, 97, 96, 99, 99	46-51, 51-55, 55-59, 63, 66-68
SPD (WG)	I	99, 97, 99	53-57, 57-61, 61-65
Catholics (Fr)	II	90, 79, 91, 50[c], 47[c]	46-51, 51-55, 55-59, 63, 66-68
CDU/CSU (WG)	II	85, 93, 78	53-57, 57-61, 61-65
FDP (WG)	II	72, 96, 78	53-57, 57-61, 61-65
Democrat (USA-House-Senate)	III	below 67	49-70, yearly
Radical (Fr)	III	56, 61, 43, 85[c], 90[c]	46-51, 51-55, 55-59, 63, 66-68
Republican (USA-House-Senate)	III	below 67	49-70, yearly

[a]Numerals under "voting cohesion" refer to the percentage of roll call votes upon which 90 percent or more of the legislative party voted with the party. The numeral 99 means at least 99 percent and up to and including 100 percent. Legislative party refers to backbenchers in Great Britain and roll call votes to two- or three-line whipped divisions. Figures for France from 1945 to 1958 are from Duncan MacRae, Jr., *Parliament, Parties, and Society in France, 1946-1958* (New York: St. Martin's Press, 1967), p. 56, fourth column on Table 3.6. For the figures we compiled, deviation by abstention, where known, was included for the European parties.

[b]Numbers indicate the years, each referring to its respective numeral under "voting cohesion."

[c]Figures so designated deviate from the level of voting cohesion ascribed to the party.

Notes

[1]Citations of some general works dealing with political parties may be found in the bibliographical section at the end of the book.
[2]See also Julius Turner, *Party and Constituency; Pressures on Congress*, rev. ed. Edward Schneier, Jr. (Baltimore, Md.: Johns Hopkins Press, 1970), Chapter 2, for another discussion of legislative party cohesion in France, Germany, Britain, Canada, New Zealand, and Australia.
[3]The selected years were 1947, 1948, 1953, 1959, 1961, 1965, and 1970.
[4]*Congressional Quarterly* selects an average of ten to fifteen roll call votes per House per year which it considers to be important or key votes of that year. The key votes are published annually in both the *Congressional Quarterly Weekly Reports* and the *Congressional Almanac* (Washington, D.C.).
[5]See also Turner, *Party and Constituency*, pp. 16-20, 33-37; and W. Wayne Shannon, *Party, Constituency and Congressional Voting* (Baton Rouge, La.: Louisiana State University Press, 1968), Chapter 3. If we examine all roll calls, the percent of votes upon which a majority of one party opposed a majority of the other markedly declines. From 1968 to 1974, the average was 36 percent.
[6]This is based on *Congressional Quarterly's* composite "Party Unity Scores" and "Opposition to Party Scores." Totals do not add up to 100 percent since failure to vote lowers both scores.
[7]Turner, *Party and Constituency*, Ch. 3. A similar conclusion has been reached by use of a variety of research methodologies. See David Mayhew, *Party Loyalty Among Congressmen* (Cambridge, Mass.: Harvard University Press, 1966); Aage Clausen, *How Congressmen Decide: A Policy Focus* (New York: St. Martin's Press, 1973), pp. 87-118; and John L. Sullivan and Robert E. O'Connor, "Electoral Choice and Popular Control of Public Policy: The Case of the 1966 House Elections," *American Political Science Review* 66 (December 1972): 1256-69.
[8]Readers are referred to the ranking of Congressmen on the liberal Americans for Democratic Action (ADA) index and the conservative Americans for Constitutional Action (ACA) index. These are found each year in the *Congressional Quarterly Weekly Reports*.
[9]Julius Turner, *Party and Constituency Pressures on Congress* (Baltimore, Md.: Johns Hopkins Press, 1951) pp. 23, 145. Turner perhaps overstates the case by using the term "pressure." At this point in our discussion, we are concerned with citing the degree of cohesion and differences on issues in American legislative parties. There are many other works that find party to be of significance. See, for example, David Truman, *The Congressional Party* (New York: John Wiley and Sons, 1959); Donald Matthews, *U. S. Senators and Their World* (New York: Random House, 1960), Chapter 6; Randall Ripley, *Party Leaders in the House of Representatives* (Washington, D. C.: The Brookings Institution, 1967), especially Chapter 6 and Appendix A; Roger Davidson, *The Role of the Congressman* (New York: Pegasus, 1969), Chapter 5; and, Duncan MacRae, *Dimensions of Congressional Voting* (Berkeley and Los Angeles: University of California Press, 1958).
[10]Since our analysis of party voting covers major or large parties, our conclusions will not necessarily apply in the same way to small (third) parties such as the Liberal party in Great Britain or the West German Liberal party (FDP). For further discussion of this point, see pp. 149. In addition, our analysis of party voting is confined to systems which contain at least one major party. As a consequence, our conclusions will pertain to this type of system and not necessarily to systems in which there is no major party.
[11]See, for example, Sullivan and O'Connor, "Electoral Choice and Popular Control of Public Policy"; Allan Kornberg and Robert C. Frasure, "Policy Differences in British Parliamentary Parties," *American Political Science Review* 65 (September 1971): 694-703; Samuel H. Barnes and Barbara Farah, "National Representatives and Constituency Attitudes in Germany and Italy" (Paper presented at the 1972 Annual Meeting of the American Political Science Association, Washington, D.C.); Jeff Fishel, "Parliamentary Candidates and Party Professionalism in Western Germany," *Western Political Quarterly* 25 (March 1972): 64-80; and William H. Hunt, "Legislative Roles and Ideological Orientations of French Deputies" (Paper presented at the 1969 Annual Meeting of the American Political Science Association, New York) pp. 9-11.
[12]According to Joseph Cooper and Gary Bombardier's study, "Presidential Leadership and Party Success," *Journal of Politics* (November 1968), the party loyalty scores of southern Democrats have "declined steadily and substantially over the past decade" (p. 1022). See also Shannon, *Party, Constituency, and Congressional Voting*, especially p. 174.
[13]Malcolm Jewell and Samuel Patterson, *The Legislative Process in the United States* (New York: Random House, 1966), p. 434.
[14]Several studies indicate that northern Democrats are more cohesive than either Republicans or southern Democrats. See, for example, Shannon, *Party, Constituency and Congressional Voting*, pp. 71-75. Hubert R. Fowler, *The Unsolid South* (Birmingham: University of Alabama: Bureau of Public Administration of University of Alabama, 1968), Chapter 1.
[15]H. Douglas Price, "Are Southern Democrats Different? An Application of Scale Analysis to Senate Voting Patterns," in *Politics and Social Life*, ed. Nelson W. Polsby, Robert Dentler, and Paul A. Smith (Boston: Hough Houghton Mifflin, 1963), p. 755.

For other discussions of northern Democrat southern Democrat differences on issues relating to civil rights, agricultural policy, social welfare, and foreign policy, including foreign aid and foreign trade, see: MacRae

Dimensions of Congressional Voting, (1958); Gerald Marwell, "Party, Region, and the Dimensions of Conflict in the House of Representatives, 1949-1954," *American Political Science Review* 61 (June 1967): 380-99; Charles Andrain, "A Scale Analysis of Senators' Attitudes Toward Civil Rights," *Western Political Quarterly* 17 (September 1964): 488-503; George Grassmuck, *Sectional Biases in Congress on Foreign Policy* (Baltimore, Md.: Johns Hopkins University Press, 1951); Leroy N. Rieselbach, *Roots of Isolationism* (Indianapolis, Ind.: Bobbs-Merrill, 1966); Shannon, *Party, Constituency and Congressional Voting*, Chapters 4 and 5; and Clausen, *How Congressmen Decide*, esp. p. 107.

[16] For the 1971 scores, see *Congressional Quarterly Weekly Report*, April 29, 1972, pp. 932-33.

[17] See Turner, *Party and Constituency* rev. ed., Chapter 7.

[18] Ripley, *Party Leaders in the House of Representatives*, p. 155.

[19] Leroy N. Rieselbach, "Congressional Vote on Foreign Aid, 1939-1958," *The Congressional System: Notes and Readings* (Belmont, Calif.: Wadsworth, 1970), pp. 372-88.

[20] S. E. Finer, H. B. Berrington, and D. J. Bartholomew, *Backbench Opinion in the House of Commons, 1955-1959* (Oxford: Pergamon Press, 1961), pp. 14-75. See also Richard Rose, *Politics in England* (Boston: Little, Brown and Company, 1964), pp. 145-46.

[21] Kornberg and Frasure, "Policy Differences in British Parliamentary Parties," p. 703.

[22] For the effect of the Algerian issue on cleavage from 1958 to 1962, see David M. Wood, "Majority vs. Opposition in the French National Assembly, 1958-1965. A Guttman Scale Analysis," *American Political Science Review* 62, (March 1968): 88-109; and Jean Charlot, *L'U.N.R.: Étude du pouvoir au sein d'un parti politique* (Paris: Armand Colin, 1967), pp. 58-84.

[23] While disagreeing on economic and social policy, these members supported the Gaullist conception of power and authority reflected in the Constitution of the Fifth Republic. Some also tended to align themselves with Gaullist foreign policy. A brief examination of divisions over policy within the Gaullist parliamentary party based on interviews also found division on economic and social questions. See William H. Hunt, "Legislative Roles and Ideological Orientations of French Deputies," p. 9.

[24] Finer, Berrington, and Bartholomew, *Backbench Opinion in the House of Commons*, p. 123.

[25] Kornberg and Frasure, "Policy Differences in British Parliamentary Parties," p. 702.

[26] Robert T. Holt and John E. Turner, "Change in British Politics: Labour in Parliament and Government," in *European Politics II: The Dynamics of Change*, ed. William G. Andrews (New York: Van Nostrand Reinhold Company, 1969), pp. 23-113. Based on their research, Holt and Turner observed: "Different ideological predispositions, contrasting class backgrounds, and varying socialization experiences lay the basis for potential disagreements over major policy in the organization" (p. 93).

[27] A "Conservative Coalition" vote is defined by *Congressional Quarterly* as a vote in which a majority of southern Democrats and a majority of Republicans vote in opposition to the stand taken by a majority of nonsouthern Democrats. Following is the percentage of recorded votes for both houses of Congress on which the Conservative Coalition appeared: 1961 (28); 1962 (14); 1963 (17); 1964 (15); 1965 (24); 1966 (25); 1967 (20); 1968 (24); 1969 (27); 1970 (22); 1971 (30); 1972 (27); 1973 (23); 1974 (24). From 1961 to 1974 the coalition was victorious on an average of about 63 percent of the times it formed. The lowest score was 25 percent in 1965.

[28] For example, the effect size of community has had on attitudes about conformity and civil liberties is shown in Samuel A. Stouffer, *Communism, Conformity, and Civil Liberties* (Garden City, N.Y.: Doubleday, 1955), p. 109. Stouffer found that people from small towns and rural areas were less tolerant of the civil rights of nonconformists than were people from larger towns and cities, even when region was held constant. For the connection between these attitudes about conformity and civil liberties and a conservative political ideology in general, see Herbert McClosky, "Conservatism and Personality," *American Political Science Review* 41 (March 1958): 33. The relationship between size of community and hard-line attitudes toward law and order is shown in Stephen E. Bennett and Alfred J. Tuchfarber, "The Social Structural Sources of Support for 'Hard-Line' Law and Order Policies" (Mimeographed paper, University of Cincinnati). For the relationship between size of community and extremist conservative ideology, see William Kornhauser, *The Politics of Mass Society* (New York: The Free Press, 1959), p. 144, and Seymour Martin Lipset, *Political Man* (Garden City, N.Y.: Doubleday, 1960), pp. 145-46 and 165.

[29] Leroy N. Rieselbach, "Congressmen as 'Small Town Boys': A Research Note," *Midwest Journal of Political Science* 14 (May 1970): 321-30. Rieselbach, too, regards size of birthplace to be an indicator of policy orientation along a conservative-liberal continuum. See Leroy N. Rieselbach, *Congressional Politics* (New York: McGraw-Hill, 1973), p. 272.

[30] Barbara Hinckley, *Stability and Change in Congress* (New York: Harper & Row, 1971), p. 56.

[31] John W. Kingdon, *Congressmen's Voting Decisions* (New York: Harper & Row, 1973), pp. 73,76.

[32] Kingdon, *Congressmen's Voting Decisions*, pp. 77-78.

[33] Finer, Berrington, and Bartholomew, *Backbench Opinion in the House of Commons*, p. 123.

[34] Matthews, *U.S. Senators and Their World*, p. 121.

[35] Ripley, *Party Leaders in the House of Representatives*, p. 141; also see pp. 197-99; Davidson, *The Role of the Congressman*, pp. 143-61.

[36] For example, see E. Stotland, "Identification with Persons and Groups" (Final report on Grant M-2423 to the National Institute of Mental Health, U.S. Public Health Service, October 1961). For the relationship between group orientation and conformity, see J. Thibaut and L. Strickland, "Psychological Set and Social

Conformity," *Journal of Personality* 25 (1956): 115-29. The connection between a person's background attributes (such as race, economic class, religion, or sex) and one's preference for other persons or groups sharing the same attributes has frequently been demonstrated. Some of the many studies are Bernice Neugarten, "Social Class and Friendship Among School Children," *American Journal of Sociology* 51 (1946): 305-313; T.M. Newcomb, "The Prediction of Interpersonal Attraction," *American Psychologist* 11 (1956): 575-86; and A. B. Hollingshead, *Elmtown's Youth* (New York: John Wiley and Sons, 1949).

[37] An excellent analysis of the class roots of the Conservative and Labour parties in the voting public can be found in David Butler and Donald Stokes, *Political Change in Britain: Forces Shaping Electoral Choice* (New York: St. Martin;s Press, 1969), pp. 65-94. In 1963, as an example, 79 percent of those persons identifying themselves as middle class expressed a preference for the Conservative party. On the other hand, 72 percent of those persons identifying themselves as working class expressed a preference for the Labour party (p. 63). See also Robert Alford, *Party and Society: The Anglo-American Democracies* (Chicago: Rand McNally, 1963).

[38] See both Butler and Stokes, *Political Change in Britain*, and Alford, *Party and Society*.

[39] For the similarity in the class structure of voters' party preferences in France and Great Britain, see Jean Charlot, *The Gaullist Phenomenon: The Gaullist Movement in the Fifth Republic* (London: George Allen and Unwin, 1971), pp. 71-73. For the occupations and family socioeconomic backgrounds of deputies, see Charlot, *L'UNR*, p. 197; William H. Hunt, "Careers and Perspectives of French Politicians" Ph.D. dissertation, Vanderbilt University, 1966, p. 73; and Roland Cayrol, *Le Député français* (Paris: Armand Colin, 1973), Chapter 3, especially p. 53.

[40] John E. Schwarz and Geoffrey Lambert, "Career Objectives, Group Feeling, and Legislative Party Voting Cohesion: The British Conservatives, 1959-1968," *Journal of Politics* 33 (May 1971): 404-6.

[41] For example, see Anthony Sampson, *Anatomy of Britain* (New York: Harper & Row, 1965), especially chapters 4, 5, 12, and 13, and Hugh Thomas, *The Establishment* (London: Anthony Blond, 1962).

[42] Byrum E. Carter, *The Office of Prime Minister* (London: Farber & Farber, Ltd. 1956), p. 145. Italics ours.

[43] Holt and Turner, "Change in British Politics," pp. 110-11.

[44] For comparisons of the societal rooting of parties in terms of the class voting structure of party preference in the United States and Great Britain (based on these we will then treat West Germany), see Robert Alford, *Party and Society*, especially p. 102. Alford found the class basis of parties to be decidedly lower in the United States than in Great Britain. By subtracting the percentage of nonmanual workers voting for the left party from the percentage of manual workers voting for the left party, Alford arrived at a class voting score of 40 for Great Britain (from 1952 to 1962) and of 16 for the United States. Using a similar measure for the CDU/CSU (percentage of workers subtracted from percentage of nonworkers supporting the CDU/CSU), we would calculate the class basis of CDU/CSU support to have ranged roughly around 15 to 22 for three elections we examined (1949, 1953, and 1965). Data on one or more of these elections can be found in Juan Linz, "Cleavage and Consensus in West German Politics: The Early Fifties," in *Party Systems and Voter Alignments: Cross National Perspectives*, ed. Seymour Martin Lipset and Stein Rokkan (New York: The Free Press, 1967), p. 287; and Lewis Edinger, *Politics in Germany* (Boston: Little, Brown and Co., 1968), p. 248.

[45] For backgrounds of Senators and Representatives by party, see Matthews, *U. S. Senators and Their World*, p. 36 and Davidson, *The Role of the Congressman*, p. 47.

[46] In this regard, aside from the comparisons we have offered, worthy of at least some mention is the long-run historical comparison that the voting unity of the British Conservative parliamentary party has itself increased since the first decade of this century, that is, since the full emergence in British politics of a decidedly contrasting socioeconomic party, the Labour party. Even though party voting had increased in the House of Commons during the latter half of the nineteenth century, by the first decade of the twentieth century the members of the Conservative parliamentary party still displayed only a moderate level of voting cohesion and a level quite comparable to that of the contemporary CDU/CSU. For comparable party voting scores, see Samuel H. Beer, *British Politics in the Collectivist Age* (New York: Alfred A. Knopf, 1966), p. 257 and Gerhard Loewenberg, *Parliament in the German Political System* (Ithaca, N. Y. : Cornell University Press, 1967), p. 357.

[47] Joseph A. Schlesinger, *Ambition and Politics: Political Careers in the United States* (Chicago: Rand McNally, 1966), p. 6. See also David Mayhew, *Congress: The Electoral Connection* (New Haven, Conn.: Yale University Press, 1974).

[48] Martin Redmayne and Norman Hunt, "The Power of the Whips," in *British Politics: People, Parties, and Parliament*, ed. Anthony King (Boston: D. C. Heath and Company, 1966), p. 145.

[49] Robert J. Jackson, *Rebels and Whips: An Analysis of Dissension, Discipline, and Cohesion in British Political Parties* (London: Macmillan, 1968), pp. 245-46.

[50] Redmayne and Hunt, "The Power of the Whips," p. 145.

[51] Schwarz and Lambert, "Career Objectives, Group Feeling, and Legislative Party Voting Cohesion," p. 402.

[52] Our examination of rebellions included all divisions upon which 5 percent or more of the Labour backbenchers rebelled (crossvoted or purposively abstained) as gleaned from newspaper accounts.

[53] Austin Ranney, *Pathways to Parliament: Candidate Selection in Britain* (London: Macmillan, 1965), pp. 129-93 and especially pp. 191-92. Michael Rusk, in a different study, found one exception, although here the

local association defended its position on the grounds that the MP had neglected his duties and not on grounds of the loyalty of the MP to the policies of the national party. See Michael Rush, *The Selection of Parliamentary Candidates* (London: Thomas Nelson and Sons, 1969), p. 163.

[54]Ranney, *Pathways to Parliament*, p. 281. See also Austin Ranney, "Candidate Selection and Party Cohesion in Britain and the United States," in *Approaches to the Study of Party Organization*, ed. William J. Crotty (Boston: Allyn and Bacon, 1968), pp. 138-58.

[55]On occasion, if a loyal member needed protection either to assure his renomination or his election, the central party has been able to locate a new constituency for the member. This has usually been done in cooperation with the local federation rather than by using force.

[56]Henry W. Ehrmann, *Politics in France* (Boston: Little, Brown, and Co., 1968), p. 232.

[57]Loewenberg, *Parliament in the German Political System*, p. 73.

[58]Karlheinz Kaufmann, Helmut Kohl, and Peter Molt, *Kandidaturen zum Bundestag* (Cologne: Kiepenheuer and Witsch, 1961), passim.

[59]Kaufmann, Kohl, and Molt, *Kandidaturen zum Bundestag*, pp. 69-70.

[60]George L. Rueckert and Wilder Crane, "CDU Deviancy in the German Bundestag," *Journal of Politics* 24 (August 1962): 479.

[61]See also Frank Dishaw, "Role Call Vote Deviancy of the CDU/CSU Fraktion," in *Sozialwissenshaftliches Jahrbuch für Politik*, ed. R. Wildenmann (Munich: Günter Olzog Verlag), p. 543.

[62]For a comparison of the party voting loyalty scores of committee chairmen to those of all party members, see George Goodwin, Jr., "The Seniority System in Congress," *American Political Science Review* 53 (June 1959): 427. Goodwin found that Democratic chairmen or ranking minority members had slightly lower party support scores than did the average Democrat and that Republican chairmen or ranking minority members had approximately the same party support scores as did the average Republican. For similar findings covering the period 1935-70, see Randall B. Ripley, *Congress: Process and Policy* (New York: Norton, 1975), p. 128.

[63]In distributing party leadership posts, weight has been given to selecting persons who were not closely identified with any wing or bloc within the party. See Matthews, *U. S. Senators and Their World*, Chapter 6, and Truman, *The Congressional Party*, Chapter 6.

[64]An example of this was Democratic Senator Frank Lausche's conservative voting record and high party opposition scores which helped lead to his defeat.

[65]Frank J. Sorauf, *Party Politics in America*, 2d ed. (Boston: Little, Brown, 1972), pp. 217-29.

[66]Of course, these kinds of favors have also been available to the parliamentary party leaders of governing parties in Britain, France, and West Germany. For a pointed illustration, see Nigel Nicolson, *People and Parliament* (London: Weidenfeld and Nicolson, 1958), p. 67.

[67]The quote is from Ripley, *Party Leaders in the House of Representatives*, p. 143.

[68]Cited by Louis Koenig, *Congress and the President* (Chicago: Scott, Foresman, 1965), p. 46. In chapters 5 and 9, we examine in detail the connection between party voting in Congress (both loyalty and deviation) and the districts Congressmen represent.

[69]See Warren E. Miller, "Majority Rule and the Representative System of Government," in *Cleavages, Ideologies and Party Systems: Contributions to Comparative Political Sociology*, ed. Erik Allardt and Yrjo Littunen (Helsinki: The Academic Bookstore, 1964), p. 364. Remember, however, that no more than 25 percent of all Congressmen are from marginal seats.

[70] Citations of literature on the Presidential coattails effect are found in Chapter 2, footnote 42.

[71]Donald E. Stokes and Warren E. Miller, "Party Government and the Salience of Congress," in *Elections and the Political Order* (New York: John Wiley and Sons, 1966), pp. 204-6. Nevertheless, the Presidency is a key political office, and actions by members of the President's party that prove embarrassing to him can prove harmful to the party's chances of retaining the Presidency. They can also spill over into Congressional elections. The sheer unpredictability may be sufficient to prompt legislators from the President's party to support the President when they can.

[72] Wolfgang Hirsh-Weber and Klaus Schütz, *Wähler und Gewählte* (Berlin: Verlag Franz Vahlen, 1957), and Lewis J. Edinger and Paul Luebke, Jr., "Grass-Roots Electoral Politics in the German Federal Republic," *Comparative Politics* 3 (July 1971): 463-98. As one analyst observed: "[the CDU/CSU has been] long inclined to present itself to the electorate through the image of its leaders." See George K. Romoser, "Change in West German Politics After Erhard's Fall," in *European Politics II:The Dynamics of Change*, ed. Eilliam G. Andrews (New York: Van Nostrand Reinhold Company, 1969), p. 209

[73]Anthony Barker and Michael Rush, *The Member of Parliament and His Information* (London: George Allen and Unwin, 1970, pp. 177-78.

[74]Philip M. Williams, *The French Parliament: Politics in the Fifth Republic* (New York: Praeger, 1968), p. 105. Emphasis ours. The same point is made by Nicolas Wahl in "The French Parliament: From Last Word to Afterthought," in *Lawmakers in a Changing World*, Elke Frank ed. (Englewood Cliffs, N. J.: Prentice-Hall, 1966), p. 57.

[75]Charlot, *L'U.N.R*, p. 89. An analysis of French opinion polls supporting this conclusion is set forth by Jean Charlot, *The Gaullist Phenomenon*, pp. 43-60.

[76]Redmayne and Hunt, "The Power of the Whips," p. 145.

[77]Matthews, *U. S. Senators and Their World*, p. 126.

[78] Leon D. Epstein, "A Comparative Study of Canadian Parties," *American Political Science Review* 58 (March 1964) : 56.
[79] See Kornberg and Frasure, "Policy Differences in British Parliamentary Parties," especially p. 703.
[80] *Tribune*, February 26, 1965. See also Michaëla Székely, "La Gauche travailliste et gouvernment Wilson," *Revue Française de Science Politique* 31 (June 1971): especially p. 587 and 613-14.
[81] Barnes and Farah, "National Representatives and Constituency Attitudes," p. 17. That Bundestag deputies also view there to be major ideological differences between the parties is documented in Fishel, "Parliamentary Candidates and Party Professionalism", pp. 75-76.
[82] The West German constitutional provision that a Bundestag vote against the government can require the government to resign only if the Bundestag is capable of forming a majority around a new government may give parliamentarians of the government party somewhat greater freedom of action than in a parliamentary setting where a defeat of the government on the floor would automatically cause the government to resign. Nevertheless, as we pointed out above, a major defeat of governmental policy on the floor of the Bundestag or several defeats on lesser issues indicating that the government had lost its majority and would face further reversals would likely have led the government to resign or to arrange for dissolution of the Bundestag.
[83] Evidence on these views is found in Charlot, *L'U.N.R*, pp. 293-94.
[84] Charlot, *L'U.N.R.*, p. 294.
[85] Charlot, *L'U.N.R.*, p. 144.
[86] Charlot, *L'U.N.R.*, p. 89.
[87] Philip M. Williams, *The French Parliament*, p. 115, referring to the views of André Philip, a left-wing Gaullist.
[88] See the findings and discussion in Oliver Woshinsky, *The French Deputy: Incentives and Behavior in the National Assembly* (Lexington, Mass: D. C. Heath, 1973), esp. pp. 69-72, 76-77, 105-6 and 177-79.
[89] Calculated from data gathered and made available to us by William H. Hunt. We wish to thank him.
[90] Davidson, *The Role of the Congressman*, p. 145 and p. 198.
[91] Charlot, *The Gaullist Phenomenon*, p. 126.
[92] Ibid.
[93] Samuel H. Beer, *British Politics in the Collectivist Age* (New York: Alfred A. Knopf, 1966), p. 96, quoting L. S. Amery.
[94] Beer, *British Politics in the Collectivist Age*, p. 83.
[95] Beer, *British Politics in the Collectivist Age*, p. 87. See also Kenneth Bradshaw and David Pring, *Parliament and Congress* (London: Constable and Co. Ltd, 1972), pp. 32-33.
[96] Beer, *British Politics in the Collectivist Age*, p. 87.
[97] Beer, p. 81. Nevertheless, unlike Conservative theory where the electoral mandate is thought to be given to the leaders, the mandate according to Socialist theory is thought to be given to the party that wins the election. As such, the power to make basic policy decisions could be considered to rest in the party as a whole, including the extraparliamentary party organization. But, the theory simultaneously conceives of elections as having also given the parliamentarians and their leaders a mandate not simply to carry out a concrete program, but also "to interpret what it means and how best to carry it out" (Beer, p. 89). The lack of precision in the Labour theory has led to some heated battles between and within the extraparliamentary party and the parliamentary party over which should be, in the end, the source of authority within the party.
[98] Leon D. Epstein, *Political Parties in Western Democracies* (New York: Praeger, 1967), pp. 318-19.
[99] Allan Kornberg, *Canadian Legislative Behavior: A Study of the 25th Parliament* (New York: Holt, Rinehart and Winston, 1967), p. 135.
[100] See Kornberg, *Canadian Legislative Behavior*; Fishel, "Party Professionalism in West Germany"; and Oliver H. Woshinsky, "How Incentives Shape Political Behavior: The Case of the French Deputies," (Paper delivered at the Annual Meeting of the American Political Science Association, September 1973). For example, Woshinsky, in studying the principal motives generating the behavior of individual French deputies, found political ambition or status motives to be dominant in the case of only 20 percent of the deputies in his sample. Ideological motives were principal to 38 percent of the deputies in his sample. Woshinsky called these "mission" deputies. The motive to solve problems and devise workable policy alternatives was dominant in the case of 28 percent of the deputies (called "program" deputies). Finally, deputies whose principal motive was broadly one of role conception, of seeking to live up to one's beliefs of how men should act (called "obligation" deputies), constituted 14 percent of the deputies. See Woshinsky, pp. 2-3. See also his *The French Deputy*.
[101] Woshinsky, "How Incentives Shape Political Behavior," pp. 26-27.
[102] See Loewenberg, *Parliament in the German Political System*, especially pp. 159-72, and Jürgen Domes, *Merheitsfraktion und Bundesregierung* (Cologne and Opladen: Westdeutscher Verlag, 1964).
[103] Loewenberg, *Parliament in the German Political System*, pp.170-72.
[104] Loewenberg, *Parliament in the German Political System*, p. 172.
[105] James J. Lynskey, "The Role of British Backbenchers in the Modification of Government Policy: The Issues Involved, the Channels Utilized, and the Tactics Employed" (Ph.D. diss. University of Minnesota, 1966). p. 43.
[106] Lynskey, "The Role of British Backbenchers in the Modification of Government Policy," p. 25.
[107] Charlot, *L'U.N.R.*, p. 165.
[108] On this, see also Kornberg, *Canadian Legislative Behavior*, pp. 132-33.

Chapter 5
Legislators and Their Political Parties: Another Perspective

In Chapter 4 we dealt mainly with differences in the levels of voting cohesion maintained by four European and the two Congressional parties. Here we will examine party voting from another perspective. Chapter 4 emphasized the comparatively low voting cohesion of the American Congressional parties. Yet, we also observed that party has been a strong correlate of voting even among American Congressmen. In the first section of this chapter, we will examine party voting loyalty as a significant correlate of Congressional behavior. We want especially to explore how such loyalty to party in the Congress relates to the framework we used in the previous chapter to help explain the comparatively low level of voting cohesion of the Congressional parties.

Another point Chapter 4 emphasized is that some legislative parties exhibit an extraordinarily high level of voting cohesion. One of the most cohesive has been the British Conservative parliamentary party. Yet, looking at the reverse side of the coin, rebellions, some of them involving substantial numbers of parliamentarians, are known here as well. Why do rebellions occur in a party that normally votes so cohesively, and how do the rebellions relate to the framework that underlies our study? An answer to this question will occupy our attention in the second section of this chapter.

Accounting for Party Loyalty in the United States Congressional Parties

With all the forces that lead to intraparty disagreement and deviant voting in the Congress, it is still true that party is one of the most important predictors of how a Congressman will vote. This fact requires some explanation. In particular, we need to ask whether party voting among United States legislators is consistent with the hypotheses and findings we reported in Chapter 4 or not.

Congressmen and their Constituencies

Why is it that, on a broad range of issues, Democrats vote fairly consistently in one policy direction and Republicans vote fairly consistently in another? In an attempt to answer this question we begin by looking at the ties members of the Congress have with their constituencies. In addition to party, one of the competing centers of a Congressman's loyalty is his constituency. We suggested in Chapter 4 that a legislator's survival in the United States is influenced more by local considerations and less by national party considerations than appears to be the case in either of the British parties or in the French Gaullist party. Miller and Stokes go so far as to say that "by plying his campaign and servicing arts over the years, the Congressman is able to develop electoral strength that is almost totally disassociated from what his party wants in Congress. . . ."[1]

Actually, the links between Congressmen and their constituencies can arise from several dispositions. One of these is the desire to survive.[2] Although a high percentage of Congressmen do survive, far fewer escape having at least one election in which their vote falls below 55 percent. Beyond this, as was also suggested in Chapter 4, many Congressmen consider representing constituency interests to be an integral element of their role, even if this should lead them to deviate from their Congressional party. Finally, the legislator's own policy convictions can be an important factor linking him to his constituency. As Kingdon has observed, "It is fair to say that William Colmer would not have been elected in New York City, nor would Emanuel Celler have been recruited in Mississippi. Different districts simply recruit people of different attitudes to run for Congress. Before the congressman casts a single vote, the broad pattern of his voting has already been determined by this [recruitment] process."[3]

More than a few members of Congress look upon party deviation in order to align themselves with constituency interests as perfectly acceptable, at times even desirable. Interviews of Congressmen give some indication of how they feel about their ties with their constituencies. For example, when asked, "If a bill is important for his party's record, a member should vote with his party even if it costs him some support in his district. (How do you feel?)," only 35 percent of the Congressional respondents agreed (or tended to agree) that the member should vote with his party, whereas 52 percent disagreed (or tended to disagree).[4]

Others have also found through interviewing members of Congress that constituency is considered a principal reason for not going along with the party.[5] Such attitudes are expressed by members of both parties from all sections of the country. A northern Democrat said: "I want to help all I can—especially on the less visible issues where there is less passion in the district."[6] A southern Democrat responded: "I would like to vote with the leadership on more things but I just can't. My constituency won't permit me."[7] A "solid party man" who was a Republican member of the House Ways and Means Committee commented: "I was with the party on everything *but* things that affected my district."[8] In an interview with the authors, a liberal Democrat and advocate of greater party purity[9] said he usually voted with his constituency when the constituency had a clear interest, unless major "principles" were at stake. He observed that reelection had to be uppermost in a legislator's mind, that he also looked at his job as partly one of representing his constituency's interests, and that constituency interests might well cause one to go against the party position.

Party leaders recognize the legitimacy of a Congressman opting for constituency, and they try to minimize the times they go to him to ask for a vote against his constituency. Party leaders usually ask for such a vote only when absolutely necessary to win a major battle.[10] After all, the party's success at election time and the ability of its members to survive determines who will control the individual houses and committees of Congress.

How, then, are the parties able to act as cohesively as they do? One answer to this question is that local demands and legislative party demands are not always in conflict. A response to perceived local interests may result in party voting cohesion if the kinds of districts represented by one of the parties tend to be *different* from the kinds of districts represented by the other party in ways that are related to the differences between the parties' general policy orientations.[11] Such differences are present in the districts held by the two American parties and appear to be partly responsible for the voting cohesion each of the two parties maintains. Froman argues: "It seems a fair inference that Democrats have more liberal voting records [than do Republicans] partially, at least, because they tend to come from more liberal constituencies."[12]

It is useful to summarize Froman's research. Froman examined differences between Democrats and Republicans representing northern districts (inclusive of districts in all parts of the country outside the South). He began by showing that there was a considerable difference in the voting behavior of northern Democrats on the one hand and northern Republicans on the other in the following areas: (1) the Kennedy Support Score on Domestic Policy (percentage support for President Kennedy's stances on fifty roll call votes on issues of domestic policy upon which President Kennedy personally took a position); (2) the Kennedy Support Score on Foreign Policy (percentage support on ten roll call votes on issues of foreign policy that President Kennedy personally urged); and (3) the Larger Federal Role Support Score (percentage support on ten roll call votes which would increase the federal government's role in various aspects of our economy and society, for example, aid to education, housing, minimum wage). Table 5.1 shows that voting differences between Republicans and Democrats for 1961 were rather substantial along these lines. The differences in the voting records are comparable to differences found between the parties in other years (reported in Chapter 4).

We should note, parenthetically, that for each of the three policy scores reported in the above table, the southern Democrats would lie between the average scores of northern Democrats and Republicans. Thus, the southern Democrats' scores aver-

Table 5.1
Voting Differences between Northern Democrats and Northern Republicans 1961 (in percent)

	Kennedy Support Score Domestic Policy	Kennedy Support Score Foreign Policy	Larger Federal Role
Northern[a] Dem.	83.8	83.9	92.7
Northern[a] Rep.	34.3	53.3	17.3

Source: Lewis Froman, *Congressmen and Their Constituencies* (Chicago: Rand McNally, 1964) p. 91.
[a]Northern includes all except the eleven southern states of the old Confederacy.

aged 56.7 percent on Kennedy's domestic policy, 57.2 percent on Kennedy's foreign policy, and 56.4 percent on a larger federal role.

Froman went on to hypothesize that Congressmen from constituencies that were urban, densely populated, having a large nonwhite population, and a low percentage of owner-occupied houses or dwelling units (people who owned their houses) would be more likely to be liberal and to support Kennedy programs and a larger role for the federal government. He found that northern Democratic districts differed demographically from the Republican districts in exctly these ways. The differences between the Republican and Democratic constituencies for 1961 can be seen on Table 5.2

Table 5.2
Comparison between Northern Democrats and Northern Republicans on Four Constituency Variables

Region and Party	Mean Average on Constituency Variables			
	Owner-Occupied in percent	Nonwhite in percent	Pop. 1 Sq. Mile Av.	·Urban in percent
Northern[a] Democrats	55.5	12.6	11,032	74.5
Northern[a] Republicans	67.1	3.8	1,667	65.1

Source: Froman, *Congressmen and Their Constituencies*, p. 92.
[a]Northern includes all but the eleven former Confederate states.

Thus, Froman argued, "factors usually associated with 'liberalism' (urban, lower socio-economic status, non-white, and densely populated areas) are the factors actually associated with the more liberal party."[13] This is the Democratic party. The same can be said for the Republican party. The characteristics of its constituencies are generally more "conservative" (less urban, higher socio-economic status, and so forth), which builds and supports a general "conservative" Republican voting record in Congress. As a consequence, Congressional party cohesion in part reflects a certain homogeneity of the constituencies each party represents.[14]

Quite a few other studies have found a relationship between constituency and party, on the one hand, and the voting of representatives sent to Congress on the other.[15] Ripley, for example, found that Republican representatives from rural constituencies have tended to be more loyal to the party. For the Democrats, it is the representatives from urban or suburban districts who have been more loyal.[16] Key, too, uncovered a relationship between the degree of liberalism of Democratic representatives and the degree of urbanization in their districts.[17] Also, using several aggregate indicators of the socioeconomic status of Congressional districts (urban-rural, owner-occupied housing, nonwhite population, blue collar labor, and median family income), Shannon concluded: "To a very large extent . . . the two congressional parties reflect the socioeconomic relationship of the constituencies."[18]

While constituency characteristics can provide a source of cohesion for the two parties, they may also contribute to intraparty conflict and deviant voting behavior.

The degree of deviant voting bears some relationship to the representation of constituencies that are atypical of the party. Froman found, for example, that the more "liberal" the constituency characteristics, the more both northern Democratic *and* Republican Congressmen supported Kennedy's programs.[19]

A look at support for the Conservative Coalition in the House revealed the same tendency. Examining northern Democrats and Republicans on twenty three Conservative Coalition roll call votes, Froman observed:

> Among the Democrats who come from conservative districts, 81 percent voted with the Conservative Coalition on [one or more] of these twenty-three issues. Among the Democrats who come from liberal districts, only 31 percent ever voted with the coalition. Similarly, among the Republicans who come from liberal districts, 56 percent voted with the Conservative Coalition at least 70 percent of the time. Among Republicans who come from conservative districts, 75 percent voted with the coalition at least 70 percent of the time.[20]

David Mayhew's analysis of party loyalty in the House of Representatives over a fifteen-year period found deviant voting behavior to be rather consistently associated with members who came from party-atypical districts. For example, Republican representatives from constituencies considered more liberal (urban, low ownership-occupancy) were markedly more likely to vote with the majority of Democrats on housing issues than were Republicans from districts with a higher percentage of homeowners. In this regard, he also found that Republicans from liberal (urban low ownership-occupancy) constituencies strengthened their electoral appeal back home the more they deviated from the Republican majority on housing issues.[21] The relationship Mayhew detected between representing party-atypical districts and deviant voting behavior held not only on housing issues but also on other urban issues, labor legislation, and farm policies as well (his findings are detailed in Chapter 9).

Southern Democratic district characteristics have resembled Republican districts more than those of northern Democrats. That is, as a group, the southern districts have not been "typical" Democratic districts. As we have seen elsewhere, southerners as a group have voted less loyally with the party than have the northern Democrats. Constituency characteristics seem at least partly an explanation of greater southern deviation and opposition. In addition, southern Democrats have probably been subject to greater cross-pressures from constituency and party than most Republicans and other Democrats, perhaps helping to explain why their voting behavior as a group has also exhibited less internal cohesiveness (on most everything except civil rights for Blacks).[22]

On the other hand, Shannon's study of constituency characteristics and intraparty voting differences has argued that the ability of constituency characteristics to explain party deviation is more limited. He found that

> constituency factors will account in part for some deviant party voting. Party members from atypical constituencies are rather more likely in some cases to be disloyal to party majorities than their colleagues from more typical districts. There are, however, many party differences that *cannot* be adequately explained by aggregate constituency characteristics.[23]

Thus, Shannon found no clear relationship existed between party opposition scores for

Democrats and Republicans and the socioeconomic characteristics of the constituencies they represented.

However, when he examined the constituency characteristics of extreme deviants, or very disloyal members of each party, clear tendencies did develop.[24] For example, the extreme Democratic deviants (among northern Democrats) came disproportionately from rural districts with a relatively low blue-collar population. The districts were also interior ones located in the Midwest or border states similar to those represented by the Republicans. An examination of extreme differences in the Republican party found that on 1964 party-unity roll calls, the rural, native, interior Republicans voted with the Republican majority 82 percent of the time while the urban, foreign, coastal Republicans supported the party only 44 percent of the time.[25] As for the southern Democrats, Shannon noted that there has been some relationship (though not as strong as expected) between a lower party opposition score and a higher percentage of urban population.[26] Finally, other investigation has concluded that rural, native, Black Belt constituencies "showed the least loyalty to the Democratic program, while the metropolitan foreign constituencies in the North produced the highest average loyalty."[27]

Research on the Senate also suggests the importance of constituency for party voting. Matthews found that while Senators from the same party and state have tended to agree, Senators from states which were less "homogeneous" deviated more than did Senators from more "homogeneous" states. Matthews attributed these differences in voting records, particularly in the less homogeneous states, partly to the different coalitions of support Senators built in their states in order to secure election.[28] Using a more complex research methodology, Jackson's study of constituency pressures in the Senate found that constituency characteristics explained variations in Senate voting, including party loyalty and deviation, to a rather high degree.[29] His "general" conclusion was that "certain socio-economic variables can be significant in explaining the roll call behavior of Senators. In the majority of the cases they accounted for 50 to 80 percent of the variance. These results support the hypothesis that Senators' voting is responsive to their constituency environments."[30]

The tie between members of Congress and their constituencies can help to explain both party voting loyalty and party voting deviation. On the one hand, "liberal" districts (according to demographic characteristics) tend to elect Democrats, and "conservative" districts tend to elect Republicans. The fact that Congressional Democrats tend to vote in one direction on such matters as economic and social policy and that Republicans tend to vote in another direction can to some extent be explained by differences in the districts the two parties represent.[31] On the other hand, not all Democrats come from "liberal" districts, and not all Republicans come from "conservative" districts. As we have seen, this diversity in the districts that each party represents bears some relationship to the deviant voting behavior that occurs in each of the Congressional parties.

Party Identification

Yet, legislative behavior toward party is not a product solely of constituency differences between or within the parties. Particularly important is the point that, on the whole, most Congressmen from party-atypical districts have been more loyal to their party than would be expected on the basis of constituency alone. As Shannon pointed out, "many party differences *cannot* be adequately explained by aggregate constituency characteristics."[32] We noted above, for example, that the northern Democrats from "liberal" districts rarely deviated from their party to join the Conservative Coalition. Yet, Republicans from "liberal" districts frequently joined the Conservative Coalition and thereby remained loyal to their party majority. For the twenty-three issues examined, 56 percent of the Republicans from "liberal" districts supported the Conservative Coalition (along with their party majority) at least 70 percent of the time, whereas only 31 percent of the northern Democrats from "liberal" districts ever deviated from their regional party majority to support the Conservative Coalition. As this suggests, legislative behavior toward party must be seen as considerably more than the simple product of constituency differences.[33]

Beyond the possible coincidence of constituency and party pressures and policy positions, there is the second factor of party identification that can lead to party loyalty on the part of individual legislators. As we pointed out in the previous chapter, feelings of party identification are by no means entirely absent among American Congressmen and Senators. Donald Matthews observed that "Party 'discipline' may be weak but party 'identification' is strong."[34] A sense of party "spirit" develops among the members of the same party. In each house Democrats sit with Democrats, Republicans with Republicans. Democrats eat together, as do Republicans; they relax and converse in the Democratic lounge or cloakroom and Republicans relax and converse in the Republican lounge or cloakroom. Thus, "Members of the House tend to know the members of their own party better than members of the opposition, and close friendships with other Representatives tend to be limited to members of their own party"[35] Congressmen interviewed by Clapp agreed "it is much easier to become acquainted with party colleagues than political opponents."[36]

The habitual patterns of alliance and interpersonal friendship help produce a feeling of party unity that will influence how the legislator perceives and acts.[37] Ralph Huitt, a close observer of the Congress for many years, remarked, "The party usually has an *emotional* appeal for its members that is reinforced by the sharing of common hazards under its banner at election time."[38] Hinckley also noted the "socialization" into party loyalty by one's past political career.[39] Party is "within" the legislator as a "series of internalized loyalties and frameworks. . . . "[40] This affects how the legislator perceives, evaluates, and responds. Programs of his own party and requests from fellow party members are likely to carry more weight. Loyalty to the party, both at roll call time and at various other stages of the legislative process, springs partly from the group life and shared identity of the legislative party members.

Various studies support the view that most legislators want to go along with their party and do not feel at ease voting with the opposition party. According to Ripley, nearly three-fourths of the sixty Democrats and Republicans he interviewed identified strongly with their parties.[41] About four-fifths of the remaining legislators saw party as an important consideration in reaching decisions. Members of the regional groups within each party that were most disloyal in voting behind party (that is, northeastern Republicans and southern Democrats) expressed the weakest party sentiments, but even here somewhat over half of the legislators voiced strong party feelings (57 percent of southern Democrats and 56 percent of northeastern Republicans). Ripley also found that, more generally, the members who indicated the strongest party feelings were in fact the most loyal.[42]

Some sample quotations will help capture the flavor of the responses of those who had the strongest feelings about their desire to go along with their party. Note the variety of parties and sections of the country represented by these quotes.

> I go through great throes when I cannot go along with my party. It is not an easy choice to vote against your party. (a southern Democrat)
> Yes I want to go along with the party. I am a team man. (western Republican)
> There is a natural desire to go along . . . Very few consciously try to be mavericks. (northeastern Republican)
> My policy is to accept everything Democratic unless it is terrible. (western Democrat)
> I have a general conviction that my party is right. (a northern Democrat)[43]

Thus, interviews reveal that many members of Congress, despite all the various pressures and loyalties competing for their attention, give party serious consideration.[44] For many of the members, loyalty to party "is instinctive; they feel uncomfortable when acting contrary to the wishes of fellow party members or leaders."[45] And, party leaders can use this feeling as a resource. In his study, Ripley found that 43 percent of the Democrats and 28 percent of the Republican House members interviewed indicated that "isolation" was a potential weapon in the hands of the party leaders.[46]

A broadly similar conclusion can be drawn from policy case studies. To cite an example, Bauer, Pool, and Dexter's study of the trade legislation found that while most Congressmen did not specifically express "party interest" as the criterion for their response to the issue, they did prefer "to act in ways helpful to the party" whenever and wherever possible.[47]

There are significant psychological and social pressures to support the party.[48] Politicians, like most people, desire the esteem of their colleagues. Even those who deviate are concerned with maintaining the understanding of their party colleagues, which likely includes many of their close friends. Party members are expected to "stretch a point" occasionally to help the party or to be willing to compromise and bargain to reach a party position.[49] Ripley remarks that "acting against the party involves a substantial amount of personal discomfort which can even be expressed physically. The only Republican to vote against his party's recommittal motion on a major administration bill in 1963 answered the roll call while crouching behind the rail on the Democratic side of the House Chamber. He explained: 'It's 190 degrees over there' (pointing to the Republican side)."[50] Another Republican who opposed his colleagues on a vote indicated he didn't even go into the Republican cloakroom anymore; he felt he could no longer talk to his older colleagues.[51]

The psychological pressures of not being accepted are important to many Congressmen and derive partially from members' feelings of identification with their party and their party colleagues. These feelings can be and are utilized by party leaders in attempting to build party voting unity, for they afford leaders what Ripley calls "psychological rewards and preferment." That is, to use the words of another analyst of Congress, "The desire to 'belong' is not merely a passive but also an active instrument in the hands of the leadership. . . . Independence can be lonely and uncomfortable if one feels that one's colleagues and 'natural' allies are increasingly cold."[52] In their efforts to build party unity, party leaders are thus able "to appeal both to the sense of solidarity the member is likely to feel with his party and to the fear of possible ostracism, which means the immediate loss of psychological preferment and a possible loss of tangible preferment."[53]

Career Advancement

In our explanation of party cohesion in the previous chapter, we also pointed to a third factor that contributes to high levels of voting loyalty. This factor is the control of offices by the party leaders and their distribution on the basis of loyalty, which limits the independence of those legislators who aspire to higher office. That is, career advancement, the improvement of one's political status or institutional power base, is tied very closely to behavior supportive of the party.

Although voting loyalty is not as strong a factor in distributing such rewards in Congress, and there is a greater possibility of developing centers of power that are independent of party loyalty, this is not to say career advancement in Congress is totally divorced from such considerations. In a significant way party "rewards" and "deprivations" with regard to career advancement—to the degree there is any "choice" available to the legislative party—are based on members' past or expected support for party and on members' compatibility with the "center of gravity" of the individual parties.[54] There are two institutional status bases in the Congress: the party organization positions and committee posts (including membership on preferred committees as well as subcommittee and committee chairmanship positions). The few studies that have been done indicate that attitude toward party and support of one's party is of some importance especially in regard to attaining party leadership positions and securing membership on preferred committees.

Party leaders tend to be selected from those who occupy the ideological center of gravity for each party in each house.[55] Nevertheless, interviews find that party leaders have the highest favorable party orientations of any single group in the House.[56] Their party support scores, especially on key "party" legislation, are also above the average for their party. Southern Democrats who have gained party organization positions show a pattern of voting quite unlike the average southerner. For example, the late Hale Boggs (D., La.), who was the majority party leader of the House, usually had party support scores above 75 percent and was annually among the highest of the southerners in Conservative Coalition opposition scores. Sam Rayburn and Carl Albert in the House and Lyndon Johnson in the Senate are other southern leaders whose party support scores were above average. Even assistant whips, as a group, show greater party support than the party average. An analysis of seventeen key votes in Congress disclosed that "assistant whips tended to be more loyal to the administration than all Democrats, and variations in their individual loyalty tended to reflect the normal variations by zone. Analysis of the performance of Republican assistant whips produce the same general conclusions."[57]

Party leaders are subject to challenge by groups within the party. For example,

Republican House leaders Joseph Martin and Charles Halleck were dumped by their Congressional party conferences. Boggs, the "heir apparent" to the House majority leader position in 1968 faced opposition from Morris Udall of Arizona. Hugh Scott, Republican leader in the Senate, has also been challenged. Not only the actual defeats of party leaders but also the continuing possibility of challenge tend to make leaders more responsive to the majority in their parties. Party leaders, to a degree greater than committee chairmen, can be held accountable by the party majority.[58]

The party also has some control regarding assignments to the other institutional base of power in the Congress, the Congressional committees. One of the tangible rewards (or deprivations) in the hands of party leaders is the ability to affect assignments and reassignments to select and standing committees, particularly the "important" committees. A major study of majority leadership covering ten Congresses concluded: "virtually all majority party leaders in both houses in all of the Congresses studied sought to have some influence over the assignment to standing committees."[59] All of the leaders met some success in this regard, although the degree of success varied with different leaders. John Manley notes two reasons why party leaders desire to influence committee assignments:

First, to the degree that the leadership affects assignments it has an important resource for doing favors for individual members, for rewarding members for past favors, and for establishing bonds with members that may provide some leverage in future legislative situations. Second, committee assignments are vital to the policy for which the leadership is responsible.[60]

In the Senate the Democratic majority leader has had substantial influence over the Steering Committee which is responsible for making committee assignments. Lyndon Johnson used his influence as majority leader in 1953 to get his party to give each freshman Senator a major committee assignment before senior Senators had two. Stephen K. Bailey comments on this change: "Johnson's action through his leadership of the Democratic Steering Committee in modifying the seniority principle was to strengthen the centripetal forces in the Democratic Senate."[61] The Republicans later adopted a similar principle for their freshmen members. When acting on transfers in committee assignments, the Senate Democratic Steering Committee, though guided by seniority, has not been bound by seniority.[62] However, the Senate Republican Committee on Committees, which is not led by the floor leader, has been required to allocate transfer assignments on the basis of seniority.[63] This means, of course, that the Democratic floor leader, both by strategic institutional location and the slightly greater leeway allowed in committee membership allocation, could potentially have greater impact on committee assignments and could thus give some edge to those who cooperated with party leaders. But the actual use of this potential for power has varied. Mike Mansfield, the present Senate Democratic majority leader, is regarded as less influential on the Steering Committee than Johnson was. Johnson used his power more regularly. For example, he would "inspire applications for committees from the Senators he favored for the openings."[64]

Whereas practically no careful empirical studies have been done on the significance of party voting loyalty for committee assignments in the Senate, the House committee assignment system has begun to receive a great deal of attention from political scientists. Three general conclusions emerge from these studies.[65] First, party leaders can exercise significant influence over appointments to committees, especially important committees. Second, successful movements to requested committees, particularly to important ones, are related to actual or anticipated party support scores on roll call votes. Third, Congressmen perceive that not only are committee assignments a power resource in the hands of party and party leaders to encourage party loyalty but also that party leaders do in fact use them for that purpose. We shall now discuss each of these findings in greater detail.

First, though today's party leaders in the House do not approach the almost absolute power of Speaker Cannon in 1910-11, they do have significant influence on committee assignments and reassignments.[66] This influence tends to be focused on the most important committees and on spot intervention rather than continuing attempts to control all committee assignments.[67]

One of the most important and prestigious committees has been the Ways and Means Committee. Influence over assignment to this committee has been especially vital since the committee has been the arena for many of the major conflicts between the parties. Until the Ninety-fourth Congress, it also served as the Committee on Committees for the Democrats. Although Democratic members serving on Ways and Means have been elected by the party Caucus, only three times in recent decades have candidates won who did not have the support of the Speaker and the party leadership.[68] Often the leadership's support went well beyond backing particular candidates seeking assignment to the committee. It sometimes also included active recruitment of responsible party men. On the occasion of the death of John Nance Garner, John McCormack reminisced how Garner, as Speaker thirty-five years earlier, had helped him get selected to the Ways and Means Committee even though he had sought Garner's help to move to the Judiciary Committee.[69] In his study of recruitment to the Ways and Means Committee, John Manley observes that leadership influence has been the rule rather than the exception:

The leaders were unanimous in their role in the recruitment process and thirteen of the eighteen Democrats interviewed mentioned the leadership as playing an important role in their successful candidacies. In at least six known cases. . . the leadership took the initiative by asking the members to go on Ways and Means, and with others the members made a call on leadership a first or second priority in their campaign for the committee.[70]

Since Ways and Means was also the Committee on Committees, the degree to which a Democratic Speaker got his men on Ways and Means affected his influence over the composition of other committees. For example, in the 1950s Rayburn was able to liberalize the House Education and Labor Committee "by asking for appointment of specific junior Democrats."[71] In an indirect maneuver with the Committee on Committees (the Ways and Means Committee) in 1949, he was also able to get two Democrats, who had supported a third-party Presidential candidate in 1948, removed from the House Un-American Activities Committee.[72]

In the case of the House Rules Committee as well, both Democratic and Republican Speakers have generally been able to influence their party's new appointments to the committee during their tenure.[73] Indeed, in cooperation with President Kennedy, Rayburn sought and was able to win a decision to enlarge the size of the House Rules Committee in 1961 in order to maximize the success of the Democratic administration's program. Another major committee has been Appropriations. Here again Speakers have usually exercised some control over new party appointments, although Republicans somewhat more so than Democrats.[74] Aside from these important committees, recent leaders have only intervened at strategic points and on rare occasions.[75]

Not only have party leaders exercised some control over assignments to important committees, but their choices and those of the Committee on Committees have also been influenced significantly by actual or anticipated party support on roll call votes. Loyal Congressmen have been more likely to get their first choices in committee assignments than have less loyal Congressmen. For the Eighty-eighth Congress, of the twenty-one incumbent Democratic Congressmen seeking new committee assignments, the Congressmen who got their first committee choices had an average party loyalty voting score of 67 percent. Those Congressmen who did not succeed in getting their first choices had an average party loyalty voting score of 34 percent[76]

Similarly, in recent years, southerners, usually regarded as the least loyal and least liberal subgroup in the Democratic party, have not been as successful in getting their committee choices. Of eight southerners who sought committee reassignments in the Eighty-eighth Congress, only two were successful—a 25 percent success rate as opposed to a 71 percent success for northerners and 67 percent for westerners.

Expected performance is also important. Southerners are expected to be less liberal and less loyal. Looking at the sixteen freshmen Democrats who applied earliest for committee assignments, before the Committee on Committees met, the only two who were unsuccessful were southerners who had campaigned for office in opposition to the Democratic administration's programs.[77]

A look at the membership of the Ways and Means Committee supports the thesis that those with demonstrably greater party support scores have generally been more succcessful in getting preferred committee assignments. Manley compared the average party unity score for all House Democrats with scores of the twenty-four Democrats who were appointed to the Ways and Means Committee from 1951 to 1966. Nineteen of these members had higher party unity scores previous to their appointments than the average for the Democratic members of the House. Moreover, of the four Democrats appointed to the Ways and Means Committee in 1949 (prior to the time that the *Congressional Quarterly* computed the average party score), three had very high party unity scores. Hale Boggs of Louisiana scored 87 percent; J. M. Combs of Texas, 95 percent; and John Carroll of Colorado, 91 percent. Taken together, twenty-two of the twenty-eight members from 1949 to 1966 for whom scores were available would be classified as party regulars *prior* to their transfer to the committee.[78] One of the twenty-two was Phillip Landrum of Georgia. In 1963 Landrum was defeated in the party Caucus for a vacated seat on the committee despite the backing of the party leadership. W. Pat Jennings of Virginia, who was from the same state as the departing member and had a more loyal party voting record, won the seat. However, Landrum won a seat in 1965 after he had demonstrated greater party loyalty. As one Democratic Ways and Means Committee member summed it up, "To get on Ways and Means, you have to be pretty much in favor of the administration, what the administration wants."[79] (Of course, the quoted member was referring to a Democratic administration.)

The situation has been quite similar for the Republicans. In response to a question about the factors that were important to secure a Ways and Means assignment, one Republican committee member commented:

It is hard to generalize. There are a lot of factors—region, seniority. Then of course there are certain key issues that you want to be sure a member is pretty much a party-line type of member. You want to be sure he will go along with the party on certain things, you want to be sure he's safe on some things.[80]

Several other members responded in a similar vein.[81]

Republican party regulars have been assigned in disproportionate numbers to the Ways and Means Committee. Only two of the fourteen Republicans who gained a transfer to the Ways and Means Committee between 1951 and 1966 had scores below the party unity average for all House Republicans. Of the four members who transfered since 1967, three had very high party voting scores (91 percent, 96 percent and 88 percent), and the remaining one a respectable 71 percent. Thus of the eighteen Republican members for whom scores exist, fifteen had high party scores.[82]

Less research is available on the relationship between party voting loyalty and committee transfers in the Senate. However, one study has examined the Senate committee transfers from 1968 to 1972. It emerged with findings similar to those for the House. Party voting loyalty and transfers to the six most prestigious Senate committees were found to be positively correlated, with a gamma of + .35.[83]

A third conclusion regarding committee assignments is that party members *perceive* committee assignment to be a potential power resource for party leaders to employ against those who are not loyal to the party. Not only do the more loyal party members, both absolutely and in relation to their regional subgroupings, tend to be more successful in committee assignment requests, but they also know that the granting or withholding of a committee assignment is used by party leaders and the Committees on Committees to reward or punish a Congressman for his degree of party voting and cooperation with party leaders. After interviewing Appropriations Committee members, Fenno observed that the members had a pretty accurate understanding that party loyalty was one reason why they had been chosen.[84] Ripley's research supports the same conclusion. In response to a question about what party leaders could do if Congressmen gave support to their position, two-fifths volunteered the information that loyal members would get the best assignments to standing, special, and select committees.[85] Members' awareness of the use of committee assignments as a "reward" available to the leadership has thus been found to be rather widespread.[86] Landrum's reversal on party loyalty and federal role support scores indicates he picked up the right "cues."

Interesting differences in perception among subgroups emerge from Ripley's interviews with Congressmen. For example, seniority seems to have made a difference, with the weapon of committee assignment appearing more salient to the junior than to the more senior members.[87] Moreover, if we break down the respondents by party, we find that Republicans were somewhat more likely than Democrats to feel that committee assignments were utilized as rewards and punishments.[88] This is partly a result of the different committee assignment systems used by the two parties,[89] for the fact is that Republicans have employed committee assignments "more consistently than Democrats to reward the faithful and punish the less than faithful,"[90] even though the Democratic leadership structure has been more centralized.[91]

Let us now recapitulate. Our aim in this section has been to bring to bear some of the factors we considered in Chapter 4 in an attempt to account for the fact that party is an important correlate of voting in the United States Congress. We have taken into consideration members' ties with their constituencies (which, as we argued toward the beginning, partly taps members' own policy views and role concepts as well as their desires to survive); members' attachments to their party and their party colleagues; and members' aspirations to receive preferred legislative assignments. We argued in the previous chapter that these factors do not, in a comparative sense, prompt members of Congress to act toward their parties with a high level of voting loyalty. Our analysis here, as well, suggests that these factors work to build party voting unity in Congress differently for different members and different issues. Yet, while the ties members of Congress have with their constituencies can lead members to deviate from their parties in Congress, we have seen that they also provide a source of party voting loyalty. As we observed, too, members' aspirations for preferred legislative assignments and members' feelings for their party and their party colleagues provide additional bases for party voting loyalty. The analysis of the chapter thus suggests that factors employed in Chapter 4 to explain the comparatively low voting cohesion of the Congressional parties at the same time operated to help lay foundations that promoted and encouraged party as a factor in Congressional voting.

Accounting for Party Deviation in the British Conservative Parliamentary Party[92]

Our problem in the previous section was to consider why one's party has been a correlate of voting among American Congressmen even though, comparatively, the level of voting cohesion of the American Congressional parties is rather low. In this section we will take up an opposite problem. We will look at a party with very high voting cohesion, the British Conservative parliamentary party, and will attempt to explain why voting dissidence occurs in that party. We will do so by using factors similar to those we focused upon in dealing with the Congressional parties. That is, we will examine party voting deviation by Conservative backbenchers as it relates especially to the legislator's ambition for advancement, his ties with his constituency, and his identification with his party. While focusing on the same kinds of factors, however, our method of analysis will differ.

Rebellions among the Conservatives

Despite its extraordinarily high level of voting cohesion, rebellions have occurred within the Conservative parliamentary party. Between 1959 and 1968, for example, there was a series of eight rebellions upon which at least 5 percent of the backbenchers deviated on a two or three-line whip, in addition to another which found such deviation when the whip was off (but the leadership had officially and publicly taken a position). There were also numerous more minor voting rebellions.

Our examination here focuses on the eight major rebellions when the whip was on as well as the additional rebellion when the whip was off. Seven of the rebellions took place on two- or three-line whips during the 1959-64 Parliament when the Conservatives controlled the government. Again, in each of these instances, 5 percent or more of the backbenchers rebelled (that is, voted with Labour or deliberately abstained).[93]

The seven votes were on corporal punishment (1961), the Wedgwood Benn issue (two votes, 1961), the Common Market (1961), the Profumo affair (1963), and the resale price maintenance controversy (two votes, 1964). A total of 123 different Conservative MPs rebelled on at least one of these seven divisions (votes). This accounts for 38 percent of the backbench population.

Let us begin by describing these rebellions. The largest backbench rebellion during the 1959-64 Conservative government took place in 1961 over the issue of whether to reinstate corporal punishment for young offenders or not. A total of sixty-nine right-wing Conservatives jumped a government two-line whip which would have required Conservative backbench MPs to vote against reinstating corporal punishment.[94] (Our operational definition of "Left," "Center," and "Right" is in the Appendix to this chapter.) This rebellion was followed shortly thereafter by two more over the issue of whether Mr. Anthony Wedgwood Benn, a Labour MP, should be allowed to sit in the House of Commons or not. A special committee set up by the Conservative government had recommended that Wedgwood Benn be required to succeed his father as Viscount Stansgate, which would have prevented him from sitting in the House. The government put on a two-line whip, but even so, major backbench rebellions took place on two separate votes. On a Labour motion that Wedgwood Benn be allowed to address the House, fourteen Conservative backbenchers voted with the opposition. A total of fifteen Conservative backbenchers rebelled on another vote that would have required the government to facilitate the renunciation of peerages.[95] Although some of the rebels were from the Center and the Right, they were predominantly from the Left.

There was a fourth major rebellion during 1961. This rebellion took place over the question of whether Britain should apply for membership in the Common Market or not. The government asked the House to approve its application and backed it with a three-line whip. Still, twenty-two Conservative backbenchers rebelled.[96] The rebels were from the party's right wing.

Another serious rebellion occurred over the Profumo affair in 1963. John Profumo, the War Minister, resigned while admitting that his previous denial of illicit relations with Miss Christine Keeler was a lie. Not only did some people see this as a serious moral issue, but the fact that another of Miss Keeler's affairs had been with an attaché at the Soviet embassy raised grave fears about the country's security. Harold Macmillan, then the Conservative Prime Minister, was held partly responsible for the breach in the nation's security system and for his incompetence in dealing with Profumo's original denial. As a result, the Labour party tabled an adjournment motion, which implied no confidence in the government. A total of twenty-seven MPs from all sections of the Conservative backbenches disregarded their leaders' three-line whip and abstained.[97]

The final two major revolts in the 1959-64 Parliament were over the abolition of resale price maintenance in 1964 (see Chapter 3). The bill, upon which the government placed a two-line whip, was designed to end informal and formal price controls on retail goods. However, many persons both inside and outside the Commons felt that the abolition of resale price maintenance would ruin small shopkeepers. On the bill's second reading, twenty-one Conservative backbenchers from the Center and Right voted "no"; an additional seventeen abstained. A little later, during the grueling committee stage of the bill, an amendment to exempt medicine and drugs from the act nearly defeated the government. The Labour party, joined by thirty-one Tory crossvoters, cut the government's majority to one.[98]

Most of these rebellions appear to have had at least some political impact. Ronald Butt, for example, argues that the rebelliousness of Conservative backbenchers over the issue of Common Market entry helped force Macmillan into attaching several significant amendments to the British application.[99] Butt also points out that backbench opinion against the elimination of resale price maintenance was one reason the government had waited a number of years to introduce the 1964 bill.[100] In addition, the two Wedgwood Benn rebellions apparently gave added impetus to the pressure for reform of the peerage, which eventually resulted in legislation supporting the rebels' position.[101] Finally, the Profumo rebellion, which is thought by some to have been the most serious challenge to the leadership during this period,[102] appears to have made matters considerably more uncomfortable than they already had been for Harold Macmillan.[103] Macmillan resigned as Prime Minister less than four months later.

Two additional rebellions took place from 1965 to 1968 while the Conservatives were in opposition. The first was an extraordinarily widespread division that arose in the party over the question of the sanctions the Labour government wished to apply against Rhodesia in 1965. A total of eighty-one Conservative backbenchers from all parts of the party rebelled against their party leadership's position of abstention.[104] The leadership made its position known publicly but at the last moment withdrew the whip. Another rebellion took place on two votes in 1967. The issue at stake was the Conservative leadership's support of the Labour government's request to apply for membership in the Common Market. Although the whip was on, twenty-six Conservative backbenchers rebelled.[105]

Accounting for the Rebellions: Career Advancement, Survival, and Party Identification

What accounts for rebellions such as these? To what extent can they be explained in terms of the variables brought forth earlier? We suggested in Chapter 4 that the voting unity of the British Conservative parliamentary party depended, in part, on the operation of three dispositional constraints: (1) the control of offices by the parliamentary party leaders and their distribution on the basis of loyalty, which keeps in check those backbench MPs who aspire to higher office; (2) checks on a member's career survival imposed by his constituency party organization; and (3) the member's feelings of identity with the party.

But we need not assume that all Conservative backbench MPs were affected equally by each of these three dispositional constraints. For example, we need not assume that all backbenchers had exactly the same career aspirations. Some MPs might not aspire as strongly to governmental office as would others, and we would expect those with lower career aspirations to be among the most likely to join the backbench rebellions and those with higher aspirations to be among the least likely to join the rebellions.

We can indicate career aspirations by whether an MP had held or could expect to hold governmental office or not. Besides examining MPs according to whether they had already been rewarded with higher office, we also need to consider whether those MPs yet to receive a first promotion had served less than five years in the Commons or not and whether they were below the age of fifty or not. The use of years of service in the Commons and age as an indicator of career aspiration may seem surprising. It was chosen because very few MPs gained a first reward after fifty years of age or after five or more years of service in the House of Commons.[106] This is suggested in Table 5.3, which shows the considerable difference between the percentage of all backbenchers and the percentage of backbench promotees which these MPs constituted. Since they were considerably less likely to be given promotions even if they remained loyal, (see also below), we inferred that these MPs might look upon rebellion as having less costly implications than would the other MPs. Hence, we hypothesized that career aspirations would not constrain these MPs as greatly as they would the other MPs and, in turn, that these MPs would be among the most likely to join the major backbench rebellions.

Nor is it the case that all potentially rebellious MPs could expect to face similar problems involving renomination and survival when dealing with their constituency party associations. It is known that most MPs from marginal seats were less vulnerable to renomination challenges, and their survival more certain, because infighting in the party association could cause the loss of the seat.[107] Party associations in marginal constituencies were thus less likely to proceed against a rebellious MP than were party associations in safe constituencies. From 1956 to 1964, seven rebellious Conservative backbenchers were not renominated by their constituencies' party association. Six of the seven rebellious MPs who were not renominated came from safe seats (the sole

Table 5.3
The Conservative Backbench: Age, Number of Years in the Commons without a First Reward and Promotions to Governmental Office (in Percent)[a]

	1959-1963		1959-1964	
	Percent of Backbench (N 268)	*Percent of Promotees (N 17)*	*Percent of Backbench (N 269)*	*Percent of Promotees (N 31)*
Age: Over 50	42.5	5.9	43.0	9.7
Five Years or More in the Commons without a First Reward	40.0	11.8	40.5	19.3

[a]The number of backbenchers is based on all backbench MPs, excluding former ministers, who served during the period under consideration. Backbench promotions considered were to any ministerial office or any whip office. Since promotions were made starting in 1960, both age and years in the Parliament were calculated as of 1960.

Labour MP purged during the period was also from a safe seat). The only Conservative exception was Dr. Johnson, whom Rasmussen says was so atypical as to defy any generalization.[108]

The fact that some MPs were less likely than others to face renomination challenges because they came from marginal seats meant that they were on the whole potentially less vulnerable than the other MPs. We would thus expect MPs from marginal seats to have been among those most likely to join the backbench rebellions. Conversely, MPs from safe seats should have been among the least likely to join the backbench rebellions.[109]

Of the constraints considered in this analysis, potential career vulnerability is the only one to have been the subject of previous testing. Two divisions were used with results that supported the importance of this constraint.[110] Our analysis in this section goes beyond these findings both by using seven additional divisions and by assessing the relevance of this particular constraint in light of our findings for the other constraints.

Finally, we will consider feelings of identification with one's party and one's party colleagues. We argued in Chapter 4 that most British MPs identify strongly with their parties. Still it is possible that not all MPs share this feeling equally. Certain socialization experiences, in particular, may inculcate especially intense feelings of identification with party and one's party colleagues. As we suggested in Chapter 4, particularly significant in this regard for Conservative backbenchers may be educational background. The most prestigious educational institutions in Britain are two of the Clarendon public schools (Eton and Harrow) and the "Oxbridge" universities (Oxford and Cambridge). Conservative MPs who have attended these institutions have also generally come from a social atmosphere in which a "natural" identity as Tories is quite often strongly in-bred even before schooling begins. Moreover, a strong network of cross-cutting family and social ties usually forms both in these institutions and in the Conservative party. Pursuing them through school and beyond, these friendship networks act to reinforce a sense of group identity. There is considerable evidence indicating that the life experiences of persons who have attended one of these institutions have tended to intensify their sense of group feeling and their Conservative identity.[111]

It is possible, then, that MPs who had *not* attended any one of the four most prestigious educational institutions shared this sense of group identity somewhat less intensely than other MPs. If voting loyalty is a function of group feelings, our inference about the importance of educational background would lead us to conclude that MPs who had not attended any one of the four educational institutions would have been more likely than the other MPs to join the backbench rebellions.

Thus far we have noted indicators that help to tap variations in several constraints thought to be significant for voting behavior: they are career aspirations, career vulnerability, and prior socialization into group feeling and party identity. We will employ these indicators to differentiate backbenchers most strongly affected by each constraint from backbenchers who were less affected. Application of the indicators shows that Conservative backbench MPs differed considerably in regard to how many and which combination of constraints affected them most strongly. Table 5.4 presents these data for Conservative backbenchers who served during the 1959-64 Parliament.

Table 5.4
Configurations of the Constraints and Conservative Backbenchers, 1959-64

Career Vulner- ability	Prior Social- ization	Career Aspira- tions	N	Number of Constraints	Total N	Percent
+	+	+	73	Three high	73	22.5
−	+	+	25			
+	−	+	31	Two high	117	36.0
+	+	−	61			
−	−	+	22			
−	+	−	14	One high	107	33.0
+	−	−	71			
−	−	−	28	Zero high	28	8.5
					325	100.0

This table is useful not only for descriptive purposes. It also delineates both the various configurations of the three constraints and the number of MPs in each configuration that provide the bases of our analysis of Conservative backbench voting behavior in the upcoming section.

Before turning to an analysis of voting behavior, we would like to remind the reader that inferences were required to arrive at the indicators we selected. The arguments we have presented support these inferences. Moreover, we shall find that the hypotheses yielded by these inferences are strongly corroborated by the data. Finally, our position is supported by an analysis of some potential alternative variables which we feared these indicators might have been tapping. This analysis can be found in the Appendix to this chapter.

Analysis of the Rebellions

We would suggest that the voting behavior of the Conservative backbenchers on the eight rebellions that took place on two- or three-line whips was a function of variations in member's career aspirations, their prior socialization into the party, and their potential career vulnerability. Let us examine first the seven rebellions that took place during the 1959-64 Parliament.

Each of these constraints is examined, individually, without holding the others constant, in Tables 5.5, 5.6 and 5.7. One can see that the degree of voting loyalty among MPs was related to the strength of career aspirations and prior socialization.[112] Those MPs with lower career aspirations or with less prior socialization were more likely than other MPs to rebel. Those consistently loyal accounted for 72 percent of the MPs with higher career aspirations as against 53 percent of the MPs who had lower career aspirations; they accounted for 71 percent of the most intensely socialized MPs and 53 percent of those who were not as strongly socialized.

Table 5.5
Conservative Backbenchers: Career Aspirations and Voting Behavior, 1959-64

	Consistently Loyal	One Rebellion	Multiple Rebellion
Higher Career Aspiratoins (N 151)	72.2	17.2	10.6
Lower Career Aspirations (N 174)	53.4	22.5	24.1

P < .001

Table 5.6
Conservative Backbenchers: Prior Socialization and Voting Behavior, 1959-64

	Consistently Loyal	One Rebellion	Multiple Rebellion
More Strongly Socialized (N 173)	70.5	17.9	11.6
Less Strongly Socialized (N 152)	52.6	22.4	25.0

P < .001

Table 5.7
Conservative Backbenchers: Potential Career Vulnerability and Voting Behavior, 1959-64

	Consistently Loyal	One Rebellion	Multiple Rebellion
Higher Potential Vulnerability	63.6	21.6	14.8
Lower Potential Vulnerability (N 89)	58.5	15.7	25.8

P < .1, p < .001

Less impressive are the figures pertaining to career survival. Although the pattern is in the expected direction, the difference in consistent voting loyalty between those MPs who were potentially vulnerable and those who were less vulnerable was only 5 percent. However, multiple rebels accounted for 26 percent of the less vulnerable group of MPs and only 15 percent of the potentially more vulnerable group.

From Table 5.8 one can examine the effects of variations in each of the three constraints on loyalty independent of variations in the other constraints. The table is based on the configurations presented earlier in Table 5.4, and the values represent the percentage of MPs within each configuration who remained consistently loyal. The eight marginals of the table show that the percentage of consistent loyalists declined whenever *either* career aspirations *or* prior socialization was reduced to a lower level, regardless of the levels of the other two constraints. This decline in loyalty occurred in every instance. The rates of decline shown in the marginals ranged from a minimum decline in percentage of 11 for each constraint to a maximum decline in percentage of 21 for prior socialization and 28 for career aspirations. The conclusion these results warrant is that career aspirations and prior socialization each had a marked (and substantially equal) effect on loyalty and rebellion among Conservative backbenchers, an effect which cannot be accounted for by variation in the other two constraints.[113]

Table 5.8
Effect of Career Aspirations, Prior Socialization, and Potential Career Vulnerability on the Voting Behavior of Conservative Backbenchers, 1959-1964[a]

	Higher Career Vulnerability		
	Higher Prior Socialization	*Lower Prior Socialization*	*Effect of Socialization*[b]
Higher Career Aspirations	(a) 75.3	(b) 64.5	−10.8
Lower Career Aspirations	(c) 63.9	(d) 50.7	−13.2
Effect of Aspirations[b]	−11.4	−13.8	
	Lower Career Vulnerability		
	Higher Prior Socialization	*Lower Prior Socialization*	*Effect of Socialization*[b]
Higher Career Aspirations	(a) 80.0	(b) 63.6	−16.4
Lower Career Aspirations	(c) 57.1	(d) 35.8	−21.3
Effect of Aspirations[b]	−22.9	−27.8	

[a]N for each cell is shown in Table 5.4.
[b]The marginals reflect difference in percentages.

There is a second way in which the impact of career aspirations on voting behavior can be examined. Since career aspirations were subject to change over time, their impact on voting loyalty can be examined in longitudinal terms (comparing the same MPs from one time period to another). It is significant in this regard to note the considerably higher degree of rebellion among the *same* MPs as their career aspirations diminished over time. There were seventy high aspirants in the 1955-59 Parliament who by virtue of length of stay in the Commons or change in age became low aspirants in the 1959-64 Parliament. Comparing the eight 1955-59 divisions upon which backbench rebellion was most widespread[114] to the seven 1959-64 divisions, rebellion within this group of MPs grew by a factor of 3. Only 13 percent of these MPs rebelled on any of the eight divisions during the earlier period, whereas after their career aspirations had diminished, rebellion within this group of MPs increased to 39 percent. In combination with the findings reported above, this finding lends strong support to the hypothesis that differences in the level of career aspirations had an important effect on the loyalty and dissidence of Conservative backbench MPs. The finding also appears to support our assumption that *in most cases disappointed career aspirations created rebellion rather than the reverse.*

The third constraint, potential career vulnerability, appears to have had a considerably weaker impact than either of the other two constraints. One can see this by comparing the cells of the upper half of Table 5.8 to their counterparts on the lower half of the table. The comparison shows that the largest decline in the number of consistent loyalists when potential career vulnerability was reduced to a lower level was 14.9 percent (comparison of cells [d]). No other decrease in loyalty amounted to as much as 10 percent, since the impact of career vulnerability became consistently weaker as MPs became increasingly subject to the other two constraints. The effect of potential career vulnerability was thus considerably less than that of either of the other two constraints.[115]

While it appears that the effect of potential career vulnerability was at most modest,

Table 5.9
**Conservative Backbenchers: Variation in
The Operation of the Number of Constraints
and the Voting Behavior, 1959-64 (in Percent)**[a]

	Consistently Loyal	*One Rebellion*	*Multiple Rebellion*
Three Constraints High (N = 73)	75.3	19.2	5.5
Two Constraints High (N = 117)	67.5	20.6	11.9
One Constraint High (N = 107)	54.3	16.8	28.9
No Constraint High (N = 28)	35.8	32.1	32.1

[a]Comparing multiple rebels to the others, gamma = .47.

its influence, along with the more consistent and sizable effects of the other two constraints, suggests a total effect on backbench voting behavior which should be substantial. Table 5.9 verifies this belief. The table examines the effect of the three constraints on voting rebellion by the number of constraints acting on each MP.

The results reported on Table 5.9 show the marked relationship that existed between variation in the operation of the three constraints and Conservative backbench rebellion from 1959 to 1964. Backbench rebellion consistently increased as the number of constraints operating strongly on backbenchers diminished. Indeed, the voting behavior of MPs upon whom all three constraints were operating strongly was almost the polar opposite of the voting behavior of MPs upon whom none of the three constraints were operating as strongly. The former group of backbenchers approached almost complete support for the leadership on these seven highly divisive votes, with 94 percent remaining loyal on at least six of the seven divisions and 75 percent remaining loyal on all seven divisions. The latter group of backbenchers, on the other hand, was about as likely as not to rebel against the leadership. Over 30 percent of these MPs rebelled on two or more of the seven divisions, and 64 percent rebelled at least once.

These findings, which indicate a close relationship between the operation of the constraints and backbench behavior on votes subject to the whip, raise the question of what effect the removal of discipline might have on backbench voting. In such a situation, one would not necessarily expect variations in the operation of these party-oriented constraints to be as striking, since removal of the whip at least partially transforms the question so that it becomes less a party issue.

For this reason a comparison of the two major backbench rebellions from 1964 to 1968, when the Conservatives were in opposition, is especially interesting. These rebellions were over Rhodesia (1965) and the Common Market (1967—two votes). Each vote dealt with a foreign policy issue closely related to the question of sovereignty, and the Conservative leadership had taken a unified public position on each vote. However, an important difference between the votes was that the whips were not applied in the Rhodesia case, whereas the whips were applied on the Common Market votes.

An examination of the Rhodesia vote shows that the effect of the constraints practically disappeared. A total of eighty-one backbenchers rebelled on this vote against their party leadership's position of abstention,[116] but there was only a slight

Table 5.10
Conservative Backbenchers: Each Constraint and Voting Behavior on Rhodesia and the Common Market, 1965-67 (percent rebels)

	Rhodesia Level of Constraint		Common Market Level of Constraint	
	High	Low	High	Low
Career Aspirations	31.5	30.5	5.4	17.7
Prior Socialization	29.7	32.5	5.1	22.1
Career Vulnerability	30.2	32.2	9.9	14.1

Table 5.11
Conservative Backbenchers: Number of Constraints and Voting Behavior on Rhodesia and the Common Market, 1965-67 (percent rebels)

	Rhodesia	Common Market
Three Constraints High	32.4	2.1
Two Constraints High	27.2	6.8
One Constraint High	34.3	18.0
No Constraint High	33.3	29.3

difference in the degree of voting loyalty and rebellion among backbenchers, regardless of the configurations of the constraints. These points are demonstrated on Table 5.10 and Table 5.11. Approximately 30 percent of the MPs with two or more constraints operating at their highest levels rebelled, whereas 34 percent of the backbenchers with either none or one of the constraints operating at their highest level rebelled.[117]

While the whips were off in the Rhodesia case, they were on once again during the two Common Market votes in 1967. It is therefore significant that voting behavior on these two divisions once again followed in almost every respect the pattern of the seven major rebellions of the 1959-64 Parliament. A total of twenty six MPs rebelled on the two Common Market votes.[118] Unlike the Rhodesia vote, variation within each of the constraints again had an impact on voting behavior (with potential career vulnerability, as usual, having less influence than the other two constraints). This is shown in Table 5.10. Table 5.11 shows, moreover, that as the number of constraints operating at highest levels decreased, voting rebellion during the Common Market divisions increased from a low of 2 percent to a high of 29 percent.

The Common Market votes and the Rhodesia vote thus add further support to our earlier findings on the salience of the three constraints. First, the effect of these constraints on backbench cohesion and rebellion was the same in virtually every respect for the 1967 Common Market votes as it was for the earlier 1959-64 votes. Second, when there was reason to believe that a division was not entirely regarded as a party vote, as was the case on the Rhodesia issue, backbench voting behavior changed, and the effect of the constraints was greatly diminished.

We suggested in Chapter 4 that the cohesion of the British Conservative parliamentary party has depended in part on the operation of three constraints. These constraints are: (1) the control of offices by the parliamentary party leaders and their distribution on the basis of loyalty, which keeps in check those backbench MPs who aspire to higher office; (2) checks on a member's career survival imposed by a member's local party; and (3) group feeling and Conservative identities transmitted by educational and social processes.

Our analysis in this section has supported the significance of these constraints by showing the close relationship that existed between variation in the operation of the constraints and backbench voting behavior. We established this relationship mainly through an examination of the nine largest rebellions to face the parliamentary party between 1959 and 1968. When major rebellions occurred, the backbenchers who were most likely to join them were those who had lower career aspirations, weaker socialization into Conservative identities and group orientations, and lower vulnerability to renomination challenges.

The seven major rebellions from 1959 to 1964 revealed that variations in each constraint had an effect on the loyalty and dissidence of backbench MPs. This was true even when the other constraints were held constant.[119] In addition, the constraint most subject to change over time (career aspirations) was examined longitudinally, by use of the major 1955-59 rebellions, and was again found to have a considerable effect on backbench rebellion.

When the three constraints were examined in combination, their effect on the voting behavior of backbenchers was substantial. Thus, only about 25 percent of those MPs for whom the three constraints operated strongly rebelled on any of the seven 1959-64 votes, while 64 percent of the MPs for whom none of the three constraints operated as strongly rebelled. The operation of the three constraints also had a marked effect on the propensity of MPs to dissent on more than one issue.

The pattern of voting behavior in the Rhodesia and Common Market rebellions after the Conservatives left power again revealed the influence of the constraints. Although the leadership took a united position in both cases, the whip was not applied on the first vote, but it was applied in the latter case. Backbench behavior when the whip was on exhibited the same pattern in virtually every respect as it did on the seven votes from 1959 to 1964, whereas the effect of the three constraints diminished considerably when the whip was off.[120]

Summary

We have focused in this chapter on two subjects regarding legislators' behavior toward their parties. These subjects intrigued us because they deal with the "other side" of the questions posed in Chapter 4. Our principal interest in Chapter 4 was to account for differing levels of party voting unity. This interest led us to examine the Conservative parliamentary party as a highly cohesive party and the American legislative parties as ones of relatively low cohesion. We attempted to explain the difference in voting cohesion partly through reference to certain dispositions that, we argued, may lie behind the individual actions of legislators.

We examined these parties from a different perspective in this chapter. Rather than examining the Conservative parliamentary party as one of high voting cohesion, we focused instead on the rebellions that have occurred in the party. Rather than examining the comparatively low level of voting cohesion present in the Congressional parties of the United States, we focused on the voting unity these parties have been able to muster. Our objective was to determine whether the dispositions relevant to explaining the typically high cohesion of the Conservative parliamentary party might also help to account for those rebellions which did arise. Furthermore, we wanted to know whether an analysis of these dispositions, which helped us to explain the comparatively low cohesion of the American Congressional parties, might also help to account for the fact that party remains a strong correlate of voting even in the United States Congress.

We argued in Chapter 4 that career aspirations and party identification were two dispositions upon which the extraordinarily high voting cohesion of the Conservative parliamentary party was based. We have observed in this chapter that the operation of these dispositions is also consistent with the fact that major rebellions have, upon occasion, occurred in the Conservative party. We inferred from our evidence that the strength of career aspirations and of party identification was not the same for all Conservative MPs. It was the MPs with lower career aspirations and lower party identification who were most likely to join rebellions. The effect of these factors on voting rebellion was found to be substantial.

We also argued in Chapter 4 that members' career ambitions and party identification did not provide the basis for a comparatively high level of party voting unity in the American Congressional parties. Despite this, we have seen that an examination of these factors enables us better to understand the degree to which members of Congress do vote along party lines. A considerable body of evidence suggests that identification with one's party and party colleagues is present to some degree in American legislative parties and that the operation of this disposition encourages party voting loyalty. Moreover, we have seen that legislators' ties to their constituencies are not necessarily inconsistent with voting along party lines. Indeed, they, too, help generate party support. The available research indicates that party voting loyalty in Congress and the different stances parties take in Congress are partly a consequence of the differences between the parties in the constituent policy interests each party represents. Finally, we have seen that career advancement is related in some important respects to evidences of party loyalty in Congress. If the point is also considered that the policy attitudes of most members of the two parties differ along a number of dimensions (see Chapter 4), these factors in combination suggest the variety of sources from which party voting unity arises and why party is a major predictor of the voting behavior even of members of the American Congress.

Appendix 5.1

The indicators we have selected for the British study face the criticism that they may in fact measure other variables. This is especially true for indicators of career aspirations (age and length of service in the Commons without a reward) and of early socialization (educational background).

Use of educational background, for example, might be criticized because of its apparent association with career aspirations. It could be argued that an MP's attendance at one of the four most prominent educational institutions and his subsequent voting loyalty was a function of career aspirations rather than of stronger prior socialization into group orientations and Conservative identities. Although comprising only 58 percent of the backbench, those MPs who attended one of the four educational institutions constituted approximately 75 percent of the MPs who attained governmental office from October, 1959, through October, 1964. Still, it is important to note that MPs attending one of the institutions were likely to attain governmental office, *whether they were loyal or not.* Only two multiple rebels were advanced to governmental rank after 1959. Both of these MPs had attended at least one of the institutions. Indeed, only 11 percent of the group of MPs having gone to at least one of the four institutions were promoted to governmental rank after 1959 (they represented 67 percent of all MPs promoted). Yet, 13 percent of this group who were multiple rebels were subsequently promoted. In addition, of the twenty-eight rebels on the well-known Suez votes, only two were subsequently elevated to governmental rank. Again, both of these MPs had attended at least one of the four institutions. Thus it would seem that rewards given to this group of MPs were less contingent on voting loyalty than were rewards for other MPs. Hence, if education had been an indicator of career aspirations instead of prior socialization, one could not have predicted correctly that voting loyalty among these MPs would be higher than that for other MPs.

It is also possible that length of service in the Commons without rewards is as much an indicator of an MP's propensity to rebel as are his career aspirations. It could be argued consistently with our hypotheses that those MPs who rebelled did not get rewarded. The failure of these MPs to get rewards over a five-year period in the Commons might thus only have been because of their tendency to rebel. If that were so, we would no longer require the notion of a reduction in career aspirations to explain the rebelliousness of these MPs.

Our earlier analysis of the effect of a change over time in a member's career aspirations on his voting loyalty provides an answer to this criticism. It was found in this analysis that as the career aspirations among the same MPs diminished over time, there followed a threefold increase in their rate of rebellion. Moreover, when these MPs had high career aspirations (1955-59), rebellion among them was remarkably low (13 percent). It would thus not appear that our indicator for career aspirations was instead tapping either similar or high rates of rebelliousness on the part of the MPs at a time prior to the 1959-68 period.

Finally, one can argue that our indicators of aspirations and prior socialization may be revealing ideological orientations instead and that rebellion was a function of ideology. It is of course possible that the older MPs had different ideological orientations than the younger MPs or that ideological tendencies of MPs varied according to educational background.

In order to deal with this problem, it was necessary to develop a measure of ideological orientation. Our measure was based on each member's record of *signing* early day motions in the 1959-64 Parliament.[121] If a member signed a motion criticizing his leader's policy, he was given a score of +1 if the motion was to the left and −1 if it was to the right. If the motion applauded or maintained the leader's policy, it was scored 0. A motion was considered to be to the left for the period of time covered if it criticized the leadership by favoring a greater role for the government in social welfare or economic management, disengagement from imperial or colonial postures, a pro-European stance, or greater penal liberalization. A motion which criticized the leaders by favoring policies toward the opposite pole was considered to be to the right.

Using these criteria, each backbench MP was accorded a net score computed from the number of motions signed and which motions they were. The score furthest to the left totaled +8 and the score furthest to the right totaled −48. Dividing the backbench according to ideological tendency into two wings as equally as possible, those MPs tending toward the left had scores of +8 to −1; those MPs tending toward the right had scores of −2 to −48.

The application of this measure of ideological orientation suggests that the indicators of career aspirations and of prior socialization were *not* good indicators of ideology. About 48 percent of the left (80 of 166) and about 45 percent of the right (71 of 159) had high career aspirations. About 60 percent of the left (100 of 166) and 46 percent of the right (73 of 159) were educated at Eton or Harrow or Oxford or Cambridge. If one excludes the center (score of +1, 0, −1), about 56 percent of the left (40 of 72) and 45 percent of the right had high career aspirations. Sixty-nine percent of the left (50 of 72) and 46 percent of the right had stronger prior socialization. While these figures suggest a modest tendency for Conservative MPs on the left to have higher career aspirations and stronger prior socialization, as *indicators* of leftist tendency, both career aspirations and prior socialization would obviously contain considerable error. Table 5.12 summarizes the situation. A value approaching +100 suggests a perfect direct relationship and −100 a perfect inverse relationship. Values closer to 0 suggest no value as an indicator.

We can conclude from this table that the relationships we found between career aspirations and prior socialization on the one hand and backbench voting behavior on the other are apparently not vulnerable to the criticism that the indicators of the former two variables might instead have been denoting differences in ideological orientation.

Table 5.12
Career Aspirations and Prior Socialization as Indicators of Leftist Ideological Tendencies

	Career Aspirations	*Prior Socialization*
Left and Center (N 166)	−04	+20
Left without Center (N 72)	+12	+38
Right (N 159)	+10	+08

Notes

[1] Donald Stokes and Warren Miller, "Party Government and the Salience of Congress," in *Elections and the Political Order*, ed. Angus Campbell et al. (New York: John Wiley and Sons, 1966), p.210. See also David R. Mayhew, *Congress: The Electoral Connection* (New Haven, Conn.: Yale University Press, 1974).

[2] There is growing evidence to indicate that the alignment of a Congressman's voting behavior with particular charateristics of his district can affect his ability to get reelected. See, for example, David Mayhew, *Party Loyalty Among Congressmen: The Difference Between Democrats and Republicans, 1947 - 1962* (Cambridge, Mass.: Harvard University Press, 1966), pp. 75-78, who points out the relationship between ownership-occupancy of housing in districts, Congressional voting behavior on housing, and reelection. See also our discussion of percentage of farmers in districts, Congressional voting on farm policy, and reelection (Chapter 9). There is also evidence that the alignment of a Congressman's voting behavior with expressed opinions of his constituents has an effect on his ability to get reelected. For example, see David R. Segal and Thomas S. Smith, "Congressional Responsibility and the Organization of Constituency Attitudes," in *Political Attitudes and Public Opinion*, ed. Dan D. Nimmo and Charles M. Bonjean (New York: David McKay, 1972), pp. 562-68, and our discussion of this topic in Chapter 10.

[3]John W. Kingdon, *Congressmen's Voting Decisions* (New York: Harper & Row, 1973), p. 46.

[4]Roger Davidson, *The Role of the Congressman* (New York: Pegasus, 1969), p. 198. See also Julius Turner, *Party and Constituency: Pressures on Congress*, rev. ed. by Edward V. Schneier, Jr. (Baltimore, Md.: Johns Hopkins Press, 1970), pp. 227-34. Recall that when asked a similar question, almost 80 percent of the Gaullist deputies said that the member should follow his party (see Chapter 4, p. 147).

[5]Randall B. Ripley, *Party Leaders in the House of Representatives* (Washington, D. C.: The Brookings Institution, 1967), pp. 143-45, 199.

[6]*Ibid.*, p. 144.

[7]*Ibid.*, p. 144.

[8]John F. Manley, *The Politics of Finance: The House Committee on Ways and Means* (Boston: Little, Brown and Co., 1970), p.39.

[9]That is, he prefers greater ideological and programmatic commonality or consensus among party members. He wouldn't object if the southern Democrats went where they "belonged," that is, to the Republican party.

[10]See, for example, Joe Martin, *My First Fifty Years in Politics* (New York: McGraw Hill, 1960), pp. 182-83, and Ripley, *Party Leaders in the House of Representatives*, p. 73.

[11]An assumption underlying this line of thinking is that the characteristics of districts, such as income level or occupational and racial mix, are indicative of policy demands likely to emanate from these districts. We thus "impute" or infer attitudes based on demographic characteristics of the district.

[12]Lewis Froman, "Inter-Party Constituency Differences and Congressional Voting Behavior," *American Political Science Review* 57 (March 1963): 59.

[13]Lewis Froman, *Congressmen and Their Constituencies* (Chicago: Rand McNally, 1963), p. 92.

[14]Froman, *Congressmen and Their Constituencies*, pp.95-96. See also Kingdon, *Congressmen's Voting Decisions*, pp. 113-14.

[15]Examples are : Ripley, *Party Leaders in the House of Representatives;* Mayhew, *Party Loyalty Among Congressmen*; Turner and Schneier, *Party and Constituency*; Duncan MacRae, Jr., *Dimensions of Congressional Voting* (Berkeley and Los Angeles: The University of California Press, 1958); W. Wayne Shannon, *Party, Constituency and Congressional Voting* (Baton Rouge: Louisiana State University Press, 1968); Leroy N. Rieselbach, *The Roots of Isolationism* (Indianapolis, Ind.: Bobbs-Merrill, 1966), especially p. 138; and Barbara Deckard, "Political Upheaval and Congressional Voting: The Effects of the 1960s on Voting Patterns in the House of Representatives" (Paper presented at 1975 Annual Meeting of the Midwest Political Science Association), pp.13-17.

[16]Ripley, *Party Leaders in the House of Representatives*, pp. 155-56. Also Deckard, "Political Upheaval and Congressional Voting."

[17]V. O. Key, Jr., *Public Opinion and American Democracy* (New York: Knopf, 1964), pp. 484-86.

[18]Shannon, *Party, Constituency, and Congressional Voting*, p. 116; see also p. 129. Given the numerical enormity of the issues they are called to vote upon, Congressmen may take cues from other Congressmen who generally face political problems similar to their own. For this reason, as well as others, Congressmen quite often vote with and frequently take cues from the party delegation from their state. See, for example, Donald Matthews and James Stimson, "Decision-Making by U. S. Representatives," in *Political Decision-Making* , ed. S. Sydney Ulmer (New York: Van Nostrand Reinhold, 1970), and Aage Clausen, "State Party Influence on Congressional Policy Decision," *Midwest Journal of Political Science* 16 (February 1972): 77-101.

[19]Froman, *Congressmen and Their Constituencies*, p. 94.

[20]Froman, *Congressmen and Their Constituencies*, p. 95. The Conservative Coalition is defined as the coalition of a majority of Republicans and a majority of southern Democrats against a majority of northern Democrats.

[21]Mayhew, *Party Loyalty Among Congressmen*, pp. 76-78.

[22]For an examination of the relationship between constituency characteristics, constituency electoral behavior, and the voting behavior of southern Congressmen, see Thomas A. Flinn and Harold Wollman, "Constituency and Roll Call Voting: The Case of Southern Congressmen," *Midwest Journal of Political Science* 10 (May 1966): 192-99. See also Deckard, "Political Upheaval and Congressional Voting."

[23]Shannon, *Party, Constituency and Congressional Voting*, p. 116, also pp. 133-38; and Aage Clausen, *How Congressmen Decide: A Policy Focus* (New York: St. Martin's Press, 1973), especially pp. 142-49.

[24]Shannon, *Party, Constituency and Congressional Voting*, pp. 138-40, 146.

[25]Turner and Schneier, *Party and Constituency*, p. 225.

[26]Shannon, *Party, Constituency and Congressional Voting*, pp. 147-48.

[27]Turner and Schneier, *Party and Constituency*, p.223.

[28]Donald Matthews, *U. S. Senators and Their World* (New York: Random House, 1960), pp. 231-34.

[29]One of the most statistically sophisticated studies relating "imputed" constituency attitudes (that is, using demographic characteristics) to Congressional votes is John E. Jackson's "Some Indirect Evidences of Constituency Pressure on the Senate," *Public Policy* 16 (1967): 253-70. See also his *Constituencies and Leaders in Congress: Their Effects on Senate Voting Behavior* (Cambridge, Mass.: Harvard University Press, 1974), especially pp. 128-29.

[30]Jackson, "Some Indirect Evidence of Constituency Pressure on the Senate," pp. 269-70.

[31]Turner and Schneier, *Party and Constituency*, p. 223. At this point, the reader should be reminded that we

have focused on aggregate constituency characteristics with the assumption that these characteristics are broadly indicative of the types of demands likely to emanate from the districts. The relationship between the expressed opinions of constituents and the voting behavior of Congressmen will be considered in Chapter 10, pages 387-389.

[32] Shannon, *Party, Constituency and Congressional Voting*, pp. 116 and 156. See also Clausen, *How Congressmen Decide*, pp. 142-49.

[33] See also Clarence Stone, "Inter-Party Differences and Congressional Voting Behavior: A Partial Dissent," *American Political Science Review* 57 (September 1963): 665-66; *idem*, "Issue Cleavage Between Democrats and Republicans in the U. S. House of Representatives," *Journal of Public Law* 25 (May 1963): 324-32. These studies point out that different Congressmen representing the same district at different times, but who are from different parties (and, to a lesser extent, even from the same party), do not exhibit similar voting records.

[34] Matthews, *U. S. Senators and their World*, p. 123. See also Turner and Schneier, *Party and Constituency*, p.234-35.

[35] Ripley, *Party Leaders in the House of Representatives*, p. 9. See his Appendix A. pp. 197-204. See, also, Frank Smith, *Congressman from Mississippi* (New York: Capricorn, 1967), p. 147, and Davidson, *The Role of the Congressman*, p. 146.

[36] Charles Clapp, *The Congressman: His Work as He Sees It* (Garden City, N. Y.: Doubleday, 1963), p. 15. A Republican said, "The system seems to prevent one's forming strong friendships on the other side of the aisle" (p. 16). A Democrat commented, "I don't know more than a very few Republicans by sight" (p.16).

[37] Turner and Schneier, *Party and Constituency*, pp. 234-35.

[38] Ralph K. Huitt, "Congressional Organization and Operations in the Field of Money and Credit," in *Fiscal and Debt Management Policies*, Commission on Money and Credit (Englewood Cliffs, N.J.: Prentice-Hall, 1963), p. 419. Emphasis ours.

[39] Barbara Hinckley, *Stability and Change in Congress* (New York: Harper & Row, 1971), p. 108. See also Ripley, *Party Leaders in the House of Representatives*, p. 203, and James Barber, "Leadership Strategies for Legislative Party Cohesion," *Journal of Politics* 28 (May 1966): 352,358.

[40] Frank Sorauf, *Party Politics in America*, 2d ed. (Boston: Little, Brown and Co., 1972), p. 347-48; See also Davidson, *The Role of the Congressman*, p. 146.

[41] Ripley, *Party Leaders in the House of Representatives*, p. 141-42. In response to the question "Do you want to go along with your party?" 74 percent of Democrats and 72 percent of Republicans answered "Yes, strongly" as opposed to "Yes, weakly." None said no.

[42] Ripley, *Party Leaders in the House of Representatives*, p. 141-42.

[43] All of the quotations are from Ripley, *Party Leaders in the House of Representatives*, pp. 142-45.

[44] Ripley, *Party Leaders in the House of Representatives*, p. 144-45. As one would expect, votes that concern party interest and procedural issues elicit the greatest unity on roll call votes. See Turner and Schneier, *Party and Constituency*, Ch. III; and Lewis Froman and Randall Ripley, "Conditions for Party Leadership: The Case of the House Democrats," *American Political Science Review* 59 (March 1965): 52-63.

[45] Ripley, *Party Leaders in the House of Representatives*, p. 194. See also Froman and Ripley, "Conditions for Party Leadership."

[46] Ripley, *Party Leaders in the House of Representatives*, pp. 151-54. See, also, Clem Miller, *Members of the House* (New York: Charles Scribner's Sons, 1962), p. 111 , and George Norris, *Fighting Liberal* (New York: Macmillan, 1945), pp. 105, 134-35.

[47] Raymond A. Bauer, Ithiel de Sola Pool, and Lewis Anthony Dexter, *American Business and Public Policy* (New York: Atherton, 1968) , p. 449; see also pp. 421-23.

[48] See the following: Davidson, *The Role of the Congressman*, p. 146 and Ripley, *Party Leaders in the House of Representatives*, pp. 158-59, 194-95, Appendix A.

[49] Ripley, *Party Leaders in the House of Representatives*, p. 159, and Nicholas A. Masters, "Committee Assignments in the House of Representatives," *American Political Science Review* 55 (June 1961): 345-57.

[50] Ripley, *Party Leaders in the House of Representatives*, p. 159.

[51] *Ibid*.

[52] Robert Dahl, *Congress and Foreign Policy* (New York: Harcourt, Brace and World, 1950), p. 50.

[53] Ripley, *Party Leaders in the House of Representatives*, p. 159. See also David Truman, *Congressional Party* (New York: John Wiley and Sons, 1959), pp. 190-91.

[54] One's career in United States politics can be enhanced by running for alternative positions. For example, a legislator may run for President, Vice-President, Governor or even the other house. Our concern here is with career enhancement within a given house. In the United States there is an alternative route to executive power not available in a system such as in Britain.

[55] Matthews, *U.S. Senators and their World*, p. 119. See also Truman, *The Congressional Party*, Chapters 4 and 6.

[56] Davidson, *The Role of the Congressman*, p. 150. Ripley, *Party Leaders in the House of Representatives*, also indicates that "The leaders may be intense partisans, but they are not usually intense ideologues" (p. 161).

[57] Ripley, *Party Leaders in the House of Representatives*, p. 39. See also his article "The Party Whip Organizations in the United States House of Representatives," *American Political Science Review* 18 (Sep-

tember 1964): 561-76. Note that this high degree of loyalty is even more significant if one keeps in mind that the power to appoint and replace Democratic whips rests exclusively with state delegations within a particular zone.

[58] See Randall Ripley, *Power in the Senate* (New York: St. Martin's Press, 1969), Chapter 4, and his *Party Leaders in the House of Representatives*, pp.54-61, Chapter 7. However, the persistence of William Knowland (R. Cal.) in his party leadership role in the Senate despite his unenthusiastic support of President Eisenhower's policies indicates removal is not easy. It also points to the independence of the Congressional party from the President.

[59] Randall Ripley, *Majority Party Leadership in Congress* (Boston: Little, Brown and Co., 1969), p. 177. The Congresses studied were the Fifty-ninth, Sixty-second, Sixty-third, Sixty-seventh, Sixty-ninth, Seventy-third, Eightieth, Eighty-third, Eighty-sixth, and Eighty-eighth. His study, *Party Leaders in the House of Representatives*, revealed the same thing for minority party leaders in the House.

[60] Manley, *The Politics of Finance*, p. 24. See also Louis P. Westerfield, "Majority Party Leadership and the Committee System in the House of Representatives," *American Political Science Review* 68 (December, 1974): 1593-1604.

[61] Stephen K. Bailey, *Congress in the Seventies* (New York: St. Martin's Press, 1970), p. 44; also see George Goodwin, *The Little Legislatures* (Amherst: University of Massachusetts Press, 1970), pp. 88-90. Wayne Swanson in "Committee Assignments and the Non-Conformist Legislator: Democrats in the U. S. Senate," *Midwest Journal of Political Science* 13 (February 1969): 84-94, argues that the Johnson rule has modified the seniority system in such a way as to help support the "Establishment." However, strictly speaking, this does not contradict Bailey; it rather points to the significance of who holds the leadership positions.

[62] Ripley, *Power in the Senate*, p. 97. See also Goodwin, *The Little Legislatures*, pp. 85,88; and Matthews, *U.S. Senators and Their World*, Chapter 5.

[63] Ripley, *Power in the Senate*, p. 102.

[64] Ripley, *Power in the Senate*, p. 98. See also John G. Stewart, "Two Strategies of Leadership: Johnson and Mansfield," in *Congressional Behavior*, ed. Nelson Polsby (New York: Random House, 1971), pp. 61-92.

[65] The first two parallel Manley's discussion of the Ways and Means Committee, *The Politics of Finance*, p. 3l). The third is suggested by Ripley, *Party Leaders in the House of Representatives*, p. 9.

[66] In the revolt against Speaker Cannon, the Speaker was stripped of the power to control chairmanships and committee membership and his seat on the Rules Committee. Ripley notes that two post-1910 Speakers, Republican Nicholas Longworth (1925-31) and Democrat Sam Rayburn (1940-61) were particularly effective in influencing the composition of committee membership. *(Party Leaders in the House of Representatives*, pp. 21-22).

[67] See Martin, *My First Fifty Years in Politics*, p. 181; Ripley, *Party Leaders in the House of Representatives*, pp. 57,61; Goodwin, *The Little Legislatures*, p. 76; and Masters, "Committee Assignments in the House of Representatives," p. 375.

[68] Ripley, *Party Leaders in the House of Representatives*. p. 56; See also Manley, *The Politics of Finance*, pp. 23-38, and Richard Fenno, *Power of the Purse* (Boston: Little, Brown and Co., 1966), pp. 56-57.

[69] *Congressional Record*, November 7, 1967 (daily edition), H 14704. The appeal by McCormack also indicates the perceived influence of the Speaker's power.

[70] Manley, *The Politics of Finance*, p. 25. See also Richard Fenno, *Congressmen in Committees* (Boston: Little, Brown and Co., 1973). pp. 25-26; *idem*, *Power of the Purse*, pp. 66-67.

[71] Ripley, *Party Leaders in the House of Representatives*, p. 22.

[72] Ripley, *Party Leaders in the House of Representatives*, p. 22. For a further discussion of the maneuver see *New York Times* for January 2, 9, 16, and 18, 1949.

[73] Ripley, *Party Leaders in the House of Representatives*, p. 57; Goodwin, *The Little Legislatures*, p. 73.

[74] Ripley, *Party Leaders in the House of Representatives*, p. 57; Goodwin, *The Little Legislatures*, pp. 75f; Fenno, *Power of the Purse*, pp.56f.

[75] It should be noted that the power of party leaders, including the Speaker, has been limited or somewhat circumscribed on *both* important and lesser committee assignments. For example, Manley's discussion of the Ways and Means Committee (in *The Politics of Finance*) indicates not only that the Speaker and party leaders of both parties lost in some rare instances in their attempt to place their men on the Ways and Means Committee, but also that they often had to negotiate with various individuals and groups, including state delegations. The "same state" rule (which applies about 50 percent of the time) coupled with the "seniority" rule within the delegation has limited the Speaker's choice of new members.

[76] Ripley, *Party Leaders in the House of Representatives*, p. 60. See also Turner and Schneier, *Party and Constituency*, p. 183.

[77] Ripley, *Party Leaders in the House of Representatives*, p. 61. Applying early is usually considered important for getting your first choice.

[78] Manley, *The Politics of Finance*, pp. 2-30. No scores were available for the fourth Democrat, Stephen Young, who served before scores were available. However, his later voting record showed him to be a party loyalist.

[79] Quoted in Manley, *The Politics of Finance*, p. 29.

[80] Quoted in Manley, *The Politics of Finance*, pp. 38-39.
[81] *Ibid.*
[82] These data and findings are from Manley, *The Politics of Finance*, pp. 41-42. Another conclusion emerging from Manley's study is that members selected to certain important committees, such as the Ways and Means Committee, tend to overrepresent their party's ideology. See also Ripley, *Party Leaders in the House of Representatives*, p. 61; Fenno, *Congressmen in Committees*, pp. 25-26; Masters, "Committee Assignments in the House of Representatives," pp. 354-55; Clapp, *The Congressman*, pp. 228-30; Bauer, Pool, and Dexter, *American Business and Public Policy*, Chapter 6.

[83] John Quistgaard, "The Applicability of the Apprenticeship Norm to Membership on and Transfers to Prestigious Senate Committees: 1968-1972" (Mimeographed, University of Arizona), p. 41. Committee prestige was measured according to the procedure found in Matthews, *U.S. Senators and Their World*, pp. 148-50.

[84] Fenno, *Power of the Purse*, pp. 69-70.

[85] Computed from information found in Ripley, *Party Leaders in the House of Representatives*, p. 150; 152-53.

[86] For other evidence, see Ripley, *Party Leaders in the House of Representatives*, pp. 152-53.

[87] Ripley, *Party Leaders in the House of Representatives*, p. 156.

[88] Ripley, *Party Leaders in the House of Representatives*, p. 150.

[89] See Masters, "Committee Assignments in the House of Representatives," pp. 345-50; Ripley, *Party Leaders in the House of Representatives,* Chapter 3, and pp. 150, 191-92.

[90] Ripley, *Party Leaders in the House of Representatives*, p. 191.

[91] Ripley, *Party Leaders in the House of Representatives*, p. 192.

[92] This section of the chapter is a revised version of John E. Schwarz and Geoffrey Lambert, "Career Objectives, Group Feeling, and Legislative Party Voting Cohesion: The British Conservatives, 1959-1968," *Journal of Politics* 33 (May 1971): 399-421.

[93] Earlier debates, newspapers, and commentaries were used to calculate deliberate abstentions. The method is similar to that used by Jorgen S. Rasmussen, *The Relations of the Profumo Rebels with Their Local Parties* (Tucson: The University of Arizona Press, 1966).

[94] See 638 House of Commons Debates (H. C. Deb.), Column 57 and 145, April 11, 1961; *Manchester Guardian* April 12, 1961; and *Daily Telegram*, April 12, 1961.

[95] See 638 H. C. Deb., Col. 561 and 635, April 13, 1961, and *Manchester Guardian*, April 14, 1961.

[96] See 645 H. C. Deb., Col. 1777-1884, August 3, 1961; *Manchester Guardian*, August 4 and 5, 1961; and Anthony Sampson, *Macmillan: A Study in Ambiguity* (New York: Simon and Schuster, 1967), pp. 214-15.

[97] See 679 H. C. Deb., Col. 169, June 17, 1963; *Manchester Guardian*, June 18 and 19, 1963; *Daily Telegraph*, June 18 and 19, 1963; Randolph Churchill, *Fight for the Tory Leadership* (Boston: Houghton Mifflin, 1964), p. 76.

[98] See 691 H. C. Deb., Col. 377-380, March 11, 1964; *Times*, March 11 and 12, 1964; *Sunday Times*, March 15, 1964; and 692 H. C. Deb., Col. 339-404, March 24, 1964; Ronald Butt, *The Power of Parliament* (New York: Walker and Co., 1967), pp. 251-74.

[99] Butt, *The Power of Parliament,* pp. 233-40.

[100] Butt, *The Power of Parliament*, Chapter 9.

[101] Bernard Crick, *The Reform of Parliament* (London: Weidenfeld and Nicolson, 1970), pp. 134-44.

[102] Robert Jackson, *Rebels and Whips: An Analysis of Dissention, Discipline, and Cohesion in British Political Parties Since 1945* (New York: St. Martin's Press, 1968), p. 169.

[103] Robert McKenzie, *British Political Parties*, 2d ed. (New York: St. Martin's Press, 1963), p. 594a, and Churchill, *Fight for the Tory Leadership*, pp. 76-77.

[104] See 722 H. C. Deb., Col. 2053-2058, December 21, 1965; *Manchester Guardian*, December 23, 1965; and *Daily Telegraph*, December 23, 1965. The right wing had fifty rebels and precipitated the vote.

[105] See 746, H. C. Deb., May 11, 1967; *Daily Telegraph*, May 12, 1967; and *The Guardian*, May 12 and 13, 1967. The twenty-six rebels were the same on both votes.

[106] For an historical account of the relationship between age and ministerial rewards, see Phillip W. Buck, *Amateurs and Professionals in British Politics* (Chicago: University of Chicago Press, 1963), p. 117.

[107] Leon Epstein, *British Politics in the Suez Crisis* (Urbana: University of Illinois Press, 1964).

[108] Rasmussen, *The Relations of the Profumo Rebels*, p. 47.

[109] Our operational definition of safeness of seat was whether or not the candidate had won his previous contest by at least a 10 percent plurality.

[110] Epstein, *British Politics in the Suez Crisis*, and Rasmussen, *The Relations of the Profumo Rebels*.

[111] See Anthony Sampson, *Anatomy of Britain* (London: Hodder and Stoughton, 1966), especially Chapters 4, 5, 12 and 13; and Hugh Thomas, ed., *The Establishment* (London: Anthony Blond, 1962).

[112] The exact measure of aspiration was calculated on the basis of the month and year of the first major rebellion following a general election. These were April, 1961, for the 1959-64 Parliament, December, 1965, for the 1964-66 Parliament and May, 1967, for the 1966 Parliament.

[113] The independent impact of each constraint became greater as MPs were increasingly less subject to the other two constraints. This can be demonstrated by examining the marginals of Table 5.8. Doing so for career

aspirations shows that, as the number of other constraints declined, the impact of career aspirations on loyalty rose from 11.4 percent, when both of the other constraints were high, to 27.8 percent when neither of the other constraints was high. The intermediate points showed differences in rates of loyalty of 13.8 percent and 22.9 percent. The same procedure applied to prior socialization shows that its impact also increased as MPs were less subject to the other two constraints—from 10.8 percent to 21.3 percent with intermediate points of 13.2 percent and 16.4 percent.

[114] The votes were on rents, Suez (three), Cyprus, coal, NATO, and the economic situation. Rebellions on the whitefish and cotton industry divisions were not included because they were regional in nature.

[115] Although the renomination of some MPs was publicly challenged, the fact that local associations did not generally challenge the renomination of their MP for joining major rebellions probably explains why this was the weakest of the three constraints. The relative lack of challenges may have been due to the fact that most rebels were from the right wing and thus were less susceptible to local challenge (that is, they did not join the opposition).

[116] See 722 H. C. Deb., Col. 2053-2058, December 21, 1965; *Manchester Guardian,* December 23, 1965; and *Daily Telegraph,* December 23, 1965. The right wing had fifty rebels and precipitated the vote.

[117] It should be noted that the Conservatives do not appear to apply discipline as much when in opposition as when in power. In addition to the Rhodesia case, other examples are the Kenyan and race relations rebellions of 1968. In these cases discipline was so relaxed that two members of the Conservative shadow cabinet not only joined the rebellion but went unpunished. Examination of the rebels suggests that, like the Rhodesia rebellion, the three constraints did not influence backbench voting behavior in either the Kenyan or the race relations divisions.

[118] See 746 H. C. Deb., May 11, 1967; *Daily Telegraph,* May 12, 1967; and *The Guardian,* May 12 and 13, 1967. The twenty-six rebels were the same for both votes.

[119] Recall that potential career vulnerability had decidedly the least effect of the three constraints.

[120] In a later chapter, we will examine the effect of these constraints on backbench supervision of the government, especially as it pertains to putting oral questions. See Chapter 8.

[121] For an earlier application of early day motions to the study of backbench thinking, see S. E. Finer, H.B. Berrington and D. J. Bartholomew, *Backbench Opinion in the House of Commons,* (Oxford: Pergamon Press, 1961).

Chapter 6
Legislative-Executive Relations In The Making of Legislation

As a typical high school civics textbook depicts the political system, the center of power and influence in the making of legislation lies in the legislature. It is the legislature that makes the laws. The executive stands at the periphery. At the opposite pole is the argument that this view is excessively formalistic (looks too much at formal constitutional powers) and does not take into account the realities of twentieth-century politics. According to this second view, the executive has become the center of power and influence in regard to the making of laws. It is the legislature that stands at the periphery. While the legislature may pass the laws, the development of policies that the legislature considers has become centered increasingly in the hands of the executive. Noting this trend as it relates to the United States, Senator George McGovern has said "Fundamentally we have experienced an exhaustion of important institutions in America. Today, only the President is activist and strong, while other traditional centers of power are depleted."[1]

The two views just outlined could hardly be at greater odds with one another. In this chapter, the first of three on the legislature and the executive, we examine legislative-executive relations in the four societies of our study with the objective of describing the relative roles of the legislature and the executive in the process of making legislation. By legislation we mean authoritative public decisions that have been specifically subjected to legislative action.[2] We want to assess how central or peripheral the four legislatures typically have been vis-à-vis the executive in the initiation and development of policies contained in such decisions.

Our examination covers the four legislatures included in the study under six different governing parties. These are the American Democratic and Republican parties, the British Labour and Conservative parties, the French Gaullist party, and the West German CDU/CSU.

We shall begin by establishing some general guidelines for examining relations between the legislature and the executive. Then, with the purpose of arriving at comparisons and conclusions about the relative roles of the legislature and the executive, we will draw upon the case studies presented in Chapter 3, supplementing them with additional evidence forthcoming both from other case studies and other relevant data. Using this evidence, we first take up relations between the legislature and the executive in the three European systems. Included here is a discussion of both the making of legislation and, related to it, the politics of parliamentary selection of the executive. Following this analysis, we will take up relations between the executive and the Congress of the United States. Our analysis will then proceed to a comparison of decision-making as it applies to foreign and domestic policy in the four systems. A final section will summarize the major conclusions of the chapter.

Of course, relations between the legislature and the executive do not end with the passage of legislation. How the executive applies legislation, as well as other decisions it makes, are also important aspects of the policy process. After our discussion in this chapter of legislative-executive relations in the making of legislation, we will turn our attention in Chapter 7 to legislative supervision of the executive in the application and implementation of policy.

Finally, in Chapter 8, we take up the question of what factors appear to mold and shape relations between legislators and the executive. This chapter will include a discussion of variables affecting: (1) the extent to which the four legislatures have been central to the development of policies contained in legislation; (2) differences in levels of influence each of the legislatures exerted across domestic as contrasted to foreign policies; and (3) the extent to which legislators engaged in activities pertaining to overseeing and supervising the executive.

The evidence and findings we present in this chapter can be viewed in the context of an argument frequently made regarding the four legislatures under consideration. The argument is that, compared to the executive, the legislature has become rather peripheral to the initiation and development of legislation and is confined instead essentially to authorizing and legitimizing policy initiatives formulated primarily by the executive. At most, according to this argument, the legislature has been central mainly in the sense of blocking, obstructing, or amending action proposed by the executive.[3]

Circumstances surrounding domestic legislation passed during recent years lead to a somewhat different conclusion. Beyond the power to authorize legislation, the four legislatures have differed appreciably in the extent to which they have been integral to the development of legislation. Particularly the Congress, but also the Bundestag, have been central to the development of key policies contained in domestic legislation more so than has been the case for the other two legislatures. Indeed, it is fair to conclude that the Congress has been an essentially equal and coordinate partner with the Presidency in the process of making domestic legislation. We mean this not simply in the sense that Congress can and does substantially alter or defeat executive proposals but also that the Congress has been a significant arena in which the origination and initiation of successfully enacted policies has occurred.

On the other hand, the argument that legislatures have become rather peripheral to the making of decisions has had greater general validity in the area of foreign and defense policy. Each of the legislatures, including the Congress and the Bundestag, ordinarily has been discernibly less effective in influencing foreign and defense policy decisions than decisions relating to domestic policy. Still, even here we will find a level of legislative involvement and influence that ought not be neglected.

Some Preliminary Remarks

Our discussion begins with some general conceptual points about the policy process.

First, it should be noted that the executive arena may encompass more than the chief executive and cabinet, just as the legislative arena may encompass more than legislators. In the case of the executive, for example, the policies it adopts frequently might be more properly and accurately attributed to lower executive officials and agencies than to the chief executive or cabinet officials. However, unless otherwise indicated, executive policy will be taken to include policy developed in the executive bureaucracy if it received the tacit or explicit approval of the chief executive or cabinet officials. Similarly, policy suggested and developed by legislative staff will be attributed to the legislature providing that such policy was advocated by legislators.

In examining executive-legislative relations, we will divide the policy process into three stages; first, the stage of policy formulation and initiation of proposals into the legislative institutions; second, the stage of deliberation and authorization (or legitimation); and third, the implementation stage (which we examine in the following chapter).

This reduces somewhat the "steps" usually alluded to in decision-making theory.[4] Under the stage of initiation we include the gathering of information and intelligence, along with consideration of various policy alternatives leading to the formulation of a specific option. Also included is the recommendation of that specific policy alternative. The second stage includes the deliberation on and/or struggle involved in securing "approval" or authorization for the alternative. The third stage, implementation, involves the embodiment and application of the authorized policy in the form of concrete government actions and programs. Here legislative supervision becomes relevant. After having enacted a policy, decision makers continue to be concerned about the adopted policy and may supervise its application to see whether or not it fulfills the expectations and objectives for which it was enacted. Negative appraisal and feedback about the policy and/or shifting power resources may set the policy process in motion again, resulting in alteration or negation of the previous policy.

As this suggests, however, the activities of initiation, deliberation, and supervision can be interspersed, meshed, often occurring simultaneously and performed by different participants. Supervising policy implementation may be carried on, for instance, partly through the ongoing process of initiating and deliberating on legislation. For example, Congressional legislation limiting Presidential powers to impound funds, adopted in 1974, was aimed at controlling the implementation of policy through the process of initiating and enacting legislation. One activity can blend into another. Though there is a distinction between the three activities cited above, they need not necessarily be undertaken separately.

A special word needs also to be said about initiation. Legislative scholars generally agree that executives initiate most major legislation. Unfortunately, this idea sometimes carries with it the equating of initiation with power and dominance. Initiation may well be an advantage in the policy process, but surely it does not guarantee dominance.[5] To respond to initiatives (whether by amendment, approval, or rejection) is not necessarily to play a peripheral or even subservient role.

Furthermore, "executive initiative" somewhat oversimplifies the reality of the process of initiating policy. Executive policies proposed today are not proposed simply by the executive; they may be the result of a bewildering array of forces, multiple power centers, and compromises in which the legislature, itself, may have played an important part.

The term executive initiative may oversimplify the reality of the birth of policy ideas by focusing on a narrow time span. Nelson Polsby draws our attention to this point with his observation that:

> It is a cliché of academic political science that in legislative matters, it is the President who initiates policy, and Congress which responds, amplifying and modifying and rearranging elements which are essentially originated in the executive branch. Not much work has been done, however, on following this river of bills-becoming-and-not-becoming-laws back to its sources. Where do innovations in policy come from *before* the President "initiates" them?
> Old Washington hands know the answer. There is very little new under the sun. . . . In the heat of a presidential campaign or when a newly inaugurated president wants a "new" program, desk drawers fly open all over Washington. Pet schemes are fished out, dusted off, and tried out on the new political leaders.
> There is often a hiatus of years—sometimes decades—between the first proposal of the policy innovation and its appearance as a presidential "initiative"—much less a law.[6]

Polsby speaks of an "incubation" period for new policy proposals. It may be years after an idea is sounded out in a legislature before it gets enough widespread support or, in time, becomes "ripe" for enactment. The legislature may play a vital role during this incubation period. According to Ralph Huitt:

> What is easy to miss is the origin of many bills which in time pick up enough support to become "Administration Bills." One or more members of Congress may have originated the idea and done all the spade work necessary to make it viable. One thinks of the lonely voice of George Norris in the 1920's calling for a Federal River Project which became, in a different political climate, the Tennessee Valley Authority.[7]

This example along with the Federal Reserve system, Medicare, civil rights bills, the peace corps, and revenue sharing are but a few illustrations of legislation proposed by individual Congressmen before they were "initiated" by the executive. Later we will cite similar examples from the European legislatures.

While important legislation may originate in the legislature, and basic groundwork for its passage be laid by legislators, it is the executive that frequently focuses the energy necessary to make significant policy proposals a viable possibility.[8] Our general point is simply that "executive initiation" does not necessarily mean that legislators (or other actors in the political arena) have never thought of the idea. Indeed, they may have both originated the idea and helped lay much of the foundation necessary for passage before the idea became an executive "initiative."

The phrase executive initiative sometimes also overlooks the fact that, during the process of executive initiation, there may have been consultation with legislative leaders or other legislators that resulted in significant adjustment of executive proposals before their initiation into the legislature. In some of the systems under examination, such consultation regularly occurs during the initiation as well as the deliberation stage, and there frequently are continuous interchanges between legislators, their aides, private persons, or pressure groups, and relevant executive personnel who are concerned with specific types of policy.[9]

Finally, executive initiation, as it is usually used, with its accompanying equation of initiation and power, tends to overlook what has been called the "rule of anticipated reactions."[10] The executive, in formulating policy proposals, may have to keep in mind the ideas of legislators, past actions by the legislators, competing policy priorities, the nature of the legislative process, and the internal legislative power structure.

In determining the influence of a legislature, our starting point will ordinarily be the formulation of the proposal upon which legislative deliberation takes place rather than the original source of the idea. This will lead us often, although in the end less than some would suspect, to focus on the executive. When the formulation and initiation of policy takes place within the executive, we will also ask whether the content of the initiated proposal appears to have been influenced by policy demands from within the legislature. This might be a result either of the direct participation of legislators or of executive anticipation of pressures that would arise in the legislature. In addition, we will want to look at the influence of legislators during the deliberation stage. Are the original proposals as sponsored by the executive changed during the deliberation stage or, indeed, even accepted? How much does opposition arise within the legislature and how successful is such opposition in shaping the content of policy?

As these remarks suggest, we will examine influence from many different sides. As we proceed, our analysis will progressively focus on the following question: to what extent has the legislature, as opposed to the executive, been the central arena for developing the basic policies contained in legislation? This will require us to look at the extent to which the four legislatures, as compared to their respective executives, were central to the formulation and initiation of successful legislation as well as the extent to which the legislatures seemed capable of independently determining both the modification and eventual fate of executive-formulated legislation. We also will distinguish between different policy areas and will concentrate particularly on the influence of the legislature in the making of domestic policy as compared to foreign and defense policy.

Executive-Legislative Relations in Great Britain, France, and West Germany: General Patterns

Our discussion turns first to executive-legislative relations in the Western European systems. Three conclusions will emerge from the discussion. First, the initiation of most adopted legislation has come not from the legislature, but from the executive. This conclusion flows both from aggregate data on the introduction of legislation and from a series of case studies that we will consider toward the close of this section. Second, in constructing their proposals, governments in all three systems have been sensitive to the legislature, certainly to their followers in the legislature, in the sense that legislators' attempts to influence government legislation have frequently met with at least some success. Finally, evidence drawn from the case studies will suggest that the three legislatures have differed in the degree to which they have been central to the development of policies contained in legislation. The Bundestag has played a more substantial part than the House of Commons or the National Assembly. This difference, in turn, provides some perspective on variations in the policy-making impact legislatures can have, a perspective to which the experiences of Congress will add later in the chapter.

While the contemporary relationship between the executive and the legislature is the primary object of our analysis, as we begin our discussion we ought to note, if only briefly, that the political importance of each of the institutions has been quite different at different times. In Great Britain, for example, we will find that the contemporary executive is a very strong institution in its relations with the House of Commons. Its strength has grown rather steadily from the later nineteenth century, although occasionally meeting challenges in the House to "redress" the balance. In the middle of the nineteenth century, however, the executive was in a much weaker position. More than a few governments during the period found their support in the Commons to be far less dependable than it is under usual circumstances today. Substantial changes in France and Germany have also occurred. But, instead of rather steady change as in Britain, in both France and Germany there have been sharp swings toward legislative dominance in one period and away from it in another. For example, since the middle of the nineteenth century in France there have been periods of strong legislatures (for example, 1946-58, under the Fourth Republic, and, for the most part, 1875-1940 under the Third Republic) and sharp swings to strong executives (1959 to the present) or even dictatorial executives (the Vichy regime during World War II).

Despite these changes, it has been customary for the executive to play an important part in the formulation of policy for initiation into the legislature even during periods of strong legislative influence. The process of formulating policy stands within the executive can be long, arduous, and complex and can involve consultations with many groups and actors. Indeed, as we will observe in Chapter 9, consultations with interest groups constitute a significant element of the process of formulating legislative proposals within the cabinet and administration and, therefore, constitute a significant element of the legislative process itself. In some systems, especially Great Britain and France, these consultations may sometimes exclude the actual participation of legislators, as was the case for French agricultural policy and, for the most part, resale price maintenance in Great Britain (see Chapter 3).

The contemporary cabinets have different structures in the different systems, especially regarding the powers and prerogatives of the leader of the cabinet. Some are quite decentralized.[11] Within the cabinet, the Prime Minister, Chancellor, or Premier is in a situation of dealing with other cabinet members many of whom have their own political base. Many of them may be politicians in their own right. To the degree cabinet ministers get substantively involved in the development of policy, they may also have a source of information from their ministry that exceeds that of the leader of the cabinet.[12] However, the leader of the cabinet also has resources which help him to influence and coordinate the policy process. These resources relate especially to the selection and dismissal of ministers as well as the organization and functioning of the cabinet. In addition to resources such as these, the leader of the cabinet has a personal staff or a staff made available to him through his party. However, how well the leader can influence and coordinate the policy process in the cabinet to his advantage depends not only on these resources but also upon his own political support within and outside the cabinet and Parliament, the force of his personality, and his skill in using these factors.

Unlike the United States, the government in Great Britain, France, and West Germany is politically responsible before a house of the legislature (the House of Commons, the National Assembly, and the Bundestag). Because of this, as we observed in Chapter 2, the government participates directly in legislative debates and can be questioned directly. It also participates directly in the deliberations of the legislative committee system. However, in the French Fifth Republic (as in the United States), members of the legislature cannot simultaneously be members of the executive. This is not the case in Great Britain and West Germany. Many members of the cabinet (now always including the Prime Minister in Britain) are also members of the legislature. Thus, when we refer to *legislators*, as distinct from the *executive*, in the British and German systems, we will be referring to legislators who are not also members of the executive; in our terminology, relations between the executive and the legislature in Britain and West Germany denote relations between the executive and legislators who are not members of the executive.

Aggregate Data

In each of the Western European systems under consideration, the executive has been the major place for introducing most of the bills adopted by the legislature. This has been the case whether we refer to Great Britain, or West Germany, or France. Thus, somewhat over 75 percent of the legislation adopted by the House of Commons from 1957 to 1969 was introduced by the government; in West Germany, also, approximately 75 percent of the legislation passed by the Bundestag during this period was introduced by the executive; and, in the French Fifth Republic, the executive was responsible for the introduction of about 90 percent of the legislation passed by the National Assembly.

On the whole, the legislation introduced by the executive has also been more significant legislation than that introduced by nonexecutive legislators. Indeed, significant pieces of legislation introduced by backbenchers and passed by the British House of Commons over the past decade have been few and far between. Of the few instances, some of the more notable have been abolition of capital punishment and restructuring legislation on homosexuality, both of which were a result of private member bills. There are also some examples of rather important pieces of legislation adopted by the Bundestag which were not introduced by the government. Some illustrations are legislation that increased financial aid for the housing of mine workers, exempted agricultural products from the industrial transportation tax, supported the concept of "people's capitalism" (through profit sharing and by changing rules or other conditions so as to enable low-income persons a greater opportunity to purchase stocks), and changed some aspects of the public health insurance system. Still compared to initiatives the government introduced, relatively few significant legislative proposals adopted by the Bundestag have been introduced by members of the Bundestag outside the government.

A glance at the figures in Table 6.1 indicates, as well, that the executive has gotten most of its legislative initiatives adopted, whereas backbenchers have not. The differences between the percentages are striking.

To say that the executive has been the locus for the introduction of most adopted legislation, and much of the most important legislation, suggests the major part it has played in the policy process. However, it does not take into account the influence

Table 6.1
Legislative Success in Three Western European Political Systems

	Percent of Executive-Sponsored Bills Approved	Percent of Non-Executive-Sponsored Bills Approved	Percent of All Adopted Bills Which Were Executive-Sponsored
Britain (1957-69)	96	27	77
West Germany (1949-69)	89	39	76
France (1961-66)	81	04	93

legislators may have had both during the stage in which executive policy was being formulated and during the stage after it was introduced (the deliberation stage).

For example, government-initiated legislation occasionally has been the result of legislative pressures for action. The parliamentary and public pressures leading up to the government's initiation of legislation covering fair trade and other consumer practices in late 1972 is just one of a number of examples that can be cited for Great Britain.[13] Illustrations from France include proposals forwarded by the government to extend social security coverage to professional persons as well as to self-employed shopkeepers and merchants and legislation to reform industrial works committees.[14] And, examples from Germany where Bundestag pressure preceded government initiatives have occurred in a number of areas including transportation, agriculture, tariffs, and cartels.[15]

Indeed, whether during the stage of policy initiation or of policy deliberation, legislative action has quite often been successful in influencing executive policy in each of the three European systems. One of the most complete studies of backbench influence on government policy in Britain covered the years 1945-57.[16] The study attempted to locate all rebellions by governing party MPs and to measure their effect. Rebellion was defined so as not only to include the act of voting against the policies of the government but also to include signing early day motions critical of the government or speaking out in other ways against government policies. The research, carried out by Lynskey, uncovered thirty rebellions by Labour backbenchers when their party controlled the government from 1945 to 1951 and twenty-seven rebellions by Conservative backbenchers from 1951 to 1957 when their party controlled the government. Lynskey found that many of these rebellions were successful either in whole or in part in influencing both government proposals and the policies finally adopted by the House. The activities of Labour backbenchers successfully altered the policies of the Labour government from 1945 to 1951 in 47 percent of the cases (fourteen of thirty cases). Conservative backbenchers influenced the policy stances of the Conservative government from 1951 to 1957 in 78 percent of the cases (twenty-one of twenty-seven cases). The results for the two parties combined, by degree of success and importance of issue, are found in Table 6.2.

Analysis of amendments proposed in debate by CDU/CSU parliamentarians again reveals the high percentage of success parliamentarians can achieve. We examined two legislative periods, 1957-61 and 1961-65. Only amendments that conflicted with policies initiated or advocated by the government, which was controlled by the CDU/CSU, were included. CDU/CSU parliamentarians were successful in getting 56 percent of their amendments adopted during the two periods. This degree of acceptance came about either because the government was brought to concur in the amendments or because the government was in effect defeated.[17] A similar study of the amendments put by Conservative backbenchers during the 1959-64 Parliament, when the Conservatives were in power, found that Conservative backbenchers were successful in getting the government and Commons to adopt their amendments on 75 of 244 attempts, or 31 percent of the amendments.[18] The figure rises to approximately 40 percent if amendments which Conservative backbenchers withdrew are excluded. Another study discovered that almost 50 percent of the amendments posed by the opposition in 1968-69 (which, by then, was led by the Conservatives) were successful, although this was true for only about 25 percent of the more important of these amendments.[19] Finally, in his study of the French Assembly, Williams reports that amendments proposed to the budget by deputies from 1958 to 1962 were adopted fully or partly by the Assembly at the following rate: for the Gaullists, 50 percent; for the Conservatives, 60 percent; and for the Communists, 28 percent.[20] A rough count of the amendments to the 1968 education bill, which is described more fully below, also indicates the success of amendments presented by deputies in the Assembly. In this case, according to our count, the Gaullist deputies and the Assembly Committee on Cultural, Family, and Social Affairs offered about 140 amendments. Just over 50

Table 6.2
The Influence of Labour Rebellions on Government Policy from 1945 to 1951 and of Conservative Rebellions on Government Policy from 1951 to 1957, by Importance of Issue

Degree of Success	Importance of Issue			
	Major	Intermediate	Minor	Total
Complete	12	2	7	21
Partial	4	0	10	14
Failure	7	6	9	22
Total	23	8	26	57
Complete success	52%	25%	27%	37%
Complete or partial success	70%	25%	65%	61%

Source: Lynskey, "The Role of British Backbenchers," p. 73, 90.

percent of these amendments were adopted by the Assembly, 31 percent were withdrawn before a vote, and 18 percent were defeated (the success of deputies from other parties was lower, however).

Nor has the influence of parliamentarians been limited to insignificant matters. A number of the successes cited in the evidence above occurred on decisions of major consequence. For instance, Lynskey's study on the House of Commons from 1945 to 1957 offers many examples. From these we will cite just four. Lynskey found that pressure from Labour backbenchers from 1945 to 1951 was instrumental in moving the Labour government to give priority to nationalizing the iron and steel industry and also led the government to propose a plan fully to socialize the British civilian airlines industry. During and after 1951, pressure from Conservative backbenchers appears to have prompted a reluctant Conservative government to propose denationalization of the road haulage industry as well as to propose legislation to create commercial television instead of allowing the BBC to have a monopoly. Indeed, another glance at Table 6.2 will show that on the issues of major importance that backbenchers from the government party tried to influence from 1945 to 1957, the backbenchers were completely successful about 52 percent of the time.[21]

Examples can also be cited from the experience of the Bundestag and the Assembly. For instance, let us cite just several illustrations from our analysis of CDU/CSU amendments in the 1957-61 Bundestag. One illustration is the government's tax proposals of 1961. These were amended in committee and on the floor of the Bundestag by CDU/CSU members in such a way as to reduce the government's proposed taxes on small business by an estimated $100 million yearly. Another example is the committee and floor action in the Bundestag during 1959 to protect the ailing coal industry that led to raising tariffs on coal to 20 percent, well beyond the 5 percent the government had proposed. A number of other illustrations could be offered, as well, including the fate of the government's public health insurance proposals (described in Chapter 3) or the complete reformulation in the Bundestag of the government's bill on federal broadcasting in 1960-61. A similar example in the French National Assembly was the ability of Assembly critics of the government's value-added tax proposals of 1965 to get the government to accept amendments which reduced revenue from the tax by almost $200 million.[22]

Case Studies

From the discussion thus far we can see that legislators' challenges to executive stands have rather frequently had some success in gaining adoption. While their actions could influence the process, however, an important question to ask is: to what extent has the process of making legislation actually centered in the legislature as contrasted to the executive? Were the policies basic to decisions that the legislature adopted normally developed by the legislature? Or, were they normally developed by the executive, instead? These questions require us not only to look at where policies for legislation were actually formulated for initiation but if formulated within the executive, also to examine how much these proposals were changed as they progressed through the legislative process. Is the legislation that was adopted similar to the initial proposals, or was it fundamentally different?

In attempting to answer these questions, we will focus on a series of case studies to help us compare the relative roles of the legislature and the executive in the development and making of specific pieces of legislation. Each of the case studies investigates the resolution of policy issues over which the legislature's assent was necessary at some point, and each also provides information allowing us to gauge the executive's control over the processes of legislative compromise. Taken together, we located thirty-three case studies of this type, including nine for the British system, eleven for the French system, and thirteen for the German system. Rather than describing all of these cases, we will briefly outline a few of them and summarize the remainder. (There also are detailed descriptions of three of the cases in Chapter 3.)

We begin by looking at the British system with a few remarks about the resale price maintenance case study presented in Chapter 3. In this case, we found that while backbenchers influenced the resolution of the issue, making some compromise by the government necessary, the government nevertheless remained the central policy-making arena in two respects. First, the formulation and initiation of the RPM proposals centered almost exclusively in the government and administration. Second, despite changes made to the bill due to parliamentary criticism, the principles of the bill as they were proposed by the government were maintained and adopted.

The reader may recall from the case study that the Conservative government's decision not to act on RPM for a period of about five years may have been partly due to widespread opposition on the Conservative backbenches against abolishing RPM. However, we also observed that, initially, the member of the government responsible for policy in this area may not have felt strongly about pressing the issue, having himself been opposed to such legislation at an earlier point (even the Prime Minister was opposed to such legislation). When he was replaced by a member who did feel strongly (Edward Heath) and there was also a new Prime Minister, we saw that, despite the opposition on the Conservative backbenches, the government quickly introduced legislation to abolish RPM. It also did so with little parliamentary consultation.

Conflicting views within the government took backbench feeling into account. The legislation the government formulated and introduced in early 1964 contained certain compromises within what government proponents for the bill considered the spirit and purposes of the bill. The major compromise was that RPM would be abolished, although firms could within a prescribed period seek exemption before a judicial tribunal. In the case of these firms, RPM agreements could be legally maintained until the tribunal made a ruling.

Despite this compromise, the bill met strong opposition from Conservative backbenchers during the deliberation stage. The reason for this is clear, for the government bill still undercut RPM agreements. After introducing the bill, a series of discussions ensued between members of the government and backbenchers from the government's parliamentary party. The discussions took place in the parliamentary party Trade and Industry Committee and the 1922 Committee. The discussions, combined at times with criticism from the opposition party, led the government once again to alter its proposals. Feelings were intense on all sides of the issue, and this became clear during the meetings of the Trade and Industry Committee and the 1922 Committee. Even so, the changes the government drafted into its proposals were rather small. Nor did the government substantially revise its policy when its representatives later met with representatives of the backbenchers in a bargaining context. The backbench representatives got much of what they wanted but by this time they were no longer pressing for revisions of a fundamental nature.

In this case, proposals for initiation were formulated almost entirely in the government, and the government was able to gain adoption of a bill that was resented by many of its backbenchers. The strong position of the government is summarized well by Mackintosh: "The amazing fact," he argues, " is that the Conservative leadership was able, at a time when defeat was staring them in the face at a general election due in a few months, to force through a measure which so deeply disturbed many of their backbenchers."[23] Indeed, not only did the government get the bill through, but it also was able to do so in a period of but six weeks. As Butt observes, "almost certainly the officers of the Trade and Industry Committee, having failed in their original plan to get Heath to put off his abolition plan . . . realized that the ultimate solution must be essentially the one that the Minister wanted, decorated with gestures of appeasement to the rebels."[24]

This case also suggests that the government probably could not have gotten any bill through the Commons, and we have seen that the government did compromise both in formulating its initial proposals and, to a lesser extent, in responding during the deliberation stage. This is, itself, significant. Nevertheless, throughout the government remained in a strong position. As already indicated, the government gained adoption of the basic principles of the bill. In so doing, it was a focal point for determining which changes to the bill would be unacceptable; the changes it found acceptable were, in the end, the only compromises the House adopted. Despite the protests from its backbenches during the Commons committee and third reading stages, the Commons rejected each amendment to which the government remained firmly opposed.

Besides the RPM issue that climaxed in 1964, there are eight additional case studies to which we can refer. These cases cover the establishment of the national health system in the middle and latter 1940s, capital punishment in the latter 1940s and 1950s, the founding of commercial television in Great Britain in the mid-1950s, British policy in Suez in 1956-57, the Rent Act of 1957, the decision to apply for membership in the European Common Market in the early 1960s, legislation covering Commonwealth immigration of 1962 and of 1964-65, and the Parliamentary Commissioner Act of 1967.[25]

Of these cases, the government did not or was unable to control the process of legislative compromise basic to the final policy decision in the Commons only in the cases of commercial television and capital punishment. Let us take commercial television as an example.[26] In this case, a small group of Conservative backbenchers organized a backbench following to oppose the government's intention to extend for ten years without change the British Broadcasting Corporation's monopoly over radio and television. The group's first success came during a November (1951) meeting with Conservative leaders in the backbench 1922 Committee. After this meeting, the Conservative cabinet decided to extend the British Broadcasting Corporation's charter, but only for a period of six months, to June (1952), instead of its earlier intention of ten years. During those six months, meetings between the group and the party leadership in the government as well as negotiations between a committee representing the backbenchers and the leadership brought forth a proposal for competition. By 1954, the Conservative government had acceded not only to competition but also to commercial advertising on an independent television station. Its bill to create an Independent Television Authority was introduced in March, 1954, and became law five months later.

However, this and the capital punishment cases were the only cases of the nine (including RPM) in which the House of Commons fundamentally altered the government's position on legislation. The relatively limited role of the government in the commercial television case, moreover, seems to have been dependent upon the position of the Prime Minister. Professor Wilson observes: "There is general agreement among all those directly involved that had Sir Winston felt strongly and wished to do so he could have quashed the backbench movement for commercial television."[27] In five of the other cases, the government, although certainly influenced by the House, was the dominant center of decision-making on policies basic to the cases in both the initiation and deliberation stages. The case of resale price maintenance is an example. Other examples are the Commonwealth Immigrants Act of 1962 and of 1964, the decision to apply for Common Market membership, the Rent Act, and legislation establishing a British ombudsman. In the remaining two cases, members of the Commons, other than the government, played a rather small part in the shaping of the decisions.

Cases on French policy-making during the Fifth Republic exhibit a similar tendency. We have already observed in Chapter 3 that French parliamentarians, although surely influencing the government's proposals on agricultural reform and delaying their passage for over a year, were unable to get the government to change its basic policy stance during either the formulation or deliberation stages. Instead, the Assembly went on to adopt the essentials of the government's policy, which it had initially opposed. Indeed, in this case the policy not only originally developed in the executive, but also with little communication with Assembly members until interest groups had been fully consulted.

There are ten additional cases on the Fifth Republic that we should consider. Among these cases are legislation introduced in 1960 and adopted in 1965 regulating the production of nontaxable alcohol, a practice that was widespread in France and that had become a major health problem (well prior to the Fifth Republic) if not also a social problem; a bill in 1965 to alter the French taxation structure to a value-added tax system (TVA); a bill in 1963 to prohibit strikes until a specific warning period had passed; legislation in 1964 to put the organization of broadcasting on a legal footing; and a bill in 1965-66 to redefine conditions enabling adults to adopt children.[28] The five other cases[29] are legislation in 1968 that restructured the higher education system in France; passage of the fifth economic plan in 1964-65; French policy in Algeria; legislation toward the outset of the Fifth Republic to subsidize private schools; and French nuclear policy up to 1964.[30]

In only three of the eleven cases (including the agricultural reform case) did the Assembly in the end appear to determine the content of policy outside the basic principles and parameters set by the executive, either during the process of policy initiation or during the stage of deliberation. In one of these cases, as we saw above, the Assembly was able extensively to alter the government's value-added tax proposals of 1965 to the point, as Williams observed, that pressed the government "to and beyond the limit of reasonable conciliation."[32]

In several of the other cases, the pressure of Assembly members also led the executive to reconsider and to change some of the provisions of its proposals. But, other than final authorization, the decisional arena in these cases still remained centered mainly in the executive. We have already described the agricultural case and we briefly outline here one further example, that of the legislation restructuring higher education in 1968.

In May of 1968, the most violent uprising to occur in France since the early 1960s was initiated by university students who were joined by trade unionists. Although there were a number of issues involved, several dealt with the authoritarian structure of the university system, its elitism, and the restrictions put upon what students felt were legitimate political and organizational activities. In response, the government proposed measures that appeared to many right-wing Gaullists both outside and inside the parliamentary party to be too liberal. The legislation included the following features: (1) entry into universities would not be selective beyond the requirement that the *baccalauréat* be passed; (2) the universities would be administered by councils in which staff and students would be represented equally; and (3) political and trade union activities would be permitted.

Given the opposition among its own supporters, the government proceeded to discuss these proposals at length with Gaullists both inside and outside the parliamentary party. A series of discussions took place between leaders of the government and a Gaullist parliamentary party study group, which had been developed as an ad hoc committee to examine university reform. The government leaders included the Premier (Maurice Couve de Murville) and the Minister of Education (Edgar Faure).

These discussions, and others, aired objections that were voiced by many,[33] especially the Gaullists on the right. There was opposition to the policy of open entry; there were fears that student political and trade union activities would lead to the politicization of the universities and that they should not be permitted; and there was feeling that the students should not have equal representation on the university councils. Indeed, there was some sentiment that the councils should not include any student representation. Others argued that voting for the council members should be compulsory, lest the student activists control the outcome of elections.

However, the meetings with the Gaullist parliamentary study group moved the government leaders only to reconsider rather than to change their proposals. In a meeting with the parliamentary group held a few days later, Faure stood by and defended the proposals once again in a discussion lasting three hours. He made only one important concession, and this was a procedural rather than a substantive concession. He was willing to ask the government to allow the Assembly to vote on all amendments rather than to request a package vote (see Chapter 2).

Having agreed not to request a package vote, attention was focused on debates between the government leaders and the Assembly Committee for Cultural, Family, and Social Affairs, which had jurisdiction over the proposed legislation. Attention was also focused on deliberations in the Gaullist parliamentary group. Pressures coming from these quarters were strong. After discussing the situation with de Gaulle, the government agreed to alter its stand somewhat. Open entry would be retained, and political and trade union activities were still to be permitted. But the government was willing to compromise to a degree on the question of student representation. Professors would be given half the representation on the councils, with the other half divided among the remaining teachers, other university staff, and students. Moreover, in order for students to obtain their full representation, the percentage of students voting had to reach a quorum of 60 percent. Beyond this, the government was unwilling to move. Ending the meeting, Couve de Murville appealed for unity within the majority on the new governmental proposals. The details of the points upon which the government was willing to compromise were to be worked out between the Minister of Education and the parliamentary group.

The next day the Assembly debated the proposals. It was expected that groups on the left, excluding the Communists, would support the bill. But the government also obtained virtually the unanimous support of its own parliamentary group despite the opposition of many of its members to several important provisions in the proposals. No Gaullist members voted against the bill, and only six abstained.

In this case, the government responded to pressures from within the Assembly by compromising and by adjusting its proposals. Indeed, as we observed earlier, the Assembly adopted about half of the amendments put by the Gaullist deputies and the Assembly committee. The case also illustrates the various arenas in which discussions between the government and the Assembly can take place before the general debate. Included among these arenas were the Gaullist study groups, the Gaullist caucus, and the Assembly standing committees.

Finally, the case indicates the general nature of the relationship that has developed between the executive and the Assembly under the Fifth Republic. Although there may be compromise, typically the executive has not only been the focal point for the initiation of policy in dealings with the Assembly but also a center in which decisions have been made as to what constitutes acceptable compromise. This relationship, in which the executive may compromise while at the same time controlling the limits of compromise, was summed up in the Gaullist *La Nation*: "Certainly the Government has, in accordance with its responsiblities, demostrated the limits beyond which it cannot go without endangering the very spirit of the bill. But the Government has also shown a certain understanding of the anxieties expressed by men whose loyalty cannot be questioned. The text which will be voted on is the result of collaboration between the Government and the Assembly."[34]

Indeed, the influence of the Assembly in this case was perhaps greater than in seven of the other ten cases. In cases such as the broadcasting bill, the fifth economic plan, and French policy toward Algeria, either the Assembly's influence was very slight or the Assembly played hardly any part at all. In only three of the eleven cases did the Assembly become an arena central to the development of policy basic to the cases.

The extent to which the executive has been able to act efficaciously in the Fifth Republic Assembly is indicated by other evidence as well. It has, in the first place, been able to gain passage of a considerably greater percentage of its legislation than were Fourth Republic executives. Thus, according to Chandernagor, 81 percent of government-sponsored bills were passed in 1961-66 as against, in the Fourth Republic, 57 percent from 1947 to 1950, 60 percent from 1951 to 1955, and 54 percent from 1956 to 1958.[35]

Williams points out, secondly, that a number of pieces of legislation which the

Fourth Republic governments could not bring the Assembly to pass were passed in the Fifth Republic. Speaking about five of the cases we have cited, Williams says:

> It is significant enough that Parliament could pass these acts at all—mostly by the normal procedure and all without a vote of confidence. For all five subjects had been under discussion for many years. A law on strikes was promised in the constitution of the Fourth Republic but never passed; alcoholism was the most notorious scandal of that regime; its Parliament discussed none of the 16 bills proposed to regulate broadcasting; adoption and the TVA, though newer topics were under debate well before 1958. The Fifth Republic could deal with them because the government could exercise effective leadership—*and could therefore impose its own wishes if it chose....*[36]

Although our last case study occurred in 1968, there is little reason to believe that the relations between the executive and the Assembly changed in the period from 1968 to 1973, when the President and the government had their largest majority in the Assembly. Numerous commentaries are available to indicate that the executive maintained at least the influence in dealing with the Assembly that we have seen it to have had in the years before 1968.[37] Indeed, its influence may well have been augmented as a consequence of the 1968 Assembly elections.[38]

Both the British and the French cases, as well as the other evidence we presented, illustrate that the executive may indeed compromise and change its policies to account for objections arising, or likely to arise, from within the legislature. It may do so during the process of formulating its proposals or during the stage of policy deliberation in the legislature. The politics of bringing its parliamentary party into line may prompt the government into repeated discussions of its proposals with its party members in parliament, such as we observed in the RPM case and in the case of the French higher education bill. It would be a mistake to suggest that the government does not need to be sensitive to the legislature and especially to its own followers in the legislature. On this the evidence has been very clear.

Nevertheless, an equally important point to be drawn from the twenty case studies we reviewed is that the legislature was not usually the place in which policies basic to the decisions adopted by the legislature were developed. In this regard, fifteen of the twenty cases had three characteristics in common. First, the executive was the principal arena in which the legislation was formulated for initiation. Second, in each case the legislation was adopted. Third, the principles of the legislation as proposed by the executive remained mainly intact.

When we turn to the West German system, an examination of case studies suggests the presence of a rather different relationship between the executive and the legislature. The case of the proposals on health insurance presented in Chapter 3 illustrated that the arena for determining policy during the initiation and deliberation stages passed from the German government to decision-making centers, and especially to the committee and party structures, in the Bundestag. We recall that the government was unable to get the Bundestag's Social Policy Committee to act favorably on its proposals, due to the opposition of SPD and some CDU members. Instead, both before and after defeating these proposals, the committee (later also the CDU/CSU parliamentary party) developed proposals of its own that had little relation to the proposals the government was formulating. These proposals then passed the Bundestag.

Twelve additional cases were available to us for inspection dealing with relations between the German executive and the Bundestag. Each of the cases occurred within the period 1949-66 when the CDU/CSU controlled the government and the SPD was in opposition. Loewenberg's analysis of the Bundestag presents five cases. These include the development of a small volunteer military force in West Germany, regulation of travel to Berlin, the establishment of a fee structure for court-appointed attorneys, legislation on the state's ability to requisition private property in emergencies, and proposals for child welfare benefits.[39] Braunthal has documented three additional cases, two covering transport policy and another covering an agreement between West Germany and the Soviet Union in 1955 (which opened diplomatic relations between the two countries and led to the release of several thousand German prisoners), and Stammer examined legislation on the representation of federal personnel.[40] Finally Bethusy-Huc covered bills dealing with agriculture and with the organization of banking, and Domes described the case of legislation on developing workers' financial estates.[41]

Including the health insurance case, we have then a total of thirteen cases. On seven of these thirteen cases, the determination of policy decisions basic to the cases during the initiation or the deliberation stage shifted from the government to decision-making arenas within the Bundestag. This happened on the proposals to regulate travel to Berlin, to reorganize the banking system, the highway relief bill, legislation to establish a volunteer military cadre, the personnel act, legislation for developing workers' financial estates, as well as on the reform of health insurance. In each of these seven cases, at least one of the following occurred: the Bundestag acted on government initiatives but only by adopting a diametrically different policy during the deliberation stage (which the government was brought to accept) or by making fundamental alterations to which the government was not a party and remained opposed; government proposals were completely rejected in committee and were not resuscitated; or, although the Bundestag adopted a bill officially introduced by the government, the participation and influence of Bundestag members were so pervasive during the initiation stage that the government was not essentially the primary arena of initiation. Moreover, on one of the remaining six cases, the child benefits bill, the government consulted members from its parliamentary party extensively (as it did in several of the other cases) during the process of formulating its proposals and initiated the bill into the Bundestag only after having received the explicit approval of the parliamentary party.

One example of a governmental proposal passing the Bundestag, but only with compromises and alterations adopted over the objections of the government, is the legislation establishing a volunteer military cadre.[42] This bill had the purpose of enabling volunteers to enlist to form a military security force until legislation providing for an army was adopted. Before introducing its proposals, the government consulted with leaders of the CDU/CSU parliamentary party and had secured their support for the proposals. To get their support, the government in turn was brought to accept a short time limit of about eight months on the validity of the legislation.

Based on the assurances of support from the parliamentary party leaders, the government introduced its proposals into the Bundestag. Still, a series of questions arose in the Bundestag, from both the majority and the opposition, that led eventually to an entire reworking of the bill. Two of the many issues raised during the deliberation stage were whether the final organization of the defense establishment should be the subject of legislation or not and the method by which the Personnel Commission (designed in part to protect the rights of recruits in the face of conflicts with their military superiors) was to be appointed.

The debate on the government's proposals centered in the Bundestag Committee on European Security (chaired by Richard Jaeger of the CDU/CSU and under the deputy chairmanship of Fritz Erler of the SPD). The government argued that subjecting the final organization of the defense establishment to legislation was unconstitutional. Similarly, it argued that the requirement that the Bundestag approve members of the Personnel Commission was an unconstitutional interference with the government's power of appointment. In both cases, opposition within the committee prevailed over the continued objections of the government, and the committee's position was adopted by the Bundestag. Indicative of the part the committee played in the policy process on the Volunteers Bill are Loewenberg's comments about the resolution of the issue as to how the Personnel Commission ought to be appointed. He observed: "Negotiations between Erler and Jaeger, and within the subcommittee of the Security Committee, without the participation of representatives of the government, produced the necessary compromise."[43] Loewenberg went on to say, "The Volunteers Bill which was reported out of committee . . . was an entirely different measure from the one the Government had presented."[44]

There is little doubt that the government was not without influence in this case or in most of the other cases. However, the point is that in this case, and in six of the remaining twelve cases, the development of policy decisions fundamental to the cases could not be said to have been centered primarily in the executive. Rather, the Bundestag also became an arena in which the policies underlying these cases were both developed and determined. Moreover, there appear to be numerous other examples which, if further research were done on them, would reveal the same conclusion. Taking only significant government proposals over the second Bundestag and the third Bundestag, five examples are: (1) legislation providing a new model for progressive income taxation in 1954; (2) the coal import tariff bill of 1958-59; (3) the free-market housing bill of 1960; (4) the legislation restructuring taxes on business of 1961; and (5) the Federal Broadcasting Law of 1960-61. Many of these cases found a division within the CDU/CSU as to the economic philosophy which would prove "best" in approaching the problem. The second and third reading debates or newspaper accounts indicate in each case that the government opposed major policy changes advocated by the responsible Bundestag committee or individual parliamentarians which the Bundestag went on to adopt over the government's objections.[45]

The case studies available on West Germany cover the period 1949-66, while the CDU/CSU controlled the executive in coalition mainly with the FDP. However, other analyses indicate that the pattern emerging from the case studies did not end when the coalition fell but continued under the succeeding CDU/CSU coalition with the SPD as well.[46]

Moreover, the conclusion the case studies suggest, that the Bundestag played a more prominent part in the development of legislation during the period covered than did the other parliaments, is also suggested by quantitative studies on the policy-making role of the Bundestag and the House of Commons. These studies endeavored to locate all successful attempts either by individual members or groups of the government party in the Bundestag and the Commons to bring about significant modification of governmental policies. The findings indicate that a markedly greater incidence of such attempts, and of successful attempts, occurred in the Bundestag as compared to the House of Commons. Thus, in a study of the activities of the CDU/CSU *fraktion* in committee and on the floor, Domes found that individual members or groups of the *fraktion* successfully brought about considerable ("*stark*") changes in a total of 177 government proposals for legislation during the eight years (1953-61) covered by his study.[47] On the other hand, in an analysis of the Commons covering a longer span of time (1945-57), Lynskey found far fewer cases of successful attempts to effectuate modification in governmental policies by members or groups of the governing parliamentary party in the Commons. His research located a total of 35 such cases,[48] a figure that is also in line with the results of other research.[49]

One factor that helps to account for this difference is that Domes found a decidedly greater number of CDU/CSU attempts to effectuate significant modification of policy, encompassing a total of 223 separate governmental bills over the eight-year period, than was the experience for governing parliamentarians in the House of Commons, where 57 such cases were found. Another, though lesser factor, is that CDU/CSU members were successful in exerting influence in about 80 percent of the cases upon which they made attempts as opposed to a success ratio of about 60 percent for governing party parliamentarians in the Commons.[50]

An additional point regarding the Bundestag that should be mentioned here has to do with the initiation of legislation. Although not usually the primary arena for the initiation of legislation, our review of case studies and other evidence on the Bundestag would lead us to anticipate that it might often be involved in the process of initiation. Indeed, Domes's study found it frequently to be the case that the political concepts behind government initiatives for legislation were developed in meetings involving not only ministers and civil servants but also representatives of policy working groups from the CDU/CSU parliamentary party. Sometimes these meetings included representatives from the opposition party in the Bundestag as well. According to Domes, government consultation with parliamentarians in the formulation of initiatives, which were then further developed in the administration and brought to the Bundestag by the cabinet, was the rule rather than the exception during the eight-year period he examined.[51]

Our discussion of relations between the European legislatures and their executives regarding the making of legislation (policies that require legislative approval) leads to several conclusions. First, the aggregate data presented toward the beginning of this section suggested that the initiation of most policies adopted by each of the three legislatures has centered not in the legislature, but in the executive. For the most part, even regarding the Bundestag, the available case studies reinforced this conclusion. The case studies contained some exceptions: the commercial television and capital punishment cases in Britain; health insurance, workers' financial estates, and the highway relief bill in Germany; and perhaps the legislation to subsidize private schools in France. But, outside these principal exceptions, the government appears to have been the main arena in which the proposals for initiation were formulated in the thirty-three case studies we reviewed.

Second, legislators have not been impotent in influencing executive-sponsored policies. Both the case studies and other types of data showed that the policies formulated and initiated by the government in all three systems frequently took into account resistance the government anticipated it would face in the legislature and/or were adjusted during the deliberation stage to accommodate the views of parliamentarians.

Third, the case studies suggest that the three legislatures were not equally central as an arena where the development of legislation occurred. A set of thirty-three case studies cannot permit firm conclusions, but tendencies did emerge. The tendencies indicate that the Bundestag was more frequently a principal policy-making arena than either the House of Commons or the National Assembly. Combining both the initiation and deliberation stages, the Bundestag under the CDU/CSU became central to the development of policies basic to seven of the thirteen cases considered while in only five of twenty cases did the House of Commons or the Assembly play such a part. Other case study data reviewed on the Bundestag and the House of Commons also warranted the conclusion that the Bundestag more frequently played a prominent policy-making part than did the House of Commons.

These general observations should not be taken to mean that in each system relations between the legislature and the executive were static. Influence could and did change over time and with varying circumstances. This is also illustrated by the case studies which showed that the importance of a particular legislature to the development of policy could alter considerably in regard to specific instances.

Both long- and short-run changes in influence have occurred. As we indicated at the beginning of this section, the influence of backbenchers in the House of Commons has undergone a long-run change since the mid-nineteenth century, when backbenchers enjoyed a more critical position and when party cohesion was considerably lower than it is today.

Influence has also changed over the short run as is suggested by the rather sharp alterations in legislative power that have marked French and German history during this century. Even during the time period we covered, data suggest that executive influence over the Fifth Republic Assembly was not as great during the initial period of the Fifth Republic, from 1959 to 1961, as it was during the period after 1961.[52] The executive's influence over the Assembly increased as the new institutional structures of the Fifth Republic began to take hold, when the Algerian question was settled[53] (removing it as an issue which divided the government's majority), when the size of the government's majority grew, and as de Gaulle's increased potential to influence legislative election outcomes was reflected by the substantial increase in the size of the Gaullist party in the Assembly in 1962. The significance of the size of the majority in the legislature for the ability of opponents within the government party to influence the government is also suggested by experience in Great Britain. Thus, Lynskey found that rebellious backbenchers were more likely to achieve success when the government's majority was rather small than when it was working with a large majority. When the majority was small (Labour 1950-51; Conservative 1951-55), backbenchers achieved complete success on eleven of the twenty-two cases upon which rebellions took place. The rebels achieved complete success on only ten of thirty-five cases when the government's majority was larger (Labour 1945-50; Conservative 1955-57).[54]

Furthermore, the influence of the executive over the legislature may change, while generally remaining within the bounds typical for executive influence, depending upon such factors as the personality and style of the executive and perceptions as to the permanence of a particular executive in office. For instance, although not going beyond the bounds typical of backbench influence, the fact that backbenchers were as influential as they were on the RPM legislation may have been in part due to the perception that the Douglas-Home government was only a caretaker government.

Finally, it is possible that legislatures are usually more capable of exerting influence in some policy areas than in others. This possibility has interested many persons, especially as it pertains to domestic policy as compared to foreign policy. We will deal with this possibility in some detail later in the chapter.

Parliamentary Selection of the Executive

For now, we wish to turn to another facet of parliamentary activity, a facet that can have an important bearing on the making of policy. This is the parliamentary function of selecting the executive. The question we raise in this section is whether the greater prominence of the Bundestag as compared to the Commons and the Assembly in the process of developing legislation may have come about because the latter two legislatures exerted greater influence on the selection of the executive itself. In an attempt to answer this question our analysis will cover three phases of executive leadership selection : the selection of the leader of the government, his choice of other cabinet members, and the retention of the leader in office. We will concentrate here on the two pure parliamentary systems in our study, Great Britain and Germany.

One way of looking at the impact of the parliamentary method of leadership selection is to inquire into who participates in the selection of the leader and the criteria used in making the selection. Let us look first at the British system. From 1945 to 1974, leadership changed hands in the British parliamentary parties six times (Labour 1955 and 1963; Conservative 1955, 1957, 1963, and 1965). Only in the case of the Conservative change of leaders in 1955 was there no contest for the leadership. In three of the other cases (Labour 1955 and 1963; Conservative 1965), the party was in opposition when it changed leaders. Thus, the party was not selecting a new Prime Minister. Rather, it was selecting a new shadow leader who would become Prime Minister if the party won the next election. In the two remaining cases where there was a contest for the leadership (Conservative, 1957 and 1963), the party was in power and was in effect selecting a new Prime Minister.

How were the selections made in the Labour and Conservative parties, and what kind of men did the parliamentary parties choose? As for the two Labour selections, each made when the party was in opposition, a vote of the entire parliamentary party determined who would be the leader. In 1955, Hugh Gaitskell replaced Clement Atlee by defeating Aneurin Bevan and Herbert Morrison on the first ballot vote. Gaitskell won the support of an absolute majority of the parliamentary party on the first ballot with 157 votes to 70 for Bevan and 40 for Morrison. Gaitskell died in 1963, and the contest for leadership fell to Harold Wilson, George Brown, and James Callaghan. On the first ballot, Wilson received 115 votes to 88 for Brown and 41 for Callaghan, thus requiring a second ballot. Wilson won this vote against Brown, 133 to 103.

The sole occasion when the Conservative parliamentary party chose a new leader by vote of the parliamentary party was also when the party was out of power.[55] In 1965, Sir Alec Douglas-Home resigned, and Edward Heath became leader by winning 150 votes to 133 for Reginald Maudling and 15 for Enoch Powell. This was the first occasion in the history of the Conservative party when the leader was chosen by formal election.

The remaining two Conservative selections, when there was a contest, were made by more informal procedures. Here the Conservatives were in power and were selecting a new Prime Minister. Having been stung by the Suez crisis and other difficulties which divided the party in 1956, the leadership of Anthony Eden was called into question. He resigned as Prime Minister on grounds of ill health in late 1957. Two senior cabinet ministers, Lords Salisbury and Kilmuir, consulted all of the cabinet ministers, the chief Conservative whip, and the leader of the Conservative 1922 Committee. After these consultations, Salisbury and Kilmuir advised the Queen that there was overwhelming support for Harold Macmillan in preference to Richard Butler. Macmillan was thereby selected. He remained Prime Minister until 1963, when it became clear that his leadership was no longer effective. Britain had been refused membership in the Common Market, prices were rising, and the party was rocked by the Profumo scandal. Macmillan resigned in 1963, again on grounds of ill health. After he had recovered from an operation, Macmillan engaged in the most thorough canvassing in the history of the party before he made his recommendation to the Queen. He and several others interviewed all candidates for the premiership, all cabinet members, some backbench MPs and party officials, and even constituency association leaders. The result of the canvassing led to the selection of Sir Alec Douglas-Home as Prime Minister over Butler, Lord Hailsham (Quintin Hogg), Reginald Maudling, Ian Macleod, and Edward Heath.

Since 1945, then, parliamentary party election of a new leader has occurred only when the party was in opposition. When in power and choosing a new Prime Minister (which only the Conservatives have done), more informal canvassing methods were used. Under the canvassing method, a most important part was played by the cabinet, with backbenchers playing a more secondary role. Each time all cabinet ministers were consulted whereas this was not the case for backbenchers. The opinions of backbenchers were sought but usually indirectly. This was done through both the chief whip and the chairman of the backbench 1922 Committee. In 1963, some backbenchers were consulted directly.

What kind of persons were selected to be leader? Perhaps a necessary condition for assuming the position of Prime Minister or shadow prime minister is having had considerable experience in prestigious political positions. The most serious candidates have previously been Chancellor of the Exchequer, Foreign Secretary, Leader of the House of Commons, or shadow minister in a key post. It is not insignificant that of the five leadership choices we have considered, four choices devolved upon persons who had either been Chancellors of the Exchequer or shadow chancellors. Each of the five leaders chosen had also occupied other leadership posts. The importance of the criterion of experience means that Prime Ministers are not likely to be young. Until Heath and Thatcher only one Conservative under the age of fifty had been chosen Prime Minister or shadow prime minister in well over a century. Since 1867, the average age of all incoming Prime Ministers has been about sixty. The combination of experience and age that appears so crucial to leadership selection has led Kenneth Waltz to term the British system an "apprentice" system.[56]

Other candidates, even if they lost, became more serious contenders if they had demonstrated administrative competence in a cabinet-level position. Almost all of the serious contenders have held such positions. The only exception was in 1963 when two of the three major contenders in the Labour party (Brown and Callaghan) had not held ministerial positions in the cabinet for any length of time. Both lost to Harold Wilson, who had been a cabinet minister for four years from 1947 to 1951.

Having held senior political office is not sufficient to gain the confidence of the parliamentary party, however. Also important is how responsibly the candidate is perceived to act and how well the candidate can unite the parliamentary party. In 1957, for example, Butler was a leading contender to become the Conservative Prime Minister after Anthony Eden resigned. The *Economist* went so far as to argue, in 1956, that "if Sir Anthony were to lay down the Premiership tomorrow, there is really no doubt that the Queen would be constitutionally bound to send for Mr. Butler."[57] But a sounding of all the Conservative ministers, the chief whip, and the chairman of the backbench 1922 Committee indicated that there were questions within the parliamentary party regarding both Butler's ability to be a strong and decisive leader and his ability to unify the party. The right wing of the Conservative parliamentary party considered Butler to be far too leftish on both domestic and foreign policy. The unacceptability of Butler to the right wing threatened to divide an already badly torn party and was an important factor leading to Macmillan's victory over him. Similarly, Bevan lost out to Gaitskell in 1956 partly because he was too much the representative of one wing of the party. Furthermore, questions about George Brown's leadership capabilities were decisive in Wilson's victory over him in 1963. Brown had a reputation for "impulsiveness, truculence and insensitivity which more than offset his other qualities."[58] The *Guardian* summed up by saying that "his judgment was too hurried, his knowledge too limited, his words too offensive and his tactics too erratic."[59] In each of these cases, the unacceptability of the candidate to a segment of the parliamentary party led to his defeat.

The relevance of parliamentary party factors for the selection of a Prime Minister or shadow minister is admirably illustrated by a comparison of who was selected to the preferences of the general public. Public opinion polls in 1956 consistently showed that the Conservative public preferred Butler over Macmillan, and yet it was Macmillan who became the new Prime Minister.[60] Similarly, the public preferred Butler, Hailsham, and Maudling over Lord Home in 1963, but Lord Home was the preference of the party leaders and backbenchers.[61] It was thus Home who became Prime Minister.

Beyond influencing the selection of the leader, the parliamentary party can also influence the leader's choice of his other cabinet members. In his choices, the leader cannot normally ignore currents of opposition within and outside the parliamentary party. Nor can he ignore leading figures within the parliamentary party. These factors impinge upon his choice of other cabinet members.[62] Nevertheless, the leader does have a considerable degree of freedom of action. This is especially so regarding which men to choose for which posts and exactly how much representation in the cabinet a particular current of opinion will secure.

There is little reason to believe that a Conservative Prime Minister or shadow prime minister is given less freedom than this in selecting his cabinet, and he may have even more.[63] However, evidence is more readily available on the Parliamentary Labour Party because, when in opposition, it elects a Parliamentary Committee. The elections give an indication of the support for individual members from within the parliamentary party.[64] We can then compare the election results to the Labour leader's shadow cabinet selections. The leader's selection of the frontbench members in the shadow cabinet has borne some relationship, but by no means a perfect relationship, to the membership elected by the parliamentary party to the Parliamentary Committee. Members elected to the Committee have been appointed in disproportionate numbers to the shadow cabinet. Yet, not only have some members on the Parliamentary Committee failed to gain frontbench positions in the shadow cabinet, but those appointed from the Parliamentary Committee have not necessarily received the more important frontbench positions. Furthermore, changing parliamentary party support for individual Parliamentary Committee members (as revealed by subsequent elections to the Committee) has not been an important factor in changes the leader made in the shadow cabinet. Thus, the leader has promoted some members to more important posts even though the support for them, relative to others in the parliamentary party, had declined, and the leader has demoted some members to less important posts despite an increase in parliamentary party support for them. Altogether, then, this evidence suggests that the Labour shadow prime minister has looked to Parliamentary Committee members the party elected (although by no means exclusively) but, like his Conservative counterpart, has had considerable leeway in whom he appointed to which position.

Another possibility is that the preferences of the parliamentary party, including backbench opinion, can influence whether the leader remains Prime Minister. The leader can become vulnerable to loss of support while in office. Such a factor might affect his ability to retain office. Here it is pertinent that two Prime Ministers have resigned since 1945, Eden in 1957 and Macmillan in 1963, and both instances were preceded by troublesome events that clouded opinion about the leader in his parliamentary party. It is possible that diminished confidence the Conservative parliamentary party had in Eden in 1956-57 and in Macmillan in 1963 was partly responsible for their decisions to resign. On the other hand, in neither case did the resignations appear to be forced by the parliamentary party. Almost certainly in the case of Eden, and probably also in Macmillan's case, the decisions to resign were principally ones of personal choice.[65]

At this point it would be useful to take up leadership selection in the German CDU/CSU, the party providing the Chancellor from 1949 to 1969, and compare the situation there to the two British parties. As in the British parties, party leaders and leaders of subgroupings in the CDU/CSU parliamentary party have weighed heavily in the selection of a new CDU/CSU Chancellor. Nevertheless, the selection in the end has depended upon obtaining the express support of the entire parliamentary party more so than it has in the British case. Since 1945, a formal vote on who shall become leader in the British case has taken place only when the parliamentary party was in opposition. Such a vote has taken place in the CDU/CSU even when it was a governing party. Thus, the CDU/CSU caucus elected Erhard as leader in 1963 by a vote of 159 to

47, with 19 abstentions, to replace Konrad Adenauer as Chancellor. With the support of the FDP, Erhard became the new Chancellor. When Erhard resigned in 1966, the caucus, on the third ballot, elected Kurt Kiesinger, who became Chancellor, by a vote of 137 to 81 for Schroeder and 26 for Barzel. Besides his experience in cabinet office and his success in leading what has been known as the German "economic miracle," a primary consideration in the caucus' acceptance of Erhard was his public popularity at a time when the popularity of the CDU/CSU appeared to be declining. Kiesinger was selected partly because it was felt that he could unite a badly divided party better than could either Schroeder or Barzel and because he was acceptable to the SPD, with whom the CDU/CSU formed the governing coalition.[66]

The resignation of the CDU/CSU Chancellors also appears to have resulted more from explicit pressure than has been the case for the resignations of British Prime Ministers. Each of the British leaders who resigned did so partly out of choice rather than solely because of explicit pressure brought to bear on them. The two CDU/CSU Chancellors who resigned, however, appear to have had little choice. The pressure brought to bear on them was so substantial that they could not have continued to lead even had they wanted to.[67]

The selection of the Chancellor in Germany and the potential to force his resignation are not the only ways CDU/CSU parliamentary leaders and backbenchers influenced the composition of the executive. They also exerted influence on the Chancellor's choice of cabinet members and their offices. Adenauer's selection of cabinet members during the 1957-61 Bundestag serves as an example, although by no means the only example.[68] One area of conflict occurred over the possible reappointment of Fritz Schaeffer as Minister of Finance. The Bavarian wing of the parliamentary party strongly supported Schaeffer's reappointment, but he was opposed by a group of CDU parliamentarians representing the business wing of the party. They disliked his taxation policies and his unwillingness to place certain public enterprises back into private ownership. As a result of this conflict, Adenauer agreed to retain Schaeffer as Minister of Justice instead of Minister of Finance. Adenauer also agreed to appoint Theodor Blank as Minister of Labor (despite ten deviations by Blank in the 1953-57 Bundestag) after conversing with a negotiating committee representing the CDU/CSU labor parliamentarians. Moreover, Adenauer's retention of Heinrich Luebke as Minister of Agriculture, over the objections of the Bauernverband (the major farmer's organization) was directly dependent upon the widespread and strong backing Luebke had in the CDU/CSU parliamentary party. In addition, Adenauer's dismissal of Theodor Oberlaender as Minister of Expellees, Refugees, and War Victims in 1960 came as a result of concerted parliamentary pressure. Finally, since the CDU/CSU formed its governments in coalition, the Chancellor also had to undertake extensive negotiations with the coalition parliamentarians before appointing his cabinet.

We have indicated that the parliamentary leaders in both British parties and in the CDU/CSU played a central part when a new leader of the government was being selected in between elections. At the same time, it appears that the impact of the CDU/CSU parliamentary party has been based upon a broader segment of the parliamentary party in selecting the leader and also seems to have been more determining in each of the other two phases of leadership choice we examined: the leader's selection of his cabinet and the retention of the leader in office. Backbenchers in the

CDU/CSU, through their vote, have been brought more directly into the process of selecting a new CDU/CSU Chancellor than has been the case for backbenchers in the selection of a new Prime Minister in Great Britain. In addition, CDU/CSU parliamentary party leaders along with leaders and members of organized groups in the parliamentary party have played a more active part (to the point of entering negotiations with the Chancellor) and have had a more decisive impact on the Chancellor's selection of cabinet members for particular posts than appears to have been the case for leaders and backbenchers in either British parliamentary party. Finally, the CDU/CSU parliamentary party has been able to exert a more decisive influence on whether the Chancellor would be retained than seems to have been the case for the parliamentary parties in the Commons.

We began this section by suggesting that the lesser role the House of Commons has played vis-à-vis the government in the making of legislation, as compared to the Bundestag, may have been due to a greater influence on its part in selecting the government. Our discussion in this section suggests that this was not the case. Instead, as it played a greater role in the development of legislation, so the impact of the Bundestag under the CDU/CSU appears to have been greater on the selection of executive leadership. Why differences such as these arise is an appropriate question which will occupy our attention in a later chapter (Chapter 8). For the moment, however, we wish to continue our description of relations between the executive and the legislature by turning now to a discussion of the American situation.

Executive-Legislative Relations in the United States

Since the earliest days of the Republic, there seems to have been an almost inevitable tension between the executive and the legislature that has resulted, over time, in the locus of power oscillating between the two branches.[69] The greatest concentration of executive power was probably under Lincoln, who seemed to act quite independently of the Congress, assuming almost dictatorial powers.[70] After Lincoln's death, the pendulum made its most dramatic swing to the other extreme. Only two decades later Woodrow Wilson, who was a political scientist before he entered politics, appropriately referred to the American political system as "Congressional government" whose real locus of political power was the standing committees of Congress, primarily the House of Representatives.[71]

Oscillations have continued, but the general trend has been toward greater and more continuous involvement by the Presidency and its bureaucracy in the legislative process. Even Eisenhower, sometimes regarded as the weakest President since 1932, recognized the inevitable involvement of the executive in policy-making when he said, "I am part of the legislative process."[72] With his increased involvement, the President has become known as the "chief legislator."[73] The rather narrow expressly constitutional bases of the President's legislative power (for example, giving Congress information on the "state of the Union," recommend measures, right to call special sessions of Congress, and qualified veto)[74] have been supplemented with various statutory bases and institutional procedures for Presidential intervention in the legislative process. However, formal powers and institutions are only potential resources for influence; actual influence also varies with the particular President's persuasive abilities, reputation, and prestige in conjunction with the political setting in which the President acts.[75]

Of the constitutional bases of Presidential power in the legislative process, one that should be singled out for discussion is the veto. By requiring the Congress to pass by two-thirds vote what it otherwise could adopt by majority vote, the veto can give the President significant influence over the entire process of making legislation. Not only is the successful invocation of this power an example of Presidential influence, but the mere threat or even suspicion of intense Presidential hostility provides the President with a bargaining weapon. President Richard Nixon vetoed 43 pieces of legislation passed by the Democratic-controlled Congresses; he was overridden only 6 times. Neither Presidents Johnson (with 30 vetoes) nor Kennedy (25) were ever overridden. Eisenhower had 3 of 201 vetoes overridden and Truman 12 of 250. Franklin Roosevelt, the most prolific user of the veto with 631, had only 9 overridden. From 1913 to 1974, only about 3 percent of over 1300 vetoes were overriden.

Of course, the veto is a power that, at least formally, can be utilized only at the final stages of the legislative process, after the Congress has adopted a piece of legislation. Presidents have also become highly active at earlier stages of the legislative process and recently have come to assume the responsibility of initiating and advocating openly a "legislative program or package." Indeed, the increased role of the Presidency in initiating and advocating legislation has been a principal development in the relationship between the Congress and the Presidency in the twentieth century.

From time to time, through State of the Union messages and speeches, Presidents had become associated with particular issues, but it was not until Theodore Roosevelt that the President began with some regularity to supplement his messages with actual drafts of bills. As Koenig notes, "Although Theodore Roosevelt, mindful of the merits of the separation of powers, was a trifle sheepish and clandestine about it all, Wilson did it openly. . . . Since then all Presidents, even Calvin Coolidge, despite his strict Constitutionalism and tired blood, have drafted bills."[76]

It was even later before a comprehensive, specifically defined "Presidential program" became customary. Richard Neustadt writes:

Presidential reports and recommendations to Congress were as old as the Constitution; Presidential sponsorship of specific measures, highlighted in special messages and spelled out in Administration bills, had been a commonplace in Franklin Roosevelt's time and by no means unknown much earlier. But the elaborate paraphernalia of a comprehensive and specific inventory, contents settled and defined as regards substance no less than finance, *presented in detailed fashion and packaged form at the opening of each session of Congress*—this was a "custom" scarcely nine years old [in 1954], a postwar phenomenon evolving under Truman and now carried forward under Eisenhower.[77]

Accompanying the assumption of greater initiative on the part of the President has been two other developments: increased executive staff to aid the process and the establishment of machinery within the executive branch for central clearance and coordination of the legislative program package.[78] Prior to 1921, the various agencies or departments went to Congress directly with their budget proposals, with little knowledge or concern as to how they related to those of other executive subunits. The first major step in the development of central clearance of a President's program as we know it today came with the Budget and Accounting Act of 1921. With this act, agencies and departments at least on paper lost their historic freedom to determine their needs alone and to approach Congress directly for appropriations. The President was to decide on needs and to make requests to Congress. A new staff agency, The Bureau of the Budget, was created to aid him. The aim was to bring income and expenditures into some sort of sensible and coherent relationship.

Central clearance of the budget worked haphazardly over the next decade. When Franklin Roosevelt became President, he initiated a different kind of clearance: "policy clearance in substantive terms."[79] FDR told the National Emergency Council meeting in December, 1934, that he had been "quite horrified—not once but half a dozen times—by reading in the paper that some department or agency was after this, that or the other without my knowledge."[80] He announced he would cease having uncoordinated requests for all legislation; he (and his aides) would rule on all proposals to Congress. FDR thus not only incorporated the earlier financial clearance system but also went well beyond the budget process. He "intended to protect not just his budget but his prerogatives, his freedom of action and his choice of policies, in an era of fast growing government and of determined presidential leadership."[81]

The process of routinization or institutionalization of central clearance was interrupted by World War II and the consequent adjustments of the policy-making machinery in wartime. However, the post-World War II period saw central clearance—from beginning to end of the legislative process—firmly entrenched.

Beginning in 1947, the Legislative Reference Division of the Bureau of the Budget, in consultation with the Presidential aides (with Truman's approval), began to review and coordinate into a comprehensive program all agency requests, suggestions and recommendations. Some research suggests that the influence of the Budget Bureau has recently been declining in favor of the White House staff.[82] Fisher comments that:

> The final step toward centralization of control under the President began in March 1970, when President Nixon proposed that the Bureau of the Budget be replaced by an Office of Management and Budget (OMB). The President explained that the dominant concern of the new agency would not be preparation of the budget but rather assessing the extent to which programs are actually achieving their intended results, and delivering the intended services to the intended participants.[83]

The OMB aids the President in the formulation of his proposals, serving as a clearinghouse to sort out and evaluate various department and agency requests, consulting with Congressmen, coordinating the drafting of the President's Congressional messages, and drafting specific bills.[84] The OMB also acts as a clearinghouse during legislative consideration of the President's program and often even helps prepare veto messages for the President.

Presidents now routinely propose comprehensive and detailed statements of legislative needs for annual presentation to Congress. Moreover, the President is expected to take initiative in proposing legislation. Matthews notes from his extensive interviews in the U. S. Senate that:

Modern Presidents are expected to lead Congress. This expectation, with all its ambiguities, is as widespread on Capitol Hill as anywhere else. . . . Few if any senators expressed opposition to Presidential leadership as such; rather if they objected at all, it was to the direction, ineffectiveness or lack of legislative leadership from the White House.[85]

Neustadt explains why Congressmen consider Presidential initiative a service rather than a threat:

In practical effect they represent a menu whereby Congress can gain from outside what comes hard from within: a handy and official guide to the wants of its biggest customer; an advance formulation of main issues in each session; a work load ready to hand to every legislative committee; an indication, more or less, of what may risk the veto; a borrowing of presidential prestige for major bills—and thus a boosting of publicity potentials in both sponsorship and opposition.[86]

The late Clinton Rossiter, in noting this shift of initiative away from the Congress toward the President, called it a "revolution" because it has established beyond the "point of no return" the President's right to executive leadership on behalf of his legislative program.[87] Voters as well as legislators expect him to be a legislative leader. His campaign platform's fulfillment depends upon legislative enactment. We often judge our "successful" Presidents by how many programs they get through Congress.[88]

Aggregate Data

How successful is the President in getting his viewpoint and his proposals adopted in the Congress?[89] One way of approaching this question is to examine the President's success on Congressional roll call votes upon which he took a stand. We do this on Table 6.3.[90]

As the table suggests, Presidential success scores on these roll call votes ranged all the way from 93 percent in 1965 for Johnson, who had an overwhelmingly Democratic Congress, to 52 percent in 1959 for Eisenhower and 51 percent in 1973 for Nixon, both of whom had a Congress controlled by the opposition party. Overall, Presidential success averaged about 75 percent between 1953 and 1974.

A look at the most important (key) votes (Table 6.4), selected by *Congressional Quarterly*, yields a similar result. The average success for Presidents Johnson and Nixon on key roll calls from 1964 through 1973 was 74 percent.

Presidential success rates such as those just reported deal with individual roll call votes rather than success in getting legislation sent to Congress passed. Presidential success in this area has been considerably less, at least if measured on a yearly basis. Thus, the percentage of Presidential proposals enacted into law in some recognizable form by Congress averaged about 44 percent each year from 1954 through 1974.[91] Again, the most successful year was in 1965 under President Johnson, when the Democrats also controlled both houses of Congress by the largest majority either party had held since World War II. During that year, Congress passed 69 percent of Johnson's proposals. President Eisenhower's most successful year was 1954, the only

Legislative-Executive Relations   221

Table 6.3
Presidential Success on Roll Call Votes

Year	Pres.	Both Chambers Combined No. Roll call tests	% Roll calls Pres. Success	House No. Roll call tests	% Pres. Success	Senate[a] No. Roll call tests	% Pres. Success
1974	Ford[b]	122	58	68	57	54	59
1974	Nixon[b]	136	60	83	54	53	68
1973	Nixon[b]	310	51	125	48	185	52
1972	Nixon[b]	83	65	37	81	46	54
1971	Nixon[b]	139	75	57	82	82	70
1970	Nixon[b]	156	77	65	85	91	71
1969	Nixon[b]	119	74	47	72	72	75
1968	Johnson	267	75	102	83	165	69
1967	Johnson	292	79	127	76	165	81
1966	Johnson	228	79	103	91	125	69
1965	Johnson	274	93	112	94	162	93
1964	Johnson	149	88	52	88	97	88
1963	Kennedy	186	87	71	83	115	89.6
1962	Kennedy	185	85	60	85	125	85.6
1961	Kennedy	189	81	65	83	124	81
1960	Eisenhower[b]	129	65	43	65	86	65
1959	Eisenhower[b]	175	52	54	55	121	50
1958	Eisenhower[b]	148	76	50	74	98	76
1957	Eisenhower[b]	117	68	60	58	57	79
1956	Eisenhower[b]	99	70	34	73.5	65	68
1955	Eisenhower[b]	93	75	41	63.4	52	84.6
1954	Eisenhower	115	78	—[c]	—[c]	—[c]	—[c]
1953	Eisenhower	83	89	—[c]	—[c]	—[c]	—[c]

Source: *Congressional Quarterly Almanacs* for relevant years
[a]Includes Supreme Court nominations
[b]Congress (both Houses) controlled by opposite party.
[c]data not available

year from 1954 to 1960 when the President's party had a majority in both houses.[92] Congress adopted 65 percent of Eisenhower's proposals during that year. The least successful year for the President was in 1971 when the Congress, controlled by the opposition party, adopted 20 percent of the initiatives proposed by Nixon. The percentages for the 1954-74 period are found on Table 6.5, and more specific data dealing with what happened to Presidential proposals in Congress during four selected years are found on Table. 6.6.

Of course, Table 6.5 shows that the Congress also adopted sizable numbers of Presidential proposals, even if the percentages were not as high as on roll call votes.

Table 6.4
Presidential Success on Key Votes

Year	Pres.	Both Chambers				House				Senate			
		# Key Votes	# with Pres. Position	# votes with Pres. success	% Pres. success	# Key Votes	# with Pres. Position	# votes with Pres. success	% Pres. success	# Key Votes	# with Pres. Position	# votes with Pres. success	% Pres. success
1973	Nixon	31	18	8	44	15	9	4	44	16	9	4	44
1972	Nixon	30	14	8	57	12	6	4	67	18	8	4	50
1971	Nixon	28	18	14	78	14	7	6	86	14	11	8	73
1970	Nixon	28	15	11	73	14	9	7	78	14	6	4	67
1969	Nixon	18	13	9	69	12	8	6	75	6	5	3	60
1968	Johnson	25	22	17	77	13	11	8	73	12	11	9	82
1967	Johnson	24	18	13	72	12	11	6	55	12	7	7	100
1966	Johnson	24	20	15	75	12	12	9	75	12	8	6	75
1965	Johnson	36	33	30	91	18	17	15	88	18	16	15	94
1964	Johnson	21	19	16	84	10	9	8	89	11	10	8	80
1964-73		265	190	141	74	132	99	73	74	133	91	68	75
1964-68	Johnson	130	112	91	81	65	60	46	77	65	52	45	86.5
1969-73	Nixon	135	78	50	64	67	39	27	69	68	39	23	59

AS SELECTED BY CONGRESSIONAL QUARTERLY (These also included nomination for the Supreme Court and votes to override vetos, [which require 2/3's votes]).

*Congress controlled by opposition party

Table 6.5
The Action of the Congress on the President's Legislative Program 1954-1974

Year	(Pres.)	Proposals Submitted	Approved by Congress (both houses)	Percent Approved
1974	Ford[a]	64	23	36
1974	Nixon[a]	97	33	34
1973	Nixon[a]	183	57	31
1972	Nixon[a]	116	51	44
1971	Nixon[a]	202	40	20
1970	Nixon[a]	210	97	46
1969	Nixon[a]	171	55	32
1968	Johnson	414	231	56
1967	Johnson	431	205	48
1966	Johnson	371	207	56
1965	Johnson	469	323	69
1964	Johnson	217	125	58
1963	Kennedy	401	109	27
1962	Kennedy	293	133	45
1961	Kennedy	355	172	48
1960	Eisenhower[a]	183	56	31
1959	Eisenhower[a]	228	93	41
1958	Eisenhower[a]	234	110	47
1957	Eisenhower[a]	206	76	37
1956	Eisenhower[a]	225	103	46
1955	Eisenhower[a]	207	96	46
1954	Eisenhower	232	150	65

Source: *Congressional Quarterly Almanac* for relevant years.
[a] Congress controlled by opposition party

From 1954 through 1974 the Congress approved in some form an overall average of about 125 Presidential proposals each year. Concerning particular Presidents, the Congress adopted an average of 247 Presidential proposals each year under Johnson, 135 proposals under Kennedy, 105 proposals under Eisenhower, and only 60 proposals under Nixon. Thus, with the exception of the Nixon Presidency, the Congress approved on average over 100 Presidential proposals per year.

One might ask why Presidential success percentages should be higher on roll call votes than on passage of legislative proposals. As indicated in Table 6.7 part of the reason is the bicameral nature of the legislature. A President's legislative proposal is sometimes victorious in one house only to be defeated for final passage by the other. Another part of the reason may be that if the President's measures can get to the floor where party influence, leadership and organization are strongest, he stands a better chance of success. On the other hand, evidence suggests that measures which do not get to the floor, that are rejected or held up in committee, frequently would have had a

Table 6.6
The Congressional Treatment of Presidential Proposals

Year	Proposals #	Requests Approved #	%	Passed by Senate & House in different forms & died waiting compromise #	%	Passed by either Senate or House but not both #	%	Request reported from committee but not come to a vote #	%	Requests receiving committee hearing but not reported #	%	Requests receiving no action at all #	%	Requests receiving unfavorable reaction through rejection in committee or on floor #	%
1960	183	56	31	2	1.1	18	9.8	6	3.5	17	9.3	43	23.5	41	22.4
1965	469	322	69	8	1.7	20	4.3	3	.6	20	4.3	40	8.5	55*	11.7
1966	371	207	56	4	1.1	20	5.4	7	1.9	23	6.2	38	9.7	74	19.9
1967	431	205	48	3	.7	49	11.4	12	2.8	43	10.0	47	10.9	72**	16.6

*4 that were rejected could be brought up again, 51 were rejected finally or completely.

**15 that were rejected could be brought up again, 57 were rejected finally or completely

Source: *Congressional Quarterly Almanac* for relevant years.

lower probability of passage on the floor or would not have passed without substantial changes.[93] Thus, some of the President's legislative package may be lost in committee, and that loss would be reflected in a lower success score for passage of his legislative proposals; however, the probable defeat on the roll call is never recorded, thus leaving his roll call success score unaffected.

General Surveys of Case Studies

The figures presented thus far give only a brief overview of the relationship between the President and the Congress in the making of legislation. For a greater depth and subtlety than these figures allow, it is necessary to examine case studies. We begin with general surveys of cases compiled by others.

On the basis of careful weighing of the information available on ninety different cases, Lawrence Chamberlain investigated the period between 1880 and 1945 and found that Congress played a critical role in determining policy outcomes in either the policy formulation stage or the policy deliberation stage or both in the majority of the cases.[94] He found that about 40 percent of the final legislation was chiefly the product of the Congress and another 30 percent was the product of joint Congressional-executive influence. In less than 30 percent of the cases (including 20 percent for which the President is given chief credit) did the Congress not constitute a critical factor in the outcome of the legislation.

Regarding the formulation of legislation, Chamberlain found that seventy-seven of the ninety laws examined were originally introduced without administration sponsorship. Twelve of the nineteen cases for which Chamberlain assessed the President as eventually dominant were bills of this type as were twenty-six of the twenty-nine joint "Presidential-Congressional influence" bills. Thus, many of the bills allocated to the category of "presidential influence" had their earliest roots in Congress. Nelson Polsby made a similar observation, pointing out the existence of an "incubation period" for a measure before the President picks it up.[95] Examples of such legislation were cited earlier (p. 195).

The results of Chamberlain's study suggest the fully joint character of the American policy process, at least until 1945.[96] Referring to the overall figures forthcoming from his compilation of cases, Chamberlain concluded:

These figures do not support the thesis that Congress is unimportant in formulation of major legislation. Rather, they indicate not that the President is less important than generally supposed, but that Congress is more important.[97]

Ronald Moe and Steven Teel attempted to "replicate, to some degree," Chamberlain's approach. They used as their data the major legislative acts from 1940 to 1967 in order to determine "whether in the years since Chamberlain's work appeared, Congress has maintained its influence over the substance of the legislation it handles, or whether the 'legislative roots of most important statutes' have . . . been entirely displaced by the resources of executive innovation."[98] They relied on other authors' case studies (some of which we cite in our more detailed analysis of individual pieces of legislation later). Their coverage of the cases was broad, encompassing twelve issue areas (economic policy, tariff, labor, transportation, urban problems, technology, agriculture, conservation, immigration, civil rights, national defense, and foreign policy).

Moe and Teel did not present their findings in tabular form, as Chamberlain did. However, our own calculation based on an interpretation of their commentary regarding the various cases in the twelve issue areas indicates that in approximately 50 percent of the cases the Congress was the major contributor to the legislation with a further 25 percent attributable to joint efforts involving the Congress.

The evidence offered by Moe and Teel's survey of legislation from 1940 to 1967, in addition to Chamberlain's work, suggests that the Congress has been vastly underrated as a major influence on the making of public policy. Moe and Teel, too, conclude that the evidence "challenges the conventional wisdom that the President has come to enjoy an increasingly preponderant role in national policy-making. . . . The evidence suggests that Congress continues to be an active innovator and very much in the legislative business. Thus the findings . . . tend to confirm the findings Chamberlain made a quarter of a century ago."[99]

Finally, Randall Ripley surveyed decisions by the Congress on President Kennedy's major legislative proposals upon which the Congress took action from 1961 through 1964. Ripley did not examine the influence of the Congress on the formulation of these proposals. His research focused only on the deliberation stage. Yet, during the deliberation stage alone, Ripley found that Congress made substantial alterations to about 20 percent of Kennedy's major proposals before passage and went on to defeat a further 25 percent of the proposals.[100]

Individual Case Studies

Discussion of several individual case studies can be useful in providing greater dimension to the evidence presented thus far, which suggests the essentially joint Presidential-Congressional character of the policy process. One of the best of these studies examined the Employment Act of 1946.[101]

This case shows Congress taking the early initiative. The Act had its beginnings when Senator James E. Murray and his War Contracts Subcommittee staff took up the "Patton amendment" to the Kilgore bill, calling for full employment as a potential solution to reconversion after the war. During the summer of 1944, an election campaign was in progress, and Murray was not ready to call the controversial amendment up for a vote. President Roosevelt had also deleted a request for full employment from a Chicago speech as too controversial. After the elections Murray appointed his subcommittee staff director to prepare a draft of a full employment bill for inclusion as an appendix to the subcommittee report and later to be introduced as a new bill. With the opening of the Seventy-ninth Congress, Senator Murray set about lining up sponsors. He secured both Senator Wagner of New York and Elbert Thomas of Utah to attract liberal support because they were chairmen of two powerful Senate committees. He also enlisted the help of Senator O'Mahoney, a respected Democrat who was an authority on economics.

During all of this maneuvering, the President had been noticeably absent, despite the use made of the executive department and the assistance of federal economists in the drafting process. Although there was no reason to feel the President opposed such a bill, his desire for Congressional unity in terms of his goal to create a United Nations organization kept him from endorsing a plan that might muddy the water. He felt that specific plans for full employment had better come from Congress itself. Thus, it was a matter of priorities that prevented aggressive executive sponsorship of some bill in the employment area.

After a series of close votes in the Banking and Currency Committee, the bill was reported out favorably 13 to 7. On the floor, Democrats tried to hold the line while Republicans tried to modify the measure in a more conservative direction. By this time, Truman had succeeded to the Presidency, and with the end of the war, Truman indicated he wanted "full speed ahead" on full employment legislation. In the floor action, after several compromises, the bill passed 71 to 10.

In the House, with 14 conservative members (from both parties) of 21 on the Expenditures Committee, strong executive pressure was needed to get the bill reported out of committee. Yet, even with the increasing leadership role the executive was taking, the House voted down the original bill and drafted a House version that clearly rejected the central ideas of the Senate version. The administration, however, requested that liberals dissatisfied with the substitute bill not make it an issue in the hope that some kind of bill would be reported out of the House. The bill might then be strengthened in conference. The final floor vote was 255 to 126. Many House liberal sponsors felt the President had let them down and that the party had lost prestige among its liberal supporters. The "liberal-labor" lobby suggested that the President veto the conference bill if it did not measure up. Two weeks later Truman appealed to the people by radio to request "real full employment legislation." His message to Congress three weeks later represented the strongest Presidential pressure for a liberal bill that came from the White House during the entire course of the struggle. Yet, Truman signed the compromise bill that emerged from the conference, since it was clear Congress would not adopt any other alternative.

In this case, the Presidency was not a primary initiator of policy (the Congress was), but it was still due partly to his efforts that some bill got through Congress. Yet, even here, as Bailey notes, "the forces which shaped and modified the legislation were far beyond his [Truman's] control."[102] Certainly this case does not picture Congress as a subordinate branch in the policy process.

An issue area that has become highly visible in the past decade is the urban crisis facing many of the country's cities. Frederick Cleaveland has brought together seven case studies on Congress and the policy process covering the 1950s and early 1960s in this issue area.[103] In an overview Cleaveland notes:

In five cases—aid to airports, air and water pollution, food stamps, and urban mass transit —Congress provided the leadership, the continuity, the persistence in formulating new policies and programs and guiding them through the political thicket of the legislative process to final decision. In most of these cases, it is true, there were important assists from interest group representatives or executive agency professionals. In contrast, however, these same cases reveal executive department leaders, the White House, and the Bureau of the Budget for the most part either hesitant and divided, resulting in halting and sporadic initiative, or frankly opposed, resulting in outright obstructionism.[104]

Cleaveland further observes that when strong legislative initiatives came from within Congress—either on substance or strategy—they tended to be generated by senior members who were openly acknowledged to be experts in the field of the legislation.[105] However, the case studies also found two relatively junior members at that time, Williams (on mass transit) and Muskie (on clean air), playing a decisive role.

Valuable contributions, of course, also came from outside Congress. In one case, Attorney General Robert Kennedy rescued the juvenile delinquency bill by a call to Representative Smith, conservative chairman of the House Rules Committee, with whom he was on surprisingly good terms. On the urban mass transit bill, lobbyists acted to encourage the Democratic Congressional leadership to reach a floor vote. At many points there was also participation by interest group professionals both in providing "technical help," compromising their interests, and mobilizing support and sympathy. The studies suggest that interest group professionals, House and Senate staff, and executive agency legal and technical experts were likely to be especially important when bills involved "complex technology and problems of regulation, as, for example, in the Clean Air Act of 1963."[106]

Most of the initiatives with which Cleaveland dealt originated and were rather fully developed in Congress during the Eisenhower administration when the Democrats controlled Congress and the Republicans controlled the Presidency. After Kennedy's election, the Presidency took up and strongly pushed a number of proposals. Yet, two areas in which Congress was to continue to be the center of initiative, even after Kennedy became President, were mass transit and air pollution.[107]

Another issue area that gained momentum in the 1950s was civil rights. The case study of the 1964 Civil Rights Bill (discussed extensively in Chapter 3) found that Congress may have been partly responsible for the President's decision initially to stress other policy concerns and not to introduce legislation on civil rights. However, when the President began to give priority to civil rights in 1963, legislative initiative centered mainly in the administration rather than in Congress. The proposals the administration introduced contained some compromises designed to help insure adoption by Congress. For example, the failure to include a Fair Employment Practices Commission was done in the hope of enhancing the possibility of gaining Republican support to replace the loss of southern Democrats.

Once in Congress, the administration was forced to accept a series of amendments to get the bill out of the House Judiciary Committee. These amendments were sufficiently significant that the President felt they might well kill the bill on the House or Senate floor. The intensity of political struggle over the bill is indicated by the fact that it took almost five months to get the bill out of committee and onto the House floor. By the end of 1963, still no bill had passed Congress.

With the assassination of President Kennedy in late 1963, the political situation changed dramatically. The assassination appeared to create new sympathy for the Kennedy legislative program that helped Lyndon Johnson, the new President, muster bipartisan strength to overcome a filibuster in the Senate. The result was that the Congress adopted much of the administration's package. Yet, even then, President Johnson was dependent for passage upon the willingness of Everett Dirksen, the leader of the opposition party in the Senate, to support the program.

Unlike civil rights, federal aid to improve primary and secondary education was a priority item for President Kennedy from the beginning. The debate in Congress over federal aid to education centered upon proposals formulated mainly within the Kennedy administration. Once again, the proposals the administration forwarded to Congress contained a series of compromises suited to the realities of Congressional politics. In trying to lure the support of southern Democrats, for example, Kennedy reduced the amount of aid to be given from about $1.5 billion yearly to about $800 million yearly while simultaneously recommending criteria for distributing aid that were favorable to the South. Moreover, the funds granted would not depend on racial integration in schools.

But these compromises did not tackle the issue of aid to nonpublic schools. Kennedy's position was that federal aid to nonpublic schools was unconstitutional, but the President's support in the Congress was based primarily in the urban northeast, where Catholics constituted a significant portion of the population. The Catholic Church, moreover, was prepared to fight the President on this issue. It argued that nonpublic schools constituted an important component of the national educational system.

Initially, Kennedy stood his ground, but as Catholic pressure began to mount, it seemed clear that a measure not containing something for the Catholic interests could not survive in Congress. As a consequence, Kennedy shifted his position to one that would permit federal loans for certain purposes to nonpublic schools.

This change in position did not improve matters. A number of Protestant leaders and groups from all sections of the country objected vehemently to the inclusion of any provision for aid to nonpublic schools. They were joined by a handful of Catholic Democrats in Congress who would not support the Kennedy compromise if it might block aid to public schools. Not even the Catholic Church appeared to find the compromise acceptable. Finally, there were some forces in and out of Congress that were opposed in principle to federal aid in the area of education. One of these was Howard Smith, chairman of the House Rules Committee.

Given this constellation of forces, it is hardly surprising that Kennedy's aid-to-education proposals were in trouble in the House. In fact, they did not survive the House Rules Committee, where they were defeated by a close vote of 8 to 7. Five Republicans, two Democrats from the South, and a northern Democrat from a Catholic district combined to defeat the President's initiative. Later, a motion to extract the bill from the Rules Committee and to consider it on the floor of the House was defeated by 242 to 170. Despite the priority he gave to federal aid to education, Kennedy was unable to get Congress to adopt his proposals.

Federal aid to education was also a high priority for President Johnson. His style led him to seek some sort of compromise position on the part of the major education interest groups, especially the NEA and the United States Catholic Conference. The "main issue" was religion. His overwhelming electoral victory in 1964, along with a sharp increase in Democrats in Congress (a pickup of about 40 seats in the House), provided favorable conditions for his successful push for the bill. After the election, Johnson asked his Commissioner of Education, Francis Keppel, for an education bill that would avoid a church-state fight. Johnson delegated to Keppel and two other key members of his staff, Lawrence O'Brien and Douglas Cater, the working out of legislative details. The administration thus took the initiative in bringing together the people and groups in and out of government who shared an interest in that particular policy area. Keppel had a series of meetings with representatives of the interest groups and three key Democratic members of the relevant House subcommittee in which they were able to negotiate an "acceptable" solution. There was not only a concern within the executive to work out a formula that would be accepted by major interest groups but one that would also be accepted by Congress, that is, that could be passed. Keppel played a major role in leading the factions to agreement. Authors of a major study of this bill note: "It is clear that the important agreements that were necessary before the House could give favorable consideration to a federal elementary and secondary aid bill, were made *outside* Congress and, furthermore, with the explicit authorization of committee Democrats."[108] They add:

The explanation for this particular "surrender" of Congressional authority in a vital sphere in the decision-making on the education bill is deceptively simple. The Congress, and particularly the members of the committee who had experienced education fights before, feared they would have to resolve the church-state issue on Capitol Hill. The political consequences of taking sides on the "religious issue" was the greatest concern of most members . . . .
In effect the Democrats on the committee wanted and expected the Administration to work out the necessary agreements (whatever they might be) so that the principal factions were satisfied.[109]

General Discussion

The individual cases we have looked at mirror the results of the aggregate data and the general surveys of cases we presented above. The cases provide examples of Presidential dominance, Presidential defeat, joint Presidential and Congressional influence, Congressional initiative on its own, and Congressional initiative and leadership lying behind legislation later taken up by the President. The general surveys of cases and the aggregate data, coupled with the individual case-study illustrations, suggest an overall picture of the process of making legislation. This overall view is that both the Presidency and the Congress have been arenas integral to the development of policies contained in legislation as well as to the determination of which policies will and will not prevail. The cases point out that how central the Presidency and the Congress are varies according to the particular case cited. But, on the whole, both have been central arenas rather than one being substantially dominant over the other.[110] Additional evidence still to be considered will further reinforce this conclusion.

It is especially important to note that the influence of the Congress has by no means been confined to the deliberation stage. In the first place, the case studies we presented show that the Presidency often molded its own initiatives in anticipation of the necessities of winning majority support in the committees and on the floors of Congress. Going further, the individual case studies (such as the employment and urban cases) as well as the general surveys of cases revealed a level of Congressional participation in the initiation of proposals for legislation that constituted an important dimension of Congressional activity. This is supported by the admittedly crude measure of the origin of legislation. Considerably less than half of the public legislation the Congress enacted during the ten year period, 1963-72, was sponsored by the President.[111]

Contrary to the traditional view that the Presidency provides the motor in the process of policy initiation and the Congress provides the brakes,[112] in certain ways the Congress may have served more capably in the formulation and initiation stage than the Presidency. For example, after investigating fourteen cases of innovative economic and social legislation adopted by the Senate during the zenith of the Johnson Presidency (1965-66), David Price found that the Senate enjoyed a number of advantages relative to the Presidency in the process of formulating and initiating legislation. It is true that Congressional formulators usually required some assistance from administrative bureaus and that getting a bill on the President's agenda would achieve greater visibility than any other move. But the case studies also found that the Senate often displayed greater flexibility and permeability. Thus, Price concluded:

A proposal could become visible much more quickly in the legislative branch. This not only gave legislators and their staffs an incentive to assume the instigator role; it also made it likely that instigators from outside . . . would seek Congressional alliances. A legislator with a permissive chairman and access to committee resources could develop a proposal and get it into the newspapers with relative ease. Ideas rose to the top with more difficulty in the executive branch . . . .[113]

Price's study covered fourteen bills (including one rider) found to be the most major pieces of legislation reported to the floor under the jurisdiction of three Senate committees in 1965-66. The fourteen bills included twelve cases where President Johnson had advocated legislation at some point before final Congressional action occurred. In one of these cases neither the executive and administration nor the Senate served as a primary arena of policy formulation (interest groups did). Of the remaining eleven cases, Price found that members or committees of the Senate were intimately involved at some point in the stage of formulating and initiating eight of the eleven bills and were equal to or more dominant participants than the executive and administration in the initiation of at least four of the eleven bills.[114] These included the Fair Packaging and Labeling Act, the Campaign Finance rider, the Traffic Safety Act, and the Veterans Readjustment Benefits Act. Taking those major bills President Johnson advocated where the initiative for legislation lay in the Johnson administration and/or the Senate, then, Price found that the Senate was equal or more dominant in the initiation of about 40 percent of the legislation and was intimately involved at some point in the initiation of well over half of the bills.

Price's analysis also included two other major bills where Presidential advocacy was not involved. On one of these bills, the Senate was again a central arena of initiation. In the other case, while members of the Senate were active, the Federal Trade Commission became the primary formulator of the legislation.

Although Price's case studies covered only two years, they were years at the zenith of Presidential political strength in Congress. His finding that the Congress continued to play a significant role as an initiator of policy reaffirms the conclusions of the other research we have reviewed covering the period prior to 1966.[115]

The role of Congress in the initiation of legislation was no less apparent under the Nixon administration. The period abounds with illustrations. From 1969 through 1973, policy initiatives which centered in or were produced primarily by the Congress (in comparison to the White House), to mention but a few examples, would include legislation on war powers (which the President unsuccessfully vetoed); tax reform in 1969; the Environmental Policy Act of 1969, as well as legislation on both coastal zone planning in 1971 and water conservation in 1972 (which the President unsuccessfully vetoed); establishment of an independent Consumer Products Safety Commission; various social policies including comprehensive child day care (which was vetoed by the President), substantial expansion of public service jobs (which was vetoed by the President), and increases in levels and coverage of both minimum wages and Social Security; extension and redrafting of the Hill-Burton hospital construction program (which the President unsuccessfully vetoed); the Intergovernmental Personnel Act; and campaign broadcasting and financial reporting reforms.

In addition, Congressional activities over the years have been central to the development of many significant proposals that later became identified with the President. This has already been suggested by some of the urban case studies reviewed above, where a series of proposals the Kennedy administration came to sponsor had been developed in the Congress and had advanced some distance prior to Kennedy's victory.

In fact, the role of elements of the Democratic party in Congress during this period as an innovator and initiator of policy to be put before the country, generating greater legislative input than could normally occur in a responsible party system, extended well beyond the area of urban policy alone. This has been ably described by James Sundquist in his study, *Politics and Policy: The Eisenhower, Kennedy, and Johnson Years*.[116] As Sundquist points out, Presidential programs of the 1960s, such as federal aid to education, medicare, area redevelopment, manpower development and training, and a more activist civil rights posture, had their roots in an earlier period. Looking at the "major legislative measures" of the immediately prior period (1953-60), during the Eisenhower administration, Sundquist found that the party battle in Congress on these issues could be characterized as one of "Democratic initiative and Republican response."[117] As Sundquist noted, "Except in civil rights, the initiative was almost wholly with the Democrats."[118]

Indeed, much of Kennedy's program was inherited from the Congressional (especially the Senate) Democrats combined with other activists usually associated with the "progressive" wing of the Democratic party. A number of the proposals had been adopted by the Senate *before* Kennedy's victory. Even so, after Kennedy's inauguration people no longer spoke of "the Democratic policy program"; instead they spoke of "Kennedy's legislative package" and later "Johnson's legislative package."

But, if the part the Congress has played in the initiation of policy ought not be minimized, neither do we want to minimize the role of the Presidency. In the case of Kennedy's program, for example, it is true that much of the program was "inherited." At the same time, the President and administration contributed substantial resources that were instrumental in gaining Congressional enactment, and especially enactment in the House, for those elements of the program to which the President gave priority.[119] In addition, it remains the case that some of the proposals incorporated into the Kennedy and, even more so, the Johnson package were almost entirely the product of the Presidency and administration with the Congress playing a decidedly peripheral part. Finally, insofar as concerns major initiatives from within Congress, seldom have such initiatives been successful where the President has stood firmly opposed. Normally at least a relative neutrality on the part of the President has been required for such initiatives to survive.

What emerges from the research we have reviewed, then, is not that one of the branches of government has been characteristically integral and the other peripheral as an arena of policy initiation. Instead, what emerges is the need each has had for the other, the use each has made of the other, and the overall significance and vitality of each—both the Presidency and the Congress—to the stage of initiating successfully adopted legislation.

Having made these points about the formulation and initiation of legislation, let us offer a few final comments about relations between the President and the Congress during the stage of Congressional deliberation and decision on Presidentially sponsored or supported proposals. As we observed above, the President's legislative program, which may itself heavily bear the mark of previous Congressional activity or of anticipating Congressional response, is something like a menu from which the Congress, also influenced by the Presidential priorities, makes decisions on legislation to enact. Thus, on a yearly average the Congress does adopt in some form a large number of executive-initiated or -supported proposals. At the same time, again on a yearly average, these proposals constitute slightly less than 50 percent of all legislative initiatives the President submits to the Congress. (See Table 6.5).

As a consequence, the Congress rather frequently rejects Presidential proposals for legislation. Also, extensive modifications to administration proposals are frequently made in committee or on the floor. We cite several budgetary illustrations under the Nixon administration to give an idea of how substantial Congressional modifications can be. These include Congressional increases of almost $1 billion to the Presidential education appropriations proposals of 1970 (which the President unsuccessfully vetoed); an almost tenfold Congressional increase in outlays for revenue sharing compared to the conception as initially proposed by President Nixon; a threefold Congressional increase in funds for water conservation (which the President unsuccessfully vetoed); and Congressional reductions of $3 billion and $5.2 billion, respectively, in the fiscal 1972 and 1973 defense budgets.[120] In addition, a series of major proposals supported by the President were defeated outright. Five of the most noteworthy examples under the Nixon administration were defeats in Congress on initiatives the President supported to reform the welfare system, to reorganize the administration, to substitute his own proposals in place of extending the Voting Rights Act, to fund supersonic transport, and to set a $250 billion ceiling on federal spending. Although not involving legislation, the Senate losses President Nixon suffered on his nominations of Haynsworth and Carswell to the Supreme Court also would be classified as major defeats.

Of course, President Nixon was not alone insofar as concerns such outcomes. For example, Ripley's research led him to find that from 1961 through the 1964 elections, the Congress either rejected or substantially altered almost 50 percent of the major legislative proposals that President Kennedy's administration was involved in initiating.[121] Nor did President Johnson escape such difficulties. Perhaps the most extreme instance of Congressional modification under the Johnson administration was the Congress's adoption of the President's proposal for a 10 percent tax surcharge only when the President simultaneously accepted an $8 billion reduction in the federal budget.

Thus, even if we limit our attention to the influence of Congress by way of its activity (or anticipated activity) during the deliberation stage, we find that the Congress was still able to play a rather considerable part in the policy process. Indeed, as Manley has put it, "Granting the power of initiation to the President . . . is not equivalent to granting him a preponderant share of influence on policy: it is often possible for Congress to be secondary in time but primary in influence."[122]

We are now in a position to summarize. The compilations of cases and much other evidence suggests that in many areas of legislation, an understanding of how ideas for legislation arose and the forces that led to the final policy outcomes would not be nearly complete without bringing Congressional initiative or subsequent involvement as a central factor into the analysis. The evidence leads us to conclude that the contemporary relationship between the President and the Congress in the making of legislation, especially domestic legislation, continues to be a coordinate relationship, essentially symmetrical in nature, rather than one which is characterized by dominance and subservience. While Congressmen themselves may regard the executive as the most influential factor in the making of public policy,[123] the view from the White House may be much less confident. Referring only to one dimension of Congressional power, the power to grant or deny Presidential initiative, President Kennedy, himself a former legislator, said during an interview at the end of 1962:

> The fact is, I think, the Congress looks more powerful sitting here than it did when I was there in Congress. But this is because when you are in Congress you are one of a hundred in the Senate and one of 435 in the House, so that the power is so divided. But from here I look at Congress and I look at the collective power of Congress, particularly the bloc action, and it is a substantial power.[124]

Foreign and Domestic Policy

Up to this point we have been describing legislative-executive relations mainly in rather general terms without regard to policy sectors. It is possible, however, that relations between the executive and the legislature vary according to policy areas. It is often said, for example, that legislatures are typically less influential in the area of foreign policy than they are in the area of domestic policy.[125] To what extent does evidence bear out this contention?

There is an element of arbitrary judgment in the classification of policy as foreign or domestic. The distinction between foreign policy and domestic policy is not absolute. Both the issues involved and the processes of making policy for each are interrelated. Yet it is also clear that some issues and decisions tend to be oriented toward internation political or economic relations or to the military protection and defense of the state from outside intervention. It is these kinds of decisions that we will classify as constituting foreign policy.[126]

We begin by looking at the European legislatures. The constitutional powers of each of the European legislatures are subject to various restraints that apply only to foreign policy matters or that apply more so to foreign policy than to domestic policy. Whereas legislatures have the power to "negotiate" agreements between groups of citizens or individual citizens and then to "ratify" these agreements by law, in no case do legislatures negotiate international treaties or agreements. In this sense, legislatures have less power to become involved in the process of making foreign policy than they have in the area of domestic policy. Furthermore, the legislature does not necessarily have to authorize or ratify certain executive actions in the area of foreign policy. Perhaps the most extreme case of this is in Great Britain, where the declaration of war does not require the consent of Parliament.[127] Then, too, the British executive, as well as the French and West German executives, can enter into arrangements with foreign powers that are less formal than treaties, which must be approved by the legislature. They are called agreements and do not ordinarily require legislative assent.[128] Finally, the executive can exercise some control over foreign policy by using its powers as commander of the armed forces. By virtue of how it exercises its powers to command the armed forces, as well as how it conducts negotiations, the executive can aggravate diplomatic relations, if it so chooses, or ease them, depending upon its own policy goals.

When one looks at executive-legislative relations in practice, one finds that each of the European legislatures has ordinarily been less influential in the area of foreign policy than domestic policy. The research on Great Britain indicates that this has been the case for the House of Commons. The reader will recall Lynskey's study of rebellions against the government by governmental backbenchers in the House. Lynskey uncovered thirty-one rebellions by Labour backbenchers from 1945 to 1951, when Labour controlled the government. Eleven of these thirty-one rebellions were on foreign and defense policy. The remaining twenty rebellions were on domestic policy issues. To what extent did the rebels achieve success in the foreign policy area as compared to the domestic policy area? The evidence shows that the rebels were less successful in their attempts to influence the foreign policies of the government. While fully or partly successful in altering government policy on twelve of the twenty domestic policy cases, they achieved such success on only two of the eleven foreign policy cases.[129]

Lynskey also uncovered twenty seven rebellions by the backbenchers of the Conservative party from 1951 to 1957, when the Conservatives were in power. Twenty three of these rebellions were on domestic issues, and four were on foreign policy.[130] Lynskey concluded that the backbenchers were fully or partly successful in influencing the government on twenty of the twenty three domestic issues, whereas they were fully or partly successful on only one of the four foreign policy issues.[131]

Data we gathered pertaining to the fate of the amendments of Conservative backbenchers from 1959 to 1964, when the Conservatives were in power, support a similar conclusion. From 1959 to 1964, a total of 198 bills which passed the House could be classified as being in the area of domestic policy; 42 bills which passed the House could be classified in the area of foreign policy.[132] Of the amendments posed on domestic policy bills (we speak here of amendments requesting substantive changes in the government's policy), 37 percent were adopted. On the other hand, the House adopted (or the government agreed to) only 18 percent of the amendments posed on foreign policy bills.

The British system is not the only example of the diminished impact of the legislature on the making of foreign policy. Another example is to be found in the operation of the French Fifth Republic. We concentrate on the period to 1969 when de Gaulle was in power, but there is little evidence to indicate that the role of the Assembly in the area of foreign and defense policy changed in any fundamental sense during Pompidou's Presidency from 1969 to 1974.[133]

One indication of the lesser role of the Assembly in the area of foreign and defense policy is that, within the governing Gaullist parliamentary party, the committees which were regularly active and influential in the policy process were all in the domestic policy area. Thus, Charlot found that neither of the two Gaullist parliamentary party committees dealing with foreign and defense policy was active or influential.[134] Moreover, unity among Gaullist members behind the party leaders appears to have been somewhat stronger on foreign and defense policy questions than on domestic policy issues. For the three years we examined (1963, 1966, and 1967), the voting cohesion score of the Gaullists was 99.2 on foreign and defense policy as compared to 96.3 on domestic policy.

Perhaps the clearest illustration of the rather minimal impact of the Assembly in the area of foreign policy, however, is a case that did generate heated opposition within the Gaullist party. This was de Gaulle's policy toward Algeria. De Gaulle was able successfully to achieve his policy of Algerian self-determination despite considerable division in the Gaullist ranks and despite the belief at the outset, among many of de Gaulle's advocates, that he would act efficaciously so as to accomplish exactly the opposite result. As de Gaulle's policy became clearer, a number of leading Gaullist parliamentarians who energetically opposed it either were expelled or resigned from the party. The Assembly was kept at the periphery during the entire process of establishing Algerian independence. It debated the Evian accords at length in a special session but did not in the end have a final say in the matter. De Gaulle secured adoption of his policy of Algerian independence, instead, by appealing to the nation in a referendum held in April of 1962.[135]

Similarly, de Gaulle was able to secure the adoption or acceptance of virtually all of his major foreign policies. Included among these were his policies toward European integration and NATO. The important point, however, is that, unlike many areas of domestic policy, neither the Assembly nor parliamentarians of the majority were consulted or in any way brought into the decision-making process. They became involved only after the decisions had been made and announced.[136] Moreover, despite the explicit opposition in 1962 of a majority of Assembly members to the general line of de Gaulle's policies on European integration (a total of 293 Assembly members, constituting a majority, signed what was known as the European Manifesto, which was a declaration opposing the policies of de Gaulle on European integration), the Assembly was unable to change those policies. Not even the resignation of the MRP ministers did so. No new initiatives were taken by de Gaulle to develop a political federation in Western Europe, and even more important, de Gaulle vetoed the British application to enter the Common Market.

Our observations on the British and French experiences would appear to apply to West Germany as well, with the possible exception of the middle 1960s. Our analysis here will focus on the period 1949-62, although the conclusions that emerge from this period seem in the main appropriate also to the period since at least 1969. Throughout the period we will focus upon, Adenauer was Chancellor and the CDU/CSU was the major governmental party.

At least until the early 1960s, Adenauer's dominance in foreign policy matters was apparently considerably greater than we have seen in the area of domestic policy. Members of the CDU/CSU were decidedly more willing to line up behind their leader on foreign policy than on domestic matters. According to Heidenheimer, "In the face of repeated Socialist attacks ever since rearmament was first broached in 1950, the CDU/CSU parliamentary party came to stand solidly behind the government's policy, and has almost unanimously defended it as the best and only feasible way of meeting the 'threat from the east'."[137] Voting unity within the CDU/CSU during this period appears to have been greater on matters relating to foreign policy than it was on domestic policy issues. For example, from 1957 to 1961, voting unity within the CDU/CSU was 98.9 percent on foreign policy as compared to, for instance, 90.2 on social expenditures, 88.8 on agricultural policy, and 82.3 on labor policy.[138]

It is true that there were differing opinions on foreign policy within the CDU/CSU parliamentary party and the views of the parliamentary party leadership and members entered into many questions relating particularly to the buildup of the German armed forces, including the development of the army during its early stages, the length of military conscription, and how quickly the size of the army would be expanded. Sometimes the Chancellor's policies were fundamentally altered, but in an overall sense, especially regarding German relations with other countries, the priority Adenauer gave to foreign policy issues and a somewhat different relationship between constituencies and their Bundestag members on foreign policy than on domestic policy left members "with little choice but to close ranks in support of a [foreign] policy to which [Adenauer] was absolutely determined to commit the party's fortunes."[139] The Chancellor also used his influence over ministerial positions to reward CDU/CSU members who were loyal to his foreign policy, whereas members who deviated on domestic policies were able to secure ministerial positions.[140] Moreover, Adenauer's stature with the public was perceived by members as salient to public confidence in the CDU/CSU. To undermine confidence by speaking against Adenauer on the policies to which he was most committed might affect the electoral success of both the member and the party. According to Heidenheimer, "When after the first rearmament crisis public opinion polls began to note a swing back towards Adenauer, the parliamentary party 'thanked the Chancellor for the persistence and toughness with which he [had] pursued his policy. Only in this way could success be achieved'."[141] In addition, the cases of which we are aware in which CDU/CSU constituency organizations failed to readopt their members on grounds of opposing national party policy appear to have occurred disproportionately in the foreign policy area.

As a result of this convergence of forces, the Chancellor began to assume the loyalty of his followers on foreign policy proposals "even on issues which had not been fully explained.... The Chancellor ... frequently made it clear that he did not consider a full understanding of his policies a necessary prerequisite for loyalty to them."[142] Thus, the high level of voting cohesion of the CDU/CSU on foreign policy during this period is not to be explained by consensus achieved through consultation. Rather, it seems better explained by greater deference to the Chancellor in this area.

After 1961, the parliamentary party, and particularly the leaders, began to penetrate the area of foreign policy more regularly.[143] The bases for Adenauer's supremacy had withered. In the first place, Adenauer's electoral appeal had diminished. Second, the policies he had pursued over the previous decade were not successful in bringing West Germany closer to reunification with East Germany. Third, de Gaulle's policies toward the United States and the United States' decreasing emphasis on nuclear deterrence within NATO raised basic questions as to whether West Germany should continue to rely as heavily on NATO for her security or should instead give greater attention to ties with Western European countries as a basis for German security in the future. The third problem, in particular, divided the CDU/CSU. The Protestant wing generally supported ties with the more Protestant Atlantic nations while the Catholic wing supported ties with Western Europe (and especially France), where Catholicism was more prevalent.

Thus, by 1962, the very foundations of German foreign policy had come into question, and Adenauer no longer had the necessary stature within the party to lead it, united, in a new direction. The struggle that ensued involved both the ambitions of politicians and the clash of ideas. In the wake of the struggle, Adenauer was undermined in favor of the pro-Atlanticist Erhard, who, in turn, fell in 1966 amid the competing CDU/CSU groups. He was replaced by Kiesinger and a new coalition with the SPD that began a more concerted effort to develop new initiatives toward the East.

Yet, until the foundations of German foreign policy came into question around 1962, the evidence suggests that the Bundestag inserted itself effectively into the making of foreign policy only infrequently. From 1949 to 1962, the Chancellor exerted a level of control over his parliamentary party in the area of foreign policy that he either did not desire or was unable to exert in the area of domestic policy. A rather similar conclusion would apparently hold for the period after 1968 as well.[144]

Evidence on the United States, too, suggests that the impact of Congress has generally not been as great on foreign policy as on domestic policy. During hearings before the Senate Preparedness Committee in 1966, Secretary of State Dean Rusk remarked:

No would-be aggressor should suppose that the absence of a defense treaty, congressional declaration, or U. S. military presence grants immunity to aggression.[145]

Senator Fulbright, referring to this statement, pointed out that not only did it convey to a potential aggressor that he should not count on American inaction or indifference in the event of an aggressive act; it also conveyed another implicit and significant message to Congress: "that, regardless of any previous Congressional action or inaction, . . . the executive would act as it saw fit in response to any occurrence abroad which it judged to be an act of aggression."[146] He went on to note that it was unlikely that Rusk "consciously intended that the congressional action was irrelevant; it seems more likely that this was merely assumed, taken for granted as a truism of American foreign policy in the 1960's."[147]

This assumption or "truism" of American foreign policy is not without some foundation in fact. Despite the formidable constitutional provisions providing the bases for Congressional participation in foreign policy decision-making (e.g., Senate approval of treaties and diplomatic appointments, Congressional right to declare war, general appropriation and legislation powers), the effective authority and role of

Congress, which only intermittently has been substantial, eroded during the cold war until it became clear that the executive dominated the foreign policy process—both the formulation and deliberation stages. As Holbert Carroll notes, "The central fact remains: the conduct and care of international affairs is a special preserve for the President."[148] Only recently has a reversal begun to take place.

Presidential ascendency over foreign policy in the United States has firm roots in the constitutional tradition. The Supreme Court, in 1936, emphasized the inherent and independent Presidential authority in foreign affairs, maintaining a "fundamental" distinction between the President's power in domestic affairs and foreign affairs with the latter's "important, complicated, delicate, and manifold problems," and affirming "the very delicate, plenary, and exclusive power of the President as the sole organ of the federal government in the field of international relations."[149] Other court decisions have also generously favored the President (such as upholding the use and binding nature of executive agreements).[150] Treaty commitments, vaguely worded and often open-ended Congressional resolutions, and an accumulation of emergency statutes in conjunction with the considerable constitutional powers of the President (such as the Commander-in-Chief section) have provided the legal justification for the expansion of Presidential power in foreign and defense policy—even to the point of sanctioning commitment of troops and/or involvement in full-scale war without Congressional approval.[151] Bipartisanship has been the bedrock of the Administration's strategy throughout most of the post-World War II period; the appropriate Congressional committee members and leaders were coopted. The committees that theoretically were to monitor, criticize, and challenge the executive were the allies of the Administration.[152]

Aaron Wildavsky has characterized the American political system as having "two presidencies"—one for domestic affairs and one for foreign policy making. The President's record since World War II has been remarkably more successful in his dealings with Congress in foreign policy than in domestic policies. Wildavsky notes: "In the realm of foreign policy there has not been a single major issue on which Presidents, when they were serious and determined, have failed."[153] He cites as "victories" NATO, the Marshall Plan, Indochina (through the 1960s), aid to Poland and Yugoslavia, entry into the UN, and the test-ban treaty. Though receiving criticism from time to time, seldom has the President had a serious setback on foreign policy (that is, in his "struggle" with Congress). Of the examples just cited, Presidential policy toward Southeast Asia since 1970 would provide the only exception.

Table 6.7, covering Presidential proposals and final Congressional action on those proposals from 1948 to 1964, shows that the President had a much better record in foreign policy and defense policy than in the domestic area. The President succeeded 73.3 percent of the time on defense policy, 58.8 percent on foreign policy, and 70.8 percent on treaties. In contrast, on domestic policy his success score was 40.2 percent. Immigration and refugees has traditionally also been considered a "domestic concern," and Congress in fact tends to dominate policy in this area, as well.

If we were to look at the roll call tests (not the same as proposals submitted) on Presidential stands for individual Presidents, the same general conclusion would be sustained. The President prevailed more often on foreign policy than domestic policy. Let us take just a few examples. In 1962 Kennedy "won" on 98 percent of the foreign

Table 6.7
Congressional Action on Presidential Proposals from 1948 to 1964

Policy Area	Congressional Action % Pass	% Fail	Number of Proposals
Domestic policy (natural resources, labor, agriculture, taxes, etc.)	40.2	59.8	2499
Defense policy (defense, disarmament, manpower)	73.3	26.7	90
Foreign policy	58.5	41.5	655
Immigration, refugees	13.2	86.0	129
Treaties, general foreign relations, State Department, foreign aid	70.8	29.2	445

Source: From data in Congressional Quarterly Service, *Congress and the Nation, 1945-1964*, vol. 1 (Washington, 1965), in Wildavsky, "Two Presidencies," p. 231.

policy tests and 81 percent of those on domestic policy; in 1961 his "wins" were 93 percent and 78 percent respectively. Eisenhower was 86 percent successful on foreign issues and 57 percent successful on domestic policy in 1960. In 1959 his score was 76 percent on foreign policy and 44 percent on domestic affairs, and it was 95 percent and 59 percent, respectively, in 1958. Whether judged by percentage of proposals adopted by Congress or on actual roll call test cases, the President prevailed more often on foreign policy-related issues than on domestic issues.

The reader may recall the case studies by Chamberlain cited earlier. These studies led him also to conclude that in contrast to domestic policy, "The President has been consistently strong in the field of national defense legislation."[154] However, Chamberlain pointed out that, on four of thirteen occasions, Congress was influential. Two of these—the National Defense Act of 1916 and the Selective Service Act of 1940—were of particular importance. A study by Robinson focused on an additional twenty-two foreign policy cases. On sixteen of them, executive influence was found to be dominant. Furthermore, Congress only initiated or formulated three of the twenty two policies Robinson examined, and where the Congress did initiate or dominate, Robinson observed, it was usually on "marginal and relatively unimportant issues."[155] Samuel Huntington's study, the *Common Defense*, reached a similar conclusion regarding Congress and military strategy: "The administration in power originated and decided upon major changes in the strategic balance. Public opinion, non-government experts, the press and Congress played peripheral roles in determining overall strategy."[156] Russett, in *What Price Vigilance?*, observed: "once the executive branch has reached agreement on its defense request from Congress, not once in the last quarter century has the legislature voted down a major weapons system proposal. It has always provided virtually everything asked of it and sometimes more."[157]

Indeed, there are more than a few significant foreign policy decisions in which the Congress played hardly any, if any, part at all. In the Cuban missile crisis of 1962, no official information was given Congressmen until after the policy decision had been made and two hours before JFK went on television to announce the executive decision. Nor did the earlier Bay of Pigs decision include a Congressional role. Truman told the Congressional leaders *after* he had ordered American ground troops to the defense of the Republic of Korea.[158] The Dominican intervention of 1965 also lacked Congressional consultation. Fulbright notes that the leadership in Congress was summoned to the White House in the afternoon before the intervention and "told that the Marines would be landed in Santo Domingo that night for the express purpose of protecting the lives of American citizens."[159] According to Fulbright, this was not the "real purpose," and when he voiced his criticisms in the later Dominican hearings, he stirred a debate not so much "on the validity or substance of the criticisms, but on the appropriateness of having made them."[160] The decision to escalate the war in Vietnam, as Eidenberg points out, did not involve a significant role for Congress.[161] In an instance where there was Congressional involvement—the Gulf of Tonkin Resolution—it was only perfunctory. Fulbright, who helped pilot the resolution, notes that he and others made an error "in making a personal judgment when we should have made an institutional judgment."[162] They "trusted" Johnson too much. Many of the so-called "consultations" with Congress on behalf of the executive were simply briefings or pre-press releases. Fulbright gives an example of this when the administration called interested Senators to tell them American planes were *en route* to the Congo. The "final" decisions on war and peace rest with the President.

However, we must be careful not to overstate our case and leave the reader with the impression that Congress and the European legislatures simply "rubber stamp" executive foreign policy decisions without offering any challenges or alternatives to executive policy. In regard to the Congress, even those scholars who recognize the subordinate role of Congress vis-à-vis the President in the area of foreign policy variously refer to the Congressional involvement as "vital,"[163] "significant,"[164] "expanded,"[165] and, in some aspects, "decisive."[166] Although the Congressional role is less than in domestic policy, nonetheless that role has been more than minimal, far more than a simple "rubber stamp."

Scott and Dawson note that "Congress is intimately involved, and its power and prerogatives are central to the form and substance of foreign policy decisions, especially *to certain kinds* of decisions . . . But the Executive is involved in *all* of these decisions."[167] Roger Hilsman has suggested a useful categorization of foreign policy decisions that will allow us to highlight the "certain kind of decisions" in which Congress and also the European legislatures are more likely to participate.[168] Hilsman's threefold classification includes: (1) crisis policy decisions, (2) declaratory or anticipatory policy decisions, and (3) program policy decisions. Scott and Dawson, who develop and illustrate this typology, note that in the first two kinds of action—crisis and declaratory—"the Executive clearly dominates." It is in the program policy decisions that the influence of Congress "is most visibly present."[169]

The Cuban missle crisis represents a crisis policy. Congress was not involved in the decision. "Secrecy, speed, unity of action and purpose"—all of which are the requisites for coping with a crisis situation—tend to be uncharacteristic features of the legislative process.[170] Malcolm Jewell observes: "A review of the post war period suggests that when foreign crises arise the President has ample resources for inducing the necessary degree of Congressional support."[171] It should perhaps be noted that what is a crisis depends partly on perception and on the President. As with Johnson and the Tonkin Gulf Resolution, the President is frequently in a position to manipulate perceptions of reality as well as precipitate and call attention to a crisis.[172]

Declaratory foreign policy also finds Congress on the edge of decision-making but with the potential of Congressional dissent or modification. Scott and Dawson cite the 1963 decision to establish a NATO nuclear force with the commitment of U. S. Polaris submarines armed with Polaris missiles. This is a declaratory policy "in the sense that it constitutes no basic change in the nature of American obligations assumed under the NATO Treaty. It was a modification of the implementation of that obligation but within the framework of an existing consensus within the United States."[173] However, there are instances when firm consensus among the politically relevant decision makers does not exist; in such instances, as the resolutions asked for by Eisenhower on the defense of Formosa and Eisenhower Doctrine for the Middle East, the President may seek to associate Congress more closely and formally with declaratory policy decisions. From time to time, Congress may issue its own declaratory policy statements (for example, its early concurrent resolution against admission of Communist China to the UN); however, these are usually aimed at the President.

Program policy decisions "call for a change in the allocation of resources, for the creation of a new framework of consensus or both."[174] The "operationalized" forms of such decisions usually require appropriations, statutes, or treaties (over which Congressional Senate assent is required). In such instances, there is at least greater potential for Congressional involvement and influence. Thus, the Senate played an important role in the Japanese peace treaty,[175] the North Atlantic treaty,[176] and United States governmental action relevant to participation in the United Nations.[177] Congressional involvement in decision-making leading up to the Marshall Plan was high.[178] Furthermore, foreign aid debates have often served as an occasion for both Congressional criticism and assertion of power, with cuts in Presidential request ranging up to two-fifths.[179]

Even in defense policy, the Congress has exerted influence on program decisions. An impressive study of defense policy from 1945 to 1963, in the words of the author, "draws a picture of Congress' exercise of its purse power that, while not complementary in many respects, contrasts with the commonly expressed view that Congress has contributed little of benefit to defense policy since 1945."[180] The study found that Congress's review of Defense Department appropriations, especially reviews carried out by Congressional defense appropriations subcommittees, has had a "perceptable impact" on debate over the doctrines which should guide defense strategy, weapons systems procurement, and defense economics; in fact, it has achieved a "remarkable record."[181] Congressional initiative or intervention in defense policy was a persistent characteristic of the latter Eisenhower period, whereas it had been "episodic and desultory" before.[182] The changes in the overall orientation of defense policy that took place under President Kennedy, when United States defense policy did take a new and different direction, "grew essentially out of the latter 1950's. Congress stood closer to the center of these controversies than ever before."[183] With Kennedy and McNamara's forceful leadership and centralization of decison-making, Congressional influence in foreign policy began to decline in the early 1960s.[184]

Recently, however, the Congress, and particularly the Senate, has again entered more actively into the making of foreign and defense policies. There has been an attempt to reassert legislative influence in the area of foreign and defense policy and in so doing to curb the power of the Presidency.[185] Disappointed with the inaccurate perceptions and apparent deceptions of the executive branch, increasingly judging executive policies to have failed, and challenging the previous consensus that regarded almost every Communist move as a security threat, the Senate Foreign Relations Committee, which formerly ran "interference" for the administration, became a defiant and vociferous critic of Presidential policies.[186] Though passed in favor of the President, legislative opposition in 1970 to the antiballistic missile system served notice that Congressional approval of executive defense policies would not be automatic.[187] This point was further driven home with increased Congressional reductions of the President's defense budget, beginning with President Johnson's last budget and culminating with reductions of $3 billion for fiscal 1972 and $5.3 billion for fiscal 1973 in President Nixon's defense budgets. Legislation was also introduced and passed over President Nixon's veto to confine the President's war powers, and funds were terminated for bombing in Cambodia and aid to Turkey. It has been proposed to limit the President's power to conclude executive agreements, as well. Thus, as Wayne Moyer observes, "[The] past half dozen years have seen a great resurgence of congressional interest on defense questions, obviating many of the earlier findings . . . that the legislature tends to rubber stamp the executive."[188]

Moreover, many challenges from Congress, especially in the field of defense policy, have had programmatic characteristics in the sense that they concerned the broad allocation of resources within the defense field (certain kinds of defense programs receiving more immediate favor than others) and/or the broad allocation of resources that should be devoted to defense policy relative to domestic policy.[189] On the other hand, when Congress has reduced funds for defense, there is some dispute as to how much it has mounted successful challenges against at least eventually (if not immediately) meeting the policy objectives of particular armaments projects.[190]

The allocation of resources and the direction of foreign and defense policy have frequently lay behind challenges within the European parliaments. For example, almost all of the Labour rebellions on foreign and defense policy since 1945 have challenged resource allocation or underlying principles of policy, including nuclear armament, the level of defense spending, conscription, the basic posture Britain took in relating to the Soviet Union and the United States, and whether Britain should enter the Common Market or not. Since 1960, entry into the Common Market has also been a major cause of rebellions in the Conservative party, as has the question of the relationship between Great Britain and Rhodesia. Furthermore, the last resignation of a Prime Minister due to diminishing support from his parliamentary party was caused by opposition to the basic orientation he was pursuing in the area of foreign policy. This was Neville Chamberlain's policy toward Germany in the latter 1930s. And one of the two resignations of a Prime Minister since 1945 which may have partly had to do with pressure from the Prime Minister's parliamentary party, the resignation of Anthony Eden, involved a particular foreign policy issue: objections to Eden's military policies toward Suez.

In France, too, challenges to basic approaches and directions of policy have weighed heavily in the National Assembly's consideration of foreign and defense policies. For example, almost 40 percent of the motions of censure put in the National Assembly have dealt with the basic orientation of Gaullist foreign and defense policies and, in particular, the priority given to developing a French nuclear capability. Furthermore, the issue that most divided the Gaullists themselves was the question of the basic approach the nation should take regarding Algerian independence.[191] And, in West Germany, the fundamental question of how the government's foreign policy ought to provide for the nation's future security and for the unification of Germany was one factor that brought the political and parliamentary downfall of both Chancellors Adenauer in 1963 and Erhard in 1966. These were the only two Chancellors from 1949 to 1974 who resigned while their party remained in office without an intervening election.

Indeed, the resignations of executives in both Great Britain and West Germany suggest the significance fundamental issues of foreign policy can have for the relations between the executive and the legislature. Such issues were at least partly responsible for the fall of one and perhaps two British Prime Ministers who resigned since 1939 and for each of the two West German Chancellors who resigned from 1949 to 1974. They were also integral to Chancellor Brandt's decision in 1972 to call for a vote of confidence in the Bundestag and for the subsequent dissolution of the Bundestag, the only time this has occurred since 1949.

Let us briefly summarize. We have concerned ourselves in this section with the relative impact of legislatures in policy processes relating to foreign policy decisions (broadly defined to encompass internation political, economic, and defense issues) as contrasted to domestic policy decisions. The evidence from the four legislatures is consistent in indicating, in each case, that the impact of legislatures has as a whole been lesser on foreign policies than it has on domestic policies. While the Congress has participated in the area of foreign policy, the fact remains that the foreign policy process within the United States, even concerning matters over which Congressional assent is required, has ordinarily been more heavily executive-centered than has the process of making domestic policy. As we have seen, this has generally also been the case in each of the European systems.

At the same time, we have cited an array of examples of Congressional influence in the area of foreign policy and have pointed to the relevance of foreign policies for legislative activity and pressures preceding the resignations of Prime Ministers and Chancellors in both Great Britain and West Germany. As these examples suggest, there have been significant legislative attempts to influence foreign policy, or to hold men responsible for failure, and these attempts have not been entirely without success.

Overview

This chapter, concerned mainly with the making of legislation, has covered the four legislatures under six different governing parties: the Democratic and Republican parties, the British Labour and Conservative parties, the French Gaullist party, and the West German CDU/CSU. There has been growing skepticism during this century about how relevant the representative legislature is to the making of public policy. Part of this skepticism has stemmed from the authority that legislatures have delegated to executives over the years. Skepticism has also arisen because of the increasing influence of the executive in the making of legislation itself. Despite this skepticism about the relevance of the contemporary legislature to the making of legislation, we have seen that two of our legislatures, the American Congress and the West German Bundestag, have been vigorous and vital parts of the political process at least in the area of domestic legislation.

Whether one refers to the Nixon years or earlier, it is clear that the Congress has been a highly active, integral, and influential factor in the making of legislation, especially legislation in the domestic area. The fact that the White House plays an important part in much policy initiation and that the Presidency is active during Congressional consideration of legislation is of obvious importance. But it does not deny the political significance the Congress has retained. Instead, it indicates the need for the kind of collaboration that has come to characterize the process of making legislation.

Several points need to be stressed. In the first place, we observed that the Congress has itself remained a prominent arena of initiation in the policy process without the lead or help of the White House. Indeed, its role in this regard during the Nixon years, certainly no less than during the three prior administrations, was a substantial one. In addition, the Congress has been an important arena of policy incubation. By this we mean that many contemporary examples of innovative-legislation, which were adopted with the collaboration of the Presidency, both originated in and were nurtured and developed principally by the Congress before they acquired the active support of the President. The Congress's "negative" action on Presidentially sponsored or supported proposals suggests the significance of its presence in the process of making legislation, as well. We have seen not only that Presidentially proposed or supported initiatives could be extensively altered in the process of gaining Congressional support and approval but also that outright defeat of Presidential initiatives in the Congress was certainly not a rare phenomenon.

As the case studies and other evidence we reviewed suggest, an understanding of the forces that led to policy outcomes across a wide variety of domestic legislation would not be nearly complete without bringing the involvement of Congress as a central factor into the analysis. Indeed, with regard to the making of domestic legislation, our findings covering the contemporary record of Congress would generally sustain the observation that Huitt and Peabody made that the Congress "has remained the coordinate branch the Founding Fathers meant it to be."[193]

Our examination of the Bundestag found that it was in many respects also active and influential in the process of making legislation. Once again, this conclusion pertains principally to domestic legislation. The government has been the primary arena in which the formulation of most significant legislation occurred, and the Bundestag has adopted a high percentage of that legislation in some form. On the other hand, especially in the domestic area, the Bundestag repeatedly had to be taken into serious account as the government formulated its proposals for legislation.[194] As part of this, members or small working groups of the parliamentary majority were often extensively involved with the executive in the process of developing proposals for initiation. Furthermore, during the deliberation stage, the Bundestag was quite willing (and able) to determine compromises on government-sponsored legislation independent of, as well as over the objections of, the government. Thus, we found that combining the initiation and deliberation stages, the Bundestag frequently became an arena in which policy basic to the cases we reviewed was developed and determined. From this it is understandable, too, that pressures arising from within the Bundestag would be and were significant in determining the selection and dismissal of government ministers as well as Chancellors, men who play such a central part in formulating legislation and pressuring for its adoption.

Despite the influence of the Bundestag, the evidence suggests that the role of the Congress in the process of making legislation has been a stronger one. The development of executive-sponsored legislation serves as an example. The case studies on the West German system indicate that the formulation of successful executive-sponsored legislation occurred primarily within the executive. This is not to say the executive took no account of the legislature. The initiation of some of this legislation was not only preceded by legislative pressures for action and by executive anticipation of legislative response, but often there were extensive consultations with the legislative majority as initiatives for legislation were being developed or before they were introduced. Still, despite such involvement, and with some exceptions, the case studies showed that the executive remained the primary arena in which the legislation it sponsored was formulated and developed.

The Congress, on the other hand, seems to have entered more so into the formulation of executive-sponsored initiatives. As in the Bundestag's case, close interaction between executive officials and members of Congress combined with executive anticipation of Congressional response have played important parts in shaping the executive's own proposals. But going further, the evidence pointed out that when the President advocated legislative initiatives, the Congress often was either equal to or more dominant than the executive in the actual development and formulation of the proposals during the initiation stage. For example, Price's study, reviewed above, showed that this occurred in almost 40 percent of the specific cases he examined for 1965-66, a high point of Presidential strength. The findings of other case studies and specific policies we reviewed covering the period since 1945 provided additional support for this conclusion.

The relative roles of the Congress and Bundestag might also be indicated by the percentage of executive-initiated proposals that the legislature passed. Here it is pertinent that each legislative period the Bundestag adopted, although sometimes in a substantially amended form, a high percentage of proposals the executive sponsored (about 90 percent). On the other hand, the Congress adopted a yearly average of less than 50 percent of the proposals the President sponsored. While the President certainly had some influence over which of his proposals the Congress would adopt, the Congress, not the Presidency, was the arena in which these legislative priorities were determined.

Admittedly, the figures just cited are crude rather than precise if only because the figures are yearly for the Congress and encompass several years for the Bundestag. Still, covering a four-year period for Congress (1961-64), it was found that the Congress adopted in some form only about 75 percent of the legislation to which President Kennedy gave priority. This included Congressional enactment of Kennedy programs during the first year of the Johnson administration.[195]

The experiences of the Congress and the Bundestag lead to a number of observations, two of which we wish to underline at this point. First, the involvement of the contemporary legislature in the decision-making process is not necessarily limited essentially to the deliberation stage and to responding to executive initiatives, as is often thought to be the case even for the stronger legislatures. The evidence reveals that neglecting the successful involvement of the Congress, or of the Bundestag to a somewhat lesser degree, in the stage of initiating legislation would be to ignore a significant area of legislative activity and of the contemporary legislative record.

A second observation pertains to the operation and practice of parliamentary systems. There has been some question as to how possible it is under a parliamentary system for a stable government to exist alongside a strong parliament, since the experience of our systems has frequently been one of relatively strong parliaments combined with unstable governments (for examples, the French Fourth Republic and the German Weimar Republic[196]) or of relatively weak parliaments combined with stable governments (for examples, the British and the French Fifth Republic systems). In this light, the experience of the contemporary West German system is of note, for its experience offers an example of a parliamentary system that has successfully combined governmental stability with a relatively strong parliament.

With these observations in mind, we can turn to some concluding remarks about House of Commons and the National Assembly. Executive control has been more important to the making of legislation in these two legislatures than in the Congress or the Bundestag. This is not to say that parliamentarians in the Commons and the Assembly have been unable to influence the making of legislation. There is much evidence to show that the executives of these two systems have compromised and agreed to modification of policy in response to legislative criticism, especially criticism from their own followers. Nevertheless, whether during the initiation or deliberation stage, the evidence suggests that the development of decisions fundamental to outcomes in these two legislatures has centered more heavily in the executive or governmental arena. Such a conclusion takes us back to the notion that the legislature is now only atypically central to the development of key policies contained in legislation. If there is validity to this notion, the evidence we reviewed indicates that it is more appropriate to the experience of the House of Commons and the Assembly than it is to the experience of either the Bundestag or the Congress.

Notes

[1] Quoted in Lewis Chester et al., *Watergate* (New York: Ballantine, 1973), p. 267.

[2] Thus, we will not ordinarily consider decisions that have not been specifically subjected to legislative action at some point, such as executive orders, decisions of independent regulatory agencies, or decisions made by courts. Discussion of legislative supervision of executive policy-making is found in Chapter 7.

[3] On the United States, representative of this argument are Samuel P. Huntington, "Congressional Responses to the Twentieth Century," in *The Congress and America's Future*, ed, David B. Truman, 2d. ed. (Englewood Cliffs, N. J.: Prentice-Hall, 1973) especially pp. 6-7; and Robert A. Dahl, *Democracy in the United States: Promise and Performance*, 2d. ed. (Chicago: Rand McNally, 1972), especially p. 180. On the European legislatures, see Alfred Grosser, "The Evolution of European Parliaments," *Daedalus* 93 (Winter 1964): 156-79; Lewis J. Edinger, *Politics in Germany* (Boston: Little, Brown and Co. , 1968), especially p. 300; Bernard Crick, *The Reform of Parliament* (London: Weidenfeld and Nicolson, 1970), and Philip M. Williams, *The French Parliament: Politics in the Fifth Republic* (New York: Praeger, 1968).

[4] See for examples: Harold D. Lasswell, "The Decision Process: Seven Categories of Functional Analysis,"

in *Politics and Social Life*, ed. Nelson Polsby, Robert Dentler, and Paul Smith (Boston: Houghton Mifflin, 1963), pp. 93-105; James Robinson, *Congress and Foreign Policy-Making*, rev. ed. (Homewood, Ill.: The Dorsey Press, 1967), Chapter 1; and Randall Ripley, *Kennedy and Congress* (Morristown, N. J.: General Learning Corp., 1972), pp.2-4. The most neglected stage in terms of scholarly analysis is the implementation stage. See Jeffrey Pressman and Aaron Wildavsky, *Implementation* (Berkeley: University of California Press, 1973), p. xiii.

[5] See the incisive discussion of the relationship between initiative and influence in David A. Baldwin, "Congressional Initiative in Foreign Policy," *Journal of Politics* 28 (November 1966): 754-73.

[6] Nelson Polsby, "Policy Analysis and Congress," *Public Policy* 18 (Fall 1969): 65. See also: John S. Saloma III, *Congress and the New Politics* (Boston: Little, Brown and Co., 1969), pp. 93-97, and Thomas E. Cronin, "The Textbook Presidency and Political Science" (Paper Presented to the Annual Meeting of the American Political Science Association. September 1970), pp. 31-33.

[7] Ralph K. Huitt, "Congress, the Durable Partner," in *Lawmakers in a Changing World*, ed. Elke Frank (Englewood Cliffs, N. J.: Prentice-Hall, 1966), p. 17.

[8] Polsby, "Policy Analysis and Congress," p. 67.

[9] Huitt, "Congress the Durable Partner," refers to this as a "policy system" (p. 19). See also, J. Leiper Freeman, *The Political Process: Executive Bureau-Legislative Committee Relations*, 2d. ed. (New York: Random House, 1965), and Eugene Eidenberg and Roy D. Morey, *An Act of Congress* (New York: Norton, 1969) Chapters 1 and 8.

[10] Carl J. Friedrich, *Constitutional Government and Democracy* (Boston: Little, Brown and Company, 1941), pp 589-91.

[11] On the trend toward decentralization of the British cabinet, see Colin Seymour-Ure, "The Disintegration of the Cabinet and the Neglected Question of Cabinet Reform," *Parliamentary Affairs* 24 (1971): 196-208.

[12] An excellent example of this is found in the relationship between the Minister of Agriculture and the Premier in formulating the agricultural reforms of 1962. See Gaston Rimareix and Yves Tavernier, "L'Elaboration et le vote de la loi complémentaire á la loi d'orientation agricole,"*Revue Française de Science Politique* 13 (1963): 389-425.

[13] For other illustrations, see James J. Lynskey, "The Role of British Backbenchers in the Modification of Government Policy: The Issues Involved, the Channels Utilized, and the Tactics Employed" (Ph. D. diss., University of Minnesota, 1966). The dissertation is summarized in James J. Lynskey, "The Role of British Backbenchers in the Modification of Government Policy," *Western Political Quarterly* 23 (June 1970) : 333-48. Citations below will be to the dissertation.

[14] Jean Charlot, *L'U.N.R.: Étude du pouvoir au sein d'un parti politique* (Paris: Armand Colin, 1967), pp. 162-63.

[15] For a discussion of the role of collaboration between individual members and groups in the Bundestag, on the one hand, and the government and administration, on the other hand, in formulating proposals for initiation, see Jürgen Domes, *Mehrheitsfraktion und Bundesregierung* (Cologne and Opladen: Westdeutscher Verlag, 1964). This account covers the experience of the Bundestag under the CDU/CSU, especially from 1953 to 1961.

[16] Lynskey, "The Role of British Backbenchers," especially pp. 1-107. See also Ronald Butt, *The Power of Parliament* (New York: Walker and Co. 1967).

[17] Some illustrations of government defeats during this period may be found in Domes, *Mehrheitsfraktion und Bundesregierung*, pp. 125-33.

[18] Amendments to which the government gave favorable assurance were categorized as having been successful.

[19] Valentine Herman, "Backbench and Opposition Amendments to Government Legislation," in *The Backbencher and Parliament: A Reader*, ed. Dick Leonard and Valentine Herman (London: Macmillan, 1972), pp. 151-154.

[20] Williams, *The French Parliament*, p. 79.

[21] For the period since 1957 (extending to 1966), see also Butt, *The Power of Parliament*, Several additional examples for the period after 1966 can be found in John P. Mackintosh, *The Government and Politics of Britain* (London: Hutchinson and Co., 1970), pp. 137-38.

[22] Williams, *The French Parliament*, pp. 93-94.

[23] Mackintosh, *The Government and Politics of Britain*, p. 55.

[24] Butt, *The Power of Parliament*, p. 269.

[25] See Harry Eckstein, *Pressure Group Politics: The Case of the British Medical Association* (Stanford, Calif: Stanford University Press, 1960);James B. Christoph, *Capital Punishment and British Politics: The British Movement to Abolish the Death Penalty, 1945-57* (Chicago: University of Chicago Press, 1962); H. H. Wilson, *Pressure Group: The Campaign for Commercial Television* (London: Secker and Warburg, 1961); Leon Epstein, *British Politics in the Suez Crisis* (Urbana, : University of Illinois Press, 1964); Malcolm Joel Barnett, *The Politics of Legislation: The Rent Act of 1957* (London: Weidenfeld and Nicolson, 1969); Eric A. Nordlinger, "Britain and the Common Market: The Decision to Negotiate," in *Modern European Governments*, ed. Roy C. Macridis (Englewood Cliffs, N.J.: Prentics-Hall, 1968), pp. 47-67; Butt, *The Power of Parliament*, pp. 233-40; Paul Foot, *Immigration and Race in British Politics* (Baltimore, Md. : Penguin, 1965); and Frank

Stacey, *The British Ombudsman* (Oxford: The Clarendon Press, 1971), which covers the enactment of the Parliamentary Commissioner Act of 1967. A case we have not included in our analysis or our tabulations deals with the development of a national economic council. We have not included it because the decision did not require legislative assent, and our discussion in this chapter is confined to relations between the executive and the legislature on those decisions that do require legislative assent. See James B. Christoph, "The Birth of Neddy," in *Cases in Comparative Politics*, ed. James B. Christoph (Boston: Little, Brown and Co., 1965), pp. 44-89.

[26] This case is described in H. H. Wilson, *Pressure Group*.

[27] Wilson, *Pressure Group*, p. 100.

[28] Each of these cases is found in Williams, *The French Parliament*, pp. 84-97.

[29] Jean Charlot, *The Gaullist Phenomenon: The Gaullist Movement in the Fifth Republic* (London: George Allen and Unwin, 1971), pp. 152-55; Edwin L. Morse, *Foreign Policy and Interdependence in Gaullist France* (Princeton, N. J.: Princeton University Press, 1973), pp. 304-313; Bernard E. Brown, "The Decision to End the Algerian War," in *Cases in Comparative Politics*, ed. Christoph, pp. 154-80; Bernard E. Brown, "The Decision to Subsidize Private Schools," in *Cases in Comparative Politics*, ed. Christoph, pp. 131-53; and Roy C. Macridis, "The French Force de Frappe, in *Modern European Governments*, ed. Macridis, especially pp. 83-91.

[30] In Philip M. Williams and Martin Harrison, *Politics and Society in de Gaulle's Republic* (Garden City, N. Y.: Anchor Books, 1973), the authors treat the role of the National Assembly in a series of other cases that we do not include here. These cases are not included because five of our eleven cases are drawn from Williams' work elsewhere and because the additional cases reach substantially the same conclusions as the five we have cited. Another case study on French policy toward NATO is not considered here because it was handled within the realm of executive decisional power. See Roy C. Macridis, "DeGaulle and NATO," in *Modern European Governments*, ed. Macridis, pp. 92-115. Finally, we have excluded a case study carried out by Lord, who purposefully presented the case as atypical of the role of the Assembly. See Guy Lord, *The French Budgetary Process* (Berkeley: University of California Press, 1973), pp. 178-86.

[31] Williams, *The French Parliament*, p. 95.

[32] See Charlot, *The Gaullist Phenomenon*, pp. 152-55 and Williams and Harrison, *Politics and Society in de Gaulle's Republic*, pp. 379-85.

[33] See the discussion in Bernard Lavergne, "La loi d'orientation universitaire de M. Edgar Faure réproduit presque integralement le projet de la commission paritaire de Faculté de Droit de Paris," *L'Année Politique et Economique* 41 (December 1968), especially p. 426.

[34] Quoted in Charlot, *The Gaullist Phenomenon*, pp. 154-55.

[35] André Chandernagor, *Un Parlement, pour quoi faire?* (Paris: Gallimard, 1967), p. 58. For the Fourth Republic, see Jean Grangé, "La Fixation de l'ordre du jour des assemblées parlementaires," in *Etudes sur le Parlement de la VeRépublique*, ed. Eliane Guichard-Ayoub, Charles Roig, and Jean Grangé (Paris: Presses Universitaires de France, 1965), p. 244.

[36] Williams, *The French Parliament*, p. 97. Emphasis added.

[37] For example, see *Le Monde*, July 14, 1971, p. 1; November 16, 1971, p. 1 and p. 13; and October 31, 1972, p. 1 and p. 13. See, also, Michel Poniatowski, "Un Parlement nouveau pour un Etat nouveau," *Preuves* 4 (1972); and Jean Charlot, *The Gaullist Phenomenon*, pp. 125-26. Our thanks to Lowell G. Noonan for his assistance on this matter.

[38] How much the relationship will alter due to the much reduced Gaullist majority in the 1973 elections and the Gaullist defeat in the 1974 Presidential elections, is, unfortunately, still uncertain.

[39] Gerhard Loewenberg, *Parliament in the German Political System* (Ithaca, N. Y.: Cornell University Press, 1967), pp. 291-373.

[40] Gerhard Braunthal, *The West German Legislative Process: A Case Study of Two Transportation Bills* (Ithaca, N. Y.: Cornell University Press, 1972); Gerhard Braunthal, "An Agreement with the Russians," in *Cases in Comparative Politics*, ed. Christoph, pp. 256-87; and Otto Stammer et al., *Verbände und Gesetzgebung: Die Einflussnahme der Verbände auf die Gestaltung des Personalvertetungsgesetzes* (Cologne-Oplanden: Westdeutscher Verlag, 1965).

[41] Viola Gräfin von Bethusy-Huc, *Demokratie und Interessenpolitik* (Wiesbaden: Franz Steiner Verlag, 1962), and Domes, *Mehrheitsfraktion und Bundesregierung*, pp. 136-51. We were not able to guage the extent to which Bundestag action was central to outcomes in one of the cases. This was the case on cartels as reported in Bethusy-Huc and in Gerhard Braunthal, "The Struggle for Cartel Legislation," in *Cases in Comparative Politics*, ed. Christoph, pp. 241-55. As a consequence, we have not included this case in our analysis.

[42] See Loewenberg, *Parliament in the German Political System*, especially pp. 290-92, 310-15, 335-41, and 361-63.

[43] Loewenberg, *Parliament in the German Political System*, p. 339.

[44] Loewenberg, *Parliament in the German Political System*, p. 340.

[45] An overall view of the role of the Chancellor in the politics of the CDU/CSU during this period and the limits on his influence can be found in Peter Merkl, "Equilibrium, Structure of Interests, and Leadership: Adenauer's Survival as Chancellor," *American Political Science Review* 56 (September 1962): 634-50. For general over-

views of relations between the government and the Bundestag, see also both Domes, *Merheitsfraktion und Bundesregierung*, and Loewenberg, *Parliament in the German Political System*.

[46]See, for example, Gerhard Lehmbruch, "The Ambiguous Coalition in West Germany," in *European Politics: A Reader*, ed. Mattei, Dogan and Richard Rose (Boston: Little, Brown, 1971), pp. 557-59 and Heinz Rausch, "Parliamentary Consciousness and Parliamentary Behavior During the Grand Coalition", *International Journal of Politics* (Winter 1971-72).

[47]Domes, *Mehrheitsfraktion und Bundesregierung*, especially pp. 133-34. Recall that Domes's figure encompasses changes brought about solely in committee and on the floor. Changes brought about during the precommittee formulation stage are not included.

[48]Lynskey, "The Role of British Backbenchers," especially p. 73 and p. 90.

[49]Lynskey's findings on the total number of attempts by governing party backbenchers to effectuate significant modification in government policies (he located fifty seven cases from 1945 to 1957) are quite similar to those reported in other research. See, for example, Robert J. Jackson, *Rebels and Whips: An Analysis of Dissension, Discipline, and Cohesion in British Parliamentary Parties* (London: Macmillan, 1968), who covers the 1945-64 period. An exception to these findings might be the 1967-69 period, in which the Labour government experienced an abnormally high number of rebellions. In Chapter 4, we discussed some of the factors that may have contributed to the increased level of rebellion during this period.

[50]Recall that our examination of amendments also found a higher success ratio on the part of members of the governing party in the Bundestag as compared to members of the governing party in the House of Commons. See page 200.

[51]Domes, *Mehrheitsfraktion und Bundesregierung*, pp. 153-57.

[52]Whereas 81 percent of government-sponsored legislation was adopted between 1962 and 1965, only 65 percent was adopted between 1959 and 1961. See also the politics of alcohol tax reform before and after 1962 as described in Williams, *The French Parliament*, pp. 85-89, and the politics of agricultural policy in which the government was able to get the Assembly to accept principles by 1962 which the Assembly had rejected in 1960 (Rimareix and Tavernier, "L'Elaboration et le vote," p. 418).

[53]The importance of the Algerian issue for politics in the 1958-62 Assembly is discussed and described in David M. Wood, "Majority vs. Opposition in the French National Assembly, 1956-1965: A Guttman Scale Analysis, " *American Political Science Review* 62 (March 1968): 88-109, especially 108-9.

[54]Lynskey, "The Role of British Backbenchers," p. 95 and p. 98.

[55]As this study was about to go to press, a second occasion arose. In February, 1975, Margaret Thatcher defeated the incumbent leader, Edward Heath, by a vote of 130 to 119 of the parliamentary party.

[56]Kenneth N. Waltz, *Foreign Policy and Democratic Politics: The British and the American Experience* (Boston: Little, Brown and Co., 1967), p. 47.

[57]*The Economist*, December 22, 1956.

[58]Robert T. McKenzie, *British Political Parties: The Distribution of Power Within the Conservative and Labour Parties*, 2d. ed. (New York: St Martin's Press, 1963), p. 631.

[59]*Manchester Guardian*, February 1, 1963.

[60]Waltz, *Foreign Policy and Democratic Politics*, p. 48

[61]Waltz, *Foreign Policy and Democratic Politics*, p. 49.

[62]See G. W. Jones, "The Prime Minister's Power," in *European Political Processes: Essays and Readings*, ed. Henry S. Albinski and Lawrence K. Pettit (Boston: Allyn and Bacon, 1968), pp. 288-90.

[63]John P. Mackintosh, *The British Cabinet* (Toronto: University of Toronto Press, 1962), pp. 384-85; McKenzie, *British Political Parties*, pp. 55-56.

[64]The following discussion on the Labour party is derived from R.M. Punnett, "The Labour Shadow Cabinet, 1955-1964," *Parliamentary Affairs* 18 (Winter 1964-65): 61-70.

[65]See McKenzie, *British Political Parties* pp. 585-86. On Macmillan, see Mackintosh, *The Government of Britain*, pp. 85-86.

[66]George K. Romoser, "Change in West German Politics After Erhard's Fall," in *European Politics II: The Dynamics of Change*, ed. William G. Andrews (New York: Von Nostrand Reinhold Co., 1969), pp. 208-9.

[67]See Romoser, "Change in West German Politics After Erhard's Fall," pp. 200-208, who describes in detail the situation Erhard faced in 1966. In the case of Adenauer, see Loewenberg, *Parliament in The German Political System*, p. 254.

[68]On 1957-61, see Loewenberg, *Parliament in the German Political System*, pp. 252-54. For added examples, see also, pp. 254-59.

[69]See Grant McConnell, *The Modern Presidency* (New York: St. Martin's Press, 1967), especially Chapter 3; Rowland Egger, *The President of the United States* (New York: McGraw-Hill, 1967), Chapter 7, especially p. 138; Wilfred E. Binkley, *The President and Congress*, 3d. ed. (New York: Random House, 1962); Richard Neustadt, "Presidential Government," in *International Encyclopedia of the Social Sciences*, ed. David Sills (New York: Macmillan and Free Press, 1968), vol. 12, pp. 451-56; Nelson Polsby, *Congress and the Presidency*, 2d. ed. (Englewood Cliffs, N. J.: Prentice-Hall, 1971); and Arthur M. Schlesinger, *The Imperial Presidency* (Boston: Houghton-Mifflin, 1973).

[70]See Binkley, *The President and Congress*, Chapter 6, especially pp. 134 and 159.

[71]Woodrow Wilson, *Congressional Government* (New York: Meridian Books, 1956).

[72]Quoted in Louis Koenig, *The Chief Executive*, 3d. ed. (New York: Harcourt, Brace and World, 1975), p. 161.

[73]See, for example, Lawrence Chamberlain, "The President as Legislator," *Annals of the American Academy of Political and Social Sciences* 283 (September 1952): 94-103.

[74]Other constitutional provisions (e.g., Commander in Chief) may serve indirectly to legitimize the President's legislative involvement.

[75]Richard Neustadt, *Presidential Power: The Politics of Leadership* (New York: John Wiley, and Sons 1960), especially Chapter 3.

[76]Koenig, *The Chief Executive*, p. 165.

[77]Richard Neustadt, "Presidency and Legislation: Planning the President's Program," *American Political Science Review* 49 (December 1955): 981.

[78]Richard Neustadt, "Presidency and Legislation: The Growth of Central Clearance," *American Political Science Review* 48 (September 1954): 641-71.

[79]Neustadt, "The Growth of Central Clearance," p. 648.

[80]Quoted in Neustadt, "The Growth of Central Clearance," p. 649.

[81]Neustadt, "Growth of Central Clearance," p. 650.

[82]See Robert S. Gilmour, "Central Legislative Clearance: A Revised Perspective" in *Congress and the President: Allies and Adversaries*, ed. Ronald C. Moe (Pacific Palisades, Calif.: Goodyear Publishing Co., Inc., 1971). pp. 109-20, esp. p. 117. For a summary of Presidential resources to aid him in formulating his program, see Thomas E. Cronin and Sanford D. Greenberg, eds., *The Presidential Advisory System* (New York: Harper & Row, 1969) and Aaron Wildavsky, ed., *The Presidency* (Boston: Little, Brown and Co. 1969), pp. 486-700.

[83]Louis Fisher, *President and Congress, Power and Policy* (New York: The Free Press, 1972), p. 105.

[84]For a good brief summary of the budgetary process, see Polsby, *Congress and the Presidency*, Chapter 6, and Wildavsky, *The Politics of the Budgetary Process*.

[85]Donald Matthews, *U. S. Senators and Their World,* (New York: Random House, 1960), pp. 140-41. See also Neustadt, *Presidential Power*, p. 9.

[86]Neustadt, "Planning the President's Program," p. 1014.

[87]Clinton Rossiter, *The American Presidency*, rev. ed. (New York: The New American Library, 1960).

[88]See Roger H. Davidson, David Kovenock, and Michael O'Leary, *Congress in Crisis: Politics and Congressional Reform* (Belmont, Calif.: Wadsworth, 1966), Chapter 2.

[89]For descriptions of how the Presidency interacts with the Congress, the following are recommended: Abraham Holtzman, *Legislative Liaison: Executive Leadership in Congress* (Chicago: Rand McNally, 1970); Edward de Grazia, "Congressional Liaison: An Inquiry into its Meaning for Congress," in *Congress: The First Branch of Government*, ed. Alfred de Grazia (Garden City, N. Y.: Doubleday, 1967), pp. 281-322; Stanley Kelley, Jr., "Patronage and Presidential Legislative Leadership," in *The Presidency*, ed. Aaron Wildavsky, pp. 268-277. On legislative liason in the Ford administration see *Congressional Quarterly Weekly Report*, February 1, 1975, pp. 226-28.

[90]The table, based on data found in the *Congressional Quarterly Almanac* for the relevant years, regards a Presidential issue as one on which the President (by press conference or other public statement) makes it clear he personally supports. Excluded by *Congressional Quarterly* are those measures that have been so significantly amended on the floor of Congress that it is impossible to say whether it is a Presidential victory or defeat. Furthermore, except on foreign aid appropriations and votes to increase or decrease specific funds requested in the Presidential budget message, roll calls on passage of appropriation bills generally are not included, "since it is rarely possible to determine the President's position on the overall revisions Congress almost invariably makes in the sums allowed." *(Congressional Quarterly Weekly Report*, Jan. 18 1975, p. 151).

[91]Note the figures do not include issues unless they were the subject of messages to Congress. For example, the vote on confirmation of Nixon's Supreme Court nominees, Carswell and Haynsworth, even though these were two of his significant defeats during his first Administration.

[92]The *CQ* tabulated scores differently before 1954, and thus Truman's scores are not quite comparable to the other Presidents on the table. However, it should be noted that compared to Eisenhower's of 1953—on the same scoring system—Truman's scores were lower—47.7 (1947); 45.7 (1948); 44.1 (1949); 44.2 (1950); 40.4 (1951); 34.9 (1952).

[93]See Chapter 8, pp. 297-300.

[94]Lawrence Chamberlain, *The President, Congress and Legislation* (New York: Columbia University Press, 1946). Chamberlain bases his allocation on a "weighing of the relative influence of the executive and Congress in its total effect upon the law in question. In some cases the initiative has lain with one, but the proponderant influence in the completed statute has been ascribed to the other. Allocation is based upon a careful weighing of all evidence" (p. 448). He recognizes that there is an element of judgment involved and cautions that his information may be incomplete and thus affect his judgment.

[95]Polsby, "Policy Analysis and Congress," p. 67.

[96]Robinson, *Congress and Foreign Policy-Making*, points out that Chamberlain's figures suggest the impact

of Congress may have declined over time. He contends: "An extension of Chamberlain's study from 1945 to 1965 would be expected to show that this collaboration has now yielded to virtually exclusive initiation by the executive. The decline in Congressional power has been especially acute with respect to its innovative or creative contributions to public policy" (pp. 174-75). Our discussion below will suggest that Robinson somewhat overstates and certainly oversimplifies the real executive-legislative relationship. See also Saloma, *Congress and the New Politics*, p. 97.

[97] Chamberlain, *The President, Congress and Legislation*, p. 454.

[98] Ronald C. Moe and Steven C. Teel, "Congress as Policy Maker: A Necessary Reappraisal" in *Congress and the President*, ed. Ronald Moe, p. 35. While a much needed study of legislative-executive relations, unfortunately, the findings are not as complete, systematic, or detailed as Chamberlain's. Thus, exact comparison is difficult.

[99] Moe and Teel, "Congress as Policy Maker," p. 50.

[100] Randall Ripley, *Kennedy and Congress*, (Morristown, N.J.: General Learning Press, 1972), esp. p. 12.

[101] Stephen K. Bailey, *Congress Makes a Law* (New York: Random House, 1964). The narrative below relies heavily on Bailey.

[102] Bailey, *Congress Makes a Law*, p. 237.

[103] Frederick N. Cleaveland, ed., *Congress and Urban Problems* (Washington, D.C.: Brookings Institution, 1969).

[104] Cleaveland, *Congress and Urban Problems*, pp. 354-55.

[105] Cleaveland, *Congress and Urban Problems*, p. 351.

[106] Cleaveland, *Congress and Urban Problems*, p. 353.

[107] See Royce Hanson, "Congress Copes with Mass Transit," and Randall Ripley, "Congress and Clean Air" in *Congress and Urban Problems*, ed. Cleaveland.

[108] Eidenberg and Morey, *An Act of Congress*, p. 77. Emphasis ours.

[109] Ibid.

[110] See Chamberlain, *The President, Congress and Legislation*; Moe and Teel, "Congress as Policy Maker"; Cleaveland, *Congress and Urban Problems*; Bailey, *Congress Makes a Law*. In addition, see John Manley, *The Politics of Finance: The House Committee on Ways and Means* (Boston: Little, Brown and Co., 1970), and Lawrence C. Pierce, *The Politics of Fiscal Policy Formation* (Pacific Palisades, Calif.: Goodyear Publishing Co., 1971), especially pp. 135-78, for studies of the impact of Congress on fiscal policy and taxation. An excellent study of the influence Congress has had on policy outcomes in the area of housing and the central role Congress has played, is found in Helen Ingram, "Congress and Housing Policy" (Ph.D. diss., Columbia University, 1967). See also Roger H. Davidson, *The Politics of Comprehensive Manpower Legislation* (Baltimore, Md.: Johns Hopkins University Press, 1972); Theodore R. Marmor, *The Politics of Medicare* (Chicago: Aldine, 1973); E.E. Schattschneider, *Politics, Pressure and the Tariff* (Englewood Cliffs, N.J.: Prentice-Hall, 1935); Raymond Bauer, Ithiel de Sola Pool, and Lewis Anthony Dexter, *American Business and Public Policy: The Politics of Foreign Trade* (New York: Atherton Press, 1968), also on tariff policy; Gary Orfield, *Congressional Power: Congress and Social Change* (New York: Harcourt, Brace, Jovanovich, 1975) regarding racial change, aid to education, and jobs programs; Dennis Brezina and Allen Overmeyer, *Congress in Action: The Environmental Education Act* (New York: The Free Press, 1974); and Eric Redman, *The Dance of Legislation* (New York: Simon and Schuster, 1973).

[111] From 1963 to 1972, Congress adopted 3,518 public laws. In so doing, it adopted 1,443 Presidential proposals (see *Congressional Quarterly Almanac*, Washington, D.C., 1972, p. 21). Unfortunately, this is a crude measure if only because we cannot simply subtract the Presidential proposals passed from the total of public laws passed in order to ascertain the number of laws enacted which were not Presidential proposals, for it is usually the case that several Presidential proposals are enacted into a single law. Thus, the number of laws that the President sponsored is fewer than the number of Presidential proposals cited above.

[112] For some citations, see footnote 3.

[113] David Price, "Who Makes the Law" (Ph. D. diss., Yale University, 1969), p. 490. See also his *Who Makes the Laws? Creativity and Power in Senate Committees* (Cambridge, Mass.: Schenkman Publishing Co., 1972). Our discussion in the paragraph following the quote is drawn from the Price book. See, as well, John R. Johannes, *Policy Innovation in Congress* (Morristown, N. J.: General Learning Press, 1972) and Helen M. Ingram et al., *Institutional Fragmentation and Policy Innovation: The Case of Federal Water Pollution Control* (Tucson, Ariz.: Institute of Government Research, 1975).

[114] As part of the initiation of legislation, we include the phases of the process Price calls "formulation," "instigation and publicizing," and "information-gathering."

[115] See particularly the series of cases in Moe and Teel, "Congress as Policy Maker," Cleaveland, *Congress and Urban Problems*, and Manley, *The Politics of Finance*.

[116] (Washington, D.C.: The Brookings Institution, 1968).

[117] Sundquist, *Politics and Policy* p. 389.

[118] Sundquist, *Politics and Policy*, p. 388 and 390-91. For a similar view regarding proposed programs covering food stamps and juvenile delinquency, see Cleaveland, *Congress and Urban Problems*, p. 355.

[119] Sundquist, *Politics and Policy*, pp. 489-90.

[120] For further data on Congressional influence over budgetary appropriations, see Chapter 7.
[121] Ripley, *Kennedy and Congress*, p. 12.
[122] Manley, *The Politics of Finance*, p. 327.
[123] Lester Milbrath, *The Washington Lobbyist* (Chicago: Rand McNally, 1963), pp. 351-54.
[124] Quoted in Koenig, *The Chief Executive,* (New York: Harcourt, Brace and World, 1964), p. 126. Cronin's research, "The Textbook Presidency and Political Science" (Paper Presented to 1970 Annual Meeting of the American Political Science Association), finds that a sample of advisors who served Kennedy and Johnson had tempered assessments of Presidential determination of public policy (p. 36). Over 50 percent considered Presidential influence to be either relatively little or only selective (p. 38).
[125] In the early part of the previous century, Alexis de Tocqueville, the author of *Democracy in America,* sounded a theme that has expressed a perennial dilemma for democracies: "It is especially in the conduct of their foreign relations that democracies appear to me decidedly inferior to other governments. . . . Foreign policies demand scarcely any of those qualities which are peculiar to a democracy; they require on the contrary, the perfect use of almost all those in which it is deficient." (quoted in Malcolm E. Jewell, *Senatorial Politics and Foreign Policy* (Lexington: University of Kentucky Press, 1962), p. 1. See also: Waltz, *Foreign Policy and Democratic Politics,* esp. pp. 308-9, and Arthur Schlesinger, Jr., "Congress and the Making of American Foreign Policy," *Foreign Affairs* 51 (October 1972): 78-113.
[126] See Leroy N. Rieselbach, *The Roots of Isolationism: Congressional Voting and Presidential Leadership* (Indianapolis, Ind.: Bobbs-Merrill, 1966), pp. 35-38. He notes: "There exist in Congress clusters of issues, foreign and domestic, which are sufficiently distinguishable to be considered as distinct segments of congressional activity" (p. 38).
[127] Peter G. Richards, *Parliament and Foreign Affairs* (London: George Allen and Unwin, 1967), pp. 37-38.
[128] Richards, *Parliament and Foreign Affairs*, pp. 41-42, and Maurice Duverger, *La Cinquieme République* (Paris: Presses Universitaires de France, 1968), pp. 154-55. For a discussion of the differences in legislative powers on domestic as contrasted to foreign policy see also David Vital, *The Making of British Foreign Policy* (New York: Praeger, 1968), pp. 47-49.
[129] Lynskey, "The Role of British Backbenchers," p. 73.
[130] Lynskey, "The Role of British Backbenchers," p. 90. The greater number of rebellions on foreign policy in the Labour party as compared to the Conservative party is probably attributable to a higher level of ideological cleavage in the PLP on such issues. See, for example, S.E. Finer, H.B. Berrington, and D. J. Bartholomew, *Backbench Opinion in the House of Commons, 1955-1959* (Oxford: Pergamon Press, 1961), pp. 48-59. Many of the issues Finer et al. isolated as creating cleavage in the PLP persisted beyond 1959 and were also present before 1955 (especially the "pacifist" sentiments held by those on the Left). From 1945 to 1951, six of the eleven rebellions on foreign policy in the PLP involved matters specifically related to armaments, defenses, and defense expenditures. From 1959 to 1969, six of the twelve voting rebellions on foreign policy in which 5 percent or more of the Labour backbenchers defected involved defense expenditures.
[131] Lynskey, "The Role of British Backbenchers," p. 90.
[132] These figures do not include the yearly finance bill.
[133] See Elijah Ben-Zion Kaminsky, "The French Chief Executive and Foreign Policy" (Paper presented to the 1973 Annual Meeting of the American Political Science Association).
[134] Charlot, *L'UNR*, pp. 160 and 165.
[135] For a description of the role of the Assembly in the resolution of the Algerian issue, see Bernard B. Brown, "The Decision to End the Algerian War," pp. 154-81. See also Williams, *The French Parliament*, pp. 25-26, and Charlot, *L'UNR*, pp. 45-84.
[136] On the French withdrawal from NATO, for example, see Macridis, "De Gaulle and NATO," pp. 110-13.
[137] Arnold J. Heidenheimer, "Foreign Policy and Party Discipline in the CDU," in *The Democratic Political Process: A Cross National Reader,* ed. Kurt L. Shell (Waltham, Mass.: Blaisdell, 1969), p. 245.
[138] Loewenberg, *Parliament in the German Political System*, p. 358.
[139] Heidenheimer, "Foreign Policy and Party Discipline in the CDU," p. 245.
[140] On foreign policy, see Heidenheimer, "Foreign Policy and Party Discipline in the CDU," p. 247. On the overall relationship between deviation and appointments to ministerial positions (remembering that over 90 percent of the deviation was on domestic policy matters), see Chapter 4, pp. 139-40.
[141] Heidenheimer, "Foreign Policy and Party Discipline in the CDU," p. 245.
[142] Heidenheimer, "Foreign Policy and Party Discipline in the CDU," p. 247.
[143] Indeed, the declining influence of Adenauer was detectable even before the early 1960s. For example, see the interesting study by Karl W. Deutsch and Lewis J. Edinger, *Germany Rejoins the Powers: Mass Opinion, Interest Groups and Elites in Contemporary German Foreign Policy* (Stanford, Calif.: Stanford University Press, 1959), pp. 195-216.
[144] See Abraham Ashkenasi, "The Federal German Chief Executive and Foreign Policy Process" (Paper presented to the 1973 Annual Meeting of the American Political Science Association).
[145] Quoted in J. William Fulbright, "Congress and Foreign Policy" in *Congress and the President,* ed. Moe, p. 197.
[146] Ibid.

[147]Ibid.
[148]Holbert N. Carroll, *The House of Representatives and Foreign Affairs*, rev. ed. (Boston: Little, Brown and Co., 1966), p. 322. See also, Robert Dahl, *Congress and Foreign Policy* (New York: Norton, 1950), p. 58; H. Bradford Westerfield, "Congress and Closed Politics in National Security Affairs," *Orbis* 10 (Fall 1966): 737-53; Roger Hilsman, *The Politics of Policy Making in Defense and Foreign Affairs* (New York: Harper & Row, 1971), Chapter 2 and p. 74; Andrew Scott and Raymond Dawson, eds., *Readings in the Making of American Foreign Policy* (New York: Macmillan, 1965), pp. 148 and 207; Holbert Carroll, "The Congress and National Security Policy," in *Congress and America's Future*, rev. ed., David Truman (Englewood Cliffs, N.J.: Prentice-Hall, 1973); Dorothy Buckton James, *The Contemporary Presidency*, 2d. ed. (New York: Pegasus, 1974), Chapter 8; and Erwin C. Hargrove, *The Power of the Modern Presidency* (New York: Knopf, 1974).
[149]*U. S. v. Curtis-Wright Export Corp.* 299 U.S. 304 (1936).
[150]*U. S. v. Pink* 315 U. S. 203 (1942). Executive agreements can be made unilaterally by the President without Congressional approval or direction. However they are as binding and legal as treaties. From 1940 to 1970 there were 310 treaties as compared to 5,653 executive agreements (Fisher, *President and Congress*, p. 45). For limitations on the President's freedom to enter executive agreements, see Fisher, pp. 45-47. Fisher observed: "The disturbing fact about executive agreements is not so much their wide range, for that partly reflects the growing interdependence among nations and the heightened international responsibilities of the United States. Of much greater concern is the failure to report executive agreements to Congress" (p. 47). For example in 1969 Congress learned of a secret agreement negotiated in 1964-65 that would commit American troops to Thailand in case of external attack. The same year, it was also discovered that the Eisenhower, Kennedy, Johnson, and Nixon administrations had pledged to "instantly repel" any armed attack on the Philippines, both bypassing the treaty process and failing to inform Congress. In 1972, however, Congress limited such secrecy.
[151]The war powers of the President are currently under debate. See for example: Fisher, *President and Congress*, Chapters 6 and 7; William Spong, Jr., "Can Balance Be Restored in the Constitutional War Powers of the President and Congress," *University of Richmond Law Review* 6 (Fall 1971): 1-47; *Hearings on War Powers Legislation before the Committee on Foreign Relations*, United States Senate, Ninety-second Congress, First Session, March 8, 9, 25; April 23, 26; May 14; July 26, 27; October 6, 1971; Schlesinger, *Imperial Presidency*; Jacob Javits with Don Kellerman, *Who Makes War: The President Versus Congress* (New York: William Morrow, 1973.
[152]See for example, Cecil V. Crabb, Jr., *Bipartisan Foreign Policy* (New York: Harper & Row, 1957); Jewell, *Senatorial Politics and Foreign Policy*; Samuel Huntington, *The Common Defense: Strategic Programs in National Politics* (New York: Columbia University Press, 1961), p. 390; David Farnsworth, *The Senate Committee on Foreign Relations*, Illinois Studies in the Social Sciences, vol. 49 (Urbana: University of Illinois Press, 1961).
[153]Aaron Wildavsky, "The Two Presidencies," in *The Presidency*, ed. Wildavsky, p. 231. The respected journalist James Reston makes a similar statement: "I cannot think of a single major foreign policy move any President wanted to make since the Second World War that he was unable to carry through because of the opposition of the press or of Congress."["The Press, the President and Foreign Policy," *Foreign Affairs* 44 (July 1966): 560].
[154]Chamberlain, *The President, Congress and Legislation*, p. 145.
[155]Robinson, *Congress and Foreign Policy-Making*, p. vii.
[156]Huntington, *The Common Defense*, p. 113. See also p. 174.
[157]Bruce Russett, *What Price Vigilance: The Burdens of National Defense* (New Haven, Conn.: Yale University Press, 1970), p. 26; Carol Goss, "Congress and Weapons Procurement" (Paper presented at annual meeting of the American Political Science Association, 1970), especially pp. 9, 16, 18; Lawrence J. Korb, "The Defense Budget Process in the United States, 1953-1970" (Paper presented at the annual meeting of the American Political Science Association, 1971; Lewis Dexter, "Congressmen and the Making of Military Policy," in *New Perspectives on the House of Representatives*, ed. Robert Peabody and Nelson Polsby (Chicago: Rand McNally, 1963), pp. 305-24; and, Bernard Gordon, "The Military Budget: Congressional Phase," *Journal of Politics* 23 (November 1961), pp. 689-710; Huntington, *The Common Defense*, p. 134.
[158]Glenn D. Paige, *The Korean Decision: June 24-30, 1950* (New York: The Free Press, 1968), p. 262. See also Kenneth M. Glazice, "The Decision to Use Atomic Weapons Against Hiroshima and Nagasaki," *Public Policy* 18 (Summer 1970): 463-516.
[159]Fulbright, "Congress and Foreign Policy, " p. 201.
[160]Ibid.
[161]Eugene Eidenberg, "The Presidency: Americanizing the War in Vietnam," in *American Political Institutions and Public Policy*, ed. Allan P. Sindler (Boston: Little, Brown and Co., 1969). Other similar examples were Johnson's decision to call a bombing halt in 1968 and Nixon's decision to invade Cambodia. See Philippa Strum, *Presidential Power and American Democracy* (Pacific Palisades, Calif.: Goodyear, 1972), pp. 96-126.
[162]Fulbright, "Congress and Foreign Policy," p. 204.
[163]Huntington, *The Common Defense*, p. 145. Huntington specifically adds "although not decisive role in the process of strategy-making."

[164]Scott and Dawson, *Readings in the Making of American Foreign Policy*, p. 151.

[165]Cecil Crabb, *American Foreign Policy in the Nuclear Age*, 2d. ed. (New York: Harper & Row, 1965), p. 91. See also Theodore J. Lowi, *Legislative Politics U.S.A.*, 2d ed. (Boston: Little, Brown and Co., 1965), pp. xiv-xv.

[166]Roger Hilsman, *Politics of Policy Making*, p. 82.

[167]Scott and Dawson, *Readings in the Making of American Foreign Policy*, p. 148.

[168]Roger Hilsman, "The Foreign Policy Consensus: An Interim Research Report," *Journal of Conflict Resolution* 3 (December 1959): 361-82; idem, "Congressional-Executive Relations and the Foreign Policy Consensus," *American Political Science Review* 52 (September 1958). The latter is reprinted in Scott and Dawson, *Readings in the Making of American Foreign Policy*, pp. 184-205.

[169]Scott and Dawson, *Readings in the Making of American Foreign Policy*, p. 148. The following discussion relies on their analysis.

[170]Scott and Dawson, *Readings in the Making of American Foreign Policy*, p. 149. Others who note the dominance of the executive in crisis include: Theodore J. Lowi, "Making Democracy Safe for the World: National Politics and Foreign Policy," in *Domestic Sources of Foreign Policy*, ed. James N. Rosenau (New York: The Free Press, 1967); Carroll, "The Congress and National Security"; Robinson, *Congress and Foreign Policy-Making;* and Dexter Perkins, *The American Approach to Foreign Policy*, rev. ed. (Cambridge, Mass.: Harvard University Press, 1962), Chapter 8.

[171]Jewell, *Senatorial Politics*, p. 203.

[172]Alfred de Grazia, "The Myth of the President," in *Congress and the President*, ed. Moe, p. 101.

[173]Scott and Dawson, *Readings in the Making of American Foreign Policy*, p. 150.

[174]Ibid.

[175]Bernard C. Cohen, *The Political Process and Foreign Policy: The Making of the Japanese Peace Settlement* (Princeton, N. J.: Princeton University Press, 1957), Chapters 8 and 11; also Jewell, *Senatorial Politics*. Robinson, *Congress and Foreign Policy-Makings* also rates Congressional involvement as "high"(p. 65).

[176]R. H. Heindel, T. V. Kaljarvi, and F. Wilcox, "The North Atlantic Treaty in the United States Senate," *American Journal of International Law* 43 (1949): 633-55.

[177]Crabb, *Bipartisan Foreign Policy*, pp. 44-53; Jewell, *Senatorial Politics*, Chapters 6 and 7.

[178]Joseph M. Jones, *The Fifteen Weeks: February 21- June 5, 1947* (New York: Viking Press, 1955). Note also Robinson, *Congress and Foreign Policy-Making*, p. 65.

[179]John D. Montgomery, *The Politics of Foreign Aid* (New York: Praeger, 1962); Congressional Quarterly Service, *Congress and the Nation* vol. 2 (Washington, 1969), p. 50; Baldwin, "Congressional Initiative in Foreign Policy," pp. 760-70.

[180]Edward A. Kolodziej, *The Uncommon Defense and Congress, 1945-1963* (Columbus: Ohio State University Press, 1966), p. viii. He also argues Congress can assume a "more positive, active, and informed role."

[181]Kolodziej, *The Uncommon Defense and Congress*, pp. 263-64.

[182]Kolodziej, *The Uncommon Defense and Congress*, p. 270.

[183]Kolodziej, *The Uncommon Defense and Congress*, p. 262, also see p. 487 and Chapter 6.

[184]Kolodziej, *The Uncommon Defense and Congress*, Chapter 7, especially pp. 419-29. See also John C. Ries, *The Management of Defense: Organization and Controll of the U. S. Armed Services* (Baltimore Md.: John Hopkins University Press, 1964).

[185]See Francis O. Wilcox, *Congress, the Executive and Foreign Policy* (New York: Harper & Row, 1971); Fisher, *President and Congress*; Schlesinger, "Congress and the Making of American Foreign Policy."

[186]President Nixon, too, moved away from the "Thucyidian" approach which viewed the Communist bloc as monolithic and which regarded every increment of influence by a Communist nation, no matter which nation or where the increment of influence lay, as a security threat.

[187]Even so, the ABM issue provides an example of the President's program being influenced by "anticipated reactions from the Congress." See Morton Halperin, "The Decision to Deploy the ABM" (Paper presented at the Annual Meeting of the American Political Science Association, 1970).

[188]Wayne Moyer, "House Voting on Defense," in *Military Force and American Society*, ed. Bruce Russett and Alfred Stepan (New York: Harper & Row, 1973), p.107.

[189]See Arnold Kanter, "Congress and the Defense Budget: 1960-1970," *American Political Science Review* 66 (March 1972): 129-43, and Bruce M. Russett, "The Revolt of the Masses: Public Opinion and Military Expenditures," in *Peace, War and Numbers*, ed. Bruce M. Russett (Beverly Hills, Calif.: Sage, 1972).

[190]See Lawrence J. Korb, "Congressional Impact on Defense Spending, 1962-1973: The Programmatic and Fiscal Hypotheses" (Paper presented to the 1973 Annual Meeting of the American Political Science Association).

[191]See Charlot, *L'UNR*, pp. 45-84, and Wood, "Majority vs. Opposition in the French National Assembly."

[192]Hanreider, "German Reunification, 1949-1963," pp. 137-39 and Romoser, "Change in West German Politics," pp. 191-203.

[193]Ralph K. Huitt and Robert L. Peabody, "Foreward," to Charles O. Jones, *The Minority Party in Congress* (Boston: Little, Brown and Co., 1970), p. vii.

[194]Loewenberg observes: "The decision in the Bundestag—and all the forces which act upon it—... influences every step of the legislative way, both those steps which are taken before a bill reaches the House, which must anticipate Bundestag reaction, and those steps which follow." *Parliament in the German Political System*, p. 281.

[195]Ripley, "Kennedy and Congress," p. 12.

[196]The French Fourth Republic operated from 1946 to 1958. During this period the French averaged a new Premier or government every six months. The Weimar Republic was established in Germany after World War I and fell in 1933, when Hitler rose to power. Again, governmental instability was commonplace throughout most of the history of the Weimar Republic.

Chapter 7
The Legislature and Supervision of Executive Action

As our discussion of policy formulation, especially foreign policy, in the previous chapter makes clear, executives can and do make decisions without legislative consultation or legislative action. Indeed, the executive may attempt to act independently of the legislature even in regard to decisions the legislature has made. In implementing legislative decisions, as Presidential impoundments readily suggest, the executive can, if not checked, alter or perhaps completely remold those decisions. Executive personnel may decide to act entirely outside the law, as some of the Watergate revelations illustrate. With considerations such as these in mind, it is obvious that a feature central to the relations between the legislature and the executive in the policy process is the extent to which controls are placed on the executive and on its ability to undertake activities having a policy content independent of the legislative mandate it received (or did not receive).

To assure that their expectations and objectives are fulfilled with some degree of adequacy, legislators must concern themselves with the implementation stage of policy. Commentators on legislatures and legislators themselves, at least since the time of John Stuart Mill, have recognized the inescapable involvement of the bureaucracy in the political process and thus the legitimacy of legislative efforts to supervise the executive and bureaucracy. Mill states: "the proper office of a representative assembly is to watch and control the government."[1] Observing the American Congress, Lowi writes: "[The] major problem and major focus of Congress is no longer simply that of prescribing the behavior of citizens but more often that of affecting the behavior of administrators."[2] The difficulty in doing this has increased with the rapid expansion of governmental activity into new areas and the inevitable growth of governmental bureaucracies.[3] As greater responsibility for direct administration of legislation (accompanied with greater delegation of power and discretion) has shifted from legislatures to the executive bureaucracies, so the need for legislative supervision has become more acute. Supervision of the executive, if not the primary function of legislatures, today is generally recognized as a legislative task that ought to take on major significance.[4]

Legislative supervision involves legislators in the implementation and application of policy, thus involving them not only in the "what" but also in the "how" of executive action.[5] The focus of supervision may vary, including possibly: (1) the substance of a policy, (2) administrative organization and structure, (3) personnel, or (4) funding. Often it is a combination of these. Moreover, legislative supervision can occur both before and after administrative action takes place and may be carried on in part through the ongoing process of legislating. A review of the implementation of past policy frequently has as its end either new legislation or budgetary alterations.

Some authors make distinctions between types of legislative involvement in the implementation stage.

[Oversight occurs] when an individual legislator observes closely and becomes familiar with the organization and implementation of an administrative agency, or when a legislative committee by contact, observation, or investigation places itself in the posture of a "watchdog" over agency activities. [Supervision occurs] when the influence of individual legislators or legislative committees constitutes substantial involvement in the formulation or implementation of administrative policy, producing changes in policy emphasis or priority. [Control occurs] when the legislature directs administrative organization and policy, or requires legislative clearance for administrative decisions.[6]

The reader should note our use of the term supervision is inclusive of terms often used such as control, oversight, review, and the like.

The purpose of supervision have received extensive treatment elsewhere. Several key themes emerge in the literature. Supervision is engaged in by the legislature to: (1) determine compliance of administration with legislative intent; (2) ascertain if programs are being efficiently and economically implemented; (3) evaluate policy during its implementation with an eye to assessing the appropriateness and effectiveness of the policy; (4) gain a perspective from which to influence the character of administrative decisions; and (5) discover bureaucratic abuses, errors, and corruption.

In the balance of this chapter, we describe the various methods of supervision established by the four legislatures to achieve these purposes. Following this description, we attempt in Chapter 8 to delineate some of the factors that affect legislative activity in this area.

Legislative Supervision: The United States

Our description begins with the United States and an examination of Congressional techniques for supervising the executive. One of the most important arenas of formal and informal supervision in the United States Congress is the standing-committee system. Committees may engage in supervisory activity while making legislation or budgetary decisions; for example, the past activities of a bureau or agency might be used as a basis for discussing its future budgetary appropriations. Or, committees may take on supervisory functions outside the process of passing legislation as, for example, when they examine Presidential nominees (only in the Senate) or carry out investigations in regard to impeachment proceedings (see pages 274-75).

The Legislative Reorganization Act (LRA) of 1946 seemed to intend that committees function as the principal agent of supervision. Not only did this "landmark" legislation rationalize the standing-committee system (making it roughly parallel to executive departments), but it also mandated that "each standing committee of the Senate and the House of Representatives shall exercise continuous watchfulness of the execution by the administrative agencies concerned of any laws, the subject matter of which is within the jurisdiction of such committee. . . ." Appropriations committees would supervise funding; the Government Operations committees would review administrative organization, behavior, and expenditures; and the other standing legislative committees would review substantive legislation within their broadly defined areas of jurisdiction. Also significant in the 1946 LRA was the provision of professional staffs for the standing committees to aid them in their performance of the "continuous watchfulness" mandated, and Congress has several times since increased the numbers of staff made available to the committees. The professional staff grew from 93 (51 House, 42 Senate) in 1946 to 588 (269 House and 319 Senate) in 1967.[7] The 1970 LRA provided for another expansion in staff for each standing committee. It is generally conceded that since the 1946 LRA, Congress has not only enlarged its capacity for supervision, but it has in fact substantially increased its involvement in the implementation phase of policy.[8]

Although we have used the term *committee* when speaking of the supervision of the executive, we mean it to embrace the committee system, which, of course, includes the use of subcommittees. It is primarily at the subcommittee level that the supervisory function of Congress has been institutionalized. For the "legislative," or substantively oriented committees, supervisory operations are usually handled by what William Morrow calls the "more autonomous" subcommittees, while the screening of new legislation is handled by other subcommittees that are more "integrated" with those of the full committee. As for appropriations, *all* the subcommittees, which is where supervision is focused, are fairly independent and autonomous.[9]

In our discussion of the devices and techniques used by Congress and its committees to supervise the executive, the reader should keep in mind the bicameral nature of Congress and the double jurisdiction for practically all bills in each house. Since most substantive legislation needs funding, it must first be authorized by a legislative committee in each house and later "appropriated" by the respective appropriations committees of the House and Senate.[10] This means that usually there are at least four committees (or subcommittees) that can potentially supervise the executive in a given area, in addition to the Government Operations committees in each house, which are specifically admonished to keep an eye on the administrative structure and procedures.[11] Furthermore, there are some issues or concerns that do not fit neatly into one legislative committee's jurisdiction, which means, potentially, other committee arenas for consideration will also become involved. Many of the devices available to supervise the executive, such as hearings and the committee veto, are available to each of the substantive legislative (authorizing) committees as well as the appropriation committees. Some are even available to select committees (although they cannot report legislation)[12] or, in rare instances, joint committees, as in the case of the Joint Committee on Atomic Energy.[13]

At least until recently, the appropriations subcommittees, especially in the House, have carried the major supervisory burden. A 1966 report of the Joint Committee on Organization of Congress recognized that the legislative (authorizing) committees—as opposed to the appropriations committees—had been more concerned with "new legislation" rather than oversight. The appropriations committees, somewhat contrary to the intention of the LRA of 1946, have filled the vacuum. Fenno, while noting that Congressional authorizing committees have numerous devices available to watch over the executive bureaucracy, also concludes that the "power of the purse" has been the "major legislative weapon in its struggles to control executive institutions."[14] Both the process of evaluating fiscal policy[15] and the severity of the sanctions that can be invoked by relevant committees make the control over expenditures (which is firmly based in the Constitution) the most effective means of supervision of the federal bureaucracy, including the Defense Department. The appropriations committees (through their decentralized subcommittees) carry most of the burden for supervision. The legislative committees, due to the insufficient time, focus of inquiry, lack of interest, or alliances with agencies, have not done as adequate a job.[16] Michael Kirst, in his incisive study of nonstatutory controls of the appropriations committees, states: "The budget document is an excellent instrument for review of substantive policy, but it is the agenda of the appropriations committee not the legislative committees."[17] Appropriations committees have thus played a pivotal role in the supervision of public policy.

Appropriations subcommittee recommendations have been quickly accepted by the parent committees and, nearly 90 percent of the time, also by the respective houses.[18] Moreover, according to Fenno's study of thirty-six bureaus from 1947 to 1962, the administration's Budget Bureau estimates were altered by the House Appropriations Committee in about 80 percent of the instances.[19] In another study, Fenno found that the committee altered administration budget requests in over 90 percent of all appropriation bills from 1958 to 1965, that the committee changed requests by more than 20 percent in over 25 percent of the cases, and that it made changes of more than 10 percent in over 40 percent of the cases.[20]

Such selectivity in funding decisions has greatly contributed to the significance of the appropriations process in Congressional efforts to supervise the administration. But even detailed appropriation does not mean that Congress's funding decisions will be implemented. The chief executive may still attempt to prevail by eliminating programs he does not want and safeguarding others that he favors. Although there was much publicity and beating of war drums by the Senate in late 1972 when it killed President Nixon's proposal that Congress grant him the authority to slash whatever he wanted from any Congressional appropriation that brought the total budget to over $250 billion, through the use of the "impoundment," Nixon was able to "freeze" federal funds previously allocated by Congress in various areas.[21] The legal justification for such action was found in the 1950 Budget Act: "In apportioning any appropriation," it says, "reserves may be established to provide for contingencies or to effect savings whenever savings are made possible by or through changes in requirements, greater efficiency of operations, or other developments." That is, the President may withhold funds for good management and economic reasons. But the ambiguity lies in the arbitrariness of judgment that is allowed. During the last thirty years, Presidents have used the power to withhold funds from such programs as the B-70 bomber, antimissile systems, flood control and disaster relief projects, highways, super carriers, urban renewal, food stamp funds, pollution control funds, model cities, and Indian eduction.

Senator Talmadge observed that this has smacked of "one-man rule" and allowed the President to "pick and choose" what he wanted to cut (similar to an "item veto" or Nixon's 1972 budget-related proposal). An irate Senator Humphrey, pounding on a table, pointed out to Agriculture Secretary Butz during a committee hearing that more than economy or efficiency (reasons Congressmen regard as legitimate) were involved in decisions by the Nixon administration to terminate programs such as the Rural Environmental Assistance Program (REAP), which were authorized and funded by Congress.[22]

Indeed, President Nixon's defense for impoundment went beyond reasons of efficiency and economy to include reasons of controlling inflation. Central to his argument was the claim that Congress had not been sufficiently capable of controlling overall federal spending because its internal procedures at no point provided for undertaking and coordinating a comprehensive review of either overall spending or its relation to overall revenue. By this he meant that each of usually fifteen or more appropriations bills was passed separately with legislators having to decide each bill without much knowledge of the other bills or of what the other house would do. Moreover, the appropriations and taxation (revenue) decision-making processes were also formally separate from one another. Looking to procedures such as these in asserting Congressional overspending, the President claimed it was his responsibility to hold down federal spending since the Congress did not. In response to this, others argued not only that the President's real motives were to scuttle those programs he did not want but also that the way the President used the power to impound was both without precedent and indefensible either in statutory law or in the Constitution. They pointed out, in addition, that Congress had on the whole *reduced* rather than increased spending proposed in the Nixon budgets.

Cases of impoundment prior to the Nixon administration had usually been in response to fairly specific statutory directives or had been related to "prudent" use of funds in weapons procurement. However, as Louis Fisher perceptively notes:

An entirely different situation has developed under the Nixon Administration, where funds have been withheld from domestic programs because the President considers them incompatible with his own set of budget priorities. In the spring of 1971, the Nixon Administration announced that it was withholding more than $12 billion, most of which consisted of highway money and funds for various urban programs. When Secretary Romney appeared before a Senate Committee in March, he explained that funds were being held back from various urban programs because there was no point in accelerating programs that were "scheduled for termination." He was referring to the fact that Congress had added funds to grant-in-aid programs which the Administration wanted to consolidate and convert into its revenue-sharing proposal. To impound funds in this prospective sense—holding on to money in anticipation that Congress will enact an Administration bill—is a new departure for the impoundment technique. Impoundment is not being used to avoid deficiencies, or to effect savings, or even to fight inflation, but rather to shift the scale of priorities from one Administration to the next, prior to Congressional action.[23]

The reaction in Congress was intense and bitter. In response, it attempted to reorganize and rationalize its own internal decision-making processes for dealing with the budget (see Chapter 2). Furthermore, it moved against the impoundment itself. For example, on January 30, 1973, Senator Ervin, with forty-five other Senators serving as cosponsors, introduced a measure (similar to his 1971 bill) that would have required the President to release the impounded funds unless such impoundment had been approved by Congress through adoption of a resolution. In April, by a vote of 70 to 24, the Senate passed an amendment that would place strict limits on the powers of the President to pick and choose which funds he would impound. Building on these actions, in 1974 the Congress enacted legislation both to reorganize its budgetary procedures and to define the power of the President and the Congress over impoundments. Where a Presidential impoundment would have the effect of delaying (rather than reducing or eliminating) the spending of funds, the legislation specifies that Congress can force the release of the funds at any time by House *or* Senate passage of a resolution directing that the funds be spent. Where Presidential impoundment would have the effect of terminating a program or reducing total spending, the impoundment remains valid beyond forty-five days only if both the House and the Senate also act to rescind the original appropriation.

In addition, challenges against impoundment were brought into the federal courts. Nearly all the lower federal court cases on impoundments authorized by the Nixon administration ruled against the President. In February, 1975, the Supreme Court ruled on the issue for the first time.[24] It decided that Nixon exceeded his authority when he refused in 1972 to allocate to the states $9 billion in water pollution funds. However, the court's ruling appeared to be based upon the wording of the particular law (i.e., the Water Pollution Control Act of 1972) which authorized the spending. It was clear to the court that the Act gave no leeway to the President to withhold any funds, although the ruling left unresolved the question of the President's right to withhold funds provided by the legislature through the normal appropriations process. In the wake of the lower court and Supreme Court decisions, Presidents Nixon and Ford moved to release several billion dollars of impounded funds. These judicial decisions as well as the legislation enacted in 1974 indicate that limits are in the process of being placed on the President's authority to impound funds appropriated by Congress. Nevertheless, exactly how this recent and bitter executive-legislative struggle will be resolved is still to reach its conclusion.

The appropriations process has been a primary mechanism used for supervision, as will be made clearer when we discuss committee hearings. Yet we do not mean to imply that the authorization stage and the involvement of the Congressional legislative committees in this stage have been unimportant. Keefe and Ogul underline this point while also suggesting some limits to the appropriations weapon.

The authorization stage tends to be far more important than is commonly realized. "To a large extent control of expenditures over the long run lies in the area of authorizing legislation, for it is here that new activities get their start." Programs once established in legislation create fixed demands over a period of years. Thus congressional ability to control spending at the appropriations stage is somewhat circumscribed.[25]

Herbert Stephens's recent study of a House and a Senate legislative committee (the Armed Services Committee of each house) in the authorization process as distinguished from the appropriations process suggests that the authorization process has become of greater importance during the past decade.[26] The period 1961-69 reflects growth of the "direct cognizance" of the Armed Services Committees over the military budget. Note Table 7.1.

The table reveals that the Armed Services Committees significantly increased their

Table 7.1
Relationship of Authorization to Department of Defense Appropriations Requests for Military Functions, FY 1961 and FY 1969 (in millions)

Budget Program	Budget Estimate				Authorization Required			
	1961		1969		1961		1969	
	Amount	Percent	Amount	Percent	Amount	Percent	Amount	Percent
Military Personnel	11,837.0	29.2	23,014.0	29.1			953.0	1.2
Operations & Maintenance	10,527.3	26.0	22,787.0	28.8				
Procurement	13,085.0	32.3	23,254.0	29.4			14,369.6	18.2
Research & Development Test & Evaluation	3,909.7	9.6	8,015.4	10.1			8,015.4	10.1
Military Construction	1,188.0	2.9	1,430.0	1.8	895.3	2.2	1,294.0	1.6
Family Housing			602.0	.8			602.0	.8
Total	40,547.0	100	70,102.4	100	895.3	2.2	25,234.0	31.9

Source: Herbert Stephens, "The Role of Legislative Committees in the Appropriations Process," *Western Political Quarterly* 24 (March, 1971), pp. 147, 152.

authority over the military budget from 1961 to 1969. Until the early sixties the committees had fulfilled their authorization role simply by providing "general continuing authorizations" to support most programs of the military departments. In 1961 only military construction received specific, detailed line-item consideration and authorization, meaning only 2.2 percent of their jurisdiction. By 1969 the Armed Services Committees authorized 31.9 percent of the military budget, or $25,234,000,000, as compared to only $895,300,000 in 1961. Stephens expects "continued piecemeal additions" to the Armed Services Committees' control. In fact even the House Appropriations Committee members he interviewed also anticipated, although not eagerly, the House Armed Services Committee to "attempt" more extensions of the annual review requirements.[27] Stephens' study not only illustrates the growth of more careful and specific authorization by the Armed Services Committees, but also suggests that at least recently there has been a direct relationship between what the committees have authorized and what was later funded by the appropriations process in the areas of military construction and research, development, and test and evaluation items in the defense budget. In addition to demonstrating the actual impact of authorization on appropriations (an impact usually underestimated by Congressional observers), he also finds that it may be possible for most, if not all, of the legislative committees, much like the Armed Service Committees, to increase their authorization competence and through this control or supervision of the executive.

Numerous scholars have emphasized the importance of *annual* authorization (i.e., requiring action by the relevant legislative committee *each* fiscal year) as a method of augmenting legislative (as opposed to appropriations) committees' ability to supervise the executive.[28] Key, among others, pointed out that the "form" a statute takes is especially important in determining both the amount and the effectiveness of Congressional supervision.[29] This is partly because the necessity of annual approval assures annual Congressional review. When an agency is forced to return annually, it becomes more amenable to committee supervision. Agencies are, in a sense, on "good behavior" and must yearly explain and justify their activities, plans, and funding. They tend to walk warily, trying to avoid alienating Congressmen, especially members of key committees. The fact that the budget gets annual consideration may help to explain the dominance the appropriations committees have had in the performance of Congressional supervision. With open-ended, lump-sum, or multiyear authorizations, legislative committees have until recently abdicated the annual review to the appropriations committees. Fenno comments on the significance of annual appropriations:

The traditional primacy of the Appropriations Committee in implementing legislative oversight tasks derives not just from the fact that it holds the power of the purse nor from the variety of techniques available to it. *It stems also from the frequency of opportunity for control.* The fact that appropriations decisions are made annually makes the Committee more "continuously watchful" than any other.[30]

Thus, when there were conflicts between Appropriations (i.e., its relevant subcommittee) and the legislative committee in situations where there was *not* annual authorization, the agencies usually followed what they perceived to be the desires of the Appropriations Committee.

Legislative committees have increasingly replaced open-ended and multiyear authorizations with annual authorizations. If, as Huitt says, most oversight by the legislative committees occurs with hearings on new bills or authorizations, then making authorizations annual should act to heighten supervision.[31] In 1946, 98 percent of the programs were authorized on a long-term or open-ended basis; by 1965, 35 percent of the annual budget in such areas as space, foreign aid, atomic energy, and defense weapons systems required annual authorizations. Several studies attest to the effectiveness this technique has had in increasing legislative committees' supervising efforts and the impact of Congress on the executive.[32] Not only was there more supervising activity and influence, the activity itself tended to be competent, informed, specific, and constructive; not only did annual authorization increase legislative committee involvement in supervising activity and policy-making, but also legislative committees were often in a better position to monitor and influence the executive. Regular involvement by legislative committees through the technique of annual authorization strengthened the *access* of Congress to policy formulation. It also offered a *utility of focus* (an opportunity for more selective attention) that was not available to a roaming appropriations committee. Finally, partly as a result of access and focus, it provided an *expanded base of knowledge.*[33] Certainly it has been a different kind of oversight than that provided by the appropriations committees.

Despite the presumed advantages of annual authorization and, thus, the possibility of more effective annual supervision by committees concerned with substantive legislation, it still appears that the appropriations committees, especially in the House, provide the most comprehensive, intensive, and effective supervision of both the funding and the organization, personnel, and programs of the executive.

Another resource available to Congressmen is the legislative audit.[34] With the Budget and Accounting Act of 1921, Congress established the General Accounting Office (GAO) to "provide itself with a trusted source of information about the way in which public funds were being used in the executive department."[35] The General Accounting Office, which is headed by a Comptroller General, was authorized by the Act to investigate all matters relating to the receipt, disbursement and application of public funds and to report annually to Congress, including not only an audit but also recommendations on any financial legislation that the Comptroller General considers necessary. He also can make any other recommendations that will contribute to "greater economy and efficiency in public expenditures." In addition, he may be required to report from time to time on the adequacy of fiscal control practices within executive agencies and to report on the violations of law in the expending of public funds. The Legislative Reorganization Act of 1946 authorized the Comptroller General to make expenditure analyses of each executive agency so that Congress could determine whether public funds have been "economically and efficiently expended" or not. Finally, he was directed to submit the reports, including the audit, for review by the Committee on Government Operations, Appropriations, and the relevant subject matter committees. In 1970, the GAO was authorized to make cost-benefit studies of programs.

Despite the formidable body of reporting, the fairly large staff of the GAO (though actually not enough to fulfill the mandate),[36] its independence from the President, and the great deference given the Comptroller General, Congress has not and does not now utilize the agency to its fullest in the appropriations or authorization process.[37] One obstacle to effective use is the fact that Congress is not organized to cope with the reports; there is no single committee with the sole responsibility of receiving, reviewing, and acting on reports. Lack of utilization is partly attributable to the number and nature of the reports, their form and timing, and the inability of the GAO to cope successfully with the complexity of executive decisions.[38] This does not mean that the GAO does not provide useful staff assistance and information, for its staff has been helpful to committees in hearings and investigations. Individual Congressmen may make requests for studies of specific problems. However, of an average of three hundred such requests per year, a large proportion come from a few enthusiasts, such as Senator William Proxmire (D., Wis.).[39] Though its chief purpose and product —audit reports—have yet to be a vital instrument of Congressional supervision of the executive, the Nader report on Congress calls the GAO "a relatively bright spot in Congress's general prospect." Due to the chronic lack of information to combat the executive, especially the OMB, the report contends that a "reassertion of Congressional power will probably begin here."[40] Interestingly, along this line, investigations carried out by the GAO in the summer of 1972 played a central role in uncovering hard evidence linking the Watergate break-in both to officials in the White House and to the Committee to Re-elect the President. The recently established Office of Program Evaluation and Review within GAO should routinize and enhance its utility for Congress.

Hearings and investigations by the Congress itself are also principal devices used to control and supervise the executive. Few major bills ever become law and few major appointments or treaties are accepted by the Senate without first proceeding through committee hearings. The House Appropriations Committee hearings alone number about four hundred a year.

Committees have considerable discretion as to whether their meetings will be open or closed to the public. Until recently, about 40 percent of the committee hearings and meetings have been closed, including a larger percentage of House Appropriations Committee hearings and subcommittee hearings and half or more of the hearings of the committees of both houses that deal with taxation and national defense. Overall, closed committee hearings and meetings declined dramatically in the Ninety-third Congress; 25 percent of the Senate's were closed but only 8 to 10 percent of House's hearings and meetings were closed.[41] In 1974 the figure dropped to 10 percent for the House Appropriations Committee and 5 percent for the Ways and Means Committee.

Needless to say, hearings would afford greater political education to the public if even more of them were open. Even so, whether open to the public or closed, hearings serve as potent forums where members of Congress scrutinize administrators' application of legislation, including their adherence to nonstatutory committee "instructions" (instructions not specifically written into the legislation) about the implementation of legislation. "Facts" and information, as well as expert opinion independent of the executive agency, are often gained through hearings, though admittedly in many instances hearings may reinforce existing preconceptions or be "staged" to reach a foregone conclusion or get a good press on the part of committee leaders.[42] Administrators know they must be prepared not only for "informational" questions but also for a detailed defense and justification of their programs, organization, and expenditures. Sometimes they may be required by law to submit a yearly report that the committee may use as a starting point. Also, administrators expect and anticipate (partly because of the stability of committee membership and past practices) that committee members will examine whether they have followed through on their earlier informal commitments or nonstatutory instructions, including the intent of legislative reports (which will be discussed later). Administrators often even go through the practice of mock hearings within their own agency.[43]

During the course of hearings, legislative instructions are given which, while not written into public law, are for all practical purposes just as binding. Administrators realize they must come back year after year. The costs and risks of not carrying out committee instructions may be high. Congressmen may use the committee hearings not only to exert influence on administrators' future actions but also to rebuke them for failures to follow through on earlier commitments.

Kirst notes that the most frequent nonstatutory technique employed in the hearings involves "urging or prodding the executive to take a particular course of action," either in implementing a future policy or an already approved policy.[44] Another kind of nonstatutory technique employed during hearings consists of making verbal agreements with administrators or obtaining definite assurances from them as to how they will implement policy.[45]

However, Kirst observes that hearings, employed independently of other control devices, are usually confined to less important matters.[46] That is, administrative actions with broad policy significance require additional devices if supervision is to be meaningful. Instances of hearings as a "supplementary," as opposed to an independently employed device, are much more frequent. Hearings, which provide the only face-to-face confrontations of Congress with the executive, are a useful instrument to convey the intensity of feeling (possibly only by the tone of the Congressman's voice) on the part of committee members for a legislative report directive. Thus, the report device, to be discussed later (pp. 269-70) is quite often combined with the hearings.

Holbert Carroll's research reveals that Presidential administrators (in this case, the State Department), carefully read the hearings (and the reports) for they know that they are expected to comply with directives or instructions contained therein. They further know that the committees can affect the "lifeblood of any policy—money."[47] Hearings, thus, are occasions for committee members to raise problems, to seek relevant information, to evaluate a piece of legislation and its administrative implementation, to urge administrative action, to reach understandings apart from statute, and to chastise or rebuke those who fail to observe the committee's will.[48] A severe rebuke, backed by the threat of disapproval of a program or funds or possibly the inclusion of "punitive" provisions, is usually sufficient to deter future nonobservance. Obviously the "public" nature of such a rebuke—often carried by the mass media—makes such a rebuke a significant weapon in Congressional hands. It is an experience administrators try to avoid.

Several other points need to be made about hearings. First, multiple hearings (normally four) are increasingly being held on important legislation, which means that there are multiple points of access for supervision by legislators. Jahnige indicates there were twelve different hearings on NASA in one Congress,[49] meaning most facets of the operation of the agency were discussed and questioned from a number of different perspectives.* Second, what scanty research there is on hearings suggests that supervision at hearings is not completely random and haphazard. In fact, a content analysis of one subcommittee of the House Appropriations Committee from 1949 to 1963 suggests a tendency to pay more attention to those agencies (in this case the Office of Education and the Children's Bureau) that "spend the most money, whose requests have increased most rapidly, and whose behavior toward the subcommittee has deviated most frequently from the subcommittee's desires."[50] Third, the degree of scrutiny varies across committees. As Fenno points out in regard to administrators' perceptions of the appropriations process,

> The single most widely held image of the Senate Committee is that it is less thorough and less interested in examining agency activity than is the House Committee. The contrast is expressed most commonly in regard to hearings, which after all constitute the major confrontation. . . .[51]

A potentially more spectacular method of supervision available to committees is *investigations*. The McCarthy and the Watergate investigations in the Senate are two prominent examples. Actually, the procedures followed by Congressional committees for investigations are quite similar to ordinary committee hearings. It is not always possible to draw a sharp line between what we referred to previously as ordinary hearings and hearings which are referred to as Congressional investigations. And, in a sense, regular examination of legislation by Congressional committees constitutes

---

*While this development has its obvious advantages for supervision, problems may also arise if administrators can play off instructions from different members and different committees against one another.

investigation. Under the ostensible right of Congress to find out the fact and gather information, investigations have been conducted by Congress since 1792. They are not always directed at the administration, but supervision of the bureaucracy clearly has been one of the traditional purposes of investigation.

Investigations can be conducted by regular standing committees as a whole, subcommittees, and select or special committees. The language of the 1946 Legislative Reorganization Act clearly intended the major burden of investigation to be carried by the regular standing committees, and in fact, since 1946 the use of special committees has noticeably diminished, especially in the Senate. The 1946 LRA gave great impetus to investigations by rationalizing the committee structure, by directing Congress to become involved in continuous supervision, and by providing the subpoena power and staff needed. (The committee staff usually plays a bigger role in full-scale formalized investigations as compared to usual committee hearings.) Investigations, which averaged around thirty each year between the World Wars, averaged two hundred per year in the early 1950s.[52] Alongside those cited above, some of the better known post-World War II investigations include: the Kefauver and McClellan subcommittee investigation of organized crime, Congressional investigation of General MacArthur's release from his duties, and Senator Truman's investigation of the national defense program during World War II. Also, the Subcommittee on Intergovernmental Operations of the House Government Operations Committee has an impressive record in investigation and supervision of the Food and Drug Administration.[53] Recent investigations of the CIA and FBI are other examples.

Congress uses investigations not merely as an additional way of gathering pertinent facts in order to keep itself and the American people informed but also, quite consciously, to supervise the bureaucracy. Most standing committees carry on their investigations without a great deal of fanfare, but those undertaken by select committees as well as by standing committees on particular types of subjects and certain partisan-oriented investigations may gain a great deal of public attention through mass media coverage. Investigations, as Kirst points out, may be "punitive" in purpose, designed to embarrass and to arouse disapproval of an agency by the public or a subpublic or even Congress itself. Punitive investigations are usually caused not by a particular isolated administrative action but by a series of such actions, such as the constant nonobservance of a legislative committee's intent as revealed in its past hearings and legislative reports.[54] Sometimes just the threat of an investigation by one or more committee members can induce changes in administrative compliance. Also the "law of anticipated reactions" comes into play. Administrators know severe alienation of important Congressmen may precipitate an investigation of their agencies or departments. Regardless of whether anything is "wrong" or not, an investigation causes an agency to "drop everything else" to justify itself before the committee, thus altering its other principal priorities at least temporarily. Though having some of the same purposes and effects as usual hearings, investigations tend to be more concerned with examining and exposing activities after the fact. They also tend to be more "one-shot" efforts rather than continuing activities over long periods of time.[55]

Even with the subpoena power and the potential of criminal prosecutions, however, Congressional committees operate with restraints in their attempts to find out the facts. The Supreme Court has varied somewhat in the latitude allowed committees but has clearly affirmed the necessity and legitimacy of Congressional investigations.

Obviously with respect to information on the implementation of legislation by the administration, the Congress is heavily dependent on the executive itself as a source of information. Though committees (both for investigations and regular hearings) supposedly have the right of access to agency and department papers and files, executive bureaucrats can under Presidential authority withhold information which the President regards as contrary to the public interest. This executive privilege may result in Congressmen receiving an incomplete or biased view of what has really happened. Of course, based on its suspicions, the committees (or the floor) may in return reduce the level of support for the program or action in question, which will sometimes lead the President either to withdraw his claim of privilege or to respond to information requests conditionally. That is, the information will be given, but only in a closed executive session of a committee or a confidential conversation and cannot be released to the press until, and if, the executive gives its approval. This, of course, dampens Congressional attempts "publicly" to supervise and criticize administrators and the operation of programs.

Another nonstatutory control available to both appropriations and authorization committees is the committee report. The report goes one step beyond the cues and promises available from the records of committee hearings. The committee report accompanies the proposed piece of legislation recommended to the respective houses for action. The report ostensibly contains the reasoning (of the majority) behind the recommendation on that particular statute. In fact, many reports include and emphasize the committee members' intentions, admonitions, directions, and understandings (including "agreements" with bureaucrats), many of which the bureaucrats may have anticipated from the way the hearings went. It may even urge more emphasis on particular programs in the next budget year or offer "warnings" about existing programs. Committee members *expect* that agencies will take note of the legislative reports; individual committees may operate as if the reports are as binding as law (which they are not) when the agency comes around for future authorization or appropriations.[56] Of special significance is the wording of the report. Kirst's study of nonstatutory controls by the appropriations committees reveals that the choice of verbs such as "earmarks," "directs," "instructs," "expects," "urges," "feels" in its reports are cues about committee intentions and intensities—almost a code language—that agencies come to understand rather quickly.[57]

Sanctions can be and often are invoked (although not always successfully) if committee reports are ignored. There may be serious consequences for agencies that fail to comply with the reports. William Morrow's study on Congressional committees and foreign aid takes note of an instance of intense committee reaction to noncompliance expressed in a report. In its 1959 report the House Appropriations Subcommittee on Foreign Operations specifically denied funds for an Incentive Investment Program desired by the administration. The corresponding Senate subcommittee was silent about the program with the final statute, thus *not* denying funds. The administration used money from the President's Contingency Fund to begin the program—a broadening of the use of that fund from previous practice. In the subsequent hearings in 1960, subcommittee members chastised the administration representatives for what they called "nullification" by the executive of the subcommittee's suggestion in its report. The subcommittee then stipulated in its 1960 report that contingency funds could not be used for *any* program for which a separate appropriation had been requested.[58] Numerous similar instances like this could be described to show that disregarding or ignoring committee reports may lead to broad prohibitions or to sanctions ranging from hearings or rebukes to punitive investigations, "punitive provisions" on funds, more detailed appropriations, and even authorizations and appropriations cuts in later years.[59] Administrators know this and carefully read the relevant committee reports, giving priority to the appropriations subcommittees' reports and especially those of the House Appropriations Committee. Minority reports may also be filed by those disagreeing with the majority report. With a change of party control in either house of Congress these may become more important. Thus, Arthur MacMahon appropriately refers to the reports as "prime instruments of legislative oversight."[60]

Administrators, for reasons that should now be obvious, desire good working relations with the relevant Congressional committees. One way to develop this is to implement subcommittee recommendations.[61] Disregarding the language in a report assures a breakdown in the "trust" desired by committees and agencies and possibly leads to the use of specific and statutory controls, which, from the standpoint of the administrators, have a more inflexible character. Committees, especially the appropriations committees, in many instances prefer nonstatutory regulations such as the report. Kirst notes that such controls must to be employed where Congressional rules prohibit statutory regulations (for example, rules prohibiting legislation in an appropriations act).[62] Moreover, if they are contained in a report rather than an actual bill, they are likely to avoid floor debate.[63] In some instances nonstatutory techniques, especially reports, provide more effective, precise, and flexible control by the committee. Reports coupled with other informal techniques give committees an important supervisory device. The effectiveness of the report, however, depends upon a number of variables, such as the agreement or lack of agreement by other relevant committees and the conference report, hearings, contradictory language, temper of floor debates, and the nature of White House priorities.[64]

Still another method (potentially available to both substantive and appropriations committees) used by Congress to supervise the executive is *legislative* or *committee clearance*, both formal and informal.[65] Clearance goes beyond the devices which instruct, disclose, and/or review; committee clearance projects the relevant influential committees into the actual administrative decision-making process on a continuing basis. *Prior* to the execution of some authority or making of some types of decisions, executive departments are required to receive Congressional or committee approval.

The most formal type of committee clearance is the committee veto, an extension of the legislative veto which was first used in 1939 to enable Congress as a whole (both houses) to cope with President Roosevelt's executive reorganization plans by giving Congress the right to cast a negative vote within a specified time period.[66] After a modification that allowed one house to cast a negative vote by simple resolution, the step that granted the legal authority to individual committees of Congress to veto executive action in various areas was approved. The Defense Appropriations Act in 1955 contained the provision that no business enterprise run by the federal government could be terminated and transferred to private enterprise if, within a ninety-day period, *either* Appropriations Committee rejected the action.[67] When used, the committee veto provisions of a bill usually require the executive agency concerned, *before* acting on certain decisions, to do these two things: (1) submit that decision to the designated committees in the House and Senate for their consideration during some specified interval of time, such as thirty or sixty days, and (2) to consult with and obtain the approval of or "come into agreement" with such committees within some specified time.[68]

This formal legal delegation of the right of veto to a committee must be granted in a regular statute. Several Presidents, including Johnson, Eisenhower, Truman, and Kennedy, tended to oppose this. Frequently, bills incorporating such a provision have been vetoed but because of the lack of an item veto for the President, they may show up again and again, and in the press of time and need for major legislation, may become law. Once the authorizing statute is enacted, as Harris points out, the "most significant" feature of the whole process is that an action of Congress or its committees (or even subcommittees or chairmen alone) is taken that does not require the signature of the President and hence is not subject to veto.[69] Perhaps of equal importance is the fact that the full Congress or even a single house of Congress need not approve the committee action once the right is given to that committee.

Since its beginning in 1944, the committee veto has broadened and been used in a variety of significant areas such as real property transactions of military departments, public buildings, flood control, various Atomic Energy Commission activities, and so on. A study of Congress and NASA, cited earlier, indicates the potential of committee clearance to Congress's getting a foothold in supervision of the space program. By the end of the Eighty-ninth Congress, nineteen statutory provisions for the committee veto were public law, including six grants of power to the Armed Services Committees, six to the Joint Committee on Atomic Energy, three to the Public Works Committees, and two each to the Interior and Agriculture Committees.[70] All the same, another scholar, in assessing the use of the committee veto, observes that the committee veto generally "plays a relatively small part in committee supervision of administration; its significance lies not in its extent but in its portent."[71] Of greater significance and use is the informal committee clearance.

Informal committee clearance is not only earlier in usage but also much more effective and pervasive as a device to supervise the executive. Committees may develop confidential and unwritten understandings with bureaucrats, whereby various executive departments and agencies may be placed under obligation to consult or inform the appropriate committees before certain actions are taken (for example, the transferring of funds from one item to another or a significant change in plans from those presented to the committee).[72] A department may often do this quite voluntarily, especially with the appropriations subcommittees, in order to ward off trouble during the next session of Congress. Sometimes, of course, it is not the whole committee (or subcommittee) that is consulted but the committee chairman or significant members of the committee. Obviously, informal clearance does not legally bind an agency to follow the committeee's views or even take them into consideration, but it is politically unsound to ignore them. Most legislative committees expect (and agencies oblige) fairly continuous personal communication with executive personnel, especially involving new developments and major changes.

Morrow describes one of the "most idyllic relationships" from the standpoint of Congress:

William A. Jump, . . . as an employee of the Department of Agriculture, conformed perfectly to the role expectations of committee members. According to one writer, if "a question would arise as to whether or not an expenditure of funds for a given purpose was authorized by appropriations . . . Mr. Jump never took a purely legalistic approach . . . but often consulted with the chairman of the committee to find out their position." Such a relationship was developed because of Jump's moral commitment to do nothing in violation of the committee will. The result of such relationships would ideally be a "common state of mind" between administrators and committee majorities which would result in natural bureaucratic compliance with legislative will without constant official contact between the two.[73]

Sometimes there may even be a statutory requirement of advance reports of executive decisions.[74] This is supposedly for the information of the committee, but it also becomes a potential means of supervision and continuing Congressional participation in the implementation stage of policy—though there is no formal committee veto provided for.

There are also other informal acts by Congressmen ranging from personal encounters with administrators to letters, telephone calls, and staff interaction (of course, not limited to relevant committee members). These, too, may be an occasion for supervision of the executive, but it should be noted that effective informal control by Congress rests ultimately on the possibility of execution of its formal power.[75]

A final point in the legislative process that allows for supervision is floor consideration. Both the nature of floor discussion and the substance of the decision itself may be supervisory in impact. That the decision may be supervisory in impact is obvious (the approval or disapproval of an organization's plans, budget, treaty, and the like). Less obvious is the process of interaction and exchange before the decision is made. Cues may be picked up by administrators simply by the temper of debate that may give an unmistakable indication of legislative desires or on the other hand indicate the degree (or lack thereof) of legislative consensus. Unlimited debate and the ever-present possibility of filibuster in the Senate is a technique to dramatize opposition and gain concessions or to assure that policy is well publicized.

Kirst observes the significance of floor consideration in each house for the appropriations committees' supervisory potential. In each house, floor debates are usually initiated by members who do not serve on the respective appropriations committees but have a great deal of interest in and are often opposed to appropriations directives or decisions. "The most significant feature of floor consideration is the extent to which members are able to clarify, modify, reenforce, or initiate non-statutory controls."[76] Such controls, of course, are strengthened to the degree that floor debate supports or at least does not undercut the thrust of those controls. Sometimes nonstatutory controls may actually be added, as the "intent" of the committee's bill or report is clarified. Or there may be an attempt by a debater or questioner to get the Appropriations Committee to restrict the application of a nonstatutory control. If possible, the Appropriations Committee (or any other committee for that matter) and supporters of the report and bill seek to use floor consideration to reenforce appropriations directives. Legislators recognize that the amount, intensity, and consistency of legislative history has a cumulative impact that will probably increase administrators' compliance. Debate may also indicate growing discontent and put the bureaucracy on notice of future problems. Young observes that the *Congressional Record* is "culled regularly" by administrators for pertinent comments on their agency's performance.[77]

Legislative Supervision:
The West European Systems

As the previous discussion suggests, Congress has evolved and used a great a variety of procedures and techniques to supervise the implementation of legislation. These can come into play while legislation is being enacted as well as during and after its initial implementation. The primary procedures and techniques used rest mainly in the committees of Congress. They involve the authorization, appropriation, and audit processes; committee hearings and investigations; the committee report; and committee clearance. Outside the committees, floor debate and especially the informal intervention of members of Congress and their staffs in the administration can also be occasions for supervision.

Of course, the American system as well as the European systems under examination have organs other than the popularly elected legislature that are used to supervise how the executive and administration implement policy. Principal organs in the Anglo-American systems are the ordinary courts, where citizens can bring grievances of all kinds, among which can be actions against the way the administration has implemented the law. There are also some courts that deal exclusively with certain kinds of administrative decisions. Such administrative courts—courts whose specialized function is to consider executive and administrative implementation of the law—are even more prominent in the other two systems, and especially France.

Major organs for legal supervision of the administration in France are found in the administration itself. In France citizens can appeal to a series of administrative courts if they feel that administrators have made decisions going beyond their powers as prescribed by legislation, or if, in making decisions, administrators have not followed proper procedures. Again, these courts comprise a part of the administration. The administrative courts have the power to annul or to change administrative decisions that they determine have gone beyond the explicit authority prescribed in the law. They can also annul or change administrative decisions that they determine were not implicitly intended by the original legislation (which leads them to look into the motives behind the legislation) or which they feel were made on grounds that were not in the general public interest.

At the apex of the administrative court structure is the *Conseil d' État*.[78] This is a general rather than a specialized court. Although it hears claims of the first instance, increasingly it has become a court of appeals for claims first heard by regional administrative courts, called *tribunaux administratifs*. It is a simple, though often time consuming, procedure to gain access to these courts, but generally it is not expensive to bring a case before the court. While a person can employ a lawyer, the court will itself also appoint a member to investigate the problem. These are thorough investigations, so much so that they "may produce arguments which the plaintiff has overlooked or discover facts that he could not discover himself."[79]

There also exists a set of specialized administrative courts covering particular types of policy. One of these is the *Cour des Comptes*, which has postaudit responsibilities very much like the General Accounting Office. It has jurisdiction over all public accounts and the accounts of nationalized industries. Its function is to assure that the accounts are balanced correctly and that reported expenditures, as supported by documented evidence, actually have been made (preexpenditure control also takes place in the administration through members of the Ministry of Finance attached to the other ministries). Other specialized administrative courts cover such areas as social insurance systems and the educational system.

How successful the French administrative court system in supervising and controlling the administration is perceived to be can be seen in the way other political institutions in the French system respond to it. It is within the power of Parliament to exclude any and all areas from the jurisdiction of the administrative courts and to deny these courts power to make certain kinds of decisions. But, rarely has it shown a strong desire to limit the powers of the administrative court system. And, although administrative courts do find against the government and the administration, even governments have made but few attempts to curtail the powers of the administrative courts.[80]

In West Germany, too, there are organs outside both the ordinary courts and the popularly elected legislature that play an integral part in the process of supervision. In some areas, such as taxation and social insurance, administrative courts help supervise the application of federal legislation. Furthermore, the application of much federal legislation occurs through the states and their administrations rather than through the federal administration. Thus, the Bundesrat is a primary legislative organ at the federal level for gaining the agreement of state administrations to apply federal legislation and for directing them to apply it.[81] The Bundesrat serves as an arena in which, before actual administrative action occurs, state administrations are given the power to mold, determine, and agree upon the legislation they will later apply. It also has the ability to determine what instructions the federal government can transmit to the state administrations as the latter implement federal legislation.

Having made these points, let us turn to the supervisory activities of the popularly elected houses in the three European systems. It is important to observe at the outset that each of these houses has a kind of power in the area of controlling the executive which the United States Congress does not have. This is the power to force the government to resign, on almost any grounds, by a vote of censure or a vote of no confidence. While none of the houses has recently used this power on grounds of government maladministration, the fact remains that the power is there; and so is the implication that there may be occasions in which the government will not serve a full term. Indeed, there are several fairly recent precedents of Prime Ministers resigning, without having been censured by Parliament, in the context of events surrounding government excess, mishandling, or maladministration of policy. For examples, Eden did so in 1957 in the wake of Suez, Macmillan resigned in 1963 after having been stung by the Profumo scandal, and Brandt resigned in 1974 after the arrest of one of his aides on suspicion of being an East German spy.

Of course, the Congress has the power of impeachment. By this power the Congress can force the President (or other federal officials) to leave office upon vote of a simple majority of the House for impeachment and two-thirds of the Senate for conviction. However, despite the Founding Fathers' expectation that the Congress could and would use this power against Presidents, it has been carried through to a Senate vote only once, against Andrew Johnson. Even then, conviction by the Senate did not follow. Interpretation of the Constitution has been that extraordinary circumstances are required, not yet known exactly what they are, to justify use of the impeachment power against a President.[82] And, only with the case of Nixon (who would likely have been convicted) is there precedent in the American system for a President resigning office on any grounds, including grounds of Congressional or public pressure. As a consequence, pressures from Congress and the public for a President to resign likely need to be more widespread (if only because two-thirds vote is needed in the Senate) and longer in existence for the threat of impeachment to have effect. This is nowhere more clearly illustrated than in the agonizing length of the Watergate affair.

Nevertheless, while there is a difference in the immediacy of the power of impeachment held by the Congress and the power of censure held by the European parliaments, the difference should not be overdrawn. If the legal constraints and problems of precedents are not as great in the European systems as in the American system, thereby making the parliamentary power of censure a more obvious avenue of action, there can still be substantial political considerations involved which, in more "ordinary" cases of governmental excess, make it difficult for the parliamentary majority to press the government or leader of the government to resign.

Perhaps partly as a consequence of the parliamentary censure power, there is no case in the European systems to match the scale of Watergate and the kinds of allegations that were directed against President Nixon personally (nor was there previously a case like Watergate in the American system). On the other hand, there have been cases of lesser magnitude in the European systems from which insight can be gleaned. A good example is the Profumo scandal, which occurred in 1963 under the Macmillan government in Great Britain. Involving, as it did, both potentially key security leaks and confirmed lying to Parliament and the public, the Profumo scandal was a serious case of government mismanagement and maladministration. Macmillan's persistent failure to look into the allegations against Profumo, who was his Minister of War, was perceived to be equally serious,[83] leading twenty-seven Conservative MPs to abstain deliberately rather than to support a vote of confidence in Macmillan and their own government. Moreover, the scandal followed upon a hard political year for the Macmillan government, a year in which public support for the Prime Minister had fallen to the lowest level recorded since the last days of the Chamberlain government in 1940. Despite this, it was not until eight months after the matter was first raised in the House of Commons and four months after Profumo decided to leave office that Macmillan himself resigned. There was no censure by Parliament. Nor is it by any means certain that the Profumo scandal itself was responsible for Macmillan's decision to resign. Thus, Mackintosh argues:

In October 1963, hit by a prostatic obstruction which required an operation, [Macmillan] resigned. But before his illness, he had offered to go if this was thought to be in the best interests of the Party and he actually left the room so that other members of the Cabinet could discuss the situation more freely. When he did so, no one moved against him and all the members departed assuming that he would remain as leader, . . . What drove Mr. Macmillan to announce his resignation was the view, later proved wrong, that his prostate trouble was malignant and that he would be weakened or incapacitated either for a very long time or permanently.[84]

None of this is to say that in the wake of a scandal of the magnitude of Watergate, regarding both the scandal itself and the allegations directed against the President personally, Parliament would not have moved quickly and decisively. Moreover, Profumo left office well before Macmillan resigned. At the same time, the handling of the Profumo affair illustrates that substantial personal or political factors may well constrain Parliamentary use of its power to remove the Prime Minister in what would be considered a serious, but not extraordinary, instance of governmental misbehavior.

Short of censure, however, parliaments have a number of other avenues open to them for the purposes of uncovering and attempting to control governmental excess, mismanagement, and maladministration. Standing behind these, even though usually remotely, is the parliamentary potential of bringing down the government.

One of the principal devices is the parliamentary question for written or oral answer by the government. Legislators in the Commons, Assembly, and Bundestag ask their governments hundreds and even thousands of questions for written answer each year. Governments are required to answer and usually do answer written questions within certain time limits; and the answers are made public. Furthermore, legislators can also ask questions for oral governmental reply on the floor. Once again, the government is allowed a specific period of time to ready its responses to these questions (although here the degree of governmental compliance has varied across the different systems). In the Assembly, the question period (often supplemented by debate) has generally taken place during one sitting each week. On the other hand, near the beginning of each sitting of the House of Commons and the Bundestag, an hour is devoted to governmental oral replies (by the responsible minister) and for a limited number of additional questions that legislators are allowed to ask in following up their original questions. Through their questions, legislators can probe into executive activities, discern how policy is being applied, uncover or pin down maladministration and faulty judgment, and hold ministers and governments accountable for their actions before a public forum.

Of the three houses, the oral question has had great difficulty in becoming an established means of continuous legislative supervision only in the French Assembly. As we just pointed out, questions for oral response have generally been considered during only one sitting per week in the Assembly. This has been a constitutional requirement. But, more important, the government has simply not answered some of the Assembly members' oral questions. In addition, through its control of the Conference of Presidents in the Assembly, the majority (in effect, the government) has been able to determine when, and even whether, various subjects and questions put by the opposition would be placed on the agenda.[85] As a consequence of all these factors, the oral question has not proven to be an effective device for controlling or supervising the government. Indeed, the government has answered only a small number of oral questions that called for debate. As an example, over the first three years of the Fifth Republic, the government responded to an average of only fifty such questions per year.[86]

The situation has been quite different in the Bundestag. In the early 1950s, Bundestag members asked the government to respond orally to only about one hundred questions each year. By the end of the 1950s, however, the pace of questioning had quickened, with an average of between three and four hundred oral questions posed to the government each year. In the 1961-65 Bundestag, members raised almost forty-eight hundred oral questions, or about twelve hundred per year; and, from 1965 to 1972 over twenty thousand oral questions were put to the government, or about three thousand per year.[87] Thus, there has been a thirtyfold increase in the oral questioning of the government by the Bundestag from 1949 to 1972. This increase has been the result of the greater use of the oral question made by both opposition members and members of the governing parties.

The device of questioning the government had its origination in the House of Commons and became firmly established as a regularized means for supervising the government long before its establishment in the Bundestag (and also the Assembly). This historical development is still reflected in the number of questions members of the Commons put to the government for oral reply. Despite the substantial increase in use of oral questioning by Bundestag members from 1949 to 1972, members of the House of Commons require the government to reply orally each year to an even greater number of questions. Thus, members of the House receive oral reply to between four and five thousand questions during a year's sitting and ask a total of over twenty-seven thousand written and oral questions each year compared to around four thousand in the Bundestag.[88]

The oral question can be used to great political effect by the opposition when it has a good case to make, for when used well, oral questions can push the government into responding on sensitive matters to the point of publicizing its own maladministration and wrongdoings. An excellent illustration of this occurred during the *Der Spiegel* affair. A few days after Defense Minister Strauss initiated a seizure of the papers of *Der Spiegel* (a German weekly news magazine that had for some time been critical of Strauss' policies), the opposition party (the SPD) used the daily question period three days in succession to criticize Strauss and other members of the government. And, through repeated questioning, it was found that Strauss had lied in his earlier statements both to the Bundestag and to newspapers. According to Kirchheimer and Menges, "Only a political party could have taken the *Spiegel* issues to the parliamentary arena and attempted to badger the government ministers into answering the questions that the press had raised. If the party had not done this, Strauss probably would never have been caught in his lies. If the government had not destroyed its credibility by being caught in numerous bald lies to parliament, it is doubtful whether the balance of public opinion would ever have swung decisively against it in this affair."[89] Eventually Strauss was dismissed as Minister.

Of course, governments sometimes attempt to answer questions by skillfully failing to answer them. Yet even here the government may be caught if additional questions are posed with a preconceived strategy in mind. The government might also publicly embarrass itself when answers are obviously "nonanswers." Vital notes that even in the area of foreign policy questions can be used effectively. "It is unpleasant," he says, "for Ministers to be pricked and criticized, however thick their skins."[90] He goes on to cite a British example from 1966, when Labour controlled the government:

Colonial Secretary Fred Lee created enormous embarrassment for the Government when, in October, 1966, he failed to give a clear answer to questions about policy on Gibraltar in the face of a newly instituted Spanish blockade of the colony. The *Times* reported (26 October) that "Mr. Lee's performance was variously described as being blundering, inept, and devious." Later the same day it was made clear in Government quarters that the answer Mr. Lee should have given. . . .was a firm "yes"! Two days later the Prime Minister and Foreign Secretary presided at a meeting of the Parliamentary Labour Party at which Mr. Lee explained himself. And three days after that the Foreign Secretary made a fresh statement of the policy, this time in "a language . . . that both sides of the Commons have been impatiently waiting to hear for some time."[91]

The question hour is used by parliamentarians to serve supervisory purposes somewhat like those of Congressional committee hearings and investigations. As one observer put it, questioning "can provide, quickly though briefly, an unceasing stream of up-to-date facts over the whole area of the government's competence."[92] There is little doubt that, if well used, questioning can both focus a problem and bring it into public view as well as influence the actions of ministers and civil servants.[93] Questioning also subjects the executive to public accountability on a continuous basis, day after day and week after week. Even so, we would agree with Bradshaw and Pring, who conclude that "viewed . . . as a device for getting information from the executive, for influencing its decisions, and for keeping officials on their toes, it does not pack the punch of an investigative committee on American levels."[94] Not only is each member procedurally limited in the number and the scope of questions he can ask at any single point, thereby placing constraints on him not imposed upon members of Congressional committees, but he does not have the staffing to help him prepare that individual members of Congress and Congressional committees have.[95]

Then again, the question is only one device legislators use to carry out supervisory activities. Parliamentary committees can also be employed, although their success has been spotty. In the House of Commons, several kinds of supervisory committees have been developed. The Bundestag and the Assembly, on the other hand, have relied more upon their standing legislation committees, supplemented at times by committees of investigation.

Perhaps the most important and influential of the supervisory committees in the House of Commons is the Public Accounts Committee (PAC). The PAC investigates the financial accounts of the government departments. While the PAC's responsibility leads it to range over many areas of policy, it is, in another sense, a specialist committee, for it deals solely with finance, and its members (who generally have long committee tenure) are men chosen for their financial knowledge or expertise.

Besides the specialist nature and the stable membership of the PAC, another key to its influence is its connection to the Comptroller and Auditor General (or the C and AG) with a staff of over five hundred executive-grade officers who are spread through the department and whose purpose is to audit the accounts of the departments. This staff allows for an examination of accounts at the end of the fiscal year and, in effect, for a continuous and close audit throughout the year. Not only does the C and AG prepare an annual audit of the accounts to be examined by the PAC, he gives a report that involves his own opinions and recommendations. Of special concern, besides economy and extravagance, is ascertaining if Parliamentary intentions have been followed by the departments.

The PAC has the power to summon civil servants and ask them about the workings of their departments. The accounting officer of each department, usually the permanent secretary, must appear before the committee to defend the department's actions against criticisms raised by members of the PAC. The reports of the committee are judicious, factual, and restrained. Usually specific recommendations made in the reports, regarding such matters as overspending or bad judgment, are implemented without question even though the reports are not legally binding.[96]

The working of the audit system in Great Britain is perhaps superior to that of the United States in two respects. The audit in Britain ordinarily takes place for each government department on a yearly basis, and there is only one committee of the House, rather than many, to which the audit office is responsible. Because the audit ordinarily takes place for each department on a yearly basis, members of the House, and particularly of the PAC, are given greater information and aid than that the GAO has been able to offer members of Congress. Also, because the audit office is responsible to one committee of the Commons, rather than to virtually all committees as in the Congress, there is a greater procedural opportunity for its reports to be dealt with in a more coordinated manner. Yet, it is also important to note that the use of the audit has inherent limits as a technique of supervision. As Punnett observes of the PAC, the "value of the committee is . . . that it acts as a deterrent to inefficiency and extravagance by the departments, but it has the essential weakness of all accounting processes of dealing with past expenditures."[97]

The PAC is complemented by the Expenditures Committee, known before 1971 as the Estimates Committee. Its purpose is to look for economies in the estimates for public expenditures within policies being implemented by the government. The committee has organized itself into six subcommittees, each covering a different policy sector. However, the committee's work has not enjoyed the same degree of respect within either the administration or the Commons as has the work of the PAC.[98] Nor has the committee been able to draw upon a large and specialist staff such as the PAC has had through the Comptroller General. In the period 1945-65, the committee made about 150 reports covering almost all the main areas of government expenditures. Only 22 of these reports became the subject of debate in the Commons, and the House has since not demonstrated much greater concern.[99]

A third select committee of the House is the Committee on Statutory Instruments, whose function is to consider the propriety of executive orders (made in the form of statutory instruments) before they become law. These instruments are to be published and circulated forty days in advance and subject to the review of the committee. The purpose of the review is to examine the instruments for consistency with delegated authority. The reports of the committee are laid before the House.

Placing responsibility for the supervision of authority delegated to the executive in a specific committee designed for that purpose has obvious merits in an age when numerous decisions are made under delegated authority. And the committee is active, as we observed in Chapter 2. However, one commentator notes that as many as 50 percent of the statutory instruments escape the procedure of being laid before the House,[100] and most that are laid before the House are not debated. Furthermore, the committee itself is confined to very narrow limits. It has no authority to comment on the merits of the statutory instruments, only on whether the statutory instruments were within the powers delegated to the executive.

The committees we have discussed thus far are specialized in the sense that they cover certain types of decisions over general areas of policy. However, since World War II, the House has created several supervisory committees that are somewhat more specialized by subject matter. Still the most important of these is the Select

Committee on Nationalized Industries. The committee has the responsibility to examine the reports and financial accounts of those British industries that have been nationalized. These industries include (or have included) civil aviation, railroads, electricity, gas, coal, and steel. Most of the members of the Nationalized Industries Committee have had political, business, or employment experiences relevant to the committee's work. Of the eight members who had the longest tenure of service on the committee between 1956 and 1963, one had been a former chairman of the Conservative backbench Trade and Industry Committee, one was a former mine owner and a former chairman of the Conservative backbench Fuel and Power Committee, two had been mineworkers, and one had been a railway stationmaster.[101] The committee also included a former Financial Secretary to the Treasury, a former Minister of Fuel and Power and a former Parliamentary Secretary to the Minister of Transport. Thus, the committee's membership has afforded it considerable experience and expertise in the carrying out of its supervisory functions.

The Nationalized Industries Committee obtains additional information by way of inquiries into each of the industries. It has generally examined one nationalized industry each year, enabling it to inquire into that industry in depth. In the process of these inquiries, the committee hears witnesses from the Boards of the Industries, Ministries, and Treasury. However, the committee does not have the power of subpoena and cannot "hear evidence or see papers and records which the Minister decides to withhold."[102] The committee has the purpose of examining general policy such as capital investment, wages and working conditions, and uneconomic services and prices. Thus, its inquiries concentrate on these matters and generally do not emphasize the day-to-day management of the industries.

The committee has been successful in a number of ways. It has unearthed information that probably could not have been obtained through parliamentary questions. Coombes' study of the committee has demonstrated how backbenchers used it "to conduct a running inquiry into the work of the public corporations."[103] The committee's findings have led to general parliamentary debates and have caused the government "to justify its policies in public [and to] explain its position on a number of important issues, on which it might rather have remained silent."[104] The inquiries led the government on more than one occasion to reconsider policy or to formulate policy where none existed.

The success of the committee, however, has been directly dependent on the fact that it has been nonpartisan. It has not taken up issues that divided the parties. The members' party loyalties have been such that, according to Coombes, were the committee to deal with matters that divided the parties, "its proceedings would be bogged down in deliberations and debate."[105] In addition, given the government majority on the committee, the committee's decisions on partisan matters would likely have refrained from criticizing the government, so as in any case to deprive its work on these subjects from coming to any other but a predetermined outcome.

That a nonpartisan character has normally been a prerequisite for the success of British select committees is also suggested by the experiences of the Public Accounts and Estimates committees. Harold Wilson, when chairman of the PAC, once said that the committee has never been "a battleground of party faction . . . in the hundred years of its existence there are only 64 recorded divisions."[106] As chairman of the Estimates Committee from 1961 to 1964, Sir Godfrey Nicholson said, "where I feel party political argument is completely inapposite is in the actual work of the committee."[107] In explaining the nonpartisan character of committee proceedings, Johnson has argued:

> They do not pass judgment on the contentious issues which divide the parties. They operate as nonparty groups producing conclusions which have in broad terms the assent of all their members. When their conclusions diverge from those of the Government—as they do sometimes—they could be put through only as a result of the House enforcing its will on the Government, and this is just what is impossible under our present political conventions.[108]

Most of the House of Commons' committees to which we have referred were established for the special purpose of scrutinizing and maintaining oversight of executive action. This differs from Congress where supervision has been expected to occur primarily through committees established essentially for the purpose of formulating, reviewing, and acting upon proposals for legislation through either the authorization or the appropriations processes. Although included in its legislative responsibilities, supervision necessarily became only one part of the work of these committees rather than an overriding part. As a consequence, the supervisory committees of the House of Commons, if they desired and had the staff, have had the potential to undertake more continuous and penetrating oversight than the legislation committees of the Congress normally could. This is significant. Nevertheless, there have also been important constraints on these supervisory committees. They have been constrained principally by their inability, for political reasons, to look into the kinds of partisan policy areas that have produced some of the most exciting and useful investigations that the Congressional committees have undertaken. Furthermore, except for the PAC, the committees have not had adequate staffs to supervise the policies for which they were responsible. Rather, they have generally had to confine themselves each year to supervising one or a few policy concerns.

Limits imposed by partisanship have also beset special investigating committees in the Bundestag and the National Assembly. The Bundestag can convene an investigating committee by a favorable vote of one-quarter of the Bundestag members. Because of this rule, the majority party or parties ordinarily cannot block the creation of an investigating committee. However, the governing party or parties will have a majority on the committees and the presence of this majority can prevent, and has prevented, the committees from investigating highly partisan areas. Hence, investigating committees have not been a useful instrument for supervision, and, indeed, few have been created since the first Bundestag.[109]

In France, special investigatory committees to look into financial malpractices and other criticisms of the administration of policy were of significance under the Fourth Republic, but an ordinance adopted early during the Fifth Republic limited their usefulness. An investigation cannot have a duration beyond four months, and publication either of the deliberations or the acts of these committees is highly restricted.[110] Moreover, since the members of investigating committees are selected by majority vote in the Assembly, the governing parties control a majority of their memberships. As a consequence, few investigating committees have been convened by the Assembly, and those that have been convened have had their mandates confined to nonpartisan issues.[111]

Of course, neither the Assembly nor the Bundestag is solely dependent on investigatory committees to obtain committee review of executive activities. Both houses also have standing, specialized committees on legislation and budgetary committees. In their review of and influence upon proposals for legislation and appropriations, these standing committees might concurrently become involved in ongoing efforts to supervise the executive.

Despite this possibility, we have seen earlier (in Chapter 2) that many limits are placed on the powers of the standing committees of the Assembly to influence substantive legislation or appropriations. Because the granting of appropriations can be such an essential device in bringing the executive and administration to account, let us concentrate upon it. The Finance Committee of the Assembly is placed in a difficult situation. Both it and the Assembly must consider the budget within seventy days. The committee not only must work within this restrictive time period, but it also has a minimal staff available to it.[112] Furthermore, it cannot propose amendments that raise the government's proposed expenditures and it is the government's original proposals rather than the committee's drafts that come to the floor of the Assembly. Finally, the government can subject the budget to a package vote on the floor that includes only those amendments the government deemed acceptable. If the Assembly refuses to pass the budget, the government's draft would be considered adopted after the seventy-day period. With these various considerations in mind, it is not surprising that the Assembly has found it difficult to alter the budget sent to it by the government or to use budgetary outlays for the purpose of bringing the government and administration to account. In fact, the Assembly has altered budgets on the average less than 1 percent.[113]

The situation is somewhat different in the Bundestag. As we observed in Chapter 2, the standing committees of the Bundestag are granted substantial powers over legislation, and the committees can and do make effective use of these powers (see also Chapter 6). It is the committee draft of a bill that the Bundestag considers, and it usually follows the recommendations of its committees. Also, almost all of the standing committees actively scrutinize government ministers and officials not only on substantive legislation, but also on annual appropriations for the ministries. Both current proposals and past activities of the ministries are closely examined in committee deliberations.

In effect, both the proposed expenditures involved in legislation and the budgets for each ministry are usually subjected to this kind of examination in two separate Bundestag committees. The first of these, as just mentioned, is the substantive standing committee (or, sometimes, committees) responsible for the policy sector encompassed by the legislation or the ministry. The second is the Appropriations Committee.

The Appropriations Committee has been, and continues to be, an esteemed and influential committee in the Bundestag. It has been highly active. It has frequently altered the budgets of the various ministries, sometimes by over 10 percent. Indeed, because of the pressures of time for considering the budget in the Bundestag, the Appropriations Committee has been empowered to make some decisions on the budget on its own authority.

An extensive amount of work goes into the decisions and recommendations of the Appropriations Committee. The committee normally comes to its decisions on the basis of hearings with each of the other standing committees as well as with the various ministries. As in the Congress, the ability of the committee to undertake these activities over the whole range of the budget is enhanced by having a specialized subcommittee system. Each of the subcommittees, made up of a small number of members from the entire committee, is responsible for the budget and the expenditures involved in specific pieces of legislation for a single ministry.

The subcommittee system also enables committee members, especially those with greater seniority, to develop considerable expertise in dealing with budgetary proposals for particular policy sectors and in attempting to hold the various ministries to account. However, while the development of expertise on the committee is maximized through the working of the subcommittees, the availability of research assistance to back up the committee members, even after the 1969 reforms, has remained inadequate.

Lying behind the supervisory control of the Bundestag, as of the House of Commons and the Assembly, is the need the government has to retain the confidence of Parliament and of its parliamentary party. Governments can certainly be shaken by serious cases of maladministration. Nevertheless, as we earlier observed, calling the life of the government into question is, in fact, usually a remote rather than a real or immediate threat. And, it is here that the influence the Bundestag has over budgetary decisions and other legislation, through its standing committees, gains value as a technique of supervision because it enables the Bundestag continuously to back up its supervisory efforts by exerting influence over decisions of consequence to the government and ministries that runs short of calling the life of the government into question.

Despite the differences between the types of supervisory devices we have discussed and the uses to which they can or have been put, there is one feature they all have in common. This is that they arise from procedures of the houses and are played out within the houses. In this sense, they contrast with a significant form of legislative supervisory activity normally carried on outside the house. We refer to legislators' constituency case work.

Legislators spend a considerable amount of time dealing with their constituents' inquiries, a number of which involve complaints arising from dealings constituents have with the administration. American Congressmen report that they spend, on the average, about one-quarter of their time on constituency case work.[114] Combined with their correspondence, a major component of which relates to constituency case work, over one-third of a Congressman's time and almost two-thirds of the time of his staff is occupied by constituency case work.[115]

Nor are American Congressmen at all unusual in this regard. The amount of time British MPs spend responding to constituent mail (one estimate suggests that members of the House as a whole receive an overall total of more than 250,000 complaints yearly),[116] writing to ministers on behalf of constituent complaints (involving an estimated overall total of 50,000 letters each year),[117] personally intervening in the administration, and holding regular meetings with their constituents (called surgeries) is also considerable. For the average MP, such activities occupy a minimum of from forty to fifty hours a month.[118] Members of the Assembly are also highly involved in constituency case work. Indeed, most members of the Assembly return to their constituencies and hold surgeries more frequently than do most members of the House of Commons. Their involvement in handling and even seeking out problems constituents face with government authorities is substantial and has increased during the Fifth Republic as other functions of the Assembly have declined.[119] It is only in the case of members of the Bundestag that handling constituency case work does not appear to be a significant aspect of their job.[120]

As is apparent from our remarks, handling constituency case work can occupy a substantial portion of legislators' time. While legislators have voiced complaints about the amount of time they are required to spend on constituency case work, most also view this work as useful, and for a variety of reasons have jealously guarded their function of handling citizens' grievances against the administration. Perhaps they view this function as an important part of their role and as serving to make the legislature a more valuable and meaningful institution in the eyes of citizens, or perhaps they view this function as having relevance to their ability to build or retain support for themselves in their constituencies. Then, too, legislators may feel that the constant flow of information they receive from citizens' complaints is essential if they are to do an effective job of supervising the executive and administration more generally and of finding weaknesses in current statutes. Whatever the reasons, many legislators have resisted the idea of creating an organ outside of the legislature and the courts for handling constituents' complaints against the administration. For example, the idea of establishing an ombudsman in the United States at the federal level has been raised many times but has not yet met with success in the Congress.[121]

The House of Commons, on the other hand, did move to create an ombudsman, known as the Parliamentary Commissioner for Administration, in 1967, but his role was carefully defined in the 1967 Act so as not to bypass the MPs. Citizens continue to bring complaints directly to their MP, who, in turn, decides whether or not to handle the complaint through the ombudsman.[122] If the MP takes the complaint to the ombudsman and if it falls within the latter's jurisdiction, the ombudsman then undertakes an investigation. Upon completion of the investigation, the ombudsman's office draws up a report which it sends to the appropriate administrative officials, the MP, the citizen making the complaint, and any other citizen named in the complaint.[123]

To aid him in his investigations, the ombudsman has a staff of sixty and has access to all departmental documents. Ministers cannot place a veto over an investigation. Furthermore, the House created its own supervisory committee (the Committee on the Parliamentary Commissioner for Administration). Among its functions, the committee follows up the recommendations of the ombudsman to find out whether the departments have complied with them.[124]

Still, the British ombudsman system has a number of weaknesses. From 1967 until 1971, MPs brought an average of about eight hundred complaints a year to the ombudsman.[125] This is not very many when one considers the work of some other ombudsmen (for example, the German military ombudsman)[126] or when one considers that MPs are estimated to receive over two hundred thousand complaints a year.[127] Moreover, while the ombudsman can make cases public by bringing reports to the House of Commons, this power is not often used and instead has typically been left up to the MP to decide whether to publicize a case or not. Perhaps partly as a consequence of this, there is only a low level of public awareness of the ombudsman's office. A public opinion survey taken two years after the establishment of the office found that almost 70 percent of the British public either had never heard of the ombudsman or had heard of the term but did not know what it meant.[128]

Yet, the ombudsman has made a positive contribution in other ways. In particular, the ombudsman has been able in some cases to correct situations and to gain financial redress for citizens when MPs had earlier failed. Indeed, the success of the ombudsman in getting the department to follow his judgments and opinions is striking, considering that the ombudsman has no legal force behind his recommendations. During the first four years of its operation, the office of the ombudsman uncovered 164 cases of maladministration, or about 15 percent of the cases that were fully investigated. In all but one of these cases the ombudsman's judgment and recommendations were followed.[129]

The West Germans also have an ombudsman, but one very different from the British. Based on an amendment to the Basic Law in 1956, an ombudsman having authority to supervise the armed forces was established in West Germany in 1957.[130] The purpose of the military ombudsman is to help the Bundestag exercise parliamentary control over the military and to protect the basic rights of military personnel. To do this, the military ombudsman has a staff, can request oral or written information and examine files (which can be denied only by the Minister of Defense or his representative), and can personally inspect troops, administrative offices, and staffs without notice.

The military ombudsman is responsible to the Bundestag. He is selected by an absolute majority of all Bundestag members on proposal of the Bundestag Defense Committee. He can also be dismissed and replaced upon proposal of the Defense Committee and vote of the Bundestag. The military ombudsman must act upon requests for investigations by the Bundestag Defense Committee. He may also act, should he so decide, upon personnel grievances communicated to him by any other source, including by soldiers themselves. Finally, he can act on cases he has uncovered during his own inspections. Upon completion of his investigation, the military ombudsman is empowered to send a report to the appropriate organ for legal proceedings. He can, and sometimes must, also submit a report to the Bundestag. These reports are published and may become the subject of oral presentation in the Bundestag.

Numerous cases are brought before the military ombudsman, almost six thousand in 1963 and over seven thousand in 1969. Of the cases in 1969, the military ombudsman's work resulted in application of penal or disciplinary sanctions in twenty cases and various other measures in approximately four hundred additional cases.[131]

Conclusion

In each of the systems we have examined, there are numerous places from which supervision of executive action and implementation of legislation occurs. A great many persons, reaching well outside the legislature, are involved in essentially supervisory activity. Besides legislators, these include the courts and individual citizens and groups who bring grievances to legislators or to the courts. It also includes investigative journalism that has uncovered and followed through on cases of executive improprieties in all four of our systems. As a consequence, executive action and implementation of the laws is watched from many vantage points and supervisory activities originate from many sources.

In this chapter, we have reviewed a series of devices available to legislators in their efforts to supervise the executive and administration's handling of policy. These include removal of the government, committee hearings and investigations, parliamentary questioning, use of the budgetary and legislative power, personal communication by legislators with executive officials, and the creation and use of an ombudsman's office. We have seen that some of these devices are employed by all four legislatures, others by two or three, and still others by only one. Our discussion has also pointed to various advantages and limits of particular devices.

With the possible exception of the Assembly, a rather considerable amount and variety of supervisory activity has occurred in each of the legislatures. Nevertheless, regardless of the degree of activity or the number and type of supervisory devices used, another characteristic the legislatures share is that they cannot make a systemic attempt to assure that the entirety of the law is applied properly. As one author put it, "The whole system of . . . control is fundamentally a spot-check system, and it cannot be an entirely comprehensive one."[132] Although the author was referring to the House of Commons, this conclusion applies to each of the other three legislatures as well.[133]

One reason why legislatures cannot supervise in a comprehensive fashion is clear. With the growth in the amount and scope of legislation and governmental activities, the task legislatures face in supervising the implementation of legislation has become an exceedingly difficult, almost overwhelming, one. Yet for the same reason it becomes all the more important that there be a high level of legislative involvement in overseeing the administration. For, not only does a high level of legislative supervisory activity serve to uncover and adjust actual cases of maladministration, it also makes the possibility of supervision more meaningful in the eyes of the administrator, which can itself serve to keep administrators on their toes and to bring about greater administrative compliance with the law.

With this in mind, it is pertinent to question what promotes or impedes legislative involvement in activities pertaining to supervising the executive. We address this question, as well as questions about what affects legislative involvement in other areas of legislative-executive relations, in the upcoming chapter.

Notes

[1] John Stuart Mill, *Considerations on Representative Government*. Quoted by Cornelius P. Cotter, "Legislative Oversight," in *Congress: The First Branch of Government*, ed. Alfred de Grazia (Garden City, N.Y.: Doubleday, 1967), p.24.

[2] Theodore Lowi, *Legislative Politics: U.S.A.*, 2d. ed. (Boston: Little, Brown and Co., 1965), p. xvi. In a similar vein Charles Hyneman, in *Bureaucracy in a Democracy* (New York: Harper Brothers, 1950), contends: "[W]hoever controls the bureaucracy controls the activities of government" (p. 24).

[3] The United States, for example, has over two and one-half million federal civil service employees, three-fourths of whom have been added in the last thirty years.

[4] See John Saloma III, *Congress and the New Politics* (Boston: Little, Brown and Co., 1969), pp. 94, 146; Joseph S. Clark, *Congress: The Sapless Branch* (New York: Harper & Row, 1964), p. 12; Joseph P. Harris, *Congressional Control of Administration* (Garden City, N.Y.: Doubleday, 1964), pp. 1-15, 327-29; Samuel Huntington, "Congressional Responses to the Twentieth Century," in *The Congress and America's Future*, rev. ed., David Truman, ed. (Englewood Cliffs, N.J.: Prentice-Hall, 1973), pp. 6-38; Michael Ameller, ed., *Parliaments*, rev. ed. (London: Cassell, 1966), esp. p. 262; and Bernard Crick, *The Reform of Parliament* (London: Weidenfeld and Nicolson, 1970).

[5] Harris, *Congressional Control of Administration*, p. 1.

[6]Malcolm Jewell and Samuel Patterson, *Legislative Process in the United States* (New York: Random House, 1973), pp. 507-508. Harris, in *Congressional Control of Administration*, makes a distinction between control and oversight, control referring to "legislative decisions and activities prior to relevant administrative action" and oversight, strictly speaking, referring to "review after the fact," p. 9. Also on definition, see Harrison W. Fox, Jr., "Oversight: Is Congress Doing Its Job?," (Paper presented to 1974 annual meeting of the American Political Science Association), pp. 4-8.

[7]Samuel Patterson, "Congressional Committee Professional Staffing," in *Legislatures in Developmental Perspective*, ed. Allan Kornberg and Lloyd D. Musolf (Durham, N.C.: Duke University Press, 1970). See, also, Kenneth Kofmehl, *Professional Staffs of Congress* (West LaFayette, Ind.: Purdue University Press, 1962), and David K. Price, *Who Makes the Laws?* (Cambridge, Mass.: Schenkman, 1972.)

[8]See for examples: Harris, *Congressional Control of Administration*, p. 10; Ernest S. Griffith, *Congress: Its Contemporary Role*, 4th ed. (New York: New York University Press, 1967), pp. 74-75; Saloma, *Congress and the New Politics*, p. 137. On recent efforts by Congress to strengthen its ability to perform the supervision role, see Fox, "Oversight: Is Congress Doing Its Job?", pp. 4, 30-31.

[9]William L. Morrow, *Congressional Committees* (New York: Charles Scribner's Sons, 1969), pp. 160-95. See, also, Stephen Horn, *Unused Power: The Work of the Senate Committee on Appropriations* (Washington, D.C.: Brookings Institution, 1970), pp. 38-40.

[10]One student of Congress, George Galloway, estimates that nine-tenths of Congress's business deals with spending issues. Cited by Robert Ash Wallace, *Congressional Control of Federal Spending* (Detroit: Wayne State University Press, 1960), p. vii.

[11]Thomas Henderson, *Congressional Oversight of Executive Agencies* (Gainesville: University of Florida Press, 1970).

[12]Dale Vinyard, "The Congressional Committees on Small Business: Pattern of Legislative Committee-Executive Agency Relations," *Western Political Quarterly* 21 (September 1968): 391-99; V. Stanley Vardys, "Select Committees of the House of Representatives," *Midwest Journal of Political Science* 10 (1966): 364-77.

[13]Harold P. Green and Alan Rosenthal, *Government of the Atom* (New York: Atherton, 1963).

[14]Richard F. Fenno, *Power of the Purse: Appropriations Politics in Congress* (Boston: Little, Brown and Co., 1966), p. 17. See also Harris, *Congressional Control of Administration*, p. 318; V.O. Key, Jr., "Legislative Control," in *Elements of Public Administration*, ed. Fritz M. Marx (Englewood Cliffs, N.J.: Prentice-Hall, 1959); Roland Young, *The American Congress* (New York: Harper & Row, 1958), p. 221; Saloma, *Congress and the New Politics*, p. 137; Cotter, "Legislative Oversight," p. 48; Wallace, *Congressional Control of Federal Spending*; Lucius Wilmerding, Jr., *The Spending Power: A History of the Efforts of Congress to Control Expenditures* (New Haven, Conn.: Yale University Press, 1943); Arthur W. MacMahon, "Congressional Oversight of Administration: The Power of the Purse," in *New Perspectives on the House of Representatives*, ed. Robert Peabody and Nelson Polsby (Chicago: Rand McNally, 1963), pp. 325-81.

[15]This includes both the authorization stage, in which "ceilings" are set, and the actual appropriation stage of the budget which involves "line-item" consideration in each house.

[16]Michael W. Kirst, *Government Without Passing Laws* (Chapel Hill: University of North Carolina Press, 1969), p. 15. See Arnold Kanter, "Congress and the Defense Budget, 1960-1970," *American Political Science Review* 66 (March 1972): 129-43; Edward Kolodziej, *The Uncommon Defense and Congress, 1945-1963* (Columbus: Ohio State University Press, 1966). See also Congressional Quarterly Service, *Power of the Pentagon* (Washington, D.C., 1972), p. 9.

[17]Kirst, *Government Without Passing Laws*, p. 15.

[18]Fenno's research found that, of the 443 separate case histories examined, the House accepted its committee recommendations in 387, or 87.4 percent, of the cases. These figures are from "The House Appropriations Committee as a Political System: The Problem of Integration," *American Political Science Review* 56 (June 1962): 323. See, also, Donald Matthews, *U.S. Senators and their World* (New York: Random House, 1960), p. 168.

[19]Fenno, *Power of the Purse*, chs. 8, 9, 12, and especially pp. 353-54. See, also, Aaron Wildavsky, *The Politics of the Budgetary Process*, 2d. ed. (Boston: Little, Brown and Co., 1974).

[20]Richard F. Fenno, *Congressmen in Committees* (Boston: Little, Brown and Co., 1973), p. 195.

[21]For a good brief discussion of the executive's spending discretion, see Louis Fisher, *President and Congress: Power and Policy* (New York: The Free Press, 1972), pp. 110-32, and Mark Green et al., *Who Runs Congress?* (New York: Grossman Publishers, 1972), pp. 113-19. Note that we have focused here on the President's "negative" power to deny the spending of funds, but he also can "reprogram" or transfer funds within certain limits.

[22]As reported in the *Minneapolis Tribune*, Feb. 2, 1973, p. 3A.

[23]Fisher, *President and Congress*, pp. 125-26

[24]For a summary, see *Congressional Quarterly Weekly Reports*, February 22, 1975, p. 313.

[25]William J. Keefe and Morris S. Ogul, *The American Legislative Process: Congress and the States*, 3d. ed. (Englewood Cliffs, N. J.: Prentice-Hall, 1973), p. 426-27. The quote contained within the quote is from Committee for Economic Development, *Control of Federal Government Spending* (Washington, D. C.: Government Printing Office, 1955), p. 6.

[26] Herbert W. Stephens, "The Role of the Legislative Committees in the Appropriations Process: A Study Focused on the Armed Services Committees," *Western Political Quarterly* 24 (March 1971): 146-62. The Armed Services Committees have usually been characterized more as "advocates" than "overseers." See *Congressional Quarterly Weekly Report*, March 16, 1972, pp. 673-77; Congressional Quarterly Service, *Power of the Pentagon*, Lewis A. Dexter, "Congressmen and the Making of Military Policy," in *New Perspectives on the House of Representatives*, ed. Peabody and Polsby, pp. 305-24.

[27] Stephens, "The Role of the Legislative Committees in the Appropriations Process," pp. 152-53.

[28] Fenno, *Power of the Purse*, p. 73; Harris, *Congressional Control of Administration*, p. 316; Thomas Jahnige, "The Congressional Committee System and the Oversight Process: Congress and NASA," *Western Political Quarterly* 21 (June 1968): 227-39; Saloma, *Congress and the New Politics*, pp. 151-53; Raymond Dawson, "Congressional Innovation and Intervention in Defense Policy: Legislative Authorization of Weapons Systems," *American Political Science Review* 56 (March 1962): 42-57.

[29] Key, "Legislative Control," pp. 313-14. Also, see: Young, *The American Congress*, Chapter 9; Fenno, *Power of the Purse*, p. 9; Harris, *Congressional Control of Administration*, p. 316.

[30] Fenno, *Power of the Purse*, p. 19. (Emphasis added.)

[31] Ralph Huitt, "Congress the Durable Partner," in *Lawmakers in a Changing World*, ed. Elke Frank (Englewood Cliffs, N.J.: Prentice-Hall, 1966), p. 20.

[32] For example, see: Dawson, "Congressional Innovation and Intervention in Defense Policy"; Jahnige, "The Congressional Committee System and the Oversight Process"; Saloma, *Congress and the New Politics*, pp. 151-53.

[33] Dawson, "Congressional Innovation and Intervention in Defense Policy," p. 57; see also Saloma, *Congress and the New Politics*, p. 152.

[34] See Robert Ash Wallace, "Congressional Control of the Budget," *Midwest Journal of Political Science* 3 (May 1959): 151-67; Congressional Quarterly, "General Accounting Office," *Guide to the U.S. Congress* (Washington, D.C., 1971), pp. 441-46; and Harris, *Congressional Control of Administration*, Chapter 6.

[35] Harris, *Congressional Control of Administration*, p. 163.

[36] *Congressional Quarterly* estimated the GAO staff of 1971 at 4,800, about 3,000 being "professionals" (*Guide to Congress*, p. 444).

[37] Harris, *Congressional Control and Administration*, pp. 164, 165, 174-76, cites some reasons for this failure.

[38] Keefe and Ogul, *The American Legislative Process: Congress and the States*, 3d. ed. (Englewood Cliffs, N.J.: Prentice-Hall, 1973), p. 4.

[39] Green et al., *Who Runs Congress?*, p. 128.

[40] Green et al., *Who Runs Congress?*, p. 127.

[41] *Congressional Quarterly Weekly Reports*, Jan. 11, 1975, pp. 81-83; *Congressional Quarterly Almanac*, 1972 (Washington, 1972), pp. 93-95; *Congressional Quarterly Almanac*, 1973 (Washington, 1973), pp. 1074-77.

[42] For a discussion of the various uses of hearings, see: David Truman, *The Governmental Process*, 2d. ed. (New York: Alfred Knopf, 1971), pp. 372-77; Morrow, *Congressional Committees*, pp. 91-92; Keefe and Ogul, *The American Legislative Process*, pp. 205-11; Ralph Huitt, "The Congressional Committee: A Case Study," *American Political Science Review* 48 (June 1954): 340-65; Fenno, *Power of the Purse*, p. 332; Heinz Eulau, "The Committees in a Revitalized Congress," in *Congress: The First Branch of Government*, ed. Alfred de Grazia, pp. 204-43; and Horn, *Unused Power*, pp. 115-27.

[43] Wildavsky, *Politics of the Budgetary Process*, p. 85.

[44] Kirst, *Government Without Passing Laws*, p. 24-30.

[45] Kirst, *Government Without Passing Laws*, p. 26.

[46] Kirst, *Government Without Passing Laws*, p. 24.

[47] Holbert Carroll, *The House of Representatives and Foreign Affairs*, rev. ed., (Boston: Little, Brown and Co., 1966), p. 162.

[48] See Kirst, *Government Without Passing Laws*, esp. pp. 74-75.

[49] Jahnige, "The Congressional Committee System and the Oversight Process," pp. 236-39.

[50] Ira Sharkansky, "An Appropriations Subcommittee and Its Client Agencies," *American Political Science Review* 59 (September 1965): 628.

[51] Fenno, *The Power of the Purse*, p. 566. See also: Horn, *Unused Power*, pp. 205-19; Morrow, *Congressional Subcommittees*, pp. 177-78; Jeffrey Pressman, *House vs. Senate* (New Haven, Conn.: Yale University Press, 1966).

[52] See Harris, *Congressional Control of Administration*, pp. 293-94; Telford Taylor, *Grand Inquest: The Story of Congressional Investigations* (New York: Simon and Schuster, 1955); M. Nelson McGeary, *The Developments of Congressional Investigative Power* (New York: Columbia University Press, 1940).

[53] Green et al., *Who Runs Congress?*, p. 121.

[54] Kirst, *Government Without Passing Laws*, pp. 74-76.

[55] It should be noted that investigations do not always run counter to executive purposes or undercut executive power. They can be used, for example, to reenforce Presidential recommendations, help the administration gather information it needs but is not empowered or capable of securing, to help create a favorable public opinion, or to undercut other hostile investigations by more unfriendly critics of the administration.

[56] Kirst, *Government Without Passing Laws*, pp. 30-31; Fenno, *The Power of the Purse*, p. 18.
[57] Kirst, *Government Without Passing Laws*, p. 32-38.
[58] William Morrow, "Legislative Control of Administrative Discretion: The Case of Congress and Foreign Aid," *Journal of Politics* 30 (November, 1968): pp. 985-1011.
[59] Kirst, *Government Without Passing Laws*, pp. 74-81.
[60] MacMahon, "Congressional Oversight of Administration," p. 358.
[61] Kirst, *Government Without Passing Laws*, p. 64.
[62] Kirst, *Government Without Passing Laws*, pp. 84-85; also Wildavsky, *The Politics of the Budgetary Process*.
[63] Kirst, *Government Without Passing Laws*, p. 109.
[64] Kirst, *Government Without Passing Laws*, p. 79.
[65] Harris, *Congressional Control of Administration*, Chapter 8; William Morrow, *Congressional Committees*, pp. 163-66.
[66] Harris, *Congressional Control of Administration*, Chapter 8; Fisher, *President and Congress*, pp. 83-84. Joseph Cooper and Ann Cooper, "The Legislative Veto and the Constitution," *George Washington Law Review* 30 (1962); 467-516. We should note in passing that the legislative veto is more than a potential weapon in approval of executive reorganization plans; it is used between 20 and 25 percent of the time. See Congressional Quarterly Service's *Congress and the Nation*, vol. I, pp. 1456-70; vol. II, pp. 655-57. Congressional Quarterly also notes that though sixteen of the seventeen reorganization plans submitted to Congress went into effect, "it was reported that [the President] refrained from sending others to Congress when it became apparent they would run into trouble" (Vol. II, p. 655). See, also, Judith Parris, "Congress Rejects the President's Urban Development Department, 1961-62," in *Congress and Urban Problems*, ed. Frederic Cleaveland (Washington, D.C.: The Brookings Institution, 1969), pp. 173-223.
[67] Edith Carper, *The Defense Appropriations Rider* (University, Alabama: University of Alabama Press, 1960).
[68] Saloma, *Congress and the New Politics*, p. 139; Harris, *Congressional Control of Administration*, pp. 241-50.
[69] Harris, *Congressional Control of Administration*, p. 265-76; see also Saloma, *Congress and the New Politics*, pp. 140-45.
[70] Saloma, *Congress and the New Politics*, p. 140.
[71] Harris, *Congressional Control of Administration*, p. 237.
[72] Kirst, *Government Without Passing Laws*, p. 115; Harris, *Congressional Control of Administration*, p. 238.
[73] Morrow, *Congressional Committees*, pp. 162-65. The quote within the quote is from William E. Rhode, *Committee Clearance of Administration Decisions* (East Lansing: Michigan State University, 1959), p. 4.
[74] Harris, *Congressional Control of Administration*. See also John R. Johannes, "Statutory Reporting Requirements: An Assessment,"(paper presented to the 1974 annual meeting of the Midwest Political Science Association).
[75] Key, "Legislative Control," p. 313.
[76] Kirst, *Government Without Passing Laws*, p. 45.
[77] Young, *The American Congress*, p.188; see also Kirst, *Government Without Passing Laws*, pp. 45f.
[78] On the Conseil d'État see Charles E. Freedman, *The Conseil d'État in Modern France* (New York: Columbia University Press, 1961), and Margherita Rendel, *The Administrative Functions of the French Conseil d'État* (London: Weidenfeld and Nicolson, 1970).
[79] F. Ridley and J. Blondel, *Public Administration in France* (London: Routledge and Kegan Paul, 1964), p. 153.
[80] Ridley and Blondel, *Public Administration in France*, p. 158.
[81] See Herbert Jacob, *German Administration Since Bismarck* (New Haven, Conn.: Yale University Press, 1963), pp. 152-78. As Jacob observes, "The Bundesrat is the principal organ through which the federal government can supervise Land administration directly" (p. 173).
[82] However, the Congress has impeached a number of other officials.
[83] See, for example, the findings and conclusions of the judicial inquiry into the Profumo affair found in *Lord Dunning's Report* (HMSO, 1963), Cmnd. 2152.
[84] John P. Mackintosh, *The Government and Politics of Britain* (London: Hutchinson and Co., 1970), p. 86.
[85] André Chandernagor, *Un Parlement, pour quoi faire?* (Paris: Gallimard, 1967), pp. 66-67.
[86] Jean Grangé, "La Fixation de l'ordre du jour des assemblées parlementaires," in *Études sur le Parlement de la Ve République*, ed. Éliane Guichard-Ayoub, et al. (Paris: Presses Universitaires de France, 1965), pp. 266-68. On the other hand, over four thousand written questions were answered in one year alone (1965). See Chandernagor, *Un Parlement, pour quoi faire?*, p. 65.
[87] German Bundestag, *Zeitschrift für Parlamentsfragen*, Jahrgang 4, Heft 1 (Bonn: 1973), p. 6.
[88] David Judge, "Backbench Specialization—A Study in Parliamentary Questions," *Parliamentary Affairs* 27 (Spring 1974): 179.
[89] Otto Kirchheimer and Constantine Menges, "A Free Press in a Democratic State? The *Spiegel* Case," in *Politics in Europe: Five Cases in European Government*, ed. Gwendolen M. Carter and Alan F. Westin (New York: Harcourt, Brace and World, 1965), p. 132.

[90] David Vital, *The Making of British Foreign Policy* (New York: Praeger, 1968), p. 79.
[91] *Ibid.*
[92] Kenneth Bradshaw and David Pring, *Parliament and Congress* (London: Constable, 1972), p. 366.
[93] See Nevil Johnson, "Parliamentary Questions and the Conduct of Administration," *Public Administration* 39 (Summer 1961): 139-41.
[94] Bradshaw and Pring, *Parliament and Congress*, p. 370.
[95] For the limitations of the question period, see Johnson, "Parliamentary Questions and the Conduct of Administration," pp. 143-44; Bradshaw and Pring, *Parliament and Congress*, pp. 366-71; and Nevil Johnson, "Questions in the Bundestag," *Parliamentary Affairs* 16 (Winter 1962): 22-34.
[96] See Harris, *Congressional Control of Administration*, pp. 167-74.
[97] R. M. Punnett, *British Government and Politics* (New York: Norton, 1968), p. 292.
[98] Nevil Johnson, *Parliament and Administration: The Estimates Committee, 1945-1965* (London: George Allen and Unwin, 1966), p. 137.
[99] Johnson, *Parliament and Administration*, p. 30 and pp. 183-84. On later years see Hugh Heclo and Aaron Wildavsky, *The Private Government of Public Money: Community and Policy Inside British Politics* (Berkeley: University of California Press, 1974).
[100] J. E. Kirsell, *Parliamentary Supervision of Delegated Legislation* (London: Stevens, 1960), p. 19.
[101] David Coombes, *The Member of Parliament and the Administration: The Case of The Select Committee on Nationalized Industries* (London: George Allen and Unwin, 1966), pp. 86-87.
[102] Coombes, *The Member of Parliament and the Administration*, p. 203.
[103] Coombes, *The Member of Parliament and the Administration*, p. 11.
[104] Coombes, *The Member of Parliament and the Administration*, p. 189.
[105] Coombes, *The Member of Parliament and the Administration*, p. 212.
[106] Gordon Reid, *The Politics of Financial Control: The Role of the House of Commons* (London: Hutchinson, 1966), p. 108. See also Punnett, *British Government and Politics*, p. 292.
[107] Reid, *The Politics of Financial Control*, p. 108.
[108] Johnson, *Parliament and Administration*, p. 140.
[109] Gerhard Loewenberg, *Parliament in the German Political System* (Ithaca, N. Y.: Cornell University Press, 1967), pp. 418-20.
[110] Maurice Duverger, *La Cinquième République* (Paris: Presses Universitaires de France, 1968), p. 118.
[111] Philip M. Williams, *The French Parliament: Politics in the Fifth Republic* (New York: Praeger, 1968), p. 51.
[112] For the problems Assembly members have in getting information in other areas and their need for expertise, see Chandernagor, *Un Parlement, pour quoi faire?*, pp. 70-71 and 125-26.
[113] Williams, *The French Parliament*, p. 79.
[114] Saloma, *Congress and the New Politics*, p. 184.
[115] Saloma, *Congress and the New Politics*, p. 185
[116] William B. Gwyn, "The British PCA: Ombudsman or Ombudsmouse," *Journal of Politics* 35 (February 1973): 47.
[117] Gwyn, "The British PCA," pp. 47-48
[118] According to the responses of 111 MPs, the average MP spends about two hours per day dealing with mail from his constituency. See Anthony Barker and Michael Rush, *The Member of Parliament and His Information* (London: George Allen and Unwin, 1970), p. 190.
[119] Henry Ehrmann, *Politics in France* (Boston: Little, Brown and Co., 1971), pp. 292 and 301. See, also, Robert Buron, *Le Plus beau des métiers* (Paris: Plon, 1963), pp. 22-34, who discusses constituency case work.
[120] Loewenberg, *Parliament in the German Political System*, pp. 427-28. It must be remembered that the authority to administer much federal legislation is at the state rather than the federal level in Germany. This may help to explain why citizens do not often work through their members in the Bundestag. Furthermore, and perhaps more important, Almond and Verba found that Germans tend to feel more competence acting as a subject (dealing with the administration) than as a citizen (dealing with the legislature) and therefore, on the whole, possibly prefer to work through administrators rather than legislators. See Gabriel A. Almond and Sidney Verba, *The Civic Culture* (Princeton, N. J.: Princeton University Press, 1963), pp. 217-29.
[121] A concise summary of the major uses and limitations of ombudsmen offices as revealed by experiences in a variety of nations where such an office operates may be found in Samuel Krislov, "Taking up the Ombudsman's Burden," *Polity* 1 (Winter 1968) : 242-50.
[122] This process of gaining access to the ombudsman only through representatives in the legislature is an innovation of the British ombudsman procedure.
[123] Frank Stacey, *The British Ombudsman* (Oxford: The Clarendon Press, 1971), p. 246.
[124] Gwyn, "The British PCA," p. 52. The committee also supervises how the ombudsman acts and can propose modifications to the government regarding the jurisdiction of the ombudsman.
[125] Gwyn, "The British PCA," P. 49.
[126] For a case load comparison of the ombudsman in Britain and New Zealand, see Stacey, *The British Ombudsman*, pp. 307-8.

[127]Certainly one reason why the British ombudsman considers relatively few cases is that the field of his authority is considerably narrowed by the exclusion of such matters as cases involving most hospitals, police investigations, postal service, and military conduct from his jurisdiction. Moreover, the ombudsman cannot take the initiative, thereby further limiting the number of cases he considers.

[128]Gwyn, "The British PCA," pp. 55-56.

[129]Stacey, *The British Ombudsman*, pp. 324-25.

[130]See Egon Lohse, "West Germany's Military Ombudsman," in *The Ombudsman: Citizen's Defender* 2d ed., Donald C. Rowat ed. (London: George Allen and Unwin, 1968), pp. 119-26. Much of our discussion in the following two paragraphs is based on Lohse.

[131]Alfred Grosser, *Deutschbilanz: Geschichte Deutschlands seit 1945* (Munich: Carl Hanser Verlag, 1970), p. 202. In mid-1973, the French also established an ombudsman, called the *médiateur*. The office of the ombudsman has twelve civil servants to investigate citizens' complaints brought by members of the Assembly and the Senate on their behalf. Antoine Pinay was appointed as the first ombudsman.

[132]Professor John Griffiths as quoted in Bernard Crick, *The Reform of Parliament*, p. 189.

[133]An excellent set of examples of the selective nature of oversight as it applies to the Congressional appropriations process may be found in Ira Sharkansky, "An Appropriations Subcommittee and Its Client Agencies," pp. 622-28.

Chapter 8
Executive-Legislative Relations: Some Explanations

Why legislators behave as they do toward the executive is the subject of discussion in this chapter. The chapter is divided into four sections. Two of these sections build on the findings of Chapter 6. First, we attempt to account for how prominent the four legislatures have been compared to the executive in the development of policies contained in legislation. Second, we take up differences in the levels of influence each legislature exerted on domestic as compared to foreign policies and examine variables that may help to explain these differences. Third, we discuss legislative supervision of the executive, the subject broached in Chapter 7, and attempt to account for how much legislators have become involved in oversight functions. Finally, the concluding section summarizes the analyses and discusses their implications for some key criticisms regarding the policy-making role of the Congress.

The Relative Prominence of the Four Legislatures[1]

Our analysis in Chapter 6 considered relations between legislatures and their executives in the development and making of legislation (policies that were subjected to legislative authorization). It focused on the experience of the four legislatures under six different governing parties. These were the Conservative and Labour parties, the Gaullist party (UDR), the CDU/CSU, and the Democratic and Republican parties. One conclusion which emerged from the discussion was that, compared to the executive, the Congress played a more prominent part than did the other legislatures as both an initiator and molder of legislation. Also, the Bundestag was more critical to the development of policies contained in legislation than the House of Commons or the National Assembly. The differences Chapter 6 disclosed from the most to the least prominent of the legislatures were rather substantial and deserve some explanation.

If the legislature is to be important as an arena of policy-making in its relations with the executive, legislators must be both willing and able to act independently of the executive. Looking at legislative-executive relations in an overall sense, rather than distinguishing policy areas, the following kinds of variables need to be stressed: the interplay of goals and situations that affect how legislators usually behave toward their party; legislators' role conceptions regarding the relationship that should prevail between the legislature and the executive; the powers over legislation that the legislature grants to its committees; and the legislature's informational resources in relation to those of the executive (or legislators' perceptions of those resources). The thrust of these variables is in the way they affect the motivation and/or the capacity of legislators to act independently of the executive. We will commence by addressing the variables as regards the overall involvement of the legislatures in the making of legislation. Then, after having also treated the other topics of the chapter, we will take up some questions our conclusions raise concerning traditional critiques of legislative action and inaction.

Party Unity and Legislators' Role Conceptions

Let us turn first to how legislators usually behave toward their parties. The primary base of support for the executive in the legislature is the executive's own legislative party. With this in mind, consider the following hypothesis: to the extent legislators from the executive's party give less priority to concerted action, the executive will normally have greater difficulty in controlling legislative decisions. Put in other words, a legislature's prominence in decision-making can be expected to increase as the usual level of voting unity among legislators of the executive party decreases.

A brief reference to the case study and aggregate evidence found in Chapter 6 is a useful point of departure. The evidence dealing with the Congress and the Bundestag serves to illustrate. Much of this evidence pointed to the importance of shifting and diverse coalitions across parties in the legislature, rather than politics that produced executive party unity, as a factor contributing to the influence these legislatures exerted in the process of making legislation.

The hypothesis suggests that the legislature is likely to be less prominent in the development of decision-making related to legislation where executive party members consistently give high priority to supporting their party and party unity is normally high. The reasoning behind the hypothesis is that such unity among executive party members may be partly a reflection of the resources available to the executive leadership to induce concerted action. Moreover, members' "voluntary" loyalty to party that helps underlie such unity (for example, party identification) might itself be transferable as a resource to the executive leadership. To the extent that these situations prevail, the executive leadership would usually be in a strong position to control the parameters of legislative compromise. This does not mean that compromise would not occur or that the going never gets rough. But, as Mackintosh put it for the British parties, "No one reaches the leadership of a party without an excellent sense of just what will and what will not arouse objections. At the same time, the leadership knows that, in the last resort, it can survive such objections."[2] Much the same conclusion has been found to characterize the broad pattern of relations between the executive leadership and the members of the Gaullist party.[3]

This observation brings us back to the point that the prominence of the legislature as a determinant of policy can be expected to increase as the normal level of voting unity among legislators of the executive party decreases. Of course, other variables are also pertinent and may affect the relationship just cited (as will be discussed below). But, in our cases this relationship prevailed. This can be seen by comparing the relative prominence of the legislature as observed in Chapter 6 to the relative level of voting cohesion of the governing party (or major governing party) in the legislature. Levels of party voting cohesion were examined in Chapter 4. Such a comparison shows that in the most prominent of the four legislatures, the Congress, the parties (whether executive or not) exhibited the lowest levels of party voting unity. The Bundestag under the CDU/CSU followed the Congress in decision-making influence and its members exhibited a moderate level of party voting unity. Finally, in the legislatures that were least prominent vis-à-vis the executive, the House of Commons, and the Assembly, members of the governing parties exhibited the highest levels of party voting unity.

In turn, this relationship suggests that factors affecting the priority legislators of the executive party normally give to supporting their party are factors that can simultaneously help to explain the relative influence of the four legislatures in the development and making of legislation. These factors were discussed in Chapter 4. We concentrated there both on dispositions or motivations lying behind the behavior of legislators and on the kinds of political structures in which the legislators were operating. Insofar as the dispositions are concerned, our discussion considered legislators' career ambitions (dealing both with the ambition to survive and with aspirations to advance to more preferred political offices), feelings of party identification, party role concepts, and policy attitudes. The analysis examined the extent to which actions based on these goals and purposes encouraged legislators to support or to deviate from their legislative party. In this connection, we brought certain elements of the political structure into account. Our focus was both on the criteria by which career rewards were allocated in the system and on the different and more constraining set of political circumstances legislators faced in a parliamentary as contrasted to a separation-of-powers system.

Let us briefly place these factors in the context of the perspective we are presenting here. Legislators of the executive party are understandably drawn strongly toward supporting their executive leadership as career advancement weighs heavily on loyalty to the leadership's policies; as members' survival may be jeopardized rather than served by supporting the opposition; as members feel a strong sense of identification with their party and feel that, as legislators, they should support their party; and as the costs to members of defeating their party are intensified because of the type of political system in which they operate (that is, the pressures that can arise under a parliamentary as contrasted to a separation-of-powers system).

Each of these dynamics of party cohesion, especially as they are combined, tend to motivate group-centered behavior and to orient behavior in support of the executive leadership rather than independent initiative. Consistent with this, the analysis of Chapter 4 showed that these motivating forces were present to only a comparatively limited degree in the American Congressional parties. They prevailed more so in the case of the CDU/CSU as a governing party in the Bundestag and to a comparatively high degree in the British Labour and Conservative and the French Gaullist parties.

We should stress that the variable referred to here is the usual level of party voting unity and the way legislators normally behave toward their party. Thus, when a higher level of unity than is typical occurs on a particular issue area in a governing party of normally moderate or low cohesion, it may be due to greater executive influence. However, such variations in unity within a party may also be due principally to factors affecting party voting that are largely independent of the executive and of executive influence. For example, research suggests that the influence of the President on members of his Congressional party has been no greater in regard to particular domestic policy areas where his Congressional party has exhibited abnormally high levels of voting unity.[4]

Nor do legislative parties of generally high cohesion necessarily have little influence vis-à-vis their executive leaderships. Much here might depend on a second variable, the legislators' conceptions of their role toward the executive. Such conceptions are important because the extent to which a legislator's loyalty and deference to his party can be transferred into an executive resource would presumably diminish if he were oriented toward a role conception that stressed the legislative party's independence from the executive. If members of a highly cohesive legislative party generally shared such a conception and if they both organized themselves separately from the executive and controlled a sizable number of legislative rewards, such circumstances might lead to a comparatively high level of legislative influence. It is thus possible that a governing party of generally high cohesion might also be one of high influence vis-à-vis its executive leadership.

But, again, this would probably require the presence of role conceptions strongly supportive of legislative independence from the executive. In the case of our three highly cohesive governing parties, the two major British parties and the Gaullist party, evidence already reviewed in Chapter 4 does not permit the conclusion that such a role conception prevailed among the parliamentary members.[5] Additional systematic and detailed interview research has been carried out on the Gaullist deputies. It supports the same conclusion.[6]

On the other hand, it is of note that the relatively greater independence members of the American Congressional parties and the CDU/CSU exhibited toward an executive of their party may well have been reinforced and strengthened by members' role conceptions about what the relationship between the legislature and the executive ought to be. Quantitative evidence on the content of these conceptions pertains mainly to members of the House of Representatives (however, there is little reason to believe that the orientations of members of the Senate have been much different). In their interviews with Representatives, Davidson and his coauthors found that about 55 percent of the members they questioned held a view (what the authors called a "model") stipulating that the Congress ought to be dominant relative to the executive in the making of public policy and a further 26 percent espoused a role that would place Congress and the executive in an equal position.[7] Views such as these likely reflect the tradition of separation of powers found in the Constitution. In any case, more than a few analysts have detected that the particular attitudes Congressmen hold about legislative autonomy and independence have influenced how independently they behaved in dealing with both the executive and other members of Congress.[8]

There is no systematic interview evidence with which to measure role attitudes among legislators in West Germany. However, other accounts leave little question that conceptions of legislative independence have been held by many of the members. As Loewenberg pointed out about feeling in the Bundestag, the traditional German conception is "still very much alive that the Government and Parliament are entirely separate entities."[9] Braunthal also found this attitude, which he described as one of "independence," among both committee chairmen and members of the parliamentary parties.[10] Attempting to emphasize the same point, Lehmbruch noted the strained relations that have involved the government and leading members from its parliamentary parties in making policy due partly to the latter's insistence on the independence of parliament.[11] Indeed, the attitudes to which we have referred are reflected in the scrupulous care the leaders and members of each governing party in the Bundestag have taken to assure the complete organizational independence of the parliamentary party from the government.

The party unity and role variables, when combined, appear to have been rather important in forming the broad pattern of relations that emerged between the legislature and the executive in the cases we considered. While the evidence suggests the relative prominence of the legislatures to have been accompanied by these factors, this was not so for some other variables. One such variable is the partisan governing context (whether the government and legislature were controlled by one party or by a mixture of parties). An obvious example is that even when one party in the United States controlled both the executive and the legislature, like the usual British experience, the Congress remained more critical to how legislation developed than did the House of Commons. Also, the Bundestag was more critical to decision-making than the National Assembly even though the partisan governing context was similar in each case. In each case a coalition of parties rather than a single party was necessary to form the government and the legislative majority. On the other hand, we observed that the partisan composition of the legislature did have some effect in the sense that *within* a system legislative influence vis-à-vis the executive often showed some increase as the size of the governing party in the legislature diminished (see page. 211 and p. 220).

In addition, the associations cited earlier prevailed regardless of the type of electoral system that was utilized. We refer here to whether the legislature and the executive were elected in separate popular elections or not. The existence of separate Congressional and Presidential elections has sometimes been considered to be a principal factor leading to Congressional independence. Citing the rather more consistent support given to government initiatives by the House of Commons majority as compared to the support the majority in Congress has given Presidential initiatives, Koenig remarked: "The President has no dependable way, as the British Prime Minister does, to command the legislature's support."[12] An important reason for this, Koenig argued, is that since "the method of electing the President differs from the method of electing Congressmen, their constituencies and therefore their concerns and viewpoints differ."[13]

It may be true that Presidential and Congressional constituencies differ, but Koenig's hypothesis runs counter to some important evidence. For example, as in the United States the French Assembly has been elected separately (even in different years) from the French President. Even so, the Assembly's relationship with the executive has been more akin to that of the British Commons and its executive than to that of Congress and the Presidency. Nor does Koenig's hypothesis tell us why German Chancellors, such as Adenauer, encountered a greater level of effective challenge from within their own legislative party than British Prime Ministers have ordinarily faced, despite the absence of separate elections in both systems.

Having said this, there still remain other factors to be considered. The variables utilized thus far have been rooted mainly in legislators' motivations to act with or to act independently of the executive. They have not taken into account the members' *ability* to act independently and the subsequent effect that this ability can have on their motivation to do so. Indeed, it is sometimes thought that differences in legislative influence have stemmed primarily from differences in the capacity legislatures afforded their members to undertake independent action. We would like to concentrate here on two factors that are thought to be important in this regard—the strength of the legislative committee system and the policy-related informational resources available to legislators as they interact with the executive.

The committee system: fragmentation of power within the legislature

The powers and prerogatives given to standing legislative committees (aside from the policy expertise that committees may bring about, which will be treated separately in the next section) are frequently cited as a principal factor affecting the influence of legislatures vis-à-vis the executive in the process of making legislation. It is true that standing committees with the greatest powers to deal with legislation are found in the two most prominent legislatures we considered, the Congress and the Bundestag. For example, both legislatures provided that their committees review bills before floor consideration and that floor consideration be based on the committee draft rather than the executive draft. The former of these powers was not normally given to committees in the House of Commons, and the latter of the powers was not afforded committees in the French Assembly.[14]

The power given to the standing committees can enable legislators to act toward the executive in ways that they otherwise could not. The smaller, more manageable, size of committees facilitates speedy, detailed, and effective challenge. Beyond this, it is often politically easier for executive party members to act against the executive in a standing committee than on the floor. For example, members of the governing party in the Bundestag have been able to defeat the government with less risk in committee than on the floor.

But the question is more complicated than this suggests. The fact that government policy initiatives have been undercut and greatly altered in Bundestag committees over the government's objections is probably also related to other factors that affect legislators' behavior towards their party and the executive. We suggested in the case of the CDU/CSU that these factors joined to lay a somewhat greater basis for legislators' independence from executive leadership than has been so for the major British and French parliamentary parties we examined. As a consequence, the government has likely faced greater political necessity to make significant compromises and bargains, not only in the Bundestag committees but also elsewhere, as part of the process of developing and ensuring sufficient legislative support for a bill before it reached the floor. Shaw and Lees' examination of the committee system in the Bundestag and several other legislatures suggests the same conclusion. They found that the influence of the committee systems they examined was tied not simply to the kinds of powers and prerogatives granted to the committees but also to the degree to which members of the legislative majority could be subjected to effective party control.[15]

We can discuss this consideration in greater detail by examining the experience of the Congress. Perhaps the most vocal criticism of the powers and operation of legislative committees has been directed against Congressional committees, which have been accused of using their considerable prerogatives to frustrate and undermine not only Presidential leadership but also potential majorities on the floor.

There is little dispute that Congressional committees have held up, greatly altered, or entirely scuttled various Presidential initiatives, including initiatives of major importance, and evidence to this effect was presented in Chapter 6. At the same time, if Congressional committees have successfully challenged and blocked Presidential policies, it is also evident that many other factors have been at play. First, the President's position has not necessarily had smooth sailing on the floors of Congress, outside the committee rooms. The fact that the President has not even been able to count on the support of members of his own party on the floor is amply illustrated by voting records on roll calls upon which the President took a stand. On floor votes during 1967-68, the last two years of the Johnson administration, the average opposition score for Democratic members of the Senate against Johnson's position was 25, and in the House was 18, as compared to average support scores of 53 and 67 respectively. In 1971-72, the average opposition score for Republican members of the Senate and the House against President Nixon was 20. The average support scores were 65 and 69, respectively.[16] While it is true that members of the President's own party in Congress have supported the President more than they opposed him and that he has usually received more support from his party members than from the opposition party, it is also true that opposition to him from within his own Congressional parties on floor roll calls has not been insubstantial. About one out of every four votes cast on the floor by a member of the Presidential party during the four years reported above was in opposition to the stand advocated by the President.[17]

Opposition that has arisen on the floor has not been just idle. It can and has defeated Presidents' policies. As we observed in Chapter 6, the President's position has been defeated on the floor on an average of about one out of every four roll call votes. The "bipartisan" Conservative Coalition has been a particular thorn in a Democratic President's side. From 1961 to 1968, for instance, this coalition formed on the floor in opposition to the President on approximately 20 percent of all roll calls upon which the President took a stand. Although the Democrats controlled the Presidency and had solid majorities in both houses of Congress, the Conservative Coalition was successful in getting Congressional passage of its own position over the objections of the President on approximately 50 percent of these roll call votes.

The Conservative Coalition only occasionally formed against President Nixon. Other alignments, some composed primarily of liberals from both parties and others consisting of both liberals and conservatives, were more troublesome. Three highly publicized instances were the major Presidential defeats on the SST and the nominations of Haynsworth and Carswell to the Supreme Court. Some other examples were the President's inability to get his entire ABM program intact through Congress, Congressional adoption of substantially greater financial outlays for water conservation than Nixon advocated, and Congressional passage of the War Powers Act, extension of the Hill-Burton Act, and expansion of the jobs services program.

With these points about floor action on Presidential policies in mind, it is important to note other evidence suggesting that the fate of major executive sponsored legislation in committee may well reflect the depth of support for the legislation or bill on the floor. This point is particularly relevant in regard to politics in the House, for research has found that partly because of the larger size of the House, both committees and their chairmen have been somewhat more consequential to decision-making there than in the Senate.[18]

One of the committees that has been most criticized in the past for opposing and blocking executive-sponsored bills is the House Rules Committee, yet a study of legislation proposed during the Kennedy and Johnson administrations has shown that the House Rules Committee actually blocked very few bills that were of priority to the President.[19] Another analyst, Lewis Froman, found that the House Rules Committee opposed, in all, about a dozen bills per Congress.[20] And, he observed, "for the most part they are bills which have only lukewarm support. In very few cases are they bills which the leadership strongly supports."[21]

This suggests that it has not only been committee preferences but also the preferences of Congressional leaders and the support leaders were or were not able to draw from among the members of the House that have often been behind the success of the Rules Committee when it did effectively block particular bills. As Froman went on to say:

Even though the Committee on Rules is usually cooperative, there are occasions (perhaps three or four times a year) when the Committee refuses to grant a rule, delays hearings, or in some other way harasses the leadership. A battle will often ensue with the outcome dependent upon the extent and intensity of support which the leadership can assert. However, it is rarely clear, when the Rules Committee is successful in blocking further action on a piece of legislation, whether the bill would have passed on the floor of the House, even with strong leadership support.[22]

These observations may apply to other committees as well. As examples, let us take the actions of the House Ways and Means Committee on two major Presidential requests, medicare and the Johnson tax surcharge. Until 1965, despite Democratic control of both the Presidency and Congress after 1960, passage of medicare, which was being held by Ways and Means, would have been far from certain on the House floor in any case.[23] A reason for this is that the bloc of Representatives supporting the bill was fairly evenly balanced by the bloc of Representatives who could not be won over to the bill. As Manley points out, "This gave disproportionate importance to a relatively small number of votes that many people felt would be affected by the Chairman's [Wilbur Mills] position."[24] When the situation changed with the election in 1964 of an enlarged liberal contingent in the House, "the Committee, at Mills' behest, made the seemingly incongruous decision to report a bill much more liberal and costly than the one it had rejected for many years. In fact, the decision was by no means incongruous given the new liberal majority in the House. . . ."[25]

Similarly, evidence suggests that the Ways and Means' position on President Johnson's tax increase (surcharge) proposal, rather than Johnson's position, would have been sustained on the floor of the House despite Johnson's insistence on the necessity for the surcharge and the fact that a majority of his party controlled the House.[26] According to Pierce, "During the month of February, the administration and the Ways and Means Committee remained deadlocked on the tax proposal. Mills had become convinced that a tax increase was needed, and would have reported the bill immediately if he had thought it would pass. He realized, however, according to a member of the Ways and Means Committee, that the only way to get a bill through the House was to tie it to a large expenditure cut."[27] Mills' perception was supported by the fate of an Appropriations Committee proposal to reduce appropriations by around $2 billion, which was defeated on the floor of the House because it was felt to be too small a reduction. In its place, the House adopted a proposal to reduce appropriations by about $6 billion.

Indeed, as a rule a committee's overall influence and prestige in the House has apparently rested partly on its willingness to act within broad parameters set by opinion on the floor. Thus, Fenno's comparative analysis of six House committees found the most influential committees in the House to be those whose members were motivated to anticipate and willing to accommodate the major coalitions and individual member interests found on the floor.[28] Also, Kingdon's examination of Congressional voting found that, especially on the more visible issues, committees usually needed to act within boundaries set by sentiment in the House if they were to maximize their own influence.[29]

Similarly, it is the rare committee chairman who has been able to make a practice of running roughshod over his committee. Most committee chairmen have been subjected to constraints set by other committee members as well as by the wider House. During the 1960s and early 1970s, Mills was one of the most influential of committee chairmen. However, research on Ways and Means revealed that Mills' influence over his committee was in no small part based on his responsiveness to other committee members. Manley observed:

Contrary to the impression one sometimes receives from newspaper stories about the "all-powerful" Chairman Mills, he is perhaps as responsive to the Committee as the Committee is to him. Great influence with the members he no doubt has, but it is influence earned by the way he approaches his job and develops its potential. Ways and Means is highly centralized under Mills, but the Committee's policy decisions emerge from an exhaustive—and *collegial*—process. The decisions of the Committee are shaped and articulated by Mills, but if his word comes close to being law in the Committee, it is because he has listened well to the words of others. . .[30]

Fenno's comparison of House committees reached somewhat the same conclusion. As pointed out in Chapter 2, of the six committees Fenno examined, he found that only one of the chairmen operated in a manner contrary to the strategy and goals of a decided majority of the committee members. And, this chairman (Tom Murray of the Post Office Committee) eventually found himself unable to control his committee.[31]

Despite this, the many prerogatives given to the standing committees and their chairmen relating to recommending, reformulating, and blocking legislation have enabled leadership centers to form in Congress that have influenced the substance of Congressional action. The presence of a strong committee system in Congress has had a tangible effect on relations between Congress and the President. Devolvement of powers to committees has both contributed to Congressional initiative and subjected Presidential leadership to more effective challenge in Congress. As noted in Chapter 6, fragmentation of power in Congress has frequently had the positive attribute of enabling new ideas and initiatives to gain a considered hearing and become visible more quickly than occurred within the Presidency. In this sense, it is pertinent that decentralization of power within committees, to subcommittees, has been found to enhance further the vitality of Congress as a successful initiator of legislation.[32] The committee system has also afforded Congress greater capability effectively to challenge Presidential initiatives. As Wildavsky observed regarding Congressional influence in the budgetary process, "The power of Congress to control budgetary decisions depends on the power of its appropriations committees. For no large assembly of men can develop the. . .self-direction, cohesiveness, and dispatch which are necessary to do the large volume of budgetary business."[33]

Yet, as our earlier commentary suggests, the underpinning of a strong legislature in its relations with the executive also lies in the willingness and the desire of members of the entire house to act independently of the executive, including an executive of their own party. This point was made at the outset for committees in the Bundestag. In the case of Congress, we have suggested that committees often operate within some element of Congressional opinion and likely response, particularly where major issues are concerned. While committees have helped to mold Congressional sentiment, a growing body of research indicates they have also been influenced by this sentiment and that a committee's own influence has depended on its willingness to anticipate and accommodate itself to such sentiment. In addition to presenting the results of this research, we offered several examples to illustrate how the possibilities that major executive-sponsored proposals might in any case have rough sailing on the floors of Congress, and might be substantially amended or defeated there, either provided an environment conducive to successful committee action that opposed the President or in fact helped influence the decisions that the committees made.[34]

Our discussion of committee politics has had the purpose of fixing upon the relevance of a powerful committee system to legislative influence in relations with the executive. It is pertinent that the two legislatures we examined with the most powerful committee systems were also the legislatures most central to the development of policy decisions in their relations with the executive. On the other hand, while the evidence indicates these committee systems facilitated effective legislative involvement, it equally suggests that other forces apart from the committee system also lay behind the independence and involvement of the two legislatures. Concerning these cases, we would argue that among the other forces that promoted such independence and involvement, the party and role factors discussed at the outset of this chapter would be important elements.

Informational capacity

In addition to considering the effect of the legislative powers that are given to the committee system, we also need to consider the extent to which policy-related informational resources have been available to legislators as they interacted with the executive in the policy process. This, too, may be partly a function of the committee system.

The ability to obtain, handle, and coordinate "technical" information upon which policies can be developed and defended is thought to be one of the determinants of influence in the legislative process. An assumption behind this argument, with which we basically agree, is that the justification of policy through reference to information and expertise is important to many legislators and is a disposition that affects their behavior. It may be that legislators feel they ought to act in ways that they can justify to themselves, both in the present and in the future. Or, justification may be a means to another end, such as not wanting to look foolish to their colleagues or their constituents.

Until the middle of the nineteenth century, problems requiring legislation were relatively few, and they were relatively simple. Since then, there has been a great change in the political setting, both domestically and internationally. The technological advances of expanding industrial societies and the increasing urban densities of populations have created new problems and demands for more and broader government activities. The enlarged scope of government and the growing complexity of problems has called for coordinated, technical decision-making. As problems proliferate, both the amount and complexity of relevant knowledge required to solve problems increase radically, as does the perceived need to coordinate information across policy areas. In commenting on executive-legislative relations in the United States, Robinson notes that a significant factor behind executive influence relative to the legislature is the character of information and intelligence in modern policy making.[35]

With the numbers of its personnel, its continuous involvement in the application of policy, and its specialized and hierarchically coordinated structures, the executive is frequently perceived to be superior to the legislature in the amount of information it can bring to bear in formulating proposals, especially where large amounts of data are available. According to Robinson, for example, it has been the executive more than the legislature that has "developed resources for the accumulation of large amounts of factual data about policy problems."[36]

Legislative attempts at influence can meet particular difficulty in areas where the executive has come to assume a heavily dominant position in the collection and aggregation of information. For here an additional source of power accrues to the executive through its influence over how the information will be used and disseminated. As Eidenberg and Morey put it: "The network of transactions that characterize the policy process is profoundly influenced by the choice of what is to be transmitted."[37] To the extent that this occurs, the executive can firmly take the initiative and control the offense. The burden of proof is on the legislature.

In dealing with this problem, most legislatures have provided some means for developing expertise among their members. These means include fostering policy specialization (generally through the standing committee system or legislative party committees), establishing legislative research staffs, and gaining information from a wide variety of interested persons and groups through hearings or other contacts.

When legislators are considered to have a high level of expertise, they can use it to great effect, for it is relevent to influence in the legislature. Members in the Bundestag, for example, are quite likely to support recommendations of the experts in their own parliamentary party. As Loewenberg put it, members are "ordinarily...hesitant to challenge their experts, and particularly reluctant to vote down in public what these have negotiated in private."[38] Matthews and Stimson noted the importance of expertise in Congress: "When the Congressman is confronted with the necessity of casting a roll call vote on a complex issue about which he knows very little, he searches for cues provided by trusted colleagues who—because of their formal position in the legislature or policy specialization—have more information than he does and with whom he would probably agree if he had the time and information to make an independent decision."[39] Seeking guidance in a particular policy area, Congressmen tend to look to specialists from their own party who are on the appropriate committee, taking cues "from the experts whose ideology they usually support" or from "the specialist whose district interests (are) similar to the member's own."[40]

Both policy problems and the information relating to them are usually subject to being viewed differently from different perspectives. As the above observations suggest, a legislator's expertise can be pertinent to influencing his colleagues, although whom he influences and who looks to him are frequently conditioned by other concerns relevant to his colleagues. Among the concerns that may weigh heavily are sharing a similar party, policy outlook, and problems of political survival.[41]

As a legislator's expertise can be important to his relations with his colleagues, so it can help to shape relations between legislators and the executive. By influencing the behavior of other legislators, experts, in turn, can affect the level of support in the legislature that the executive will be able to develop for its own position. Furthermore, expertise can serve legislators well when dealing directly with the executive. For example, the House Ways and Means Committee has been noted for its expertise and has been assisted, according to Manley, "by a tax staff that is equal to the expertise of the Treasury Department."[42] As one committee member observed of relations between this informed committee and executive personnel: "They sit in there with us and sometimes we kick their teeth in. Time and time again we kick their teeth in. . . . On the tax bill they had to just sit there and recede from their position, then help us to write what we wanted."[43] Or, to offer a European example, it is instructive to consider the success achieved in the French Assembly by proponents of low-cost housing. In essence, the proponents got the government to reverse its policy and to transfer $15 million in funding for the construction of new towns to the construction of low-cost housing instead. The proponents were led by M. Royer, who had become an expert in the area by virtue of his own extensive investigations, coupled with his considerable experience with these matters as a mayor. According to Lord, Royer's success in altering the government's policy resulted primarily from his exceptional expertise, which had reached such a level that he was able to challenge the government effectively on its own ground.[44]

Nevertheless, while legislators are capable of developing expertise, and more than a few do so, the level of perceived expertise at the hands of the executive and its personnel is a factor that can also place legislators at a disadvantage. This can be true even in the case of Congress, which has provided the greatest means for its members to gain access to information.

The experience of members of the House Appropriations Committee can serve to illustrate both the potential that Congressional expertise has and the problems members face as a consequence of the need for information upon which to make policy judgments. In dealing with the budget, members of the Appropriations Committee have been aided by a permanent professional and temporary investigations staff numbering about seventy staff personnel. Members have also had available testimony given by hundreds of witnesses each year, their own personal inspections of agencies and bureaus, and knowledge gained through specialization on the committee. Thus, many members of the committee, especially the more senior members, have come to possess a high level of expertise in the substantive budgetary areas for which they are responsible. They, too, are aware of this and are respected for their expertise.[45] Partly as a consequence, the committee has regularly been willing to make independent judgments of executive budget requests and, as observed in Chapter 7, has altered the funding of about one-quarter of the executive's appropriations bills by more than 20 percent.[46]

Despite this, Appropriations members often perceive themselves to be at some informational disadvantage when dealing with specialist bureaucrats. Whereas individual Congressmen and members of the committee staff must cover numerous agencies, even at the Appropriations subcommittee level, individual bureaucrats spend much of their time on matters pertaining to their own agency. Fenno's research on the Appropriations Committee, based on in-depth interviewing as well as other techniques, led him to observe: "A committee member's self-confidence is weakened . . . by the perception that, relatively, he knows a great deal less about the agencies for which he appropriates than do agency officials themselves."[47] He went on to say that, "The committee's sense of information inferiority . . . is sufficiently widespread so that agency officials are well advised when they warn their witnesses not to talk down to the committee."[48]

Especially notable is the effect such considerations can have on the legislature's involvement in the initiation of policy. This is suggested not only by budgetary policy, an area of vast information where Congress has often sought administration initiative, but also by examination of other policy areas. For example, David Price found from his analysis of the role of the Senate in the development of fourteen legislative acts that ordinarily certain conditions involving information capacity needed to be met if the Senate (as contrasted to the executive and administration) was to become a central arena in which policy origination and formulation occurred. In his fourteen case studies, Price observed that the involvement of Senate members who wished to develop policy initiatives was often motivated by their career needs or policy outlooks. However, successful involvement usually also depended on whether the members, especially through their committee, had staffing available to them that was both willing to become competent in the area and interested in policy initiation. When this combination did not occur, the Senate generally did not become a central arena of policy initiation. Furthermore, the advantage of the executive in the information-gathering process of the policy-initiation stage tended to increase, and to become almost monopolistic, as the scale of available data in the policy area was large and its collection and analysis were necessary for the development of legislative initiatives.[49]

At the same time, it is important to remember that the staffing and other informational resources afforded members of Congress, although uneven, have not been insubstantial. In this regard, Price found that the informational resources available to members of Congress were sufficient to enable those otherwise motivated to play a central and sometimes dominant part in the initiation of about 40 percent of the legislation he considered. Additional evidence contained in Chapter 6 found that Congressional activity has remained integral to the initiation of successfully adopted legislation in numerous policy areas and that its involvement relative to the executive has been greater than for any of the European legislatures in relation to their executives. This was particularly so in comparison to the House of Commons and the Fifth Republic Assembly.

With this in mind, it is pertinent that the resources and opportunities given to members of Congress to develop policy-related expertise have been markedly greater than those made available to the European legislators. For example, let us look at the House of Commons and the Assembly. In neither of the two legislatures has the standing committee system on legislation fostered policy-related specialization among the members to the extent that the Congressional committee system has (see Chapter 2). In this respect the Assembly of the Fifth Republic has also differed from that of the Fourth Republic. Moreover, the professional research staffs available to Congressional committees on legislation have not been matched in either of the legislatures. While the permanent staff attached to a typical Congressional committee is around thirteen professional personnel in the House and twenty in the Senate, the average staff assigned to committees on legislation in the French Assembly is about four, and in the case of the standing legislative committees of the House of Commons it is only one or two. Nor have the individual members of the two European legislatures been given anything like the staff made available to individual members of Congress. Indeed, even now few individual parliamentarians have more than one secretarial assistant. Finally, the additional professional staff available to individual members of Congress through the Congressional Research Service has been approximately ten times greater than that regularly available to members of the Commons or the Assembly through parliamentary parties or the library or research divisions found in their legislatures. Given the relevance evidence has found expertise and information resources to have, it is a reasonable supposition that the more limited opportunities to gain expertise in the Commons and the Assembly has contributed to the degree individual legislators (especially those of the governing party) have looked and deferred to the executive in the process of making legislation.[50] Particularly significant is the effect such limited opportunities to develop expertise have likely had on the extent to which legislators could serve effectively, alongside the executive, as policy formulators during the initiation stages of the decision-making process.

Most of the staffing problems to which we have referred have also characterized the Bundestag. Yet, as Chapter 2 showed, the committee system in the Bundestag has both routinized and encouraged the development of members' own policy-related specialization on legislation to a greater extent than has the committee system in either the House of Commons or the Assembly. Furthermore, participation of deputies from the governing party in the formulation and initiation of governmental legislation has been encouraged by forming ad hoc working groups (composed of several deputies) which concentrated on particular pieces of legislation from their inception and which utilized staff made available through the parliamentary party. Where they deemed it necessary, the Bundestag parliamentary parties have also been able to reinforce expertise in various areas within their ranks through the use of list nominations.[51]

As all of this suggests, legislators have not been unaware of the importance of informational factors for influence in the policy process. Indeed, the creation of greater informational resources has frequently been a major feature of postwar legislative reforms. Certainly the most significant example is the Congressional Legislative Reorganization Act of 1946, which laid the foundation for more rationalized policy specialization in Congress and for the genesis of far greater research staffing. More recently, in 1974, the Congress adopted a major reorganization of its budgetary process, two features of which involved enlarging the professional staff available to Congress on budgetary matters and developing new mechanisms for coordinating overall appropriations and revenues. The development of greater informational capacity has been an integral feature of recent reforms undertaken by the other legislatures as well. Examples include the major Bundestag reforms of 1969 which provided over one hundred additional staff officials to the Bundestag committees and the partially successful push for the establishment of more specialized supervisory committees in the House of Commons during the middle and latter 1960s.

Nevertheless, it is fair to say that legislatures, including the Congress, have also been sluggish in their responses to the problems of inadequate informational capacity. The reforms they have undertaken frequently have not met the problem fully head on. Staffing remains insufficient, particularly in the European legislatures, and Congressional reforms have yet to make more than minimal use of computers and other kinds of sophisticated machinery that are necessary resources for storing, aggregating, and analyzing large amounts of policy-related information.

Our discussion thus far has concentrated on a series of variables and their association with how prominent we earlier found the four legislatures to be as initiators and molders of legislation. Before continuing, let us briefly summarize the variables. Some of the variables focused on legislators' motivations to act independently of the executive. One of these, inversely related to the legislature's overall prominence, was the priority legislators of the executive party normally gave to supporting their party. In turn, this association directed our attention to the goals and situations that affected the depth of legislators' ties with their party (discussed more fully in Chapter 4) as factors that could also influence how legislators behaved toward the executive. Combined with these party-related factors, legislators' role orientations also appeared to be of some importance. We refer here to legislators' conceptions about the proper relationship between the legislature and the executive and particularly how independent the legislature ought to be.

Other variables associated with the prominence of the four legislatures centered on the capacity the situation or setting afforded legislators to act independently of the executive. One variable considered here was the power which the legislature delegated to its committee system. A second pertinent variable was the informational resources and structured opportunities to gain expertise which the legislature provided its individual members.

Foreign and Domestic Policies

The preceding discussion, which concerned relations between the legislatures and their executives in terms of general or overall patterns, did not distinguish between the kinds of policy decisions involved. The legislature may be more influential in one policy field, less influential in another.

Perhaps the most poignant example of this is the contrast between domestic and foreign and defense policy issues.[52] In Chapter 6 we observed that in each of the four systems the impact of the legislature has generally been greater on decisions relating to domestic policy than on decisions relating to foreign and defense policy. The evidence referred not simply to crisis types of situations or to decisions over which legislative assent was not required, but to the field of foreign and defense policy generally.

Moreover, we recognize that there may be exceptions in the sense, for example, that the legislature may intervene on certain kinds of foreign and defense policy decisions more than on others. We will take note and discuss some exceptions later in this section. For now, when we speak of foreign policy as compared to domestic policy, we are referring to tendencies in each area rather than to uniformities.

Our description of foreign and defense policy in Chapter 6 pointed out that the relative formal and traditional powers of the four legislatures vis-à-vis the executive have as a whole been weaker in this area of policy than in most areas of domestic policy. In this sense, none of the legislatures has had the potential capacity to control or direct foreign policies, or to become directly involved in the bargaining process, to the degree that this potential has been present in most areas of domestic policy.

Yet the formal and traditional powers of the legislatures in the area of foreign and defense policy remained quite considerable. This factor alone probably has not been responsible for the deference the legislatures generally have shown the executive. Other factors affecting either the desire and willingness of legislators or their capacity to act independently of the executive need also to be taken into account. As the journalist I. F. Stone noted regarding Congressional involvement in foreign policy: "It is the will that has been lacking in the past. . . .None of the [reforms], if enacted, will make much of a difference if Congress is as supine as it has been in the past."[53]

On the whole, most of the factors that affect the desire or capacity of legislators to act independently of the executive have worked to orient legislators more to the executive in foreign and defense policy decisions than in domestic policy decisions. When we compared the legislatures in the previous section, we argued that an understanding of executive influence needed to consider the priority legislators of the executive party gave to supporting their party and how this related them to the executive. We noted that variation in these priorities from one issue area to another might also reflect changes in executive influence, though this would likely differ across issues. With this in mind, let us begin with the point that the unity of most of the governing legislative parties we considered has generally been greater in regard to foreign policy than domestic policy. In Chapter 6 we observed this to be true for the Gaullists. We also observed that the CDU/CSU acted with a higher level of unity on foreign policy matters throughout most years when it was the governing party. During periods when the Conservatives formed the government, too, it was domestic policy issues that provided the large majority of cases of significant backbench rebellion in the House of Commons.[54]

The voting unity of the Presidential party in Congress has ordinarily been higher on foreign than domestic policy issues, as well. At the same time, bipartisan support for the President's foreign policy has been more characteristic in the Congress than in the European parliaments. Even so, research has found that the President's influence, in terms of shifting or altering members' basic orientations regarding foreign policy, has mainly been effective with members of his own party in Congress rather than with members of the opposition parties.[55]

Given the differences just cited, what variables might help to explain these differences? Why has party support been greater in the area of foreign policy and how might this be tied to executive influence? In light of our discussion earlier in this chapter and in Chapter 4, we need to look at legislators' goals to see how these relate them to their party and to the executive. One relevant consideration in this regard has to do with legislators' career survival. In most cases this centers on relations between the legislator and his constituency and the effect these relations can have on his behavior toward his party and the executive. The relationship may be somewhat different on foreign than on domestic policy issues. For example, Alfred Grosser once noted: "The legislator must think about his reelection. Now, that is a function essentially of the positions he takes on domestic policies and particularly those which directly affect his district."[56] Although Grosser was referring to the Fourth Republic Assembly, research on the relationships between public opinion at the district level and the behavior of Congressmen during the latter 1950s suggests that this observation may be equally valid for the United States.[57] The positive relationships that were found were confined almost completely to domestic policy issues. There were fewer significant relationships between legislators' behavior and constituent opinion on foreign policy. Moreover, there has tended to be lesser interest group activity on foreign policy than on domestic policy issues. As Wildavsky observed: "In foreign policy matters the interest group structure is weak, unstable, thin rather than dense. In many matters affecting Africa and Asia, for example, it is hard to think of well-known interest groups."[58] A recent exception here has been American involvement in Southeast Asia since the middle 1960s. This exception will be explored in greater detail later in this section.

Although not true for every foreign policy issue, in general the likelihood is that constituent opinion and interest group activity have constrained American legislators less frequently on foreign than on domestic issues. One important result is that legislators have had somewhat greater freedom to look elsewhere for cues. One of the prime sources for cues, particularly for members of the Presidential party and members from marginal seats,[59] became the executive.

A number of factors can help to account for this tendency among members of the Presidential party. One of these, although likely a modest one, should be mentioned at this juncture. It has to do with the politics of Presidential elections.

The Presidency is, of course, a political office prized by both parties. Although foreign and defense policies usually have not been overly important in Presidential elections, they have had a tendency to be more important in Presidential elections than in Congressional elections. In addition, until recently, the President has shown substantial ability to mold public opinion in the short run favorably to his foreign policies. This may have to do with the majesty of the Presidential office being connected particularly to foreign policy or to citizens' impulses to "rally around the flag." Perhaps it is also due to the relative absence of interest group activity in foreign policy. In any case, public opinion surveys indicate that dramatic foreign policy moves by the President, no matter how unsuccessful they were (even in the case of the Bay of Pigs and throughout much of our involvement in Vietnam and Cambodia) almost always had the effect of creating greater public support for the President.[60]

With this in mind, foreign policy is an area in which the President may have been peculiarly able to gain an advantage over potential opposition party candidates. Also, it is an area where legislators have typically had greater freedom from constituency and interest group pressures. It is plausible that the President's advantage in the foreign policy area combined with both the legislators' own greater freedom of action and their partisan desires to retain the Presidency have been among the factors helping to generate greater support for the President's foreign policy initiatives, particularly from among members in his own Congressional party.

At this point, let us shift our attention briefly to the European systems. We suggested that members of the Presidential party in Congress have had somewhat greater freedom to look to executive cues on foreign policy partly because they have been less constrained by constituency and interest group demands on foreign than on domestic issues. A rather different set of circumstances has apparently faced parliamentarians in the European parties we considered. Here there has been the tendency for members to face constituency demands (generally from the party association) that carried a potential to sanction and punish those who deviated from the national party leadership on controversial foreign policy issues. Thus, large scale challenges to legislators' renominations by local party activists, or local activists working in collaboration with the national leadership, have occurred disproportionately against those who defied the national leadership in the foreign and defense policy area.

Certainly the leading cases of sanctions in the Gaullist party, perhaps even more effective because they occurred rather early in the development of the UNR, involved members who rebelled on the Algerian issue. The national leadership with the aid of local forces successfully terminated the political careers of many of the dissidents.[62] Similarly, almost all of the large-scale renomination challenges within the Conservative party since 1945 have involved MPs who rebelled on matters of foreign policy. This has been particularly so regarding members who, in rebelling, supported foreign policies advocated by the opposition. Thus, five "leftist" Conservative backbenchers were denied renomination by their local associations in the 1950s for their rebellion against the party leadership on the Suez issue.[63] The renominations of a further thirty-one "leftist" backbenchers were challenged after they rebelled on the Rhodesia issue.[64] In the CDU/CSU, too, the cases we found of renomination denials on grounds of members' deviation from the party leadership when it formed the government were also disproportionately in the area of foreign and defense policy.

As we indicated in Chapter 6, executives in each of the countries, including the United States, have also tended to give priority to matters of foreign and defense policy.[65] This, in itself, may have served to intensify support for the executive from its legislative party members, based on such feelings as party loyalty and identification.[66] Furthermore, the priority executives have given to foreign policy made it likely that the executive would use its resources disporportionately on behalf of its foreign policy aims. For example, to the extent that the executive had control over the career advancement of its legislative party members, it could use this resource as a means of rewarding members who were regularly supportive of its foreign policy and punishing those who were not. Thus, Adenauer rarely promoted to ministerial office those members who had opposed his foreign policies (see Chapter 6). On the other hand, some notable deviants on his domestic policies did receive ministerial appointments. Vital made the same point about the career advancement of British MPs when he observed that "a rebel against foreign policy is, if anything, in a more difficult situation than a rebel against domestic policy."[67]

The considerations mentioned thus far have had the potential either to tie legislators of the governing party somewhat more closely to the executive leadership or to give such legislators greater freedom to follow the executive. Of the parties we considered, only in cases where there have been rather deep and continuing ideological divisions over foreign policy among the legislative party members, as in the Parliamentary Labour Party,[68] has rebellion been a feature as common to the area of foreign policy as to the area of domestic policy. And here, with a few important exceptions, rebellions have generally tended to be further to the left of the party rather than in support of Conservative policy.

Given what we said earlier, however, the factors so far cited should take effect especially as they combine with and are reinforced by other factors. One of these is the legislators' conceptions of what their role ought to be in relationship to the executive. It is relevant that legislators may define their own role vis-à-vis the executive differently in the area of foreign policy than they do on domestic policy matters.

Discussion of this factor is particularly pertinent in the context of legislatures where the view is held that the legislature ought normally to be rather independent of the executive. Let us take Congress as a case. One reason why Congress has not influenced foreign policy to the same extent as domestic policy may be that many Congressmen feel that the Congress should not play a primary role in this policy area. Thus, Senator Sparkman, chairman of the Foreign Relations Committee, has said that "It is the constitutional duty of the President to direct foreign relations and Congress has not a great deal to do with activating foreign policy."[69] Robinson observes that there has been "a strongly held and widely accepted perspective prevailing in Congress that the executive deserves and possesses primacy in foreign policy."[70]

Supporting this view, Wildavsky found that Congressmen "do not think it is their job to determine the nation's defense policies."[71] This orientation prevailed even in places from which one would normally anticipate Congressional leadership to come. Wildavsky went on to observe that "extensive interviews with members of the Senate Armed Services Committee, who might be expected to want a voice in defense policy, reveal that they do not desire that men like themselves run the nation's defense establishment."[72] One wonders how much this sentiment has owed to the record the Congress compiled in the foreign policy area, rejecting first the League of Nations and then alliance against Hitler (both repeatedly against the counsel of the President), in the period between the two world wars.

The combination of various factors brought forth to this point, as applied to Presidential influence in Congress in the area of foreign policy, has been commented upon and given further support by way of roll call voting research. Concluding his elaborate voting analysis, Clausen observed:

Presidential influence [in Congress] is a major force on the international involvement dimension for two reasons. First, this is an area in which the president is *expected* to provide leadership; and, second, foreign policy has implications sufficiently removed from the cognitive experience of the citizen that congressmen are not tightly constrained by perceptions of constituency demands. Therefore, a congressman may shift about a bit in response to executive requests without risking his political investment.[73]

Of course, for ideological and other reasons[74] in none of the legislatures do all members of the executive's party, let alone of the opposition party, support the lines of policy the executive may wish to pursue. However, when legislators desire to undertake initiatives of their own in the area of foreign policy, or to challenge executive initiatives, they frequently run into problems of capacity and the subsequent effect limited capacity can have on motivation. Limited capacity may sometimes have to do with the narrower powers of the legislature on certain foreign policy actions, a characteristic each of the legislatures has shared.

There are also other limitations that have perhaps been even more important. Compare the resources of the legislature and the executive regarding information and expertise in the field of foreign policy and domestic policy. A significant advantage the executive has had when dealing with foreign policy, even more so than in domestic policy, is access to information. Foreign policy decisions not only demand careful, coordinated, and overall planning with the maximum of information gathered, sorted, and processed, but they also involve enormous amounts of information. The interrelationship of events in the international sphere make even seemingly minor problems worthy of considerable attention. It is thus pertinent that in some foreign policy areas the executive has held a virtual monopoly on information and that, generally, both the legislature and the public (including interest groups) have been more dependent upon the executive for information on foreign policy than on domestic policy. Through its continuous involvement in foreign policy, resulting especially from direct participation in negotiations, the executive has possessed *firsthand* information dealing with the bargaining attitudes of other nations which the legislature and the public have not had. As Vital said of the British executive in foreign policy: "It is a source of additional strength to the Ministers that they and they alone have the inside story of events; the ready access to the Treasury, the Bank of England and the Foreign Office; the means of tapping and processing information that exists in the unofficial worlds of commerce and industry and, even more so, in the official world of international relations."[75] Moreover, in each of the systems, the executive has been able, legally, to keep secret substantial bodies of information on foreign policy matters while simultaneously contending that the wisdom of its policies is based on information that cannot be made public.

Legislators and citizens can have an idea of the desire for or the effects of health care, education, or transportation programs and the like, but they have fewer firsthand observations on the likely consequences of a particular policy for the behavior of foreign nations. For example, how can legislators make a fully considered evaluation of an executive assertion such as that to eliminate the ABM would undermine our bargaining position with the Soviet Union in the Strategic Arms Limitation Talks? If we assume that legislators wish to make rational and intelligent decisions, policies that in their view will achieve beneficial results, their greater dependence upon the executive for information upon which to arrive at informed decisions can only have encouraged greater executive influence in the area of foreign policy than in the area of domestic policy.

Indeed, the importance of reaching beneficial decisions and the significance that is thereby attached to information have been reinforced in the field of foreign policy during the twentieth century by the potential consequences of "bad" foreign policy decisions. A series of such decisions could possibly lead to the total destruction of the nation making those decisions and, perhaps, to the destruction of its allies as well. It is no wonder, then, as Wildavsky put it, "In foreign affairs we may be approaching the stage where knowledge is power."[76] Nor is it surprising, in these circumstances, that "the calculation of where the public interest lies is often passed to the Executive on matters of foreign policy,"[77] for it is presumed that generally the executive has both greater access to and a greater feel for the requisite information. Yet, once again, this presumption is likely to be even stronger for members of the executive party, since we observed in the previous section that party tends to be one of the determinants of which persons legislators look to and trust regarding information and expertise.

Along with its informational resources, the executive is perceived to have advantages regarding other capacities often thought to be relevant to pursuing foreign policy successfully. Thus, unity, speed, and secrecy of action, all perceived to be advantages in carrying out foreign policy, especially in crisis situations, are usually also perceived to be qualities of a hierarchically organized institution such as the executive rather than of a more collegial and deliberative institution such as the legislature. Indeed, we observed in Chapter 6 that although the executive has normally tended to dominate foreign policy decisions, it has done so even more consistently in crisis foreign policy situations.

Yet this also suggests that legislative involvement and determination to influence foreign policy have not been completely constant. Not only has crisis made a difference, but legislative influence has shifted with time (see Chapter 6) and has also usually been greater in certain areas of foreign policy than in others. Such variations in influence can be viewed in the context of variables we have stressed here and elsewhere in the chapter.

The Congress serves as an example. Our discussion has suggested that Presidential influence in foreign policy has been particularly effective on his own party members in Congress. Thus, with divided party control, we should expect legislative involvement and influence to increase. In this light, it is of interest that alterations of defense budgets by the Congress over the past twenty years were comparatively substantial during the final Eisenhower years and throughout much of the Nixon administration.[78] In each of these cases, the Presidency and the Congress were controlled by different parties.

Furthermore, we should expect that as interest groups and constituents come to see greater connection between the direction of foreign policy and their interests regarding domestic policy, the involvement and determination of the legislature would increase in the area of foreign policy. Since the middle 1960s, for example, there has been growing popular concern in the United States over the relative resources devoted to meeting foreign and defense needs as these affect the system's ability to meet domestic needs. These growing popular concerns undoubtedly helped to stimulate the increased Congressional challenges to the size of defense appropriations over the six-year period beginning in 1968 with Johnson's last budget.[79] There have also been particular foreign policy areas of relatively high Congressional involvement over time. These have tended to be areas intertwined with the concerns of domestic interests. Four examples would be tariff, immigration, weapons procurement, and military installations legislation.

Moreover, we should expect Congressional involvement and influence to grow when confidence declines in the executive's claims to informational superiority and such claims become more vulnerable to attack. As we have seen, Congressional challenge to Presidential policies increased in the latter 1960s and early 1970s. This is indicated not only by the comparatively large reductions Congress made in defense budgets but also by Congressional decisions such as those to terminate funds for bombing in Cambodia and to limit the President's authority to undertake prolonged military action in new theaters without the explicit consent of the Congress. Congressional involvement beginning in the latter 1960s followed a sustained period in which Presidential policies had become increasingly questionable because of the differences between the overt results of a series of executive decisions as compared to the executive's pronounced goals and predictions. Similarly, Congressional involvement and influence grew in the latter 1950s when the executive's pronounced assumptions in the area of defense policy had become questionable due to overt changes in international conditions.[80]

The Congress has not been, nor is it now, a coordinate partner in the making of foreign and defense policy. Even so, there has been a renewal of Congressional activity and assertion of power in recent years. We pointed out that this change, as well as changes at earlier points in time, could be understood in the context of variables connected to our earlier analysis concerning differences between foreign and domestic policies. Our discussion suggests that this has been the case. Summarizing the variables associated with Congress's most recent renewed involvement, for example, notable among them have been divided party control, growing constituent awareness of the interconnection between foreign and domestic policies, and a greater vulnerability of the President's claim to informational superiority.

Legislative Supervision

Another important dimension of relations between the legislature and the executive involves legislative supervision of how the executive applies and administers legislation as well as how the executive uses both delegated powers and powers it has otherwise assumed. Supervision is one of the primary functions of the legislature. Chapter 7 examined different kinds of supervisory techniques available to the legislatures and we wish here to discuss factors likely to prompt legislators to become actively involved in supervisory functions.

Our analysis in previous parts of this chapter focused on a series of variables related to how legislators behave toward the executive. Particularly important have been party-related variables (including factors affecting legislators' ties to their party and the partisan composition of the legislature), legislators' conceptions of the role the legislature ought to play in relation to the executive, and factors concerning informational expertise or perceptions of expertise. Our use of these variables has been based on the notion that legislators act in ways that will maximize certain goals within the context of a given situation or setting and that these provide an underpinning for legislators' behavior toward other actors, such as the executive. Using a similar approach, we can investigate legislators' activity in the area of supervising the executive.

One of the main devices used to supervise the executive in a parliamentary system is the question period. Certainly not all questions have oversight as a purpose, but many do. Which legislators are most likely to use this device? We might expect them to be legislators who are least tied to the party of the executive—whose careers depend least on the success of the executive party or on its favors, who do not identify with the executive's party, whose policy attitudes are most likely to be in disagreement with the policies of the executive—and who are simultaneously most likely to look upon their role as one of independence and criticism of the executive. In short, hardly surprising, we would expect legislators from the opposition party or parties to be most likely to engage in supervisory activity and generally to make greatest use of the question period.[81]

Most of the evidence on questioning in the three European houses bears out this expectation. A study by Chester and Bowring, for example, found that when the Conservatives were in power in 1958 in Great Britain, Labour parliamentarians asked 74 percent of the oral questions. On the other hand, Conservative legislators asked 57 percent of the oral questions posed in 1948, when the Labour party was the governing party.[82] Of the twelve most persistent questioners in 1958, eleven were from the Labour party. Of the twelve most persistent questioners in 1948, eight were from the Conservative party. It is possible, too, that the greater tendency of the Labourites than Conservatives to pose questions to their own government has been a reflection of the persistent ideological divisions over policy within the Parliamentary Labour Party. For example, one of the four Labour members who was in the top twelve questioners in 1948 was a communist and another was a member of the Keep Left group in the PLP.

Loewenberg's study of the Bundestag from 1949 to 1965 also found that parliamentarians from the opposition party (the SPD for the period he examined) asked the highest percentage of oral questions. During the early years after 1949, SPD members asked questions at four times the rate of CDU/CSU members, and over twice the rate during the remaining years.[83]

Although members of some of the governing parties in the French Assembly have posed a number of questions proportional to the strength of these parties in the Assembly, evidence suggests that this was not the case for members of the major governing party, the Gaullist parliamentary party. In a study of questions in the French Assembly, Grangé found during the three years he covered that the Gaullist parliamentarians were the only ones not to pose as high a percentage of questions as the percentage of Assembly members they constituted.[84]

While this evidence indicates that governing parliamentary party members, on the whole, usually make lesser use of the oral question period, there are individual members of the governing parties who ask disproportionate numbers of questions. How can this be explained? One factor that may be involved is members' ideological and policy concerns, as we suggested in the case of the Labour party. But other factors are also pertinent, as a glance at individual questioners in the Conservative parliamentary party indicates. The reader may recall our analysis in Chapter 5 of the effect of lower career aspirations and diminished party identification on the voting behavior of Conservative backbenchers from 1959 to 1968.[85] We found that these backbenchers were the most likely to rebel. Similarly, these backbenchers were more likely to put oral questions to their government. Three years during the period were examined

(1961-64). Although the members with lower career aspirations comprised 54 percent of the Conservative backbenchers, they constituted 68 percent of the backbenchers who raised thirty or more oral questions during any one of the three years under examination.[86] The Conservative backbenchers who were least socialized into Conservative group feelings and identity also asked questions at a higher rate than did their more intensely socialized colleagues. The less socialized group comprised 45 percent of the backbenchers, but 60 percent of the Conservative members who asked thirty or more oral questions during any single year.

One can see from Table 8.1 that these tendencies remain, and in some cases become even more pronounced, when we examine the effect of career aspirations and party identity together. Ninety-three percent of the Conservatives who ranked high on both these dispositions asked an average of eight or fewer oral questions yearly, whereas this was the case for only 60 percent of the Conservatives who ranked low on both dispositions. In addition, only 5 percent of the former group asked thirty or more oral questions in any single year, whereas 22 percent of the latter group asked that many oral questions in a single year. It is interesting, too, that the only Conservative who was among the top twelve questioners in the Commons in 1958, Mr. Nabarro, ranked low on both dispositions according to our measurements.

Returning now to the effect of partisan affiliation (whether members were of the governing party or not), the significance of this factor for legislative supervisory activities is also to be seen in the workings of committees that have had a supervisory function. From Chapter 7 we recall that investigatory committees in the French Assembly and Bundestag generally proved to be ineffective instruments for supervising the government partly because the majority on the committees, who were of the governing parties, were anxious or willing to insulate their parties and their leaders from public exposure on potentially embarrassing matters. As a consequence, investigatory committees were restricted mainly to issues of a less partisan nature. In Great Britain, too, we found that supervisory committees shied away from partisan topics. The reasons are clear.[87] Given the forces producing party unity behind the government and the presence of a majority from the governing party on each committee, a committee would be unlikely in any case to decide against the government on partisan issues. Moreover, if the government opposed the committee's decisions, it could be

Table 8.1
Career Aspirations, Party Identification, and Oral Questioning by Conservative Backbenchers from 1961 through 1963 (in percent)

Aspirations and Identification	Averaged Eight or Less per Year	Averaged Nine or More but less than Thirty per Year	More than Thirty in One Year	Total
Both High	93	02	05	100
One High	86	10	04	100
None High	60	18	22	100

Number of Questions

made to follow those decisions only if the Commons accepted them. Due to the forces producing party unity behind the government, however, it is highly unlikely that a committee could bring the House to undertake such action. Realizing that the committee could not be successful in supervising partisan areas, each of the supervisory committees we examined in the Commons chose to avoid these areas and to concentrate instead on investigating nonpartisan policies over which they might have some effect.

Supervision by Congressional committees has also been influenced by partisan considerations. After examining the supervisory activities of one Senate and two House committees, Scher made the following observation: "leaders can be expected to involve. . .resources in studies of agency performance if and when the likely gains in things valued by Congressmen is gauged as greater than any prospective loss in those things."[88] Under what conditions did the leaders or other members perceive that gains outweighed prospective losses?

Scher found that supervisory activities occurred "when the leadership of the majority party in Congress believes that it can cause sufficient embarrassment, with accompanying profit for itself, to a past or current *opposition* President who is held responsible for the perfomance of his agency appointees."[89] Moreover, since the "successes or failures of the 'independent' as well as the executive agencies will be publicly credited to or blamed on the President. . . .the President's allies in Congress tend to assume a posture of support and protectiveness toward his appointees in whatever agency."[90] Thus, Scher found that several committee reviews of agencies that began while Eisenhower was President were quietly concluded by the Democratic Congress as President Kennedy's appointees took over positions in these agencies. As in the three European legislatures, partisan affiliation and estimates of party gains or losses have apparently contributed to whether members undertook or attempted to scuttle oversight activities.

At the same time, partisan affiliation needs to be viewed alongside other factors that affect legislators' ties with their own parties and that might lead them to deviate from their party. Countervailing constituency influences have been especially important. Jewell and Patterson observed that "since American legislators are predominantly constituency oriented, legislator-bureaucrat contact tends to be motivated by demands from the legislators' constituents."[91] Scher similarly concluded: "when the committee leadership or powerful committee members believe that constituent or group interests important to them cannot be satisfied by routine personal intercessions between Congressmen and agency, committee review tends to be used as a substitute."[92] He found that committee members were most concerned with the effects of particular agency acts on important group interests in their districts: "Committee Democrats and Republicans alike viewed NLRB activity largely in terms of how the agency treated 'my people.' "[93] Moreover, when Congressmen themselves shared the values of the interests back home, their reaction was likely to be particularly intense.[94] Oversight tended to intensify, then, when constituent interests coincided with the policy attitudes of the legislator. Not surprisingly, in attempting to enhance constituent support, members of Congress have been prone to review those agencies that were more in the public eye[95] as well as to shy away from action where the member perceived a review would "provoke costly reprisals from powerful economic interests regulated by the agencies."[96] Congressmen were likely to think twice about engaging in oversight if they feared that such activities might lead the agency's clientele back home to work for an opposing primary candidate or to support the opposition in a general election. Thus, by developing a close relationship with the groups they were supposed to regulate, agencies could protect themselves to some extent from investigations and close committee review.[97]

Legislative supervision has apparently also been influenced by the legislators' role conceptions—how they viewed their own work and the work of their committees. For example, an analysis of the Senate Banking and Currency Committee found that the chairman and most subcommittee chairmen viewed the role of the committee "primarily in terms of processing legislation" rather than in reviewing the application of that legislation.[98] In turn, such views tended to reduce the activities of the committee as an agent of supervision. A similar conclusion has been suggested by research in other legislative contexts, such as in the House of Commons.[99]

In addition to the factors just cited are others involving informational considerations and especially the member's perception of his capacity effectively to understand and handle the problems that require oversight. Relevant in this regard is Scher's finding that a number of Congressmen view agencies "as impenetrable mazes," leading them also to believe "that any serious effort at penetrating them poses hazards for the inexpert Congressman which outweigh any conceivable gain to him."[100] Scher alluded to the remarks of one member of a House committee: "The (regulatory) agencies' work is pretty technical. Most of us just don't know enough about it to even begin to ask intelligent questions."[101]

In order to overcome this problem, and successfully to undertake an in-depth review, Bibby's study of the Banking and Currency Committee found that certain kinds of conditions may be required. These include decentralization of both staffing and power within the committee, giving subcommittees and their chairmen the resources and freedom to act independently. Thus, Bibby found that the Housing Subcommittee of the Banking and Currency Committee, which was the most active of its subcommittees in reviewing the administration of policy, also had the greatest freedom to act independently and the largest specialized staff with which to do so.[102] Where staff was less available, on the other hand, review of agencies was restricted. Bibby suggests: "For example, Senator Proxmire, the chairman of the Small Business Subcommittee, has attempted to oversee carefully the SBA; but because he has only minimal staff assistance, his activities have been limited both in scope and effectiveness."[103]

The point made here, especially regarding the relevance of having expertise as a prerequisite for sound, in-depth supervision, is suggested as well by evidence from the Western European legislatures. For example, the success of committees such as Nationalized Industries or Public Accounts in supervising the administration of policy may well be attributed to the fact that these committees specialize both in a particular policy concern and in supervision. Perhaps more important, the most successful committee by reputation, which is Public Accounts, is aided through the office of the Comptroller by a staff far larger than that available to any of the other committees. The relevance of specialization and staff to the capacity of the Commons to act efficaciously in the area of supervision is such as to have led Shonfield to argue:

If Parliament is to exercise an effective supervision over the great range of work which is, or ought to be, done by a modern administration, it must reequip itself for this highly technical and exacting task. The plenary session culminating in a vote taken along party lines has limited relevance to the problem. The obvious alternative is the small specialist committee, developing over a period of time a considerable degree of expertise, and supported by a professional staff of its own sufficiently knowledgeable to talk to the professional civil servants on equal terms.[104]

Research on the conditions that lead legislators to attempt to supervise the executive is only at a preliminary stage, yet the findings of much of the available research converge on similar conclusions. One of these is that how much legislators become involved in supervisory activities needs to be viewed in the perspective of how supervision relates to the achievement of their own goals and purposes, a relationship whose strength varies considerably for different legislators. Second, a variety of goals and purposes, spanning members' career objectives, affective attachments, and normative outlooks have been found to be pertinent. Finally, the motivation to undertake a thorough review of a policy area requires the expectation that the setting provides adequate resources to gain the information necessary to make a thorough review sufficiently successful to outweigh the costs that such supervision may entail.

Given the vastly increased amount and scope of executive administrative action during the twentieth century, some observers have argued that legislatures ought to expend substantially greater effort in supervising executive policy decisions.[105] Legislatures certainly have greater potential to do this in the sense that not all legislators are consistently active and some engage in rather limited supervisory activity. We have attempted in our analysis to delineate some of the reasons why legislators do or do not undertake supervisory functions. To the extent these reasons go back to the supervisory devices and the resources the legislature affords its members, mechanical reforms can be helpful. Yet the reasons are not rooted in such factors alone, but also in the legislators' goals and purposes and how the achievement of these relates to involvement in supervisory functions. It is this dimension that is not subject to easy or predictable mechanical reform. Because this is true, mechanical reforms within the legislatures in the area of oversight are likely to have only a muted effect in eliciting more thorough and intense legislative supervision than that which currently prevails.

Conclusions

This chapter has focused on relations between legislators and their executives and on variables helpful to understanding these relations. We examined this subject from a variety of perspectives. First, we compared the overall place of the four legislatures relative to the executive in the making of legislation. A second perspective was to break down policy areas in order to look at domestic as contrasted to foreign and defense policies. These have been areas of notable differences in the impact of the legislature relative to the executive. Third, the activities of legislators in supervising and overseeing the executive were examined.

To help account for legislative behavior toward the executive a series of variables were considered. Major variables discussed were how legislators behave toward their party (first introduced in Chapter 4) and the factors underlying this behavior; legislators' conceptions about the role or job of the legislature in relation to the executive; and legislators' capacity to act effectively, particularly as shaped by the informational resources available to them and the organization of power within the legislature.

Our study of legislative behavior began in Chapter 4 by pointing out that how legislators behave toward their party, and the factors underlying this behavior, could serve as a useful point of departure in helping us to understand phenomena such as how legislators behave toward the executive and interest groups. Our consideration of legislative-executive relations in the present chapter found this to be true in each area of activity we treated. Thus, party-related variables were helpful toward understanding legislators' overall involvement in the development and making of legislation, involvement in foreign as compared to domestic policy, and involvement in the oversight function. The party variables encompassed both partisan affiliation and the priority legislators of the executive party gave to supporting their party. Various goal and situational factors discussed in Chapter 4 as affecting the magnitude of these priorities were detectable in each area of activity as well.

Combined with these party-related factors, legislators' role attitudes about the proper relationship between the legislature and the executive also appeared to be an influencing factor. Conceptions regarding legislative independence of the executive were useful when considering the overall prominence of the four legislatures and the contrast between legislative involvement in foreign and domestic policies. More relevant to oversight activity were attitudes about how integral oversight was to the legislative task. Indeed, research on both the Congress and the House of Commons has suggested that the failure of many legislators to view detailed supervision as an essential part of the job of legislating has been an important force restraining legislative supervisory efforts over what they otherwise might be.

Other variables of importance centered on legislative capacity. In this regard, the informational resources available to legislators relative to the executive as well as their perception of these resources and the informational requirements of a policy sector were pertinent to relations between legislators and the executive in each area of activity we considered. In addition, how broadly powers were distributed within the legislature had some impact. Research indicated that the effect of power distribution needed to be understood within the context of the other variables shaping legislative motivation and capacity. Nevertheless, the legislatures that were more central to the making of legislation were those whose powers were most widely spread and dispersed among the standing committees. Evidence also suggested that dispersal of power within committees, to subcommittees, tended further to heighten legislative activity, including legislators' involvement both in the initiation of policy and in supervision of executive action.[106]

Finally, relations between the legislature and the executive were associated with another capacity variable, the legislature's formal or traditional powers to act relative to those of the executive. The contrast between executive-legislative relations in domestic as compared to foreign policy provides a principal illustration. At the same time, the lesser influence of the legislature in the area of foreign policy was by no means attributable simply to the lesser powers of the legislature in this field. That is, the generally diminished influence of the legislature in foreign policy also arose from the play and effect of the party, role, and informational variables considered earlier.

The variables treated in this and the preceding two chapters have spoken to a number of propositions regarding relations between the legislature and the executive. It is fitting to close by commenting on perhaps the most important of these propositions, which also represents a major criticism that has been levied against the Congress. The proposition is that disunity among members of the executive party along with internal fragmentation of the legislature's powers and resources are likely to produce legislative "obstructionism."

How accurately does this proposition describe the cases we covered? If we take obstructionism to mean that the legislature becomes an arena in which executive initiatives are likely to be negated or challenged with greater effect, the proposition held true in our cases. The two legislatures (the Congress and the Bundestag) whose executive party showed greatest voting disunity and whose internal powers were most fragmented also were most likely to oppose executive policies effectively. On the other hand, we found in Chapter 6 that the legislatures which were more central in the sense of "obstructionism" still usually adopted sizable numbers of executive initiatives. Also, when compared to the other legislatures, these legislatures were found to be more actively involved and effective vis-à-vis the executive in the development of successful policy initiatives.[107] Thus, there is another side of the coin that needs recognition. For, if disunity among members of the executive party combined with fragmentation of power and resources within the legislature was related to legislative "obstructionism," it was simultaneously associated with an increased vitality and significance of the legislature, itself, as an arena of policy initiation.

Why was this so? We would argue that the forces that diminish cohesion among legislators of the executive party equally stimulate greater numbers of such legislators to act independently of the executive. This independence can be expressed in terms of working to obstruct or block executive proposals. Yet, legislators can also attempt to express this independence through their own initiatory activity—by formulating and moving on their own proposals and to build their own record in this way. If power and resources are fragmented and dispersed within the legislature, a greater number of individual legislators are simultaneously afforded a base helpful to engaging in such activity. Furthermore, given the wider prevalence of the motivation to act independently of the executive, the likelihood is raised that legislative as contrasted to executive coalitions can win. In essence, then, the forces that produce party disunity, when combined with internal fragmentation of the legislature's powers and resources, may contribute to legislative initiative in a three-fold way. They may do so by maximizing the numbers of legislators motivated to become involved in policy initiation independently of the executive; by enlarging the numbers of legislators who have resources enabling them to pursue these activities more efficaciously; and finally, by raising the likelihood that legislative-centered winning coalitions can be nurtured and successfully constructed.

Notes

[1]The reader should recall that, for purposes of examining legislative-executive relations when members of the legislature can also be members of the executive, we defined the legislature as inclusive of all nonexecutive members. Members of the legislature may simultaneously be members of the executive in Britain and West

Germany (this was also the case for the French Fourth Republic), whereas simultaneous membership is not possible in the United States or the French Fifth Republic.

[2]John P. Mackintosh, *The Government and Politics of Britain* (London: Hutchinson, 1970), p. 75.

[3]For example, in referring to the effect of the package vote, Williams makes essentially this point for the Assembly and its Gaullist majority. According to Williams, the package vote "is a small-scale variant of the vote of confidence procedure, which can allow the Government to carry a controversial bill for which there is no majority in [the] house provided only that fewer than half the deputies are willing at the moment to overthrow the Government and face a general election." See Phillip Williams, "Parliament Under the Fifth Republic: Patterns of Executive Domination," in *Modern Parliaments: Change or Decline?*, ed. Gerhard Loewenberg (Chicago: Aldine-Atherton, 1971), p. 106. See, also, Guy Lord, *The French Budgetary Process* (Berkeley: University of California Press, 1973), especially p. 152.

[4]For example, this point is suggested by Aage Clausen's analysis in, *How Congressmen Decide: A Policy Focus* (New York: St. Martin's Press, 1973), pp. 192-212.

[5]See pp. 147-149 of Chapter 4.

[6]See Oliver Woshinsky, *The French Deputy: Incentives and Behavior in the National Assembly* (Lexington, Mass.: D. C. Heath, 1973), especially pp. 69-72, 76-77, 105-9, 177-79.

[7]Roger H. Davidson, David M. Kovenock, and Michael K. O'Leary, *Congress in Crisis: Politics and Congressional Reform* (Belmont, Calif.: Wadsworth, 1966), p. 70.

[8]See, for examples, John F. Manley, *The Politics of Finance: The House Committee on Ways and Means* (Boston: Little, Brown and Co., 1970), pp. 325-26; Lawrence C. Pierce, *The Politics of Fiscal Policy Formation* (Pacific Palisades, Calif.: Goodyear Publishing Co., 1971), pp. 155-57; and Richard F. Fenno, Jr., *Congressmen in Committees* (Boston: Little, Brown and Co., 1973), pp. 277-79.

[9]Gerhard Loewenberg, *Parliament in the German Political System* (Ithaca, N.Y.: Cornell University Press, 1967), p. 307.

[10]Gerhard Braunthal, *The West German Legislative Process: A Case Study of Two Transportation Bills* (Ithaca, N.Y.: Cornell University Press, 1972), pp. 138, 146.

[11]Gerhard Lehmbruch, "The Ambiguous Coalition in West Germany," in *European Politics: A Reader*, ed. Mattei Dogan and Richard Rose (Boston: Little, Brown, and Co., 1971), p. 558.

[12]Louis Koenig, "More Power to the President (Not Less)," in *Congress and the President: Allies and Adversaries*, ed. Ronald C. Moe (Pacific Palisades, Calif.: Goodyear Publishing Co., 1971), p. 70.

[13]Ibid.

[14]A detailed discussion of the committee system found in each legislature may be found in Chapter 2.

[15]Malcolm Shaw and John D. Lees, "Committees in Legislatures and the Political System" (Paper presented to the Ninth World Congress of the International Political Science Association, 1973).

[16]Presidential support and opposition scores are from the *Congressional Quarterly Almanac*, 1969 (p. 1041) and 1972 (p. 43).

[17]Interview research by John Kingdon during the first year of the Nixon administration found that the position of the administration was either of no importance or minor importance in almost 70 percent of the roll call voting decisions of the Republican Representatives he examined. See John W. Kingdon, *Congressmen's Voting Decisions* (New York: Harper & Row, 1973), p. 176.

[18]See the analysis of House and Senate committees in Richard F. Fenno, Jr., *Congressmen in Committees*, pp. 146-47.

[19]Douglas M. Fox and Charles H. Clapp, "The House Rules Committee and the Programs of the Kennedy and Johnson Administrations," *Midwest Journal of Political Science* 14 (November 1970): 667-72.

[20]Lewis A. Froman, Jr., *The Congressional Process: Strategies, Rules, and Procedures* (Boston: Little, Brown and Co., 1967), p. 54.

[21]Ibid.

[22]Froman, *The Congressional Process*, pp. 54-55. In our case study on federal aid to education (found in Chapter 6), the House, by a vote of 242 to 170, sustained the House Rules Committee decision not to report the bill. The politics behind the willingness of the Rules Committee in the end to report legislation desired by the House is found in the case study on civil rights discussed in Chapter 3.

[23]Manley, *The Politics of Finance*, p. 214. As Manley observes, "Medicare, of course, was 'bottled up' in the Ways and Means Committee for several years, but one primary reason the Committee never reported it was that the bill would not have passed the House.... Whatever the substantive arguments against medicare, there was a strong political argument against reporting the bill: lack of votes" (pp. 214-15).

[24]Manley, *The Politics of Finance*, p. 217.

[25]Ibid.

[26]Pierce, *The Politics of Fiscal Policy Formation*, p. 161. See also pp. 158-59.

[27]Pierce, *The Politics of Fiscal Policy Formation*, p. 161.

[28]Fenno, *Congressmen in Committees*, pp. 46-80, 278-79.

[29]Kingdon, *Congressmen's Voting Decisions*, pp. 126-35.

[30]Manley, *The Politics of Finance*, p. 150. Emphasis ours.

[31]Fenno, *Congressmen in Committees*, especially Chapter III.

[32]See David Price, *Who Makes the Laws: Creativity and Power in Senate Committees* (Cambridge, Mass.: Schenkman Publishing Company, 1972), especially his conclusion on p. 318. Another demonstration of the contributions fragmentation of power makes to policy initiation from within Congress is found in Helen M.

Ingram et. al., *Institutional Fragmentation and Policy Innovation: The Case of Federal Water Pollution Control* (Tucson, Ariz.: Institute of Government Research, 1975).

[33] Aaron Wildavsky, "Toward A Radical Incrementalism: A Proposal to Aid Congress in Reform of the Budgetary Process," in *Congress: The First Branch of Government*, ed. Alfred deGrazia (Garden City, N.Y.: Doubleday, 1967), pp. 134-35.

[34] See also the findings reported in Julius Turner and Edward V. Schneier, Jr., *Party and Constituency: Pressures on Congress* (Baltimore, Md.: Johns Hopkins University Press, 1970), pp. 212-14. Examining party voting in committees and on the floor of the House for the "twenty-five bills on which the same basic questions were raised both on the floor of the House in the form of roll-call vote and in committee," they found that party voting in committee ordinarily was quite similar to party voting on the floor.

[35] James A. Robinson, *Congress and Foreign Policy-Making*, 2d ed. (Homewood, Ill.: The Dorsey Press, 1967), pp. 6-9.

[36] Robinson, *Congress and Foreign Policy-Making*, p. 7.

[37] Eugene Eidenberg and Roy D. Morey, *An Act of Congress* (New York: Norton, 1969), p. 225. See also Raymond A. Bauer, Ithiel de Sola Pool, and Lewis Anthony Dexter, *American Business and Public Policy* (New York: Atherton Press, 1968), p. 405.

[38] Loewenberg, *Parliament in the German Political System*, pp. 351-52. See also p. 355. See also Hans-Hoachim Arndt, *West Germany: Politics of Non-Planning* (Syracuse, N.Y.: Syracuse University Press, 1966), p. 67.

[39] Donald R. Matthews and James A. Stimson, "The Decision-Making Approach to the Study of Legislative Behavior: The Example of the U.S. House of Representatives" (Paper presented at the Annual Convention of the American Political Science Association, September 1969), p. 15.

[40] Matthews and Stimson, "The Decision-Making Approach to the Study of Legislative Behavior," p. 16. See also Kingdon, *Congressmen's Voting Decisions*, pp. 72-88.

[41] Also pertinent here are, John S. Saloma, III, *Congress and the New Politics* (Boston: Little, Brown and Co., 1969), p. 217 and Kingdon, pp. 70-79.

[42] Manley, *The Politics of Finance*, p. 339.

[43] Manley, *The Politics of Finance*, p. 326.

[44] Guy Lord, *The French Budgetary Process*, pp. 186-87.

[45] Richard F. Fenno, Jr., *The Power of the Purse: Appropriations Politics in Congress* (Boston: Little, Brown and Co., 1966), p. 344.

[46] Fenno, *Congressmen in Committees*, p. 195.

[47] Fenno, *Power of the Purse*, p. 345.

[48] Fenno, *Power of the Purse*, p. 347. Members of Congress, generally, perceive information inferiority to be one of the major problems Congress faces. See Davidson, Kovenock, and O'Leary, *Congress in Crisis*, p. 77.

[49] David E. Price, *Who Makes the Laws: Creativity and Power in Senate Committees* (Cambridge, Mass.: Schenkman, 1972), p. 293.

[50] Henry W. Ehrmann, *Politics in France* (Boston: Little, Brown and Co., 1971), p. 281.

[51] For a discussion of list nominations, see Chapter 2.

[52] The distinction between foreign policy issues and domestic policy issues can be found in Chapter 6, p. 234.

[53] I. F. Stone, "Nixon's War Powers," *The New York Review of Books* 20 (April 19, 1973), p. 22.

[54] See Robert J. Jackson, *Rebels and Whips: An Analysis of Dissension, Discipline, and Cohesion in British Political Parties* (New York: St. Martin's Press, 1968).

[55] See Clausen, *How Congressmen Decide*, Chapter 8 and pp. 196-208, and Mark Kesselman, "Presidential Leadership in Congress on Foreign Policy: A Replication of a Hypothesis," *Midwest Journal of Political Science* 9 (1965): 401-6.

[56] Alfred Grosser, *La IV République et sa politique extérieure* (Paris: Armand Colin, 1961), pp. 79-80.

[57] Warren E. Miller and Donald E. Stokes, "Constituency Influence in Congress," in *American Legislative Behavior*, ed. Samuel Patterson (Princeton, N.J.: D. Van Nostrand, 1968) and Warren E. Miller, "Majority Rule and the Representative System of Government," in *Cleavages, Ideologies, and Party Systems: Contributions to Comparative Sociology*, ed. Erik Allardt and Yrjo Littunen, (Helsinki, Finland: The Academic Bookstore, 1964). See also Malcolm E. Jewell, *Senatorial Politics and Foreign Policy* (Lexington: University of Kentucky Press, 1962), p. 205 and 210.

[58] Aaron Wildavsky, "The Two Presidencies," in *Introductory Readings in American Government: A Public Choice Perspective*, ed. Robert S. Ross and William C. Mitchell, (Chicago: Markham, 1971), pp. 154-55.

[59] Clausen, *How Congressmen Decide*, Chapter 8; Miller, "Majority Rule and the Representative System of Government," p. 364.

[60] For additional examples of this phenomenon and reasons for it, see John E. Mueller, "Presidential Popularity from Truman to Johnson," *The American Political Science Review* 64 (March 1970): 18-34.

[62] Ehrmann, *Politics in France*, p. 232.

[63] See Leon Epstein, *British Politics in the Suez Crisis* (Urbana: University of Illinois Press, 1964).

[64] Peter G. Richards, *Parliament and Foreign Affairs* (London: George Allen and Unwin, 1967), p. 121.

[65] On the United States, see also Wildavsky, "The Two Presidencies," p. 154, and John H. Kessel, "The

Parameters of Presidential Politics" (Paper presented at the 1972 Annual Meeting of the American Political Science Association), pp. 8-9.

[66]Clausen, *How Congressmen Decide*, p.227.

[67]David Vital, *The Making of British Foreign Policy* (New York: Praeger, 1968), p. 77.

[68]See S. E. Finer, H. B. Berrington, and D. J. Bartholomew, *Backbench Opinion in the House of Commons, 1955-1959* (Oxford: Pergamon Press, 1961), pp. 48-59.

[69]*Arizona Daily Star*, June 17, 1974, p. 6.

[70]Robinson, *Congress and Foreign Policy-Making*, p. 169. See also Holbert Caroll, *The House of Representatives and Foreign Affairs* (Boston: Little, Brown and Co., 2nd ed., 1966), p. 24.

[71]Wildavsky, "Two Presidencies," p. 155.

[72]Wildavsky, "Two Presidencies," p. 155. For a summary statement of how variation across committees regarding members' views about playing an independent role affected their relations with the executive, see Fenno, *Congressmen in Committees*, especially p. 277.

[73]Clausen, *How Congressmen Decide*, p. 212 Emphasis added.

[74]For example, see Robert A. Bernstein and William A. Anthony, "The ABM Issue in the Senate: The Importance of Ideology," *American Political Science Review* 68 (September 1974): 1198-1206; and Finer et. al., *Backbench Opinion in the House of Commons*, pp. 48-59.

[75]Vital, *The Making of British Foreign Policy*, p. 78.

[76]Wildavsky, "Two Presidencies," p. 164.

[77]Miller and Stokes, "Constituency Influence in Congress," p. 228.

[78]Arnold Kanter, "Congress and the Defense Budget: 1960-1970," *American Political Science Review* 66 (March 1972): 129-43.

[79]See Bruce M. Russett, "The Revolt of the Masses: Public Opinion and Military Expenditures," in *Peace, War, and Numbers*, ed. Bruce M. Russett (Beverly Hills, Calif.: Sage Publications, 1972), esp. pp. 317-18. For a contrasting view on the French system, see Edward L. Morse, *Foreign Policy and Independence in Gaullist France* (Princeton, N.J.: Princeton University Press, 1973) who found that the Assembly's involvement in foreign policy under a Gaullist majority did not change during the Fifth Republic as popular demands for domestic programs grew.

[80]See, for example, Kanter, "Congress and the Defense Budget," p. 137.

[81]However, Domes makes the interesting point that while the opposition is likely to make greatest use of supervision in regard to matters related directly to the government, members of the majority might well make greater use of supervision where it concerns the bureaucracy and its handling of the legislation the majority has passed. See Jürgen Domes, *Mehrheitsfraktion und Bundesregierung* (Cologne and Opladen: Westdeutscher Verlag, 1964), pp. 169-71.

[82]D. N. Chester and Nona Bowring, *Questions in Parliament* (Oxford: The Clarendon Press, 1962), pp. 196-99. In terms of the rate of questioning by individual parliamentarians, on average opposition members asked questions at twice the rate of government supporters in 1948 and three times the rate in 1958 (p. 199).

[83]Loewenberg, *Parliament in the German Political System*, p. 414.

[84]Jean Grangé, "La Fixation de l'ordre du jour des Assemblées parlementaires,", *Études sur le Parlement de la Ve République*, ed. Eliane Guichard-Ayoub (Paris: Presses Universitaries de France, 1965), p. 267. As Grangé observes of the Gaullist members of the UNR: "The parliamentarians from the UNR are not proportionally well represented among the authors of questions . . . This is not surprising: the government majority does not look to interrogate or criticize the ministers that it supports" (p. 269).

[85]The measurements of career aspirations and party identification we used were based on inferences we made from indicators rather than on the basis of direct questioning. For the indicators, see Chapter 5.

[86]For the relation of career aspirations to parliamentary supervision, see also Hugh Heclo and Aaron Wildavsky, *The Private Government of Public Money: Community and Policy Inside British Politics* (Berkeley: University of California Press, 1974), esp. pp. 260-61.

[87]On this topic see also David Coombes, *The Member of Parliament and the Administration* (London: George Allen and Unwin, 1966), p. 212.

[88]Seymour Scher, "Conditions for Legislative Control," in *The Congressional System: Notes and Readings*, ed. Leroy N. Rieselbach (Belmont, Calif.: Wadsworth, 1970), p. 402.

[89]Ibid. Emphasis ours.

[90]Scher, "Conditions for Legislative Control," p. 400.

[91]Malcolm Jewell and Samuel Patterson, *The Legislative Process in the United States* (New York: Random House, 1973), p. 509.

[92]Scher, "Conditions for Legislative Control," p. 403.

[93]Seymour Scher, "Congressional Committee Members as Independent Agency Overseers: A Case Study," *American Political Science Review* 54 (December 1960): 918.

[94]Scher, "Congressional Committee Members," p. 919.

[95]Ira Sharkansky, "An Appropriations Committee and Its Client Agencies: A Comparative View of Supervision and Control," *American Political Science Review* 59 (1965): 627.

[96]Scher, "Conditions for Legislative Control," p. 399.

[97] An agency might be protected from oversight, as well, by legislators' ideological affinities with the agency, friendships with or feelings of confidence in its personnel as a consequence of previous dealings, and other such normative and affective ties. See Scher, "Conditions for Legislative Control," pp. 396-97.

[98] John F. Bibby, "Committee Characteristics and Legislative Oversight," in *The Congressional System*, ed. Leroy N. Rieselbach, p. 429.

[99] For example, research on expenditure procedures in the House of Commons indicates that the failure of legislators to view oversight of the details of executive spending policies as an essential part of the parliamentary role has been an important factor inhibiting the legislature as a forum of effective supervision. See Heclo and Wildavsky, *The Private Government of Public Money*, pp. 261-62.

[100] Scher, "Conditions for Legislative Control," p. 395.

[101] Scher, "Conditions for Legislative Control," p. 396.

[102] Bibby, "Committee Characteristics and Legislative Oversight," pp. 420-23

[103] Bibby, "Committee Characteristics and Legislative Oversight," p. 421.

[104] Andrew Shonfield, *Modern Capitalism* (London: Oxford University Press, 1965) p. 388. See also Paul Byrne, "The Expenditure Committee: A Preliminary Assessment," *Parliamentary Affairs* 27 (Summer 1974), pp. 284-85.

[105] See, for example, Samuel P. Huntington, "Congressional Responses to the Twentieth Century," in *The Congress and America's Future*, ed. David B. Truman (Englewood Cliffs, N. J.: Prentice-Hall, 1973), and Bernard Crick, *The Reform of Parliament* (London: Wiedenfeld and Nicolson, 1970).

[106] See our discussion on pp. 230-231 of Chapter 6 and both p. 301 and 317 of this chapter.

[107] There is a substantial body of evidence supporting this conclusion in the case of the Congress. See Chapter 6, pp. 230-232. Insofar as concerns the Bundestag, the evidence tends in the same direction but is less complete. On the Bundestag, see p. 210 of Chapter 6.

Chapter 9
Interest Groups and the Legislature

Fundamental to the idea of a democratic system is that people have the right to petition the government for the redress of grievances. In this chapter we will examine one of the main vehicles people have used to exercise this right. This is the interest group. By an interest group we mean any private organization or collection of persons with shared attitudes or goals who consciously seek to influence political decision-makers on public policies. While interest groups and parties may overlap, they are not identical. As we shall see below, one strategy an interest group may use is to attempt to influence the recruitment and election of political office holders by contributions of time, money and so on, and some office holders may indeed be members of the interest group. However, an interest group does not officially enter election contests and campaign under its own banner. If it were to do so, and the more it engaged in this activity, the group would then be defined as a political party.[1]

The decisions legislatures make are frequently surrounded by bargaining and logrolling where interest groups are, with others, important actors in the process. Our objective in this chapter is to examine the relations between interest groups and members of the legislature. We will begin by reviewing the varieties of interest groups present in our four systems, attitudes about the legitimacy of interest groups, and the kinds of strategies interest groups employ in attempting to influence the legislative process. This will be followed by a discussion of some factors that are important in determining how legislators behave toward interest groups. Then we will both summarize the findings and consider what the findings tell us about the extent to which the actions of individual legislators tend to be dominated by the pressures of interest groups.

Types of Interest Groups and Their Legitimacy

One of the characteristics common to the four political systems is that each comprises a great number of interest groups. To begin the discussion, we simply wish to give the reader an idea of the great variety of interest groups as well as a feeling for the size of some of these groups.

Among the more visible kinds of interest groups are labor, business, farm, and professional groups. In the United States,[2] examples of major groups in these areas are the AFL-CIO and the Teamsters; the National Association of Manufacturers, the Chamber of Commerce of the United States, and other trade or financial associations, such as the American Bankers Association; the American Farm Bureau, the National Grange, and the National Farmers' Union; the American Medical Association, the National Education Association, and the American Bar Association. And one could either continue this list or cite groups in other areas (the American Legion, Veterans of Foreign Wars, the American Automobile Association, the National Rifle Association, the National Association for the Advancement of Colored People, and Women's Lobby, Inc., for examples). In the latter part of the previous decade, environmental groups (e.g., Sierra Club) and public interest groups (e.g., Common Cause) appeared on the Washington scene. All these groups cited, and others like them, have a number of different purposes, but for each, one of their purposes is to influence decisions of the political system that concern their group.

Many of the groups to which we have just alluded are large-scale operations. This is suggested by membership figures. The AFL-CIO, for example, has a membership of 16 million. The American Legion has 3 million members. The American Farm Bureau has a membership of 1.6 million, and the Chamber of Commerce has over three thousand affiliate chapters.

Nor is the United States alone in the large number of interest groups it has or in the size of some of the groups.[3] In Great Britain, for example, it has been estimated that there are about twenty-five hundred trade associations and seven hundred trade unions.[4] The major labor union is the Trades Union Congress (TUC), which has about eight million members belonging to around two hundred smaller unions. Examples of important business groups are the Federation of British Industries and the National Union of Manufacturers, the former representing "big" industry and the latter representing smaller manufacturers. The National Farmers' Union, with over two hundred thousand members, is the major farm group. Some of the many professional groups of importance include the National Union of Teachers and the British Medical Association. There are, in addition, thousands of groups outside these areas—religious or social action groups such as the Lord's Day Observance Society or the National Temperance Federation or the Howard League for Penal Reform.

There are numerous interest groups in France as well. Labor is represented through three major unions: the Confédération générale du travail (a Communist union with over one million members); the Force Ouvrière (a Socialist union numbering around 350,000); and the Confédération française et démocratique du travail (a union with approximately 500,000 members stemming from the Catholic workers movement). Business has organized itself into two central or peak organizations, one representing large business and the other representing smaller business. They are the Conseil national du patronat français (CNPF) and the Confédération générale des petites et moyennes enterprises (CGPME), respectively. As we have seen in the case study presented in Chapter 3, two major agricultural forces in France are the Fédération nationale des syndicats d'exploitants agricoles (FNSEA) and its subsidiary but rather independent organization, the Centre national des jeunes agriculteurs (CNJA). There are also farm groups covering specific products as well as other more general farm groups organized on the basis of political ideology. Professional organizations repre-

There are literally dozens of groups that have members in the legislature associated with them. The study on the House of Commons from 1951 to 1955 found 101 such groups were represented in the Commons. These groups ranged from the major business and trade union groups, to local government groups, to religious groups, to social-cause groups. All told, over 30 percent of the members of the House of Commons were associated with one or another of the interest groups. Data covering 1962-72 suggest this figure has not declined.[7] A study on the Bundestag from 1957 to 1961 found approximately the same percentage of members (30.4 percent) who could be called "interest representatives," and another study indicated that as many as 45 percent of the Bundestag deputies from 1949 to 1971 had an interest affiliation.[8]

Thus, when we deal with the European legislatures, we are examining a situation in which interest group activities in the way of attempting to influence individual legislators and the outcomes of legislative decisions is an expected and legitimate activity. However, this does not mean that it is felt to be proper for a member to act solely on the basis of what interest groups want. As studies on German politics reveal, appearing to be an instructed delegate is considered improper. Braunthal observes: "The BDI [Federation of German Industry] makes it clear to the deputies that they must not be tagged as tools of industry . . . ."; instead, the BDI considers it more advantageous "to support a lawyer or tax expert who is not generally identified with industry but who can give hard support to its goals . . . . One representative of big business put it this way: 'I learned my lesson in the Bundestag in the first few months. I spoke up on some matter involving my company's interests. Since then I do not "identify" myself.' "[9]

As these remarks suggest, there is some feeling in the Bundestag that the actions of members should not be completely dominated by interest groups. While these statements were drawn from West Germany, they could easily have come, even more strongly, from Great Britain. In the words of Herbert Morrison, "The first duty of Members of this House is to their constituents and the nation, and it is wrong that they should be fettered in their judgment by any outside interest."[10] Or, from the other side of the House is the position of Sir Ian Fraser: "If every group were to press its claims by undue pressure and if Members yielded to this there would be a breakdown of Government."[11]

In France, too, the propriety of interest group determination of policy decisions is questioned. A suspicion of interest groups has long-standing historical roots in France going back at least as far as Rousseau. Rousseau suspected that interest groups might intervene between the individual and the state in such a way as to inhibit the state from acting upon the general will and the common interest. The fact that interest groups might also help the state to reach beneficial decisions or could help individuals resist "unjustified" decisions the state might attempt to impose was not considered by Rousseau to be as important as the negative effects these groups would have. Thoughts similar to those of Rousseau are reflected in statements made by the leading men of the Fifth Republic. For example, without placing the legitimacy of organized groups representing special interests fully in question, de Gaulle nevertheless emphasized the limits of their legitimacy when he rejected the demand of a majority of Assembly deputies to convene the Assembly for a special session to discuss agricultural problems. He said, "It appears to be beyond question that their claims result mainly from demands made by the leaders of a professional group. Now, however representative sent such diverse areas as law, medicine, teaching, journalism, and local government functions. An example is the Fédération de l'éducation nationale (FEN), which is a major peak association of teaching personnel. There are also a great number of religious and social action groups in France. Two of the major groups involved in the struggle over whether state funds should be used or not for religious schools in France, for example, have been the anticlerical Ligue française de l'enseignement (the Teachers League) and the Secrétariat d'étude pour la liberté de l'enseignement (the League for the Defense of Freedom in Teaching), which was pro-Catholic.

As in the other systems, a diversity of organized interest groups is equally present in West Germany. The Deutscher Gewerkschaftsbund (DGB) is the largest trade union, representing sixteen national unions with a total of over six million members. The DGB is made up primarily of manual workers. There are two other unions, which encompass civil servants (the Deutscher Beamtenbund) and other salaried workers (the Deutsche Angestelltengewerkschaft). Two business groups that are highly active politically are the Bundesvereinigung der deutschen Arbeitgeberverbände (the BDA) and the Bundesverband der deutschen Industrie (the BDI). There are also numerous individual business groups organized around specific economic sectors (transportation, banking, and so on) and organizations of independent craftsmen. Very powerful in West Germany are the agricultural groups, which have almost three million members in national and product-based organizations. The strongest of these associations is the Deutscher Bauernverband, which led the fight for the establishment of rather high price supports for German farmers and which has also had considerable influence on German agricultural policy toward the European Common Market. The Bauernverband has over two million members. The two major churches, Roman Catholic and Protestant, are also politically active in West Germany, and there is the usual myriad of professional, veterans, and social-cause groups operating in West Germany.

The fact that there are so many openly active organized groups in each of the four systems suggests that such groups enjoy a certain degree of legitimacy. Attitudes about the legitimacy of interest groups in the legislative process may be indicated by characteristics and views of the legislators themselves. In the three European legislatures, it is quite normal for members of the legislature to be officially associated with interest groups. A leading example is found in the members who have been trade union officials or employees. In 1966, for example, there were 50 union officials or employees in the Commons and over 100 members who were sponsored by trade unions. Of the 519 Bundestag members in 1961, about 45 were officials or employees of trade unions and 200 were members of trade unions. The French Assembly of 1967 included 37 members with trade union affiliations.

Nor are trade unions the only groups having employees or members in the legislature. A study of the House of Commons from 1951 to 1955 found more than thirty members who held elected or appointed honorary positions in the National Chamber of Trade and twenty members with similar positions in other leading business groups.[5] Executives from economic associations totaled twenty members of the Bundestag in 1957 and seventeen members in 1961. Also, a study of the 1953 Bundestag found that twenty three of the CDU/CSU members were honorary or paid officials of agrarian interest groups. Of these, ten were executives of national or regional farm associations.[6]

the group might be of the particular economic interests which it promotes, it is nevertheless, according to the law, completely devoid of political authority and responsibility."[12]

Much of what we have said about conflicting attitudes toward interest groups in the three European systems is also true for the United States. Several scholars have interviewed Congressmen in order to elicit their feelings about interest groups. Matthews found in his study of the Senate that there was "little hostility on Capitol Hill to lobbying in general."[13] Davidson's interviews of members of the House of Representatives found that "few Congressmen deny the legitimacy of organized interest groups."[14] Only 15 percent of the respondents felt that Congress would work better without the activities of interest groups. As for the role Congressmen said they adopted towards groups, however, only 29 percent of the Congressmen classified themselves as "facilitators" of interest groups. Forty-nine percent were classified as "neutrals" and 21 percent as "resisters."[15] While Congressmen tend to view interest groups as legitimate and do not look upon them in a hostile manner, the interest group roles they adopted suggest that many of them, too, have some reservations as to how influential interest groups should be.[16]

Strategies and Techniques of Influence

We have seen that there are numerous interest groups in each of the four systems and that, on the whole, interest groups are thought to be legitimate organizations in society. However, there is no certain attitude about what the exact limits of interest group influence in the legislative process should be. Because interest groups are clearly not ruled out of participation in the political process, it is relevant to ask how they do participate (what strategies they use) and especially how they go about attempting to influence legislators and legislative decision-making.

Interest groups employ an almost bewildering array of strategies in attempting to influence legislators. These can be divided broadly into two types: those that involve contacting the legislator directly and those that lead to indirect communication with the legislator. We can also distinguish between two types of indirect strategy: those that concentrate on influencing the legislator by way of gaining grass roots support for the group and those that concentrate on influencing the legislator by way of influencing the legislator's party or the executive.

Let us first consider some of the methods interest groups employ to gain direct contact with legislators. We have already observed one tactic used frequently in Britain, France, and Germany. This is the tactic of getting members elected to the legislature who are affiliated with the group. This is frequently done by sponsoring the member's candidacy to help him win his party's nomination or the general election. An interest group also might offer an incumbent an honorary office in the interest group or attempt to secure his agreement to serve on its parliamentary panel. As we have seen, in the European legislatures, often 30 percent or more of the members have an interest group affiliation. Through its members, an interest group may be better placed to propose legislation, amendments, motions, and to raise questions in committees and general debate. The members can also attempt informally to persuade other legislators to support their group's position. Finally, these members can be highly valuable simply by alerting the group to scheduling, how issues are developing, and other legislative matters that may affect the group.[17]

Lobbying is also a technique used in the European systems to gain direct contact with members of the legislature. A main instrumentality of lobbying is the lobbyist, who is hired by an interest group to put the group's case directly before legislators (or legislative staffs) and to keep the group informed about what is happening in the legislature. Although lobbyists may be affiliated with the group, they are not members of the legislature.

But while employed in the European systems, the use of lobbyists is undoubtedly most widespread in the United States. It is difficult to say how many lobbists there are in Washington, although there are assuredly a great many. The lobbying regulations are so vague and ineffective (due partly to the problem of defining the term, *lobbyist*) that an accurate accounting is almost impossible. However, one observer estimates that about eighteen hundred organizations actually maintain offices in Washington.[18] According to another leading journalist:

Washington swarms with lobbyists. It always has and always will. More than 1100 individuals and organizations are currently registered as lobbyists, which means that . . . they outnumber the 535 members of Congress 2 to 1. But the real ratio is much higher than that. Because the law regulating lobbying is virtually a dead letter, a horde of company representatives, public relations men, lawyers, and organizations engaged in influencing government in one way or another do not register as lobbyists. There are at least 8 to 10 lobbyists for every member of Congress.[19]

A problem that lobbyists must solve before establishing influence is to gain access to legislators. Access can be enhanced if there are friendships or personal ties between a legislator and the lobbyist.[20] The atypical social, economic, and educational background of Congressmen favors greater communication and access for some lobbyists (or groups) than others, since persons with life experiences similar to those of Congressmen are likely to gain greater access.[21] Milbrath, among others, has noted a bias for previous governmental experience in the recruitment of lobbyists, thus indicating the importance of one's "contacts" and of knowing one's way around the government. Admittedly, the popular image of large numbers of ex-Congressmen stalking the halls of Congress appears to be largely untrue.[22] But no doubt, with other things equal, being a former Congressman is an asset to a lobbyist. Such a status, as with many of the other relationships (such as common educational backgrounds) tends to affect the atmosphere (i.e., becoming more "chummy," less pressure-packed) and to expand the arenas for lobbying beyond the halls of Congress to, for example, the golf course, or the club, or even, at times, to the Congressman's home.

To secure and maintain direct access to legislators, a variety of economic payoffs may also be used. Despite the occurrence of widely publicized instances of bribery (one of the most recent being the conviction of former Maryland Senator Daniel Brewster for accepting $24,500 from his client, Spiegel, Inc., in return for votes on postal legislation favorable to Spiegel),[23] respected students of American politics, lobbyists, and Congressmen agree that the flagrant direct bribe is not a major factor in lobbyist-legislator relationships today.[24] Though the purpose may be similar, the disguised payoff, or "indirect bribery" as Milbrath calls it, typically comes in much more subtle, sophisticated, and "soft sell" forms. For example, instead of money going directly from a lobbyist into a Congressman's pockets with an open quid pro quo arrangement prevailing, the Congressman may be given a "tip" on a business investment or perhaps a low-interest loan from a bank, his law firm may be retained on a continuing basis, or he may be hired as a consultant or given a large honorarium for speaking at interest group gatherings.[25] In various small ways, such as theater tickets, small gifts, free rides or weekend cruises, free meals, entertainment, and so forth the lobbyist seeks to ingratiate himself to Congressmen and their staffs. Former Illinois Senator Paul Douglas describes the technique this way:

> The enticer does not generally pay money directly to the public representative. He tries instead, by a series of favors, to put the public official under such a feeling of personal obligation that the latter vradually loses his sense of mission to the public and comes to feel that his first loyalties are to his private benefactors and patrons. . . . Throughout this whole process the official will claim and may indeed believe that there is no causal connection between the favors he has received and the decisions which he makes. He will assert that the favors were given or received on the basis of pure friendship unsullied by worldly considerations.[26]

No single gift or favor even approaches the style or magnitude of what would be considered a meaningful bribe, but it is the intent of the lobbyist that the accumulation of favors over time will create a sense of indebtedness. Actually the wining and dining and entertainment are not as widespread, or thought to be as effective, as the popular folklore projects.[27] But it doesn't hurt, and at a minimum it does help to keep the doors of communication open, an important first step for actual influence to occur.[28]

The cost of running legislative campaigns is extremely expensive and interest groups know this very well. Financial contributions given directly to campaigns or other forms of financial support (such as the provision of supplies) can be of considerable significance in efforts to open or maintain access and gain influence. In the European systems, contributions are made primarily to party organizations. We observed in Chapter 2 that substantial sums of money may be contributed. For example, in the case of the CDU/CSU in 1969, the party received about $6 million in private contributions, much of it from the business community. As we will observe later in this chapter, organizations that made financial contributions to the CDU/CSU may well have been anticipating, among other things, that such contributions would be helpful in influencing nominations within the party. We have also seen that some nominated candidates in each of the systems are sponsored by interest groups, which frequently means that the interest group provides financial contributions through local party organizations to help support their campaigns. In addition, we observed that interest groups may carry out their own campaigns, costing thousands or even hundreds of thousands of dollars, in an effort to help one party or discredit another.

Interest groups in the United States are also actively involved in supporting and helping to finance election campaigns. A great deal of money comes from business and producer organizations, individual businessmen, farming, labor, and others as well. Edward Maher, newsletter editor for the BIPAC, which is the political committee of the National Association of Manufacturers and relies heavily on campaign donations, once stated: "If you get the right group down there, you don't have to lobby."[29] However, interest groups usually talk in less lofty terms, suggesting that their contributions are intended to "buy an ear" or give them the "right to dialogue." A spokesman for Union Carbide, pointing out why it gave funds to help candidates in districts in which it had production facilities, said, "When we have problems as constituents, we go talk. Therefore, they (candidates) have a right to ask (for funds at election time.)"[30] As one would suspect, political contributions tend to be given to those legislative candidates having "considerable similarity in outlook and interests" with the donor.[31]

If they are "wise shoppers," firms and organizations will concentrate on giving financial aid to those legislators who hold legislative posts that are relevant to their concerns. An example is Ling-Temco-Vought, a major defense contractor, whose political contributions have been made through a fund called CITIGO. According to Walter Pincus, writing in 1972:

Our limited research turned up a not surprising emphasis by CITIGO on defense-related legislators: $1,000 to Mollohan for Congress Committee (Representative Robert H. Mollohan, Democrat of West Virginia, a member of the House Armed Services Committee); $500 to Citizens for Minshall (Representative William E. Minshall, Republican of Ohio and ranking GOP member on the Defense Appropriations Subcommittee); $500 to Californians for Murphy (former Senator George Murphy, Republican of California and a member, before his defeat, of the Senate Armed Services Committee). There also were contributions of $2,000 to House Minority Leader Gerald Ford of Michigan. . . .[32]

In turn, Congressmen do seem to find time in their busy schedules to "listen" to their large campaign donors' problems and opinions—usually in an atmosphere characterized variously as "fraternal," or "chummy," or one of "good will."[33]

In their efforts to gain direct access, lobbyists and interest groups are concerned with getting to the "right" legislators. Whom one has access to can be important to the eventual success or failure of the interest group's policy goals. As one ex-lobbyist put it, "In Washington, it is the quality not the quantity of one's connections that counts. . . ."[34] Go where the power is, all the way to the top if possible. The success of the oil industry in maintaining the favorable oil depletion allowance was in no small way attributable to the powerful internal legislative positions of its Congressional allies, such as Lyndon Johnson, Sam Rayburn, Robert Kerr, and Russell Long. The infighting that has occurred among interest groups to locate friendly legislators in key parliamentary and parliamentary party posts, especially in the CDU/CSU, indicates the importance that German groups have attached to the quality of their connections.

Along the same line, lobbyists and interest groups attempt to establish direct contact with legislators whose major field of interest is of concern to the group. One of the principal means is for the group to establish communication with the members of relevant specialized committees. The group can do this by sending written communications to members and by testifying at committee hearings. It can also attempt to develop and cultivate informal contacts with members and try to place legislators affiliated with the group, or otherwise friendly to the group, on the committees.

Working through relevant committees is of such value to interest groups when using a legislative strategy that some years ago the British National Farmers Union stopped sponsoring candidates and establishing panels of parliamentarians who agreed to help the group in favor of working closely with the agricultural committees in the Labour and Conservative parliamentary parties. As Stewart observed, "If the Union succeeds in having good relations with the party committees other means of contact are unnecessary."[35] Such methods of contact are perceived to be valuable in the other legislatures as well. In Germany, groups frequently contact members of the relevant specialized party or Bundestag committees on important pieces of legislation. The frequency of contact that can occur is illustrated by the deputy who recalled seeing about ten interest group officials weekly during consideration of a particular bill.[36] As indicated earlier, interest groups also actively attempt to place their own representatives on the Bundestag committees of concern to them. As will be shown below (p. 352), these efforts have met with a good measure of success. In France, one of the reasons for changing the committee system of the Fourth Republic Assembly to that of the Fifth Republic was the feeling that interest groups had gained inordinate influence through connections with members of the specialized committees of the Fourth Republic Assembly. Although now diminished in power, interest groups still work through the Assembly committees as well as through committees within the parliamentary parties.

Interviews with American lobbyists also show that they look upon contacts with Congressional committees as an important part of their strategy. Efforts are made by groups to locate members friendly to them on the relevant Congressional committees. Groups also establish communications by presenting their cases at committee hearings. Of thirteen techniques lobbyists were asked to rank in terms of effectiveness, they ranked testifying at hearings as third in importance and presentation of research results (which often takes place in the context of the relevant specialized committees) as second in importance.[37] Congressmen seem to agree with this judgment. Scott and Hunt found in interviewing Congressmen that only 3 percent felt that group contact through committee hearings was ineffective. Over half the Congressmen they interviewed felt testimony given by interest groups during committee hearings was a very effective method for gaining favorable action. A further 41 percent felt it to be moderately effective or at times effective.[38]

The interest group techniques we have discussed thus far all involve, in one way or another, attempts to establish direct access to legislators, especially at key points of decision-making in the legislature. There are also ways in which interest groups may try to exert influence that do not rely on direct contact. The grass-roots campaign, which has received greater emphasis in recent years, is an obvious example.[39] A grass-roots campaign may attempt to get constituents to write to or otherwise communicate with their own representatives. If so, the group often works through its local membership (or local branches) or through people at the local level whose interests coincide with those of the group. Medical groups have frequently used this tactic. In 1945-46, the British Dental Association (BDA) objected to certain parts of the proposed National Health Service Bill and attempted to stir constituents into writing directly to their MPs. Its tactic was to advise dentists to make their patients aware of the BDA's opposition and to encourage their patients to write their MPs.[40] It has not been unknown for medical associations in the other three countries to follow a similar strategy, such as in the American Medical Association's long-standing attempt to prevent Congress from enacting "socialized" medicine programs.

The use of a constituency grass-roots campaign can also be observed in the coordinated action of oil companies to protect the oil depletion allowance and the import quotas on oil. According to Knoll, "By pooling their efforts, the companies are able to marshal formidable forces. In the carefully orchestrated campaign against reducing the depletion rate, for instance, one concern urged all of its stockholders to write to members of Congress; another focused on mobilizing its retired employees; a third concentrated on service station operators; a fourth sent brochures to its credit card holders."[41] Oil companies have also tried to work through groups that are indirectly connected to oil interests at the district and state levels. For example, in several of the "oil states," the companies have received the support of teachers' associations, which may have been so moved because of the relationship they perceived between the profits of oil companies in their states and state expenditures on education (or private donations to education).

The grass-roots campaign frequently goes beyond attempts to get constituents to communicate directly with their own representatives. A group may also attempt, through grass-roots activity, to communicate its strength to the legislature as a body rather than to individual representatives. This is what several educational groups in France endeavored to accomplish when, in opposition to the education reform law of 1959, they obtained over ten million signatures on a petition urging repeal of the law.[42] The French Teachers' League staged several mass rallies in an attempt to forestall the adoption of the same law. French farmers, especially from the poorer regions, have frequently staged mass demonstrations in attempts to get higher price supports. In an effort to get the British government to commit itself to equal pay for women, several different interested organizations established the Equal Pay Co-ordinating Committee and the Equal Pay Campaign Committee. These committees organized a number of mass rallies, culminating in one staged on "Equal Pay Day." The committees also presented Parliament with a petition upon which there were more than one million signatures.[43] Similarly, between 1948 and 1950 the Scottish Covenant League secured over two million signatures on its parliamentary petition for greater home rule for Scotland. In the United States, the civil rights sit-ins in the United States and the 1963 march on Washington had the purpose of demonstrating to Congress as a whole the depth and breadth of public feeling favoring the enactment of legislation on civil rights. Organized mass marches were also used to voice opposition to American policy in Vietnam. The examples we have cited are simply some of the more spectacular cases of the kind of grass-roots strategy that is meant to appeal to the legislature as a body and that go beyond attempts by groups to get constituents to communicate directly with their individual representatives.

Each of these examples, however, deals with concrete decisions a group or groups wanted to assist or oppose. Grass-roots campaigns need not necessarily limit themselves to specific decisions. There may also be prolonged campaigns having the purpose of cultivating generally favorable public attitudes that might later be used in specific instances. This kind of activity has been particularly characteristic of business groups through commercial advertising and other forms of public relations campaigns.[44]

Another indirect way of contacting legislators and of attempting to influence them is through the executive and administration. As we observed previously, interest groups are likely to try to gain access at significant points of decision-making in the legislature.

The importance groups attach to gaining access to the executive and administration is based on the same principle. Perhaps the best example of this principle at work was the change in the strategy of French interest groups as power shifted toward the executive and away from the Assembly from the Fourth to the Fifth Republics. While interest groups still attempted to influence parliamentarians directly and still undertook grass-roots campaigns, in the Fifth Republic groups began to devote more effort to strategies and tactics that would appeal to the executive and administration. According to one close observer: "The shift of power to the prime minister, president and civil service has generally brought, not a diminution of pressure group activity, but rather a corresponding shift in tactics or techniques . . . . The most profound change in style was brought about by the increased importance of the civil service. Wealthy organizations hired researchers, economists and even ex-civil servants in order to present their case to the appropriate department in the most effective possible manner."[45]

Because of the importance the executive and administration has come to assume in the formulation of major legislation in each of the four systems, one of the primary strategies of a group is to be consulted by the executive and administration during its process of formulating legislation and other policies. Executive consultation of interest groups occurs in each of the four systems. It has become formalized, especially the European systems, through the creation of a myriad of specialized advisory and ad hoc administrative committees that bring together on a continuing basis members both of the executive and administration on the one hand and representatives of the major interest groups concerned on the other hand. Discussion in these administrative committees may take on the character of formal negotiations and may become the sole strategy employed by the group at least until the negotiations are completed. Witness the remark of the Labour MP, Roy Mason: "on occasions trade union M.P.s are actually gagged. When a deputation from a trade union is in negotiation with a Government Department, all too often a hint is passed to the union's M.P.—'No questions in the House on this issue, please. They might be embarrassing.' "[46] Consultation has become formalized in the three European systems to such an extent that in some cases groups have come to regard being consulted as a formal right.

Despite the rather highly formalized nature of the executive consultative process in these systems, it is not the case that a particular group invariably will be consulted. Presumably, this would be even more so the case in a system like the United States, in which the process of consultation, though present, is somewhat less institutionalized. Except as required by legislation, whether a group is consulted or not is, in the end, determined by the executive and administration. For example, in our case study of the reform of French agriculture we saw that the executive did consult major agricultural groups during the process of policy formulation. On the other hand, it was not until 1968 that the French government engaged in consultations with most major educational groups during the process of formulating education reform legislation. In 1959 the government refused to consult with the High Council of National Education during the development of its proposals for educational reform of that year. The government again ignored several important educational groups in developing the Fouchet Plan during 1964 and 1965.[47]

Because consultation is to some extent dependent upon the agreement of the executive, which is influenced by political considerations, the conditions that lead particular groups to achieve a consultative status and to be influential during consultation are variable. Research on our four systems, however, indicates some relevant factors to be: the size of the group's membership along with the percentage of its clientele included within its membership, the importance of the group to the health of significant sectors of the economy and society, the social status of the group, the group's political orientation, the informational expertise at the command of the group, and the financial status of the group.

Behind such factors as the size of the group, the percentage of clientele the group includes, and the relevance of the group for the health of significant sectors of the economy may be such considerations as voter appeal and the potential ability of the group to undermine the successful application of legislation covering the group's interests. Social status may also indicate voter appeal (perhaps by way of the deference given to the group by the public).

Social status may again be relevant because, as with legislators, access to the executive and administration appears to be partly a function of whether interest group representatives and administrators share a common background or not—common schooling, a common social milieu, and so forth.[48] As one observer said of interest group relations with the administration in the Fifth Republic: "Increasingly there is a dialogue between the 'men of the big lobbies' and the technocrats, who speak the same language and usually come from the same social class."[49]

The financial strength of an interest group is an important source of influence during the consultative process partly because such strength can afford the group greater ability to develop expertise helpful to presenting its case to administrators. Even so, the financial strength of the group, as it attempts to influence the consultative process, needs also to be viewed in the context of actual or potential campaign contributions. Contributions groups make directly to the chief executive or to his party (rather than to individual legislators or local party organizations) surely have as one purpose gaining or maintaining access to the executive and administration in order to influence decisions of concern to the group. Indeed, there may be attempts at a direct quid pro quo. It is not known how prevalent or successful these attempts are, but financial contributions to the Nixon campaign amounting in the hundreds of thousands of dollars by the Dairymen's Association and the subsequent alteration of decisions on milk price supports by the Nixon administration to favor dairymen created suspicions that a quid pro quo had been exacted. And, the Watergate investigation has revealed a series of other such questionable dealings. The activities of the Federation of German Industry (BDI), too, are relevant here. It is worth quoting Braunthal at length:

Evidently industry is not willing to aid the conservative parties out of pure altruism. Explicitly or implicitly it wants assurance, first of all, that they will pursue economic and social policies in harmony with its own goals; second, that they will support the candidacy of Bundestag deputies who are sympathetic to the BDI. The way in which industry has attached strings to its financing activities may readily be seen from several cases which have been publicized by the press or by the opposition, and of which there has been no official denial. . . . In 1960, according to one news story, the Chancellor yielded to strong pressure from steel executives who threatened to reduce their contributions to the CDU and to increase those to the FDP unless he reversed himself on the question of prohibiting Sunday work in the steel mills. Another report has it that in 1961 the monthly check for 100,000 DM . . . was suddenly withheld because of Berg's annoyance at Adenauer for having gone back on a promise not to revalue the currency.[50]

As this remark and much of the foregoing discussion suggests, interest groups attach considerable weight to influencing decisions made in the political system. And it is not surprising that interest groups should take such a position, for the stakes that they have in these decisions can be quite high.

Our discussion thus far has been focused on providing an overview of different kinds of strategies interest groups use in attempting to influence the decision-making process and particularly decisions in the legislature. Insofar as concerns these decisions, interest groups employ both direct and indirect strategies, with each of these in turn having numerous variations. Because a number of different groups are typically competing in their efforts to influence legislative decisions, it is the rare group that employs only one of the strategies. Almost all groups make use of several tactics, including direct contacts, grass-roots efforts, and attempts to influence executive and party leaders. They will perhaps emphasize a single tactic at one point in time and others at different points, depending upon the success they have achieved, who is the target of influence, and the phase of the decision-making process involved. But, whichever strategy they use or however many they use, the purpose remains the same. This is to secure favorable action on decisions that are important to the group either by getting the "right" legislators elected or by influencing them once they are in office.

The Responses of Legislators to Interest Groups

Keeping in mind this review of the kinds of strategies interest groups use in attempting to influence legislators, let us turn to examining the success groups have in getting legislators to support their aims. What factors are likely to maximize a group's success? We begin by looking at legislators' relations with interest groups in the context of their relations with their party and the executive. Then we will turn to relations between interest groups and individual legislators outside the context of executive and party influence. Here we will consider evidence dealing with legislators' goals and purposes, along with relevant interest group resources, as these pertain to interest group effectiveness. The discussion will focus on legislators' policy attitudes, desires to make informed decisions, ambitions to survive in office, and role orientations toward constituents.

Indirect Relations between Interest Groups and Legislators

We can begin with the point that a legislator's response to an interest group may be indirect. By influencing the party leadership or the executive, an interest group may increase the probability of influencing ordinary legislators of that party (or of the executive's party), even legislators whom the interest group has not directly contacted. Of course, interest groups are well aware of this. The importance interest groups attach to being consulted by the executive in the process of policy formulation is certainly partly due to their knowledge that the policy stance the executive takes will, in turn, influence legislative decisions. Thus, Hirsch-Weber observed of interest groups in West Germany that "In addressing cabinet members, interest groups see in them not always the heads of the administration, but also party leaders able to control or influence their friends in parliament. . . ."[51]

As our discussion in earlier chapters showed, there is little question that both party and the executive help shape how legislators behave. This can benefit an interest group if its position has gained support from these quarters. It equally can place limits on the interest group if opposition is forthcoming from these quarters.

Where legislators of the governing party vote with a high degree of cohesion, it is not difficult to imagine that the influence of an interest group might depend upon how successful it was in influencing governmental or party leaders. The case of the efforts of interest groups to influence legislative outcomes on French agricultural policy revealed quite clearly that success depended very much on influencing the posture of the President and key members of the government (see Chapter 3). A similar phenomenon also applies to Great Britain. A number of examples could be cited where party leadership support for the objectives of a group brought about greater support for those objectives among ordinary parliamentarians of the party.[52] It would be equally easy to cite examples where the objectives of an interest group to which an MP was associated ran counter to the policy position of his party, with the MP ending up by supporting his party. Here is one example of the latter situation:

Mr. Charles Royle found himself [in such] a situation when the Labour Party published its proposals for the nationalization of the importing and the wholesaling of meat. As Vice-President of the National Federation of Meat Traders' Associations he was placed in a very difficult position. At its annual meeting . . . a resolution was passed instructing the Executive to take early action to combat nationalization of the wholesale meat trade. After it had also been resolved that no money be granted from the Parliamentary and Defense Fund to any member . . . of the House of Commons who supported nationalization of the meat trade, Mr. Royle announced his resignation and said that his political party had declared itself in favor of nationalization of wholesale meat distribution and that the time had come when political issues could not be divided from the trade point of view.[53]

Indeed, when British MPs have supported their party over an interest group to which they were affiliated, as in the above case, they appear to have been rather well insulated from interest group retaliation, at least retaliatory efforts in the sense of group attempts to prevent the renomination of the legislators. There have been few serious attempts of this kind, and even fewer have been successful.[54]

Where the forces of party and the executive have been weaker, they have still often played some part in how legislators behaved toward interest groups. Speaking about the calculations that influenced his actions toward interest groups, a member of Congress said: "Now, of course, if you are a member of the Administration party, then you try to get the viewpoint of the President. You have to know whether something under consideration is in line with the President's program and with what the Bureau of the Budget sends up. That's the first thing to find out."[55]

The fact that members may wish to know the views of the party and the executive (if of their party) and that this may affect their own actions is seen in the case of health insurance reform in West Germany and especially in the behavior of the labor union members of the CDU/CSU at the early stages of the fight over financing the reforms. According to Safran, "Although many of these men opposed some forms of cost sharing, they felt constrained to be silent about their disapproval because they were expected to identify with the CDU position on the issue. . . ."[56]

Ties to party may in the end lead legislators to behave quite differently from the way they otherwise would. Take, for example, the support urban Democratic Congressmen gave to the farm programs advocated by their party despite the lower costs attending the programs proposed by the Republican administration. One of the factors that helped induce support from the urban Democrats for their party's farm policy is suggested by the observations of one of its members:

> the leadership attempts to exert a personal persuasive influence. I have experienced this on two issues, one of which was the farm bill just prior to the 1956 election. My district opposes the party position on farm policy. The Speaker called me and said, 'This is very vital to the party, particularly with the national election approaching. Can you possibly go along with us?' It was a personal appeal from the Speaker on the day of the vote. . . . Friends told me he talked to them also. In effect he buttoned the thing up by that type of personal appeal.[57]

Thus, how legislators behave toward various interests can be shaped by, and must be seen in the context of, the legislators' ties to their party and/or to the executive. Indeed, by gaining the active support of the executive or party leaders, an interest group's influence can, in essence, have a multiplier effect that reaches beyond the support given by the executive or party leaders to the legislators they are able to influence.

Yet, for a multiplier effect to occur in the first place, interest groups must be able to influence the executive or party leaders. This raises other questions. How much are interest groups able to shape the policies of a strong executive backed by a cohesive legislative majority? Are interest groups able to do so to the same degree that they can influence the decisions of a legislature characterized by shifting coalitions and the wide dispersal of power among individual committees and legislators? The limited amount of research that has been carried out suggests that they can and do. Thus, a comparison of the operation of the French Fifth Republic to its predecessor, the French Fourth Republic, found that overall interest-group success in influencing policies has been about as great since the system enabled the President and government to dominate legislative decision-making as it was in the Fourth Republic, where the legislature's powers were more decentralized and policy outcomes in the legislature were determined by shifting and diverse coalitions.[58] Several comparisons of Britain and the United States go further to suggest that in a more party- and executive-dominated system, such as in Great Britain, the overall influence of interest groups on policy outcomes may well normally increase.[59]

As we pointed out earlier in the chapter, how much influence an interest group achieves in the process of executive decision-making depends upon a variety of factors. There are, of course, electoral requirements that involve the executive's attempt to maintain and enlarge its bases of electoral support (including its means of political financing). Furthermore, members of the executive and administration who are occupied in developing policy have their own policy convictions as well as their own identifications and friendships that lead them to give preference to some groups, or to representatives of those groups, over others. Moreover, considerations of making workable policy decisions may require the cooperation or acquiesence of certain interest groups as well as their expertise. As a consequence of factors such as these, there exists an interplay between interest groups and the executive which, probably no less than in the legislature, enables interest groups to exert influence on executive policies and leads some groups to be treated more preferentially than others.

Direct Relations between Interest Groups and Legislators

In the same vein, the success of interest groups in their relations with individual legislators ultimately depends on the goals of the legislators and the compatibility of these goals with favorable action toward the interest group. Since the influence interest groups exert by way of their direct relations with individual legislators has frequently been the subject of concern and criticism, it is proper to discuss the nature of these relations in some detail.

In this regard, several different kinds of goals can influence the way legislators behave toward interest groups. One goal that is often thought to be quite significant is the legislator's career ambitions, and the rewards and sanctions interest groups can apply in this connection. However, while we would not deny the relevance this factor can have (as we will point out further along in the chapter), career ambition is only one of several goals that may shape how legislators behave.

The influence of normative considerations Among the other goals relevant to determining relations between a legislator and interest groups, and perhaps even more fundamental, are the legislator's normative dispositions and especially his own policy attitudes. That is, how a legislator behaves in dealing with a given interest group, and whether it is useful for an interest group to establish direct contact with the particular legislator or not, is likely to depend upon how compatible the group's policy interests are with the legislator's own policy outlook.

Let us review some of the main research findings dealing with the American Congress. Summarizing the results of their interviews with Representatives on the influence of interest groups and lobbyists in Congress, Scott and Hunt concluded: "In addition to group contacts, many other stimuli impinge upon a congressman . . . The personal outlook of a congressman is often a vital factor in influencing his vote; he, like other men (and more than most men), will have policy preferences, and he has ample opportunity to give them play."[60] Zeigler, too, was led to conclude after his intensive examination of interest groups that "the influence of interest groups in the legislative process depends more on the harmony of values between the group and the legislators than it does on the ability of the group to wield its 'power' either through skillful techniques or presumed electoral influence."[61] Cohen also detected that a factor characteristic of most effective interest groups was that their interests coincided with the basic ideologies of most Congressmen.[62] Finally, an examination by Bauer, Pool, and Dexter found that the legislators' own stands were usually more critical than interest group activity for the development of legislation in the area they studied, which was tariffs. They offered these comments:

> Indeed, in many instances, and the most important ones, the relation between officeholder and lobby is exactly the reverse of what the public thinks. The protectionist leadership in the United

States clearly lay inside the United States Congress. Congressmen Richard Simpson and Cleveland Bailey and Senators Malone and Eugene Millikin were far more important defenders of a waning ideology than were the more-or-less inert American Tariff League or the clamorous but relatively unsophisticated Strackbein committee. The business interests that sought protection were, of course, an essential ingredient in the picture. . . . It was the congressman, however, who opened the path to business pleas, and it was he who stimulated and guided the protectionist lobbies in their every effective move. The lobby became the congressman's publicity bureau. Indeed, without a congressman working with it, a lobby found it difficult to do anything the press would consider newsworthy.[63]

As one Congressman, in another context, argued: "Lobbyists are effective when they are urging what you are for and not effective when they are urging what you are not for."[64]

John Kingdon's analysis of the voting decisions of members of the House in 1969, covering fifteen diverse issues, examined the influence of the members' own policy attitudes alongside a series of other factors that might influence their behavior on floor votes.[65] In addition to the Congressman's policy attitudes, these factors included interest groups, constituency, the administration, the party leadership, fellow Congressmen, and the staff of the Congressman. Kingdon determined the policy position of these factors largely by interviews or published statements. For reasons we will mention momentarily, he found that about half of the time there was little direct conflict among the factors as they related to the voting decisions of individual Congressmen. However, taking the cases where the individual Congressman's own policy attitudes did conflict with the policy direction in which either all or all but one of the other factors (including interest groups) were going, Kingdon found that Congressmen voted in line with their own policy attitudes somewhat over 70 percent of the time.[66] On the other hand, taking those cases where the position of the interest group conflicted with the policy direction in which either all or all but one (always including the Congressman's own attitudes on the issue) of the other factors were going, Kingdon found *no* instance in which Congressmen voted in line with the interest group. Thus, when a legislator's policy attitudes differed from the stances of interest groups, the findings again point to the value of the Congressman's own attitudes to the way he behaved.

Partly because of the importance of the Congressman's policy dispositions, the primary function of lobbying has been more one of attempting to reinforce legislators than of attempting to convert them. Thus, lobbyists have tended to contact those who typically supported the group and its aims, which helps to explain why Kingdon often found little conflict between a Congressman's policy attitudes and the interest groups that lobbied him. Similarly, Matthews's study of Senators found that, "the vast majority of all lobbying is directed at senators who are already convinced."[67] Scott and Hunt also observed that people who have been in Congress over a period of time and have made their positions known were rarely bothered by opposition pressure groups.[68] And, according to Bauer, Pool, and Dexter, "lobbyists fear to enter where they may find a hostile reception. Since such uncertainty is greatest precisely regarding those who are undecided, the lobbyist is apt to neglect contact with those very persons he might be able to influence. . . . It is much easier to carry on activities within the circle of those who agree and encourage you. The result is that the lobbyist becomes in effect a service bureau for those congressmen already agreeing with him, rather than an agent of direct persuasion."[69]

It is probable that legislators' policy attitudes have been important to their relations with interest groups not only in a lobbying context but also in situations where legislators have been associated with interest groups through formal affiliation or sponsorship. Numerous British, French, and West German legislators have been interest-group affiliated or sponsored in one way or another. It is likely that in many of these cases the members' policy attitudes have coincided with, or at least been sympathetic toward, the broad aims of their groups. As Stewart observed about interest groups and their MPs in Britain, "The group enters into a relationship knowing that the M.P. is sympathetic with it. . . ."[70] Referring to affiliated and sponsored members in the Bundestag, Eschenburg noted the very close policy attachments that have linked many of the members to their groups and that have worked, in turn, to predispose their support for the kinds of policies that served the groups.[71] Indeed, in attempting to further certain policy ideas to which they have been committed, it has not been uncommon for such members to have led, organized, and in effect used their groups rather than awaiting for initiatives to come from them.[72]

This is not to say that the policy stands of affiliated members always coincided with the interests of their groups. The comments of some of the industry (BDI) representatives in the Bundestag are instructive along this line. One remarked that his willingness to go to bat for the BDI was tempered by whether, "the BDI had a good case and I was personally convinced of it. . . ." Another industry representative said, "On three key issues I voted against the industrial point of view. I told my industry friends: 'Listen, it is a question of conscience.' "[73] Observations such as these indicate that matters of conscience may enter into how intensely an affiliated member supports the position of his interest group and even whether the member lends his support to that position or not. Along a similar vein, legislators' own attitudes on party issues have been thought to be a very important factor in determining, for example, whether British MPs decided to become active on behalf of an interest group or not, including groups to which the MPs were affiliated.[74]

The observation of the BDI member cited above, who spoke of the importance of being convinced, suggests that this might have been partly determined by the effectiveness of the group's case, presumably by how reasoned the case was and the evidence it brought to bear. In previous chapters, we found that expertise, or perceived expertise, has been a resource that influenced relations among legislators as well as between legislators and the executive. It is also a resource that has influenced interest group success. Perhaps this is one reason why interest groups may not be content simply with the number of sponsored legislators they have, but also care about the ability of these legislators to be persuasive: as the BDI put it, having representatives with sufficient economic expertise to be "able consistently and convincingly to look after the interests" of the group;[75] or as an official of the German Catholic Labour Movement told one of the authors, having "members whose views are respected by their colleagues."

Evidence regarding information and expertise as a resource affecting relations between interest groups and legislators is found particularly in research on the United States Congress. David Truman found that an important factor determining whether an interest group obtains access to a legislator or not "is created by the legislator-politician's need of information and a group's ability to supply it." In making policy decisions, and for numerous other purposes, Congressmen need information. Truman pointed out that "Access is likely to be available to groups somewhat in proporation to their ability to meet this need."[76] The authors of *The Legislative System*, too, concluded, "Pressure groups are most welcome in the legislative arena when they go beyond a mere assertion of demands and interests and present information and data which help legislators work out compromises and adjustments among the most insistent demands of groups on the basis of some vague conception of the public interest against which particular claims can be judged."[77] Information gained from interest groups serves as a supplement and alternative to the other sources available to the legislators. The value of this is enhanced by the difficulty legislators sometimes have in getting information from the executive. A great many students of the Congress have concluded that the influence of an interest group on Congressmen is based at least partly on the usefulness of the information the interest group is able to supply.[78]

As we observed earlier, the provision of information and data has certainly been thought by practitioners (both lobbyists and members of Congress) to be an effective way of influencing Congressional behavior. For example, lobbyists ranked the presentation of research results as the second most effective of thirteen techniques of influence. Testifying at hearings was ranked third. Each was thought to be more effective in gaining favorable Congressional action than public relations campaigns (ranked fifth) or communicating with members through close friends (ranked seventh).[79]

Arndt has said that "the problem of obtaining information . . . is the distinctive problem of the Representative of today," enabling interest groups to wield greater influence than they otherwise might.[80] Evidence suggests that an interest group's access to American Congressmen and its influence on legislative response may well be affected by the ability of the group to provide technical and political information useful to the making of decisions. However, Arndt was not basing his observation on American legislative politics. Rather, his observation was based on his years of experience in the German Bundestag.[81]

Of course, the ability of an interest group to gain favorable responses and action from legislators on the basis of the information and expertise it supplies also has limits. Two limits are that other groups may present competing information and that there usually are sources of information, or perspectives on that information, outside those of interest groups. A further limit is that legislators do not act solely on the basis of information and expertise. Not only may a legislator give other dispositions equal or greater priority, but the validity he attaches to the information he receives may itself be a function of these other dispositions, such as for example his own policy attitudes.[82]

The available evidence dealing with the normative concerns considered thus far suggests that such concerns have been prominent in influencing legislators' relations with interest groups. Previous discussion indicated that party and executive influences have also been important factors. Of course, building upon members' ties to their party and to an executive of their party, upon their own policy attitudes, and upon their desire to make informed decisions by no means exhausts the ways interest groups attempt to develop favorable legislative response. Indeed, the factors discussed thus far have not yet brought to the fore what some feel is perhaps the most important factor shaping direct relations between individual legislators and interest groups. This is the bearing that interest groups have on the success with which legislators pursue their individual career objectives.

Interest group influence through the electoral process Particularly relevant in this regard is the ability of interest groups to affect the political survival of individual legislators. Here our principal concern is the relations that evolve between interest groups and legislators as a consequence of rewards or sanctions affecting survival that interest groups have at their disposal. We thus want to focus on the cases included in our study where the literature suggests that interest group intervention, including their financial contributions, has had greatest impact on the nomination and/or election outcomes of individual legislators. This leads us to concentrate especially on members of the two American parties and the West German CDU/CSU.

We begin with the American Congress. In the case of Congress, interest groups can turn to a variety of resources in an effort to influence individual election outcomes. These include the sizes of their clienteles, contributing work or organizational machinery to election campaigns, and making financial contributions to these campaigns. They can attempt to use such resources either in primaries or in general elections. Certainly we hear a great deal about the part interest groups play in elections and especially about the influence their financial contributions exert on how Congressmen behave.

How much an interest group is able to gain a favorable response from Congressmen because of their dependence on the group's resources at election time is difficult to measure precisely. Some evidence suggests that the ability of groups to affect elections is not as great as we might first anticipate. One of the earliest studies, by V. O. Key, attempted to determine whether the way Congressmen voted on legislation of importance to the American Legion had any bearing on how well Congressmen went on to do in elections. He found that the voting record of Congressmen made little difference for their electoral fortunes: "The Legion's general effect on the outcome was almost completely negligible."[83] On the other hand, a study of how well candidates supported by labor did in Congressional elections of 1948 reached a somewhat different conclusion. Of the 215 candidates labor endorsed, 144 were elected. Twenty-six of the labor-endorsed candidates defeated Congressmen who had held their seats for three or more terms. An additional 61 defeated Congressmen had held a seat for one term.[84] The contrasts in the evidence just cited led David Truman to observe that "The effects of interest group activity upon the outcome of elections are . . . highly variable. They are, moreover, easily exaggerated. The difficulty of obtaining incontrovertible evidence that a group has wielded influence at the polls facilitates this tendency toward overestimation of the group's effectiveness."[85]

A more recent illustration of the difficulty in determining the effect of interest group activity on Congressional elections concerns the financial contributions of a major business organization, BIPAC,[86] during the 1970 elections to the House of Representatives. During this election, BIPAC contributed from $1,000 to $5,000 to the campaigns of each of forty-eight nonincumbent candidates for the House, all Republicans.[87] A total of 19 of these candidates, or about 40 percent, were victorious. Facing nonincumbent Democratic candidates, the nonincumbent Republicans BIPAC supported did quite well, winning seventeen of twenty seven races, or 63 percent of the races. However, checking the 1968 outcomes, we found that the Republicans had also held 63 percent of these districts in 1968. Each of the remaining candidates BIPAC supported faced an incumbent. Of these 21 candidates, only two were victorious. From this record, it would be tenuous to conclude that BIPAC contributions made a noticeable difference for the election outcomes of the candidates it supported. On the other hand, neither do we know what would have happened in these races had BIPAC refrained from making any contributions at all.

What, then, do the practitioners think is the effectiveness of interest-group electoral resources in influencing Congressional behavior? Both lobbyists and Congressmen seem to agree that the technique of influencing Congressmen through either financial contributions to campaigns or campaign work is of value, but only of moderate value. Presented with a choice of thirteen techniques by which to influence legislators, lobbyists in Washington ranked campaign work eighth and financial contributions to campaigns tenth.[88] Congressmen have also been asked how they would estimate the effectiveness of financial contributions to campaigns in getting favorable Congressional action. Six percent of the respondents said campaign contributions were very effective in stimulating favorable Congressional action, a further 30 percent said either that they were moderately effective or that they could be effective, and 18 percent were unsure. The remaining 46 percent said that they were not very effective. Congressmen responded somewhat similarly to the question of how effective campaign work was in getting favorable Congressional action.[89]

One of the advantages for the group that is often obtained through financial contributions to campaigns or active campaign work is gaining access to the Congressman. According to one observer, "When the lobbyists themselves are asked to define the chief value of campaign contributions in their work, they frequently reply with one word: access. . . . Since it would be unrealistic to expect the lobbyist to describe his campaign contributions as attempts at influence, the access explanation may be, in some cases, a cover story. In the majority of instances, however, it is probably the truth or close to it."[90]

Nevertheless, it appears that the influence of campaign contributions, when they are known to a Congressman, can be greater than simply affording the group access. Campaign contributions may make it more difficult for the legislator to act strongly against the group. One Congressman observed that you don't have to do anything your contributors tell you to do, but he went on to say, neither do you "kick your contributors in the face."[91] Congressmen do their best not to hurt their contributors.[92] Another Congressman looked at campaign contributions as a more positive resource: "Campaigns cost more and more, and if you are going to have any influence on the candidate, you are going to help him in his campaign contributions. Now I don't think that a congressman looks back and votes according to campaign contributions received, but he can't help being indirectly influenced by what his friends think. He knows that his friends are the ones who back him financially in a campaign so indirectly they are going to influence his decisions."[93]

Why, then, should campaign work and campaign contributions be felt to be only moderately effective as techniques for getting Congressmen to respond favorably. The most important reason may be that, as Truman observed above, "the effects of interest group activity upon the outcome of elections are . . . highly variable."[94] If a Congressman perceives that the effect of the interest group will not be significant for his reelection, he will be less likely to respond to the group on those grounds. Scott and Hunt suggest that:

Those Congressmen who minimized the importance of campaign activity remarked that while spokesmen for an organization might say the organization would work for him (or, far more rarely, against him), the organization was rarely able to deliver. The reason for this, it was suggested, is that organizations do not have the machinery to work in the field for a congressman, often do not have the resources, and are rarely sufficiently concerned about an individual candidate to make a significant effort for or against him."[95]

Financial contributions, too, have certain limits. In the first place, a contributor works within a two-party system. Because it is a two-party system, the choice the contributor has in whom to support, at least after the primaries, may be rather restricted. It is understandable, for example, that a far greater portion of the contributions from business and financial interests goes to Republican candidates than to Democratic candidates and that the reverse is true for contributions from labor unions.[96] And, to the extent that the contributor's choice is confined, he becomes as dependent upon the candidate to whom he contributes as the candidate may be dependent upon his contribution. Second, the choice the contributor has may be even more severely restricted because of the incumbent's advantage in gaining reelection. Contributors gain little access by contributing to a loser. It is not surprising, then, that incumbents sometimes receive financial contributions from potential rival interests.[97] Third, most incumbents, particularly in the House, are not especially dependent on large contributions ($1,000 or more).[98] Moreover, whether in the House or Senate, most candidates receive financial contributions from a sizable number of different sources. Because candidates usually do receive contributions from many different sources, it is frequently difficult to say, as the BIPAC illustration indicated, that contributions from a particular source, even large contributions, had a noticeable impact on an election outcome or that it was a particularly crucial factor in bringing about victory.

As this also suggests, money is in any case only one resource in the politics of winning an election. It is difficult to say how valuable money is compared to other resources, but it is clearly not the sole factor that determines election outcomes. Indeed, it is not always clear whether spending beyond a certain amount in a campaign has much effect at all (the exact amount would depend, of course, on the size and "safeness" of the constituency as well as whether the opponent is an incumbent or a nonincumbent). For example, comparing cases in which nonincumbents ran against each other during the 1972 House elections, *each* of the four highest spenders *lost* his bid for election despite the fact that each spent, on the average, $100,000 more than did his opponent.[99] This was also the fate of the candidate in 1970 who spent $2 million in an attempt to win election to the House.[100] An interesting illustration on the Senate side is the case of Senator Albert Gore's defeat in 1970. This would seem on the surface to be the obvious example of money talking, since Gore's opponent, William Brock, spent three times more than did Gore in winning this 1970 Tennessee election, but one seasoned observer takes another view. According to Richard Harris, "While Brock outspent Gore by three to one, Gore ended up spending more than half a million dollars—more than enough for him to get his message across to the voters. Several of Gore's aides put his defeat down, most of all, to his failure during his last term to mend his fences back home—with county chairmen, precinct workers, prominent supporters, and ordinary voters—and thereby cut down the resentment toward him that had obviously been building up over the years. 'Bill Brock didn't win, Albert Gore lost,' one of the Senator's aides said the day after the election."[101]

All of the above considerations, taken together, might lie behind the assessments of both Congressmen and lobbyists that financial contributions to campaigns generally are of moderate, but only moderate, effectiveness in influencing Congressional behavior.[102] Yet the difficulty of calculating how important certain financial contributions might be to winning the next election or of how effective a group will be through campaign work cuts both ways. On the one hand, it may allow the legislator greater freedom of response. On the other hand, it is a consideration the legislator may have to take into account in deciding how to act. His decision might well rest on how much he thinks responding favorably to the group will affect voting support for him in his district. If, for example, the Congressman perceives the group may be able to deliver at the polls, this is a factor he probably will tread lightly. One Congressman put it this way: "When you measure pressure, you measure it in terms of what the groups do in an election period. In my area, railway labor's Political League is one of the most aggressive and active campaign organizations I know. It really does a job of informing its members of who has been friendly to railroad labor. Their activity, of which they gave tangible evidence during a campaign, is certainly a factor to think about when you look at a group's position on a bill affecting it."[103]

If this is the case, we ought to find that how a Congressman behaves on legislation upon which an interest group has a stake would be related to the potential support for the group's stands in his district. Both the visibility and salience of the particular issue and the connection between the group's interests and the Congressman's constituency ought to be relevant. Along this line, Kingdon's study of the House reached exactly this conclusion. The study involved an analysis, through interviews, of over two hundred individual voting decisions in 1969 by members of the House on fifteen different issues. Among the issues covered were the tax reform bill, the ABM, amendments to the poverty program, farm payment limitation, water pollution abatement, elementary and secondary education, the cigarette bill, and foreign aid. The research found that in order for interest groups to be of major importance to Representatives' voting decisions, the issue in question ordinarily had to be one of high visibility or salience. Five of the fifteen issues were of this type. In addition, the research showed that on issues of high visibility, interest groups located outside the district were of little importance to the voting decisions of individual Representatives unless the group's position was consistent with the Representative's perception of the direction of active opinion located within his constituency.[104]

Numerous illustrations could be cited to attest to the importance of constituency considerations for the way members of Congress behave toward various interests. Farm policy is an example. Investigating six important roll call votes from 1947 to 1962 covering agricultural policy, Mayhew attempted to determine which Congressmen supported the more costly farm policy (based on higher price supports and greater governmental intervention) advocated by the Democratic leadership and which Congressmen supported the less costly farm policy (favoring lower price supports and less governmental intervention) urged by the Republican leadership and generally also by the American Farm Bureau. He examined Congressmen both according to party and according to whether they came from a farm or nonfarm electorate. This was measured by the percentage of persons involved in farm work in the district.

The results of the six roll calls found that, notwithstanding the position of the American Farm Bureau, the Democrats representing farm districts were highly unified in support of the agricultural policy of their party (which gave greater financial support to agriculture than the Republican alternative did). Although the Democrats from nonfarm districts also tended to support their party, they were far less cohesive as a group. The total party vote of the Democratic Congressmen representing farm districts on the six roll calls was 395 to 13 (a party voting score of .96) as contrasted to 633 to 215 from the Democratic Congressmen representing nonfarm districts (a party voting score of .75).

Looking at the Republicans, Mayhew found that the main defectors from their party to support the Democratic farm policy, as we would expect, were the Republicans from farm districts. In fact, the Republicans from farm districts supported the Democratic policy more than they supported the policy of their own party (their party voting score was only .36). On the other hand, the Republicans from the nonfarm districts voted rather solidly behind their own party's farm policy. Their party voting score was .85.[105] Thus, the voting patterns for both parties indicate that Congressmen deviated from their party in large numbers only if such deviation was consistent with the type of electorate the Congressmen represented.

The Republicans from farm districts who voted with the Democrats discovered in 1954 that they were politically well advised to do so, for the Republicans from farm districts who had gone along with their party found themselves locked in stiff battles for survival in the 1954 Congressional elections. There were nineteen Republicans from farm districts who deviated from their party in 1954 to support the Democratic agricultural policy. Only two of the nineteen were defeated in the 1954 Congressional elections, and these two had the misfortune to face Democrats who were extremely active in their opposition to Republican agricultural policies.[106] There were an additional nineteen Republicans from farm districts who remained loyal to their party on agricultural policy. Eight of these Republicans, or 42 percent, were defeated in the 1954 election.

Another area that Mayhew's analysis covered was labor legislation. His analysis in this regard examined thirteen roll call votes that found labor in opposition to business and most Democrats (supporting labor) in opposition to most Republicans (supporting business). If support for labor at the district level was a relevant factor (measured by the percentage of blue-collar workers in the district), one would expect that the Democrats most likely to support the prolabor position of their party would be the Democrats from the labor districts and that the Democrats least likely to unite behind their party would come from nonlabor districts. Similarly, we would anticipate that the Republicans most likely to support the probusiness position of their party would be the

Republicans from nonlabor districts and that the Republicans least likely to unite behind the party would come from labor districts.

An examination of the voting indicates that this is what happened. Highest party support came from Democrats representing labor districts, with a party voting score on the thirteen roll calls of .85 and from Republicans representing nonlabor districts, with a party voting score of .87. Democrats from nonlabor districts and Republicans from labor districts were less likely to unite behind their parties on these thirteen roll call votes. Thus, Democrats from nonlabor districts had a party voting score of only .57, and Republicans from labor districts had a party voting score of .75. On the basis of these voting patterns, Mayhew observed that Congressional behavior on labor legislation could be partially explained in the following terms: "Conflicting party pressures superimposed on conflicting constituency pressures produced unity among labor Democrats and nonlabor Republicans, disunity among nonlabor Democrats and labor Republicans."[107]

At least in the fields of agricultural and labor legislation, it would appear that how Congressmen voted was related to the size of the interested group in the electorates the Congressmen represented. Unless an interest could build on likely support for its position in Congressmen's electorates, its ability to get Congressmen to shift their responses away from their party's position was noticeably weakened. Indeed, the pull of party was often apparent, although to a lesser extent, even for Congressmen who faced possible countervailing group pressures at the district level.

Perhaps one additional illustration would help to underline these points. In mid-1971, the House of Representatives voted on a controversial proposal to grant an emergency loan guarantee to the Lockheed Aircraft Corporation. A diverse set of political forces was operating in this case. Both President Nixon and George Meany, President of the AFL-CIO, supported the loan guarantee, while a number of others (such as General Electric, several other labor leaders, the ADA, and the ACA) either strongly or conditionally opposed the guarantee. Conflicting forces such as these helped pave the way for a highly divided vote within the House as a whole (192 to 189), within each party (Republicans were divided 90 to 60, Democrats 102 to 129), and within the northern and southern Democratic delegations (northern Democrats were divided 55 to 95, southern Democrats 47 to 32).

One of the major contracts upon which Lockheed was working was the Tri-Star Project. The corporations that were major suppliers to this project were located in 34 different Congressional districts. Not only the corporations, but also their employees, might have suffered harmful effects were Lockheed to fail. It is interesting, then, that the Congressmen from these districts consistently supported the loan guarantee more so than did their party or their regional colleagues. Whereas 57 percent of the Congressional Republicans from outside Tri-Star districts supported the guarantee, 81 percent (13 of 16) of the Republicans from Tri-Star districts supported the guarantee (one Republican did not vote); whereas 36 percent of the northern Democrats from outside Tri-Star districts supported the guarantee, 45 percent (5 of 11) of the northern Democrats from Tri-Star districts supported the guarantee; and whereas 58 percent of the southern Democrats from outside Tri-Star districts supported the guarantee, 83 percent (5 of 6) of the southern Democrats from Tri-Star districts supported the guarantee.

As with the agricultural and labor cases we reviewed, then, the success particular interests had in getting legislators' support, compared to the support given by the members' party (or regional) colleagues, was related to the possible support these interests could develop in the Congressman's district. Other policy areas with similar tendencies could also be cited.[108] The cases help to illustrate Kingdon's findings (reported above) on the fifteen issues he studied that interest groups were an important factor in the voting decisions of Congressmen principally when the group's position was consistent with the Congressman's perception of his constituency's position. In this context, one can see why, as Milbrath observed, "A smart lobbyist tries to demonstrate to a member that following a particular course of action will help him in his constituency."[109] If the group can back up its claims, and especially if the issue is a visible one, this strategy does appear to be rather effective.[110]

At the same time, the evidence indicates that constituency factors usually are *not* strong enough to overwhelm the party and normative influences discussed earlier as determinants of Congressional behavior. For example, roll call analyses reviewed above and in Chapter 5 revealed that party influences on members' behavior were still quite detectable even in the face of potentially conflicting constituency pressures. Additional evidence is available as regards legislators' normative concerns, and especially their policy attitudes, in relation to constituency factors. Much of this evidence shows that constituency considerations, while significant, have by no means been solely determining when examined alongside the legislators' policy attitudes. Once again, when conflict has occurred between them, the legislators' policy attitudes have been found overall to be about as important in explaining legislators' behavior as constituency considerations.[111] The analyses thus suggest that when constituency factors are pertinent, they normally enter into legislators' actions in conjunction with the party and normative influences discussed earlier rather than having the effect of replacing or supplanting them as explanatory variables.

One further point also to be made. This deals with the possibility that particular interest groups can exert disproportionate influence in the Congress if individual legislators favorable to the group (for electoral or other reasons) are located in key Congressional positions. As we suggested earlier in this chapter, there is little doubt that this does occur. At the same time, there are other factors to be considered. In particular, recall that the ability of legislators to use key positions effectively itself depends upon taking into account major coalition and individual member interests that are found on the floor (on this, see our discussion of committees and their chairmen in Chapter 8). The same point emerges from analysis of cueing in Congress. Especially on issues outside his own areas of specialization, we have seen that a Congressman tends to look to other members for guidance. He "cues" on other members, often members from the substantive committee appropriate to the policy area. But how much influence committee members can exert by holding such posts greatly depends upon their colleagues' own normative motives and electoral needs. Thus, among the most prominent of the factors in determining which member(s) a Congressman chooses to cue upon is whether he shares similar interests with the member arising from similar policy attitudes or from similar electoral problems.[112] As one Congressman put it, in deciding whom to follow, the basic principle is to "Choose those you agree with."[113] A further consideration of importance as a Congressman selects another member to cue on is credibility stemming from the member's reputation for knowing his subject, "for being well prepared."[114] Hence, both the experiences of committees and the factors affecting cueing suggest that influence in the Congress arises not only from the powers attending the position or office a member holds but also from how he handles that position in the context of the views and needs of other members.[115]

While these findings add to the perspective, more central to the concern of our discussion has been the influence interest groups have directly on individual legislators by way of their ability, or potential ability, to influence the electoral process. In this regard, prior to summarizing Congressional tendencies, it would be helpful to be able to examine its experience in the perspective of the case of the CDU/CSU parliamentary party. Here, too, interest groups are thought to play a major role in the recruitment and survival of individual legislators.

A general statement which the evidence warrants is that there is a high degree of interest-group activity in the process of nominating CDU/CSU candidates to run for the Bundestag. The principal resources of groups are money, campaign work, and voter support. Through resources such as these, rather close links may be developed between interest groups and CDU/CSU parliamentarians. If a group controls the process by which an elected member has been nominated, it is not only likely to get a representative whose survival depends on the group, but also a representative whose views about policy are sympathetic toward those of the group.

The ability of business organizations and industrial firms to affect the nomination process in the CDU/CSU is based chiefly on financial contributions. The party's dependence on the economic associations that donate money has been a very real one. According to Safran, "Although the political parties occasionally complain of blackmail, they have been quite willing to offer their services for sale to the highest bidder."[116]

Some concrete examples of the influence of financial contributors on CDU/CSU nominations may prove helpful. Braunthal supplies the example of the CDU local executive committee in Kiel that forwarded the party secretary as its nominee. When objections arose in the party meeting by a group opposed to the secretary, the party chairman disclosed that representatives of business, who had made financial contributions, wanted the secretary. It was he who in the end was chosen at the state convention.[117] Braunthal offers another example, the case of Hans Dichgans, a leading iron and steel industrialist who was a German representative to the European Coal and Steel Community. Despite his financial connections, the Rhineland CDU committee decided not to give Dichgans a safe place on the state list. At this point, a prominent banker and party leader, Robert Pferdmenges, and another notable in the steel industry, Hans-Günther Sohl, met with the leader of the Rhineland CDU (Wilhelm Johnen). During the meeting, Sohl threatened to terminate the steel industry's contributions to the CDU. The result was that Johnen capitulated and "Dichgans received seat number 35 and won the election."[118] Still another example is the case of Wolfgang Pohle, who in 1969 failed to gain a safe place on the Westphalia list. However, through the intervention of Franz Josef Strauss and others, he got a CSU-list nomination in Bavaria and was elected. When Pohle died in 1971, *Der Spiegel* suggested that Strauss and the CSU had given Pohle a safe place on the list due to Pohle's close links with business in an effort to generate financial contributions for the CSU.[119]

The bidding that takes place in order to obtain the financial support of business is nowhere more clearly illustrated, however, than in a case Dübber cites. Here the CDU went to the Hanover mechanics' guild with the formula that for every mechanic it nominated as a candidate, the guild would be asked to contribute approximately $12,000 to the party.[120] Another revealing example is quoted by Uwe Kitzinger: "The Chief Association of German Retail Traders sent a letter to its Land member organizations asking for money to help place one particular candidate high up on the Lower Saxon list." Part of the letter read as follows: "This as usual presupposes the supply of election finance. . . . Mr. Meyer-Ronnenberg informs us that it will be necessary to secure additional money so as to place him in a correspondingly promising position."[121]

It is not only business that is able to penetrate the nomination processes of the CDU/CSU. Examples can also be drawn from farming and labor groups. For instance, a study by Kauffman, Kohl, and Molt of the CDU nomination process in three states contains several examples of the influence of farming associations in making constituency nominations. In one case, farming groups felt that the incumbent Bundestag member had not looked after the farming interests of the constituency. In particular, he had not joined the Green Front in the Bundestag. He was opposed for renomination by the vice-president of the Bauernverband in Baden-Württemberg, who promised faithfully to represent farming interests. The incumbent was defeated at the constituency party meeting by a vote of 111 to 64.[122] In another constituency, a farm-oriented incumbent was opposed by a faction in the local party, but his renomination was protected due to the support of the local farming associations.[123]

A potential advantage of having representatives of one's group in the Bundestag is that they can gravitate to the Bundestag committees of significance to the group and through the committees attempt to influence policy decisions of concern to their group. It is no coincidence, for example, that from 1961 to 1965 the Bundestag committee with the highest percentage of deputies from business and industry was the Economic Affairs Committee. While business and industry deputies constituted only about 15 percent of the total Bundestag membership, they held twelve of twenty-seven positions on the committee, including the chairmanship.[124] Indeed, twelve of the sixteen CDU/CSU and FDP members on the committee were business and industry deputies. Moreover, on the Bundestag trade committee, nine of sixteen CDU/CSU and FDP members on the committee were business and industry deputies.[125]

Business and industry had no representatives, on the other hand, on committees such as agriculture, family, or health.[126] Or, to cite another example, members of the labor group accounted for 23 percent of the CDU/CSU parliamentary party in 1961, but 55 percent of the CDU/CSU seats on two of the most relevant Bundestag committees to its concerns, social policy and labor.[127]

Getting the chairmanship of and members on key committees can be quite helpful to the group in its efforts to influence the policy process. Walter Eckhardt, for example, said that while he was chairman of the turnover tax subcommittee in the Bundestag, not a single change was made in these taxes without the assent of the entire business community.[128] It is little wonder that the BDI has stressed that "it is simply a matter of vital importance for business whether it is duly represented in parliament by experienced deputies."[129]

These examples indicate that interest groups are able by acting through the nomination process to gain "direct representation" in the CDU/CSU parliamentary party. Moreover, the representatives attempt to get assignments in the Bundestag that are advantageous to their groups. As this suggests, the ties between interest groups and parliamentarians that come about through the electoral process are often close. Their influence was stressed by one Bundestag member who, in deciding not to run again, pointed to "the predominance of interested politicians" in the Bundestag.[130]

Yet the dynamics of the relationship between interest groups and the behavior of CDU/CSU parliamentarians are rather more complex than the picture just presented. First, the ability of an interest group to determine the nomination of CDU/CSU candidates does not depend solely on its financial contributions to the party. Influence depends also on the size of the group at the state or constituency level. Second, the group's influence on its representatives in the Bundestag is not uniform, for there may be competing factors at play. Third, there are limits on the extent to which these representatives can influence CDU/CSU deputies who are not affiliated with the group.

While financial contributions to the party undoubtedly serve to increase a group's leverage in the politics of nomination, they are clearly not the only consideration. We presented a series of vivid examples of business attempts to influence nominations, yet it is also significant that in several of these examples a state or local party was willing to forego a potential nominee's financial connections in order to make its own choice. After all, Wolfgang Pohle had first failed to receive a place on the Westphalia list before finding a place on the Barvarian list. And, in the end, the candidate (Meyer-Ronnenberg) whom the retailers wished to place on the Lower Saxon list was not given a place at all. Examples such as these are hardly rare. For instance, in the cases Kaufmann and his coauthors studied, it was discovered that industry, wholesale trade, and banking groups were frequently unsuccessful with their candidates.[131] Instead, these authors found that a factor of equal, and perhaps greater, importance was the grass-roots strength of the interest group in terms of its party membership at the state or constituency level. Their analysis of the politics of nomination led to the conclusion that often "the only interest groups which can exercise real influence are those strongly represented in the party membership."[132] And, it is possible that the passage in the 1960s of legislation providing federal funding for political parties has worked further to reinforce the importance of this factor, as opposed to financial contributions, in the determination of party decisions on nomination.

Nor would we offer a balanced picture of the relationship between interest groups and the CDU/CSU parliamentary party without reiterating that there have been certain limits to the ability of interest groups to gain the uniform support of their own representatives.[133] It is true that the bonds linking representatives to the groups that sponsored them have frequently been strong. Nevertheless, these bonds have not been equally intense for every member or on every issue. For example, while the policy attitudes of affiliated representatives may often have coincided with the specific positions taken by their groups, this has not invariably been so. Interviews of BDI representatives, cited earlier, indicated that such conflicts could affect the support members gave to their group. Indeed, Braunthal points out that not even Pohle or Hellwig, both highly active in business circles, followed the industrial line 100 percent.[134] Some others were found to give no more than marginal support.[135] Furthermore, representatives have ties with their party that may encourage behavior along somewhat different lines than those desired by the group. Members both develop a feeling of attachment to their parliamentary party and their colleagues as they do battle with the opposition and become aware of their continuing need for support from these quarters if they are to gain their own legislative ends. Speaking of industry representatives in the CDU/CSU parliamentary party, Braunthal observed that "at the outset of his career . . . a legislator identifies himself closely with his firm or association, but as the legislative term progresses he becomes more self-assertive and develops a sense both of party loyalty and of parliamentary identity."[136] Other research has similarly found such factors to reduce the degree of allegiance members show toward their groups.[137]

The relationship between a given interest group and the CDU/CSU parliamentary party also unfolds in a situation in which many parliamentarians are not affiliated with or sponsored by the group. Indeed, about 50 to 60 percent of the members of the CDU/CSU parliamentary party cannot be classified as having been affiliated with or sponsored by any interest group.[138] Furthermore, numerous different interest groups have sponsored the remaining 40 to 50 percent of the parliamentarians. The result of this configuration is that power has to an important extent been shared. For example, the fact that business seems to have held considerable sway on turnover taxes is important and should not be neglected, but it is also significant that labor has had substantial leverage in a number of social policy areas.

Because each group has had a limited number of representatives in the CDU/CSU parliamentary party and in the Bundestag, its ability to influence policy decisions through its representatives has hinged on a number of considerations. A group's influence has not only been affected by the obvious factor of its success in getting the support of its own members but also by the willingness of other noninterested members to support or at least acquiesce to the group's preferences. In turn, the success a group has had in gaining the support or acquiescence of members not affiliated with the group has generally depended upon whether the group obtained the backing of party leaders or a party caucus stand favorable to the group. There are various incentives that prompt members to support their party and their party leaders (see Chapter 4) and because of this party ties have been particularly decisive for members when their own group interests were not at stake. Indeed, Braunthal's research on CDU/CSU members found the party leadership usually to be dominant in determining the behavior of members whose group interests were not involved.[139] Similarly, analyses of voting behavior have found the voting records of those CDU/CSU members not sponsored by an interest group to have been markedly more loyal to party stands than the records of the sponsored members.[140] We have thus come full circle, for this directs our attention again to the importance interest groups attach to gaining the support of party leaders and the executive, which is the subject we broached at the outset of this section of the chapter.

This area of our study has considered settings in which the influence of interest groups on the recruitment and survival of individual legislators has been most noted. Certain tendencies that bear some similarity can be suggested. In the case of the Congress, we observed that unless an interest group was able to build on likely support for its position within a member's local electorate, its ability to get the member to deviate from his party's stand was appreciably weakened. Somewhat analogously in the case of the Bundestag, evidence just cited indicated an increase in party influence on those CDU/CSU parliamentarians whose survival at the local level bore no connection to an interest group's sponsorship as well as on parlimentarians whose own group interests were not at stake. Furthermore, as an interest group's effectiveness with members of Congress often depended on its size or potential popular appeal at the local level, so this has likely been of some importance in the case of sponsored Bundestag members. For grass-roots strength has been among the factors found to affect group success in determining nominations. Also, recall that how Congressmen behaved even toward the interests of sizable groups located in their own electorates was tempered quite greatly by other considerations. For example, party and normative influences have usually been quite discernible even in these instances. The evidence suggests that factors beyond interest group influence have also played a part in the case of sponsored CDU/CSU members. Partly because these factors have not always coincided with behavior favorable to their group, few sponsored members have been unswervingly loyal to their group. While there has been a clear tendency among these members to be supportive, the pattern of support has been found to be neither uniform nor complete and in some cases no more than marginal. In both the American and West German cases, then, the influence on legislative behavior of interest group resources potentially relevant to recruitment and survival has been apparent. At the same time, there have also been perceptible limits to their effectiveness even on those members subject to them. Finally, to the extent such resources have been effective, evidence on each system indicated that a group's membership size or its potential popular appeal has been among the pertinent considerations.

Another Normative Consideration A further point to be made is that whatever importance an interest group's potential to affect nomination and election outcomes has as a resource, it is not likely the only factor that works to move legislators to support particular interests located in their electorates. As alluded to earlier, legislators' conceptions of their roles as representatives may act as another factor. That is, if the legislator's conception of his role leads him to feel a sense of duty to his constituents as part of his job, it is possible that this orientation, in turn, will lead him to support the interests of particular groups in his constituency, even groups that have little electoral influence.

How can we determine whether role conceptions of responsibility to one's constituents influence the way legislators behave toward groups located in their districts? We need to look at a situation in which other important factors, such as career survival and policy views, are held constant. This can be accomplished by isolating issues upon which most legislators had generally the same attitude toward the policy aims of a group; the group was located in some districts and not in others; and the group did not appear to have been an electoral determinant for legislators from these districts. If we isolate such cases, we can examine which legislators have become active on behalf of the group and then determine whether there is any relationship between the particular legislators who became active and the presence of the group in their particular districts. If such a relationship emerges, we cannot explain it as a consequence of problems of survival, for we will have argued that legislators did not face such problems. Nor can we explain it as a consequence of the legislator's policy outlook, for we will have argued that most legislators began with similar attitudes on the issue. One alternative explanation is that the relationship results from the legislator's representative role orientation regarding his district. This explanation will be particularly attractive if we also have reason to suspect that the legislators felt some sense of responsibility to their constituents.

Cases such as these are not easy to find. We might begin, however, by looking at a system in which local electoral factors (aside from national electoral swings) are usually of rather minor consequence to the survival of most legislators, but where the conception that the legislator's job is partly to look after the constituency has some foundation. One such system is the British system.

We observed in Chapter 4 that due to the strength of national electoral forces, individual MPs do not normally need to orient their behavior on policy issues to the special concerns of groups located in their constituencies in order to gain reelection (see Chapter 4). While there are issues that provide exceptions, whether an MP is reelected or not will depend almost entirely upon the stands and the successes of his national party rather than on his individual stands on issues or his individual popularity. Nor is there the necessity to cater to local groups in order to secure renomination, for members can be virtually assured of renomination if they remain loyal to their national party policy, and this assurance is rarely challenged by the local associations.

We also observed in Chapter 4 that constituency role orientations, as distinct from party role orientations, are probably not dominant in Great Britain. However, this does not mean that the conception of representing one's constituents is completely absent. In fact, it is not. For example, Stewart observes, "Members of Parliament exist in a distinctive atmosphere. In it, certain ideas and principles are taken for granted. One of them is that a member has a duty to his constituents."[141]

This combination of the presence of some conception of constituency role and the absence, generally, of the necessity to cater to local groups in order to survive leads us to look at the British system. An analysis of constituency-oriented behavior in this system can help us to assess how much (or whether) role conceptions of responsibility to constituents make any difference for how legislators behave toward groups back home.

Since we know, however, that the policy attitudes of a member may also affect his behavior toward particular groups, we would want to focus on an issue upon which most legislators of a given party had rather similar views. An illustration of this kind appears to be the issue over whether Britain should retain an elite school system or should adopt in its stead a comprehensive school system (all children in a locality going to the same school) somewhat like that operating in the United States.

Britain has a long-established elite school system in which the elite schools are of two types: "public" schools such as Eton and Harrow, which are funded privately, and "grammar" schools, which are dependent upon public funding, usually from the local level. Of the grammar schools, the most prestigious (as a class of schools) are the direct-grant schools. These schools receive financial support directly from London. This support complements local funds, private funding through tuition, and private contributions. Many of these schools originally were "public" schools.

When Labour took office in 1964, there were numerous rumors that the government was making plans that, in effect, would dismantle the elite school system in order to replace it with a comprehensive school system. If it was not to go this far, an intermediate step would be to try further to develop comprehensive schools along side the elite schools (a process that had slowly been taking place since World War II) and to make comprehensive schools out of some of the elite schools. Interviews we undertook with officials of education groups indicated more than a few felt that the elite schools that would likely first be affected under this policy were the direct-grant grammar schools, the schools that were subsidized in part by the national government.

As far as we can discern, almost all Conservative MPs agreed that, at most, no more than a few elite schools should be converted into comprehensive schools and that, if this were done, it should be done provisionally for experimentation so that they could be converted back to elite schools, should the experiment fail. There was uniform opposition to any widespread comprehensive school proposal. Our interviews with a dozen Conservative MPs, coupled with an examination of the motions and series of debates on this issue in the 1964 Parliament, suggest a general consensus in the parliamentary party on this issue. Thus, the early day motion of December 1964, signed by 108 Conservative MPs, argued that it was premature to accept a reasoned judgment on comprehensive education and that therefore any proposal for the imposition of the comprehensive system on local authorities by the government was to be deplored. This view was reiterated again and again by a series of Conservative speakers in the Commons's debates, and every Conservative MP we interviewed shared a similar view.

Despite the general consensus of outlook among the Conservative MPs, it is interesting that those who signed the early day motion of December, 1964, and/or who participated in the Commons's debates of late 1964 and early 1965 disproportionately represented constituencies in which the direct-grant grammar schools were located.[142] There were 68 such Conservative MPs. Of these MPs, 56 percent either signed the 1964 motion or spoke in debate or did both. Of the remaining Conservative members, only 33 percent used one or the other instrument to voice their views. Moreover, the fact that members were not making electoral calculations in responding to this issue is suggested by the similarity of the behavior of MPs from safe and marginal constituencies. As Table 9.1 shows, the margin of electoral victory in the previous election (more or less than 10 percent) made only little difference to the behavior of Conservatives from the direct-grant grammar school constituencies. Each of the two groups of MPs from the direct-grant grammar school constituencies was disproportionately active on this issue.

The consensus within the parliamentary party suggests that the disproportionate activity of MPs from the direct-grant grammar school constituencies was not a consequence of a difference in policy outlook. Nor would electoral considerations back home appear to have been a determining factor. It is also fair to say that almost all of the MPs were well aware of the issue, whether they represented a direct-grant grammar school constituency or not. We are thus led to infer that the disproportionate activity of the MPs from the direct-grant grammar schools may have involved an attitude about representing one's constituency and one's constituents.

Surely more research is required in this area, but if there are circumstances in which

Table 9.1
Type of Constituency and Active Support in Parliament by Conservative Backbenchers for Elite Secondary Schools, 1964-65 (in percent)

	Type of Constituency			
	Safe		Marginal	
Parliamentary Activity	Direct Grant	Nondirect Grant	Direct Grant	Nondirect Grant
Activity (N = 115)	58	34	54	25
No Activity (N = 179)	42	66	46	74
	100	100	100	100

British legislators act on public policy issues partly on the basis of a representative role orientation toward the constituency, it is likely that legislators in the other systems do as well.[143] This is particularly true for the American system where, as we observed in Chapter 4, the concept of being a representative of a district rather than of a party is quite well developed. A suggestion along this line is contained in an analysis of the views of members of the United States House of Representatives towards interest groups, where Kingdon found that a Representative's conception of the legitimacy of a particular group was closely tied to whether or not a group was in some way connected to his district. The analysis disclosed that Congressmen ordinarily considered groups having no such connection to be less legitimate.[144] Kingdon also observed that the lesser legitimacy with which most legislators looked upon these groups partly explained why such groups in fact had less success in influencing the legislators' behavior.[145]

Conclusion

In this chapter we have discussed relations between interest groups and legislators. We reviewed the kinds of interest groups present in each of the four systems, feelings about interest groups, the diverse strategies interest groups employ, and factors that help determine the effectiveness interest groups have in gaining favorable legislative responses.

We have seen that legislators' behavior toward interest groups is shaped by, and must be viewed in the context of, the ties they have with their party and an executive of their party. Although Chapters 4 through 8 showed that the force of these ties has been stronger on legislative members of the two British parties and the Gaullist party, their influence was still quite apparent on relations between interest groups and legislators in both the Congress and the Bundestag. As a consequence, interest groups in all four systems have attempted to maximize their impact on a large bloc of legislators by using strategies that concentrated on influencing the executive and/or the legislative party organization. The seemingly favorable response of individual legislators to an interest group successfully using this strategy thus was not to the interest group per se but to other political actors (i.e., the executive or the legislative party organization).

The principal focus of the chapter has been on direct interaction between interest groups and individual legislators. Our point of departure was to examine how interest groups and their strategies related to the goals and purposes of the legislators. Along this line, we reported evidence dealing with legislators' policy attitudes, desires to make informed decisions, career ambitions, and role orientations toward constituents and looked at the significance of these goals and purposes to the way legislators behaved toward interest groups. Consideration of these goals and purposes also led us to examine certain resources interest groups might employ in an attempt to alter legislative behavior, such as the provision of policy-relevant information or the use of resources that might have a bearing on legislators' nominations and elections.

The conclusions that have emerged from the discussion are relevant to some of the major criticisms directed at the legislature. We will summarize these conclusions specifically as they pertain to the Congress. At the same time, it is important to add that our discussion of the European legislatures, in those situations comparable to the Congress, found that they experienced broadly similar tendencies.

In making their "Case Against Congress," Drew Pearson and Jack Anderson spoke of interest group influence in the following terms: "Their influence cuts across sectional boundaries and party lines; they have established, in effect, an invisible super-government that shapes national policies to gratify the moneyed interests."[146] This popular image portrays interest-group influence as pervasive and views Congressmen as bowing before and surrendering to the pressures of these groups and, especially, to the financial rewards and sanctions they apply.

We have seen that the effect of financial rewards and sanctions cannot be dismissed, that major contributors to legislators' campaigns for nomination and election have greater access than the average citizen, and that their access is taken more seriously. Even so, there are additional considerations to be viewed alongside the effect of financial sanctions and rewards. For example, if financial contributions to campaigns should not be discounted as an influencing factor, we also observed that their influence has been dampened by various limitations.[147] The evidence indicated as well that interest group influence in dealing directly with individual legislators, at least on the diversity of issues considered, was often related to the popular size or potential appeal of the interest group at the constituency level. As significant, we observed that normative concerns of legislators were quite prominent in establishing the character of relations between members of Congress and interest groups. Of chief importance here were the legislators' own policy attitudes and, within this context, an interest group's ability to provide relevant information and expertise. Some evidence equally pointed to the possibility that legislators' constituency role concepts or orientations have been important in shaping their attitudes and behavior toward specific interest groups.

With the exception of the last finding, a broad range of evidence was brought forth in the chapter to support these conclusions. It is significant that even the Nader Report, while accusing the Congress of "surrendering its enormous authority and resources to special interest groups . . . " also admits that "Congress is still the most responsive and open branch of the government" and alerts us to the "danger" that with "increased presidential power is the *even greater* amount of pandering to private interests it encourages."[148] Indeed, such a conclusion coincides with other evidence we cited on our systems suggesting that overall interest group influence on legislative policy decisions has been as great (and perhaps greater) in executive and party-dominant situations.

Notes

[1] See Graham Wooten, *Interest Groups* (Englewood Cliffs, N.J.: Prentice-Hall, 1970), Chapters 1-3, for a discussion of the variety of definitions of the term "interest group" and problems involved in defining and analyzing the term. See, also, Maurice Duverger, *Party Politics and Pressure Groups* (New York: Thomas Y. Crowell, 1972).

[2] For a listing of major literature on interest groups in the United States, see the bibliographical note at the conclusion of the book.

[3] For a listing of major literature on interest groups in the European systems, see the bibliographical note at the conclusion of the book.

[4] Samuel Finer, "Interest Groups and the Political Process in Great Britain," in *Interest Groups on Four Continents*, ed. Henry Ehrmann (Pittsburgh: University of Pittsburgh Press, 1958) p. 118.

[5] J. D. Stewart, *British Pressure Groups: Their Role in Relation to the House of Commons* (Oxford: The Clarendon Press, 1958), pp. 250-57. For more detailed information on the companies and occupations represented by MPs, see Andrew Roth, *The Business Background of MPs* (Old Woking, Surrey: The Gresham Press, 1972). A tabulation for the period 1962 to 1972 is found on p. 24.

[6] Wolfgang Hirsch-Weber, "Some Remarks on Groups in the German Federal Republic," in *Interest Groups on Four Continents*, ed. Henry Ehrmann, p. 110.

[7] See Roth, *Business Background of MPs*.

[8] Gerhard Loewenberg, *Parliament in the German Political System* (Ithaca, N.Y.: Cornell University Press, 1967), p. 126, and Gerald G. Watson, "Social and Political Factors in Parliamentary Recruitment: The West German Bundestag, 1949-1971" (Paper delivered at the 1973 Annual Meeting of the Western Political Science Association), p. 13.

[9] Gerhard Braunthal, *The Federation of German Industry in Politics* (Ithaca, N.Y.: Cornell University Press, 1965), pp. 160-61.

[10] Stewart, *British Pressure Groups*, p. 199.

[11] Stewart, *British Pressure Groups*, p. 186

[12] L'Institut d'Études Politiques, *L'Année Politique* (Paris: Presses Universitaires de France, 1960), p. 640. It should be noted that neither Rousseau nor De Gaulle (not even James Madison in Federalist Paper Number 10) was thinking of interest groups in a restricted sense. Interest groups from their perspective would also include political parties (in the case of De Gaulle, "irresponsible" political parties such as those of the French Fourth Republic).

[13] Donald R. Matthews, *U.S. Senators and Their World* (New York: Random House, 1960), p. 177. See also Eugene McCarthy, "A Senator Looks at the Lobbies," in *Readings on the American Political System*, ed. L. Earl Shaw and John C. Pierce (Lexington, Mass.: D. C. Heath, 1970) pp. 280-86.

[14] Roger H. Davidson, *The Role of the Congressman* (New York: Pegasus, 1969), p. 164. See also Charles L. Clapp, *The Congressman: His Work as He Sees It* (Garden City, N.Y.: Doubleday, 1963), pp. 184-85, 206, and Andrew Scott and Margaret Hunt, *Congress and the Lobbies: Images and Reality* (Chapel Hill: University of North Carolina Press, 1966), pp. 31, 32, 36, 37, 48, 56.

[15] Davidson, *The Role of the Congressman*, p. 166.

[16] Davidson, *The Role of the Congressman*, p. 165

[17] On the activities of affiliated and "interested" members, see John H. Millett, "The Role of an Interest Group Leader," *Western Political Quarterly* 9 (1956): 915-26; Stewart, *British Pressure Groups*; Safran, *Veto Group Politics: The Case of Health Insurance Reform in West Germany* (San Francisco: Chandler Publishing Co., 1967); Viola Gräffin von Bethusy-Huc, *Demokratie und Interessenpolitik* (Wiesbaden: Franz Steiner Verlag, 1962); Otto Stammer et al., *Verbände und Gesetzgebung: Die Einflussnahme der Verbände auf die Gestaltung des Personalvertretungsgesetzes* (Cologne and Opladen: Westdeutscher Verlag, 1965); Braunthal, *The Federation of German Industry in Politics;* and Braunthal, *The West German Legislative Process: A Case Study of Two Transportation Bills* (Ithaca, N.Y.: Cornell University Press, 1972).

[18] William Keefe and Morris Ogul, *The American Legislative Process: Congress and the States*, 2d. ed. (Englewood Cliffs, N.J.: Prentice-Hall, 1968), p. 328.

[19] James Deakin, *The Lobbyists* (Washington, D.C.: Public Affairs Press, 1966), pp. 1-2. In 1971, about three hundred groups and individuals filed such reports with spending calculated by *Congressional Quarterly Weekly Report* (August 19, 1972, p 2067) to be $6,524,849. The incomplete registration as well as the incomplete reporting of the registered means the dollar figure cited above is perhaps only the tip of the iceberg. See, for

example, the discussion in Deakin (Chapters 1, 2, and 9); he refers to it as a "billion dollar a year business" (p. 224).

[20] Although there is but scanty systematic evidence dealing with the effect of members' friendships and identifications, several examinations of members of Congress indicate that friendships can make a difference in regard to how individual members respond to particular interests or to representatives of those interests. Yet the research also indicates that friendships are not routinely a determining factor and that when they do come into play it is usually in regard to rather narrow or specific policy items rather than broad policy questions. See Lewis A. Dexter, *How Organizations Are Represented in Washington* (Indianapolis, Ind.: Bobbs-Merrill, 1969), pp. 113-17; Matthews, *U.S. Senators and Their World* p. 191; and Lester Milbrath, *The Washington Lobbyists* (Chicago: Rand McNally, 1963), pp. 243-44. In his interviews with lobbyists, Milbrath found that lobbyists ranked contacts by close friends of members of Congress to be the eighth most effective technique in influencing Congressmen of the thirteen techniques which were ranked. On the other hand, members of Congress looked at the technique as being more effective, ranking it fourth. See Milbrath, *The Washington Lobbyists*, pp. 213, 240, and 257.

[21] For a similar proposition regarding the bureaucracy, see Joseph La Palombara, *Interest Groups in Italian Politics* (Princeton, N.J.: Princeton University Press, 1964), pp. 22-23.

[22] Milbrath found only 3 former members of Congress in his sample of 114. Nevertheless, about half of the sample did come from government, including 41 former employees of the executive branch. (Milbrath, *The Washington Lobbyists*, pp. 67-69). See, also, Green et al., *Who Runs Congress?* (New York: Grossman Publishers, 1972), pp. 43-46 and Congressional Quarterly Service, *Legislators and Lobbyists* (Washington, D.C.: Congressional Quarterly, 1968), pp. 45-49.

[23] For discussions of recent investigations, indictments, and convictions of Congressmen and their staff members, see *Congressional Quarterly Weekly Report*, May 27, 1972, pp. 1181-82, and Green et al., *Who Runs Congress?*, pp. 143-59. On the European scene, a recent instance of bribery has been revealed in the case of the vote of a deputy on a crucial confidence motion in the Bundestag.

[24] Deakin, *The Lobbyist*, p. 7; Milbrath, *The Washington Lobbyists*, p. 275; Clapp, *The Congressman*, p. 185; McCarthy, "A Senator Looks at the Lobbies," p. 281; Green et al., *Who Runs Congress?*, p. 6. An ex-lobbyist, Robert Winter-Berger, seems to take exception to this in his book *The Washington Payoff* (New York: Dell, 1972), which is heralded as an exposé of influence-peddling in Washington. A close reading reveals very few new cases other than the well-known ones.

[25] Milbrath, *The Washington Lobbyists*, pp. 278-86; Green, et al., *Who Runs Congress?*, pp. 40-42; Drew Pearson and Jack Anderson, *The Case Against Congress: A Compelling Indictment of Corruption on Capitol Hill* (New York: Simon and Schuster, 1968), Chapter 12, esp. pp. 312-24; and Winter-Berger, *The Washington Payoff*, p. 30.

[26] Quoted in Pearson and Anderson, *The Case Against Congress*, p. 312.

[27] Matthews, *U.S. Senators and Their World*, p. 180; Milbrath, *The Washington Lobbyists;* pp. 270-74. It is interesting that the Nader Report (Green et al., *Who Runs Congress?*) felt this area was not worth giving even two complete pages of attention.

[28] Milbrath, *The Washington Lobbyists*, pp. 270-74; Matthews, *U.S. Senators and Their World*, p. 180.

[29] Quoted in Green et al., *Who Runs Congress?* p. 24.

[30] Walter Pincus, "Silent Spenders in Politics: They Really Give at the Office," *New York*, January 31, 1972, p. 40.

[31] Milbrath, *The Washington Lobbyists*, p. 283; Alexander Heard, *The Costs of Democracy* (Chapel Hill: University of North Carolina, 1970), pp. 72-88; David W. Adamany, *Financing Politics: Recent Wisconsin Elections* (Madison: The University of Wisconsin Press, 1969), pp. 86-89, 203-12; and David W. Adamany, *Campaign Finance in America* (North Scituate, Mass: Duxbury Press, 1972), esp. pp. 126-74.

[32] Pincus, "Silent Spenders in Politics," p. 40.

[33] Green et al., *Who Runs Congress?*, pp. 24-25.

[34] Winter-Berger, *The Washington Payoff*, p. 13. Milbrath, *The Washington Lobbyists*, also notes the tendency of lobbyists to concentrate on a few key contacts (pp. 264-65).

[35] Stewart, *British Pressure Groups*, p. 159.

[36] Braunthal, *The West German Legislative Process*, p. 161. See also both Safran, *Veto-Group Politics*, and Stammer et al., *Verbände und Gesetzgebung*.

[37] Milbrath, *The Washington Lobbyists*, pp. 213, 240, 257.

[38] Scott and Hunt, *Congress and Lobbies*, p. 78. Scott and Hunt also found that while the visibility of interest groups to Congressmen was low on the whole, visibility was relatively higher in the area of a Congressman's working interest (p. 55).

[39] Congressional Quarterly, *The Washington Lobby* (Washington D.C.: Congressional Quarterly, 1971), p. 6; Lester Milbrath, "Lobbying as a Communication Process," *Public Opinion Quarterly* 24 (September 1960):53.

[40] Stewart, *British Pressure Groups*, pp. 95-96.

[41] Erwin Knoll, "The Oil Lobby Is Not Depleted," in *Introductory Readings in American Government: A Public Choice Perspective*, ed. Robert S. Ross and William C. Mitchell (Chicago: Markham Publishing Company, 1971), p. 301. Knoll goes on to say that, "The companies claimed all these efforts as deductible

business expenses, but the Internal Revenue Service is, at the request of Senator William Proximire of Wisconsin, examining those claims." (p. 301).

[42] Pierre-Bernard Marquet, "L'oeuvre scolaire de la Ve république," *Revue politique et parlementaire* (September 1968): 62.

[43] Allen Potter, "The Equal Pay Campaign Committee: A Case-Study of a Pressure Group," *Political Studies* 5 (February 1957) :49-64.

[44] Keefe and Ogul, *The American Legislative Process*, 3d ed. (1973), pp, 371-74.

[45] Bernard E. Brown, "Pressure Politics in the Fifth Republic," *Journal of Politics*, 25 (August 1963): 524-25. For a comparison of the strategy of British and American interest groups using this principle, see Samuel H. Beer, "Group Representation in Britain and the United States," *The Annals of the American Academy of Political and Social Science* 319 (September 1958): 130-40.

[46] John P. Mackintosh, *The British Cabinet* (Toronto: University of Toronto Press, 1962), p. 470.

[47] For a brief critical account of the Fouchet Plan, see, L'Institut d'Études Politiques, *L'Année Politique 1965*, p. 407.

[48] See Henry W. Ehrmann, *Organized Business in France* (Princeton: Princeton University Press, 1957); Brown, "Pressure Politics in the Fifth Republic," p. 525; La Palombara, *Interest Groups in Italian Politics*, pp. 262ff; Harry Eckstein, *Pressure Group Politics: The Case of the British Medical Association* (Stanford, Calif.: Stanford University Press, 1960); and David Truman, *The Governmental Process, Political Interests and Public Opinion*, 2d ed. (New York: Alfred A. Knopf, 1971), p. 265.

[49] Brown, "Pressure Politics in the Fifth Republic," p. 525, referring to a comment by Viansson-Ponte.

[50] Braunthal, *The Federation of German Industry in Politics*, pp. 129-30.

[51] Hirsch-Weber, "Some Remarks on Groups in the German Federal Republic," p. 112.

[52] On this, see the suggestive analysis in J. Roland Pennock, "Responsible Government, Separated Powers, and Special Interests: Agricultural Subsidies in Britain and America," *American Political Science Review* 56 (September 1962): 621-33.

[53] Stewart, *British Pressure Groups*, 187. Three additional studies of interest here are Millet, "The Role of an Interest Group Leader"; William D. Muller, "Union-MP Conflict: An Overview," *Parliamentary Affairs* 26 (Summer 1973): 336-55; idem, "Trade Union Sponsored Members of Parliament in the Defence Dispute of 1960-1961," *Parliamentary Affairs* 23 (Summer 1970): 258-76.

[54] See, for example, the results Muller presents in his "Union-MP Conflict" and his "Trade Union Sponsored Members," both cited in footnote 53.

[55] Scott and Hunt, *Congress and Lobbies*, p. 87. *Congressional Quarterly Weekly Report* suggests that the support of the Nixon administration for some of business' positions was partly responsible for the success business had in lobbying the Congress (Oct. 14, 1972, p. 2635).

[56] Safran, *Veto-Group Politics*, pp. 81-82.

[57] Clapp, *The Congressman*, p. 326.

[58] For an excellent study in this regard, see Brown, "Pressure Politics in the Fifth Republic." On the United States, Pendleton Herring, *Presidential Leadership: The Political Relations of Congress and the Chief Executive* (New York: Farrar and Rinehart, 1940), pp. 28-29, noted some time ago: "A fact overlooked and still generally disregarded is that transfer of power from the legislative to the executive branch does not eliminate the drives of special interests; it only forces them to seek different channels. Their demands and their bargaining are no longer plainly visible tactics. Instead of getting legislators to do their logrolling on the floor of the assembly, special interest representatives and administrators do their bargaining in the privacy of their own office." See also Theodore J. Lowi, *The End of Liberalism* (New York: Norton, 1969), For a contrary view as applied to West Germany, see Bethusy-Huc, *Demokratie und Interessenpolitik, pp. 128-30*.

[59] See Pennock "Responsible Government, Separated Powers, and Special Interests"; Samuel H. Beer, "Pressure Groups and Parties in Britain," in *Legislative Behavior: A Reader in Theory and Research*, ed. John C. Wahlke and Heinz Eulau (Glencoe, Ill.: The Free Press, 1959) pp. 165-78.

[60] Scott and Hunt, *Congress and Lobbies*, p. 94.

[61] Harmon Zeigler, *Interest Groups in American Society* (Englewood Cliffs, N.J.: Prentice-Hall, 1964), p. 274.

[62] Bernard C. Cohen, *The Influence of Non-Governmental Groups on Foreign Policy-Making* (Boston: World Peace Foundation, 1959), p. 14.

[63] Raymond Bauer, Ithiel de Sola Pool, and Lewis Dexter, *American Business and Public Policy: The Politics of Foreign Trade*, (New York: Atherton, 1968), p. 477. Additional evidence supporting this view may be found in David E. Price, *Who Makes the Laws: Creativity and Power in Senate Committees* (Cambridge, Mass.: Schenkman Publishing Co., 1972).

[64] Quoted by Milbrath, *Washington Lobbyists*, p. 337.

[65] John W. Kingdon, *Congressmen's Voting Decisions* (New York: Harper & Row, 1973).

[66] Data for the figures in this paragraph were taken from Kingdon, *Congressmen's Voting Decisons*, p. 236, Table 10-1.

[67] Matthews, *U.S. Senators and Their World*, p. 182.

[68] Scott and Hunt, *Congress and Lobbies*, p. 94.

[69] Bauer, Pool, and Dexter, *American Business and Public Policy*, pp. 352-53; see also Matthews, *U.S.*

Senators and Their World, pp. 182-83.

[70] Stewart, *British Pressure Groups*, p. 185.

[71] Cited in Braunthal, *The Federation of German Industry in Politics*, p. 159.

[72] Some examples of this are found in Braunthal, *The West German Legislative Process*, pp. 109-12 and 166-67, and Bethusy-Huc, *Demokratie and Interessenpolitik*. For some British examples see both Millet, "The Role of an Interest Group Leader," and Stewart, *British Pressure Groups*.

[73] Both quotes are found in Braunthal, *The Federation of German Industry in Politics*, p. 163.

[74] For example, see James J. Lynskey, "The Role of British Backbenchers in the Modification of Government Policy: The Issues Involved, the Channels Utilized, and the Tactics Employed" (Ph.D. diss., University of Minnesota, 1966), pp. 47-48; Millet, "The Role of an Interest Group Leader," and Stewart, *British Pressure Groups*, p. 187.

[75] Braunthal, *The Federation of German Industry in Politics*, p. 151.

[76] Truman, *The Governmental Process*, pp. 333-34.

[77] John C. Wahlke et al., *The Legislative System* (New York: John Wiley and Sons, Inc., 1962) pp. 338-39. See also Scott and Hunt, *Congress and Lobbies*, p. 58, and Zeigler, *Interest Groups in American Society*, pp. 270-71.

[78] Besides the research we have cited, additional support for this conclusion can be found in Dexter, *How Organizations are Represented in Washington*, pp. 122, 130; Green et al., *Who Runs Congress*, p. 31; Clapp, *The Congressman* pp. 183-86; and Milbrath, *The Washington Lobbyists*, p. 142.

[79] Milbrath, *The Washington Lobbyists*, pp. 213, 227-32, 257, 285-296. Lobbyists work hard to acquire a reputation for reliability, avoiding intentionally misleading a legislator with information or advice. See Matthews, *U. S. Senators and Their World*; Abraham Holtzman, *Interest Groups and Lobbying* (New York: Macmillan, 1966), p. 77.

[80] Quoted in Loewenberg, *Parliament in the German Political System*, p. 56.

[81] The dependence of the individual legislator on the information and expertise of any single interest group is likely to be greatest when he wishes to initiate a piece of legislation. This is particularly the case for European legislators who do not have staffs of their own and even more for legislators who do not have the instrument of specialized legislative committees through which to work. In order to initiate a piece of legislation, legislators may come to depend upon a single interest group both for subject-matter expertise in the area of the legislation and, in the case especially of European legislators, for legal expertise in how to draft an acceptable bill.

[82] Indeed, Kingdon, *Congressmen's Voting Decisions*, suggests that the primary effect of information may normally be to reinforce the direction of the legislator's policy attitudes rather than to change their direction (pp. 250-52).

[83] Truman, *The Governmental Process*, p. 317, concludes this from V. O. Key, Jr.'s study, "The Veterans and the House of Representatives: A Study of a Pressure Group and Electoral Mortality," *Journal of Politics* 5 (February 1943): 27-40.

[84] Truman, *The Governmental Process*, pp. 315-16. See also Judith G. Smith, ed., *Political Brokers: People, Organizations, Money and Power*. (New York: Liveright, 1972)

[85] Truman, *The Governmental Process*, p. 318.

[86] The Business-Industry Political Action Committee.

[87] The following paragraph is based on data regarding BIPAC contributions found in Jonathan Cottin, "Business-Industry Political Action Committee," in, ed. Judith G. Smith, *Political Brokers*, pp. 141-43.

[88] Milbrath, *The Washington Lobbyists*, pp. 213, 240, 257.

[89] Scott and Hunt, *Congress and Lobbies*, p. 82.

[90] Deakin, *The Lobbyists* p. 101.

[91] Scott and Hunt, *Congress and Lobbies*, p. 83.

[92] Milbrath, *The Washington Lobbyists*, p. 284.

[93] Quoted in Clapp, *The Congressman*, pp. 187-88.

[94] Truman, *The Governmental Process*, p. 318.

[95] Scott and Hunt, *Congress and Lobbies*, pp. 82-83.

[96] Adamany, *Financing Politics*, pp. 86-89, 203-12; idem *Campaign Finance*, pp. 126-74.

[97] Pincus, "Silent Spenders in Politics."

[98] Adamany, *Campaign Finance*, pp. 127-31 and 159. See also John P. White and John R. Owens, *Parties, Group Interests, and Campaign Finance: Michigan, 1956* (Princeton, N.J.: Citizens' Research Foundation, 1960).

[99] Compiled from Common Cause Campaign Monotoring Project, Release, September 13, 1973, Appendix C. The four losing candidates averaged about $275,000, and the four winning candidates averaged about $170,000. Of the House races between nonincumbents cited by Common Cause, seven of the eleven *highest* spending candidates lost the election.

[100] See Jeff Fishel, *Party and Opposition: Congressional Challengers in American Politicis* (New York: David McKay, 1973), p. 199

[101] Richard Harris, "Annals of Politics: How the People Feel," *The New Yorker*, July 10, 1971, p. 54.

[102] Besides the sorts of limits on the effectiveness of resources which we have already delineated, we ought

also point out that there are frequently further limits having to do with problems of interest-group unity and organization. Evidence of these problems as they pertain to individual interest groups and of the subsequent problems interest groups have in using financial and other resources to exert pressures on members of Congress is found in Bauer, Pool and Dexter *American Business and Public Policy*; David Price *Who Makes the Laws?*, especially pp. 322-23; and Milbrath, *The Washington Lobbyists*, p. 348. On the European systems, see Braunthal, *The West German Legislative Process*, especially p. 176-77; Bethusy-Huc, *Demokratie und Interessenpolitik*; and Gaston Rimareix and Yves Tavernier, "L'Élaboration et le vote de la loi complémentaire à la loi d'orientation agricole," *Revue Française de Science Politique* 13 (June 1963): 389-418. Eckstein's case study on the passage of the national health insurance system in Great Britain is also instructive in this regard. See his *Pressure Group Politics*.

[103] Quoted in Clapp, *The Congressman*, p. 187.

[104] Kingdon, *Congressmen's Voting Decisions*, pp. 140 and 145. In relying on Representatives' perceptions of constituent opinion, Kingdon points to the problem that Representatives may instead have been perceiving the position of constituency elites. However, he goes on to suggest that it is particularly on issues of high visibility and salience (those upon which interest groups were most influential) that Representatives' perceptions of general constituent opinion in their district were likely to be most accurate (p. 298).

[105] The data for the analysis of agriculture are found in David R. Mayhew, *Party Loyalty Among Congressmen: The Difference Between Democrats and Republicans 1947-1962* (Cambridge, Mass.: Harvard University Press, 1966), p. 30.

[106] Wesley McCune, "Farmers in Politics," *The Annals of the American Academy of Political and Social Science* 319 (September 1958): 48.

[107] Mayhew, *Party Loyalty Among Congressmen*, pp. 121. Figures in the above paragraph were calculated from data found in Mayhew on p. 123.

[108] For example, see the suggestive analysis of the impact of constituency factors on the politics of oil in Congress found in Bruce Ian Oppenheimer, *Oil and the Congressional Process: The Limits of Symbolic Politics* (Lexington, Mass: D.C. Heath, 1974), especially pp. 57-59.

[109] Milbrath, *Washington Lobbyists*, p. 335. Interestingly, Winter-Berger, *The Washington Payoff*, who plays up the power of influence peddlers in Washington, also comes to the conclusion that pressure groups back home rank in the first order of importance in influencing Congressional votes (p. 315). For the United States Senate, see Matthews, *U.S. Senators and Their World*, p. 180.

[110] Although this conclusion is based on evidence apart from the views of lobbyists, most lobbyists share the view that large membership or otherwise popularly supported organizations are the most influential. See Milbrath, *The Washington Lobbyists*, pp. 348-49.

[111] See Kingdon, *Congressmen's Voting Decisions*, Chapter 10 and especially Table 10-1 (p. 236); Warren E. Miller and Donald E. Stokes, "Constituency Influence in Congress, "*American Political Science Review* (March 1963): 45-56; Warren E. Miller, "Majority Rule and the Representative System of Government," in *Cleavages, Ideologies, and Party Systems*, ed. Erik Allardt and Yrjö Littunen (Helsinki: The Academic Bookstore, 1964), pp. 343-77; and, on information and expertise as a normative concern compared to constituency contacts and pressures, see Milbrath, *The Washington Lobbyists*, pp. 213, 240, and 257.

[112] See both Kingdon, *Congressmen's Voting Decisions*, pp. 72-79, and Donald Matthews and James Stimson, "Decisionmaking by U.S. Representatives: A Preliminary Model," in *Political Decision-Making*, ed. S. Sidney Ulmer (New York: Van Nostrand Reinhold, 1970), pp. 14-43.

[113] Kingdon, *Congressmen's Voting Decisions*, p. 72.

[114] Kingdon, *Congressmen's Voting Decisions*, p. 79. See also Manley, *The Politics of Finance*.

[115] Besides the citations already mentioned in this paragraph, further support for this point may be found in our discussion and references cited on pp. 298-300.

[116] Safran, *Veto-Group Politics*, p. 96. See also Arnold Heidenheimer, "German Party Finance: The CDU," *The American Political Science Review* (June 1957): 369-85, especially p. 379. The hold business can achieve on the CDU/CSU through financial contributions may be somewhat greater than the effect of contributions in the United States, because German business can with some credibility threaten to contribute to the FDP instead of to the CDU/CSU.

[117] Braunthal, *The Federation of German Industry in Politics*, p. 142

[118] Braunthal, *The Federation of German Industry in Politics*, p. 142-143.

[119] *Der Spiegel*, November 15, 1971.

[120] Ulrich Dübber, *Parteifinanzierung in Deutschland* (Cologne: Westdeutscher Verlag, 1962), pp. 27-31.

[121] Uwe Kitzinger, *German Electoral Politics: A Study of the 1957 Campaign* (Oxford: Oxford University Press, 1960), p. 72.

[122] Karlheinz Kaufmann, Helmut Kohl and Peter Molt, *Kandidaturen zum Bundestag* (Cologne and Berlin: Kiepenheuer and Witsch, 1961), p. 72.

[123] Kaufmann, Kohl, and Molt, *Kandidaturen zum Bundestag*, pp. 156-57.

[124] Braunthal, *The Federation of German Industry in Politics*, p. 170.

[125] Braunthal, *The Federation of German Industry in Politics*, p. 171.

[126] Braunthal, *Ibid*.

[127]Loewenberg, *Parliament in the German Political System*, p. 199.
[128]Braunthal, *The Federation of German Industry in Politics*, p. 172.
[129]Braunthal, *The Federation of German Industry in Politics*, p. 151.
[130]Braunthal, *The Federation of German Industry in Politics*, p. 162, quoting Dr. Hans Wellhausen.
[131]Kaufmann, Kohl, and Molt, *Kandidaturen zum Bundestag*, p. 212.
[132]Kaufmann, Kohl, and Molt, *Kandidaturen zum Bundestag*, p. 74. For the relevance of the popular size of an interest group to its impact on behavior in the Bundestag, see also Bethusy-Huc, *Demokratie und Interessenpolitik*, especially pp. 126ff.
[133]Of course, a group can be effective in gaining a favorable response from its representatives only to the extent that these representatives are not affiliated to two groups that make competing claims or to a group that is itself fragmented. A chief CDU/CSU spokesman for labor, Bernhard Winkelheide, faced competing demands on the sickness insurance issue from groups that supported him. He was, on the one hand, president of the CGD which generally opposed cost-sharing, while, on the other hand, he was an official of the KAB (Catholic Workers Club) which favored the principle of cost-sharing. (Safran, *Veto-Group Politics*, p. 83) Or, take the dilemma of the industry deputy, who commented: "It is like walking a tightrope over Niagara Falls. If I represent my firm too much, its competitors will complain. If I represent my industry, I am labelled a tool of industry. If I were to represent the 'general interest' only, my firm and industry would be dissatisfied" (Braunthal, *The Federation of German Industry in Politics*, p. 162).
[134]Braunthal, *The Federation of German Industry in Politics*, p. 160.
[135]Braunthal, *The Federation of German Industry in Politics*, p. 163.
[136]Ibid.
[137]Safran, *Veto-Group Politics*, p. 81-82, pp. 181-82, and pp. 185-86.
[138]Loewenberg, *Parliament in the German Political System*, p. 126, and Watson, "Social and Political Factors in Parliamentary Recruitment."
[139]Braunthal, *The Federation of German Industry in Politics*, p. 163.
[140]Frank H. Dishaw, "Roll Call Deviancy of the CDU/CSU Fraktion in the West German Bundestag," in *Sozialwissenschaftliches Jahrbuch für Politik*, ed. R. Wildenmann (Munich: Günter Olzog Verlag, 1971), esp. pp. 548-54.
[141]Stewart, *British Pressure Groups*, p. 218. On this, see also Anthony Barker and Michael Rush, *The Member of Parliament and his Information* (London: George Allen and Unwin, 1970), especially pp. 173-204.
[142]The constituencies chosen were based on the actual location of a direct-grant grammar school in the constituency, with an enrollment above 400 students, and not on the entire service area of the school. An exception was made when a direct-grant grammar school formally or informally bore the name of a city for which there was more than one constituency. In these cases, all of the constituencies from the city having Conservative MPs were included.
[143]For several examples suggestive of the relevance of such representative role orientations to the activities of members of the French Assembly, see Mark Kesselman, *The Ambiguous Consensus: A Study of Local Government in France* (New York: Knopf, 1967), pp. 79-83.
[144]Kingdon, *Congressmen's Voting Decisions*, p. 144.
[145]Kingdon, *Congressmen's Voting Decisions*, pp. 144-45.
[146]Pearson and Anderson, *The Case Against Congress*, p. 103.
[147]In discussing limits on the influence of interest group financial rewards and sanctions, our analysis concentrated on the impact such resources have by way of legislators' campaigns for nomination and election. However, such resources might be more influential if used to benefit the Congressman personally. Here preliminary attempts to analyze recent available data indicate that possible financial benefits in the form of a representative's personal business or financial status (frequently called conflict of interest) were only very unusually correlated with either legislators' membership on pertinent Congressional committees (the exception being in the area of banking) or with legislators' substantive action on legislation (no significant correlations were uncovered). See Association of the Bar of the City of New York's Special Committee on Congressional Ethics, *Congress and the Public Trust* (New York: Atheneum, 1970) and James W. Lundeen and Shirley A. Lundeen, "Conflict of Interest in the U.S. House of Representatives: Some Preliminary Findings" (Paper presented at the Annual Meeting of the Midwest Political Science Association, 1973).
[148]Green et al., *Who Runs Congress?* pp. 95 and 105-6.

Chapter 10
Representing Citizen Opinion In The Legislature

No matter what the influence patterns within democratic political systems are, the systems are based on the assumptions that decisions on public policy should be made in the interest of the citizenry and that an essential step toward ensuring that such decisions will be made is to involve citizens and their views in the political process. To help achieve this end, Western democracies enable the citizenry, in periodic and competitive elections, to select officials who will be vested with public decision-making authority. If elected representatives stand in place of the citizenry in exercising decision-making authority, an appropriate question to ask from the perspective of democratic theory is how reflective these representatives are of citizen opinion. In order to assess how representative a system is, it is important not only that there be elections, but it is also necessary to judge the behavior of those who are elected. In this sense, representation involves more than formal intitutional (electoral) mechanisms. It is also a substantive matter.[1]

What is meant by substantive representation? By substantive representation we mean that "the people of a nation are present in the actions of its government"[2] and that, in acting, policy-makers are responsive to and/or reflective of the substantive preferences or opinions found within the general public.

This is not to say that the idea of representation excludes the notion that representatives take into account their own judgments and convictions. As Pitkin points out, this is also an essential aspect of representation.[3] It is to say that the idea of representation includes, as well, a responsiveness to and a reflection of the opinions of the represented and the incorporation of such opinion to some degree into the decision-making process.[4]

In the previous analytical chapters, we have been concerned mainly with factors that affect how legislators behave. Our analysis has focused upon legislators' dispositions and how these, in combination with the political setting, work to affect their behavior. From an evaluative standpoint, however, it is essential to determine how consistent actions based on these dispositions are with actions that can be defined and described as substantively representative. It is also important to know whether particular kinds of political structures are likely to produce a higher level of substantive representation than are others.

Since World War II, there has been a great deal of criticism of the United States

Congress as a representative institution.[5] Many of the critics have favored a stronger Presidency. They viewed the President, the only nationally elected official (with the exception of the Vice-President), as the leader best situated to represent the public. While the President has been responsible to the entire public they contended that members of Congress, or at least many of them, represented essentially partial and parochial or local interests. As a consequence, the Congress as a whole was not viewed as attuned to the pulse of national opinion. Furthermore, even if the Congress was representative, its committee leaders, chosen through the seniority system, certainly were not. Finally, critics argued that because of the decentralization of Congressional power resulting from the Congressional committee system, the divisiveness of the parties in Congress, and the localism of many Congressman, the Congress was rendered unable to undertake the constructive action necessary to meet the expressed needs of a growing and increasingly complex national society.

Offering solutions to these problems, the critics have proposed various alternatives. Some have called for the establishment of a stronger President backed by a national Presidential party in Congress but still within a separation-of powers and checks-and-balances system (what might be called an executive-force solution). Others have advocated a party-responsibility parliamentary system that would closely resemble the British system.[6] The desired effect of each of the proposed solutions is to make the legislature more responsive to national opinion and concerns by strengthening executive or executive party leadership over the legislature.[7] Of course, this reflects the argument that has often been used to defend the proposals, that the Presidency is better situated than the Congress to represent the national electorate. Such an argument not only frequently appeared during the Democratic administrations over the past thirty years, but proponents for a stronger Presidency during Republican administrations regularly made similar claims.[8]

It is thus proper to ask whether the assertion that the Presidency is a superior representative of national opinion, advanced by those favoring increased executive influence in Congress, has been valid or not. Have Congressional critics been correct in their claims that, compared to the proper functioning of their proposals for reform, the Congress has been inadequately representative of the national electorate?

As we suggested, many critics proposed turning either to a party-responsibility or an executive-force system. Davidson and his coauthors have pointed out that the party responsibility system is in many respects the logical extension of most proposals for an executive-force system[9] and would perhaps be the end result of these executive-force proposals.[10] As a consequence, we will compare substantive representation of citizen opinion in Congress to what a party-responsibility system likely accomplishes, although the conclusions we draw from such a comparison could be applied to the executive-force proposals as well.

The party-responsibility system, as it is frequently set forth by critics of Congress, is based on a majoritarian model or theory of representation.[11] The system is supposed to operate in such a way that the public is given choices among alternative policy programs covering a series of issues and presented by competing political parties. Furthermore, it should operate so as to enable the party advocating the program preferred by a majority in national popular elections to gain a majority of the seats in the legislature and to determine who will lead the legislature. Through discipline and cohesion of the majority party, this majority can then captain the legislature and infuse its program into the decison-making process. Thus, the party-responsibility system is based on the idea that the majority and its leadership, having received a popular mandate for its program over the competing alternatives, should be able to exercise control over the decision-making process. A rather similar characterization could be made of most executive-force proposals.[12]

However, there is a second model of substantive representation that differs from the majoritarian model, yet whose operation, if the standards of the model are met, can be considered equally representative. This can be called the consensual model.[13] In this model, like the majoritarian model, the purpose of national elections is to produce a relatively close correspondence between the percentages of the public choosing the available general policy alternatives and the election of legislators advocating those alternatives. The policy alternative preferred by a majority of the public should thus receive a majority of the legislative seats.

However, the consensual model does not call for legislative leadership to be drawn almost exclusively from legislators representing the majority alternative. Instead, leadership should be drawn from legislators who proportionally represent the various competing alternatives according to support for these alternatives in the public. Nor are decisions in a consensual model usually resultant from a single cohesive majority in the legislature. Rather, they are made by differing majorities arising from diverse and shifting sets of coalitions encompassing the entire legislature.

Rather than decision-making being controlled by the majority, then, the idea behind the consensual model of representation is that advocates of the different policy alternatives should be effective in determining legislative decision-making proportional to support in the citizenry for the alternatives. This requires that both the legislative leadership and the legislature as a whole be proportionally representative of the alternatives, with legislative decisions based not on one disciplined and cohesive majority but on majorities stemming from varying alliances ranging across the whole legislature.

Our analysis will utilize these two models to assess representation in the Congress. In so doing, the analysis will address the question of whether or not the Congress has been less representative of national public opinion than a party-responsibility system would be, the solution offered in some form by many critics of Congress.

Representation and the
Party-Responsibility System

Before turning to Congress, we need to discuss the operation of the British party-responsibility system, the principal example cited by critics of Congress. We want briefly to make several points relevant to understanding representation in this system. Ideally, to maximize substantive representation across a series of issues rather than on a single issue, the party-responsibility system is expected by critics of Congress to enable voters to choose between distinct policy programs that are quite specific and well defined in content. This does occur to some extent in the British system. There are contrasts between the programs as well as the actions of the parliamentary parties on a number of issues. At the same time, it is pertinent to note that somewhat less than half the British public finds a good deal of difference between the parties.[14] Moreover, while specific and well defined on some issues, the typical program is also rather vague on other issues. A glance at almost any party program indicates this.[15] One result is that it is at times difficult to say whether legislative action by the victorious parliamentary party lies within or outside its party program.

Let us assume for the moment that each element of the winning party's program is well defined and consistent with all other elements of the program and that the party's program also differs from the other programs on many issues. Even if this is so, it obviously remains the case that substantive representation will be realized on these issues only to the extent that the policies of the victorious party program on the issues are agreeable to a majority in the electorate.

This requirement leads to another problem. The problem is that voters may have different elements of a party's program in mind when they vote for the party. Because of this, it is not necessarily true that there is a majority in the country that favors any given element of the program of the party winning the election.[16] For example, Labour won both the 1964 and the 1966 elections despite the fact that the majority of the public seems to have opposed its stance on the question of renationalizing the steel industry.[17]

A further problem arises as to what to do about elements of the party program that are not as valid after an election as they were before the election, or about matters that were not included in the program. We all know that unforeseen events after an election may change the desirability of elements of the program upon which the party ran during the campaign or may create new problems not considered in that program. When this occurs, as it frequently does, the governing party and its leaders may need to deviate from the original program or to develop policies not included in that program in order to confront the unforeseen events.

It is important to recognize that these problems of substantive representation do not apply solely to a party-responsibility system. They apply equally to representation through Presidential elections, as Dahl long ago demonstrated.[18]

However, critics of the Congressional system can argue that if the party-responsibility system does not necessarily represent public opinion on each individual issue, it does give the public choices between two or more parties advocating programs that contrast in general direction over a series of issues, what we might call "general policy alternatives" or, loosely, "ideological alternatives." From these the public can then select the alternative toward which it has greatest overall affinity, although likely disagreeing with some parts of it. In the British case, the contrast between the alternatives does subsume a number of important issues, even though by no means all of them. It is true that campaign oratory aside, the policies of the two major parliamentary parties in Britain frequently have not differed in their essentials on such varied issues as entry into the Common Market (such as from 1963 to 1970), relations with the United States, nuclear disarmament, immigration (since 1963), and regionalization of power. On the other hand, the postwar differences along a Left-Right dimension between the Labour and Conservative programs, as well as the parliamentary parties, on such issues as social welfare and pensions policies, nationalization of industry, education reform, and British military presence east of Suez illustrate that contrasts in general orientation between the parties are present to some degree.

Through the device of national popular elections, the public is given an opportunity to select the party whose policy direction or orientation (general policy alternative) it feels closest to, given the competing alternatives. Again, this is not to say that the public subscribes completely to the orientation of the party it selected, nor is it to say that the public agrees with each specific policy (whether part of the overall orientation or not) of the party it elected or that the party leadership later undertakes. We have seen, for example, that the public elected the Labour party to office in 1964 and 1966 despite its disenchantment with Labour's policy to renationalize the steel industry. To cite another example, in 1971-72 the Conservative government and Parliament agreed to join the Common Market even though this policy was opposed by a majority of the nation.

Nevertheless, if the election results in accurate proportional representation, then the overall alternative to which the majority of the public felt closest (despite disagreement with aspects of it) would secure a majority of the seats in the legislature. According to the party-responsibility model, through discipline and cohesion the party winning the majority could then control the legislature and infuse its general alternative, supported by a popular majority, into the process of decision-making.

Note, however, that this characterization makes an assumption that elections faithfully produced proportional representation in the legislature. Ideally, if substantive representation is to be maximized, the party that wins an absolute majority of the seats in the legislature (thereby giving it control of the legislature) ought also to have won an absolute majority of the popular vote. At least in the British case, this has not occurred since World War II. In the first of the 1974 elections, no party won an absolute majority in the House of Commons. And, as observed in Chapter 2, in each of the other elections since 1945, the party that did win an absolute majority of the seats in the House of Commons did *not* win an absolute majority of the popular votes.[19] This was the product of the single-member-district electoral system in combination with the presence of a third party, the Liberals. Because of this combination, the party winning a plurality of the votes was sufficiently overrepresented in the Commons to receive an absolute majority of the seats.[20] As a consequence, though usually representing a plurality of the voters, the governing parties in Britain have not necessarily represented a majority of the voters. Whether they have or not would depend upon whether those who voted for the Liberals (or smaller fourth and fifth parties) actually preferred the governing party as contrasted to the major opposing party. The implications of this particular point (a point that again applies to many Presidential elections)[21] for substantive representation in the British as compared to the Congressional system will be explored later in this chapter.

Leaving this aside for the moment, certainly one of the attractive features of a party-responsibility system is its potential to represent the proximity of the citizenry to competing policy programs that span a number of important issues, what we have called general policy alternatives. With this in mind, our analysis of substantive representation in Congress will give some consideration to Congressional representation of general policy alternatives. Such an analysis needs to assess the extent to which citizen proximity to these alternatives received proportional representation within each of the houses of Congress. Furthermore, it needs to examine Congressional leadership and how representative it has been of public support for the different alternatives. As an added test, it might investigate how well Congress has represented policy alternatives espoused by a minority that has suffered from demographic underrepresentation. Finally, to complement these various investigations, analysis ought also to consider individual issues for which data are available and examine how well the Congress reflected citizen opinion on these individual issues. This is what we will attempt to do.

The Level of Representation in Congress as a Composite Body and in its Leadership

Perhaps the conflict over general policy alternatives most often thought to be central to American politics over the past several decades is the division, broadly defined, between liberals and conservatives. While certainly not encompassing all issues, this division has subsumed a number of important issues, including federal regulation of business, economic and social welfare policies, civil rights, and states' rights. This is not to say that all liberals or conservatives agree with their respective groups on each of the issues. It is to say that there is a perceptible tendency toward agreement within these groups. Thus, differences on issues such as those mentioned above have been found to distinguish both liberals from conservatives in the Congress[22] and liberal identifiers from conservative identifiers in the public.[23]

Instead of examining divisions concerning party, then, our analysis will concentrate on divisions within the Congress and the public as they pertain to support for liberalism and conservatism. This requires that we locate measures that can tap such support. In the case of the Congress, we will employ measures compiled by groups associated with the two persuasions. The measures are the ADA (liberal Americans for Democratic Action) index and the ACA (conservative Americans for Constitutional Action) index. Each of these measures is based on the voting records of Congressmen. With regard to the public, self-identification will be used as a method (on pp. 387-389, later we will also discuss research results based on other methods of measuring public opinion). By this method, citizens are classified as liberal or conservative according to how they identify themselves. Gallup opinion polls will serve as our base of reference.

Admittedly, self-identification constitutes a rough measure of opinion. Yet, as indicated above, this measure has been found to correlate with citizen attitudes along a liberal-conservative scale over a series of issues.[24] It has also been found to correlate with the vote. In the 1972 Presidential elections, for example, self-identification as liberal or conservative was associated considerably more closely with decisions to vote for McGovern or Nixon than was party identification.[25] Seen in absolute terms, 83 percent of those strongly or moderately strongly liberal by self-placement voted for McGovern, whereas this was so for only about 8 percent of those strongly or moderately strongly conservative by self-identification.[26]

Our discussion of the party-responsibility model earlier in this chapter pointed out that persons who support a candidate or a party do not necessarily agree completely with the policy orientation or each individual policy of that candidate or party. The presumption at most in the model is that support indicates the likelihood of being closer to the policy of one's candidate or party as compared to the other candidates or parties. Similarly, we do not assume here that persons identifying themselves as liberals share exactly the same views as legislators who are liberal. Nor do we make this assumption for conservatives. The assumption we make is that, given a choice between a liberal Congressman and a conservative Congressman, most persons who identify themselves as liberal would on the whole prefer the orientation of the liberal candidate and most persons who identify themselves as conservative would on the whole prefer the orientation of the conservative candidate.

With this in mind, we turn to the data on the public and the Congress. The data pertain to the public in 1963, 1969, and 1970 and to the Congress in 1963-64, 1970, and 1971. The former two periods were chosen according to a widely read and cited analysis of changes in American public opinion carried out by Scammon and Wattenberg.[27] The latter period was the latest for which the ADA and ACA indexes were available at the time our research was carried out (Winter, 1972). Each of the Congressional periods follow immediately upon the periods used to measure public opinion.

Inspection of the 1969-70 and 1970-71 data on the House and the public reveals for both periods a rather close correspondence between the ideological composition of the House membership (as measured by ADA and ACA scores) and of the public (as measured by self-identification). In mid-1970, the Gallup polling organization found that 62 percent of the American public considered itself to be conservative and 38 percent considered itself to be liberal.[28] According to our measures of conservatism and liberalism in the House, 59 percent of the members of the House in 1971 were conservative in their voting behavior and the remaining 41 percent of the House members had liberal voting records.[29]

Examining the data for 1969-70, as we might anticipate, we again find a fairly close correspondence between the House and the public. A Gallup poll carried out in the middle of 1969 found that 61 percent of the public considered itself to be conservative and 39 percent considered itself to be liberal.[30] According to our measures of liberalism and conservatism in the 1970 House, we found that the voting records of 58 percent of the House members were conservative while 42 percent of the House members had liberal voting records.[31]

Of course, it is possible that 1969-71 was an atypical period. It might be argued that the correspondence between the public and the House occurred because the public had by 1969-71 turned in a conservative direction and had, in a sense, "caught up" with the conservatism of the House. This argument would lead to the conclusion that the correspondence between the ideological composition of the House membership and the public would disappear or be greatly reduced when liberal persuasions were more prevalent in the public.

In order to evaluate this possibility, we examined public opinion in 1963 and the behavior of the members of Congress in 1963-64. The Gallup public opinion poll taken in the summer of 1963 revealed that 51.5 percent of the American public considered itself to be liberal and 48.5 percent of the public considered itself to be conservative.[32] Using the ADA and ACA indexes from 1963-64, we found that 50 percent of the members of the House of Representatives in 1963-64 were liberal in their voting behavior and the remaining 50 percent had conservative voting records.[33] Thus, the more liberal tendency of the public in 1963-64 as compared to 1969-71 was reflected in the House of Representatives. And, once again, there was a rather close correspon-

Table 10.1
Conservative and Liberal Orientations Found in the American Public and in the House of Representatives, 1963-64, 1969-70, and 1970-71 (in percent)

Year		Liberal	Conservative
1969	Public	51.5	48.5
1963-64	House	50.0	50.0
1969	Public	39.0	61.0
1970	House	42.0	58.0
1970	Public	38.0	62.0
1971	House	41.0	59.0

dence between the mixture of ideological leanings in the public and in the House. The results for each year are presented on Table 10.1.

We should point out, parenthetically, that the ideological composition of the House and the public also remained quite close when there was a slight upsurge of liberalism in the public during the following year. Thus, the Gallup poll taken in 1964 found that approximately 53 percent of the public considered itself to be liberal, while 47 percent of the public considered itself to be conservative.[34] Use of the 1965 ADA and ACA scores reveal that 54 percent of the members of the House had a liberal voting record and 46 percent of the members had a conservative voting record.[35]

When we examine the Senate, however, a different pattern emerges. According to our measures, it is a pattern that is rather less representative (Table 10.2). Whereas persons identifying themselves as conservative constituted 62 percent of the public in 1970 and 61 percent of the public in 1969, we found that only 50.5 percent of the members of the Senate had conservative voting records in 1971 and 49.5 percent in 1970.[36] Going back to the 1963-64 period, we found that 58 percent of the members of the Senate had liberal voting records, whereas only 51.5 percent of the public considered itself to be liberal.

Nevertheless, we should note that as the public became increasingly more conserva-

Table 10.2
Conservative and Liberal Orientations Found in the American Public and in the Senate, 1963-64, 1969-70, and 1970-71 (in Percent)

		Liberal	Conservative
1963	Public	51.5	48.5
1963-64	Senate	58.0	42.0
1969	Public	39.0	61.0
1970	Senate	50.5	49.5
1970	Public	38.0	62.0
1971	Senate	49.5	50.5

374 *The Congress in Comparative Perspective*

tive from 1963 to 1971, so did the Senate membership. Thus, while conservatives composed only 42 percent of the Senate in 1964, by 1970 conservatives had come to constitute 49.5 percent of the Senate and in 1971 constituted a narrow majority of 50.5 percent of the Senate.

The figures reviewed thus far relate to the ideological composition of the public (as measured by self-identification) and of the membership of Congress (as measured by the ADA and ACA indexes). Based on these measures, the figures suggest a rather close correspondence between the overall composition of the House and of the public during the time periods examined. A greater divergence emerged when the overall composition of the Senate and of the public were compared, although changes in the composition of the Senate over time appear to have been broadly commensurate with changes that occurred in the public. Additional support for these conclusions through use of other kinds of measures will be presented later (pages 387-388).

Of course, models of substantive or preferential representation take into account more than the legislature as a composite body. They also take into consideration the leadership of these bodies. One of the main criticisms of the Congress is that its leaders, and especially its committee chairmen, who have been selected according to the rule of seniority, have been unrepresentative of general trends of opinion within the public. The prevailing feeling of the critics is that committee chairmen have overrepresented conservatives, thereby making it difficult for the Congress to enact liberal programs. With this criticism in mind, we decided also to examine the ideological orientations of committee chairmen and to compare these to the orientations with which citizens identified themselves.

Figure 10.1
The Majoritarian Model of Representation: Ideological Orientation of the Electorate, the Legislature, and the Legislative Leadership of the Majority Party

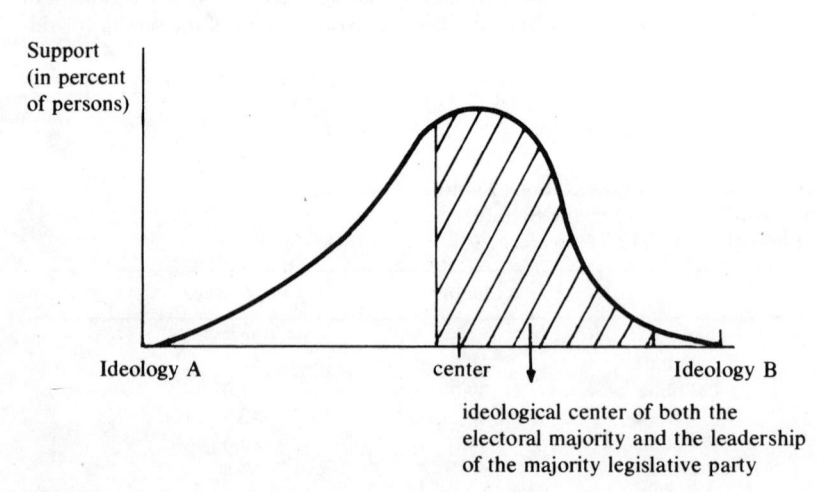

As we suggested earlier in this chapter, the correspondence we should expect between the orientation of legislative leaders and of citizens depends upon the assumptions we make about representation. We could look at representation with the majoritarian idea that the leadership should represent the majority that elected it to power. This would mean that the orientation of the legislative leaders should be at or near a center point within the orientations of the majority party electorate. Figure 10.1 illustrates this point.

The consensual model of representation, on the other hand, would suggest that legislative leadership, like the legislative body as a whole, ought to reflect proportionately the mixture of ideological orientations within the whole electorate. If this were the case, legislative leaders as a composite would be at the center of the ideological spectrum of the entire public rather than at the center of the ideological spectrum of the majority. This is suggested by Figure 10.2.

Presumably, any leadership that meets the ideal of either of these two competing models, or is at some point in between the ideals of the two models, could be considered representative. This means that there is a range within which legislative leaders as a composite must fall to be considered representative and that a leadership which falls outside that range would be considered unrepresentative.

With this in mind, we can refer to Figure 10.3. Let us say that point (b) is the ideological center of the electorate as a whole and that point (c) is the ideological center of the electorate of the majority party. Given our discussion above, any leadership whose ideological orientation fell on or between points (b) and (c) could be defended as representative leadership. Any leadership that fell outside this range, that is, to the

Figure 10.2
The Consensual Model of Representation: Ideological Orientation of the Electorate, the Legislators, and the Legislative Leadership of the Majority Party

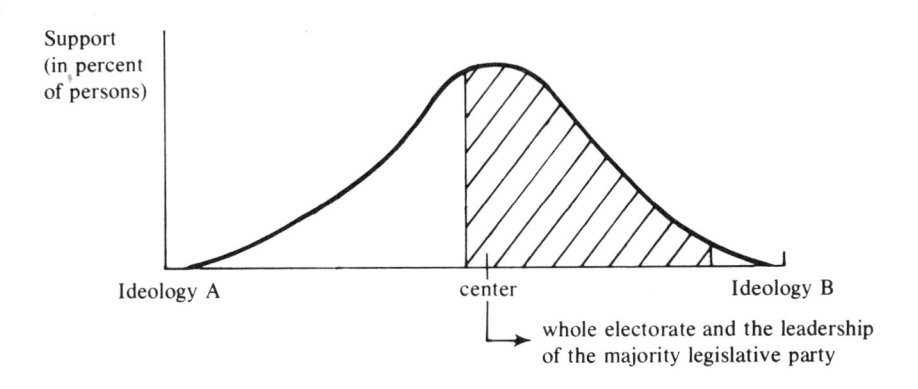

Figure 10.3

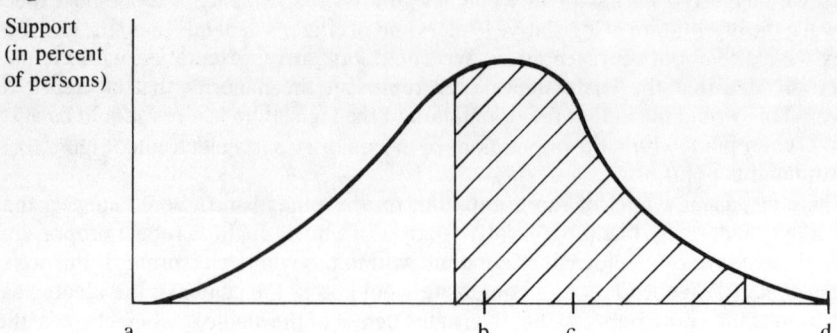

Support
(in percent
of persons)

a   b   c   d

▨ ideological preference of the electorate and the legislators of the majority party

left of (b) or to the right of (c), would not be representative. Moreover, the greater the distance between the ideological center of the leadership and this range, the more unrepresentative the leadership would be.

Let us now turn to the representative character of Congressional committee chairmen. What we wish to determine is whether the ideological center of committee chairmen as a composite fell at or between the ideological centers of the public as a whole and of the majority party electorate. In order to calculate the ideological center of committee chairmen as a composite, we will take the *percentage* that conservatives (or liberals) constituted of the committee chairmen. For example, if 75 percent of the committee chairmen are conservative, we will describe the ideological center of committee chairmen as a composite to be 75 percent conservative.

In examining the ideological makeup of the committee chairmen, we used the ADA and ACA indexes, employing them in the same manner as we did to measure the ideological composition of the House and the Senate. However, we did not treat control of each committee as being of equal value. Committees differ in their importance, and we wanted this to be reflected in our analysis. We did this by weighting the committees in each house and by assigning a value of 3 to control of the most important committees, a value of 2 to control of the committees second in importance, and a value of 1 to control of the least important committees.[37]

To determine the ideological center of the population as a whole and of the majority party electorate, we once again took the percentage of conservatives and liberals within the two publics. The data available for the majority party electorate, the Democrats, focus on party identifiers rather than on actual voters for the Congressmen of the majority party. It is probable that the actual voters for Democratic Congressmen were somewhat more liberal than the party identifiers. According to this assumption, independents and Republicans who voted for Democratic Congressmen probably were disproportionately liberal and those Democrats who did not vote for Democratic Congressmen probably were disproportionately conservative. We wanted to take this into account and have done so with the very rough estimate that party identifiers might underrepresent liberals who actually voted for Democratic Congressmen by about 10 percent.[38]

We can assess the representative character of the committee chairmen for the 1970 House and Senate by referring to Table 10.3. According to the points we made above, the range within which the committee chairmen would need to fall to be considered representative is set by the ideological center of the public as a whole and of the voters for the majority party. Thus, according to the table, any leadership in which liberals constituted from about 39 percent of the leadership (thereby matching the public) to about 59 percent of the leadership (thereby matching our estimate of voters for the majority party) would be considered as representative. The committee chairmen in each house seem to have met this requirement. The division of chairmen in the House, weighted for the importance of the committees, was 50 percent liberal in 1970. It was 47 percent liberal in the Senate.[39]

A similar result occurs for the committee chairmen in the 1971 House and Senate. This can also be seen on Table 10.3. According to the table, liberals would have to constitute from about 38 to 58 percent of the committee chairmen, again weighting for the importance of the committees, in order to fall within the range set by the population and the voters for the majority party. Once again, the committee chairmen met this requirement. The weighted division of chairmen in the 1971 House was 39 percent liberal and 47 percent liberal in the 1971 Senate.

Nor do these results seem to have occurred because of the decrease in the percentage of liberals in the population by 1969-71 as compared to 1963-64. Referring back to

Table 10.3
Conservative and Liberal Orientations Found in the American Public, the Democratic Voting Public, and the Committee Chairmen of the House and Senate for 1969-70 and 1970-71 (in Percent)

	Conservative	Liberal
1969-70		
Population (1969)	61	39
House Chairmen (1970)	50	50
Senate Chairmen (1970)	53	47
Democratic Voters (estimate—1969)	41	59
1970-71		
Population (1970)	62	38
House Chairmen (1971)	61	39
Senate Chairmen (1971)	53	47
Democratic Voters (estimate—1969)	42	58

1963-64, liberals constituted 53 percent (weighted) of the committee chairmen in the Senate, almost exactly the percentage of liberals in the population in 1963 (51.5 percent). In the case of the House, liberals constituted 70 percent (weighted) of the committee chairmen in 1963-64 (see Table 10.4), thereby approximating the percentage of liberals within the House Democratic party in 1963-64 (79 percent) and our estimate of the percentage of liberals among Democratic voters (78 percent).[40]

The findings we have presented for the committee chairmen do not deal with representation as a procedural or electoral mattter.[41] Rather they treat representation as general substantive matter, as a matter of legislative leadership reflecting general orientations found within the citizenry. Within the context of the measures we used, we found that the ideological composition of committee chairmen consistently fell within the range requisite for satisfactory substantive representation set by the consensual and the majoritarian models of representation. It is true that committee chairmen would have constituted different percentages of liberals or conservatives from the ones we observed had either the majoritarian or the consensual model been applied to the exclusion of the other. The point is, however, that a leadership that meets the standards set by either of the two models or by any combination of the two models, as our findings suggest the committee leadership did, can be considered as having achieved an equivalent level of substantive representation.

Earlier we argued, too, that the House as a whole (but less so the Senate) approximated the requirement of proportional substantive representation appropriate to both the majoritarian and consensual models of representation. Again within the context of the measures we used, this assessment was suggested by the rather close correspondence we consistently found between the ideological composition of the House membership and the ideological leaning with which the public identified itself.

Further Comments on Majoritarian Representation

With these points in mind, we are in a position to raise several additional questions we have thus far ignored about substantive representation through a majoritarian system.

Table 10.4
Conservative and Liberal Orientations Found in the American
Public, the Democratic Voting Public, and the Committee
Chairmen of the House and Senate for 1963-1964 (in Percent)

	Conservative	Liberal
Population (1963)	48.5	51.5
House Chairmen (1963-64)	30.0	70.0
Senate Chairmen (1963-64)	47.0	53.0
Democratic Voters (estimate—1963)	22.0	78.0

In particular, it is important to note that a strictly majoritarian legislature may encounter certain nagging representational problems that are less applicable either to the Congress or to a strictly consensual legislature. The problems flow from two assumptions contained in the majoritarian model of representation. While the same assumptions are made by the consensual model of representation, we will suggest that the implications of the assumptions are different for a consensual legislature than for a strict majoritarian legislature.

According to the majoritarian and consensual models of representation, at least two assumptions need to be met if the fullest policy linkage between electorates and legislatures by way of election outcomes is to occur. One assumption is that citizens vote for a candidate or a party based upon preference for the policy views of that candidate or party over those of the competing candidates or parties. A second assumption is that the electoral mechanism produces a legislature that is similar to the popular vote. While there is growing research to indicate that many voters do vote for a candidate or a party in a way that is consistent with their own policy preferences,[42] it is nevertheless the case that by no means all voters act in this manner. Nor does the electoral mechanism necessarily lead to an exact correspondence between the vote and percentages of seats won in the legislature. Both are true not only for the United States but also for a majoritarian system such as that in Great Britain.[43] If only because the two assumptions are not fully met in either system one can expect some discrepancy to occur in each between popular preferences for general policy alternatives and the proportional representation of these preferences in the legislature.

Yet the point that there is not likely to be a perfect correspondence carries with it certain implications regarding the overall representativeness of the consensual as contrasted to the majoritarian and party-responsibility or executive-force models of representation. If a perfect correspondence is not likely to occur, it would seem plausible that representation of the policy preferences of the public would be maximized better by that legislature which is least dependent upon the fully accurate proportional reflection of these preferences in the legislature. This is the consensual legislature.

When a majority is elected to a strictly majoritarian legislature, it controls and leads the legislature. The majoritarian system enables a defined legislative majority to control 100 percent of the leadership and of the decisions. Given this level of control, the potential capacity for misrepresentation in a strictly majoritarian system is considerable if the majority elected to the legislature does not actually represent the general policy orientation preferred by the majority of the voters.

When a majority is elected to a consensual legislature, on the other hand, it does not exercise complete control. Instead, leadership is drawn also from those holding the general policy preference of the minority in the legislature, and the particular coalition of legislators that determines any given legislative decision varies according to the issue. Because a single majority does not control 100 percent of the leadership or of the decisions, the potential consequences of inaccuracies in representation are not necessarily the same for a consensual system as for a majoritarian system.

This point can be made by contrasting the operation of the two systems in a hypothetical situation. Assume that 47 percent of the public preferring one policy direction over the alternative ended up electing 52 percent of the legislators. Under a strictly majoritarian system, this 52 percent of the legislators would provide 100 percent of the legislative leaders and would be the coalition that determined 100 percent (or almost 100 percent) of the legislation.[44] Under a consensual system, however, this 52 percent of the legislators would provide considerably less than 100 percent of the legislative leaders and, through the operation of shifting coalitions characteristic of a consensual legislature, would determine considerably less than 100 percent of the decisions. As a consequence, the misrepresentation of popular preferences for general policy alternatives that could result from the factors we outlined above would not be exaggerated nearly as much (and perhaps not at all) in a consensual legislature as compared to a majoritarian legislature.

In the situation just described, one might conclude that a *strict* majoritarian operation of the legislature was rather highly unrepresentative of public preferences for general policy alternatives, given the fact that 47 percent of the public determined the alternative that comprised 52 percent of the legislature and provided 100 percent of the leadership and the requisite support for nearly 100 percent of the legislation. Such a conclusion would not be as pertinent to the strictly consensual legislature if 47 percent of the public ended up determining, let us say, about 52 percent of the leadership and the support that decided about 52 percent of the legislation.

Obviously, it is better if the legislature contains a majority of members holding the same general policy orientation as that preferred by the majority of the public, but when there is a close division in the public, the consensual legislature might still be considered reasonably representative if there is a close division in the legislature, even if the narrow majority in the legislature differs from the narrow majority in the public.

This suggests, too, that a consideration worth taking into account in examining the operation of substantive representation through a nominally majoritarian kind of legislature is whether leadership within the legislature takes on some of the characteristics of consensual leadership or not. Indeed, leaderships in supposedly majoritarian legislatures may need to assume consensual characteristics for the purposes of achieving substantive representation. With this in mind, it would be useful to look at leadership in a majoritarian legislature and especially the British system, which critics of the Congress have frequently cited as a worthy alternative to the Congress.

The principal systematic research done on the policy views of the leadership of the two parties in the House of Commons was carried out by Kornberg and Frasure on the 1966 Parliament.[45] According to their findings, the policy views of the leadership groups of the Labour and Conservative parliamentary parties, each taken as a composite, did *not* coincide with the ideological center of the party each group led. The differences between the leaders of the two major parliamentary parties on the ideological issues examined were not only "noticeably less intense" but also encompassed a lesser number of issues than the differences that divded backbenchers of the two parliamentary parties. That is, the findings suggest that the policy views of the leadership groups in the Commons did not conform completely to the majoritarian model. Instead, not totally unlike the American experience, the policy views of the leaders also exhibited some of the characteristics one would expect of leadership groups in consensual legislatures.[46]

Minority-Group Representation in the House*

Let us return, then, to the idea of the consensual model and take it a step further in assessing substantive representation through the House of Representatives. In particular, we want to examine the extent to which the policy preferences associated with a minority and demographically underrepresented group of House members were substantively represented in the House in proportion to an estimate of popular support for such preferences. Our objective is to assess whether or not the preferences were proportionally represented with regard both to the House membership as a whole and the leadership structure and decision-making processes in the House.

Our attention centers on the representation of Black policy preferences in the 1971 House of Representatives. We chose to examine the Blacks partly because of the significance this group has had for public debate in the United States over the past two decades and partly because the group has quite obviously been demographically underrepresented in the House. Whereas Blacks account for 11 percent of the American population, with twelve Representatives (all members of the Black Caucus) they accounted for only 2.8 percent of the House in 1971. We chose to examine the 1971 House as the latest year for which data appropriate to our earlier analyses were available.

In our examination, we will investigate preferences the Black Caucus members supported in opposition or contradistinction to preferences supported by a majority of the group of which they were all members, the northern Democrats. Our procedure will be to differentiate these preferences and then to gauge both the support for the preferences and the political strength of that support in the House. Having done this, we will then compare the results to an estimate of support for the preferences among the general public.

We begin by isolating the roll call votes upon which a majority of the Black Representatives deviated from the majority of the remaining northern Democrats. During the 1971 House, these roll call votes totaled 45, or about 14 percent of the 320 roll call votes recorded in 1971. As might be anticipated, the forty-five roll call votes revealed a set of policy preferences that called for significant change in the priorities of the federal government in all areas of policy, foreign and domestic. As examples, the deviant votes expressed preferences such as the desire to reduce military expenditures substantially (eleven roll calls) as well as to terminate our involvement in Indochina (five roll calls); to reduce expenditures devoted to major technological or other "nonsocial" programs (nine roll calls); to increase greatly financial support for the poor, for antipoverty programs, and for the unemployed (six roll calls); to restrict business in various ways as well as to provide greater consumer protection (seven roll calls); to terminate or reduce economic relations between the United States and governments that officially discriminated against Blacks (three roll calls); and to prevent powers from being given to the District of Columbia government that might be

---

* The following analysis relies on John E. Schwarz and Lee Ridgeway, "Black Representation in Congress: An Examination of the 1971 House of Representatives" (Mimeographed paper presented to the Annual Convention of the Midwest Political Science Association, 1973).

used to the disadvantage of Blacks (two roll calls).[47] Many of the concerns and aims expressed in these votes were again in evidence in a list of sixty-one recommendations that the Black Caucus drafted and presented to President Nixon in 1971.[48]

What support did such preferences receive in the House? Were the Black Caucus members practically alone in their stands on the forty-five roll call votes? Or were they supported by non-Black members of the House? If the Caucus found support among the non-Blacks, how many non-Blacks generally gave their support and what was the degree of support they gave?

Recall that on each of the roll calls the Black Caucus voted against the majority of non-Black northern Democrats. As would be expected, with few exceptions it opposed majorities of all other party, regional, and demographic groupings. We define support for the Black Caucus to mean that at least a majority of the votes a member cast on these roll calls was in support of the position taken by the Black Caucus. The percentage of favorable votes a member cast can be defined as a Black Caucus support score. In turn, the "Black Coalition" can be defined as consisting of all members whose Black Caucus support scores were greater than 50 percent.

The Black Caucus support scores of the northern Democrats, including the Black northern Democrats, are presented on Table 10.5. Defining the "Black Coalition" as those whose Black Caucus support scores were greater than 50 percent, we find from the table that a total of 39 of the 164 northern Democrats (including the Blacks) belonged to the Black Coalition (the support scores of these 39 members ranged from 51.5 to 97.2). According to these voting records, approximately 24 percent of the northern Democrats, also constituting 9 percent of the entire House, were members of the Black Coalition. In addition, there were two Congressmen from outside the northern Democratic group who supported the Black Caucus preference on at least 50 percent of their votes. One of these was a southern Democrat, with a support score of 63, and the other was a Republican, with a support score of 57. Including the 12 Black Caucus members, then, there were 41 members with a support score above 50, or about 9.5 percent of the House.

Table 10.5
Black Caucus Support Scores of the Northern Democrats in the 1971 House of Representatives

Support Score	Non-Black Members	Black Members	Total
0-9	26	0	26
10-19	41	0	41
20-29	31	0	31
30-39	17	0	17
40-49	12	0	12
50-59	3	2	5
60-69	10	1	11
70-79	10	1	11
80-89	2	4	6
90-100	2	4	6

How strong was the support of the 29 non-Black members for the policy positions the Black Caucus members backed? On the forty-five roll calls, the average Black Caucus support score of the 29 non-Black members was 72 percent as compared to about 24 percent for the remaining non-Black northern Democrats. The average support score for the twelve Black members was 84 percent. So, while there was some difference between the voting patterns of the 12 Black and 29 non-Black members of the Coalition, the level of support of the non-Blacks for the Black Caucus was not far removed from that of the Blacks.

Another way of assessing the support of the 29 non-Black members for the Black Caucus is to examine the extent to which the majorities of the two groups voted together on the forty-five roll call votes. The majorities of the two groups aligned on thirty-six of the roll calls and differed on the remaining nine roll calls. Thus, a majority of the non-Black members did not join with the Black Caucus 100 percent of the time the Caucus majority followed a course of action separate from that of the northern Democrats. But, the non-Black and Black members of the Coalition did come together on 80 percent of the occasions.

As these figures show, the voting record of the Black and non-Black members of the Coalition on the roll calls was not the same. While the differences were not substantial, they should not be neglected.

We also need to consider how integral Black Coalition supporters were to the decision-making process. What was the political significance of the forty-one members of the Black Coalition in the 1971 House of Representatives?

One aspect of political significance that immediately comes to mind is whether or not a group plays a part in the decisional process of the House equal to the percentage who support the group in the House (its percentage in the House, in turn, should be related to the size of the group in the wider public). One approach here is to measure the extent to which the votes of the forty-one members of the Coalition were critical to the outcome of decisions of the House and to ask whether the decisions for which the Coalition's votes were critical were at all relevant to the objectives pursued by the Black Caucus or not.

There was a total of 320 roll call votes during the 1971 session of Congress. Of these, the votes of the members of the Black Coalition made the difference on 15, or about 5 percent, of all roll calls. However, a number of the 320 roll call votes had a nonpartisan character. Of all roll calls, 148 were partisan, and of these, how the members of the Black Coalition voted made the difference on 14, or about 9.5 percent. When partisan conflict occurred, then, the Black Coalition votes were instrumental in determining the outcome on about 1 of every 10 roll calls.

It is important to ask whether these decisions were at all related to the objectives of the Black Caucus. In fact, a number of them were of considerable significance in regard to Black Caucus's attempts to change the budgetary and policy priorities of the federal government. For example, without the votes of the Black Coalition members, funding for the SST (Supersonic Transport) would have passed the House, the House would not have decided to limit farm subsidies to $20,000, the House would have been prevented from accepting in conference the Mansfield amendment relating to the withdrawal of troops from Vietnam, and child day-care legislation would have been defeated in the House. On each of these roll calls, all relevant to the objectives of the

Caucus, the votes of the Black Coalition members made the difference in the House between victory and defeat.

Another way of looking at political significance is positional. This type of analysis focuses on the extent to which a particular group in the legislature holds important decision-making positions. Using this approach, we examined the percentage of committee and subcommittee chairmanships the Black Coalition members held. We also looked at specific committees central to the achievement of the Black Caucus's overall objectives, asking the percentage of seats on these committees occupied by Black Coalition members.

The Black Coalition members did not do well in regard to committee chairmanships. In fact, not one of the 21 committee chairmen in 1971 was a member of the Black Coalition. On the other hand, 13 of the 120 subcommittee chairmen, or 11 percent, were members of the Black Coalition.

We also examined seven committees that we felt were especially critical to the achievement of the Black Caucus's objectives. These were Appropriations, Ways and Means, Rules, Armed Services, Foreign Affairs, Judiciary, and Education and Labor. Of the total of 250 members on these seven committees, 28, or 11 percent, were Black Coalition members. The members were overrepresented on three of the committees (Judiciary, Education and Labor, and Foreign Affairs), had approximate proportional representation on two of the committees (Appropriations and Ways and Means), and were underrepresented on the remaining two committees (Rules and Armed Services).

No single measure or set of measures can provide a full description of political significance. The decisional and positional measures we have used can only be suggestive. With the important exception of committee chairmanships, few of the measures uncovered a marked disparity between the percentage of the House the Black Coalition constituted and the political significance of its members. In this sense, both the decisional outcome and positional measures of political significance tend in the same direction. Constituting about 9.5 percent of the entire House, the votes of the Black Coalition determined 5 percent of all roll calls and 9.5 percent of the partisan roll calls. The members of the Black Coalition also held 11 percent of all House subcommittee chairmanships. Finally, Coalition members occupied about 11 percent of the seats on seven House committees we considered most central to the objectives the Black Caucus wished to pursue.

Having assessed support in the House for Black Caucus preferences and having examined some measures of the political strength of its supporters, let us now consider citizen support. The policy preferences to which we have referred in our examination of Congressional support cover a variety of issues and of particular stands on these issues. The best measure of public support would be a survey of public opinion across these particular issues. However, we are not aware of any public opinion poll that both includes a sufficient number of these issues with sufficient specificity to enable us to caluclate from the poll the percentage of persons in the public who would support a majority of the issue positions the Black Caucus took.

Nevertheless, the question of whether or not these issue positions were being adequately represented in the House is of sufficient significance that it merits a provisional answer even if the method necessary to reach that answer is somewhat unorthodox. In an effort to obtain such an answer, we begin by making certain assumptions that help to delineate those segments of the public likely to support the Black Caucus. Based on the size of these segments of the public, we can then estimate the percentage of the public from which support was likely to be forthcoming. Thus, our objective is to obtain an estimate of likely popular support and to do so on the basis of assumptions that seem reasonably valid.

We begin with the assumption that the general policy direction of the Black Caucus was strongly liberal. This assumption cannot be proved to be entirely correct, yet the particular policy preferences of the Black Caucus, which called for a substantial change in public priorities, including marked income redistribution through greatly increased financial support for the poor and a marked decrease in spending on defense and "nonsocial" items, seem to us to have been more than moderately liberal preferences. We would categorize these preferences as very liberal. This categorization gains some credence from the fact that not one moderate liberal Congressman (ADA score of 51 to 75), nor any conservative Congressman, supported the position of the Black Caucus on a majority of the forty-five roll call votes. According to the ADA scores, each of the Congressmen who supported the Black Caucus was strongly liberal.

With this in mind, we will assume that support for the preferences of the Black Caucus from within the non-Black population would draw from persons who were very liberal and would include all such persons. However, this assumption takes into account only ideological alignment. It fails to include the possibility of potential alignment through identification. Thus, for the Black segment of the population, we will go further to assume that all persons who were not conservative might potentially support the Black Caucus. That is, we assume that the base of possible support from within the Black population for the Black Caucus preferences may come from moderately liberal and centrist persons as well as from strongly liberal persons.

To determine the strength of liberal and conservative persuasions within the public, we once again employed self-identification as a measure, as we did in our previous analysis. In the case of the Blacks, public opinion polls taken in 1970 show that from 25 to 30 percent of the Black population considered itself conservative.[49] Let us make our calculation according to the minimum percentage of Blacks considering themselves to be conservative, 25 percent. Using our assumptions, the remainder of the Black population would constitute the base of support from within the Black population for the Black Caucus. This encompasses 75 percent of all Blacks. Since Blacks make up 11 percent of the population, 75 percent of all Blacks would constitute 8.3 percent of the total American population.

Our assumptions for the non-Black population lead us to focus on the percentage of very liberal persons within the population. The poll that taps the percentage of very liberal persons (using those words) closest to the period we are covering was taken in October, 1970.[50] According to this poll, persons identifying themselves as very liberal constituted 4 percent of the total non-Black population, or about 3.6 percent of the total American population.

However, measuring extremes of public opinion by self-identification can be subject to error that underrepresents the extreme. There is the possibility that some people may be hesitant to identify themselves with extremes of opinion. In order to take this possibility into account, let us assume a 10 percent error that consistently underestimates the percentage of persons who properly belong in the "very liberal" category. This would lead us to place in the very liberal category 10 percent of the persons who identified themselves as fairly or moderately liberal. According to the 1970 poll, 10 percent of the persons identifying themselves as fairly liberal would comprise 1.5 percent of the non-Black population, or 1.3 percent of the entire population. With the addition of this possible error, the base of support for the Black Caucus from the non-Black population would constitute from about 3.6 (our original figure) to about 4.9 percent of the entire population.

A similar procedure applied to Blacks who identified themselves as conservative (25 percent) would lead us to add an additional 2.5 percent of the Black population as potential supporters of the Black Caucus, or 0.3 percent of the total population. Thus, Black support would constitute from 8.3 (our original figure) to 8.6 percent of the population.

We can now put our estimates for the Black and non-Black segments of the population together. Within the Black population, we have estimated likely support to have included around 8.3 to 8.6 percent of the entire American population. Within the non-Black population, our estimate suggests that support comprised from 3.6 to about 4.9 percent of the entire American population. Putting these figures together, our estimate suggests that support for the preferences of the Black Caucus during the period we covered constituted from around 11.9 to 13.5 percent of the American public.

How does this estimate of popular support for the preferences of the Black Caucus, constituting from 11.9 to 13.5 percent of the public, compare to the level of support we found for these preferences in the House of Representatives? As we observed previously, Black and non-Black Congressmen who regularly supported the Black Caucus constituted 9.5 percent of the House. This figure is somewhat below our estimate of support from within the public. Yet, the figure also comes within fairly close range of the support we estimated the policy preferences had within the public and at least suggests the presence of a decidedly higher degree of representation than would have been anticipated judging from the demographic representation of Blacks in the House. Based on demographic representation, the Blacks deserved forty-eight members in the House (11 percent) and instead had only twelve (2.8 percent). According to our estimate of preferential representation, the Black Caucus deserved the support of from fifty-two to fifty-seven members in the House and instead had the support of forty-one.

To summarize, then, the results of this analysis flow in a direction broadly consistent with our earlier analyses covering the House of Representatives. The measures we used suggest that out of substantial demographic underrepresentation emerged a greater correspondence between an estimate of popular support and both support in the House for Black Caucus preferences and the political strength of that support in the decision-making processes of the House.

Even so, we need to note again that the indicators we have used are rough. They are intended as suggestive, not conclusive. Moreover, we found that overall support for Black Caucus's preferences was somewhat less than our estimate of support in the citizenry and that non-Black members of the coalition supported the Black Caucus with slightly less regularity than did members of the Caucus. In addition, while fully proportionally represented in many aspects of the House decision-making process (including membership on key committees, chairmanship of subcommittees, and determination of outcomes on partisan votes), coalition members were not proportionally represented with regard to committee chairmanships.

Finally, we should stress that representation of policy preferences is not in any case the sole reason why one might advocate greater demographic representation of Blacks. For example, the election of a larger number of Black officials may be necessary if Blacks are to develop a feeling that they constitute a meaningful element of the American political community. Allied to this, demographic representation may be instrumental to the growth among Blacks of feelings of political self-worth. Although these are different objectives than the proportional representation of policy preferences, each might be thought to be appropriate objectives of legislative representation.

Application of Other Opinion Measurement Methods

To this point, our discussion of substantive representation has been based on inferences we have made about public opinion from self-identification measures of opinion. While we have attempted to defend these inferences, we should also assess the findings in the light of more detailed data about the specific opinions of the public as compared to Congress on particular issues. Unfortunately, very little research of this kind is available. We have located only one published survey using a national sample of public opinion on several specific issues and a comparison of opinion revealed by the

Table 10.6
Comparison of Public and Congressional
Opinion on Key Policy Issues, 1970[a]

	Public	U.S. House Members	U.S. Senators
1. Vietnam: Percent agreeing with, "speed up our withdrawal"	27	30	45
2. Defense: Percent agreeing with, "place less emphasis" on military weapons programs	30	37	45
3. Guaranteed Income: percent approving at least "$1600 for a family of four or more"	48	65	76
4. Civil Rights: Percent who agree that the "government should go farther to improve blacks' conditions"	53	58	76
5. Law and Order: Percent who disagree that too much consideration is given to rights of people suspect of crimes	29	36	56

Source: Robert Erikson and Norman Luttbeg, *American Public Opinion* p. 257.

[a] Except for question 5, the questions asked the public sample and the Congressmen were not exactly identical, although close enough to each other to allow rough comparison.

survey to the opinions on each issue of all House and Senate members.[51] The results of the study, undertaken in 1970, are presented in Table 10.6. They are largely consistent with the conclusions for the House and the Senate we have reached. This is true in three respects. First, inspection of the table shows that the complexion of opinion in the House was in fairly close correspondence with public opinion on four of the five issues. Second, the complexion of opinion in the Senate was generally further removed from public opinion than was the case for the House. Third, the complexion of opinion in the Senate was found to be more liberal than in either the House or the public. Each of these conclusions coincides with the results of our analysis earlier in the chapter (see pp. 372-374).

In addition to this study, another on the House of Representatives was undertaken in 1958 by the Michigan Survey Research Center.[52] It covered a sample of House members and examined the relationship between the voting records of these members and the opinions of constituents in the members' districts. Three issues treated were civil rights, social welfare policy, and foreign involvement.

The study was based on a probability sample of 116 House members and a small number of constituents in each of their districts. Included in the study were sample surveys of the opinions of these constituents on the three issues, interviews with the Representatives of the districts covering the Representatives' own attitudes about the issues as well as their perceptions of the opinions of their constituents, and measures of how the Representatives voted on the three issues. Each of these components of the study (constituent opinion in each district, each Representative's own attitudes, each Representative's perceptions of constituent opinion in his district, and each Representative's voting behavior) was categorized as being favorable (i.e., pro-civil rights, pro-social-welfare policy, pro-foreign involvement), neutral, or unfavorable (i.e., anti-civil rights, anti-social-welfare policy, anti-foreign involvement). The resulting correlations could range from +1.0 (which would mean complete agreement, for example, between the behavior of Representatives and the opinion of the respective constituents) to −1.0 (which would mean complete disagreement between the behavior of Representatives and the opinion of the respective constituents).

Taking the issues individually, the results of the 1958 study are quite compatible with the results and conclusions we have reached regarding representation in the House. Respectable positive correlations emerged between the behavior of Representatives and the specific opinions of their constituents both on the civil rights and the social-welfare policy issues. Looking at these issues, Miller and Stokes, the authors of the study, reported that "the correlation of congressional roll call behavior with constituency opinion on questions affecting the Negro was about +.65"[53] and that "on questions of social and economic welfare there is considerable agreement between Representative and district, expressed by a correlation of approximately +.4."[54] On neither of these issues was there complete agreement between Representatives and their districts. However, constituent opinion and the behavior of Representatives on each of the issues did move, in the aggregate, rather firmly in the same direction. Such was less the case for the third issue, foreign involvement, where the correlation between constituent opinion and the behavior of Representatives was slightly less than +.2.[55]

While a measurable congruence between Representative and district occurred on two of the three issues taken separately, it is possible to examine the three issues together from an ideological perspective in order to determine whether a measurable congruence between Representative and district also prevailed along ideological lines or not. In an effort to do this with the 1958 data, Segal and Smith uncovered a liberal-conservative scale both of constituent opinion and of Representatives' voting behavior on the civil rights, social-welfare policy, and foreign involvement issues.[56] Rather than treating each issue separately, the scales the authors used encompassed all three issues. Based on these scales, Segal and Smith attempted to correlate strength of constituent ideological leanings with the strength of ideological leanings exhibited in the voting behaviors of the respective Representatives.

Segal and Smith's findings show the correlaton between the ideological leanings found among constituents and the behavior of the respective Representatives to have been only a slightly positive +.18.[57] On the other hand, not all the Representatives were reelected in the 1958 Congressional elections. After taking account of those incumbents not reelected in 1958 (whose voting behavior correlated with constituency opinion at −.63), Segal and Smith found the correlation between constituency opinion and the voting behavior of the remaining Representatives to be +.43.[58]

Clearly, if all incumbents are considered, the authors did not uncover agreement between constituent opinion and the behavior of Representatives that would be consistent with the conclusions we have reached for the House. On the other hand, the results dealing with those Representatives who were reelected are considerably more compatible with our earlier conclusions. Thus, if one considers the Representatives who were reelected, which includes 84 percent of all the incumbents the authors examined, a rather respectable correlation did arise between the ideological leanings shown in the voting behavior of these Representatives and the ideological orientations held by the respective constituents.

Conclusion

A few conclusions are now in order. The chapter has been devoted to an examination of the representation of public opinion in Congress. Much of the analysis was carried out from the perspective of two contrasting models of representation. These were the majoritarian (incorporating the party-responsibility and executive-force proposals for reform) and consensual models of representation.

Let us summarize the results of our inquiry as they apply to the House of Representatives. First, the measures we used to tap the general direction of ideological leanings in the public and in the House consistently revealed, for the years we covered, a rather close similarity in the percentages of persons identifying themselves as liberals or conservatives in the public and percentages of Representatives having liberal or conservative voting records in the House. Second, we observed that the ideological composition of the House shifted over time according to shifts that occurred in the ideological composition of the public. Third, we saw that the ideological composition of committee chairmen consistently fell within the range of satisfactory substantive representation set by the majoritarian and the consensual models of representation. Moreover, the ideological composition of the committee chairmen, like the House as a whole, also shifted in line with shifts that occurred in the ideological composition of the public. Fourth, we found that support in the House for the policy preferences associated with a minority group, the Blacks, came within fairly close range of the support we estimated these policy preferences had within the public. Finally, we examined studies of the House based on other methods of inquiry and found that the thrust of most findings forthcoming from these researches were compatible with the findings that emerged from our analysis of the House.

Within the context of the measures we used and placed alongside the models of representation we described, we would conclude that the House of Representatives achieved a rather impressive record of substantive representation during the years we covered. The measures suggest that the House achieved a level of representation appropriate to a combination of the majoritarian and consensual models of representation. If the two models are viewed as being of equal value in terms of substantive representation, it follows that the House performed in this area as effectively as could be expected of the main alternative that has been proposed by the critics of the Congress. This alternative is the majoritarian model. Indeed, we observed that when there was a close division in the public, the House was probably in a more advantageous representative position to the extent that it operated closer to the consensual model as contrasted to the majoritarian alternative.[59]

While these conclusions appear to be appropriate for the House, they are less appropriate for the Senate. The principal reason for this is that the ideological composition of the Senate membership was consistently at greater variance with the ideological composition of the public than we observed for the House. Again this was reconfirmed by alternative methods of analysis. In certain other ways, however, we found the Senate to be quite representative. Thus, as for the House, it is important to note that changes in the ideological composition of the Senate as a whole paralleled changes that took place in the public. In addition, the Senate committee leadership consistently met the standards for substantive representation set by a combination of the majoritarian and consensual models of representation.

Notes

[1] Hanna Fenichel Pitkin, *The Concept of Representation* (Berkeley: University of California Press, 1967), pp. 209-40. See, also, Robert Y. Fluno, *The Democratic Community: Governmental Practices and Purposes* (New York: Dodd, Mead and Co., 1971), p. 156.

[2] Pitkin, *The Concept of Representation*, p. 235.

[3] Hanna Fenichel Pitkin, "The Concept of Representation," in her *Representation* (New York: Atherton Press, 1969), p. 22.

[4] Pitkin, "The Concept of Representation," in *Representation*, p. 22.

[5] A presentation and summary of arguments may be found in Joseph S. Clark, Congress: *The Sapless Branch* (New York: Harper & Row, 1964); James A. Burnham, "The Case for Congress," in *Congressional Reform: Problems and Prospects*, ed. Joseph S. Clark (New York: Thomas Y. Crowell, 1965), pp. 29-44; James MacGregor Burns, *The Deadlock of Democracy: Four-Party Politics in America* (Englewood Cliffs, N.J.: Prentice-Hall, 1963); James MacGregor Burns, *Congress on Trial: The Legislative Process and the Administrative State* (New York: Harper & Brothers, 1949); The Committee on Political Parties, American Political Science Association, *Toward A More Responsible Two-Party System* (New York: Rinehart and Company, 1950), pp. 1-37; Roger H. Davidson, David Kovenock, and Michael K. O'Leary, *Congress in Crisis: Politics and Congressional Reform* (Belmont, Calif.: Wadsworth Publishing Company, 1966), pp. 7-37; and, Samuel Huntington, "Congressional Responses to the Twentieth Century," in *The Congress and America's Future*, 2d ed., David B. Truman (Englewood Cliffs, N.J.: Prentice-Hall, 1973), pp. 6-38.

[6] For a summary of the executive-force and party-responsibility proposals, see Davidson, Kovenock, and O'Leary, *Congress in Crisis*, pp. 25-37; Burnham, "The Case for Congress"; Committee on Political Parties, *Toward A More Responsible Two-Party System*, pp. 37-96; and John S. Saloma, III, *Congress and the New Politics* (Boston: Little, Brown and Co., 1969), pp. 28-56.

[7] Davidson, Kovenock, and O'Leary, *Congress in Crisis*, pp. 28-33 and p. 36; Saloma, *Congress and the New Politics*, pp. 38-40 and p. 72.

[8] Arthur M. Schlesinger, Jr., *The Imperial Presidency* (Boston: Houghton Mifflin, 1973), pp. 252-55.

[9] Exceptions here are certain executive-force formulations under the Nixon administration that had a rather different and lesser idea of executive responsibility and accountability to the legislature than the usual executive-force or party-responsibility proposals.

[10] Davidson, Kovenock, and O'Leary, *Congress in Crisis*, p. 30-31

[11] Davidson, Kovenock, and O'Leary, *Congress in Crisis*, pp. 32-33; Saloma, *Congress and the New Politics*, p. 72.

[12] Davidson, Kovenock, and O'Leary, *Congress in Crisis*, p. 28

[13] See Robert A. Dahl, *A Preface to Democratic Theory* (Chicago: University of Chicago Press, 1956), Chapter 5, and his *Pluralist Democracy in the United States: Conflict and Consent* (Chicago: Rand-McNally, 1967), and Willmoore Kendall and George Carey, "The 'Intensity' Problem and Democratic Theory," *American Political Science Review* 62 (March 1968): 5-25

[14] David Butler and Donald Stokes, *Political Change in Britain: Forces Shaping Electoral Choice* (New York: St. Martin's Press, 1971) pp. 466, 482, and 496. For an analysis of the diminishing policy differences between parties in West Germany and other Western systems, see Otto Kirchheimer, "Germany: The Vanishing Opposition," in *Political Oppositions in Western Democracies*, ed. Robert A. Dahl (New Haven, Conn.: Yale University Press, 1966), pp. 243-48, and Otto Kirchheimer, "The Waning of the Opposition in Parliamentary Regimes," in *Legislative Behavior: A Reader in Theory and Research*, ed. John C. Wahlke and Heinz Eulau (Glencoe, Ill.: The Free Press, 1959), pp. 43-55. For a theoretical treatment, see Anthony Downs, *An Economic Theory of Democracy* (New York: Harper & Brothers, 1957).

[15] See A. H. Birch, *Representation* (New York: Praeger, 1971), pp. 99-100.

[16] A theoretical discussion of this problem is found in Kenneth J. Arrow, "Political and Economic Choice," in *Game Theory and Related Approaches to Social Behavior*, ed. Martin Shubik (New York: John Wiley and Sons, 1964), pp. 135-40.

[17] Figures for British public opinion on the nationalization of industry for 1963, 1964, and 1966 can be found in Butler and Stokes, *Political Change in Britain*, p. 176.

[18] Robert A. Dahl, *A Preface to Democratic Theory*, pp. 124-31.

[19] R. L. Leonard, *Elections in Britain* (London: D. Van Nostrand Company, 1968), pp. 162-63.

[20] An exception occurred in 1951 when the party that won a majority of the seats in the Commons (the Conservatives) did not even win a plurality of the vote. See Leonard, *Elections in Britain*, p. 162. For an analysis of the general effect of single-member-district and proportional electoral systems, see Douglas Rae, *The Political Consequences of Electoral Laws* (New Haven, Conn.: Yale University Press, 1967).

[21] This particular point would apply to the executive-force alternative whenever a President was elected by a plurality rather than by an absolute majority of the vote. This has happened in three Presidential elections since 1945 (1948, 1960, and 1968).

[22] See Chapter 4 and especially the citations for the Congress in notes 11, 13, and 15.

[23] Using public samples, Free and Cantril examined the relation between self-identification as conservative or liberal and views on such matters as states' rights, federal government power, and preserving the free enterprise system (which the study termed ideological concerns). Of those respondents the study classified as either liberal or predominantly liberal regarding these ideological concerns and who identified themselves as liberal or conservative, 74 percent identified themselves correctly as liberal. Similarly, of those respondents Free and Cantril classified as either conservative or predominantly conservative regarding these ideological concerns and who identified themselves as liberal or conservative, about 78 percent identified themselves correctly as conservative. See Lloyd A. Free and Hadley Cantril, *The Political Beliefs of Americans: A Study of Public Opinion* (New York: Simon and Schuster, 1968). The percentages cited here were calculated from their figures on ideological spectrum found on page 224 weighted, where needed, according to the proportion of respondents in the ideological spectrum categories as shown on page 23.

Several other studies also document a close association between self-identification and one's policy views. The rather strong relationship between respondents' self-placement as conservative or liberal and their views on a wide range of issues (including the Vietnam, military, urban, minorities, busing, campus unrest, and marijuana issues) is shown in Arthur H. Miller et al.,"A Majority in Disarray: Policy Polarization in the 1972 Election" (Mimeographed paper presented to the 1973 annual convention of the American Political Science Association), and James W. Clarke and Joseph Egan, "Social and Political Dimensions of Campus Protest Activity," *The Journal of Politics* 34 (May 1972): 500-23.

[24] See note 23 and especially, Arthur H. Miller et al., "A Majority in Disarray."

[25] Arthur Miller et al., "A Majority in Disarray," p. 66

[26] Arthur Miller et al., "A Majority in Disarray," p. 23

[27]Richard Scammon and Ben Wattenberg, *The Real Majority* (New York: Coward-McCann, 1970), especially pp. 72-73.

[28]*The Gallup Opinion Index: Political, Economic and Social Trends*, May 1970, p. 8. The figures we present divide those having no opinion according to the percentages of persons identifying themselves as conservative and liberal. We did not use a Gallup poll that was taken closer to the 1970 election, in October of 1970, because "middle of the road" was offered as a choice along side "conservative" and "liberal." The total percentage of persons who identified themselves as liberal or conservative in this poll was markedly less than in the polls we employed. Since we wanted to determine tendency more than strength of tendency, the polls we did use were capable of giving us more complete information in this regard than could the October, 1970, poll.

[29]The ADA and ACA measures as applied to members of the House and the Senate in 1971 can be found in *Congressional Quarterly Weekly Report*, April 29, 1972, pp. 932-33. Members were ranked as liberal if they scored higher on the ADA index than on the ACA index. Members were ranked as conservative if they scored higher on the ACA index than on the ADA index.

[30]Scammon and Wattenberg, *The Real Majority*, p. 72. The figures we present divide those having no opinion according to the percentages of persons identifying themselves as conservative and liberal.

[31]The ADA and ACA measures as they applied to the members of the House and the Senate in 1970 can be found in *Congressional Quarterly Weekly Report*, April 16, 1971, pp 865-67. For our method of categorizing members as liberal or conservative, see footnote 29.

[32]Scammon and Wattenberg, *The Real Majority*, p. 72. The figures we present divide those having no opinion according to the percentages of persons identifying themselves as conservative and liberal.

[33]The ADA and ACA measures as they applied to members of the House and of the Senate in 1963-64 can be found in *Congressional Quarterly Weekly Report*, April 16, 1971, pp. 865-67. For our method of categorizing members as liberal or conservative, see footnote 29.

[34]George H. Gallup, *The Gallup Poll: Public Opinion 1935-1971* (New York: Random House, 1972), p. 1907. The figures we present divide those having no opinion according to the percentages of persons identifying themselves as conservative and liberal.

[35]The ADA and ACA measures as they applied to members of the House and the Senate in 1965 can be found in *Congressional Quarterly Weekly Report*, February 25, 1966, pp. 472-73. For our method of categorizing members as liberal or conservative, see footnote 29.

[36]The percentage of Senators for 1971 and for 1963-64 was calculated on a base of less than 100, since two Senators received the same score on both the ADA and the ACA index.

[37]We ranked the House committees according to whether members on a committee were allowed to belong to more than one committee (a nonexclusive committee) or were not allowed to belong to more than one committee (an exclusive committee). Nonexclusive committees were ranked as the least important and given a score of one, semiexclusive committees were given a score of two and exclusive committees received a score of three. We ranked the Senate committees according to the ranking found in Donald Matthews, *U.S. Senators and Their World* (New York: Random House, 1060), p. 149, with the top three committees receiving a score of three, the next eight committees receiving a score of two, and the lowest five committees (including Aeronautical and Space Sciences, added since Matthew's study) receiving a score of one. The number of committee chairmanships held by the liberals (conservatives) multiplied by the importance of each of the committees and then taken as a percentage of the total number of committee chairmanships multiplied by the importance of the committees constituted the percentage to which the liberals (conservatives) controlled the committee chairmanships. For example, if liberals in the Senate controlled one of the top three committees (3 points), three of the next eight committees (6 points), and two of the lowest five committees (2 points), the liberal score would be 11 divided by a total possible score of 30 ($3 \times 3 + 8 \times 2 + 5 \times 1 = 30$.) In this case, control over the Senate committee chairmanships would be 37 percent liberal.

[38]Percentages were calculated on the basis of the results for ideological orientation according to party identification found in the Gallup polls we have used.

	1963-64		1970		1971	
Position	ADA	ACA	ADA	ACA	ADA	ACA
Senate Majority Leader	80	7	75	29	78	11
Senate Majority Whip	97	1	84	5	26	45
House Majority Leader	80	4	48	16	54	14
House Majority Whip	88	9	48	16	78	11

Only the post of Senate majority leader was occupied by the same man (Mansfield) throughout the time period indicated. Obviously, as expected, there is a "liberal" bias for the party leadership of the Democratic party in Congress.

[40]Gallup, *The Gallup Poll*, p. 1845.

[41]While we have treated committee chairmen from the perspective of substantive representation, there is

also the matter of formal representation to consider—that is, the ability of the public to control through elections who will become committee chairmen. This is done through Congressional elections in a manner that, in one important respect, is similar to parliamentary elections. That is, by voting for party, the electorate in effect also determines which of two alternative sets of leaders will control the committees. Moreover, the public is given a choice in the sense that the percentage of liberals and conservatives that would constitute the Democratic and Republican committee chairmen usually differs by from 30 to 40 percent. Finally, it should be noted that the majority Congressional party has the power, should it so choose, as the House Democrats have recently done, to remove and replace a committee chairman. Perhaps a reason why it has rarely used this power is that the committee chairmen as a composite could have been viewed as being substantively representative.

[42]Insofar as concerns Congressional elections, see David R. Segal and Thomas S. Smith, "Congressional Responsibility and the Organization of Constituency Attitudes," in *Political Attitudes and Public Opinion*, ed. Dan D. Nimmo and Charles M. Bonjean (New York: David McKay, 1972), pp. 562-68, and Warren E. Miller and Donald E. Stokes, "Constituency Influence in Congress," in Angus Campbell et al., *Elections and the Political Order* New York: John Wiley and Sons, 1966), pp. 359-60. On Presidential elections, see Arthur Miller et al., "A Majority in Disarray," and also David RePass, "Issues Salience and Party Choice," *The American Political Science Review* 65 (June 1971): 389-400.

[43]On voting behavior in Britain, see Butler and Stokes, *Political Change in Britain*, and on the effects the electoral mechanism has on election results, see our Chapter 2, pp. 000.

[44]This example may seem somewhat extreme because the majority parliamentary party may contain some legislators who share the general policy direction of the opposite party. However, it should be noted that to the extent that this occurs, the system would increasingly be taking on the characterisitcs of the consensual model and increasingly losing the characteristics of the consensual model and increasingly losing the characteristics of the majoritarian model.

[45]Allan Kornberg and Robert C. Frasure, "Policy Differences in British Parliamentary Parties," *American Political Science Review* 65 (September 1971): 694-703.

[46]Kornberg and Frasure, "Policy Differences in British Parliamentary Parties," pp. 700-701 and 703. As Kornberg and Frasure point out, this finding was not unexpected, given the similar conclusions Robert McKenzie had reached in his pioneering study on the Labour and Conservative parties, *British Political Parties* (New York: St. Martin's Press, 1963).

[47]The remaining two roll calls had to do with a vote on the proceedings and on native claims in Alaska.

[48]For the recommendations, see "The Black Caucus and Nixon," *The Black Politician* 3 (July 1971): 4-12.

[49]*The Gallup Opinion Index: Political, Social, and Economic Trends,* April, 1970, p. 17; May, 1970, p. 8; and November, 1970, p. 17.

[50]*The Gallup Opinion Index: Political, Social, and Economic Trends,* November, 1970, p. 17.

[51]See Robert Erickson and Norman Luttbeg, *American Public Opinion: Its Origins, Content and Impact* (New York: John Wiley and Sons, 1973), p. 257.

[52]Miller and Stokes, "Constituency Influence in Congress."

[53]Miller and Stokes, "Constituency Influence in Congress," in *Elections and the Political Order*, ed. Campbell et al., p. 359.

[54]Ibid.

[55]Ibid.

[56]Segal and Smith, "Congressional Responsibility and the Organization of Constituency Attitudes," in *Political Attitudes and Public Opinion,* ed. Nimmo Bonjean, pp. 562-68.

[57]Segal and Smith, "Congressional Responsibility and the Organization of Constituency Attitudes," p. 567.

[58]Ibid.

[59]Some may suggest that if the Congress represents, it cannot act. Evidence relating to this suggestion, much of it disconfirming, has already been presented and discussed. See Chapter 6.

Chapter 11
Conclusion

Our initial interest in undertaking an analysis of the United States Congress and the West European legislatures was precipitated by the contemporary importance of the subject. Some years ago, Woodrow Wilson wrote: "The whole purpose of democracy is that we may hold counsel with one another, so as not to depend on the understanding of one man, but to depend on the counsel of all."[1] Yet despite the centrality of the legislature to early modern democratic theory and the enormous formal or constitutional powers allocated legislatures in Western political systems, numerous scholars and other observers have found the contemporary legislature to be in a stage of crisis. Many, including mid-twentieth-century liberals, have rather enthusiastically cited a decline in legislative influence. Criticism of the legislature as a representative institution has also been rife.

This study has focused principally on the American Congress. At the same time, our analysis has treated several parliamentary legislatures in an attempt, where possible, to avoid parochial descriptions and conclusions. In this way the experience of Congress could be given some perspective and generalizations about behavior, or exceptions to them, could be revealed. As a consequence, we have brought into the analysis experiences of the British House of Commons, the West German Bundestag, and the French National Assembly.

Much of our description and explanation of legislative behavior has been founded on the framework introduced in the first chapter. Following his study of the United States Senate, David Price pointed out that to explain legislative behavior one must denote both the legislators' "intentions and goals in their own right" as well as the "limiting or enabling conditions which have a determinate impact on the options and capacities" of the legislators.[2] These were ordinarily a product of the situation or setting within which the legislator functioned. Similarly, the underlying theme of our framework has been that an understanding of how legislators behave toward other actors requires both specification and knowledge of what the legislators themselves wish to achieve as well as knowledge of the relation between the meeting of their goals and the given political situation or setting.

The study has thus attempted to specify various types of goals and particular elements of the legislative setting and to show their relevance to legislative behavior. Three general types of goals have been central to the analysis. These have been legislators' career ambitions, affective attachments (with our focus particularly on feelings of party identificaton), and normative outlooks (including legislators' policy attitudes, conceptions of roles, and desires to make informed decisions).

We examined the legislator's situation or setting partly in terms of the presence of other actors and the objectives they pursued. Also important were certain features of the political structure, whose influence was considered along two dimensions. One dimension was the way the structure, in light of the legislator's goals, affected the costs and benefits of alternative courses of action he could take. Particularly relevant in this connection was the type of system (parliamentary as against separation of powers) and how career rewards regarding survival and advancement were distributed in the system (here the salient point was not who controlled rewards but the conditions or criteria pertinent to gaining and maintaining the rewards, whoever controlled them).[3] The other dimension was the way the political setting affected the legislator's capacity to act effectively on his goals. Included here were such structural features as the extent to which parties were organized internally, the informational resources available to the legislator, the powers of the legislature, and how powers were distributed within the legislature.

The findings of the study as they applied to legislators' behavior toward their parties, the executive, and interest groups were summarized in the concluding sections of Chapters 4 through 9 (see especially Chapters 4, 5, 8, and 9). The evidence in these chapters suggested that each of the structural variables was relevant to explaining legislative behavior in at least one area under consideration. Each of the motivational variables also proved to be pertinent. Especially in the case of the motivational variables, where it is sometimes considered that career ambition is the strongest force, it is of note that no single variable seems to have predominated. With few exceptions, the evidence was more consistent with the conclusion that, in the aggregate, legislative behavior could be adequately understood only by interjecting normative and affective concerns alongside career goals.

Throughout the course of the study, the variables of the framework were found to contribute to understanding Congressional behavior and to placing that behavior in the perspective of legislative experiences in the three European systems. For example, the variables highlighted and helped to explain both the strength that party alignment has had as a focus of Congressional behavior and the relative weakness of party alignment in Congress when viewed alongside the European legislative experiences. Based on this analysis, the variables helped to account for the rather balanced relationship on domestic legislation that has existed between the Congress and the Presidency, with neither being essentially dominant over the other, and to understand as well the influence and centrality of Congress (particularly its significant role in policy initiation) that emerged when Congress was compared to the European legislatures. Also, the variables helped to delineate the strengths and weaknesses of interest group influence on individual members of Congress and to bring to light roughly similar tendencies that have characterized relations between interest groups and European parliamentarians in analogous settings.

These examples could be supplemented by others throughout the study, some showing differences between the Congressional and European experiences and others highlighting areas of broad similarity, which our analysis has described and sought to understand. The examples equally illustrate the varying perspectives from which one can attempt to comprehend Congress—the configurative perspective, which focuses almost exclusively on Congress within the American system, and the comparative perspective, which considers Congress in relation to other legislatures.

Utilizing descriptions and explanations of legislative behavior as bases for evaluation has also been a concern of the study. How one moves from descriptions and explanations to evaluation depends to a significant degree upon the judgmental criteria one utilizes. A commentator's own values often play a leading part in determining the "grade" the legislature receives.[4] For example, this helps to account for the different positions on the Congress of James MacGregor Burns, a liberal, and James Burnham, a conservative.[5] Often an individual unhappy with the particular policy outputs of the legislature or the allocation of power within it (i.e., the "bias" is mobilized against his "side")[6] may condemn the legislature, while those sympathetic toward the policy outputs may praise the legislature. The fact is there is no general agreement (nor is there likely to be) on the values that are proper to use in making judgments about the legislature.

Yet, our concern about evaluation gains special relevance considering the many substantial criticisms that have been levied against the legislature. We outlined a number of the key criticisms in the introductory chapter. Our summary comments regarding evaluation are directed at these particular criticisms. Within the context of the descriptions and explanations found in the study, our discussion centers on how the criticisms apply to the Congress.

One of the major criticisms raised against the Congress has had to do with its effectiveness in representing public opinion on questions of policy (what we called substantive or preferential representation). It has been argued that partly because of the disunity of its parties and the fragmentation of its power structure, the Congress has been rendered less able to represent national opinion than could alternative kinds of systems. National opinion representation could be better accomplished by a party-responsibility system, such as the British, or by an executive-force system that would accord the Presidency, a nationally elected officer, greater influence in Congress.

We investigated these arguments in Chapter 10. The chapter examined Congress in the perspective of two models of substantive representation, one called a majoritarian model and the other called a consensual model. As indicated in the chapter, the majoritarian model of representation has provided one of the underpinnings for the party-responsibility system. Similarly, it has been used to support the claim that the Presidency has been more representative of national opinion than has the Congress.

Utilizing the two models of representation, we examined the contention that the Congress has not been as representative of national opinion as a majoritarian system would be. Our analysis of the House of Representatives did not support this contention. Rather, within the context of the measures and time periods we used, the findings in Chapter 10 suggested the conclusion that the House achieved a level of national opinion representation that the majoritarian alternative would not have exceeded or perhaps even met. While this conclusion did not hold as consistently for the Senate, we observed that in a number of key areas (including both the substantive representativeness of the Senate committee chairmen and shifts in voting patterns within the Senate over time) the conclusion reached for the House was equally applicable to the Senate.

Findings presented in other chapters also bore on the question of substantive representation. These findings addressed assertions that members of Congress have been essentially subservient to the pressures of special interest groups and that the internal decisional process of the Congress, especially the role of the committee system, has itself been unrepresentative. Another element of the indictment against Congress that our analysis treated reaches beyond the question of representation, strictly defined. It is that the Congress, again because of the disunified character of its parties and the great fragmentation of power that has typified its decisional process, has been unable to play a significant leadership role in the initiation of policy. Instead, the Congress has been relegated to a role either of being dependent upon and dominated by Presidential leadership or of blocking and essentially thwarting Presidential leadership.

These criticisms are obviously quite fundamental, and we have examined research and evidence relating to each of them in various parts of the study. While each criticism has some virtue in some areas and in some cases, the evidence we have reviewed again suggests a picture rather different from the one the criticisms often convey.

For example, in face of the criticism that individual members of Congress have been subservient to interest-group pressures, the evidence in Chapter 9 disclosed that factors other than pressure have usually been quite prominent in determining the relations between interest groups and members of Congress. We refer particularly to the relevance member's own policy views and concerns have had for how they behaved toward interest groups. Various kinds of analyses were presented that supported this conclusion. At the same time, we found that a complex of factors has served to limit the effectiveness of certain interest group resources, and especially the financial sanctions and rewards available to them. Moreover, to the extent interest groups were able to alter behavior in dealing with individual legislators, the evidence indicated a mitigating factor from the standpoint of representation. This is that the influence of interest groups on the members seems frequently to have been associated with the demographic size or potential popular appeal of the group at the constituency level.

Thus, not only did the evidence suggest that legislators have interacted with interest groups with a higher degree of independence than the assertions of subservience have sometimes implied, but it also indicated that group size or potential popular appeal was frequently central to how influential groups were in their dealings with legislators. While one should not discount the effects of other kinds of group resources, such as financial rewards and sanctions, neither should one neglect the considerations just mentioned.

Criticisms have also been raised about the representativeness of the decision-making process within Congress and particularly about the powerful role of committees and their chairmen. One of the concerns of critics has been that the chairmen of committees, selected by seniority, have been unrepresentative. It is true that until recently committee chairmen have been selected through the seniority system. Even so, the models of substantive representation and the data considered in Chapter 10 consistently showed the ideological composition of committee chairmen to have been substantively representative for the time periods covered. This was the case for both the House and the Senate. Also pertinent is evidence that we presented in Chapters 8 and 9. This evidence disclosed that relations between chairmen and their committees, as well as between committees and the wider legislative body, have tended to evolve within parameters the wider body placed on the committees and both the wider body and the committees placed on the chairmen. Research covering an array of chairmen and committees has found that continuing evidence of insensitivity to the interests of a decided majority of committee members or to individual member and major coalitional concerns on the floor have usually also had the effect of undercutting the influence of the chairmen in leading their committees and of the committees in leading the wider legislative body.

A final area of criticism has been directed to the role of Congress in the making of policy. Here, with the important exceptions of foreign policy and domestic policies requiring the analysis and integration of huge amounts of available data, the evidence has not sustained the criticism that the Congress has been unable to play a significant role in the initiation of policy or that Congress has been relegated to a role either of being subservient to Presidential leadership or of frustrating Presidential leadership. Instead, the evidence revealed that the Congress has contributed substantially to the initiation of successfully-adopted policies over a broad range of domestic legislation. Moreover, its outright rejections of Presidential initiatives and the extensive modifications it has attached to some other initiatives, combined with its own record of initiative, suggests that the relationship between the Congress and the Presidency in the domestic area has typically been a coordinate one rather than one of Presidential dominance and Congressional subservience. Even with this in mind, it should be remembered that the Congress has also regularly adopted in some form a sizeable number of Presidential initiatives, one indication that its role has not been characteristically obstructionist of Presidential leadership.

In the various criticisms just addressed, certain basic features of Congress have regularly been cited as weaknesses that need correction. We refer especially to the comparatively undisciplined nature of the Congressional parties and the comparatively great fragmentation of power and resources within the Congress. Although often roundly criticized as major defects, there are also numerous ways, as our analysis has suggested, that these features have enhanced Congressional effectiveness. In particular, investigations of both the Congress, itself, and the Congress alongside the European legislatures found that each of these features contributed to Congressional effectiveness in the key areas of both policy initiation (see Chapter 8) and the representation of national opinion (see Chapter 10).

Yet, if these conclusions about the Congress in response to the various criticisms are correct, another conclusion also emerges: the record of the Congress along the lines we have discussed has been rather more respectable than its image appears to have been. And, if this is true, the Congress would do well not only to consider reforms that might help it further improve upon its record, such as those addressing informational capacity and mechanisms for policy coordination; but equally important, the Congress would do well to improve its image. In this vein, continued campaign-financing reform, stricter codes regarding conflicts of interest, opening up committee procedures to greater public view, and the like might be of great value in helping to better the image of Congress and to build the more balanced view that our study suggests the Congress deserves to have.

Notes

[1] Woodrow Wilson, *The New Freedom* (Englewood Cliffs, N.J.: Prentice-Hall, 1961), p. 164.

[2] David Price, *Who Makes the Laws? Creativity and Power in Senate Committees* (Cambridge, Mass.: Schenkman Publishing Company, 1972), p. 310.

[3] For example, the fact that there was a relatively high level of local control over nominations in both the American and British parties nevertheless led to different consequences partly because the criteria used to make these rewards were different. On this see our discussion in Chapter 4 and Austin Ranney, "Candidate Selection and Party Cohesion in Britain and the United States," in William J. Crotty (ed), *Approaches to the Study of Party Organization* (Boston: Allyn and Bacon, 1968), pp. 139-58.

[4] For a similar position see: John S. Saloma, III, *Congress and the New Politics* (Boston: Little, Brown & Co., 1969), Chapter 1, and Leroy N. Rieselbach, *Congressional Politics* (New York: McGraw-Hill, 1973), Chapter 14.

[5] See specifically James MacGregor Burns, *The Deadlock of Democracy* (Englewood Cliffs, N.J.: Prentice-Hall, 1963), and James Burnham, *Congress and the American Tradition* (Chicago: Henry Regnery Co., 1959).

[6] See E. E. Schattschneider, *The Semi-Sovereign People* (New York: Holt, Rinehart and Winston, 1960).

Bibliographical Notes

Several chapters in the text alluded to bibliographical notes that would present a larger set of citations than would be appropriate to place in a textual footnote. The introductory chapter referred to a bibliographical note on criticisms of the legislature, Chapter 4 to a note on political parties, and Chapter 9 to a note on interest groups. These bibliographical notes are found below. The literature cited in the notes is not exhaustive. It is intended to provide a selection enabling the reader using it to get a sense of the variety of work available.

1. Numerous criticisms have been made and continue to be raised about modern representative legislatures. For instance, party pressures are thought to be too great in some legislatures, while for others there is concern that political parties are not as important an organizing force as they should be. Similarly, some legislatures are reproached for being too subservient to the executive, while others are criticized for not being sufficiently compliant (at times both sides of this criticism are directed at the same legislature, though usually by different critics). Allied to this criticism is a concern that legislatures have become highly dependent on executive leadership because they are insufficiently organized or equipped to handle the policy questions confronting them. On this basis some critics argue that the legislatures should spend less time than they currently do on the details of legislation while devoting more time to debating broad issues and to overseeing government operations. Still another criticism is that legislators are influenced too much by private interests and that neither legislators as a group nor the way the legislature is organized is representative. Finally, parties within many legislatures are admonished for being too similar to one another in policy approach, thereby not giving the voter a real alternative.

Discussions of one or more of these criticisms as they apply to the American Congress are presented in Roger H. Davidson, David M. Kovenock, and Michael K. O'Leary, *Congress in Crisis: Politics and Congressional Reform* (New York: Wadsworth, 1966); John S. Saloma III, *Congress and the New Politics* (Boston: Little, Brown and Company, 1969); Samuel Huntington, "Congressional Responses to the Twentieth Century," in *The Congress and America's Future* (Englewood Cliffs, N. J.: Prentice-Hall, 1973), ed. David Truman, pp. 6-38; Joseph S. Clark, ed., *Congressional Reform: Problems and Prospects* (New York: Crowell, 1965); American Political Science Association Committee on Political Parties, *Toward a More Responsible*

Two-Party System (New York: Rinehart, 1950); Richard Bolling, *House Out of Order* (New York: Dutton, 1965); James MacGregor Burns, *Congress on Trial: The Legislative Process and the Administrative State* (New York: Harper and Brothers, 1949); James MacGregor Burns, *The Deadlock of Democracy: Four-Party Politics in America* (Englewood Cliffs, N. J.: Prentice-Hall, 1963); Arthur M. Schlesinger, Jr., *The Imperial Presidency* (Boston: Houghton Mifflin, 1973); James Burnham, *Congress and the American Tradition* (Chicago: Regnery, 1959); Alfred de Grazia, ed., *Congress: The First Branch of Government* (Washington, D. C.: American Enterprise Institute, 1966); Alfred de Grazia, *Republic in Crisis: Congress Against the Executive Force* (New York: Federal Legal Publications, 1965); Mark Green, James Fallows, and David Zwick, *Who Runs Congress? The President, Big Business, or You?* (New York: Grossman Publishers, 1972); and Drew Pearson and Jack Anderson, *The Case Against Congress: A Compelling Indictment of Corruption on Capitol Hill* (New York: Simon and Schuster, 1968).

On the European legislatures, see Alfred Grosser, "The Evolution of European Parliaments," *Daedalus* 93 (Winter, 1964): 153-79; Otto Kirchheimer, "The Waning of the Opposition in Parliamentary Regimes," *Social Research* 24 (Summer, 1957): 128-56; Gerhard Loewenberg, ed., *Modern Parliaments: Change or Decline?* (Chicago: Aldine-Atherton, 1971); Philip M. Williams, *The French Parliament: Politics in the Fifth Republic* (New York: Praeger, 1968); Bernard Crick, *The Reform of Parliament* (London: Weidenfeld and Nicolson, 1970); Andrew Roth, *The Business Back-ground of MPs* (Old Woking, Surrey: The Gresham Press, 1972); Gerhard Braunthal, *The Federation of German Industry in Politics* (Ithaca, N. Y.: Cornell University Press, 1965); and Samuel Beer, "The British Legislature and the Problem of Mobilizing Consent," and Nicolas Wahl, "The French Parliament: From Last Word to Afterthought," in *Lawmakers in a Changing World*, edited by Elke Frank (Englewood Cliffs, N. J.: Prentice-Hall, 1966). On the problems of the influence of private interests in West Germany, two additional valuable studies in German are Viola Gräffin von Bethusy-Huc, *Demokratie und Interessenpolitik* (Wiesbaden: Franz Steiner Verlag, 1962); Otto Stammer et. al., *Verbände und Gesetzgebung* (Cologne and Opladen: Westdeutscher Verlag, 1965). On the absence of real contrasts between the parties, see Manfred Friedrich, *Opposition ohne Alternative* (Cologne: Verlag Wissenschaft und Politik, 1962). For a broad survey by a French author of criticisms of the French National Assembly, see André Chandernagor, *Un Parlement, pour quoi faire?* (Paris: Gallimard, 1967).

2. There is a wealth of literature dealing with political parties and with party politics in the legislature. On the United States, quite valuable as general references are Frank J. Sorauf, *Party Politics in America*, 2d. ed. (Boston: Little, Brown and Co., 1972); V.O. Key, Jr., *Parties, Politics and Pressure Groups*, 5th ed. (New York: Crowell, 1964); and Austin Ranney and Willmoore Kendall, *Democracy and the American Party System* (New York: Harcourt, Brace and World, 1956). More detailed descriptions of various facets of the organization and working of parties in Congress are Randall B. Ripley, *Party Leaders in the House of Representatives* (Washington, D. C.: The Brookings Institution, 1967); Randall B. Ripley, *Majority Party Leadership in Congress* (Boston: Little, Brown and Co., 1969); Charles O. Jones, *The Minority Party in Congress* (Boston: Little, Brown, and Co., 1970); John F. Manley, *The Politics of*

Finance: The House Committee On Ways and Means (Boston: Little, Brown and Co., 1970), especially pp. 15-59; Charles O. Jones, *Party and Policy-Making: The House Republican Policy Committee* (New Brunswick, N. J.: Rutgers University Press, 1964); Hugh A. Bone, "An Introduction to the Senate Policy Committees," *The American Political Science Review* 50 (June 1956): 339-59; Ralph K. Huitt, "Democratic Party Leadership in the Senate," *The American Political Science Review* 55 (June 1961): 331-44; John G. Stewart, "Two Strategies of Leadership: Johnson and Mansfield," in *Congressional Behavior* (New York: Random House, 1971), edited by Nelson W. Polsby, pp. 61-91; Jean Torcom, "Leadership: The Role and Style of Senator Everett Dirksen" in *To Be a Congressman: The Promise and the Power* (Washington, D. C.: Acropolis, 1973), edited by Sven Groennings and Jonathon P. Hauley, pp. 184-223; Robert Peabody, "Party Leadership Change in the House of Representatives," *The American Political Science Review* 61 (September 1967): 675-93; Lewis Froman and Randall Ripley, "Conditions for Party Leadership: The Case of the House Democrats," *The American Political Science Review* 59 (March 1965): 52-63; and Donald R. Matthews, *U. S. Senators and Their World* (New York: Random House, 1960), pp. 118-46.

Among the excellent book-length analyses of party behavior in Congress through roll call voting are Julius Turner, *Party and Constituency,* revised edition by Edward Schneier, Jr. (Baltimore, Md.: Johns Hopkins Press, 1970); David R. Mayhew, *Party Loyalty Among Congressmen: The Difference Between Democrats and Republicans, 1947-1962* (Cambridge, Mass.: Harvard University Press, 1966); Aage R. Clausen, *How Congressmen Decide: A Policy Focus* (New York: St. Martin's Press, 1973); David Truman, *The Congressional Party* (New York: John Wiley, 1959); W. Wayne Shannon, *Party, Constituency and Congressional Voting* (Baton Rouge: Louisiana State University Press, 1968); and Duncan MacRae, Jr. *Dimensions of Congressional Voting* (Berkeley and Los Angeles: University of California Press, 1958).

A broad discussion of legislators' role beliefs, by party, is presented in Roger H. Davidson, *The Role of the Congressman* (New York: Pegasus, 1969). On the characteristics of party candidates competing for election to Congress, see Jeff Fishel, *Party and Opposition: Congressional Challengers in American Politics* (New York: David McKay, 1973); and John L. Sullivan and Robert E. O'Connor, "Electoral Choice and Popular Control of Public Policy: The Case of the 1966 House Elections," *The American Political Science Review* 66 (December 1972): 1256-69.

For general works on contemporary political parties in Great Britain, see Robert T. McKenzie, *British Political Parties* (New York: St. Martin's Press, 1963); Samuel H. Beer, *British Politics in the Collectivist Age* (New York: Knopf, 1965); Martin Harrison, *Trade Unions and the Labour Party Since 1945* (Detroit, Mich.: Wayne State University Press, 1960); and Ralph Miliband, *Parliamentary Socialism: A Study in the Politics of the Labour Party* (London: Merlin, 1965). In addition, valuable sources on party politics in the House of Commons employing quantitative evidence are Robert J. Jackson, *Rebels and Whips: Dissention, Discipline and Cohesion in British Political Parties Since 1945* (New York: St. Martin's Press, 1968); S. E. Finer, H. B. Berrington and D. J. Bartholomew, *Backbench Opinion in the House of Commons, 1955-1959* (Oxford: Pergamon Press, 1961); Robert T. Holt and John E. Turner, "Change in British Politics: Labour in Parliament and Government" in *European Politics II: The*

Dynamics of Change, edited by William G. Andrews (New York: Van Nostrand Reinhold Company, 1969), pp. 23-116; and Allan Kornberg and Robert Frasure, "Policy Differences in British Parliamentary Parties," *The American Political Science Review* 65 (September 1971): 694-703. See also John E. Schwarz and Geoffrey Lambert, "Career Objectives, Group Feeling, and Legislative Party Voting Cohesion: The British Conservatives, 1959-68," *Journal of Politics* 33 (May 1971): 399-421. On the selection of parliamentary candidates within the parties see Austin Ranney, *Pathways to Parliament: Candidate Selection in Britain* (Madison: University of Wisconsin Press, 1965); Michael Rush, *The Selection of Parliamentary Candidates* (London: Thomas Nelson and Sons, 1969); Leon D. Epstein, *British Politics in the Suez Crisis* (Urbana: University of Illinois Press, 1964); and Jorgen S. Rasmussen, *The Relations of the Profumo Rebels with Their Local Parties* (Tucson: University of Arizona Press, 1966).

Accounts of the development of political parties in the French Fifth Republic are found in Frank L. Wilson, *The French Democratic Left, 1963-69; Toward a Modern Party System* (Stanford, Calif.: Stanford University Press, 1971); Harvey Simmons, *French Socialists in Search of a Role, 1956-1967* (Ithaca, N.Y.: Cornell University Press, 1970); and Jean Charlot, *The Gaullist Phenomenon* (New York: Praeger, 1971). Two excellent sources in French are Jacques Fauvet and Alain Duhamel, *Historie du parti communiste français,* vol. 2 (Paris: Fayard, 1965) and Jean Charlot, *L'Union pour la Nouvelle République: Étude du pouvoir au sein d'un parti politique* (Paris: Armand Colin, 1967). Quantitative studies on the party behavior of legislators in the National Assembly may be found in David M. Wood, "Majority vs. Opposition in the French National Assembly, 1958-1965: A Guttman Scale Analysis," *The American Political Science Review* 62 (March 1968): 88-109; William G. Andrews, "Change in French Politics After the 1965 Presidential Elections," in *European Politics II: The Dynamics of Change,* edited by William G. Andrews, (New York: Van Nostrand Reinhold Co., 1969), pp. 117-75; and, under the Fourth Republic, Duncan MacRae, Jr., *Parliament, Parties and Society in France, 1946-1958* (New York: St. Martin's Press, 1967). For attitudinal studies of Assembly members by party, see Oliver Woshinsky, *The French Deputy: Incentives and Behavior in the National Assembly* (Lexington, Mass.: D. C. Heath, 1973) and Roland Cayrol, et. al., "L'Image de la fonction parlementaire chez les députés français," *Revue Française de Science Politique* 21 (December 1971): 1173-1206.

For overviews in English of parties and their operation and development in postwar West Germany, see Harold Kent Schellenger, Jr., *The S.P.D. in the Bonn Republic: A Socialist Party Modernizes* (The Hague: Martinus Nijhoff, 1968); Douglas Chalmers, *The Social Democratic Party of Germany: From Working-Class Movement to Modern Political Party* (New Haven, Conn.: Yale University Press, 1964); Arnold J. Heidenheimer, *Adenauer and the CDU: The Rise of the Leader and Integration of the Party* (The Hague: Martinus Nijhoff, 1960); Gerhard Braunthal, "The Free Democratic Party in West German Politics," *Western Political Quarterly* 13 (June 1960): 332-48; Lewis J. Edinger, "Political Change in Germany: The Federal Republic After the 1969 Election," *Comparative Politics* (July 1970): 549-78; Otto Kirchheimer, "Germany: The Vanishing Opposition," in *Political Oppositions in Western Democracies* (New Haven, Conn.: Yale University Press, 1966), edited by Robert A. Dahl; and Charles

Frye, "Parties and Pressure Groups in Weimar and Bonn," *World Politics* 17 (July 1965): 635-55. Discussions of the operation of parties in the Bundestag and legislators' behavior with reference to their parties may be found in Gerhard Loewenberg, *Parliament in the German Political System* (Ithaca, N.Y.: Cornell University Press, 1967); Gerhard Loewenberg, "Parliamentarianism in Western Germany: The Functioning of the Bundestag," *The American Political Science Review* 55 (March 1961): 87-102; Arnold J. Heidenheimer, "Foreign Policy and Party Discipline in the CDU," *Parliamentary Affairs* 13: 70-84; George Rueckert and Wilder Crane, "CDU Deviancy in the German Bundestag," *Journal of Politics* 24 (August 1962): 477-88; and Frank H. Dishaw, "Role Call Deviancy in the CDU/CSU Fraktion of the West German Bundestag," in *Sozialwissenschaftliches Jahrbuch für Politik*, ed. R. Wildenmann (Munich: Günter Olzag Verlag, 1971), pp. 539-61; and on the goals of Bundestag candidates by party, Jeff Fishel, "Parliamentary Candidates and Party Professionalism in Western Germany," *Western Political Quarterly*, 25 (March 1972): 64-81. Five valuable sources in German on party and party behavior with reference especially to the Bundestag are Heino Kaack, *Geschichte und Structur des deutschen parteisystems* (Opladen: Westdeutscher Verlag, 1969); and Jurgen Domes, *Mehrheitsfraktion und Bundesregierung* (Cologne and Opladen: Westdeutscher Verlag, 1964); Hans-Joachim Veen, Die CDU/CSU *im Parlamentarischen Entscheidungsprozess* (Munich: Verlag Ernst Vogel, 1974); and, on candidate recruitment, Karlheinz Kaufmann, Helmut Kohl, and Peter Molt, *Kandidaturen zum Bundestag* (Cologne and Berlin: Kiepenheuer and Witsch, 1961) and Bodo Zeuner, *Kandidatenaufstellung zur Bundestagswahl* 1965 (The Hague: Nijhoff, 1970).

Finally, from a comparative perspective, general overviews with different emphases may be found in Maurice Duverger, *Political Parties: Their Organization and Activity in the Modern State* (New York: John Wiley and Sons, 1954) and Leon D. Epstein, *Political Parties in Western Democracies* (New York: Praeger, 1967).

3. For many years interest groups have been a topic of fascination in political literature. What follows in this note is a broad sampling of the literature on interest groups in the four political systems we have considered.

Some of the more notable works on the United States, reflective of differing approaches in examining the relation of interest groups to the Congress, include the following: Raymond Bauer, Ithiel de Sola Pool, and Lewis Dexter, *American Business and Public Policy: The Politics of Foreign Trade* (New York: Atherton, 1963); Lewis Dexter, *How Organizations are Represented in Washington* (Indianapolis, Ind.: Bobbs-Merrill, 1969); John W. Kingdon, *Congressmen's Voting Decisions* (New York: Harper & Row, 1973), especially pp. 139-68; Earl Latham, *The Group Basis of Politics* (Ithaca, N.Y.: Cornell University Press, 1952); Theodore Lowi, "American Business, Public Policy, Case Studies, and Political Theory," *World Politics* 16 (July 1964): 677-715; Lester W. Milbrath, *The Washington Lobbyists* (Chicago, Ill.: Rand McNally, 1963); Peter Odegard, *Pressure Politics: The Story of the Anti-Saloon League* (New York: Columbia University Press, 1928); Andrew Scott and Margaret Hunt, *Congress and Lobbies: Image and Reality* (Chapel Hill: University of North Carolina Press, 1965); Congressional Quarterly, *Legislators and the Lobbyists* (Washington, D. C.: Congressional Quarterly Service, 1968); Judith G. Smith, ed., *Political Brokers: Money, Organizations, Power and People* (New York: Liveright,

1972); David B. Truman, *The Governmental Process* (New York: Knopf, 1955); Harold L. Wollman and Norman C. Thomas, "Black Interests, Black Groups. and Black Influence in the Federal Policy Process: The Cases of Housing and Education," *Journal of Politics* 32 (November 1970): 875-97; L. Harmon Zeigler and Wayne Peak, *Interest Groups in American Society* 2d. ed. (Englewood Cliffs, N.J.: Prentice-Hall, 1972); Donald R. Hall, *Cooperative Lobbying* (Tucson: University of Arizona Press, 1969); Donald Haider, *When Governments Come to Washington: Governors, Mayors and Intergovernmental Lobbying* (New York: The Free Press, 1974); and Bruce Ian Oppenheimer, *Oil and the Congressional Process: The Limits of Symbolic Politics* (Lexington, Mass: D. C. Heath, 1974).

General critiques are found in William Connally, "The Challenge to Pluralist Theory," in *The Bias of Pluralism* (New York: Atherton, 1969), edited by William Connally, pp. 3-34; James Deakin, *The Lobbyists* (Washington, D. C.: Public Affairs Press, 1966); Ovid Demaris, *Dirty Business: The Corporate-Political Money-Power Game* (New York: Harper's Magazine Press, 1974); Robert Winter-Berger, *The Washington Payoff* (New York: Dell, 1972); Mark J. Green, James M. Fallows and David R. Zwick, *Who Runs Congress? The President, Big Business, or You?* (New York: Grossman Publishers, 1972); Theodore Lowi, *The End of Liberalism: Ideology, Policy and the Crisis of Public Authority* (New York: Norton, 1969); Drew Pearson and Jack Anderson, *The Case Against Congress: A Compelling Indictment of Corruption on Capitol Hill* (New York: Simon and Schuster, 1968); Grant McConnell, *Private Power and American Democracy* (New York: Knopf, 1966); E. E. Schattschneider, *The Semi-Sovereign People* (New York: Holt, Rinehart and Winston, 1960); Paul Conn, "Social Pluralism and Democracy," *American Journal of Political Science* 17 (May 1973): 237-54; and Michael P. Smith, et. al., *Politics in America: Studies in Policy Analysis* (New York: Random House, 1974), parts 1 and 2.

Descriptive and analytical studies of interest groups in Great Britain and their relations with government and Parliament include Harry Eckstein, *Pressure Group Politics: The Case of the British Medical Association* (London: Allen and Unwin, 1960); Samuel Finer, *Anonymous Empire: A Study of the Lobby in Great Britain* (London: Pall Mall, 1966); Richard Howarth, "The Political Strength of British Agriculture," *Political Studies* (December 1969): 458-69; John H. Millett, "The Role of an Interest Group Leader in the House of Commons," *Western Political Quarterly* 9 (December 1956): 915-26; William D. Muller, "Union-MP Conflict: An Overview," *Parliamentary Affairs* 26 (Summer 1973): 336-55; G. C. Moodie and G. Studdert-Kennedy, *Opinions, Publics, and Interest Groups* (London: Allen and Unwin, 1970); Allan Potter, *Organised Interest Groups in British National Politics* (London: Faber, 1961); J. D. Stewart, *British Pressure Groups: Their Role in Relation to the House of Commons* (Oxford: Oxford University Press, 1958); and H. H. Wilson, *Pressure Group: The Campaign for Commercial Television* (London: Secker and Warburg, 1961).

On the politics of a variety of interest groups in France see: William Bosworth, *Catholicism and Crisis in Modern France: French Catholic Groups at the Threshold of the Fifth Republic* (Princeton, N. J.: Princeton University Press, 1962); Bernard E. Brown, "Pressure Politics in the Fifth Republic," *Journal of Politics* (August 1963): 509-25; James Clark, *Teachers and Politics in France* (Syracuse, N. Y.: Syracuse University Press, 1967); Henry W. Ehrmann, *Organized Business in France* (Princeton, N.J.: Princeton University Press, 1957); Henry W. Ehrmann, "French Bureaucracy and Organized Interests," *Administrative Science Quarterly* 5 (1961): 534-55; Val R. Lorwin, *The French Labor Movement* (Cambridge, Mass.: Harvard University Press, 1954); Jean Meynaud, *Les Groupes de pression en France* (Paris: Armand Colin, 1958); Jean Meynaud, *Nouvelles études sur les groupes de pression en France* (Paris: Armand Colin, 1962); Jean Reynaud, *Les Syndicats en France* (Paris: Armand Colin, 1963); and Yves Tavernier, *Le Syndicalisme paysan* (Paris: Armand Colin, 1969).

On West Germany are Klaus von Beyme, *Interessengruppen in der Demokratie* (Munich: Piper, 1969) which also covers other nations; Viola Gräfin von Bethusy-Huc, *Demokratie und Interessenpolitik* (Wiesbaden: Franz Steiner Verlag, 1962); Gerhard Braunthal, *The Federation of German Industry in Politics* (Ithaca, N.Y.: Cornell University Press, 1965); Gerhard Braunthal, *The West German Legislative Process: A Case Study of Two Transportation Bills* (Ithaca, N.Y.: Cornell University Press, 1972); Rupert Breitling, *Die Verbände in der Bundesrepublik* (Meisenheim: Anton Hein, 1955); Karl Deutsch and Lewis Edinger, *Germany Rejoins the Powers: Mass Opinion, Interest Groups, and Elites in Contemporary German Foreign Policy* (Stanford, Calif.: Stanford University Press, 1959); Thomas Ellwein, *Klerikalismus in der deutschen Politik* (Munich: Isar Verlag, 1956); Charles E. Frey, "Parties and Pressure Groups in Weimar and Bonn," *World Politics* 17 (July 1965): 635-55; William Safran, *Veto Group Politics: The Case of Health Insurance Reform in Western Germany* (San Francisco: Chandler, 1967); Otto Stammer et. al., *Verbände und Gesetzgebung* (Cologne-Opladen: Wesdeutscher Verlag, 1965); and Hans-Joachim Veen, *Die CDU/CSU im Parlamentarischen Entscheidungsprozess* (Munich: Verlag Ernst Vogel, 1974).

Besides the citations listed, comparisons of two or more of the systems may be found in Samuel Beer, "Group Representation in Britain and the United States," *The Annals of the American Academy of Political and Social Science* 319 (September 1958): 130-41; Henry W. Ehrmann, *Interest Groups on Four Continents* (Pittsburg, Penn.: University of Pittsburg Press, 1958); Abraham Holtzman, *Interest Groups and Lobbying* (New York: Macmillan, 1966, pp. 40-71; J. Roland Pennock, "Responsible Government, Separated Powers, and Special Interests: Agricultural Subsidies in Britain and America," *American Political Science Review* 56 (September 1962): 621-33; and Graham Wooten, *Interest Groups* (Englewood Cliffs, N. J.: Prentice-Hall, 1970). Comparative overviews of relations among broad subgroupings in the populations are presented in Gabriel Almond and James Coleman, *The Politics of the Developing Areas* (Princeton, N. J.: Princeton University Press, 1960) and Arend Lijphart, "Consociational Democracy," *World Politics* 21 (January 1969): 207-25. For a series of hypotheses that have been applied regarding interest group politics, see Joseph LaPalombara, *Interest Groups in Italian Politics* (Princeton, N.J.: Princeton University Press, 1964), especially pp. 13-26.

Credits

The authors wish to express their gratitude to the following writers and publishers who have given us permission to quote from their works: Robert S. Erikson and Norman R. Luttbeg, *American Public Opinion: Its Origins, Content and Impact* (New York: John Wiley and Sons, Inc., 1973), reprinted by permission of John Wiley and Sons, Inc. Lewis A. Froman, *Congressmen and Their Constituencies* (Chicago: Rand McNally, 1963), reprinted by permission of the author. Charles O. Jones, "Inter-Party Competition for Congressional Seats," *Western Political Quarterly* 17 (September, 1964), reprinted by permission of the University of Utah, Copyright Holder, and by permission of the author. John F. Manley, *The Politics of Finance The House Committee On Ways and Means* (Boston: Little, Brown and Company, 1970), reprinted by permission of Little, Brown and Company. Leroy N. Rieselbach, "The Congressional Vote on Foreign Aid, 1939-58," *American Political Science Review* 58 (1964), p. 578, reprinted by permission of the *American Political Science Review* and the author. Table entitled "Size of Birthplace, Constituency Type, and Support for the Conservative Coalition," p. 328, reprinted from "Congressmen as 'Small Town Boys': A Research Note," *Midwest Journal of Political Science* 14.2 (1970) by Leroy N. Rieselbach by permission of the Wayne State University Press, copyright, 1962, by Wayne State University Press, and by permission of the author. Randall B. Ripley, *Party Leaders in the House of Representatives* (Washington, D.C.: The Brookings Institution), ©1967 by the Brookings Institution, Washington, D.C. Frank Stacey, *The Government of Modern Britain* (Oxford: The Clarendon Press, 1968), reprinted by permission of Oxford University Press. Herbert Stephens, "The Role of Legislative Committees in the Appropriations Process," *Western Political Quarterly* 24 (March, 1970), reprinted by permission of the University of Utah, Copyright Holder, and by permission of the author. Aaron Wildavsky, "The Two Presidencies," *Transaction* 4 (Dec., 1966). Published by permission of Transaction Inc., from *Transaction* Volume 4 #2. Copyright © 1966 by Transaction Inc.

Index

Abram, Michael, 91
Adamany, David, 89, 361, 363
Adams, James Clark, 9
Adenaur, Konrad, 57, 92, 110, 216, 237-38, 244, 250, 296, 309, 336
Albert, Carl, 37-38, 42, 90, 100, 167
Albinski, Henry, 92, 250
Alexander, Herbert, 31, 89
Alford, Robert, 156
Algeria, 125, 204, 206, 211, 236, 253, 309, 313
Allardt, Erik, 322, 364
Allport, Floyd H., 20
Almond, Gabriel, 290, 406
Ambition, political (see dispositions of legislators)
Ameller, Michael, 286
Americans for Constitutional Action (ACA), 154, 349, 371-74, 376, 392
Americans for Democratic Action (ADA), 116, 122-23, 154, 349, 371-74, 376, 385, 392
Amery, L. S., 158
Anderson, Jack, 359, 365, 401, 405
Anderson, Malcolm, 93
Andrain, Charles, 155
Andrews, William G., 92, 155, 250, 403
Annual authorizations, 263-64
Anthony, William W., 20, 323
Apportionment, 24-26, 88
Arndt, Hans-Hoachim, 322, 343
Arrow, Kenneth J., 391
Ashkenasi, Abraham, 253
Assembly (see National Assembly, France)
Atlee, Clement, 55, 212

Bailey, Cleveland, 341
Bailey, Stephen K., 116, 168, 188-89, 226, 252
Baldwin, David A., 248
Bandura, Albert, 19

Barber, James, 10, 188
Barker, Anthony, 157, 290, 365
Barnes, Samuel H., 146, 154, 158
Barnett, Malcolm J., 95, 248
Bartholomew, D. J., 95, 155, 191, 253, 323, 402
Barzel, Ranier, 216
Bauer, Raymond A., 166, 188, 190, 252, 322, 340-41, 362, 364, 404
Beer, Samuel, 148, 156-58, 362, 401-02, 406
Bell, Roderick, 9
Bennett, Stephen E., 155
Berelson, Bernard, 20
Berger, Raoul, 88
Berman, Daniel, 96-97, 115-16
Bernstein, Robert A., 20, 323
Berrington, H. B., 95, 155, 191, 253, 323, 402
Bethusy-Huc, Viola Gräffin von, 208, 249, 360, 362-65, 401, 406
Bevan, Aneurin, 212, 214
Beyme, Klaus von, 406
Bibby, John F., 317, 324
Biddle, Bruce, 10
Biemiller, Andrew, 116
Binkley, Wilfred, 250, 251
Birch, A. H., 9, 391
Black Caucus, 381-86
Blank, Theodore, 216
Blondel, Jean, 289
Boggs, Hale, 34, 167-68, 170
Bolling, Richard, 103, 401
Bombardier, Gary, 154
Bone, Hugh, 35, 90, 402
Bonjean, Charles M., 186, 393
Bosworth, William, 405
Bowering, Nona, 314, 323
Bradshaw, Kenneth, 92, 94, 158, 290
Brandt, Willy, 57, 70, 244, 274
Braunthal, Gerhard, 94, 208, 249, 295, 321, 327, 336, 353-54, 361-65, 401, 403, 406

Breithling, Rupert, 406
Brewster, Daniel, 330
Brezina, Dennis, 252
Brock, William, 346-47
Bromhead, Peter A., 92
Brown, Bernard E., 249, 253, 362, 405
Brown, Clarence, 102
Brown, George, 212, 214
Bruner, Jerome S., 20
Buchanan, James, 10
Buck, J. Vincent, 90
Buck, Phillip W., 190
Buckley, James, 31, 33
Budget Reorganization Act, 1974, 19
Budgets, 218-19, 259-64, 304, 306
Bundesrat, West German, 2, 58, 62, 93, 111, 274, 289
Bundestag, West German, (see also Committees in the Bundestag, Elections, West German, legislative)
   agenda, 78, 80, 82
   constitutional status, 61-64, 93, 235
   influence on public policy, 77, 113, 193, 197-201, 207-211, 237-38, 244-46, 256, 292-93, 307
   influence on domestic compared to foreign policy, 193, 236-38, 244
   relation to executive, 56-58, 77-78, 197-98, 274
   staff, 77-79, 305-06
Bureau, National Assembly, France, 83
Bureau of the Budget, 219, 227, 260
Buron, Robert, 290
Burnham, James A., 390-91, 396, 399, 401
Burns, James MacGregor, 390, 396, 399, 401
Butler, David, 156, 391, 393
Butler, Richard, 213-14
Butt, Ronald, 116, 174, 190, 203, 248
Butz, Earl, 261
Byrd, Harry, 33
Byrd, Robert, 37
Byrne, Paul, 324

Cabinet (see government)
Callaghan, James, 212, 214
Cambodia, 34, 243, 308, 312-13
Campaign Reform Acts, 32
Campbell, Angus, 86, 393
Cannon, Joe, 34, 41, 46, 169, 189
Cantril, Hadley, 391-92
Carey, George, 391
Carper, Edith, 289
Carroll, Holbert, 239, 254-55, 267, 288, 323
Carroll, John, 170
Carswell, Harold, 233, 251, 298

Carter, Byrum E., 133, 156
Carter, Gwendolyn, 289
Cater, Douglas, 229
Caucus (see individual parties by name)
Cayrol, Roland, 156, 403
Celebrezze, Anthony, 99
Celler, Emmanuel, 99-100, 102-03,160
Censure, 55, 57, 62, 87, 92-93, 274-76, 321
CDU/CSU (Christian Democratic Union/Christian Social Union) Parliamentary Party (see also Party leaders in the Bundestag, Elections, West German legislative)
   caucus, 80-82, 111, 150, 215-16
   cleavages in, 81, 112, 124-25, 129, 146
   executive committee, 80-82, 150
   specialized policy committees or work groups, 80-82, 111-12, 150
   voting cohesion, 120-21, 143-44, 152-53
Central clearance, 218-19
Centre Démocrate Party, France, 60
Chalmers, Douglas A., 92, 94, 403
Chamberlain, Lawrence, 225-26, 240, 250-52, 254
Chamberlain, Neville, 243, 275
Chancellor, West Germany (see also Executive)
   powers of, 56-57, 77
   removal of, 57-58, 274
   selection of, 56-57, 70, 215-17
Chandernagor, André, 94, 206, 249, 289-90, 401
Charlot, Jean, 93, 95, 136, 148, 151, 155-58, 236, 248-49, 253, 255, 403
Chester, Lewis, 247
Chester, D. N., 314, 323
Christoph, James B., 248-49
Churchill, Randolph, 190
Churchill, Winston, 55, 204
Civil Rights Act, 1964, 96-107, 228
Clapp, Charles, 89, 165, 188, 190, 321, 360, 362-64
Clark, James, 405
Clark, Joseph S., 286
Clausen, Aage R., 151, 155, 187-88, 310, 321-23, 402
Cleaveland, Frederick, 227-28, 252, 289
Clem, Alan L., 90
Cloture, 104, 106
Cnudde, Charles, 116
Cochrane, James D., 92
Cohen, Bernard C., 255, 340, 362
Coleman, James, 406
Colmer, William, 48, 160
Combs, J. M., 170
Committees in the Bundestag

Index **411**

assignment to, 78-79, 81-82
chairmen of, 78-81, 296
influence on legislation, 79, 113, 209, 297
legislative supervision by, 281-83, 315
staff, 79, 305-06
standing committees, 78-79, 82, 283
subcommittees, 283
Committees in the Bundestag, by name,
Agriculture, 352
Appropriations, 282
Defense, 285
Economic Affairs, 352
European Security, 209
Family, 352
Health, 352
Labor, 112, 352
Social Policy, 112, 207, 352
Trade, 352
Committees in the Congress
assignment to, 37, 42-44, 142, 168-72
chairmen of, 45-49, 99, 134, 141, 157, 300, 374, 376-78, 392, 397-98
conference committees, 51-52, 92, 227
influence on legislation, 40-42, 56, 287, 297-301
joint committees, 51, 259
legislative supervision by, 258-72; 316
select committees, 50-51
Senate-House differences, 42
seniority in, 17, 43-50, 80, 141, 168, 171, 374, 397
staff, 52-53, 259, 303-06, 317
standing committees, 40-49
subcommittees, 41, 49-51, 9l, 259
Committees in the Congress, by name
Administration, House, 45
Agriculture, House & Senate, 45, 49, 53, 271
Appropriations, House & Senate, 41-45, 50, 52-53, 170-71, 259, 264-66, 270, 272, 300-01, 303-04, 384
Armed Services, House & Senate, 262-63, 271, 310, 332, 384
Banking & Currency, House & Senate, 45, 227, 317
Budget, House & Senate, 41-43, 50
District of Columbia, House & Senate, 43
Education and Labor, House, 53, 116, 169, 384
Ethics, House 41
Finance, Senate, 43
Foreign Relations, Senate, 53, 243, 310
Government Operations, Senate, 43, 259, 265, 268
Interior, House and Senate, 271
Internal Security (formerly Un-American Activities), House, 41, 169

International Relations (formerly Foreign Affairs), House, 53, 384
Interstate and Foreign Commerce, Senate, 101, 116
Joint Committee on Atomic Energy, 51, 259, 271
Joint Committee on Internal Revenue, 51
Joint Economic Committee, 51
Judiciary, House & Senate, 23, 50, 97, 99, 101, 104, 116, 169, 228-29, 384
Labor & Public Welfare, Senate, 41, 53
Post Office & Civil Service, House & Senate, 43, 47, 300
Public Works, House & Senate, 271
Rules Committee, House, 35, 37-38, 41-43, 46, 48, 50, 101-03, 106, 116, 169, 189, 229, 299, 384
Rules & Administration, Senate, 43
Small Business, House, 41, 50
Veteran's Affairs, Senate, 41
Ways & Means, House, 42-44, 169-71, 189-90, 266, 299-300, 303, 384
Committees in the House of Commons,
assignment to, 74, 76
chairmen of, 75-76
influence on legislation, 74-76, 297
legislative supervision by 278-81, 315-16
select or supervisory committees, 280-81, 315
staff, 75, 95, 281, 305, 318
standing general committees, 74-75, 79
Committees in the House of Commons, by name
Agriculture, 76
Committee on Nationalized Industries, 76, 280, 317
Committee on Parliamentary Commissioner for Administration, 284
Committee on Science and Technology, 76
Committee on Statutory Instruments, 63, 76, 279
Expenditures Committee (formerly Estimates Committee), 75-76, 279-80
Fuel and Power, 280
Public Accounts Committee (PAC), 75-76, 278, 280-81
Standing Committee on Private Member Bills, 74
Standing Committee on Scotish Affairs, 74
Trade and Industry, 202, 280
Committees in the National Assembly
assignment to, 84
chairmen of, 85-86
influence on legislation, 83-84, 297
legislative supervision by, 281-82; 315
staff, 305

standing committees, 83, 206, 259
subcommittees, 84
Committees in the National Assembly, by name
   Agriculture, 114
   Finance, 282
   Cultural, Family & Social Affairs, 201, 205
Committee veto, 259, 270-72, 289
Committee of the Whole,
   Britain, 74, 109
   U. S., 102
Common Market, 113, 173, 181-83, 203-04, 236-37, 243, 370
Communist Party, France, 65, 68-69, 83, 119, 132, 153, 200, 206
Conable, Barber, 35
Confidence, vote of, (see censure)
Conflict of interest, 365, 398
Congress (see also Committees in Congress, Elections, U.S. Legislative)
   constitutional status, 3, 21-22, 87, 238-39
   compared to other legislatures, 54-55, 86-87, 211, 247, 292
   criticisms of, 4-9, 34, 47, 192, 298, 359, 366-69, 374, 394, 396-98, 400
   influence on domestic compared to foreign policy, 23, 193, 238-43
   influence on public policy, 3-4, 193, 217-34, 238-43, 245-47, 292-93, 307
   informational capacity of, 301-06, 311-13
   relation to executive, 274-75, 302
   staff, 52-53, 259, 303-06, 317
Congressional Budget Office, 42
Congressional Research Service, 53, 305
Conservative coalition, 126-28, 155, 163, 165, 167, 187, 298
Conservative Party, British Parliamentary (see also Party leaders in the House of Commons, Elections, British legislative)
   cleavages in, 125-26, 129-30
   1922 Committee, 73, 109, 150, 202-03, 213
   specialized policy committees, 73, 109, 150
   voting cohesion in, 119, 143-44, 152-53, 156, 159, 191, 294
Constituency,
   and legislators' voting behavior, 94, 142, 147-48, 160-64, 186, 188, 308-10, 347-50, 356-58
   casework, 283-84
   and legislative supervision, 316-17
Constituency associations, 64, 137
Constitutional Council, France, 61, 93
Constitutional powers (see Executive, individual executives and legislatures by name
Conn, Paul, 405

Connally, William, 405
Conseil d' État, 273
Conway, Jack, 116
Coolidge, Calvin, 218
Coombes, David, 95, 280, 290, 323
Cooper, Ann, 289
Cooper, Joseph, 91, 154, 289
Cotter, Cornelius P., 286-87
Cottin, Jonathan, 363
Council of Elders, 78, 80, 82-83
Cour des comptes, 273
Couve de Murville, Maurice, 205-06
Crabb, Cecil V. Jr., 254-55
Crane, Wilder, 141, 157, 404
Crick, Bernard, 92, 190, 247, 286, 291, 324, 401
Cronin, Thomas E., 248, 251, 253
Crotty, William J., 399
Cue, 16, 128, 187, 302-03, 308-09, 350
Cummings, Milton, 26, 88, 90

Dahl, Robert, 10, 96, 99, 115-16, 188, 247, 254, 369, 391, 403
Davidson, Roger, 10, 20, 154, 158, 187-88, 251-52, 295, 321-22, 329, 360, 367, 390-91, 400, 402
Dawson, Raymond, 241-42, 254-55, 288
Deakin, James, 360-61, 363, 405
Debré, Michel, 148
Deckard, Barbara, 187
de Gaulle, Charles, 59, 114-14, 143, 148, 211, 236, 238, 327, 360
de Grazia, Alfred, 250, 255, 286, 288, 322, 401
de Grazia, Edward, 250
Delbeque, Léon, 125
Democratic Party, U. S. congressional, House & Senate (see also Party Leaders in the Congress, Elections, U. S. legislative)
   campaign committees, 36
   caucus conference, 34-36, 39, 42-43, 45, 151, 169-70,
   cleavages in, 120, 122-23, 126, 129, 154, 163
   committee on committees, 36, 42-44, 169-70
   policy committees, 34-35, 39, 42-43, 45-46, 151, 168
   voting cohesion in, 119-21, 144, 152-53
Democratic Research Group, 36
Democratic Steering and Policy Committee, see Democratic Party, policy committees
Democratic Study Group, House, 36, 102-03, 116
Dentler, Robert, 154, 248
Deschamps, Bruno, 95
d'Estaing, Valéry Giscard, 59
de Tocqueville, Alexis, 253
Deutsch, Karl, 253, 406

Dexter, Lewis Anthony, 166, 188, 190, 252, 254, 288, 322, 340-41, 361-64, 404
Dichgans, Hans, 351
DiNitto, Andrew, 88
Dirksen, Everett, 90, 104-06, 116, 228
Discharge motion, Senate, 41
Discharge petition, House, 41, 102
Dishaw, Frank H., 365, 404
Dissolution of parliament, 55-56, 59, 62, 92-93, 145, 158
Dispositions of legislators, 12-14
　career ambitions, 12, 18, 19, 135-45, 151, 158, 160, 167-72, 174-85, 188, 294, 308-09, 315, 344-47, 355
　desire for informed decisions, 13-14, 18, 302, 311, 317, 319
　party identification, 13, 18, 130-34, 151, 164-67, 174, 176, 294, 315
　policy preferences, 18, 121-22, 125-29, 131, 146, 151-52, 158, 160, 185-86, 311, 324, 340-43, 350, 356
　role conception, 14, 18, 147-49, 151, 158, 160, 292-96, 310, 317, 319, 355-56, 358
Dogan, Mattei, 95, 250, 321
Domes, Jürgen, 95, 116, 158, 208, 210, 248, 250, 323, 404
Donovan, John C.,
Douglas, Paul, 331
DouglasHome, Alec, 108, 212-14
Downs, Anthony, 391
Drew, Elizabeth Brenner, 105, 116
Düebber, Ulrich, 94, 352, 364
Duhamel, Alain, 403
Durkin, John, 33
Duverger, Maurice, 88, 93, 95, 253, 290, 360, 404

Early day motions, 109, 185, 191, 357
Eastland, James, 99, 101, 104
Easton, David, 10
Eccles, David, 108
Eckhardt, Walter, 352
Eckstein, Harry, 248, 362, 364, 405
Eden, Anthony, 55, 213-15, 243, 274
Edinger, Lewis J., 156, 158, 247, 253, 403, 406
Egger, Rowland, 250
Ehrmann, Henry, 9, 93, 138, 157, 290, 322, 360, 362, 405-06
Eidenberg, Eugene, 241, 248, 252, 254, 302, 322
Eisenhower, Dwight David, 32-33, 189, 217-18, 220-31, 223, 228, 232, 242, 251, 254, 271, 312, 316
Elections, British legislative, 55, 64, 69-70, 143
　campaign costs and financing, 65-66

nominations, 64-65, 94, 137-38, 157, 175-76, 191, 399
turnover in, 67
Elections, French legislative, 59-60, 64, 143
　campaign costs and financing, 65-66
　nominations, 64-65, 138-39
Elections, U.S. legislative,
　campaign costs and financing, 28, 30-32, 65, 89, 344-48, 363
　impact of interest groups on, 344-47, 351
　nominations, 27-28, 64-65, 142, 399
　qualifications for, 22-24
　turnover in, 28-29, 67
Elections, West German legislative, 57, 64, 143
　campaign costs and financing, 65-66, 69, 331, 351
　impact of interest groups on, 351-55
　nominations, 64-65, 94, 140-41, 143, 351-52
　turnover in, 67
Electoral systems,
　political consequences of, 24-25, 66-71, 88, 370
　proportional representation system, 66, 69-70
　single member district system, 23, 26, 66-70, 370
Elliot, Carl, 101
Ellwein, Thomas, 406
Employment Act, 1946, 226-227
Epstein, Leon, 92, 145, 149, 158, 190, 248, 322, 403-04
Erhard, Ludwig, 57, 92, 215-16, 238, 244, 250
Erickson, Robert, 89, 387, 393
Erler, Fritz, 209
Erroll, Frederick, 108
Ervin, Sam, 50, 101, 261
Eulau, Heinz, 9, 11, 19, 288, 362, 391
Evers, Medgar, 97
Executive (see also individual executives by name, individual legislatures by name)
　definition of, 194, 197-98, 320
　constitutional bases of authority, 218, 235, 238-39
　influence on domestic compared to foreign policy, 234-44, 255, 306-13
　influence on public policy, 192-212, 217-34, 247, 251-52, 257
Executive agreements, U.S., 239, 254
Executive privilege, 269

Fallows, James, 401, 405
Farah, Barbara, 146, 154, 157
Faure, Edgar, 205
Fauvet, Jacques, 403

414 *Index*

FDP (Free Democratic Party), West Germany, 57, 70, 78, 80, 92, 119-20, 153-54, 209, 352
Federal Constitutional Court, West Germany, 93
Feedback, 18-19
Fenno, Richard, 19-20, 40, 42, 47, 52, 90-91, 171, 189, 190, 259-60, 264, 267, 287-88, 300, 304, 321-22
Ferejohn, John A., 91-92
Festinger Leon, 20
Filibuster, 41, 99, 104-06, 128, 228, 272
Finer, S. E., 95, 116, 123, 125-26, 129, 155, 191, 253, 323 360, 402, 405
Finletter, Thomas K., 10
Fiorina, Morris, 19
Fishel, Jeff, 31, 88-89, 154, 157-58, 363, 402, 404
Fisher, Louis, 219, 251, 255, 261, 287, 289
Flinn, Thomas A., 187
Fluno, Robert Y., 390
Foley, Thomas, 45
Foot, Michael, 73, 146
Foot, Paul, 248
Ford, Gerald, 33, 37, 221, 261, 332
Foreign policy, definition of, 234
Fowler, Hubert R., 154
Fox, Douglas M., 321
Fox, Harrison W., Jr., 92, 287
Foxe, Fanne, 45
Fraktion, 80, 210
Frank, Elke, 95, 157, 248, 401
Fransworth, David, 245
Fraser, Ian, 327
Frasure, Robert, 124, 126, 129, 154-55, 158, 380, 393, 403
Free, Lloyd A., 391-92
Freedman, Charles E., 289
Freeman, J. Leiper, 248
Frey, Charles E., 404, 406
Friedrich, Carl J., 248
Friedrich, Manfred, 401
Froman, Lewis, 88, 91, 161-63, 187-88, 299, 321, 402
Fulbright, J. William, 238, 241, 253-54

Gaitskell, Hugh, 212, 214
Gallaher, Miriam, 91
Galloway, George, 287
Gallup, George H., 393
Garceau, Oliver, 19
Garner, John Nance, 169
Gaullist, French Parliamentary Parties (see also Party leaders in the National Assembly, Elections, French legislative) Ad hoc policy committees or study groups, 85

Bureau, 84-85
Caucus, 84, 150, 206
cleavages in, 125, 129-30
specialized policy committees or study groups, 85, 114, 150-51, 205,-06, 236
voting cohesion in, 119, 121, 143-44, 152-53, 294
Gerrymander, 25
Gilmour, Robert S., 251
Glaser, William, 90
Goldwater, Barry, 29, 106
Goodell, James, 31
Goodwin, George, 47-48, 91, 157 189
Gordon, Bernard, 254
Gore, Albert, 346-47
Gore, William, 89
Goss, Carol, 254
Government, formation of, 54, 56-57, 59-60, 72, 197, see executive,
Government Accounting Office (GAO), 53, 265
Grange, Jean, 94-95, 249, 289, 323
Grassmuck, George, 155
Green, Harold P., 91, 287
Green, Mark, 89, 265, 288, 359, 361, 363, 365, 401
Greenberg, Sanford D., 251
Griffith, Ernest S., 287
Griffiths, John, 291
Groennings, Sven, 90, 402
Grosser, Alfred, 291, 308, 322, 401
Guichard-Ayoub, Elaine, 249, 289
Guillotine motion, 72
Gwyn, William B., 290-91

Habib-Deloncle, Michel, 143, 147
Haider, Donald, 405
Hall, Donald R., 405
Halleck, Charles, 37, 99-100, 168
Halperin, Morton, 255
Hamilton, James, 116
Hamilton, Roy, 91
Hammond, Susan Webb, 92
Hancock, M. Donald, 9
Hanson, Royce, 252
Hargrove, Erwin C., 254
Harris, Joseph P., 274, 286-90
Harris, Richard, 347, 363
Harrison, Martin, 94, 249, 402
Hawley, Jonathon, 90, 402
Haynsworth, Clement, 298, 233, 251
Hays, Wayne, 45
Heard, Alexander, 89, 361
Heath, Edward, 55, 108-09, 113, 116, 202-03, 213, 250
Hebert, Edward, 45

Heclo, Hugh, 290, 323
Heidenheimer, Arnold J., 89, 94, 237, 253, 364, 403-04
Heindel, R. H., 255
Henderson, Thomas, 287
Herman, Valentine, 248
Herring, Pendleton, 362
Hickenlooper, Burt, 106
Hilsman, Roger, 241, 254-55
Hinckley, Barbara, 48, 90-91, 128, 155, 165, 188
Hirsch, Herbert, 9
Hirsh-Weber, Wolfgang, 157, 337, 360, 362
Hollinger, Joan, 28-29, 48, 89, 91
Hollingshead, A. B., 156
Holt, Robert T., 155-56, 402
Holtzman, Abraham, 257, 363, 406
Honors list, 72, 94
Horn, Stephen, 90, 287
House of Commons, British (see also Committees in the House of Commons, Elections, British legislative)
 agenda, 72, 94
 constitutional status, 54, 62-64, 235
 influence domestic compared to foreign policy, 235, 243-44, 253
 influence on public policy, 63, 71, 77, 197-204, 210-12, 235, 243, 246, 292-93, 307
 relation to executive, 55-56, 77, 83, 197-98, 274-75
 staff, 75, 95, 281, 305, 318
House of Lords, 2, 56, 58
Howarth, Richard, 405
Huckshorn, Robert, 88-89
Huitt, Ralph, 19, 39, 90-91, 165, 188, 195, 248, 255, 264, 288
Humphrey, Hubert, 104-06, 260
Hunt, Margaret, 333, 340-41, 346, 360-63, 404
Hunt, Norman, 95, 156
Hunt, William H., 154-56, 158
Huntington, Samuel P., 240, 247, 254, 286, 324, 390, 400
Hyneman, Charles, 286

Impeachment, 22-23, 274-75, 289
Impoundment, 194, 260-62
Incentive theory, 6-7
Independent-Republican Party, France, 59-60
Ingram, Helen M., 252, 322
Interest groups,
 access to executive, 334-37, 362
 access to legislature, 328-34, 337, 345, 351, 361
 and committees, 332-33
 definition of, 325
 effectiveness of, 308, 336-37, 339-40, 345, 347, 353-55, 359-60, 363, 394, 397
 grass-roots campaigns, 333-34
 legitimacy of, 328-29
 lobbying by, 98-99, 102-03, 106, 109, 111, 113-14, 116, 227-30, 330, 360, 397
 types and sizes of, 326-328
Interpellation, 82, 95

Jackson, John E., 187
Jackson, Robert J., 135, 156, 164, 190, 250, 322, 402
Jacob, Herbert, 88, 289
Jaeger, Richard, 209
Jahnige, Thomas, 267, 288
James, Dorothy Buckton, 254
Javits, Jacob, 254
Jennings, M. Kent, 89
Jennings, W. Pat, 170
Jewell, Malcolm, 288, 88-90, 122, 154, 241, 253-55, 287, 316, 323
Johannes, John R., 252, 289
Johen, Wilhelm, 351
Johnson, Andrew, 274
Johnson, Lyndon B., 33, 37, 39, 43, 100-02, 104, 106-07, 168, 218, 220, 223, 228-29, 232-33, 241-43, 246, 253-54, 271, 298-99, 312, 332
Johnson, Nevil, 95, 281, 290
Joint Mediation Committee, 58
Jones, Charles O., 28-29, 88-91, 94, 255, 401-02
Jones, G. W., 92, 250
Jones, Joseph M., 255
Judge, David, 289

Kaack, Heino, 92, 404
Kaljarvi, T. V., 255
Kalleberg, Arthur, 19
Kaminsky, Elijah Ben-Zion, 253
Kammerer, Gladys, 92
Kanter, Arnold, 255, 323
Kaplan, Abraham, 10
Katzenbach, Nicholas, 99-100, 103
Kaufmann, Karlheinz, 94, 140, 157, 352-53, 364-65, 404
Keef, William, 28-29, 87-89, 91, 262, 287-88, 360, 362
Kefauver, Estes, 50, 268
Kellerman, Don, 254
Kelley, H. H., 10
Kelley, Stanley, Jr., 251
Kendall, Willmore, 391, 401

Kennedy, Edward, 37
Kennedy, John F., 23, 33, 97, 99-102, 105-06, 160-61, 163, 218, 221, 223, 226, 228-29, 232-34, 239, 241-42, 246, 253-54, 271, 299, 316
Kennedy, Robert F., 23, 99-101, 106, 228
Keppel, Francis, 229-30
Kerr, Robert, 332
Kessel, John H., 322
Kesselman, Mark, 365
Key, V. O., Jr., 88, 162, 187, 264, 287-88, 344, 363, 401
Kiesinger, Kurt-Georg, 57, 216, 238
King, Anthony, 95
King, Martin Luther, 97
Kingdon, John W., 20, 89, 128, 155, 160, 186-87, 300, 321-22, 341, 347, 350, 358, 362-65, 404
Kirchheimer, Otto, 277, 289, 391, 401, 403
Kirst, Michael W., 260, 266, 268-70, 272, 287-89
Kitzinger, Uwe, 352, 364
Knoll, Erwin, 334, 361
Knowland, William, 189
Koenig, Louis, 157, 218, 251, 253, 296, 321
Kofmehl, Kenneth, 92, 287
Kohl, Helmut, 157, 352, 364-65, 404
Kolodziej, Edward A., 255, 287
Korb, Lawrence, 254-55
Kornhauser, William, 155
Kornberg, Allan, 9, 10, 92, 124, 126, 129, 149, 154-55, 158, 287, 380, 393, 403
Kovenock, David, M., 251, 321-22, 390-91, 400
Krisell, J. E., 290
Krislov, Samuel, 290
Krone, Heinrich, 112
Kuchel, Thomas, 104-05

Labour Party, British Parliamentary (see also Party leaders, House of Commons, Elections, British legislative)
 cleavages in, 123-24, 126, 128-30, 146, 310
 liason committee, 73
 parliamentary committee, 73, 150, 215
 specialized policy committees, 73, 150
 voting cohesion in, 119, 121, 143-44, 152-53, 294
Lakeman, Enid, 88
Lambert, Geoffrey, 156, 190, 403
Land, 58, 61, 69, 71, 93, 140-41
Landrum, Phillip, 170-71
Langdon, Frank C., 94
LaPalombara, Joseph, 361-62, 406
Lasswell, Harold D., 10, 247
Lathan, Earl, 404

Lausche, Frank, 157
Lavergne, Bernard, 249
Lee, Fred, 277
Lee, John, 321
Legislative Reorganization Act, 1946, 19, 35, 41, 52-53, 258-59, 265, 268, 305
Legislative Reorganization Act, 1970, 52-53, 259
Legislative supervision (see also Questions, written & oral; Ombudsman; Committees in the individual legislatures; Bundesrat; Budget)
 administrative courts, 273-74
 audits, 265, 279
 hearings and special investigations, 265-69, 281, 315-16
 legislative clearance, 270-72
Legislators (see also Dispositions of legislators, Elections to Bundestag, Congress, House of Commons, National Assembly)
 as a focus of study, 9
 influence of political setting on, 8, 16-18, 21, 87, 144-51, 294, 296-97, 302, 319, 394-95
 social backgrounds of, 23-24, 127-28, 131-34, 156, 176, 184-86
 perceptions of, 15, 20, 293, 310, 364
Legislatures (see also Bundestag, Congress, House of Commons, National Assembly)
 definition of
 relation to democracy, 1, 3-4, 366, 394
Lembruch, Gerhard, 95, 250, 296, 321
Leonard, Dick, 248
Leuthold, David, 89
Liason Committee, 84
Liberal Party, Britain, 55, 57, 68, 154, 370
Lijphart, Arend, 10, 406
Lincoln, Abraham, 217
Linz, Juan, 156
Lipset, Seymour Martin, 155-56
Littunen, Yrjö, 322, 364
Loewenberg, Gerhard, 9, 11, 19, 80, 92, 94-95, 150, 156, 158, 208-09, 249-50, 253, 256, 290, 295, 302, 314, 321-23, 360, 363, 365, 401, 404
Lohse, Egon, 291
Long, Russell, 37, 332
Longworth, Nicholas, 189
Lord, Guy, 249, 303, 321-22
Lorwin, Val R., 406
Lowi, Theodore, 15, 20, 255, 257, 286, 362, 404-05
Luebke, Heinrich, 216
Luebke, Paul, Jr., 157
Lundeen, James W., 365
Lundeen, Shirley A., 365
Luttbeg, Norman, 387, 393

Lynskey, James J., 150, 158, 199, 201, 210-11, 235, 248, 250, 253, 363

MacArthur, Douglas, 268
Mackintosh, John P., 92, 116, 203, 248, 250, 275, 289, 293, 321, 362
Macleod, Ian, 213
MacMahon, Arthur, 270, 287, 289
Macmillan, Harold, 55, 108, 173-74, 214-15, 250, 274-75
MacRae, Duncan, Jr., 154, 187, 402-03
Macridis, Roy C., 248-49
Madden, Ray, 107
Magnuson, Warren, 101, 116
Maher, Edward, 331
Manley, John, 47, 90-92, 168-69, 187, 189-90, 234, 252-53, 299-300, 303, 321-22, 364, 401
Mansfield, Mike, 35, 37, 39, 43, 104-06, 116, 168, 383
March, James, 10
Marmor, Theodore, R., 252
Marquet, Pierre-Bernard, 362
Marshall, Burke, 99, 103
Martin, Joseph, 37, 142, 168, 187, 189
Marwell, Gerald, 155
Marx, Fritz M., 287
Mason, Roy, 335
Masters, Nicholas, 44, 91, 188, 190
Matthews, Donald, 20, 23, 39, 88, 90-91, 130, 154-57, 164-65, 187-90, 219, 251, 287, 302, 322, 329, 341, 360-64, 392, 402
Maulding, Reginald, 213-14
Mavrinac, Albert, 95
Mayhew, David, 19, 88-89, 151, 163, 186-87, 348, 364, 402
McCarthy, Eugene, 360-61
McConnell, Grant, 250, 405
McCormack, John, 37, 100, 169, 189
McClellan, John, 268
McClosky, Herbert, 155
McCrone, Donald, 116
McCulloch, William, 99-100, 103
McCune, Wesley, 364
McGeary, M. Nelson, 288
McGovern, George, 192, 371
McKay, David, 363
McKenzie, Robert T., 92, 190, 250, 393, 402
McNamara, George, 242
McPhee, William, 90
Meany, George, 349
Médiateur, 291
Meller, Norman, 92
Menges, Constantine, 277, 289
Merkl, Peter, 95, 249
Meyer, John W., 90

Meynaud, Jean, 406
Mezey, Michael, 88
Micaud, Charles, 93
Milbrath, Lester, 253, 330, 350, 361-64, 404
Miller, Arthur H., 391, 393
Miller, Clem, 33, 188
Miller, Warren, 90, 116, 157, 160, 168, 322-23, 364, 388
Millet, John H. 360, 362-62, 405
Millikin, Eugene, 341
Mills, John Stuart, 257, 286
Mills, Wilbur, 45, 47, 299-300
Minister, see government, party leaders
Minshall, William 332
Mitchell, Clarence, 116
Mitchell, William C., 322, 361
Mitterand, François, 60
Moe, Ronald C., 225-26, 251-53, 321
Mollohan, Robert H., 332
Molt, Peter, 157, 352, 364-65, 404
Mondale, Walter, 30-31
Montgomery, John D., 255
Moodie, G. C., 405
Moos, Malcolm, 90
Morey, Roy D., 248, 252, 302, 322
Morrison, Herbert, 212, 327
Morrow, William, 91, 259, 268, 271, 287-89
Morse, E. L., 249, 323
Moyer, Wayne, 243, 255
MRP, Mouvement Républicain Populaire (Catholics), 60, 68, 120, 153
Mueller, John E., 322
Muller, William D., 362, 405
Murphy, George, 332
Murray, James E., 226
Murray, Tom, 47, 300
Muskie, Edmund, 228
Musolf, Lloyd, 10, 92, 287

Nader report, see Green, Mark
National Assembly, France (see also Committees in the National Assembly, Elections, French legislative)
  agenda, 83-86
  constitutional status, 59-64, 84-84, 93, 235
  influence on domestic compared to foreign policy, 236, 244
  influence on public policy, 3, 197-201, 204-07, 211, 236, 243-44, 246, 292-93, 307
  relation to executive, 59-60, 83, 197-98, 274
  staff, 94-95, 305
Neureither, Karlheinz, 92
Neugarten, Bernice, 156
Neustadt, Richard, 88, 218, 220, 250, 251
Newcomb, T. M., 156
Nicholson, Godfrey, 280

418 Index

Nicolson, Nigel, 157
Nimmo, Dan D., 186, 393
Nixon, Richard M., 33-34, 43, 218-21, 223, 231, 233, 243, 245, 251, 254-55, 260-62, 274-75, 298, 312, 336, 349, 362, 371, 382, 391
Noonan, Lowell G., 83, 95, 249
Nordlinger, Eric A., 248
Norris, George, 188

Oberlaender, Theodor, 216
O'Brien, Lawrence, 103, 229
O'Connor, Robert E., 151, 402
Odegard, Peter, 404
Office of Management and Budget, 219, 265
Ogul, Morris, 28-29, 87-91, 262, 287-88, 360, 362
O'Leary, Michael, K., 251, 321-22, 390-91, 400
Oleszek, Walter J., 90
O'Mahoney, Joseph, 226
Ombudsman,
  Britain, 76, 204, 284-85, 290-91
  West Germany, 284-85
O'Neill, Thomas, 34, 38, 90
Oppenheimer, Bruce Ian, 364, 405
Orfield, Gary, 252
Osborne, John, 108
Ottinger, Richard, 31, 65
Overmeyer, Allen, 252
Oversight of executive (see Legislative supervision)
Owens, John R., 363

package vote, 84-85, 205, 321
Packenham, Robert A., 10
Paige, Glen D., 254
Paletz, David, 89
Parliamentary systems, 54-55, 86, 145, 212, 247
Parris, Judith, 289
Parsons, Talcott, 10
Party leaders in the Bundestag (see also Chancellor, Government)
  parliamentary party chairman, 80-81
  selection of, 139-40, 215-17
  whips, 80-81, 150
Party leaders in Congress
  influence of, 37, 39-40, 99-100, 141-42, 144, 160, 167-71, 189
  Majority and minority leaders in the House, 37-39, 167-68
  Majority and minority leaders in the Senate, 37-39, 116, 168, 392
  Selection of, 34, 36-37, 39, 167-68
  Speaker of the House, 34, 37-38, 169-70, 189, 339

Whips, 37, 103, 109, 167-68
Party leaders in the House of Commons (see also Government, Prime Minister)
  influence of, 76, 148, 174
  selection of, 135-36, 212-215
  Shadow cabinet, 72, 76, 94-95, 213-215
  Whips, 72-74, 76, 135-36, 172-73, 181-82
Party leaders in the National Assembly (see also Government, Premier)
  influence of, 115
  selection of, 84-85
  President of the parliamentary party bureau, 84
Patman, Wright, 45
Patterson, Samuel, 9, 19, 28, 88-90, 92, 122, 154, 287, 316, 322-23
Payne, James L., 10
Peabody, Robert, 19, 89-90, 254-55, 287-88, 402
Peak, Wayne, 405
Pearson, Drew, 359, 361, 365, 401, 405
Pennock, J. Roland, 362, 406
Perkins, Dexter, 255
Pettit, Lawrence, 92, 250
Pferdmenges, Robert, 351
Philip, André, 158
Pierce, John C., 360
Pierce, Lawrence C., 252, 299, 321
Pierce, Melvin, 45
Pierce, Roy, 93
Pinay, Antoine, 291
Pincus, Walter, 332, 361, 363
Pinney, Edward, 93
Pisani, Edgar, 114, 138
Pitkin, Hanna, 9, 366, 390
Poage, W. R., 45
Pohle, Wolfgang, 351, 353
Policy process, conceptualization of, 194, 252
Political parties, (see also individual parties by name, Election to Bundestag, Congress, House of Commons, National Assembly)
  as contrasted to interest groups, 325
  in democracies, 118
Polsby, Nelson, 88-91, 154, 189, 195, 248, 250-51, 254, 287-88, 402
Pompidou, Georges, 59, 148
Poniatowski, Michel, 249
Pool, Ithiel de Sola, 166, 188, 190, 252, 322, 340-41, 362, 364, 404
Potter, Allan, 362, 405
Powell, Adam Clayton, 98
Power theory, 7-8, 10
Powell, Enoch, 213
Premier, France, (see also government, executive)
  removal of, 59, 274

selection of, 59
President of the Bundestag, 78, 95
President of France, (see also Executive)
  constitutional powers of, 54, 59, 62
  election of, 59, 93
President of the National Assembly, France, 83
President of the United States, (see also Executive)
  coattails, 142-43
  constitutional powers of, 22-23
  legislative, success scores, 220-225
  veto, 217-18, 227, 232-33, 243
President of West Germany, 56, 62, 92, (see also Executive)
President's Conference, National Assembly, 83
Prime Minister, Britain (see also Executive, Government)
  as party leader, 72, 77, 87
  removal of, 55, 274
  selection of, 54-55, 212-215
Private member bills,
  Britain, 77, 86, 108
  France, 83, 85-86
  West Germany, 82, 86
Press, Charles, 90
Pressman, Jeffrey, 91, 248
Price, David, 91-92, 246, 252, 287, 304, 321-22, 362, 364, 394, 399
Price, H. Douglas, 27-28, 88-89, 154
Pring, David, 92, 94, 158, 290
Profumo affair, 173-74, 274-76, 289
Proxmire, William, 265, 317, 362
Punnett, R. M., 92, 94-95, 250, 277, 290
Putman, Robert D., 20

Queen's speech, 94
Questions, oral & written/question period,
  Britain, 76-77, 95, 276-78, 280, 314-15
  France, 83, 85, 276-77
  West Germany, 82, 95, 208, 276-77, 314
Quistgaard, John, 190

Radical Party, France, 68, 119, 153
Rae, Douglas, 88, 94, 391
Ranney, Austin, 88, 138, 156-57, 399, 401
Rapporteur,
  France, 86
  West Germany, 79-80, 82
Rasmussen, Jorgen, S., 176, 190, 403
Rausch, Heinz, 250
Rauth, Joseph, 116
Rayburn, Sam, 35, 37, 101, 167, 169, 189, 332

Redman, Eric, 252
Redmayne, Martin, 73-74, 95, 109, 135-56, 144, 156
Reid, Gordon, 95, 290
Rendel, Margherita, 289
RePass, David, 393
Representation,
  as a reflection of citizen opinion, 370, 372-78, 380, 386-90
  definition of, 366
  models of, 367-75, 378-80, 393, 396
Republican Booster's Club, 31
Republican Party, U.S. Congressional, House & Senate (see also Party leaders in Congress, Elections, U.S. legislative)
  campaign committees, 36
  cleavages in, 123, 126, 129
  committee on committees, 36, 42-44, 168
  conference, caucus, 34-35, 39, 43, 45, 151
  issue differences with the Democratic Party, 120
  policy committees, 35, 39, 90, 151
  voting cohesion in, 119-121, 144, 152-53
Resale Price Maintenance, 107-110, 173-74, 197, 202-04, 207, 212
Reston, James, 254
Reuss, Henry, 45
Rhode, D. W., 91
Rhodes, John, 38
Rhodesia, 174, 181-83, 191, 203, 243, 309
Richards, Peter, 94, 253, 322
Ridgeway, Lee, 381
Ridley, F., 289
Ries, John C., 255
Rieselbach, Leroy N., 10, 88-89, 123, 127, 155, 187, 253, 323-24, 399
Riggs, Fred W., 9
Rimareix, Gaston, 117, 248, 250, 364
Ripley, Randall, 38, 90-91, 123, 130, 154-55, 157, 162, 165-66, 171, 186, 188-90, 226, 233, 248, 252-53, 256, 401-02
Robinson, James, 92, 240, 248, 251-52, 254-55, 302, 310, 322-23
Roig, Charles, 94, 249
Rokeach, Milton, 19
Rokkan, Stein, 156
Role theory, 6-7
Romney, George, 261
Romoser, George K., 92, 157, 250, 255
Roosevelt, Franklin D., 33, 218-19, 226, 270
Roosevelt, Theodore, 218
Rose, Richard, 94-95, 155, 250, 321
Rose, S., 92
Rosenau, James N., 255
Rosenthal, Allan, 91, 287
Ross, Robert A., 322, 361

Rossiter, Clinton, 220, 251
Roth, Andrew, 360, 401
Rousseau, Jean-Jacques, 328, 360
Rowat, Donald, C., 291
Royle, Charles, 338
Rueckert, George L., 141, 157, 404
Rule 16, 104
Runquist, Barry, 91
Rush, Michael, 94, 157, 290, 365, 403
Rusk, Dean, 238
Russell, Richard, 104
Russett, Bruce M., 240, 254-55, 323

Safe seats, 28-29, 48-49, 66-67, 88, 175, 190, 357
Safran, William, 116-17, 338, 361-62, 364-65, 406
Saloma, John S. III, 248, 252, 286-89, 322, 391, 393, 400
Samson, Anthony, 156, 190
Salinger, Pierre, 23
Scammon, Richard, 372, 392
Schaeffer, Fritz, 216
Schäfer, Friedrich, 95
Schattschneider, E. E., 252, 399, 405
Scher, Seymour, 316-17, 323-24
Schlesinger, Arthur Mr., Jr., 250, 253-55, 391, 401
Schlesinger, Joseph, 19, 89, 135, 156
Schleth, Uwe, 94
Schmidt, Helmut, 58
Schneier, Edward, Jr., 154, 187-88, 322, 402
Schroeder, G., 216
Schütz, Klaus, 157
Schwarz, John, 156, 190, 380, 403
Scott, Andrew, 241-42, 254-55, 333, 340-41, 346, 360-63, 404
Scott, Hugh, 39, 90, 168
Segal, David, R., 186, 389, 393
Senate, French, 2, 60-62, 93
Separation of powers system, 23-24, 86-87, 145
Seymour-Ure, Colin, 248
Shadow cabinet (see Party leaders in the House of Commons)
Shannon, W. Wayne, 154, 163-64, 187-88, 402
Sharkansky, Ira, 288, 291, 323
Shaw, L. Earl, 360
Shaw, Malcolm, 297, 321
Shell, Kurt L., 253
Shonfield, Andrew, 317, 324
Shucik, Martin, 391
Shuttlesworth, Fred, 97
Sills, David L., 19, 250
Simmon, Harvey G., 93, 403
Simpson, Richard, 341

Sindler, Allan P., 254
Smith, Frank, 188
Smith, Howard, 101-03, 106, 228-29
Smith, Judith G., 363, 404
Smith, M. Brewster, 19-20
Smith, Michael P., 405
Smith, Paul A., 154, 248
Smith, Thomas, 186, 389, 393
Smithers, William, 88
Snowiss, Leo M., 88
Socialist Party, France, 68, 119, 123, 132, 153
Sohl, Hans-Günther, 351
Sontheimer, Kurt, 92
Sorauf, Frank J., 88, 90, 157, 188, 401
Soustelle, Jacques, 125
Sparkman, John, 310
SPD (Social Democratic Party), West Germany, 57-58, 65-66, 70, 78, 80-82, 92, 110-12, 119, 133-34, 146, 153, 207-09, 216, 294, 314
Speaker of the House,
   Britain, 72, 94
   United States, (see Party leaders, Congress)
Spencer, Robert, 88-89
Spong, William, Jr., 254
Stacey, Frank, 92, 95, 240, 290-91
Stammer, Otto, 249, 260-61, 401, 406
Steiner, Gary, 20
Steiner, Gilbert, 92
Stepan, Alfred, 255
Stephens, Herbert, 262-63, 288
Stewart, John G., 90, 333, 342, 356, 360-62, 364, 402, 405
Stimson, James, 20, 187, 302, 322, 364
Stokes, Donald, 116, 156-67, 160, 186, 322-23, 364, 388, 390, 393
Stone, Clarence, 188
Stone, I. F., 307, 322
Stotland, E., 155
Stouffer, Samuel A., 155
Strauss, Franz Josef, 277, 351
Strickland, L., 155
Strum, Philippa, 254
Studdert-Kennedy, G., 405
Subcommittee Bill of Rights, House, 42, 91
Suez, 185, 191, 203, 213, 243, 274, 309
Suffert, Georges, 93
Sullivan, John L., 151, 402
Sundquist, James, 232, 252
Supreme Court, 23, 233, 262, 268
Swanson, Wayne, 189
Systems analysis, 8

Talmadge, Herman, 260
Tavernier, Yves, 117, 248, 250, 364, 402

Taylor, Telford, 288
Teel, Steven, 225-26, 251-52
Teller vote, 102
Ten minute Rule, 77
Thatcher, Margaret, 213, 250
Thibaut, J. W., 10, 155
Thomas, Edwin, 10
Thomas, Hugh, 156, 190
Thomas, Norman C., 405
Thompson, Frank, 45, 103
Torcom, Jean, 90, 402
Tribunaux administratifs, 273
Trossman, Hans, 94-95
Tower, John, 35
Truman, David, B., 20, 88, 90-91, 154, 157, 188, 247, 254, 286, 288, 324, 342-44, 346, 362-63, 390, 400, 402, 405
Truman, Harry S., 33, 50, 218-19, 227, 241, 251, 268, 271
Tuchfarber, Alfred J., 155
Tufte, Edward, 88
Turner, John E., 155, 156, 402
Turner, Julius, 121, 154-55, 187-88, 322, 402

Udall, Morris, 168
UDR (Union of Democrats for the Fifth Republic) see Gaullist parties)
UDT (L'Union démocratique du travail) (see Gaullist parties)
Ulmer S. Sydney, 20, 187, 364
UNR (Union of Democrats for the Fifth Republic) (see Gaullist parties)

Vardys, V. Stanley, 91, 287
Veen, Hans-Joachim, 404, 406
Verba, Sydney, 290
Veto, (see President of the United States)
Vietnam, 34, 241, 308, 334, 383, 387
Vinyard, Dale, 91, 287
Vital, David, 253, 277, 290, 309, 311, 323
Vogler, David, 52, 91

Wagner, Robert, 226
Wahl, Nicolas, 401
Wahlke, John, 9-11, 19-20, 362-63, 391
Wakland, S. A., 92, 116
Wallace, George, 105
Wallace, George Ash, 287-88
Walters, Richard H., 19
Waltz, Kenneth, 214, 250, 253
War Powers Act, 298
Watergate, 49-50, 257, 267, 275, 336
Watson, Gerald, 360, 364

Wattenberg, Ben, 372, 392
Weber, Max, 10
Wedgewood-Benn, Anthony, 173
Wednesday Club, 36
Wednesday Group, 36
Weimar, August, 116
Wellhausen, Dr. Hans, 365
Werner, Rudolph, 111
Westberry v Sanders, 25, 88
Westerfield, H. Bradford, 254
Westerfield, Louis P., 189
Westin, Alan, F., 289
White, John P., 363
White, Robert, 20
Wilcox, Francis O., 255
Wildavsky, Aaron, 239-40, 248, 251, 254, 287-88, 290, 301, 308, 310, 312, 322-24
Wildenmann, R., 157, 365, 404
Williams, Philip, 20, 93-95, 143, 157-58, 200, 205-07, 247, 249-50, 253, 290, 321, 401
Williams, Harrison, 228
Willis, Edwin, 103
Wilmerding, Lucius, 287
Wilson, Frank L., 93, 403
Wilson, Harold, 55, 76, 212, 214, 280
Wilson, H. H., 204, 248-49, 405
Wilson, Woodrow, 40, 90, 217, 251, 394, 399
Winter-Berger, Robert, 361, 364, 405
Wirtz, Willard, 99
Wolfinger, Raymond, 28-29, 48, 89, 91
Wollman, Harold L., 187, 405
Wood, David M., 155, 250, 255, 403
Wooten, Graham, 360, 406
Woshinsky, Oliver H., 10, 20, 149, 157-58, 321, 403
Wyman, Louis, 33

Young, Roldns, 287-89
Young, Stephen, 189

Zeigler, L. Harmon, 89, 340, 362-63, 405
Zeuner, Bodo, 94, 404
Zwick, David, 401, 405